Forging
Latin America

ALSO BY RUSSELL CRANDALL

The Salvador Option: The United States in El Salvador, 1979-1992

America's Dirty Wars: Irregular Warfare from 1776 to the War on Terror

The United States and Latin America after the Cold War

Gunboat Democracy: U.S. Interventions in the Dominican Republic, Grenada, and Panama

Driven by Drugs: U.S. Policy toward Colombia

The Andes in Focus (coeditor)

Mexico's Democracy at Work (coeditor)

Forging Latin America

Profiles in Power and Ideas, 1492 to Today

RUSSELL CRANDALL

ROWMAN & LITTLEFIELD
Lanham • Boulder • New York • London

Published by Rowman & Littlefield
An imprint of The Rowman & Littlefield Publishing Group, Inc.
4501 Forbes Boulevard, Suite 200, Lanham, Maryland 20706
www.rowman.com

86-90 Paul Street, London EC2A 4NE

Copyright © 2024 by The Rowman & Littlefield Publishing Group, Inc.

All rights reserved. No part of this book may be reproduced in any form or by any electronic or mechanical means, including information storage and retrieval systems, without written permission from the publisher, except by a reviewer who may quote passages in a review.

British Library Cataloguing in Publication Information Available

Library of Congress Cataloging-in-Publication Data

Names: Crandall, Russell, 1971- author.
Title: Forging Latin America : profiles in power and ideas, 1492 to today / Russell Crandall.
Description: Lanham : Rowman & Littlefield, 2023. | Includes bibliographical references and index.
Identifiers: LCCN 2023019668 (print) | LCCN 2023019669 (ebook) | ISBN 9781538183311 (cloth) | ISBN 9781538183328 (paperback) | ISBN 9781538183335 (epub)
Subjects: LCSH: Latin America—Biography. | Politicians—Latin America—Biography. | Reformers—Latin America—Biography. | Latin America—Politics and government.
Classification: LCC F1407 .C736 2023 (print) | LCC F1407 (ebook) | DDC 980.009/9 [B]—dc23/eng/20230425
LC record available at https://lccn.loc.gov/2023019668
LC ebook record available at https://lccn.loc.gov/2023019669

I dedicate this book to Allen Wells, longtime history professor at Bowdoin College in Maine. Adored by legions of Bowdoin undergraduates for his intellectual tenacity, cavernous recall, good humor, baseball metaphors, and reliable and wise correspondences with former students, Professor Wells embodied the essence of liberal arts inquiry and passion. For me as a rookie Latin American Studies major, he was highly demanding but fair and accessible.

And ever since my graduation from Bowdoin three decades ago, Allen has remained a rock-steady and spirited colleague—and, more vitally, friend. As has been the case with all my books, he keenly read this manuscript from start to finish; his trademark copious notations made the work *infinitely* better. Through my vocation as a professor at a Bowdoin-like institution in North Carolina, I have attempted to pay forward to my students a portion of his boundless gift.

Un abrazo muy fuerte, profe, RC

Gratitude

My oldest brother, and my best friend and best man, Bill Crandall Jr., died while I was writing this book. Bill cheerfully chopped on endless drafts of all my previous books, so it was an especially big void to not have him on the team this time around.

My long-standing, vital editor in London, Alex Goodwin, performed his trademark editing scrub—and rescrub, and, God bless him, yet one more. If you enjoyed a particularly keen turn of phrase, that was certainly Alex, not me. But heavy rouge does not do justice to what Alex's outsized abilities—intellectual no less than his mighty pen—meant for imagining the spirit of and composing the prose for this book. If he had not been on board, this book would never have seen the light of day.

Spouse and life coach, Britta H. Crandall, was an invaluable part of making this book into a reality. Britta never complained when I asked her to read yet another version of this section or that section. Her single-authored chapter on Lula is easily one of the best in the book.

The endlessly patient and wise Father Kevin O'Neil went above and beyond on all things Roman Catholic Church history and doctrine; Kevin O' has forgotten more about liberation theology in five minutes than I will learn in a lifetime.

Andy Rhodes and Ron Grim, both board members of the illustrious Washington Maps Society were fantastic helpers in getting the Waldseemüller Map into adequate shape. You can find Andy's smart Nicaragua map in the chapter on Augusto Sandino. Davidson's Little Library team was once again formidable and forgiving: Joe Gutekanst, Jayme Sponsel, Lisa Forrest, and Cara Evanson.

With generous help in various chapters were Davidson's history colleagues John Wertheimer and Ralph Levering. Hispanic Studies colleague Angie Willis read the José Martí chapter backward and forward and keenly translated "Adbala" from the Spanish; she also took the magnificent photograph of the Martí bust during her 2018 research trip to Cuba. Davidson students Kat Andersen and Grace Ayyildiz were intrepid fact-checkers. Jack Richardson's research and writing were indispensable to the Fidel Castro chapter.

Russell Crandall
Summit Coffee
Davidson, North Carolina

Contents

Introduction	1
PART I: Colonial	
1 Amerigo Vespucci: "Half the World Baptized with His Dishonest Name"	8
2 Bartolomé de las Casas: *A Short Account of the Destruction of the Indies*	16
3 Sor Juana Inés de la Cruz: Latin America's First Feminist	26
4 Túpac Amaru II and the Great Andean Rebellion	34
5 Toussaint Louverture: The Black Spartacus of the Caribbean	46
6 Simón Bolívar: The Great Liberator, Flawed Emancipator	60
PART II: Nineteenth Century	
7 Antonio López de Santa Anna: The Hero Who Lost Half a Country	76
8 Benito Juárez: Mexico's Great Reformer	89
9 Juan Manuel de Rosas and Domingo Sarmiento: The Struggle to Hatch Argentina	100
10 Dom Pedro II: Brazil's Citizen Monarch	110
11 José Martí: The Colossus of Cuba	122
PART III: First Half of the Twentieth Century	
12 José Enrique Rodó: *Ariel* and a New Vision for Latin America	132
13 José Vasconcelos: The Mexican Revolution's Cultural Caudillo	138

14	Diego Rivera and Frida Kahlo: Passion, Paint, and Politics	147
15	Berta Lutz: Brazil's Frog-Loving Feminist	160
16	Augusto Sandino versus the United States	167
17	Lázaro Cárdenas: "Nuestro Petróleo"	179
18	Rafael Trujillo: "Our S.O.B."	188
19	José Carlos Mariátegui and Victor Raúl Haya de la Torre: Peru's Long Revolution	198

PART IV: Cold War

20	Juan and Eva Perón: Peronism's Dynamic Duo	210
21	Rómulo Betancourt: Titan of Democracy	223
22	Jacobo Árbenz: A Guatemalan Spring, Interrupted	233
23	Fidel Castro: A Rebel with a Cause	245
24	Ernesto Guevara: Becoming Che	262
25	Manuel Marulanda: Founding Father of the FARC	280
26	Salvador Allende: "All Things to All Men"	289
27	Augusto Pinochet: The Unlikely Model Dictator	305
28	Eduardo Galeano: Poet of History	318
29	Gabriel García Márquez: Magical versus Social Realism	326
30	Óscar Romero: Priest, Saint, Revolutionary	342
31	The Mothers and Grandmothers of the Plaza de Mayo: Despair, Resistance, and Remembrance	354
32	Becoming Pope Francis: Jorge Mario Bergoglio and the Dirty War	362
33	Efraín Ríos Montt: From God to Genocide	371
34	Rigoberta Menchú: A Voice for the Voiceless	382
35	Abimael Guzmán and Shining Path: The Philosophy of Terror	388
36	Chico Mendes and Marina Silva: Defenders of the Amazon	399

PART V: Postmodern Age

37	Mario Vargas Llosa: Cartographies of Power	412
38	Pablo Escobar: The First Drug Lord	421

39	Subcommander Marcos: The First Postmodern Guerrilla	437
40	Hugo Chávez: The Richest Revolutionary in the World	451
41	Yoani Sánchez: Cuba's Underground Revolutionary	466
42	Michelle Bachelet: Healing Chile	474
43	Evo Morales: Reclaiming Bolivia	483
44	José "Pepe" Mujica: From Communism to Chrysanthemums	494
45	Luiz Inácio Lula da Silva: Brazil's First Working-Class President (by Britta H. Crandall)	502
46	Daniel Ortega and Rosario Murillo: Nicaragua's Toxic Power Couple	511
47	Berta Cáceres: The Guardian of the River	522

Bibliography   529
Index   559

Introduction

Created by the Mexican muralist Diego Rivera, *Dream of a Sunday Afternoon at Alameda Central Park* (1946–1947) at first glance appears to resemble the bucolic park scenes by nineteenth-century French Impressionists illustrating upper-class mores. But closer inspection reveals a much more revolutionary agenda. The painting is nothing less than a surrealist depiction of Mexico's turbulent history, read from the Spanish Conquest on the far left of the mural (where conquistador Hernán Cortés is portrayed) to the Mexican Revolution of the early twentieth century and the new postrevolution society on the far right. Amid the colorful balloons and pleasant trees are scenes of violence, struggle, and persecution: the Spanish Inquisition, the oppression of indigenous peoples, the War of Independence, and the dictatorship of Porfirio Díaz, whose brutal rule sparked the revolution. Other famous figures include Benito Juárez, the nineteenth-century president known as the "Great Reformer," the last Aztec emperor Cuauhtémoc, the Archduke Maximilian of Austria, emperor of Mexico between 1864 and 1867, and Francisco Madero, a revolutionary and first post-Díaz president who was assassinated in 1913.

But in addition to portraying famous historical figures and anonymous oppressed peoples (frequently neglected by history), there are also less expected figures, such as Sor Juana, a seventeenth-century nun and arguably Mexico's first feminist. Most striking is the depiction of artists, who are arranged at the center of the composition. Rivera appears as a boy, with his actual wife Frida Kahlo (also a painter) behind him, laying a hand on his shoulder. Close by is printmaker José Guadalupe Posada, who stands next to the figure he created that dominates the picture's focal point: the skeletal La Calavera Catrina, a satirical portrait of upper-class women in *fin de siècle* Mexico City.

Diego Rivera's Dream of a Sunday Afternoon in the Alameda (1947). It was painted in 1947 and was moved from the Hotel del Prado after it was destroyed by the 1986 earthquake. It was later housed in the Museo Mural Diego Rivera. *(John Mitchell/Alamy)*

By placing artists—and art—center stage, Rivera implied that amid all the world-historical political figures involved in the violent evolution of the nation, it is artists who are crucial to the transmission of history—how it is told, whose stories are chosen, what ideas are foregrounded. Rivera was one of the Mexican government's official artists mandated to broaden the awareness of the revolution and reimagine the nation's idea of itself (now to include all Mexico's people) via a new, distinctively "Mexican" visual language. That *Sunday Afternoon at Alameda Central Park* was installed at an upmarket hotel in Mexico City furthers the points: in the new Mexico, the revolution would be everywhere.

This book shares the same ambition as Rivera's masterpiece. Bringing together a collection of figures—some well-known, others less so—it seeks to understand the role power and ideas have played in shaping the destiny and character of Latin America, from the Spanish Conquest to the present day. Alongside profiles of the usual suspects of dictators, presidents, and guerrillas are profiles of priests, writers, artists, and activists whose ideas have influenced the region's history and defined its character.

WHOSE HISTORY?

The conceptual inspiration for this book lies in Mexican historian Enrique Krauze's *Redeemers*, which I have taught in my Politics of the Americas course at Davidson College for over a decade. In the book, Professor Krauze attempts to get to the root of the Latin American political mind via twelve profiles of major figures who lived during the late nineteenth and twentieth centuries. It's a *tour de force* of scholarship and exquisite writing and an excellent forum for debates about the various political currents at play.

This book includes many of the figures profiled by Krauze but broadens the canvas both in terms of the number of biographical sketches (fifty-two) and the span of history considered, from 1492 to the present day, allowing the reader to trace across centuries and nations the influence of certain individuals, who, for better or worse, left an indelible imprint on their time and societies. Beginning with Columbus may appear to some a crude marker to start an exploration of Latin America's political history, ignoring the millennia of sophisticated civilizations that existed prior, but it remains an inescapable (and tragic) fact that the *conquistadores* effectively destroyed the preexisting political architecture of Latin America. However, as will be seen again and again in the profiles, the precolonial heritage continued to form a potent political rallying cry during the colonial era—a story that is arguably less well-known than the conquest itself. For this reason, although the book begins in 1492, its roots go back much further.

What emerges from this polyphonic cast is a region that appears to be in ceaseless conversation with itself over its past, present, and future, reusing and reinventing a potent dictionary of symbols and ideas. We see eighteenth-century indigenous heroes like Túpac Amaru II invoked by twentieth-century Marxist groups, petroleum-fueled autocrats summoning the ghost of Simón Bolívar, and populist dictators flying the flag of an anti-*yanqui* bandit, Augusto Sandino. Unless we understand this political language, the true undercurrents of how power is used and abused in Latin America will remain obscure.

Profiling historical figures is not without its methodological hazards, of course. For centuries, history has been dominated by the "Great Man" approach, which sought to understand seminal changes as the consequence of the herculean efforts of a small pool of people—usually white, usually European, inevitably male. History has since developed to recognize the vastly more intricate and numerous factors at play, and new theoretical frameworks have helped unlock new perspectives and narratives related to race, gender, and economics that have long been neglected or downplayed. It is here that a dual focus—power *and* ideas—is most liberating, for it recognizes the contributions made by those who have long been denied access to institutional corridors of power, yet whose ideas can have a huge political impact, resonating across centuries and national borders.

It is especially crucial, given the long tradition of omission, to recognize the transformative role women have frequently played in Latin America's political development—often against impossibly daunting odds. Take, for instance, Guatemalan activist Rigoberta Menchú, winner of the Nobel Peace Prize and advocate of indigenous rights, or the fearless women of the *Plaza de Mayo* movement in Argentina, who overcame persecution to protest the "disappearances" that took place during the so-called Dirty War (1976–1982) and became a symbol of the global human rights movement in the late 1970s. And of course, some women have managed to achieve a level of fame and political influence that rivals their male counterparts, most notably Eva "Evita" Perón in mid-twentieth century Argentina, whose popular appeal and public works underwrote the success of the ideology known as Peronism.

Forging Latin America also highlights those whose influence has also been diminished or ignored by traditional categorizations of power and ideas, such as Toussaint Louverture, the redoubtable Black former enslaved person who led a revolution on the French colony of Saint-Domingue that helped create the modern state of Haiti. Chapters on Argentine Jorge Mario Bergoglio (later Pope Francis) and the martyred Salvadoran Archbishop Óscar Romero highlight the complex role the Roman Catholic Church has played in the region's history, at times acquiescent with repressive rightist regimes while at other times preaching forms of revolutionary "liberation theology" that on occasion echoed Marxist concerns regarding social inequality and repression. And then there are figures who stand opposed to or outside of the traditional power structures altogether, like Pablo Escobar, the Colombian drug lord whose vast wealth, political influence, and violent proclivities dramatically warped governance in Colombia, and who ushered in a new type of actor in Latin America's power dynamics.

As per Rivera, artists (including Rivera and Kahlo) and writers are also included, for their contribution is often to show a country what it is—and where it is failing. Two literary titans, Gabriel García Márquez and Mario Vargas Llosa, have often taken power in Latin America as their theme, and often written about it from close personal experience (García Márquez was a friend of Castro; Vargas Llosa ran for the presidency of Peru). Latin America also has a towering tradition of political writing that seeks to scrutinize what Latin America should stand for (such as José Enrique Rodó's anti-North American treatise *Ariel*) and challenge who should be represented (such as José Carlos Mariátegui's 1928 *Seven Interpretive Essays on Peruvian Reality*, which changed the perception of the Aymara and Inca indigenous peoples in Peru).

This book does not claim to be comprehensive, nor can it include all the figures who have made a significant impression on shaping Latin America—such a project would be vastly, perhaps infinitely longer. There are omissions of individuals some might argue deserve their place in this telling of Latin American history, such as Mexico's Pancho Villa and Chileans Pablo Neruda and Gabriela Mistral. Rather than produce an exhaustive catalog, this book instead aims to be illustrative of the diversity and variety of actors who have crossed the stage of this sometimes star-crossed continent. While scholars of Latin America might learn from it—especially outside their areas of specialization—the book is intended primarily for the general reader with little or only middling knowledge of Latin American history and politics.

When reading these profiles, one point that must be stressed is the need to acknowledge our own biases, especially if we are unfamiliar with Latin

America and judge developments by, say, North American political orthodoxies (although the erratic presidency of Donald Trump may have made this a less demanding task). In this regard, understanding the local and historical context is crucial if we are to truly understand why figures perceived as repressive were sometimes embraced with open arms (because, for instance, they brought improved security or stability to a country), or why there has been resistance to certain international institutions (such as the International Monetary Fund), which we might consider trustworthy promoters of economic development. It is also instructive to consider how events that originate from the Northern Hemisphere are read and manifest themselves in the south, particularly that of the US-led War on Drugs.

LATIN AMERICA, NEW AND OLD

We must not allow our historically minded approach to somehow prevent us from seeing all that is new in Latin America in the twenty-first century. Images of, say, world-beating high-tech startups in São Paulo, Brazil, should eradicate any notion that Latin America was and thus will always be a "Banana Republic," in which civil strife, poverty, and charismatic dictators known as *caudillos* hold sway from presidential balconies. This is not your father's—or your grandfather's!—Latin America.

But it would also be inaccurate to draw a hard line between a "new" and "old" Latin America. In a 2017 article, Dawisson Belém Lopes deplored "the recycling of old ideas" in contemporary Latin America, yet as these profiles show, it is astonishing how many "old ideas" have been in play in every century, and how the "recycling" process never fails to infuse them with life, urgency, and relevance to contemporary political situations, often through synthesis with new ideas. This book urges readers to visit the past with open eyes to see this history for what it was, but also for how it shaped and explains the region's contemporary nature, especially related to politics.

We begin our sketches with the life of the late fourteenth- and early fifteenth-century Italian explorer Amerigo Vespucci, who highlights the extent to which the term "America" is a nexus for competing ideas about power and identity that would form a recurring note over the region's history. Lacking Columbus's history-shifting fame (or infamy), Vespucci's words, imagination, and communication skills led his name to be attached to the mighty "fourth part" of the world.

I
COLONIAL

1

Amerigo Vespucci

"Half the World Baptized with His Dishonest Name"

Amerigo Vespucci's deeds cannot compete with the pantheon of explorers who set out for the Americas in the fifteenth and sixteenth centuries, yet in one aspect he outstrips them all. His vividly written accounts of his adventures—which some have claimed were fabricated, in whole or in part—saw him become the de facto chronicler of the Explorer Age. His writings ended up on the desk of a pair of cartographers then engaged in drawing up a new map of the world incorporating the part "discovered" by Columbus and his associates. Casting about for a name for this new land, they cited Vespucci's accounts—and so "America" was born.

As we chart Latin America's subsequent history, it is instructive to remember that part of its name is associated with one not known for daring feats of arms or the exercise of power and dominion, but for a knack for exciting the imagination and reaching outside the traditional avenues of authority to effect a transformative change. It was an ability that would be used again and again by a range of actors, great and small, in the centuries-long struggle over the identity of this mighty land, both among those descended from the Conquistadores and those whose lands had been seized.

OTRO MUNDO

On March 4, 1493, a Spanish ship, captained by the Genoese sailor Cristoforo Colombo, put in at Lisbon, Portugal, somewhat worse for wear after a stormy month-long Atlantic voyage. But despite appearances, this was a triumphant return: Christopher Columbus—as he is now better known—brought news of a massive archipelago he had "discovered" on the eastern fringes of Asia.

Columbus quickly sent word to his Spanish patrons, King Ferdinand I of Aragon and Queen Isabella II of Castille, who, while delighted, did not view the report as anything especially significant. Ships had been locating new islands throughout the Atlantic for at least a century, so it was logical, and almost expected, that intrepid explorers such as Columbus would discover more. As author Toby Lester explained, even if the Genoese sailor had made it to the Indies (an old name for Asia), this would not have increased Europe's "geographical horizons." He expands, "By sailing west to what appeared to be the Indies (but in actuality were the islands of the Caribbean), he had confirmed an ancient theory that nothing but a small ocean separated Europe from Asia. Columbus had closed a geographical circle, it seemed—making the world smaller, not larger."

But by the time of his Fourth Voyage in 1502, Columbus was very likely aware that he had encountered an *"otro mundo"* between Europe and Asia, not the Indies. Historians are not in full agreement on what Columbus thought, but a portion of the evidence bolstering this interpretation comes from the Third Voyage, in 1498. While sailing near modern-day Venezuela, Columbus remarked that "I have come to believe that this is a mighty continent which was hitherto unknown."

THE GREAT OPPORTUNIST

Colonial ventures usually impose the name of the "discoverer" onto the "discovered," regardless of whether people were living there beforehand or not. Yet in the case of America, there is an intriguing anomaly. Columbus's name lives on in Colombia, but the vast land to the west of Europe and Africa takes its name from Amerigo Vespucci, a Florentine merchant, explorer, and navigator.

On the face of it, Vespucci appears to have been a bit player in the grand undertakings. Historians debate just exactly how many voyages Vespucci made across the Atlantic. He claimed four, spanning 1497 through 1504, but only the first two expeditions are documented, and even in these two it is not at all clear what Vespucci contributed. Certainly, he pales in comparison with the pantheon of Columbus, Vasco da Gama, Balboa, and Magellan—all history-changing explorers who fall squarely in the "Great Man" tradition. This thesis, developed in the nineteenth century and most associated with Scottish philosopher Thomas Carlyle, posits that history is determined by the necessary and outsized actions of individuals (today, to eliminate the gender question, some scholars call it the "Big Beast of History") who, born with characteristics like courage and intellect, make the events bend to them, not the other way around. "The history of the world is but the biography of great men," Carlyle wrote in his 1840 tome, *On Heroes, Hero-Worship, and the Heroic in History*.

Vespucci was not what Carlyle might have termed a "Great Man," but he was good at storytelling. His best-selling series of letters from 1503 to 1505—scribed by him (or ascribed to him) and published as booklets—regaled readers with scintillating descriptions of exploration and discovery. In *Mundus Novus* ("New World")—widely printed and voraciously read throughout Europe—Vespucci described a 1501 voyage sponsored by Lisbon in which he sailed alongside a massive mainland unshown on contemporary maps. Like Columbus, Vespucci believed that the newly discovered land spanning thousands of miles south of the Equator was not part of Asia but an entirely new continent, which he called "Terra Nova":

> In the past, I have written to you in rather ample detail about my return from those new regions . . . and which can be called a new world, since our ancestors had no knowledge of them, and they are entirely new matter to those who hear about them. Indeed, it surpasses the opinion of our ancient authorities, since most of them assert that there is no continent south of the equator. . . . But I have discovered a continent in those southern regions that is inhabited by more numerous peoples and animals than in our Europe, or Asia or Africa.

The two explorers had come to similar conclusions, but Vespucci had the readers, and crucially, among those readers were two cartographers who were working on a new map.

A REVOLUTIONARY MAP

In the first years of the 1500s, sponsored by René II, Duke of Lorraine, a group of scholars assembled in a town not far from Strasburg, France. Their task was to publish a long overdue update of *Cartography*, the seminal work of Ptolemy (c. 100–170 CE), using degrees of latitude and longitude to map the known world.

Two of this project's collaborators—Martin Waldeseemüller, a cartographer, and the young Alsatian Matthias Ringmann, who dabbled in Ptolemy's classical geography—published a book they acknowledged was deeply influenced by their recent reading of Vespucci's chronicles. The 103-page book, written in Latin, was called *Introduction to Cosmography* and was published in 1507. The book contained some explanatory text stating that it was based on Vespucci's recent letters, Ptolemy's foundations, and new regional charts of the lands explored by Columbus and others. For this New World, the author, likely Ringmann, concluded, "It is found to be surrounded on all sides by the ocean." In a late chapter, the author declared:

> a fourth part has been discovered by Amerigo Vespucci (as will be heard in what follows). Since both Asia and Africa received their names from women, I do not see why anyone should rightly prevent this [new part] from being called Amerigen—the land of Amerigo, as it were—or America, after its discoverer, Americus, a man of perceptive character.

Toby Lester wonders, "How strange. With no fanfare, near the end of a minor Latin treatise on cosmography, a nameless 16th-century author briefly stepped out of obscurity to give America its name—and then disappeared again."

The book made repeated references to an attached world map that included the fourth part of the world. This was Waldseemüller's large wall-size map, the not-pithily titled *Universal Geography According to the Tradition of Ptolemy and the Contributions of Amerigo Vespucci and Others*—or what history now calls the "Waldseemüller map." Measuring four-and-a-half by eight feet and divided into twelve square sheets, and painstakingly carved from woodblock plates, the exquisite work was probably one of the largest of its time. The map gave Europeans a visual sense of the revolutionary interpretation of this four-part world. Much was patently recognizable and logical for readers: Europe and North Africa (right out of Ptolemy); Asia (from Marco Polo and Ptolemy); and Africa (from Portuguese ocean maps). But on one side of the map was an entirely novel proposition. Here is Lester, "Rising out of the formerly uncharted waters of the Atlantic, stretching almost from the map's top to its bottom, was a strange new landmass, long and thin and mostly blank—and there, written across what is known today as Brazil, was a strange new name: 'America.'"

The map originally had a printing of one thousand copies and was widely studied and emulated. In the next decades, cartographers copied the "America" designation. In his 1538 map, seminal Flemish cartographer Gerardus Mercator used the term "America" to christen the two continents—not just the southern section—with the labels: North America and South America.

The Waldseemüller Map. It is also the first map to depict a separate and full Western Hemisphere. It is often referred to as America's Birth Certificate. (Library of Congress Prints and Photographs Division, Washington, DC)

The Waldseemüller Map. This illustration shows a section from sheet #3 out of the massive twelve-sheet map. *(Library of Congress Prints and Photographs Division, Washington, DC)*

Vespucci almost certainly was never aware of the honor, seeing as the book had not yet made it to the Iberian Peninsula by the time of his death in 1512. That said, he had done well out of the expedition business, becoming the principal navigator for Spain's House of Trade of the Indies in Seville. But his historical legacy has been more complicated: starting in the 1500s and continuing through the present, the veracity of the extent of his transatlantic expeditions and even the authorship of some or all of the post-Atlantic crossings letters have been questioned.

Outspoken Spanish bishop Bartolomé de las Casas excoriated Vespucci as a charlatan who gained fame at the expense of Columbus (see Chapter 2, "Bartolomé de las Casas, *A Short Account of the Destruction of the Indies*"). Centuries later, Ralph Waldo Emerson labeled Vespucci a "thief" and "pickle dealer" who was able to get "half the world baptized with his dishonest name." Most interestingly, Waldseemüller made other New World maps, but henceforth labeled the fourth part "Terra Nova" (New World), never again using America or depicting the region with water on all sides, prompting some scholars to think these were his colleague's ideas. In 1516, Waldseemüller even offered an apology that may refer to his 1507 map:

We will seem to you, reader, previously to have diligently presented and shown a representation of the world that was filled with error, wonder, and confusion. ... As we have lately come to understand, our previous representation pleased very few people. Therefore, since true seekers of knowledge rarely color their words in confusing rhetoric, and do not embellish facts with charm but instead with a venerable abundance of simplicity, we must say that we cover our heads with a humble hood.

After the first decades following publication, copies of the map either disintegrated or were replaced by more accurate ones, so that by the end of the sixteenth century it appeared that the 1507 map had disappeared. By the 1890s, right around the time of the four-hundredth anniversary commemoration of Columbus's first crossing, the quest to find this "cartographical Holy Grail" was afoot. "No lost maps have ever been sought for so diligently as these," Britain's *Geographical Journal* wrote at the time. In 1901, a forty-four-year-old Austrian priest and history and geography buff, Father Joseph Fischer, who had for a good while already scoured public and private libraries across Europe to locate discarded or forgotten old maps, struck gold in a tower of Waldburg-Wolfegg Castle in Germany. Fischer had found a copy of the map that had originally belonged to the Nuremberg scholar Joannes Schöner before being acquired by the Waldburg-Wolfegg family and transferred to the castle, where it lay undisturbed got more than 350 years.

Reports at the time give an idea of the excitement surrounding this seismic discovery. "Geographical students in all parts of the world have awaited with the deepest interest details of this most important discovery," the *Geographical Journal* exclaimed, in early 1902, "but no one was probably prepared for the gigantic cartographical monster which Prof. Fischer has now awakened from so many centuries of peaceful slumber." A few months later, the *New York Times* celebrated: "There has lately been made in Europe one of the most remarkable discoveries in the history of cartography."

It took another century for the world to see the renowned map. It is currently housed at the Library of Congress, which, after protracted negotiations, purchased what had once been the most-searched-for map in history for the tidy sum of $10 million from the Waldburg-Wolfegg family and Berlin in 2003. Four years later, on April 30, 2007, just about five hundred years after the original was completed, Angela Merkel, chancellor of Germany, concluded the formal transfer of the map to the US government. The map is now on permanent display in the Library of Congress's palatial Jefferson Building, the focal object in the exhibition, "Exploring the Early Americas."

Of course, outside the Jefferson Building, Vespucci's name also lives on in our maps today. In the context of our history of Latin America, his role may seem merely etymological, yet his life also demonstrates the power of ideas to capture the imagination and change the course of history. Columbus may have been "first," but it was Vespucci who would have the last word.

2

Bartolomé de las Casas

A Short Account of the Destruction of the Indies

Oh, would that I could describe even one hundredth part of the afflictions and calamities wrought among these innocent people by the benighted Spanish!

—*Bartolomé de las Casas*

In 1511, Spanish commander Diego Velázquez left Hispaniola (the island that today comprises the Dominican Republic and Haiti) for Cuba. His goal was to defeat and enslave members of Taíno indigenous tribes (between one and four million of whom lived on Hispaniola, Cuba, and throughout the Caribbean) and find treasure, namely gold. A Taíno *cacique* (chief) known as Hatuey had prior fled Hispaniola for Cuba, along with hundreds of fellow tribespeople, to escape the pending Spanish wrath. Cornered and desperate, Hatuey used military smarts to evade the relentless Spanish pursuit and even killed eight enemies in the process. On February 2, 1512, however, Spanish conquistadors finally caught the mighty chief and sentenced him to death. Before the execution, a Spanish priest inquired if Hatuey would acknowledge Jesus Christ as his savior; if so, his soul would reach heaven. "Are there people like you in heaven?" responded Hatuey, to which the friar replied in the affirmative. Then, Hatuey rejoined, he'd rather go to hell, as there he would not be among such evil men.

Velázquez may have become Cuba's first governor, but it is Hatuey who is memorialized as Cuba's original national hero. And Hatuey's savage assassination would have an intense, life-altering impact on history's most famous chronicler of conquistador brutality: the Spanish friar Bartolomé de las Casas, who would become a fierce critic of the imperial project and its devastating impact on indigenous tribes.

EARLY FORAYS

Born in Seville in 1484, Bartolomé's upbringing was anything but radical or revolutionary. His father, Pedro de las Casas, was a prosperous trader whose sizable income allowed Bartolomé to study Latin and the humanities at university, as opposed to a merchant vocation like his father. Pedro and a couple of his uncles were actually on board with Columbus during the second voyage in late 1493, although history has lost any sense of the role they played in either the voyage or after landing in the Caribbean. One account describes Pedro bringing an Indian youth back to Spain so that his ten-year-old son would have a friend, but Bartolomé turned him over to Spanish officials so that he could return home to "the Indie" (the generic Iberian term for the Western Hemisphere at the time).

Then, in 1502, at the age of eighteen, Bartolomé bid farewell to Spain and, with 2,500 fellow fortune and adventure seekers, set off for the Indies on the flotilla of Nicolás de Ovando, a solider who had been dispatched to serve as the new governor of Hispaniola. Upon arrival, he was greeted by Iberian settlers, who told him "You have arrived at a good moment . . . there is to be a war against the Indians and we will be able to take many slaves." As Las Casas reflected bitterly decades later, "This news produced a great joy in the ship."

Despite a greater interest in learning the language Taíno, reading theology, and getting to know his new island home, Bartolomé's initial employment on the island was aiding his father's firm in selling supplies to the conquistadors now plundering other Caribbean islands. After about five years, Las Casas returned to Europe and was ordained in Rome as a deacon, but still full of wanderlust, he sailed back to Hispaniola, where he likely became the first person to receive holy orders (between 1510 and 1513) in the New World. In these early years in the Western Hemisphere, Las Casas came into contact with many of the most lionized conquistadors of the time, such as Hernán Cortés and Pedro de Alvarado. Serving as a chaplain, Las Casas participated in the invasion and pacification of nearby Cuba—the campaign led by Diego Velázquez and Pánfilo de Narváez, which resulted in Hatuey's execution, among myriad other abominations. Las Casas witnessed another especially wretched episode right around the same date of Hatuey's killing, described by the priest here. "On one occasion, when the locals had come some ten leagues out from a large settlement in order to receive us and regale us with victuals and others gifts, and had given us loaves and fishes and any other foodstuffs they could provide, the Christians were suddenly inspired by the Devil and, without the slightest provocation, butchered, before my eyes, some three thousand souls—men, women, and children—as they sat there in front of us. I saw that day atrocities more terrible than any living man has ever seen nor ever thought to see."

REALIZING THE HORROR

Las Casas, now based in Cuba, played a dual role for the next couple of years. The priestly side of him was baptizing indigenous babies or converting communities to Christianity through words and acts of compassion. But Las Casas was also a beneficiary of the *encomienda* system, under which indigenous tribes were forced to provide labor in "return" for the conquistador's "civilizing" Christian program, which almost invariably devolved into slavery. Las Casas had been awarded Indians and land in both Hispaniola and Cuba (including a large encomienda near the Cuban port of Xagúa) for his loyal service, and legions of indentured servants toiled in the mines and plantations day and night to pad the priest's wealth and status. Indeed, for over a decade, and despite some of his acts of kindness, he very much "lived the life of an early Caribbean conqueror, watching indigenous people die by the dozen from exploitation and disease."

Many subsequent accounts of this critical period assumed that Las Casas had a Damascene moment in which he, all at once, realized the totality and morality of the horror that was the Spanish conquest. Instead, his conversion was far more gradual, although at least one of the Spanish massacres he witnessed in Cuba in 1511 undoubtedly weighed on his conscience, moving him from a questioning encomendero/colonizer into a fierce guardian of New World Indians. He also listened to and absorbed the increasingly fiery, unrepentant words of a small coterie of radical (at least for the day) Dominican friars who had come to believe that the Spanish conquest and colonization was, in historian Lawrence A. Clayton's deft phrasing, "where justice, truth, and morality were bent and mangled by greed, prejudice, and immorality." Especially influential were the sermons of a Spanish Dominican priest, Antonio Montesinos, denouncing imperial excesses and sins. In 1511, Montesinos lamented the once "paradisiacal" lands of Hispaniola, now turned upside down by the conquerors:

With what right, and with what justice do you keep these poor Indians in such cruel and horrible servitude? By what authority have you made such detestable wars against these people who lived peacefully and gently on their own lands? Are these not men? Do they not have rational souls? Are you not obliged to love themselves?

The turning point arrived in 1514, when Las Casas, then around forty years old, delivered an excoriating sermon on Pentecost Sunday, condemning the Iberian handling of the region's native population. To back up his nascent theology and newly vocal morality, the priest renounced his encomienda (and thus his enslaved people, whom he returned to the governor of Santo Domingo) and began, with swelling ire and ardor, advocating on behalf of natives in front of local colonial authorities.

In 1515, now back in Spain, Las Casas continued to shift his attention from specific conquistador atrocities in the islands of the Indies to a broader indictment of the encomienda system itself. "The reason for the death and destruction of so many souls at Christian hands: gold, and the attempt to get rich quickly." Not surprisingly, Las Casas's denunciations of the moral inferno—now arguing that the conquest writ large was a sin—enraged local colonial officials and encomenderos, who subsequently relayed their misgivings to Madrid.

In 1516, the maverick priest received the title "Protector of the Indians" from Cardinal Francisco Jiménez de Cisneros, but in truth there was little Las Casas could do to rein in the unaccountable conquistadors. These rogue actors scoffed at lawful and religious authority, and "as lions, and tigers, hungry for a time," to use Las Casas's own words, they consumed the indigenous peoples. Constraints were long overdue and needed to come straight from the king.

Las Casas and his crusade caught a break in 1520 when Charles V (Charles I of Spain) offered Las Casas an audience to counter the allegations his colonial enemies had made against him. It was here in the royal court, where both supporters and critics of Las Casas' reform agenda were present and attentive, that Las Casas contended that the era of military occupation in the New World empire had expired, making it a necessary time for pacific conversion of the local populations. Brilliantly, over the next decades, Las Casas exploited the Spanish monarchs' own identities as upholders of Christendom, working on the idea that the conquest was outside the mandates of God.

In 1537, Las Casas's protracted campaign had a breakthrough when Pope Paul III issued an official edict that provided significant moral backing for the reform movement. The edict—known as a papal bull—clarified the Church's stance on the natives: the Indians were in fact "true men," and not subhuman as was often believed at the time, and thus were able to be legitimate Christians and, not insignificantly, hold property. Yet, given the reactionary customs and climate amid the encomendero ranks, slavery, and subjugation remained in both Spanish and Portuguese America.

Indeed, meaningful improvements in the treatment of indigenous communities were absent, even though Las Casas relentlessly described the ongoing barbarity of the settlers to an aghast royal court: "One day . . . the Spanish dismembered, beheaded or raped 3,000 Indian people. They cut off the legs of the children that ran before them. They poured people full of boiling soup. I saw all the above things . . . and numberless others." The Indians were handled with "strange cruelty," he said, with the colonizers feeding infants to dogs, hunting Indians for sport, and burning men alive. "They think no more of killing ten or twenty Indians for a pastime, or to test the sharpness of their swords."

But Las Casas could not see that, cruel as the conquistadors were, the majority of the devastation wrought by the colonizers did not come from their brutality, but from their pathogens. Like so many other Europeans arriving, he was unable to imagine the cumulative impact of these European illnesses—smallpox and measles—on human beings without prior exposure. From 1492 to 1600, the indigenous population in the Americas plummeted from likely well over fifty million to less than five million.

Despite the carnage, it took until 1542 for the king to act decisively with his "New Laws of the Indies for the Good Treatment and Preservation of the Indians"—and even then, his concerns may have been more realpolitik than altruistic, for amending his strategy, Las Casas had been holding up the notion that the encomenderos were aspiring to a rival, Indies-based variant of the Spanish aristocracy. To get back at the rogue colonists, the New Laws proscribed Indian slavery and immediately circumscribed new assignments of encomiendas, then phased them out entirely so they could no longer be inherited.

Sometime in 1544, in the aftermath of the New Laws, Las Casas voyaged to New Spain to become the Bishop of Chiapas (today's Guatemala and the Mexican state of Chiapas) which gave him a perch from which to oversee the new policies. Legend is that Rome offered him the bishopric of Peru, the most illustrious post in the Indies, but he declined, selecting instead one of New Spain's most impoverished regions. The Chiapas adventure, however, proved short-lived and exasperating. The New Laws proclamation had sparked manifest insurrection throughout the Spanish Indies, and Las Casas raised the temperature with his criticisms of Spain's claims of legitimacy in the New World. In one instance, Las Casas denied final absolution to Spanish settlers who did not liberate their slaves or pay indemnities, prompting death threats. Other priests, in cahoots with encomenderos, flouted his rule. Don Antonio de Mendoza, viceroy of New Spain, condemned Las Casas's subversion in stark terms, and it was not long after that Las Casas was recalled to Spain.

THE GREAT DEBATE OF VALLADOLID, 1550–1551

King Charles V was profoundly influenced by Las Casas's moral protestations, but Las Casas was not the only voice in the room. Other court advisors, like the eminent jurist Juan Ginés de Sepúlveda, were pushing an entirely different, and more pernicious, moral universe for Indian treatment. With so much contention in the air, the ruler, in 1550, called for a halt to new military campaigns in the Indies until the "conquests may be conducted justly and with security of conscience."

In April 1550, the king summoned a *junta* (council) of a dozen or so illustrious theologians and jurists in the northern Spanish city of Valladolid. Through an examination of just wars and Aristotelian logic as it related to American Indians, the goal was to resolve the conquest abuse and Indian rights matter once and for all. This convention turned into the "great debate of Valladolid," as history labeled it, between two giants, Sepúlveda and Las Casas.

The two renowned theologians never actually debated face to face but instead made their cases individually before the royal tribunal. Sepúlveda, who possessed a keen intellect and host of well-placed supporters at the court, argued that the conquest, slavery, and forceful conversion in the Indies was just through a series of points: the indigenous groups had committed sins by their worship of pagan deities and other inhuman practices like cannibalism and human sacrifice; the Indians' "natural rudeness and inferiority" aligned with the Aristotelian concept of "natural slavery" (or some humans being born for slavery); conquest was an expeditious and thorough way of converting Indians to Christ; subjugating the Indian tribes allowed the Spanish to protect the weakest in their ranks. Six years prior, Sepúlveda had written *Democrates Alter* (or, the Just Causes for War against the Spanish Indians), which became a seminal volume and the basis of much of what the scholar laid out in Valladolid—essentially that Indians were pre-social beings with no rights. Works like *Democrates Alter* were also used by colonizers in the New World to morally justify the status quo.

In a characteristically impassioned manner, Las Casas took five days to read his long-winded *Apologética historia* to the royal tribune, which served as his rebuttal to his brilliant adversary. The natives were not morally inferior to Europeans, but rather were human beings able to be artistically and spiritually developed despite their patent barbaric customs—and thus merited human rights.

As the debate moved into the following year before concluding, neither side was declared the official winner. However, despite the inconclusive outcome, a good share of the judges backed Las Casas's emotive, visceral case—including

Fray Bartolomé de las Casas, standing on steps of despoiled Aztec temple; dead Indian man and weeping woman at his feet. *(Library of Congress Prints and Photographs Division, Washington, DC)*

those eager to check encomendero impunity as much as promote indigenous rights—although fear of widespread opposition might have also driven their decision not to issue a judgment. Two decades later, in 1573, Philip II's ordinance using terms such as "pacification" instead of "conquest" in respect to Spanish colonization of the Philippine Islands channeled Las Casas's side from Valladolid. This well-meaning change in language, of course, would have been infinitely more consequential had the "age of great conquests" not already expired by the last decades of the sixteenth century.

DESTRUCTION OF THE INDIES

In 1551, Las Casas entered the San Gregorio monastery in Valladolid, bringing to a close his vast public career. But his cloistered existence was an especially productive time for his scholarship, including the weighty tome, *History of the Indies*, which would be officially published in 1552. Las Casas maintained a furious pace of new books and finished manuscripts long ago started. In 1552, without requesting permission from the Inquisition, Las Casas published *A Short Account of Destruction of the Indies*. Bypassing the Inquisition usually would have resulted in large sanctions for the author and publishing house, but it was likely Casas's seasoned standing, now at the ripe age of sixty-seven, that allowed him to escape this outcome.

Destruction of the Indies is known to history as one of the world's first books to document, firsthand, the Spanish conquest's destruction. Scholars today generally agree that *Destruction of the Indies*'s poignancy and timelessness lies in its implicit and explicit elevation of fundamental human rights. Written over a decade, it was an early example of what would later become known as bearing witness: "So far as to not keep criminal silence concerning the ruin of numberless souls and bodies that these persons cause," Las Casas scribed, "I have decided to print some of the innumerable instances I have collected in the past and can relate with truth." Las Casa also considered the endeavor his patriotic duty. "My deep love of Castille," he wrote at the end of *Destruction of the Indies*, "has also been a spur, for I do not wish to see my country destroyed as a divine punishment for sins against the honor of God and the true Faith."

Ultimately, Las Casas intended the book to serve as a protest in a moment when it seemed that the ravages of Spanish imperialism might be remedied and that an "earthly paradise" of natives and European settlers could still be realized, yet by the time the book was read in the 1550s, there was not much of an Eden left in the New World. Here is historian Anthony Pagden: "The Indians, their culture all but eradicated or forgotten, were already faced with the need either to become a lowly, marginalized part of the European colonial system or, as they continue to do in increasing numbers, to perish altogether."

Critics at this time in Spain and the Americas castigated the Dominican friar both for treason and for resorting to fiction and hyperbole in his depictions of atrocities, but the book found a large audience in Europe. The work was widely disseminated in translation in the key European empires England, France, and the Netherlands—there were eighteen Dutch editions alone. Of particular salience, Protestant enemies of Catholicism saw the book as proof-positive of the innate nefariousness of Spanish culture and colonies: the so-called Black Legend. Largely a product of Anglo-Dutch propaganda, the Black Legend held that Spain's conquest and colonization were cruel and inhumane, a tendency that was associated with the colonizers' Catholic faith. Las Casas would have been appalled that the Protestants, a group whom he loathed as heretics, had used his well-intended book to impugn the Catholic Church.

MORAL COMET WITH A COSMIC FLAW

Las Casas in his twilight years never ceased to be a voice for Indian humanity, even if these were not happy years given his legions of enemies at the royal court. And his legacy—as we will explore later—was inspiring, even centuries later during the Cold War, when idealistic and often radical men (and women) of the cloth became advocates of what is known as liberation theology. Las Casas himself was under no illusions that the work he had helped set in motion was finished. On his last day of life, in July 1566, he is reported to have expressed remorse for not having accomplished more for the Indians.

Yet other, more complicated aspects of his legacy must be told. During his campaign for reform, Las Casas fatefully put forth what he certainly must have assumed was an innocuous scheme in 1516, but one that would have lasting consequences. Regarding his vision of a new communal arrangement in the Indies, he said, "If necessary black slaves can be brought from Castile." Las Casas was certainly not alone in believing that Indians were morally superior to black Africans. The difference, though, was that Las Casas had already earned himself an outsized influence and thus his views carried more weight than others.

Two years later, Charles V approved the buying of enslaved people to be used in the New World. Decades hence, Las Casas would reverse his stance, but the damage was done. Religious scholar Martin Marty writes that the African slavery issue is a stark reminder that, even for the most dedicated "Lacasista," we must qualify the claims for "heroism or sainthood." Indeed, like so many historical figures (or any human, for that matter), he had his "cosmic flaw" or at least a cosmically flawed notion, one that is not especially easy for twenty-first-century readers to comprehend.

Still, it must be remembered that this relentless advocate for indigenous rights emerged at a time when the notion of dignity and equality for native peoples was unimaginable. One modern biographer, Lawrence Clayton, wrote that few figures had "flashed across human history" as Las Casas did. Here is the assessment of Professor Martin E. Marty:

> Balance is the last and least thing Las Casas sought. He was for justice, truth, and the rights of the Indians, and would stay around as long as it took to make his point. He would shout as loud as he thought necessary. He would cry not in sentimentality but in rage and sympathy as often as the tears would naturally well up, and he would plead even at the expense of his own dignity.

The largely self-educated Las Casas did not have the benefit of Enlightenment thinkers to help shape his still premodern views. A decided and valiant maverick and revolutionary who brilliantly elevated the Indians to the highest levels of the Spanish imperial project and Christian theology, Las Casas was also a monarchist who called for African slavery and never allowed that Indians could resist conversion to Christianity. He blasted Spanish conquest and cruelty, but not, as some of his fellow Dominicans did, the legitimacy of the Spanish Empire. Showing his conservative streak, he hit back at rebels whom he held undermined the "common reason of man." He went to his grave still maintaining that indigenous persons had freely relinquished their natural sovereignty to the Spanish monarch. Radical ideas, indeed, but this was a preternatural reformer, an institutionalist, and a believer in all things King and Cross. Perhaps the best categorization for Las Casas is that he was a "medieval prophet" who was one of the first to promote, albeit inconsistently, the modern idea of human rights.

3

Sor Juana Inés de la Cruz
Latin America's First Feminist

You men are such a foolish breed,
appraising with a faulty rule,
the first you charge with being cruel,
the second, easy, you decree.
—*Sor Juana Inés de la Cruz's poem, "Foolish Men," 1689*

On July 5, 1684, residents of Mexico City—the nucleus of the autocratic and theocratic viceroyalty of New Spain—came out to dance, sing, and toast the birthday of an especially special infant: José María Francisco de la Cera, the sole heir of the colony's *virey* (viceroy) and *virreina* (vicereine, or wife of the viceroy). One of New Spain's most storied voices, Sor Juana Inés de la Cruz, composed a *romance* (ballad) for the royal couple, a common custom at these sorts of regal celebrations. The nun's poem offered blessings for the child but also included a plea to cancel a prisoner's execution.

In directing her political agenda to the colony's top official, this fearless, worldly nun was punching above her weight—centuries above her weight, in fact. Through the course of her life, and especially through her pen, this brilliant autodidact confronted power and hypocrisy again and again, often in the service of elevating the condition and consciousness of her so-often-relegated fellow women. Toward the end of her life, she offered an impassioned public defense of the right of women to intellectual independence, foreshadowing Virginia Woolf's famous call for a "room of one's own." But as well as being an excellent candidate for the honor of being Latin America's first feminist, she was also a renowned poet and playwright whose fame spread across the Spanish world, although for most of her literary life she was ensconced within the stone walls of a convent in Mexico City, and her ideas and writings are still very much a part of the Mexico's literary fabric today.

A PRODIGY IS BORN

Born out of wedlock (a "natural" child, as the lingo of the time went) in either 1651 or, more likely, 1648 to a Creole (New World–born Spaniard) mother, Isabel Ramírez, and Spanish captain father, Pedro de Asbaje, Juana de Asbaje de Ramírez was the second of three daughters in a family of humble means. Growing up in her beloved maternal grandfather's hacienda near the pueblo of San Miguel de Nepantla, Juana was (by her own later account) reading and writing from an unusually early age, taught by her older sibling.

Being female, she was denied formal education, but despite this staggering impediment, she at least had access to the hacienda's library and made heavy use of it, devouring classic Greek and Latin tomes as well as the writings of the venerated Portuguese Jesuit theologian and philosopher, Father Antonio de Vieira. It was also at Nepantla that she picked up Nahuatl, the Aztec mother tongue, from the indigenous enslaved people living at the ranch. One family characteristic, unusual for the time, was the fortitude, autonomy, and spirit of its women, especially Isabel, who ran the family compound from when she inherited it from her father until her death three decades later.

After her grandfather died in 1656, her parents decided to send the gifted youth to Mexico City, where she could live with her mother's wealthy sister and her husband, who presented her at court. By 1664, her immense talents, charm, and arresting beauty had reached the attention of Antonio Sebastián Álvarez de Toledo, Marquis of Mancera and viceroy (1664–1673), and his wife the Doña Leonor de Carreto, or the *marquesa*, and this connection brought Juana into the heart of high society. The viceregal court in Mexico City was an especially artistic and learned spot of the so-called Spanish Golden Age when ornate Baroque painting, architecture, and music offered a lavish counterpoint to the stark Protestantism in other parts of Europe. The couple routinely held grand balls and soirees featuring philosophers, theologians, mathematicians, and historians. The Spanish royal pair invited Juana to live at the viceregal court as a lady-in-waiting of the marquesa. Bedazzled by Juana's brilliance, the marquesa became the precocious female poet's patron. Under the viceroys' tutelage, the burgeoning sage was able to hone her skills while charming the cultured court through bold sonnets, poems, and funeral elegies that earned her the sobriquets "the Tenth Muse" and "the Phoenix of Mexico."

Within a year, Juana composed a poem addressing the passing of Philip IV. At one point, likely in 1668, the marquis had her anomalous smarts confirmed by forty notable scholars who observed how readily she adroitly answered question after question.

IN SEARCH OF INDEPENDENCE

In another realm, Juana's next step would have been enrolling at a university, but women were proscribed. (She did attempt to dress up as a man, but the disguise failed.) The court priest and her confessor, Father Antonio Nuñez de Miranda, enlisted private tutors to continue Juana's education, including Latin. At this point, and in her own words, the adolescent had a "total disclination to marriage," preferring her desire "to have no fixed occupation which might curtail my freedom to study." Her wishes also reflected her not-inaccurate belief that entering into marriage would invariably entail a life of submission to her partner—and by extension, society.

An empathetic Father Núñez had a solution for Juana's distraught soul: pursuing life as a "wife of Christ" by joining a convent, as this would keep her away from matrimony and allow her to hone her literary gifts. In 1669, she entered the convent, the Barefoot Carmelites in Mexico City, but within three months Sor (Sister) Juana had had more than enough of the hyper-strict order, which had made her physically ill.

Not long after, on February 24, 1669, at not yet twenty-one she became a nun in the more liberal (read, less rigid) order of San Jerónimo in the Convent of Santa Paula, also in Mexico City, where she remained cloistered for the rest of her days as Sor Juana Inés de la Cruz. She even had the use of a mulatto servant and a capacious private two-floor cell—a far cry from her existence in the Carmelites' spartan quarters.

Ensconced at Santa Paula, Sor Juana passed her days in scholarly pursuits, reading and writing, teaching music and drama to girls at the convent school, and also found time to be the convent's accountant and archivist. She frequently hosted guests, including the marquise Leonor de Carreto, who remained an admirer and friend. Over the ensuing years and decades, and buoyed by her potent court sponsors whom she deftly utilized, Sor Juana painstakingly transformed her cell into one of the best private libraries in the Americas, a collection that included hundreds of books, as well as music and scientific instruments and works of art. Like the other nuns she could not

Sor Juana Inés de la Cruz. *(Library of Congress Prints and Photographs Division, Washington, DC)*

physically leave Santa Paula, but her insatiable mind's eye went outside the thick, cold walls any time she desired.

INTERNATIONAL FAME, FROM A CONVENT CELL

Sor Juana was dealt a disquieting setback in 1673 when she learned that the marquis and marquise had been summarily relieved of their duties. Worse was to come when that April, Doña Leonor de Carreto died during a provincial visit. Grief-stricken, Sor Juana scribed three baroque elegies on the sudden passing of her advocate, calling the fallen woman "Laura." Both elegy and a note, "On the Death of That Most Excellent Lady" reveal a level of intimacy that some scholars suggest indicates the couple's love was not entirely platonic. "Let them die with you, Laura, now you are dead, these longings that go out to you in vain, these eyes on whom you once bestowed a lovely light never to gleam again."

The royal couple was succeeded by Friar Payo Enríquez de Ribera, who enjoyed a cordial relationship with the vaulted nun. But a far more significant relationship prospered after 1680 when Don Tomás Antonio de la Cerda y Aragón, along with his wife, Doña María Luisa Manrique de Lara y Gonzaga, were installed as Spain's highest representatives. The viceregal couple, from especially rarefied Spanish aristocratic blood, soon took to the brilliant nun's vivacity and humanity and lavished her with sponsorship and protection.

Scholars consider the next half-decade or so Sor Juana's own "golden age," when she became a veritable literary star of the Iberian imperial realm from Quito to Buenos Aires, Madrid to Manila, half the Western World! And the variety of her literary work, according to Mexican novelist Octavio Paz who inked the seminal modern biography of our seventeenth-century protagonist, is mindboggling: "love poems, verses for songs and dance tunes, profane comedies, sacred poems, an essay in theology," among myriad others.

When the vicereine arrived back in Spain, she did not forget to bring along Sor Juana's works so that they were printed and disseminated. Philosophical and metaphysical, published in 1692, "First Dream" is widely considered Sor Juana's masterpiece. Almost one thousand lines long, "First Dream," while Baroque and thus abstruse, is concerned with the intellectual capacity of human beings. Or as Paz put it, the poem "is a confession that ends in an act of faith: not in knowing but in the desire to know."

Yet while Sor Juana furiously wrote for her royal audience, she wrote equally fervently for her own intellectual and emotional satisfaction. These were also the years when the nun broke away from her long-time confessor, Father Núñez de Miranda, who fiercely detested female education and edification; in fact, he even publicly censured Sor Juana, contending that her irrepressible learning jeopardized her ascension to journey to salvation (by this time the sisters had gained the right to sanction a confessor). In her steely missive to him, "Spirited Self-Defense," in 1681, Sor Juana advocated for her entitlement, as a woman, to be educated:

> Did not St. Catherine, St. Gertrude and my mother St. Paula study without harming their lofty contemplations, and was the latter's travail in the founding of convents impeded by her knowledge even of Greek? By having learned Hebrew? By having been instructed by my Father St. Jerome to understand and interpret Holy Writ, as the Saint himself tell us?

She was also acute on the possible real source of her confessor's ire: that she had dared express herself without seeking his prior permission: "The cause of your anger ... has been none other than the ability that God has given me in creating these wretched verses without asking permission from Your Reverence."

AN IMPASSIONED DEFENSE

The year 1690 proved to be a fateful one in Juana's remarkable life. She was swept up in a scandal after criticizing a niche theological argument made back in 1650, when a renowned Portuguese Jesuit theologian, Father António de Vieyra, whose works Sor Juana had first encountered in her childhood hacienda, delivered a sermon on "grace," the Christian concept of God's love to the unmerited. At an intellectual salon, Sor Juana outlined her disagreement with Father Vieryra over God's greatest gift to mankind, arguing (as she later expanded) that "God's greatest gift, in my opinion, was the negative benefits: that is, the benefits that God does not give us because He knows that we have to repay them."

For us contemporary readers this might seem like splitting hairs, but in the inflexible theological climate of the era, this alternate reading could easily be viewed as heresy. And while such comments might have passed in an intellectual salon, committing them to paper was another matter, although, in her defense, this was not Juana's idea. Don Manuel Fernández de Santa Cruz y Sahagún, the bishop of Puebla, was a confidant of Sor Juana, despite having a rich reputation for misogyny, and asked her to put her thoughts about Vieyra down on paper. Sor Juana duly produced the cutting, exquisite "Letter Worthy of Athena." Without Sor Juana's prior knowledge, the bishop published the letter and sent Sor Juana a copy.

A scandal erupted, magnified by Juana's fame, which ensured that more and more people (including powerful church and political figures) learned that she had attacked the illustrious Father Vieyra. Possibly encouraged by his superiors, Fernández de Santa Cruz (using the female pseudonym of "Sister Filotea," as though a woman was the best weapon to attack another woman) penned a public excoriation of Sor Juana, exhorting her to cease writing about such lofty matters. Those who continued to back her, on the other hand, lauded her grit and logic.

Before the publication of the letter, Sor Juana had been living her storied life, even if she had not ventured beyond Santa Paula's walls. Now she felt isolated and ridiculed, but equally (and characteristically) determined to fight her corner. Published in March 1691, the trenchant, exceptionally candid "Response to the Most Illustrious Sister Filotea de la Cruz" was Sor Juana's impassioned defense of her intellectual endeavors. (The letter also revealed her mortification about hearing that her original letter had been made public.) Citing historical examples such as Greek astronomer Hypatia of Alexandria, Juana's letter was a paean to women and their right to think, write, and publish their ideas—a veritable declaration of (female) intellectual independence. Part autobiography, the missive detailed her own innate "inclination to letters," as well as the obstacles she had had to overcome time and again, such as her illegitimate birth. As a child she was "inflamed by the desire to know how to read," and even abstained from eating cheese after someone told her "that it made one slow of wits."

Yet this history-altering correspondence also precipitated its author's uncharacteristic resignation to the (largely clerical) powers at hand. "You will command what I am to do," she instructed Sor Filotea de la Cruz, adding "I will weaken and dull the workings of my feeble reason." She would no longer write publicly, preside over poetry contests, or craft plays. And indeed by 1694, after signing several renunciations (one of them in blood!), a sorrowful Sor Juana ceased publishing and turned inward to singularly religious efforts, just as the Bishop of Puebla had urged.

On April 7, 1695, Sor Juana Inés de la Cruz died, just forty-seven years old (or forty-four, depending on which birth date is accepted), contracting typhoid while attending to stricken nuns during an epidemic that was ravaging the city. Her will, discovered later, asked for her books to be sold (some claim they were hawked before she passed away) and the revenue donated to aid the indigent. Her body was buried in the convent's graveyard.

The nun's epic intellectual journey might be encapsulated by one of the most enduring sentences she ever scribed, from "Response to Sor Filotea": "I suffer no blame, as I have no obligation; no discredit, as I have no possibility of triumphing and *ad impossibilita neme tenetur.*" ("No one is obliged to do the impossible.") Yet many would argue that she had achieved just that. Time and again she had challenged the standing male-monopolized intellectual backdrop of the Spanish-speaking Americas during the Golden Age and gained sizable acclaim in both the colonies and Spain itself. The remarkable nun left behind almost scores of published volumes she wrote, and (perhaps most impressively) remains widely read today; ask a Mexican scholar for a list of the nation's most famous bards, and Sor Juana will be on it. She is the greatest writer of the Spanish American colonization era.

But Sor Juana's legacy in Mexico is far more than literature; she adorns stamps and currency, and in 1979, the site of her convent, closed since the nineteenth century, was reopened as a university named in her honor. Her natal town is now called Nepantla de Sor Juana. Most of all, she is considered a thinker of singular significance, a feminist before the term was conceived. She is a testament to the power of ideas in and of themselves, outside of political power structures, and her courage in standing up to and flourishing in a male-dominated world was a truly revolutionary stance.

4

Túpac Amaru II and the Great Andean Rebellion

The years between 1780 and 1782 witnessed the apex of the North American revolution against the hated British monarch, King George III. Yet it is far less known that South America was also up in flames. Madrid, like London, faced losing one of its most lucrative and coveted foreign holdings. With the Spanish conquistador-led toppling of the formidable Incan empire in the 1530s and the subsequent unearthing of silver at the Andean lair of Potosí, Madrid had, via the viceroyalty of Peru, secured a steady stream of riches to underwrite its "empire of the Indians." But in November 1780, Madrid's hermetic grip was challenged by a minor Indian nobleman, José Gabriel Condorcanqui, later known as Túpac Amaru. While nominally declaring fidelity to both Christianity and the Spanish king, he began a campaign to fight back against colonial abuses and construct an "Andean Utopia" through the resurrection of Incan dominion.

And his was not the only insurgency. We will also see that a broader, overlapping "Great Andean Rebellion" was afoot in approximately two hundred thousand square miles of strategically vital lands at the heart of Spain's South American possessions. While there had been no shortage of uprisings and protests before, nothing had ever reached such scale before: by the time the rebellion was put down, as many as one hundred thousand Indians alone had been killed. But the mythology of its leaders would live on and become a potent force in the centuries that followed, both shaping the drive for independence from Spanish colonial rule and offering iconic examples of resistance.

MAN IN THE MIDDLE

José Gabriel was born in 1738 in the high-mountain city of Cuzco, the religious and political capital of the Incan empire which had fallen to Spanish conquistadores a little more than two centuries before. His father was a *cacique* (chief) in the Tinta region of Peru, serving as the intermediary between the Spanish colonial state and Indian communities. With their putative and manifest linkage to Incan lords, caciques were often perceived as "royal," or at least widely recognized as indigenous elites, although scholars debate as to whether Condorcanqui ("you are a condor," in Quechua) was a mixed-blood *mestizo* or pure-blood Incan.

Losing both his mother and father before he was a teenager, José Gabriel relied on relatives for his care, before embarking on a Jesuit education at the San Francisco de Borja academy, established to educate the sons of caciques, where he learned Latin and polished his Spanish. In his early twenties, José Gabriel had inherited the position of cacique, his new status and Jesuit education enabled him to shift effortlessly between the two worlds of Spanish and Incan languages and societies. After marrying the formidable Micaela Bastidas, Condorcanqui developed his reputation as a prosperous and influential merchant.

But he soon found himself in conflict with his colonial overloads and grew increasingly aghast at what he viewed as wanton abuse by the Spanish and a broader deterioration of the entire project of Spanish dominion and legitimacy in the colonies. As cacique, José Gabriel was responsible for enforcing the labor and tax burdens on the Indians, which were often brutally oppressive.

IBERIAN IMPERIOUSNESS, IBERIAN REFORM

It's worth reflecting that at this time the Spanish Empire in the Americas—and in the Andes in particular—was in a perilous condition, in part due to how the empire had been created in the first place. A key variance between their Portuguese counterparts in Africa and Asia, and to a lesser extent Brazil, Spanish colonizers were reluctant to limit their dominion to the coasts. Instead, they conquered and occupied inland indigenous cities like Cuzco and built other ones in their Iberian images, from Potosí to Zacatecas. Iberian-born colonial officials came by the thousands from Spain but so did merchants, proprietors, and adventure-seekers who sought only to "do the Americas." These settlers and bosses, over the decades and centuries, mixed with Indians, creating a new *mestizo* grouping. Over time the distinction between "colonizers and colonized" was blurred.

Both the Aztec and Inca empires, long before their Iberian conquerors arrived and colonized, practiced obligatory labor service, or tribute, and the Spanish proved more than willing to continue the tradition. The Spanish imposed their system of forced service—the *encomienda*—to build roads, citadels, churches, public buildings, and of course to work the hellish silver mines, but while this forced labor helped generate the vast wealth of empire, it was also necessary for the survival of the colonies, putting in place vital infrastructure. But there is no question that the system was heavily abused by the increasingly powerful *encomenderos*, and clamors for reforms grew louder. The encomienda was regulated and constrained (with a view to abolition) under the New Laws of 1542, before eventually being formally replaced by the *repartimiento* ("partition") in New Spain (*mita* in Peruvian Potosí) in about 1575 (although it had been in effect in places for decades). For many, however, it was the same system under a new name: while the new approach nominally made provision for limited, paid work, in practice it almost invariably devolved into forced labor.

In the eighteenth century, the Spanish crown enacted another series of reforms, known in Spain as the Bourbon Reforms (named after the ruling dynasty) and called the Pombaline Reforms in Brazil. The Bourbon monarchs had inherited, from the preceding Hapsburg dynasty, a legacy of highly baroque policies, a massively rich and potent Catholic Church, corruption (in the shape of tax evasion, illicit trade, nepotism, and embezzlement), and bloated bureaucracies. To remedy the situation, the Bourbon rulers passed a motley assortment of economic and political changes to bolster efficiencies and, of course, revenues, through increased indigenous taxes and compulsory labor.

Some of the "reforms," such as the crackdowns on caciques' autonomy, were clearly designed to reassert Madrid's control over its empire. Others, like replacing corrupt, rapacious, and once-invulnerable magistrates who ruled indigenous communities with seasoned administrators, were well intentioned and sometimes worked. But, paradoxically, this protracted effort to clean up, centralize, and modernize the colonial governance and economy ended up making the colonies more resentful. The Bourbon Reforms created a preference for Iberian-born Spaniards to govern the colonies, which meant that it was not just the overworked and overtaxed Indians who held a grudge or grievance, but also the New World–born Spaniards ("Creoles") class excluded from leadership positions.

All this time, tensions were brewing between the magistrates—already resented by the Creole elites for being Spain-born—and the caciques, fueled by the goods distribution system, which gave administrators a monopoly on the sale of certain goods—and forced indigenous communities to buy them.

Another development was that arrogant, often distant Spanish authorities were appointing nonethnic caciques, despite the long-standing custom of indigenous families like Condorcanqui's, with believed bloodlines to the Inca lords. On an ideological level, the Enlightenment ideas of self-rule, democracy, republicanism, equality, and fraternity—hatched in Europe and manifested in Old World and New World revolutions in France, the United States, and Haiti—were challenging the arcane imperial model.

Also part of the Bourbon Reforms was the creation of a new viceroy called Río de La Plata in 1776, encompassing large parts of modern-day Argentina, Paraguay, Bolivia, and Uruguay, with Buenos Aires as its capital. The new arrangement damaged the Peruvian viceroyalty: the key city of Cuzco was administratively severed from key altiplano (high plateau) areas to the south, with Lake Titicaca and the mining city of Potosí both now governed from the impossibly remote Buenos Aires. Trade was also diverted to the Atlantic and Buenos Aires from the Cuzco-Lima-Pacific corridor. In short, resentment and estrangement smoldered in the capitals, high-Andean mining communities, and port cities. And then José Gabriel struck the match that set the continent alight.

REBEL YELL

Condorcanqui was cacique of the highland region of Tinta, but he was also the subordinate of the *corregidor* (magistrate) Antonio de Arriaga. In his capacity as corregidor, the Basque-born nobleman collected taxes and managed the mita that sent workers to the colossal mine network at Potosí six hundred miles south—abuses which Condorcanqui deplored. The animosity between the two men was also heightened by the fact that the two leaders worked and lived together, with Arriaga subjecting Condorcanqui to incessant impositions and even death threats.

In 1777, Condorconqui made a fateful journey to Lima, the Peru viceroyalty capital, to make the case for the Indians in his district. For around a year, Condorcanqui argued over the abuse of the mita being extended to working in the mines. (Interestingly, all individuals or communities under Spanish control held a right of appeal up through the myriad bureaucratic layers, all the way up to the king himself. As the eminent British historian J. H. Elliott laconically wrote, "This system left room for maneuver both to the rulers and the ruled.")

The cacique returned home empty-handed but with galvanized resolve, reinforced by his exposure to Enlightenment texts. There were also works from voices inside the New World not connected to the Enlightenment that influenced Condorcanqui. For example, he purportedly read the impassioned *Royal Commentaries of the Incas* by Garcilaso de la Vega, another indigenous Inca royalty, a tome which was at the time banned by the viceroy authorities for its pro-Inca subversion and perhaps deepened Condorcanqui's sense of Incan identity and anticolonial sentiment. Either way, Condorcanqui's Incan identity played a larger part in his thinking, both about his country and himself. He began increasingly calling himself Túpac Amaru II, after his claimed ancestor Túpac Amaru (Shining Serpent), the so-called last Incan royalty who was put to a grisly death in 1572 by Spanish Viceroy Francisco de Toledo.

And then he struck. On November 4, Túpac Amaru dined with Arriaga in a pueblo not far from Tinta, a not-unusual occurrence given how frequently the pair interacted. But this time was different: after the meal, the Spanish official was captured by Túpac Amaru's associates. One mestizo adherent read a declaration in Spanish and Quechua: "Through the [Spanish] King it has been ordered that there no longer be . . . a customs house, or the Potosí mita and that Don Antonio de Arriaga lose his life because of his destructive behavior." (While patently untrue, Túpac Amaru started a habit of claiming various sorts of Spanish royal affirmation for his stances and orders.) Túpac Amaru then ordered Arriaga's scribe, Antonio Oblotas, to carry out the sentence, and Arriaga was duly executed.

His loathed superior now dispatched, Túpac Amaru proceeded with his wildly ambitious revolution: kick out the Spanish, end the despised *mita*, and establish autonomy for Indians to live in and around mestizos and Creoles. Even before the rebel cacique had reached the province of Quispichanchis, he had confiscated Arriaga's holdings and had given them to his swelling army of tens of thousands. Led by both Creoles and the mestizo middle class, the lion's share of the foot soldiers comprised male and female Indians as well as formerly enslaved Black people. (Contrary to what is often logically assumed, mestizos, Black people, Indians, and even Spaniards fought on both sides of this complex conflagration.) Seemingly overnight, the rebels controlled a wide assortment of provinces in the vicinity south of the Incan capital. There was also looting of Hispanic businesses, dwellings, haciendas, and textile mills where Indians were forced to work under harsh conditions.

A little over a week after Arriaga was executed, a seminal battle occurred in the pueblo of Sangarará that pitched insurgent forces against well over one thousand Hispanic and loyalist Indian fighters who had been deployed from

Cuzco. Before the dust had settled, 578 counterinsurgent fighters (two dozen Spanish) were slain, mostly with slingshots made from llama wool (able to hit an enemy at up to seventy yards). The town church was demolished, and weapons and booty seized in what was a morale-raising rout for Túpac Amaru's embryonic campaign.

As news of the catastrophe—including cannibalism on the enemy side—made its way back to Cuzco, Spanish officials began to realize that the rebellion posed an existential threat. Túpac Amaru and his backers were precipitously excommunicated for being heathens who destroyed churches, although Túpac Amaru was nevertheless able to utilize the support of an array of priests who were indignant about what the Bourbon Reforms had done to Church prerogatives.

In his sizable highland dominion, Túpac Amaru summarily abolished the office of corregidor, the mita, certain despised taxes, and freed indigenous prisoners. With the wind in their sails, the guerrillas expanded their campaigns, bringing destruction and death but also hope that, driven first and foremost by local disputes and grudges, the rebellion's leadership would eradicate Hispanic dominion and culture from their native lands. Within weeks, the rebellion had turned into a revolution.

In an instance of an unexpected but vital female political agency in this colonial era, Micaela Bastidas had goaded her husband at the onset to kill Arriaga; then, seeing that some cities and locales were being quickly retaken by the Spanish, she urged him to move more aggressively. She was also a chief propagandist and strategist—a veritable Joan of Arc (more acerbic critics might say Lady Macbeth) of the Andes. Túpac Amaru and Micaela Bastidas also adroitly tapped into Incan iconography: they commissioned a rebel flag and other icons portraying themselves as Inca king and queen; dressed in the garb of Incan royalty; and addressed their fighters at *huacas* (Indian shrines). The self-mythologizing worked: legions of Indians paid visits to their Inca warrior, who they received as their rightful ruler. Eminent historian Alberto Flores Galindo explains, "His orders were to be obeyed because he was the heir to the Inca empire and thought by some even to possess divine powers like the ability to resurrect those who died in his service."

THE REVOLUTION STALLS

With Sangarará subdued, by mid-December the rebel leaders turned their attention to imperial-held Cuzco, the jewel in the crown for both sides. Before the month was out, Túpac Amaru had amassed a motley yet spirited army of forty thousand near the city, while the Spanish frantically prepared defenses and prayed that overdue reinforcements from Lima would arrive soon. And, as if the Christian God had intervened, on January 1, 1781, fresh Spanish troops, albeit only two hundred but vitally with hundreds of weapons and ammunition, from the coast arrived in Cuzco with an officer, Colonel Gabriel de Avilés (who would later serve as Governor of Chile), in command. This was only a day before Túpac Amaru was set to pounce and seize the city.

Within a week, Avilés ordered probing sorties followed by a larger operation to crush the rebels—a futile effort as, once the fog—which had caused fits for both sides at various moments—literally lifted, it was manifestly clear that the insurgents had already fled. Without much of a fight, the siege of Cuzco was over, a failure that was due in no small part to Túpac Amaru's inability to seize the city before the Avilés contingency showed up.

In the first months of the new year, Micaela Bastidas, Túpac Amaru, and other insurgent leaders remained anxious about the looming harvest's potential to pull soldiers from their ranks and back to their fields. Complicating matters, the Spanish wisely offered amnesty to rebels and rescinded the despised colonial encumbrances.

Insurgent momentum stopped cold. It would now be just a matter of further military setbacks which culminated in Túpac Amaru's capture in April, in the resplendent central plaza of Cuzco. At the show trial, José Antonio de Areche, the magistrate, explained how the "horrendous crime" of the antimonarchy insurgency was the formal charge but referred to Túpac Amaru as "his excellence, highness, and majesty." Indeed, a central tension in this episode, was the captive a rightful ruler or a rebel? These notions of authority and legitimacy—for example, who gets to make the rules?—are so often central to revolution and reform.

The self-professed Inca warrior (if we forget for a moment that he was a Jesuit-trained merchant) watched Micaela and other family members being tortured and executed before he suffered the ghastly fate of being drawn (body cut up) and quartered (pulled apart by horses). When the horses could not break apart his body, the Spanish authorities ordered him to be decapitated. (According to Areche, killing in full public view was essentially given "the superstitions that led the people to believe that it was impossible to kill him because of the nobility of his character, which made him the inheritor of the Incas.")

To terrify anyone thinking of starting a similar revolt, Spanish authorities ordered that the various parts of the executed rebels be displayed in an assortment of provincial towns. The "Distribution of the Bodies, or parts thereof, of the Nine Offenders of the Rebellion, Brought to Justice in the Plaza of Cuzco, on the 18th of May 1781" listed the names of the executed insurgents and which severed body part of each killed rebels' body parts would go to what province or town. In one southern city: "Arequipa: Micaela Bastidas' arm."

While dealt a sharp setback with the death of its vaunted leader, the Túpac Amaru rebellion continued under the command of José Gabriel's cousin, Diego Cristóbal Túpac Amaru. As the fight progressed, both rebel and royalist sides turned to harsher tactics, with the insurgents pillaging and plundering along the way and killing Spaniards on site as they moved southward, closer to Lake Titicaca, and thus Upper Peru. The intrepid Spanish officer, José del Valle, had also taken off the gloves. In the mountain city of Puno on Lake Titicaca, he reported that "Everybody [the rebels] was put to the knife, no living soul being spared." Diego Cristóbal accepted an amnesty offer, although he was subsequently arrested and executed in, if at all possible, a manner more gruesome than his cousin.

A SEPARATE CACIQUE-LED REBELLION TO THE SOUTH

Our story now moves to Upper Peru, in what we now call the Bolivian altiplano. There, in the city of La Paz, some 325 miles south of Cuzco, lived Tomás Katari, a brilliant and tenacious but illiterate and non-Spanish speaking cacique, although of more humble origin than José Gabriel.

Just as José Gabriel had gone to Lima to push for reforms, so too did Katari go to Buenos Aires—a distance of over one thousand miles, all on foot—to argue for the cessation of myriad cases of abuse. And like his Peruvian counterpart, Katari returned incensed and impatient, and things quickly got worse. Upon returning home, Katari was arrested by the corregidor of Macha, a highland locality, and tortured and imprisoned before he made a series of escapes. No longer fully beholden to a legal strategy, in February 1770 Katari announced that tribute amounts would be reduced by one-third, a move that led to his return behind bars. Interestingly, Katari himself did not cease professing his "blind obedience" to King Carlos III, highlighting that at heart he remained more reformer than revolutionary.

A series of riots erupted demanding Katari's release, which finally occurred, amid much celebration, on August 30, 1780. But on January 8, 1781,

Rebellion in the Andes. *(University of Wisconsin-Madison Cartography Lab)*

just around the time of Túpac Amaru's failed siege of Cuzco, the Spanish authorities ordered Katari's re-arrest, which eventually resulted in the cacique's very public execution.

His incipient "katarist" revolt was now in the hands of his brothers, Diego and Dámaso, before their brutal public executions at the hands of royal authorities in the plaza of La Plata (today's Bolivian city of Sucre). It was now left to the illiterate, charismatic but mercurial Ayamara, Julián Apaza, to continue the insurrection and demands of reform. He now assumed the nom de guerre Túpac Katari, in honor of the martyred Túpac Amaru and Tomás Katari. (Class is a central issue in times of social revolt, it is notable how Spanish official documents routinely mention Túpac Katari's ignoble social status, unlike the respect granted to the [ostensible] Inca lord, Túpac Amaru II.)

One massive, protracted siege of La Paz utilized over forty thousand fighters, an offensive that even involved breaking a dam to flood the city with water. Scholars reckon that upward of ten thousand Hispanics and their indigenous allies died after futilely holding out, not just from rebel slings but starvation. Spanish reinforcements finally ended the siege and Túpac Katari was imprisoned and executed—brutally drawn and quartered, his parts dispatched across the empire to sow terror in the hearts of potential imitators—in November 1781. His final dying words, according to oral tradition, were "You can kill me, but I will return, and I will be millions."

The execution of Katari coincided with the end of another insurrection that had taken place at about the same time: the potent Comunero Rebellion (1780–1781) in the regions north of Bogotá, the capital of the New Granada viceroyalty. Interestingly headed by the local criollo elite, this rebellion was also brutally put down by Spanish forces, who reneged on key concessions over the opprobrious taxes that had engendered the rebellion in the first place.

END GAME

The Great Rebellion of 1780–1782, as colonial officials called it, inundated the Andes from Peru to Upper Peru, but failed to wipe away Spanish control and customs. While brutally vanquished, the insurgencies reinforced the Spanish and Creoles' (or at least the elites') wariness of the Quechua and Aymara multitudes. This led to assorted efforts to eliminate or minimize native customs—the very pre-Hispanic flags, royal garb, literature, and drama that Túpac Amaru, for one, had elevated. Caciques were officially ended to allow the Indian workers and communities to be more closely controlled by

Hispanic overseers. A proscription on speaking Quechua was revived. Most gruesomely, all sorts of individuals and groups believed to have been affiliated with the rebellions were arrested, tried, and imprisoned. In some pueblos, royal officers would assemble men in the central plaza to execute every fifth person, the vile but effective *quintado*.

The chaos and killing of the Great Andean Rebellions—and the cautionary brutality of the executions—may have made some Creoles grow more conservative and royalist, a fact which came to the fore, especially in Peru, where Creole-led independence movements started in the first decades of the next century.

Royalist authorities also offered some carrots, so to speak, by doing away with some of the most hated laws and practices that provoked the insurrections. Yet while there were patent improvements, these reforms did not put an end to Hispanic abuses; indigenous agency and prospects remained circumscribed. And it would only be a score of decades hence that the Spanish colonial project—in place for almost three centuries and long considered eternal—would effectively end.

Túpac Amaru II and Micaela Bastidas. A circa 2010 mural located in a town near Cuzco, states "Welcome to the homeland of Tupac Amaru and Micaela Bastidas." *(Hervé Hughes/Alamy)*

But although the rebellion may have failed, Túpac Amaru II continued to play an iconic role in Andean, Latin American, and even global politics and society. Renowned Chilean poet and communist, Pablo Neruda, penned a verse "Túpac Amaru 1781" (in his epic *Canto general* 1950), lionizing the heroic exploits of the rebel leader and mythologizing how his legacy has become a part of the very earth itself. Fast forward two centuries and an African American political organizer renamed her one-year-old son Túpac Amaru Shakur, who became a globally successful rap artist who criticized social inequality. Notably, a Cold War–era Peruvian Marxist guerrilla group—its revolutionary goal to overthrow the central government and establish a Communist state—adopted the name Túpac Amaru Revolutionary Movement. (This was despite the Marxist group lacking an actual indigenous linkage.)

Elsewhere, the Katari legacy resurged in 1980s Bolivia with the emergence of the Túpac Katari Guerrilla Army, which advocated "Katarism," a political ideology based on social justice. One of their coleaders, Álvaro García Linera, later became closely connected with the "Aymara rebelde" Evo Morales, who emerged as an iconic and revolutionary indigenous figure in twenty-first-century Bolivia, and explicitly evoked the legacy of Túpac Amaru II. In some eyes, the ideological orthodoxy behind Evo's power, Álvaro García Linera ultimately became his vice president. Whatever the case, with Evo Morales's presidency, a long indigenous revolution had finally succeeded, although via the ballot box.

5

Toussaint Louverture

The Black Spartacus of the Caribbean

Freedom is a right given by nature.

—*Toussaint Louverture*

The Haitian Revolution—said to be the biggest slave rebellion after Spartacus's uprising against the Roman Empire almost two millennia prior—started in 1791 in what was still called Saint-Domingue, a French colony in the Caribbean. Beginning with the cries for equality and self-government for freed people of color, the insurrection then became radicalized with the onset, in August 1791, of a mighty enslaved-person rebellion that within two years had achieved the abolition of slavery in the colony.

The revolution resulted in a slew of firsts. Haiti was the first nation in Latin America to gain independence and remains the only country to have gained independence through an enslaved-person revolt. It was also the first country to outlaw slavery and to be ruled by former enslaved persons and people of mixed race. Lasting a decade and a half, the protracted revolution was of great interest to many, including private US abolitionists who sought a case study of a stable and prosperous freed–enslaved person republic to challenge both entrenched beliefs about Black inferiority and enslavers in the American South.

It is also a case study of the power of the individual: in this case, Toussaint Louverture, a freed Black enslaved person, fearless soldier, and astute diplomat who ushered in enslaved-person emancipation and paved the way for Haitian nationhood, all the while avoiding becoming embroiled in the machinations of rivaling France and the United States and fending off British and Spanish attempts to gain control of the island. Radically, he not only challenged the myriad ruling norms of his time—racial hierarchy, slavery, imperialism, settler colonialism, and European cultural hegemony—but even coopted them, "bending them to his will," as historian Sudhir Hazareesingh deftly phrased it. His admirers called him the "Black Spartacus," the "father of the blacks," "Washington of the Antilles," "the Bonaparte of the Caribbean," and the "the Hannibal of Saint-Domingue."

SAINT-DOMINGUE, "THE IMPERIAL ENGINE"

Encompassing the western third of Hispaniola Island (around 10,600 square miles, about the same size as the state of Maryland), Saint-Domingue was claimed by Spain following Columbus's landfall in the northwest of the island in December 1492. The colony was ceded to France in 1697 and became the country's most lucrative New World possession; colloquially, it was known as the most "profitable stretch of real estate on the planet." The colony's world-leading exports of sugar and coffee (shipping more than Jamaica, Cuba, and Brazil put together, and representing 40 percent of sugar and 50 percent of the coffee ingested globally) as well as chocolate, indigo, and cotton, served as the fuel for France's "imperial engine." Ships from the Americas and Europe sailed to and from its lively ports, five hundred voyages to the United States each year. Belying its physical size, the colony's flourishing trade created more wealth for France than the thirteen North American colonies produced for Great Britain combined.

Extracting this "fuel," however, would have been impossible without the colony's massive, enslaved labor force. Comprising 480,000 enslaved Africans (by 1789, representing some 50 percent of the enslaved Caribbean population), the majority born in Africa, it dwarfed the colony's population of whites (thirty thousand) and freed persons of color (twenty-eight thousand). The colony's slavery model was considered "perhaps the most horrific . . . ever seen in human history." Amid wretched conditions with enslavers wresting the maximum labor out of their bodies, one in twenty enslaved persons died each year—worked to death to produce this massive wealth. This brutal toll fed into a nightmarish cycle whereby enslaved-person traders imported ever-greater numbers of slaves to make up for losses and drive production higher. In fact, between 1740 and 1789 that population increased fourfold.

Map of Haiti, 1800. (*Histoire of Weapons in Medicine*, Cartography Lab)

By 1789, the tiny island colony had two-thirds the number of shackled humans living in the entire United States of America. Also crucial here is that, while small and geographically removed from its European mother country, Saint-Domingue was very much connected to the era's cultural and philosophical movements. At the end of the 1780s, Le Cap Français (later Cap-Haïtien) comprised almost twenty thousand residents, a size larger than all but a handful of towns in the United States. It was a vibrant port metropolis providing residents with a standard of city living on par with New York, Philadelphia, or Havana. There were twenty bakeries, five bookstores, numerous printing presses, subscription reading clubs, a theater able to seat 1,500 (another half-dozen towns had theaters), a newspaper, literary and scientific academies, and private libraries "stacked with the latest philosophical works from Europe." Historian David A. Bell describes how readers in the colony's urban locales could "follow the events of the American Revolution in detail and even read admiring notices in their own newspaper about Guillaume-Thomas Raynal, France's most prominent critic of slavery. In short, the same cultural changes that helped bring about the revolution in Europe and North America also reached these distant shores."

THE GREAT ENSLAVED-PERSON REVOLT

Given the hyper-skewed ratio of enslaved persons to whites, as well as the abhorrent treatment by the European minority, an uprising was only a matter of time. From the 1750s onward, the enslaved-person communities had established a variety of individual and group resistance movements, and the mood grew increasingly tense. In this late colonial period "social and political conflict was rife" in Saint-Domingue; a planter acknowledged that he and his fellow enslavers "walked on barrels of gunpowder." Neither was the sense of injustice limited to enslaved persons: *gens de couleur* (free people of color) in Saint-Domingue, were also enraged by French landowners' refusal to extend them citizenship.

In late August 1791, the detonation finally came, partly a consequence of the colonial administration in Saint-Domingue collapsing after the 1789 onset of the French Revolution. Staring in the northern plains, the self-liberated enslaved persons of Saint-Domingue revolted, torching fields of cane and massacring their masters and mulattoes (persons of mixed European and African ancestry). The Haitian Revolution had begun.

Among the insurrectionists was François-Dominique Toussaint, a former domestic slave (one of the tiny fractions to be granted manumission). Trusted

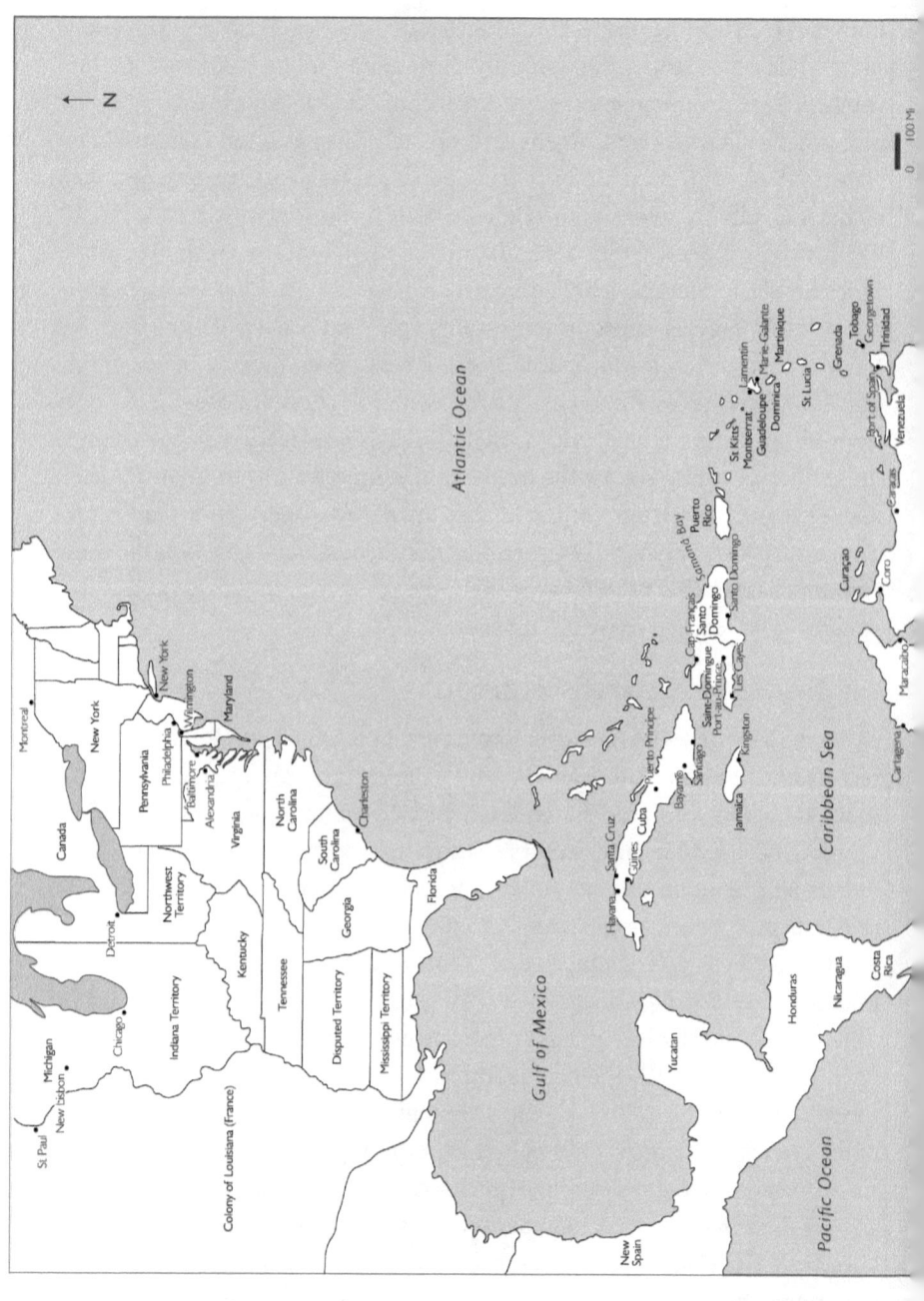

biographical particulars are scant and maddeningly contradictory and contested, but he was apparently abstemious and short in physical stature. His freedom came in 1776 at the age of thirty-three; he was married and had two children. At various points, the autodidact worked as a cattle rancher and coachman, and devoutly worshiped Roman Catholicism, not Vodou, the African diasporic religion, even if in Haiti the two beliefs were intertwined, a phenomenon often labeled syncretism. While initially equivocal about the wisdom of the burgeoning enslaved-person insurrection, Toussaint joined and became a brilliant, venerated guerrilla commander. (In 1793, he added "Louverture" ["Opening" in French] to his name, which some reckon might be linked to his military aptness.)

French administrators in Saint-Domingue were at a loss about how to check the uprising. As a form of appeasement, the radical French republic, in 1794, proscribed slavery in its treasured colony. Spain and France broke out into war that same year, which eventually led Louverture and other enslaved-person rebellion officers to join up with Spanish forces across the border in Santo Domingo, the eastern two-thirds of the island (today's Dominican Republic). But by 1794, for reasons that are not fully clear, Louverture had defected to the French in Saint-Domingue and was appointed the colony's governor general in 1796. Over the next few years, his cagey handling of political rivals in conjunction with his legendary prowess on the battlefield helped catalyze Louverture's meteoric ascent to maximum power in Saint-Domingue, even if it remained under the French flag. In one instance, the Louverture-led summary expulsion of British occupying forces from Saint-Domingue, in September 1798, prompted French colonial official, Philippe Roume, to describe the general's "rebellious" inclinations in awe-struck tones:

> This is a rebel who commands the assent of nine-tenths of the population of Saint-Domingue; a rebel whose courage, discipline and strategic intelligence in the conduct of colonial war have overcome the might and the ruses of the British; a rebel who hardly ever sleeps and seems able to multiply himself and be present in many different places at the same time; a rebel who knows the ideal locations for ambushes in every part of his territory which is littered with mountains, rivers, and passes; a rebel who commands a tireless army; that can feed itself on anything which can be digested and can even do without clothing.

Eager to capture the lucrative sugar colony, Great Britain, in 1793, deployed the largest naval expedition it had ever assembled to take Saint-Domingue.

The failed expedition against Louverture's forces resulted in more British casualties than had occurred during the American Revolutionary War.

Louverture also worked feverishly to abolish slavery on the island, as well as helping to rebuild it after years of unspeakable violence and catastrophic destruction. As a fig leaf gesture to heal the racial wounds, he permitted émigré planters to come back to the colony. Despite his visceral hatred of slavery, he autocratically reinstated the inhumane labor code—enforced by a sort of military guild—that was effective serfdom, even if it did allow the workers to share of the (restored!) plantation revenues and were not whipped anymore. (In a historical first for a country using a national identification program, in 1801 the austere Black general ruled that all citizens had to carry identity cards so that the labor code was expediently administered.) Louverture likely feared that without export revenues from the plantations his nation would be

Toussaint Louverture. Image published by the prominent African American Underground Railroad conductor, George DeBaptiste, circa 1870. *(Library of Congress Prints and Photographs Division, Washington, DC)*

reenslaved or reconquered, but he also thought that humans were innately indolent and amoral, and therefore perhaps needed strong compulsion to work. Remarkably, Louverture's imposition of the draconian labor system provided him with untold personal wealth. It's good to be the king, it seemed.

With Saint-Domingue under his dominion, in 1801, Louverture captured all of Santo Domingo where slavery persevered. He promptly freed those in bondage but, in a tribute to his political savvy, wowed Europeans and mulattoes with his high-mindedness and humanitarianism. In a precursor to Simón Bolívar's autocratic inclinations after independence had been won from Spain, Governor General Toussaint Louverture decreed a constitution—despite still being a French colony—that gave him indefinite supreme powers. (See Chapter 6, "Simón Bolívar: The Great Liberator, Flawed Emancipator.") However, keen to demonstrate his French patriotism to Paris, Louverture instituted a variety of revolutionary tenets that had at least putative concurrence: Catholicism, for example, became the official religion. Seeing as how Louverture avouched himself as a loyal French subject, then presumably there was no need for any other French colonial ruler on the island.

"IS NOT THEIR CAUSE AS JUST AS OURS?"

The world was divided as to what to make of this new Black revolutionary leader. Terrified of the prospect of a Toussaint-style revolt occurring at home, enslavers in the United States, Europe, and nearby Caribbean colonial islands excoriated this new figurehead of emancipation. For Hazareesingh, "From London and Paris through Virginia and Louisiana to Jamaica, Cuba, Brazil, and Venezuela, planters and merchants echoed these alarms and lambasted the leader of the revolution—the man they saw as the 'Robespierre of Saint-Domingue.'" In 1799, Thomas Jefferson vilified Louverture and the Black insurgents as "cannibals of the terrible Republic," asserting that their "missionaries" could elicit a "combustion in America." Two years later, British War Secretary Lord Hobart trembled at the scene of the "power of a Black Empire under Toussaint." Jamaica's richest sugar lord, Simon Taylor, "tossed and turned in his luxurious bed linen, suffering repeated bouts of fever as he imagined Toussaint and his revolutionaries arriving on his plantation and slitting his throat."

But Louverture also had his vocal backers, although decidedly in the minority. Some Pennsylvania dailies referenced him as the "celebrated African chief"; over in London, considerable liberal sentiment cheered on the "Negro

King" who was, according to the *London Gazette* in 1798, a member of the "Black race whom the Christian world to their infamy have been accustomed to degrade." A couple of years later, another London publication honored Louverture as "the major public figure of the year, and a great man." Connecticut's Abraham Bishop, a political follower of Jefferson, was forthright in his support, although perhaps over-optimistic in his assessment of the national mood for Louverture's revolt. "If Freedom depends upon colour, and if the Blacks were born for slaves, those in the West-India islands may be called Insurgents and Murderers," he declared in the Boston-published essay, "The Rights of Black Men." "But the enlightened mind of Americans will not receive such ideas," he goes on to write. "We believe that Freedom is the natural right of all rational beings, and we know that the Blacks have never voluntarily resigned that freedom. Then is not their cause as just as ours?"

LOUVERTURE'S REGIONAL *REALPOLITIK*

Between the onset of revolution in 1791 and Haiti's independence in 1804, Louverture worked feverishly to carve out a new state without provoking the great world powers of Spain, France, Great Britain, and the United States. Louverture's diplomatic calculations were especially complex when it came to navigating the competing interests of France and the United States. France had come to the nascent United States' aid in the latter's rebellion against Great Britain, but after the United States won independence, Washington promptly expanded trade with its former colonizer and declared neutrality in France's conflict with Great Britain. In a further indication of cooling ties, the John Adams administration (1797–1801) stopped paying its debts to Paris. In retaliation to these snubs, France seized a fleet of US merchant ships off the United States' East Coast, sparking what would be a two-year-long period of undeclared hostilities—known as the "Quasi-War"—from 1798 to 1800.

As the two navies duked it out in the West Indies—the conflict had the unusual character of being conducted almost exclusively on the open seas—Saint-Domingue became a locale of strategic importance. In July 1798 Congress slapped an embargo on all trade with France and its colonies—including Saint-Domingue. To repair relations with the Americans and kill the trade embargo, Louverture dispatched a discreet and capable representative, Joseph Bunel, in late December 1798 to Philadelphia for consultations with Secretary of State Timothy Pickering. Bunel, who as a white man hoped to be accepted more openly, was successful in achieving his goal: by February 1799, the US Congress gave commander-in-chief Adams the authority to exempt from the embargo any French colonies not menacing American merchantmen. The law's patent intention to apply to Saint-Domingue earned it the moniker the "Toussaint Clause."

Louverture and Bunel's success may have been helped by good timing. The New England–bred Adams was not an enslaver and was more disposed to entertain Louverture's solicitation than his predecessor George Washington or successor, Jefferson. Secretary Pickering, for his part, was an early supporter of independence, fearing that maintaining Saint-Domingue's status quo as a French colony could facilitate either its use as a base for French military action against the United States or French anti-US pressure.

In negotiating a cessation of the US embargo, Louverture also had to hash out an agreement with the British, as Great Britain's naval superiority meant that all goods flowing to Saint-Domingue passed through what were, in effect, British waters. Fortunately, British diplomat Thomas Maitland arrived in northern Saint-Domingue on May 4, 1799, with a joint agreement between the British and the United States in hand. Britain and the United States were willing to resume trade with Louverture in one or two ports if Louverture promised to not incite a rebellion in the British colony of Jamaica. Louverture readily agreed to these terms, as the resumption of trade with the United States was fundamental to his domestic agenda.

Making matters even more complex, Louverture wanted to keep the French onside as well. When speaking to the American first consul-general to Saint-Domingue, Louverture focused on Haitian independence; with Paris, he continued to profess that he was "proud to be [France's] adoptive son." But keeping the French onside was sometimes a delicate business. Using the rationale of the revolt for imperial ends, French officials pushed Louverture to promote the Declaration of the Rights of Man and of the Citizen through an attack on either the British island colony of Jamaica or the American South. (French authorities had already used former Black enslaved persons for just such a campaign on the island of neighboring Guadeloupe.) But Louverture would have none of it. According to biographer Philippe Girard, "He did not want to risk his life in some harebrained adventure overseas, even one that offered the promise of altering the course of world history. His long-term goal was not universal emancipation but abolition in Saint-Domingue, his political rise, and the colony's economic recovery, none of which could take place if he needlessly provoked the two main naval powers of the Caribbean. He chose to pursue cooperation instead."

Shrewdly, Louverture's international diplomacy not only saved the colony from becoming embroiled in a great-power struggle but also helped him solve a domestic problem in the shape of rival André Rigaud, a mixed-race general who controlled the south of the colony. Without food and guns from America, Louverture recognized that his chances of defeating Riguad were slim. But with the reopening of Cap-Français and Port Repúblicain on June 13, 1799, to US trade, matériel and supplies began to flow again, and led to his victory over Rigaud in a savage civil war that would soon be dubbed the "War of the Knives." But then came a challenge of an altogether different order.

"NO MORE GILDED AFRICANS"

In 1800, eager to return Saint-Domingue to a lucrative colony (and thus slavery needed to be reinitiated) Napoleon Bonaparte—then First Consul of France—resolved to restore French dominion over Saint-Domingue and decisively end the revolt despite the fact Toussaint was still pledging allegiance to French overlordship. He dispatched one of the largest invasion forces to sail from Europe to the New World—landing in January 1802—and comprising upwards of fifty thousand troops, and led by his gallant brother-in-law Charles Victoire ("Victory") Leclerc. The French dictator's orders to his subordinate were clear: "No more gilded Africans." Napoleon deliberately enlisted mixed-race and Black officers into his force to add credence to his public promise not to restore slavery. In a distressing harbinger of Louverture's calamity, a strong portion of Europeans and mulattoes in Saint-Domingue switched to join Leclerc's campaign.

But it was French perfidy, not French arms, that led to Louverture's downfall. In May, Louverture surrendered to General Leclerc's expedition force in exchange for what he thought was a French commitment not to reestablish slavery on the island. Months later, after being tricked into appearing at a meeting under bogus promises, the apprehended Louverture was sent to Fort-de-Joux, a castle-turned-wretched, damp prison in France's Jura Mountains. Within a year, after suffering from intense interrogations and tuberculosis, the forlorn Louverture died on April 7, 1803, never to set foot in Haiti again, nor witness his country achieve independence.

But back in Saint-Domingue, the French were fighting a losing battle. General Leclerc died of yellow fever (a fate that awaited most of his expedition); and several of the French force's Black generals mutinied. Despite a twenty-thousand-strong army of reinforcements sent in 1802 (diverted from their original mission to reestablish French control over Louisiana), the writing was on the wall. In November 1803, Haitian guerrillas fought the remnants of Leclerc's besieged force at Vertières, close to Louverture's birthplace. With the rebel troops prevailing, the French forces fled the island. Ultimately, Leclerc's failed counterinsurgency was critical to Napoleon's subsequent decision to sell New Orleans and all French Louisiana (530 million acres, at three cents per acre) to the United States, thus doubling the size of the fledgling nation. The irony, of course, is that the liberation of enslaved Haitians had now, as historian Edward Baptist put it, "delivered the Mississippi Valley to a new empire of slavery."

In 1802 France restored slavery in its empire, but Saint-Domingue was an exception. On January 1, 1804, Louverture's successor, Jean-Jacques Dessalines, a former enslaved person, put forth the Haitian Declaration of Independence, although France would not recognize Haiti until 1825 (charging Haiti 150 million francs for the enslaved persons and property lost during the revolution). Nevertheless, the Declaration in effect ended the thirteen-year revolution and proclaimed equality for imported Africans and their descendants who, as stated in the preamble, had "so unjustly and for so long a time considered outcast children." The struggle had exacted a brutal toll: upward of 350,000 Haitians and 50,000 French troops had been killed (the troops mostly from yellow fever), and the island nation's economy lay in tatters.

During his initial oration to the Haitian nation, Dessalines demanded "eternal hatred for France," but bragged that "my happy fate preserved me to serve one day as the sentinel guarding the idol to which you sacrifice: I have watched and fought sometimes alone." Ominously, he assumed Louverture's appellation of "Governor General for Life"; his military officers pledged to "obey blindly the laws emanating from his authority." (Less than a year after learning that Bonaparte had taken up an imperial title, Dessalines proclaimed himself Emperor Jean-Jacques I of Haiti, initiating an autocracy that ended just two years later with his assassination.)

Under Dessalines, Haiti became the first country in the world to permanently bar slavery. This incredible feat, however, would be somewhat tainted by Dessalines's order to wipe out the entire residual white population in the country, a genocide known as the "horrors of Santo Domingo" (and more recently, the 1804 Haitian massacre). Leaving three thousand to five thousand dead in its tracks, the massacre's victims included women and children and whites sympathetic to the new Black order. Eager to court favor with the United States, Dessalines corresponded with Jefferson, but the Virginian never replied. On the contrary, the American commander-in-chief suspended relations between the two countries from 1806 to 1808. The United States did not recognize Haiti's independence until 1862 when President Abraham Lincoln dispatched New Hampshire judge, teacher, and diplomat Benjamin F. Whidden to Haiti to present his credentials.

Despite his short rule, Dessalines had set a precedent. Haiti, across most of the nineteenth century, would exist under the rule of a slew of iron-fisted former generals who sold themselves as "providential saviors" of the nation.

"DEATH OR LIBERTY"

Louverture has been celebrated by abolitionists around the world as someone who had dealt a blow to the evil scourge of slavery. French abolitionist Victor Schoelcher's nineteenth-century biography of Louverture describes him as a "man of genius." Antislavery polymath Frederick Douglass, America's most illustrious African American in the period, vigorously applauded Toussaint, including using the Haitian's likeness in the publicity for his *New National Era* newspaper. More directly, Louverture's achievements also inspired emancipatory action in the United States. In 1800, a tradesman called Gabriel commanded a failed enslaved-person insurrection in Virginia under the slogan "Death or Liberty," while the enslaved-person revolts of African Americans Denmark Vesey (1822) and Nat Turner (1831) were also influenced by the Haitian example. Radical American abolitionist John Brown read up on Louverture's military forays when devising his own 1859 raid on Harpers Ferry, West Virginia, in an attempt to initiate an enslaved-person revolt. Yet despite this legacy, even pro-slavery voices in America praised the Haitian leader for his willingness to forgive his former masters and to force the free enslaved persons back to the plantations. According to one, Louverture was "the only true great man yet known of the negro race." People who would have never endorsed the intellectual merits of enslaved persons, or their ability to achieve self-government, could not help but admire Louverture's ability to keep his nerve when challenged by foreign powers.

Of course, beneath the bold lines of the revolutionary hero there are complexities that paint a more nuanced picture. Louverture's domestic politics were complex, contradictory, and, from a twenty-first-century perspective, sometimes very far from emancipatory: he was hostile toward his mixed-race brothers and sisters; attempted to resurrect the plantation economy by hammering out an accord with the colony's white (formerly ruling) elite; failed to redistribute lands to the peasant legions; and coerced former enslaved peoples to work for their old plantation owners. To critical scholarly eyes, the "liberator" had become the "liquidator." (More recent documentary evidence suggests that during his pre-revolution years as a freed man he owned enslaved peoples.) Louverture was a reformer who circumspectly operated within the system, and also a revolutionary who wanted to blow it up. Ends justifying the means, his diplomatic double-dealing ensured that the newly born republic survived. Overcoming enormous odds, Louverture achieved a miracle in setting his country on the path to independence and freeing countless people from the horrors of slavery.

6

Simón Bolívar

The Great Liberator, Flawed Emancipator

If Nature itself decides to oppose us, we will fight and force her to obey.
—*Simón Bolívar*

Just short of midnight on December 15, 1999, Venezuela was renamed the "Bolivarian Republic of Venezuela" in honor of the nation's independence savior. For some observers, this was simply a superficial, apolitical change amid a host of far more controversial ones in a new constitution backed by the fiery socialist President Hugo Chávez. But others argued that Chávez was audaciously coopting the legacy of Simón Bolívar as part of a self-serving cult. According to one observer in Chávez's Venezuela: "Along the streets of Caracas it became common to see murals of Chávez together with Jesus Christ and Bolívar, the Holy Trinity of the Bolivarian Revolution." While critics blasted him for cynical exploitation of the Great Liberator, Chávez had deftly tapped into a rich propaganda vein of a country obsessed with its founding father's life, utterances, and philosophies.

The truth is that Bolívar—the military genius who liberated a half dozen nations from the yoke of the Spanish Bourbon empire—is such a complex figure that he provides a ready foil for a whole host of ideologies, which is one of the reasons why his legacy has been hotly disputed. For most politically liberal academics, Bolívar's core impact was fighting royalist tyranny. For rightist nationalists going back to the middle of the nineteenth century, by contrast, he was a symbol of unyielding *patria* (homeland) and duty. Elsewhere, the Great Liberator is seen among others as a Marxist. Ultimately, any attempt to reduce Bolívar to a single ideology is doomed to fail, for he does not fit into a neat interpretative box. He was a child of the Enlightenment but shunned democracy. He understood that factionalism was poison for the newly independent countries, but also installed the rule of *caudillos*, or strongmen. He wanted freedom for Spanish Americans but was terrified about the rule by the dark-skinned. Many in these newly liberated nations wanted him to be their supreme ruler; others, by contrast, saw him as a dangerous usurper and plotted to murder him. Above all, Bolívar was inherently pragmatic—and it may be this pragmatism that is key to understanding the often-paradoxical nature of his actions and influence.

WONDER YEARS

Simón Bolívar's ancestors first arrived in the New World (in what is now Venezuela) from Spain in the late sixteenth century. Over the subsequent two hundred years, the Bolívar clan built up sizable holdings of houses and ranches, mines, cattle sugar and indigo plantations, and hundreds of enslaved persons. Born into this life of privilege on July 24, 1783, tragedy would nevertheless soon strike the young child. At the age of two, he lost his father, and his mother died several years later.

From an early age, Simón had a wild streak: in historian Enrique Krauze's keen phrasing, "willful, irascible, in obvious need of a stern hand, he became progressively ungovernable." Young Simón's formal education was not extensive; rather, occasional tutors instructed him. But things began to change when the fourteen-year-old Bolívar served as a cadet with the vaunted White Volunteers of the valley of Aragua, during which time the adolescent Venezuelan demonstrated the innate leadership that would define his life, as well as his ability to connect with all strata of society. As a relative described him, "he is always wandering the streets alone—by foot as well as on horseback. What's worse is that he's always in the company of boys who are not of his class."

Venezuela was a backwater in Madrid's vast New World empire—and certainly not a hotbed of colonial revolt. Yet atop the social and economic totem pole in this vast unknown realm, New World–born Spaniards ("Creoles") like Bolívar—"well above the mestizos (mixed bloods of Spaniard and Indian), mulattos (mixed white and black blood), and slaves toiling at the bottom of society"—nonetheless bristled at the thought of their country and peoples being at the whim of Iberian masters. A special indignity for Creoles was Spain's continued iron grip over the colonies' commerce and industry, which left the locals (read, Creoles) to "cultivate fields of indigo, grain, coffee, sugar cane, cacao, and cotton, to raise cattle on the empty plains; to hunt wild beasts in the wilderness; to mine the earth for gold to satisfy the insatiable greed of Spain."

In the late eighteenth century, the Spanish Bourbons implemented reforms intended to address a host of legitimacy and efficiency issues in the colonies. One of the central pillars of the Bourbon Reforms was a liberalization of foreign trade restraints—a development that benefited all sorts of Creole merchants— but the Crown also attempted to tighten political controls by reinforcing *peninsular* (Iberian-born officials) appointments, disenfranchising the Creole class. For the Peruvian Jesuit and pro-independence precursor, Juan Pablo Viscardo y Guzmán, Madrid's push for *peninsulares* was "to the permanent exclusion of those who alone know their own country, whose individual interest is closely bound to it, and who have a sublime and unique right to guard its welfare." Over in Venezuela, Bolívar also seethed at the omission of Creoles from all facets of government, "perhaps to a greater extent than ever before."

Still only a teenager, in 1799 Bolívar departed his native land for several years in Europe and took a long, hard look at the mother country. He was not impressed, observing that "Spain was a country of savages compared to France." Still, this antipathy for the Iberian nation did not prevent Bolívar from living the good life of a moneyed aristocrat in Spain. He also fell in love with and married (at the tender age of eighteen) María Teresa Rodríguez del Toro. Bolívar's European years also witnessed his intellectual coming of age. Voraciously reading classical texts and Enlightenment writers like John Locke, Thomas Hobbes, Montesquieu, and Jean-Jacques Rousseau, the budding philosopher and political activist could not ignore the Spanish crown's patent moral and geopolitical debilities, nor the potency of Great Britain and Napoleonic France. In one contemporary correspondence to a female acquaintance, he wrote: "I was suddenly made to understand that men were made for other things than love."

In 1802, Bolívar and María Teresa returned to Venezuela, but only months after arriving, in January 1803, María Teresa succumbed to yellow fever. In part to escape his grief, Bolívar returned to Spain. By 1807, he was back again in Venezuela, via a sailing ship that stopped off in the United States where he visited Washington, DC, New York, and Boston. According to Bolívar, "for the first time in my life, I saw rational liberty at first hand," although in the end he did not see the United States as a paradigm for Spanish American liberty. (The storied Francisco de Miranda was also laudatory of the North American paradigm, uttering in 1799 after a visit to France's radical revolution, "We have before our eyes two great examples, the American and the French revolutions. Let us prudently imitate the first and carefully shun the second.")

Bolívar believed that liberty for Spanish America was anything but a fool's errand, but this view was not shared by most of his compatriots, who had not yet reached his degree of political awareness, although it was now increasingly hard for Creoles to ignore the political and social earthquakes in North America and France. (The revolt led by enslaved people in Haiti in the 1790s, by contrast, terrified white Creoles like Bolívar who were aghast at the notion of subjugation by mestizos, *pardos* [tri-racial], and Black people.) Increasingly, Creole resentment at Iberian imperiousness in the Bourbon reform era would merge with Enlightenment philosophies of self-determination and personal liberty into the spark of rebellion.

THE BATTLE FOR VENEZUELA, AND BEYOND

In 1808, the embryonic pro-independence sentiment in Spanish America was set ablaze by precipitous events back in the Old World. France had been at war with Great Britain since 1803, but now the mercurial Napoleon sent his armies over the border to conquer Spain, which had been France's ally since 1796. Already riven by its own internecine struggle, the Spanish crown was unable to muster a suitable defense. In March, Bonaparte's forces occupied Madrid, and by May had forced King Charles IV and then his son and successor Ferdinand VII to cede the crown to Napoleon's brother, Joseph Bonaparte, who was crowned King of Spain the following month.

Anti-French resistance began manifesting itself in the form of guerrilla warfare (the word "guerrilla" actually comes from this moment in history) and the establishment of provincial *Junta* governments. By September 1808, a Supreme Central Junta was in place to govern the regions that continued to oppose rule by Napoleon's forces and allies; after this was dissolved in 1810, the Cortes of Cádiz emerged as a national legislative body, bringing together representatives from Spanish provinces and colonies. In 1812, the Cortes passed the liberal Constitution of 1812. One drawback, at least in the eyes of the Creoles back in America, was that although the Constitution deemed the New World territories members rather than colonies, the Creoles participating in the drafting were not given equal rights, and nor were the New World lands granted free commerce.

By 1814, Napoleon's military gambit in Spain had failed. Ferdinand returned to the throne with a renewed commitment to restoring Iberian control over the wayward (and at times recalcitrant) New World colonies. This time, however, some radical members of the Creole class were eager to start literal battles for independence on their native soils, and indeed the battle was already raging in Venezuela, which since 1810 had been caught up in a civil war between pro-independence Creoles and those remaining loyal to the Spanish monarchy, even before Ferdinand VI had been restored. And, over the next few years, Bolivar threw his body and mind into this anti-Spain organizing and diplomacy. In 1813, during his "Admirable Campaign," Bolívar established the Second Venezuelan Republic, and declared a "Decree of War to the Death," permitting violent acts against Spanish loyalists. In one demonstration of Bolívar's strategy, in 1814, he ordered the summary execution of just under one thousand Spanish detainees.

But a devastating reversal was not far away, in the shape of Spanish caudillo José Tomás Boves. Boves realized that his largely pardo army was more motivated by its visceral hatred of the arrogant Creoles—perceived as being engrossed with their putative nobility or perpetuating the "purity" of their bloodlines—than the distant, almost abstract notion of defending Spanish sovereignty, not to mention the fact that the canny caudillo promised to hand them the vast Creole land holdings. Biographer Marie Arana, bemoaned the fact that the pardos did not grasp "the true pyramid of oppression . . . that the roots of misery were in empire, that Spain had constructed that unjust world carefully." Bolívar also lamented the pardos' "unbelievable dementia" for "[taking] up arms to destroy [their] liberators and restore the scepter of its tyrants." Misguided or not, they were an effective fighting force: in July 1814, Boves's forces seized Caracas and, as one biographer put it, drove Bolívar's fellow Creoles into "an exodus of biblical proportions."

With Bolívar's dream of liberty stymied, the liberator turned his military sights to battle loyalist forces as a fugitive in New Granada (present-day Colombia). Within a year, after suffering more setbacks against loyal forces, he fled into exile, first in Jamaica and then Haiti. It was in Jamaica where in September 1815 he would pen his illustrious "Jamaica Letter," which would become "part of the political currency of the Spanish American Revolution."

Bolívar's letter was putatively a piece of private correspondence to an English friend living in Jamaica, Henry Cullen. After first assessing the state of the independence struggles and restating the justifications for forever removing Madrid's dominion, the Venezuelan aristocrat ended his essay with a new vi-

Simón Bolívar. *(Library of Congress Prints and Photographs Division, Washington, DC)*

sion for his native lands, an outlook deeply enmeshed in what he contended was the region's distinct characteristics, such as an underdeveloped civic culture and regional factionalism. Liberalism was less preferable to a highly centralized (read, run by Creoles like him!) federal government. Fascinatingly for our modern eyes, Haitian ruler Alexandre Pétion insisted that Bolívar eradicate slavery in his native Venezuela in return for Haitian soldiers, munitions, and money for his revolution.

Bolívar went only partway. In June 1816, returning to Venezuela from Haiti, the patriot leader abolished slavery, but only for those who would pick up arms for independence. "The new citizen who refuses to take up arms to fulfill the sacred duty of defending his freedom will remain subject to slavery, like his sons less than fourteen years old, his wife and his elderly parents." Bolívar also repeatedly expressed his deep fear of the *pardocracia*, whereby the result of independence would be governance by the majority Black people and pardos at the expense of enlightened Creole rule. One wonders the extent to which his time in Haiti—where a war of annihilation against the French slaveowners had terrified the Creoles' collective conscience—had shaped his racial outlook.

Through 1817 and 1818, Bolívar renewed the war against the royalist forces in Venezuela, now benefiting from the aid of erstwhile military rivals, including *llanero* (plainsman) José Antonio Páez. After the patriot victory at the Battle of Carabobo, on June 24, 1821, west of Caracas, effectively ended Spanish control in Venezuela, the war shifted west, across the rugged Andes range to the viceroy of New Granada. In one of the most stunning accomplishments in the history of warfare, Bolívar led a force of two thousand soldiers through an icy mountain pass known as the *Páramo de Pisba*. (páramos are high-elevation treeless plateaus.) Of these soldiers, some were English and Irish enlistees, as well as "medics, auxiliary forces, women, children, and a herd of cattle." Marie Arana describes the arduous march:

> Slipping and sliding over the wet, icy rock, the army kept on the move, ascending to thirteen thousand feet, knowing that to stop and lie down at those bone-chilling heights was to give up and die. By the time they had scaled the Páramo de Pisba, their shoes had no soles, their clothes were in shreds; hundreds had died of hypothermia.

Indeed, Bolívar, often riddled with malaria or dysentery, trekked on horse or foot over seventy-five thousand miles of formidable, sometimes inhospitable, terrain, from scorching plains to the tundra of the lethal páramos throughout his life. When in camps, the general rested, like his troops, in hammocks or on the ground or floor, never a bed, "wrapped only in a cape, curled up like a dog." Storied travel writer Wade Davis gives us a piercing sense of Bolívar's habits and idiosyncrasies that included taking a bath at the crack of dawn and two further ones throughout the day:

> Meticulous about cleanliness at the table, he carried his own silverware. Though a notorious womanizer, he rarely drank and never smoked; he was especially proud of his teeth, a complete set, perfectly aligned and brilliantly white, a rare achievement in a time of wooden dentures and toothless grins. He also had a passion for cologne, which his immediate entourage struggled to supply. His

soldiers tolerated the cloying scent as the one flaw in their otherwise exemplary and truly exceptional commander.

By August 1819, the Spanish had effectively lost their hold on what is today Colombia. With Venezuela and Colombia now both free, Bolívar turned his sights on Spanish-controlled Ecuador, which he freed in 1822. It was here in the port city of Guayaquil where he met up with José de San Martín, who had executed his own Hannibal-like performance to liberate the lands that would become Argentina and Chile. Within three years, Bolívar's military sagacity had toppled the deeply pro-royalist faction in Peru, where, in 1824, he was named dictator.

Next was Upper Peru (present-day Bolivia), the final section of South American land in royalist hands. This remaining liberation campaign was given to Venezuelan patriot general, Antonio José de Sucre—whose command had been vital to the liberation of Ecuador and Peru. By April 1825, the holdout royalist forces had surrendered. Although Bolívar did not lead the campaign, the new country was named in his honor. He could claim with much credence that his efforts, in his words, "had demonstrated to Europe that America has men who are equal to the heroes of antiquity."

Bolívar's success was perhaps only matched by his ego. A German outside of Bogotá painted Bolívar as "cold, domineering and limitlessly proud. Those around him suffer from his . . . practically childlike vanity." The sibling of a British officer affiliated with the independence armies described him as "insatiably covetous of fame." Even before his biggest military conquests, Bolívar had come to see himself as an incomparable savior. Having made it to Quito in 1822, he ascended Chimborazo, the snow-covered, 20,564-foot-high peak visible from the city—at the time believed to be the highest in the world. In a poem, "My Delirium on Chimborazo," he wrote of having "the God of Colombia take possession of me" and that "I have surpassed all men in good fortune, as I have risen above the heads of all." And despite his vast successes, the Great Liberator's ambition never flagged: "the demon of Glory will take us to Tierra del Fuego [the southern tip of Chile and Argentina]."

It was Bolívar's outsize influence (and ego) that arguably hindered the emergence of any post-independence regional solidarity. Bolívar wanted Latin American nations to stand together on their own terms, and envisioned the freshly minted republics *themselves* setting the diplomatic wheels in motion to establish a new league of Spanish American nations that would resist

Latin American Independence. *(University of Wisconsin-Madison Cartography Lab)*

common (imperial) foes and promote solidarity. In late 1824, Bolívar issued invitations for an "assembly of plenipotentiaries" to meet in Panama (then part of Gran Colombia, encompassing today's Colombia, Panama, Venezuela, and Ecuador) in June 1826, but the conference was a profound failure. Only Peru, Gran Colombia, Mexico, and the Federal Republic of Central America (today Costa Rica, Honduras, El Salvador, Nicaragua, and the southern Mexican state of Chiapas) attended the conference. Chile, "wrenched by internal conflagrations," was missing, and the United Province of Río de la Plata (parts of today's Argentina, Bolivia, Uruguay, Paraguay, and Brazil) skipped too, citing its "horror of too early a union," especially if said union was a decidedly pro-Colombia—that is, pro-Bolívar, affair, despite Bolívar's decision not to attend to reduce the chance that the outcomes could be written off as his preferences. Little emerged by way of outcome: only New Granada ratified the vacuous resolutions. Bolívar later acknowledged his foolhardiness in assuming he could bring a regional bloc together: "The institution [conference] was admirable like that mythic madman, perched on a rock in the open sea, thinking he could direct the ships' traffic."

The divisions between the new Latin American states—illuminated by the conference—were in part a consequence of the intense struggles for independence, but their futures were no less fraught. In Arana's words, "The Americas that were emerging under Bolívar's horrified eyes were feudalistic, divisive, militaristic, racist, ruled by warlords who strove to keep the ignorant masses blinkered and under bigoted control." Indeed, Latin America's much larger battle was domestic, as new leaders attempted to forge nations out of exploited colonies with profound racial and economic schisms.

FOUNDING FATHER, LIFETIME PRESIDENT, AUTOCRAT?

In 1826, Bolívar wrote a new constitution for the new nation of Bolivia, in which the long-standing tension between democracy and authoritarianism in Bolívar's thought became manifest—and leaned toward the latter. His constitution had key liberal elements like civil rights, strong courts, and abolition. However, features such as a lifetime presidency—which, ironically, he did not seek (he resigned in late 1825, holding the executive appointment for only five months, replaced by Sucre)—and voting restricted to certain classes were decidedly autocratic.

Explaining his stance, he told a British diplomat in Peru, "that his heart always beats in favour of liberty, but that his head leans towards aristocracy ... if the principles of liberty are too rapidly introduced anarchy and the destruction of the white inhabitants will be the inevitable consequences." Or to take the words of one of his subordinates, Daniel Florence O'Leary: "He sought a system capable of controlling revolutions, not theories which might foment them; the fatal spirit of ill-conceived democracy which had already produced so many evils in America had to be curbed if its effects were to be avoided." Or, perhaps more revealingly of Bolívar's real reasons for autocratic control, we might cite his 1821 correspondence with fellow independence giant, Francisco de Paula Santander of Colombia, in which Bolívar laid scorn on liberals who did not understand how difficult it would be to govern the disparate masses, encompassing "savage hordes from Africa and America."

Not surprisingly, there were many disapproving voices. French philosopher Benjamin Constant blasted the Liberator as an "outright despot." Santander, now Bolívar's vice president, dismissed the document as "absurd, a dangerous novelty." On the other hand, some thought he had not gone far enough: the former caudillo Páez urged Bolívar to end the formalities and simply call himself king of Gran Colombia. In a breathless letter from Caracas, in 1825, he warned Bolívar of the tumult in Venezuela and urged him to do exactly what Napoleon had done in Europe: "The situation in this country," he wrote,

> greatly resembles the way things stood in France when Napoleon was in Egypt [before he became Emperor], and was called upon by those great leading men of the revolution, who were convinced that a government had fallen and into the hands of the lowest rabble was not one that could save that nation. You are now in a position to say what that famous man said at the time: the intrigues are going to ruin this country. Let us go and save it.... General, this is not the land of Washington: Here people bow down to power out of terror and self-interest.

Legend has it that when the messenger gave Páez's correspondence, he responded with umbrage. Firing off a letter to Santander, Bolívar blasted Páez and a few supporters as despots since they believed that "no one can be great except in the manner of Alexander, Caesar and Napoleon." Nevertheless, upon returning to Colombia after this extended stint in Bolivia, Peru, and Ecuador, Bolívar once again pushed for more dictatorial elements in that Gran Colombia's founding document. When in 1828, the constitutional convention imploded, within months Bolívar, already president, proclaimed himself dictator as well, although he thought this was to save the republic. He ultimately decided that a Bolivian-styled constitution would be sufficient *mano dura* and crowning himself king would be rash and counterproductive. "Equality would be broken, and the people of color would see all their rights lost to a new aristocracy." Nevertheless, at this time Bolívar's shadow loomed large over the continent: for at least half a year, he was simultaneously president of Gran Colombia, president of Bolivia, and dictator of Peru.

END OF THE ROAD

As with many heroic arcs, Bolívar's apex was followed by a swift fall. In an infamous episode on September 25, 1828, that came to be known as the September Night, a band of political rivals infiltrated the San Carlos presidential palace to assassinate Bolívar. With the valiant dexterity of his lover and confidant, the Ecuadorian noblewoman and fireball revolutionary Manuela Sáenz, Simón narrowly escaped through a window and spent the night under a bridge. Sáenz was then given the moniker, "the liberator of the Liberator."

But the uprisings, machinations, and dissent kept brewing. In late April 1830, implacable opposition from liberal political actors forced Bolívar to vacate the presidency in Gran Colombia. In Venezuela, officials rescinded his citizenship, seized his property, and barred him from entering his native country. His last remaining asset was a distant copper mine, but this was tied up in a legal dispute. He was without money, salary, or even a pension, as the government would not honor his years of army service without indemnity. Here is Wade Davis, "Having committed his entire family fortune to the struggle, Simón Bolívar, 'El Libertador de la Gran Colombia,' emancipator of a continent, found himself alone on the streets of Bogotá, broke and impoverished, without sufficient means even to abandon the nation that so cruelly had abandoned him."

Soon after, the freshly arrived French ambassador, August Le Moyne, was horrified by Bolívar's appearance. When asked gently about his health, the South American liberator trenchantly quipped, "It isn't nature that has reduced me to this, but the pain gnawing at my heart. My fellow citizens couldn't kill me with daggers, so they are trying to kill me with ingratitude. When I cease to exist, those hot heads will devour each other like a pack of wolves, and what I erected with superhuman effort will drown in the muck of rebellion."

On May 8, the bitter and broken general set off from Bogotá to travel to the Caribbean coast along the sweltering, disease-infested Magdalena River. As Davis describes, "Though just forty-seven, he was little more than a bundle of bones: gaunt and frail, unable to walk, and scarcely able to breathe, so corrupted were his lungs, corroded by tuberculosis. His face hung yellow with jaundice; his eyes were dark as coal. Only his mind remained untarnished and alert, ensuring that his final days on the river, the last passage of his life, would be a torrent of regrets and recriminations." In December, not far from the port locale of Santa Marta, six hundred miles downriver to the Caribbean Sea, the despondent, hate-filled, and sickly Great Liberator died from tuberculosis. Here is how one modern Colombian admirer painted the Liberator's fate:

> Before the revolution, Bolívar was one of the richest men in the Americas. George Washington lived out his days in comfort, on vast estates, surrounded by his slaves, a wealthy man to the end. Bolívar freed his slaves, lost his land, and died in abject poverty, having committed his entire fortune to the struggle. He never wavered from his ideals, even if it meant the sacrifice of everything his family had acquired over three hundred years. The way Bolívar met his end will always be a shadow in our lives. The founder of six countries surely deserved better.

Even before the Great Liberator had his ignominious expiration, Venezuela and Ecuador had seceded from Gran Colombia, leaving New Granada (present-day Colombia and Panama) to fend for itself.

For nearly a quarter century, Bolívar's power of leadership and ambition helped secure freedom for the Spanish American people, but it also led him to personal destruction and isolation. Bolívar's Pan-American vision also came to naught, felled by political infighting and the innate preference by regional governments and actors to rule themselves. In the end, he was largely repudiated by the very nations he had willed to freedom.

But there is also another way of looking at Bolívar's legacy, particularly in terms of what we might call his inconsistent political morality. From our twenty-first-century vantage, we may struggle to reconcile the apparent contradictions in Bolívar's thought, but it is worth reflecting that in many ways, these tensions—concerning race, class, and the disposition of power—became a template for many of the struggles that would define these new republics. Bolivar may have helped Latin America secure its future independence, but he was also the product of its polarizing past. In Bolívar's brave new world, old beliefs die hard.

CODA: A SWORD AND A CEREMONY

In a brazen 1974 raid, rebels from the M-19, a Colombian Marxist guerrilla insurgency, stole Bolívar's sword and riding spurs from the Great Liberator's colonial house in Bogotá, which now contained a museum, leaving the note: "Bolívar, your sword returns to the battlefield." Over the next seventeen years, there was at least one instance when the sword spent years out of the idealistic guerrilla group's possession. One likely apocryphal tale is that the rebels presented the saber to their ideological mentor (and at least to some extent, cash and weapons provider) Fidel Castro for "safekeeping," but that the Cuban comandante would not hand it back.

Be that as it may, in early 1991 at a solemn ceremony at Bogotá's San Carlos presidential palace attended by Colombian president César Gaviria, the M-19 returned the sword to the museum, having laid down its arms and become a political party less than a year prior. "It has crossed mountains, been hidden in the homes of patriots and crossed borders," said (the now former) guerrilla Antonio Navarro Wolf. "Today it returns to the hands of the Colombian people." The spurs, however, were never returned—perhaps a fitting testament to a man who in his remarkable life never stood still.

II
NINETEENTH CENTURY

7

Antonio López de Santa Anna
The Hero Who Lost Half a Country

> Providence willed my history to be the history of Mexico since 1821.
> —*Antonio López de Santa Anna*

During the quarter century between independence in 1821 and the full-scale "gringo invasion" in 1847, the new nation of Mexico endured constant destitution, tumult, and, extraordinarily, fifty military regimes, often tacking from "federalist" (more autonomy for *state* governments) to "centralist" (mostly conservative, supporting the Church and a strong, elite *central* government), then back to federalist again. Administrations convoked five constitutional assemblies and blessed three constitutions (and numerous state constitutions), each one "driven by the notion of final, national redemption." In 1827, Mexico's legendary liberal thinker, José María Luis Mora, described his priority in shaping the structures of power in the new country:

> The most important thing... is to reduce the motives, real or imagined, which could lead to the concentration of a great accumulation of authority in power in the hands of one man.... The love of power, innate in man and always on the increase in the process of government, is much more to be feared in republic than in monarchies.

Mora hypothesized the dangers of a Mexican version of French emperor Napoleon Bonaparte, who, donning the veil of liberalism and acting as though he was serving the people, would become a dictator and turn the population into political slaves.

And this is exactly what came about with Antonio López de Santa Anna, a "creole caricature of Bonaparte" [Creoles were New World–born Spaniards] who dressed in both liberal and conservative contours and fashions (as the occasion demanded), and who had outsize influence on Mexico until 1855. As Lucas Alamán, Mexican scientist, conservative politician, and writer, commented: "The history of Mexico since 1822 might be accurately called the history of Santa Anna's revolutions. . . . His name plays the major role in all political events of the country and its destiny has become intertwined with his." But while most caudillos had little use for ideology, few were as feckless in their abandonment and shifting of policies and parties as Santa Anna.

THE PATH TO PRESIDENT

Santa Anna was born in 1794 in Veracruz, "the richest, gayest, most spendthrift and morally easygoing port in the country." Here is one insightful account of Antonio's childhood: "His father had been an army officer who was always in debt and his mother a great beauty rumored not to believe in God; he had Gypsy blood in him, and one of his uncles had seen no contradiction in being at once a priest and a bullfighter." Santa Anna's hobbies included "gambling, womanizing, cockfighting, delivering speeches, flattery, and forging commercial documents." He was a regular user of opium, along with other drugs.

Before we continue the Santa Anna saga, some brief history is to give us a sense of Mexico's idiosyncratic political climate at the time. On September 16, 1810, outspoken Catholic priest Miguel Hidalgo y Costilla, through his celebrated "Cry of Dolores" (with Dolores being the location it occurred), rang his church bell, declaring Mexico's independence movement. Despite initial successes in this battle to enact land redistribution and racial equality, Hidalgo was apprehended and executed. But his call to arms was picked up by campesino and men of the cloth commanders, notably Mariano Matamoros, José María Morelos, and Vicente Guerrero, who all led racially mixed and indigenous rebellions against the Spanish and their royalist supporters.

Ironically, it was the Royalists—comprising Mexican Creoles as well as other conservatives—who ended up achieving independence by calling for a break with Spain to maintain their prerogatives in Mexico. Unlike Hidalgo's putsch eleven years before, their rebellion was pacific and orderly, with nary a shot fired. It was led by the cagey royalist Creole landowner and former officer in the Spanish army, Agustin de Iturbide, who had opposed Hidalgo and vanquished Morelos.

Iturbide worked with his erstwhile enemy, Vicente Guerrero, a mestizo, to broker the Plan de Iguala, on February 24, 1821. Now Mexico would be a constitutional monarchy, with the Catholic Church's elevated status guaranteed. Iturbide proceeded to defeat the remaining Royalist factions who did not support this new plan. There was much joy and expectation, given the country's assumed riches. Maybe Alexander von Humboldt's prognostication would pan out. "The vast kingdom of New Spain, well cultivated, could by itself produce everything that commerce goes searching after throughout the rest of the world."

In 1822, Iturbide was proclaimed "Constitutional Emperor of Mexico," but it appeared he had decidedly mixed feelings about the job. Upon assuming the crown, he proclaimed that his subjects should not obey him if he did not follow the constitution, and just days after the ceremony, he confided in a letter to Simón Bolívar: "How far I am from considering this a benefit, when it has placed this burden on my shoulders that overwhelms me!" He then revealed, "I lack the strength needed to hold the scepter; I refused it and finally consented in order to avoid evil consequences for my country, which is on the verge of once again yielding, if not to the ancient slavery, then surely to the ills of anarchy."

But the cold reality was soon to put his ideals to the test. After only ten frenetic months in power, Iturbide realized that the "opulent empire" was anything but. The protracted independence wars had led to mines being abandoned, haciendas torched, nascent industrial development halted, and millions of dollars of capital fleeing the bankrupt country. Fatefully, Iturbide opted to suspend Congress, replacing it with an abhorred junta.

Enter Antonio López de Santa Anna. The haughty young Creole had served in the Spanish army and rose to the rank of captain; he had backed Iturbide (who thought Santa Anna was a "volcanic genius") and the independence struggle. In December 1822, Santa Anna launched an insurrection against the emperor, which Iturbide could have crushed but confusingly chose not to. Santa Anna and Guadalupe Victoria, an independence war veteran, overthrew Iturbide, with Victoria becoming the Republic of Mexico's first president. Congress sentenced Iturbide to death if he ever dared step foot again in Mexican territory. The following year, Mexico embraced the nation's first federal constitution, very much modeled after the United States' founding document, although only Catholicism was allowed.

After a few turbulent years, Santa Anna finally got a shot at the top job himself. In 1829, Madrid dispatched an expeditionary force to reconquer Mexico—something that the United States' so-called Monroe Doctrine (declared six years earlier) was supposed to have thwarted. Santa Anna, saber literally in hand, led the troops who checked the Iberian incursion at the Gulf port of Tampico. His attack on the Spanish command post, as described by Mexican general Manuel de Mier y Terán, was "a master stroke of boldness." Promoted to major general, Santa Anna, the "hero of Tampico," became a national icon, and in 1833, the self-proclaimed "Man of Destiny" was elected president with a staggering level of support.

Claiming an ailment, Santa Anna did not attend his own inauguration; like Iturbide, he too did not appear to relish the responsibilities of the highest rung, although in Santa Anna's case a lack of dedication was more to blame. Between his first election in 1833 and 1835, Santa Anna was *"el presidente"* on four very brief occasions, preferring in the main to delegate the tedious duties of governing to Dr. Valentín Gómez Farías, an illustrious liberal, who, along with advisor José Luis Mora, went to work implementing wide-ranging reforms intended to hit at the Church's entitlements as well as more modest moves to rein in the military.

Over the next months and years, the proposed reform agenda incensed entrenched army and church interests, who then frantically turned to the now quasi-retired Santa Anna, "the maker and unmaker of presidents par excellence." In 1835, he backed this embryonic insurrection against his own government. Here from the book, *The Course of Mexican History*: "Not embarrassed by lack of consistency, the embattled champion of all liberal causes since 1821 began denouncing anti-clerical atheists, York Rite masons, native federalists, subversive anarchists, Jacobins, Gómez Farías, and his liberal cohorts."

Santa Anna formed a new manifestly conservative and pro-church government which nullified the liberal 1824 Constitution and replaced it with a centralist variant. He then headed back into retirement at his beloved hacienda, *Manga de Clavo* (Sleeve of a Clove), vowing never to return to politics unless a "daring enemy" menaced the *patria* (homeland).

"REMEMBER THE ALAMO!"

Santa Anna's revocation of the 1824 Constitution had caused an uproar among liberal elites in the Yucatán and, more fatefully, in the northern province in what is now Texas, where the swelling ranks of Anglo-American colonists rejected the new constitution and launched a war of independence. The Mexican government's abolition of slavery in 1829 also provoked the settlers—overwhelmingly from the American South—who had transported their enslaved people with them.

In September 1835, Santa Anna sent a general with a small detachment of troops to put down the rebellion, but by October, the tide had turned against the Mexicans, who were forced to withdraw south of the Rio Grande. After he had been exhorted by his *paisanos* (countrymen) to come out of retirement, Santa Anna assembled a motley six-thousand-man army and recrossed the Rio Grande at the start of 1836, together with some fiery rhetoric: "I have sworn that my sword will always be the first to deliver a stroke upon the presumptions of the enemy."

An unabashed worshiper of Napoleon, he was confident that, like Napoleon's epic offensive across Europe, he would do the same in Texas. In response to rumors of US volunteers crossing the border to bolster rebel numbers, Santa Anna told the French ambassador, "If the North Americans do not behave themselves, I will march across their country and plant the Mexican flag in Washington." It would be a posture that would have consequences far beyond what even Santa Anna could have imagined. As historian David A. Clary expressed, "This vainglorious caudillo all but guaranteed that a provincial rebellion would turn into a war of independence and his country into an implacable enemy of the United States."

Yet at first, Santa Anna's campaign seemed to be successful. Even the prudent conservative figure Lucas Alamán cheered on the vanquishing Mexican general: "Señor Santa Anna has so prevailed over the Anglo-American colonists who have rebelled in Texas that we may consider the matter over and done with." And then came the Alamo, an aged, dusty Franciscan mission near San Antonio de Béxar where two-hundred-odd independence fighters were garrisoned under the command of Colonel William Barrett Travis. This group included illustrious patriots Davy Crockett (a former congressman) and Jim Bowie, inventor of the Bowie knife, but also Mexican citizens who had joined the independence movement.

Santa Anna's army began a ten-day-long siege before launching a final attack. Late on March 5, 1836, the defenders heard a bugle call from the Mexican side they did not recognize. It was the *degüello*, the ancient battle call played when the Spanish fought their centuries-long campaign to rid the Moors of the Iberian Peninsula. Ordered by Santa Anna, the degüello meant that there

Map of Texas. *(University of Wisconsin-Madison Cartography Lab)*

was to be no mercy shown to the enemy in the ensuing battle. On March 6, Santa Anna's take-no-prisoners degüello was brutally enforced: all were killed, aside from a handful of women and children and one enslaved man.

At the Battle of San Jacinto (near present-day Houston) in late April 1836, around eight hundred to nine hundred freedom fighters led by Sam Houston punched back, attacking the Mexican force of over 1,330 with cries of "Remember the Alamo!" Santa Anna, overconfident and tactically sloppy, presided over a Mexican army that capitulated in just eighteen minutes. After winning the lopsided fight that ended with 630 killed and 730 captured on the Mexican side (with only nine dead and thirty wounded on the Texan side), Texan forces captured Santa Anna the next day (he was hiding in the brush) and quickly coerced him to sign a covert pact recognizing their autonomy. The imprisoned Mexican commander signed two peace agreements with Texas President David Burnet, which, among other things, ended hostilities between the two sovereign sides and moved Mexican forces back across the Rio Grande (in Mexico, the Río Bravo).

But Santa Anna's diplomacy failed to change the standing of either side. Mexico City, contending that Santa Anna had been ousted from public office before he signed these peace accords, vehemently maintained that Texas was a renegade province, while in September 1836, Texans voted to request annexation by the United States. Back home, Santa Anna's star had fallen dramatically: a mere three months after praising the general, Lucas Alamán said that Santa Anna had put himself before his country:

> In no time at all, the political affairs of this country have taken a terrible turn. General Santa Anna, lured on, without doubt, by the idea of finishing the war himself with a decisive blow, and perhaps jealous of the glory his lieutenants had acquired, advanced with a small body of troops, rashly and without taking proper precautions, and was defeated and taken prisoner on the 21st of April. . . . General Santa Anna signed an armistice solely to gain his own freedom and as a result of this agreement he is expected soon in Veracruz.

When Santa Anna was released and back in Mexico, he once again retreated to Manga de Clavo where he scribed a "Manifesto," absolving himself of responsibility for the military debacle. He held that, underequipped and outgunned, and in inhospitable territory, his forces had little chance. He also blamed the siesta—the time-honored Mexican tradition—as his men were snoozing when

Sam Houston's forces attacked. "I never thought that a moment of rest . . . could be so disastrous."

Yet his reputation for military genius was restored in late 1838 when Santa Anna again came out of retirement to personally and valiantly lead Mexicans against the French in the wonderfully titled Pastry War. The conflict was named for its catalyst—the claim by a French pastry chef working at a restaurant near the capital that drunken Mexican soldiers ate without paying the bill and destroyed part of the establishment. The resulting indignity in Paris saw a ten-ship French force sent to seize Veracruz. It was in an early December 1838 battle that Santa Anna had several horses shot out from under him and lost half his left leg after being hit by French grapeshot. The limb was buried at his Manga de Clavo, in a religious ceremony with speeches and full military honors.

In one of the most freakish moments in his time in power, in the fall of 1842 the venerable caudillo—now president again—had the remains of his leg unearthed from its "quiet repose" and taken to Mexico City in a garish coach. A procession that included the army, presidential guard, and cadets from the Chapultepec Military Academy accompanied the limb, which was ostentatiously laid on a public memorial in an elaborate state funeral—attended by the full cabinet, diplomatic corps, and Congress—at a cemetery. It was all naturally "Santanesque." One astute historian put it this way: "the speeches, songs and poems offered in Santa Anna's honor paled all previous efforts at sanctification as the leg shattered by the French cannonball was now being offered to the fatherland."

It was during his presidency between 1842 and 1844 that Santa Anna's ego really began to get the better of him. The new theater built in the capital, which had a price tag of 350,000 pesos (a staggering sum), was opened with the name the Gran Teatro de Santa Anna. When performances were introduced, they were: "Dedicated to His Most Serene Highness, Major-General, President of the Republic, National Hero, Commander of the Great Cross of the Royal and Distinguished Order of Carlos III and Grand Master of the National and Distinguished Order of Guadalupe: Don Antonio López de Santa Anna." The presidential residence in Tacubaya, outside the city, was converted into a palace. "Salvos of artillery fire and twenty-one-gun salutes preceded the dictator and announced his presence everywhere he went." Congress, concluding that the existing head of state bodyguard details was too small for a leader of his eminence, sanctioned a new 1,200-man guard, called the Lancers of the Supreme Party. Santa Anna's Saint's Day was made into a national holiday; friends gave him presents, which in a bountiful year amounted to thousands of pesos.

But public sentiment soon soured again, especially after the fifty-year-old Santa Anna precipitously married a fifteen-year-old beauty a mere few months after the death of his long-suffering wife. Santa Anna was forced into exile, and a rowdy mob dug up his leg and made it a target of derision by dragging it through the capital, whooping, "Death to the cripple!"

THE BATTLE FOR MEXICO CITY

The animosity between Mexico and the United States over Texas was still smoldering in the mid-1840s and broke out into war by the middle of 1846. The Mexicans, however, soon found themselves on the back foot and looked to a familiar face for aid. In 1847, Santa Anna assembled a force of around eighteen thousand soldiers in San Luis Potosí and marched them just over 250 miles in five days over arduous topography. Then on February 23, 1847, he faced off in the province of Coahuila against US General Zachary Taylor's forces. While the battle ended inconclusively, the 4th Illinois Infantry did score a macabre battlefield trophy: after surprising the Mexican commander who fled on horseback, they captured Santa Anna's prosthetic leg, which they carried back to their home state. (After a stint making the rounds in country fairs it ended up at the Illinois State Military Museum, where it remains despite Mexican government requests to have the leg repatriated.)

In March, a sizable US invasion force of around thirteen thousand troops commanded by General Winfield Scott landed in Veracruz and headed westward—roughly along the route Cortés took to defeat the Aztecs—to seize Mexico's national government. By August 1847 Scott's forces had reached the outskirts of Mexico City. Santa Anna, now the supreme commander of the Mexican forces, offered the Americans a truce but did not surrender. The Americans refused and on August 20 launched a campaign to seize the capital. At the battles of Contreras and Churubusco in the city's southern environs, Scott's forces won two victories on the same day, decimating Santa Anna's army. Within a month US forces were attacking the formidable hilltop citadel Chapultepec Castle, which once was the Spanish viceroy's residency but was now a Mexican military school, with the two sides engaging in brutal hand-to-hand combat.

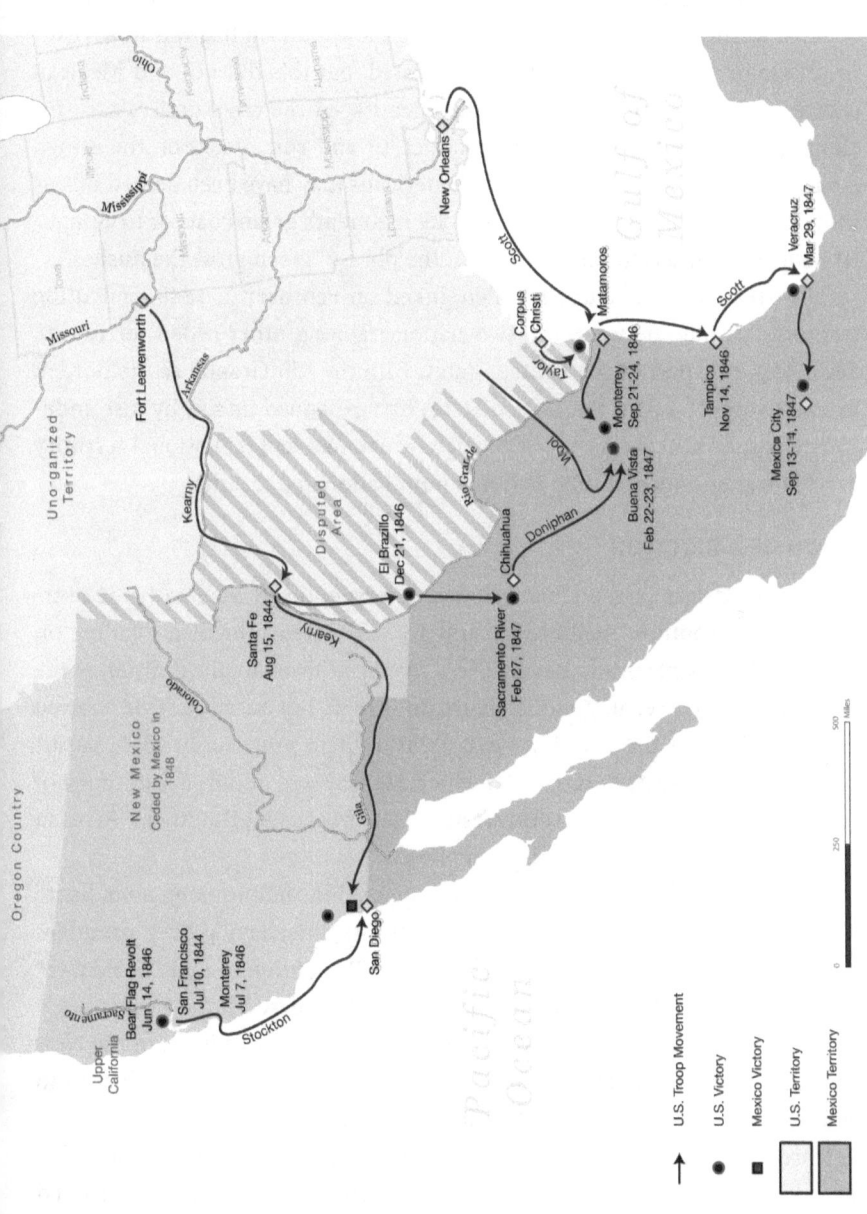

Mexican American War, 1846–1848. (University of Wisconsin-Madison Cartography Lab)

On September 13, America's siege of the fortress ended. The next day General Scott entered the central square, "resplendent in full-dress uniform, to accept the formal surrender of the city," while the American flag was flown over the National Palace. The city had capitulated, but this did not end Mexican resistance to the conflict. Santa Anna encouraged the city's underclass—including just-released inmates—to conduct hit-and-run attacks on the gringo invaders. (This disparaging term for Americans may have been coined in this war, perhaps in reference to the Kentucky regiment's green coats or to a popular song sung by US soldiers ending in the phrase "green grow the bushes.")

The Treaty of Guadalupe Hidalgo, inked on February 2, 1848, ended the territorial dispute between the two nations; among other ceded territories, Texas was now part of the United States, with the Rio Grande as the border. In one swoop of a pen, the United States had expanded its size by just under two-thirds, all at the expense of Mexico, which lost half its national territory in what was an indescribable national humiliation and trauma.

DEATH OF A DICTATOR

Despite the defeat in the United States, Intervention in Mexico (as it came to be known south of the border), and a good share of the blame falling on his shoulders, Santa Anna nevertheless managed to maintain himself as the country's most powerful political figure until 1855. But once again, he showed that his political acumen did not match his military prowess. In 1853, he authorized the Gadsden Purchase, in which Mexico sold additional millions of acres of land in present-day southwestern New Mexico and southern Arizona to the United States for ten million dollars.

The move sparked widespread liberal opposition, and not long after, Santa Anna would be removed from office for the last time, having been president on eleven distinct occasions, by liberals in the "Revolution of Ayutla." He went into exile in Colombia, Cuba, and the West Indies (where he met US Secretary of State William Seward), and also lived, demented and destitute, in the New York City borough of Staten Island for a few years. At last, he was allowed to return to Mexico a few years before he died in 1876.

Here is how one Mexican paper described the postmortem scene, "The last hours of his life inspire the saddest of reflections: the man who controlled millions, who acquired fortune and honors, who exercised an unrestricted dictatorship, had died in the midst of the greatest want, abandoned by all except a few of his friends." Another daily, *Dos Repúblicas*, had its own obituary:

Antonio López de Santa Anna. *(Library of Congress Prints and Photographs Division, Washington, DC)*

"A relic of another epoch, our generation remembered him for the misfortunes he brought upon the republic, forgetting the really eminent services he rendered to the nation. However, he may have been condemned by parties, his career formed a brilliant and important portion of the History of Mexico. . . . Peace to his ashes." His death was noted in the US presses but with little sadness or concern.

"THE TUMULTUOUS ORDER OF THE DAY"

Scholars have attempted to understand Santa Anna's appeal given all of the failures and chaos that marked his tenure in power. Certainly, Santa Anna proved himself a brave military leader, yet also one who could allow the desire for glory to cloud his reason. Liberal intellectual and physician Lorenzo de Zavala accurately characterized his persona as early as 1826: "The soul of the general cannot be contained by his body. He lives in perpetual agitation, he gets carried away by an irresistible desire to acquire glory. . . . Defeat . . . maddens him . . . then he abandons himself to a feeling of weakness though not cowardice. He pays no attention to strategy."

As a politician, Santa Anna was even more chaotic, impulsive, and contradictory: traits that would have deep consequences for a nation looking to set itself on firm ground. More from his contemporary, Zavala: "He is a man who has within him some force always driving him to take action, but since he has no fixed principles nor any organized code of public behavior, through his lack of understanding he always moves to extremes and comes to contradict himself. He does not measure his actions or calculate the results."

Alamán argued that his complete "inner lack of consistency" and "enterprising spirit which had neither a set plan nor a fixed purpose" reflected the Creole elites' condition; and by extension, we can see that Santa Anna's success was also in some part an indication of the societal fascination with those aristocratic forms of power and personal behavior. Ultimately, then, we might see the mercurial Santa Anna not only as a cause of Mexico's "restlessness, disorder, vacillation, and disorientation," but also as a result of it, its "personalized expression." Here is one early biographer, "[Santa Anna] went along with the tumultuous order of the day"; but he was the "barometer of national upheavals"; the "specter of the society, of its romanticism and megalomania." Soul of a country or not, it is undeniable that this history-making figure's "intelligence, resolution, and temperament, his sins and ambitions" set the course for mid-century Mexico.

8

Benito Juárez

Mexico's Great Reformer

During Mexico's calamitous war with the United States in the late 1840s, Benito Juárez, a thirty-something Zapotec Indian, was serving his nation as a deputy to the national Congress in Mexico City. He returned to his native state of Oaxaca, in the country's southern reaches, to serve as the interim governor, an appointment he started on October 29, 1847. Notably, Juárez was the first Indian governor since the founding of the Mexican republic following independence from Spain in 1821.

It was an extraordinary achievement, the product of a lifetime's hard work and drive to succeed. Born to rural poverty and orphaned as an infant in a mountainous region in 1818, Juárez had left home for good before he was even a teenager, trekking from his Oaxaca pueblo to the state capital where his older sister worked as a cook. The move allowed him to begin his formal studies, including learning Spanish. His sister helped the scrappy lad land a job at the residence of a Franciscan lay brother, Antonio Salanueva, who had a side gig as a bookbinder. In return for his chores around the house and at the bindery, Juárez had his tuition covered at the Council Seminary, the city's sole educational institution. Studying Latin and theology, in his early twenties Juárez had been keen on a vocation in the cloth. But for whatever reason this ardor eased, replaced by an interest in law. It was in law school where he honed his understanding and respect for Enlightenment principles: reason, secularism, and republican government, before graduating in 1831.

This was also when he first cut his teeth in the Oaxaca city council, where he quickly earned a reputation for honesty and a methodical legal mind. He later made his way to the state legislature, during which time he contributed pro bono legal work for the indigent and *campesinos* (peasants) who, among other grievances, were often contesting the sky-high rates demanded by priests for the sacraments or suing the local *hacendado* (landowner) class.

In 1848, Oaxaqueños elected Juárez to a full term as constitutional governor. That same year, vanquished and humiliated after the brutal US conquest of Mexico, the ever-polarizing General Santa Anna sought sanctuary in Oaxaca (also his native soil), but in 1848, the governor issued a persona non grata decree—a slight that the raging commander never excused. In so many ways Juárez was the polar opposite of Santa Anna. "His Most Serene Highness" was imperious, vain, and mercurial. The indigenous figure from the lowly Oaxaca pueblo of Guelatao—"with his darkness of aged bronze, his look of a stone idol"—was inscrutable and orderly. Santa Anna gave innumerable speeches that lacked even a single phrase of sincerity or veracity, all pure theater. In Juárez's rhetoric, moral sobriety is ubiquitous. Most strikingly, next to Santa Anna's antics, Juárez had a profound sense of public duty: "God and society have placed us in these positions so as to bring happiness to our communities and avoid the evils which could come to them."

Unusual for Mexico in this era, the unflagging governor oversaw the building of around fifty rural schools that promoted female attendance; paid debts in full; and trimmed red tape from the state's bloated bureaucracy. But the mere fact that he, a Zapotec Indian, was governor was revolutionary in itself, and his class-transcending confidence was further proved when back in 1843, the up-and-coming reformist liberal married, Margarita Maza, a Creole, turning the country's normal social conventions on its head.

LIBERAL REVOLUTION

In 1853, however, the tables had turned. Santa Anna was back in power, now under the guise of His Most Serene Highness, and was swift to exact his revenge on Juárez, whom he perceived as being part of the liberal threat to his rule. Forced into exile, the former Oaxaca governor wound up in New Orleans, where he started organizing with other disaffected liberals, led by Melchor Ocampo, already residing in the Louisiana city who were eager to topple the Mexican tyrant. These individuals joined up with rugged caudillo Juan Álvarez, who had fought as a patriot when Santa Anna was with the royalists.

In 1854, Álvarez led an insurrection under the banner of the Plan of Ayutla, which called for liberal policies and listed scores of grievances against the dictator. By the following year, Santa Anna, the ruler responsible for stymying liberal policies for a generation, was deposed, never to hold power again;

"Ayutla" had become a victorious armed revolution. It did not hurt that conservatives had soured on Santa Anna's ability to protect their interests; in fact, many of their elite ranks expressed sympathy or switched over to the ascendant, confident liberal forces.

The Revolution of Ayutla, as history remembers it, comprised several of Mexico's "most original and creative minds." Not cloistered academics, these were first-rate authors and intellectuals infused with a selfless spirit of public service and idealism who were eager to create a true modern Mexican nation, the only thing that could stave off the fledgling country's self-destructive tendencies—an anxiety reinforced by the catastrophic outcome of losing half of the country's territory to the United States just a quarter century after independence. With Álvarez in power, these newly repatriated liberal thinkers—led by Juárez—worked furiously as a brain trust to promulgate a serious, if initially vague, reform agenda, *La Reforma*. The movement's principal target was, predictably, the Catholic Church, an institution that the reformers viewed as hopelessly linked to conservative and reactionary sectors; along with the military, the Church's prerogatives appeared as a foul-smelling holdover from the colonial period.

Now the minister of justice, one of Juárez's first reforms was, in 1855, the eponymous *Ley Juárez* (Juárez Law) that, in addition to ending special rules absolving soldiers and priests from civil legal oversight, dissolved military and ecclesiastical *fueros* (special exemptions). Not surprisingly, Ley Juárez provoked ire amid Church and conservative ranks, but it also highlighted a dichotomy on the liberal side as moderates were inclined to pull back while the orthodox liberals pushed an unyielding line. President Álvarez would resign during the tumult, creating an opening for his successor, the more obliging Ignacio Comonfort, but the anti-church reforms kept coming. In 1856 the so-called *Ley Lerdo* (after statesman Miguel Lerdo de Tejada) went after corporate property, including *ejidos*, the communal lands held by indigenous communities. It also tackled the threat that was the Church's massive private landholdings through the declaration that, while it could keep its churches, monasteries, and seminaries, its properties not used for regular activities had to be relinquished at a public option. The plan, as its architects well understood, would have the added benefit of lining the federal government's underfunded coffers.

The crowning achievement of La Reforma was the drafting of a new constitution. A leading twentieth-century scholar of Mexico's liberal period, Daniel

Cosío Villegas, wrote that Mexico's Constitutional Convention was seminal: "Mexican history has black and shameful pages that we would love to eliminate; it has heroic pages that we would like to see printed in large letters; but our history has one unique page in which Mexico conveys the sense of being a mature country fully at home within the democracy and liberalism of modern Western Europe. And that page is the constitutional Convention of 1856."

The following year on February 5, a new constitution was promulgated. Among its dozens of articles were provisions for freedom of association and movement; abolition of debtors' prisons; gratis public defenders in court trials; the ending of nobility titles; property rights; election of magistrates to the Supreme Court; the right of habeas corpus in instances of abuse of authority; and the abolition of slavery—eight years before the United States. Prior critical reform laws, notably Ley Juárez and Ley Lerdo, were absorbed into the new charter. The Mexican framers of the Mexican Constitution of 1857 were "fiercely, proudly, arrogantly, absurdly, irrationally independent," and they remade the state as a new democratic, representative republic. Unlike its forlorn predecessor from 1824, the 1857 constitution did not establish Roman Catholicism as the state church, a move that effectively legalized other religions.

THE WAR OF THE REFORM

Liberal leaders mandated that citizens take an oath to the new founding document; civil servants who did not do so could lose their jobs. Predictably, the constitution was sternly rejected by conservatives and clergy. Bishops such as Clemente de Jesús Munguía contended that Catholics could not observe numerous articles, including freedom of speech and freedom of assembly, let alone tolerate Ley Juárez and Ley Lerdo. Pope Pius IX himself also condemned the new document. Troops who endorsed the constitution were refused treatment in Catholic hospitals. Not surprisingly, many Mexicans felt squeezed between the revolutionary liberal state's new rules and their traditional allegiances to Catholicism.

The new Constitution was supposed to bind the new country together, but it ended up precipitating a civil war. The Reform War was an especially heinous internal conflict that endured for three years, between January 1858 and January 1861. At first, conservative armies scored victory after victory. They captured Mexico City and in January 1858 removed President Comonfort, whose efforts at compromise had come to naught, prompting him to flee into exile.

Fatefully, Juárez, serving as the elected head of the Supreme Court and thus effective vice president, was now the constitutional president. Declaring his legal claim to be the legitimate head of state in the war-torn nation, he decamped his military forces to the relative sanctuary of the Gulf Coast port redoubt of Veracruz. Conservative general Félix Zuloaga was now in power in Mexico City, eventually swearing fidelity to the Vatican, and planned to smash the liberal heretics. Zuloaga closed Congress and had Juárez arrested, although the wily liberal was able to eventually make his way to Querétaro, by which time liberal backers declared him president—a sort of legitimate government in exile.

The country now had two presidents with two absolutist ideologies, backed by two armies. Conservatives, militarists to their core, had the more capable and seasoned generals and prodigious weapons caches, while the liberals had the port revenues, better communications with foreign capitals and leaders, and the indomitable figure of Juárez. The Zapotec liberal president in Veracruz indeed had his work cut out for him: continuing to resist conservative armies intent on seizing Veracruz, but also mitigating pettiness amid ambitious liberal leaders and jockeying while enacting the constitution and offering at least a veneer of societal normalcy.

A shot in the arm to the liberal cause came in the form of foreign recognition from the James Buchanan administration. Soon *yanqui* materiel was flowing to the freedom fighters in Veracruz, an interesting moment in US–Mexican relations given that, just a decade prior, US troops had used the same port to commence their march on Mexico City! American volunteers offered to join the liberal fight. By contrast, Madrid, Paris, and London by and large backed the conservatives. In fact, by 1859, both sides had incurred large foreign debts: liberals to the United States and conservatives to Spain.

Unlike the independence campaigns, *mestizo* (mixed Spanish and native) and indigenous Mexicans did not readily involve themselves in this war, something that forced both sides to resort to forced conscription. Still, the civil war never exploded on a national scale and remained at heart a conflict between governing minorities: out of a population of eight million, fewer than twenty-five thousand fighters were active. Indians fought on the liberal side for their Zapotec hero, but also on the conservative side as some groups throughout the vast countryside assumed that reform laws would abolish their ejidos, or communal land plots.

But the violence was still severe. Excitable commanders on both sides targeted civilians and executed prisoners in cold blood, one side in the name of the Holy See, and the other to uphold democracy and the rule of law. Liberals shot priests and torched churches, enraging their God-fearing enemies who vowed revenge. In one of the war's most infamous episodes, on April 11, 1858, in the town of Tacubaya, not far from Mexico City, conservative commander Leonardo Márquez killed prisoners as well as medical students attending to wounded liberal soldiers. He afterward gained the chilling sobriquet "the Tiger of Tacubaya."

JUÁREZ GOES MAXIMALIST

During 1859 and 1860, the civil war's fervor was matched by the political activity of the liberal camp. These were a series of Veracruz-issued decrees that made La Reforma policies seem like child's play. Juárez's government

Benito Juárez. *(Library of Congress Prints and Photographs Division, Washington, DC)*

was going maximalist in the anti-clerical crusade to irrevocably subjugate the Mexican Church: ecclesiastical holdings were confiscated without compensation; religious marriages annulled; monasteries and convents shuttered; the clergy made to pay taxes for the first time; religious holidays eliminated and, gratuitously, the ringing of church bells restricted. Juárez codified the separation of church and state, and guaranteed religious freedom for all Mexicans. And not least, the revenues from the church property sales helped bolster the liberal war chest.

The military tide then turned in the liberals' favor. Buoyed by a succession of battle successes in the prior weeks and months, on January 11, 1861, Juárez jubilantly reentered Mexico City. The liberal army had entered on New Year's Day, marking the end of the war and a liberal victory. Nevertheless, Church and conservative resistance to the new administration was significant, with scattered militias assassinating liberal government officials. Liberals also continued to hunt foes despite the conflict being over. One scholar chillingly coined this era "The Pickaxe of the Reform." Here is historian Enrique Krauze: "Eminent Liberals literally picked up axes to destroy altars, church facades, pulpits, and confessionals. Scenes out of the French Revolution were reenacted. Images of Saints were decapitated, shot full of holes, burned in public *autos-da-fé*; Church treasuries were robbed, archives were plundered, ecclesiastical libraries went up in flames. Bishops were stoned to death, and Church property was auctioned off." And this unspeakable savagery was exactly what conservatives had predicted would be the result of Juárez's unleashed war on Christ and country.

THE AUSTRIAN ARCHDUKE

In March 1961, just a few months after the conservatives had fled Mexico City, Juárez was elected president. Having inherited an exhausted treasury and dealing with a military and civil service waiting for its overdue pay, one of his first moves was to declare a two-year moratorium on further payments on the onerous foreign debt. By mid-December, France, Spain, and Great Britain had retaliated by collectively seizing the custom houses in Veracruz, from where funds would presumably have been used to pay off the debts. But officials from the three occupying countries were not able to come up with a resolution on debt enforcement, and a massive yet highly dubious French claim, in particular, led Spain (six thousand troops) and Great Britain (seven hundred marines) to withdraw their contingencies.

Yet France (initially two thousand troops), under the rule of the enigmatic Napoleon III, had a plan that went well beyond restarting debt collection: installing Austrian archduke Maximilian on a Mexican throne. Coming to power in 1848 and craving the imperial possessions and prestige of his illustrious uncle Napoleon I, Napoleon III held the fanciful notion, hyped to him by Mexican conservatives, that Mexico's masses would back the French forces, plus the idea that he would be restoring God and church through a new monarchy was appealing. That the United States was distracted with its own incipient civil war in the aftermath of the firing on Fort Sumter on the morning of April 12, 1861, was also a motivating factor in the French ruler's planning.

Within weeks of the Spanish and British pull-out, the French army, reinforced by an additional four thousand fighters, commenced its trek inland, the destination Mexico City. Charles Latrille, the arrogant and confident commanding general of the French expeditionary force, dispatched a missive to Paris: "We are so superior to the Mexicans in race, organization, morality and devoted sentiments, that I beg your excellency to inform the Emperor that as the head of the 6,000 soldiers I am already master of Mexico." Yet before Latrille could be master of Mexico, he had to master Puebla, the city along the route where Juárez had opted to stymie the French. Under the command of the youthful Brigadier General Porfirio Díaz, the Second Brigade scored a key battlefield win on May 5, 1862, the now-celebrated holiday *Cinco de Mayo*.

Legions of conservative monarchists and clergy were despondent. Some priests turned to urge their parishioners to abet the Catholic French against the atheist Juárez regime. The steely Juárez in turn raised the ante with orders that banned clergy from wearing their vestments when not performing services. Earlier in the year, in a move that prompted historians to label this latent "democratic dictatorship," he ordered the death penalty for those who, in the estimation of his republican government, promoted the reactionary cause.

His expeditionary force licking its wounds, Napoleon III doubled down by sending an additional thirty thousand soldiers. Now the valiant Mexican forces were hopelessly out-manned and out-gunned. Thirteen months after the stunning battle of Puebla, French soldiers marched into Mexico City, pushing Juárez and his administration, desperate and deposed once again, to the north to San Luis Potosí, and eventually Chihuahua City. On July 10, the French-appointed junta announced a Catholic Empire and offered Maximilian, Napoleon's pawn, the position of emperor. The Hapsburg monarch, just twenty-something, reportedly insisted that the Mexicans endorse his ascension, and a conservative-run (and highly dubious) referendum ensued to indulge Maximilian in the pretense of legitimacy.

Maximilian's conservative government now held the lion's share of the national territory, but Juárez's liberals were looming in the far north. An inherent moderate, and likely not as gullible as history recalls, Maximilian attempted to unite the nation's disparate factions and ideologies, but he wound up being too liberal for conservatives—and vice versa. Many conservatives felt betrayed that their monarch did not repeal La Reforma, even passing decrees backing religious tolerance. Moreover, the French invasion and coronation of Maximilian had sparked a nationalist backlash, something that Juárez would come to exploit.

GRINGO GODSEND

Help came from an unexpected quarter. The Monroe Doctrine, in which the United States had pledged to protect the Americas from outside (read, European) interference, had been patchily applied since its formulation in 1823. The American Civil War further complicated this stance, turning US political energy inward and making policy makers wary of blowback. President Lincoln's secretary of state, William Henry Seward, had been dismayed by the French incursion into Mexico but had been unable to respond out of fear that Emperor Maximilian would retaliate by increasing support to the Confederacy.

But after Civil War hostilities ceased in 1865, Seward rattled his saber, and General Ulysses S. Grant initiated covert assistance to the forces of the deposed Juárez. For good measure, he sent some fifty thousand soldiers to the Rio Grande border. Along with supplying guns to the anti-Maximilian forces, the Seward/Grant deployment helped precipitate the departure of French soldiers in early 1867, and without French protection, Maximilian was unable to uphold his empire. A key battle on early May 5, 1867, at Querétaro, a staunchly pro-monarchy metropolis, ended with a resounding victory by the large republican force that had laid siege to the city. Regional and European governments and actors pleaded with Juárez and the republicans to spare Maximilian's life, but fully aware that tens of thousands of Mexicans had died battling the French, Juárez laconically explained his decision, "I am not the one who has condemned them [to death]; it is the law, it is the people." Staring straight at his firing squad on June 19, 1867, Maximilian's last utterances included "Viva México!"

On July 15, 1867, Juárez once again set foot in Mexico City, cheered by thousands of euphoric residents. One breathless liberal journalist hailed Juárez as "the Personification of the Republic. Worthy of a thousand titles and universal respect." La Reforma had won. And despite the nation being in tatters, it was now on the dawn of its Second Independence. Scorned for their support for the foreign empire, Mexican conservatives never gained national power again, nor would the church ever have anything close to the clout it enjoyed before the liberal reformer revolution.

Juárez wasted no time in calling for general elections and five constitutional amendments (including a presidential veto and a second congressional chamber, or Senate) to the very Constitution of 1857 that so many liberals considered sacred. Concluding that proposed amendments were intended to provide the president with outsized powers, critics and even some supporters laid scorn on Juárez for his sneaky autocratic (albeit constitutional) maneuvering. In the end, Juárez was the one who blinked, and the proposed amendments went nowhere.

In the concomitant presidential vote, Juárez took home just under three-quarters of the vote, ensuring a strong mandate for his fresh term. Yet it was now he made perhaps his biggest mistake: despite Juárez's demonstrated reverence for the constitution and the failed amendments, the head of state now asked for and was granted, extraordinary powers, something necessary to forever rid Mexico of the "crabs," or monarchists, as he continued efforts to resurrect the economy and expand public education.

CIVILIAN CAUDILLO?

Despite having suffered a stroke and losing his wife Margarita in October 1870, Juárez threw his hat into the presidential ring once again in the tense 1871 election climate. Having held power (albeit sometimes in far-flung exile locales) for fifteen years, Juárez was resisting the emergence of new political figures. Could it be that Juárez, the liberal's liberal, would only leave office when he decided to? Sebastián Lerdo de Tejada, a longtime friend and trusted advisor and one of the most loyal *Juarista* advisors, opted to desert his mentor and enter the presidential horse race himself. Juárez's other opponent would be Porfirio Díaz, the brilliant Oaxacan liberal general who had won countless battles for Juárez.

Juárez won the election with just under 50 percent of the electorate, but this was easily his most controversial win given his involvement in a series of electoral "adjustments" leading to the vote. Many reformist figures invoked the principles of the Constitution against Juárez's cynical autocracy. They lampooned their erstwhile hero with terms like "the candidate of himself" or "His Majesty Benito the First." One opponent stated, "Today it is not the Constitution that the government defends, but the presidential chair." Another, escalating the rhetoric even more, professed that "Julius Caesar was a greater man than Juárez and everybody blessed Brutus for killing him." And this was the Mexican hero whom the Colombian government had just recently offered the titular appellation, *Benemérito de las Américas* ("Worthy of the Gratitude of the Americas").

Porfirio Díaz plotted a rebellion against the alleged despot, but before he could make his move, news broke on July 18, 1872, that Juárez had died of heart failure at the National Palace; he was laid to rest at the Pantheon of San Fernando in the same city. Mourners extolled the "Messiah" and "Redeemer" who had forged the true nation. His successor, Lerdo, offered the insurgents an amnesty, which Díaz took up. Four years later, Díaz would, first using force and then an election, assume the presidency. He held this position—much of it autocratic—for double the time his former ally Juárez had. In 1910, citing a similar slogan about stopping reelection that Díaz had used against Juárez, revolutionaries led by Francisco Madero rose and, the following year, overthrew the strongman Díaz in what was the start of the bloody decade-long Mexican Revolution.

Juárez left a deep mark on Mexican society and politics. Under his leadership, La Reforma, albeit in fits and starts over the decades, took hold, the French intervention was smashed, and with it any semblance of a conservative or clerical dominion in the country. There is also the infrastructure modernization—roads, rail, and telegraph—and the sweeping education expansion, all of which would endure for the last decades of the century. Equally important, Juárez paved the way for mestizos—including Díaz—to reach the commanding heights of Mexican politics just as he had overcome nineteenth-century prejudices and exclusions. Having seen the chaos of Santa Anna, he never wavered from his belief in the importance of liberal ideals, laws, and the republic, although at times it appeared he was prepared to use decidedly nonliberal means to protect them.

9

Juan Manuel de Rosas and Domingo Sarmiento

The Struggle to Hatch Argentina

Post-independence Argentina was riven by internal strife between urban and rural-based political factions. Juan Manuel de Rosas and Domingo Faustino Sarmiento were two leading figures of this period, respectively symbolizing the powerful caudillo streak and emerging democratic tendency in Argentina. Fierce rivals with egos to match, each tried to impose their idea of what an independent Argentina should look like. After Rosas was finally ousted, Sarmiento would assume the presidency and go on to radically reform the country's education system, utilizing forward-thinking ideas he had gathered on trips to the United States. When he left the presidency in 1874, there were one hundred thousand students in the country's schools compared to thirty thousand when he started, reflecting his goal to "make the whole Republic like a school."

"FEDERATION OR DEATH"

The so-called May Revolution of 1810 in Spain's Viceroyalty of Río de la Plata marked the initial phase of a protracted independence movement that would culminate in the establishment of Argentina. Great Britain recognized the new country in 1825, although Spain would not do so for several decades. Independence from Spain, though, was quickly replaced by a protracted civil war between Unitarists and Federalists. In the most elemental terms, Unitarists advocated for a centralizing (and preeminent) Buenos Aires holding a stronger grip on the remote provinces. Federalists, by contrast, pushed for an association of more autonomous provinces. Unlike their cosmopolitan, European-influenced *unitarios*, the anti-Buenos Aires federalists tended to be led by caudillos, often *gauchos*, the cowboys of the Argentine *pampas*, a vast region of fertile pastures and plains, cattle, wheat, and flax touching up against the province of Buenos Aires. The gauchos and pampas were also very much part of the nascent nation's romantic myths and legends versus the urban *porteños* of Buenos Aires.

From a rich family with unrivaled cattle holdings in the pampas, Rosas received his early education in Buenos Aires, but most of his youth was spent outside in the hinterland. As was typical of his class, Rosas was skeptical of the independence movement driven by the merchant class in Buenos Aires—the rebel execution of Viceroy Santiago de Liniers in 1810 incensed him—but by 1816, Rosas and his fellow provincials grudgingly accepted the fact of independence even if they did not support it.

After years of political tumult, in 1829 Rosas, now heading the Federalist Party and a preeminent caudillo, assumed office as governor of Buenos Aires,

A portrait of Argentine ruler Juan Manuel de Rosas, printed in *The Illustrated London News*, 1844. (Alamy Stock Photo)

the highest position in the land. After his initial three-year term ended, he departed, as a general under a new governor, to lead a brutal internal war—the scorched-earth Desert Campaign (1833–1834) against indigenous tribes of the southern pampas and northern Patagonia—and would then, assuming dictatorial powers, rule the country until his overthrow in 1852.

Rosas's seventeen-year tyranny was, despite its putative adherence to federalism, quite centralist. Elections were held, but checks on power were nonexistent or nothing more than rubber-stamp exercises to maintain Rosas's power and prerogatives, especially during the apex of his totalitarianism between 1839 and 1842. By this time, the regime ordered the majority of Unitarist porteños to march wearing red to demonstrate fidelity; both the Federalist and pro-Rosas hues became ubiquitous in the capital. Indeed, (enforced) public commitment to Rosas permeated almost every facet of life. The slogan "Long live the Federation and Death to the Unitarist Savages" became omnipresent in all newspapers, public documents, and even personal letters. A painting of his likeness was mandated to be placed on church altars and in public buildings. Those getting state salaries—priests, bureaucrats, military officers—were required to don a red badge with the engraving, "Federation or Death." Males had to sport the "federal look," consisting of a visible mustache and sideburns—forcing more than a few to wear fakes. Troops had to wear red *chiripás* (blankets used as pants), while their mounts displayed various red accessories, part of the all-encompassing cult of *rosismo*. Lackeys were the norm in senior government posts; anyone suspected of disloyalty was purged. "Do not imagine that my Ministers are anything but my Secretaries," Rosas explained, "I put them in their offices to listen and report, and nothing more." Opposition newspapers and books were ritually burned in public plazas. His newly created secret paramilitary force, the *Mazorca* (ear of corn), killed roughly two thousand real or perceived regime opponents, often Unitarists, by its signature throat-cutting and public display of severed heads. Opponents half-jokingly called the shadowy force "más horca" a play on words meaning "more hanging." Rosas defended the group's savagery with the logic that only by taking the gloves off would the still-fractured and vulnerable South American country be secure.

The socially conservative Catholic Church readily supported Rosas. The Jesuits, however, did not, which led to their expulsion. Given his pampas roots and public affinities, Rosas did not ignore the lower classes or Black people, who could help steady his public support, but he was anything but a civil rights proponent. Despite his sometimes-fiery rhetoric in defense of the lower social strata, he never embraced education or redistributed lands, and he pursued aggressive vagrancy policies. At heart, he was a gaucho *estanciero* (landowner) elite.

SARMIENTO: A UNITARIAN MAN OF IDEAS

Domingo Sarmiento's early life ran in parallel with his country's fight for independence. He came into this world in San Juan on February 15, 1811, a year after the revolution began, and joined a family of fifteen children, but would wind up being the only male of the six who survived adolescence. He lost his mother at a young age and his father rarely had a steady income. He was a precocious youth who started reading at the tender age of four, and after his original school closed following political disturbances in 1825, the now-teenager began studying and living with an uncle, a priest, who opened his mind to the value of education and personal and societal liberty. Domingo went on to help open a provincial school outside San Juan as well as work in a grocery market. He continued to read voraciously, devouring the classics given to him by a friend. At one point Sarmiento was forced to serve in a local militia, eventually becoming a second lieutenant. But a rebel and contrarian to his core, he was castigated for refusing to fulfill certain duties.

His political thinking evolved after reading French philosopher Victor Cousin, among others. Sarmiento became a Unitarist, advocating for Buenos Aires to govern the entire country's politics. This stance, and his activism in progressive political causes, was intolerable to the Rosas regime and saw him and many other leading liberal lights forced into exile. Sarmiento went to Chile in 1831; jurist and economist Juan Bautista Alberdi relocated to Montevideo, Santiago, and Paris; and Esteban Echeverría, a poet, landed in Uruguay. Known loosely as the *Generation of the '37* (1837 was the year when a literary hall they frequented was founded), this motley but formidable band of liberal thinkers firmly believed that Rosas was a bloodthirsty tyrant. Having come of age at the height of the tyranny, Echeverría, in his classic short story "El Matadero," equated Rosas's despotism to the cruelty of a slaughterhouse:

> The butchers of the slaughterhouse were the apostles who propagated the *rosista* federation at the point of a dagger. . . . They labeled as [an opponent] anyone who was not a decapitator, a butcher, a savage, or a thief; anyone who was a decent man, with his heart in the right place, any enlightened patriot

who promoted knowledge and freedom; and . . . it can be clearly seen that the source of the federation could be found in the slaughterhouse itself.

His health was devastated by typhoid fever, and in 1836 Sarmiento was permitted to return to San Juan where he believed he would die. But the young man did eventually recover, allowing him to found a high school for women in 1839—the first of its kind in his native city. His passion for the right of women to education (on which topic he would later write a book) likely was the influence of his mother, who had only a smattering of primary school education but was a firm believer in equality in education. Around this time, Sarmiento also founded and edited a paper, *El Zonda*, which published articles attacking Rosas's Federalist regime.

Diego Sarmiento. *(Library of Congress Prints and Photographs Division, Washington, DC)*

Following yet another arrest, in 1840 Sarmiento once again fled to Chile, which would become his base for the next twelve years. His goal while exiled was to use his pen to undermine Rosas. For his part, Rosas began to see the exiled Sarmiento as a formidable adversary, who himself, without a hint of modesty, described their feud as a "struggle between titans." At one point Rosas attempted to have Sarmiento extradited home, a move which only served to enhance the latter's swelling reputation.

In Chile, the extravagantly prolific Sarmiento published editorials in the most prominent newspapers, wrote three of his most celebrated literary tomes, established a normal school (a school to train teachers) in Santiago—the first in Latin America—and served in the Chilean government in a variety of roles. All this service and publicity helped him score an appointment as a faculty member at the University of Chile. In short order, the mostly self-taught Argentine had established himself in the most rarefied layers of Chilean intellectual society.

FACUNDO: UNDERSTANDING CAUDILLISMO

Sarmiento's 1845 masterpiece, titled *Civilization and Barbarism: The Life of Juan Quiroga Facundo* first came out in serial form in a Santiago daily and brought him widespread attention. Ostensibly a novelized biography of the Argentine caudillo Facundo Quiroga, it was also an exquisite blend of history, sociology, and political theory, as well as a fiery indictment of Rosas and the provincial political customs that the author believed fomented *caudillismo*.

As the title suggests, in the book Sarmiento explored the duality of civilization and barbarism, which he believed were in perpetual conflict with each other. For Sarmiento, civilization entailed urban, educated residents who respected social solidarity, republican norms and laws, and European culture; barbarism, by contrast, was the life of the ignorant savage gaucho and caudillo customs. While Sarmiento had considerable admiration for gaucho skills like horsemanship and even had a romantic image of self-reliance and stoicism, he also viewed the social customs of the pampas in general as backward and destructive: "Country life, then, has developed the gaucho's physical faculties, but none of his intelligence. His moral character is affected by his custom of triumphing over obstacles and the power of nature—his is strong, haughty, vigorous." In Sarmiento's reckoning, the Rosas regime came about because this regional barbarism was, at least for now, holding the upper hand against civilization.

Intriguingly, Sarmiento located the root of the caudillo problem in the geography of Argentina itself, stating "The disease from which the Argentine Republic suffers is its own expanse." His solution? Simply bring the city and its Western cosmopolitanism out to the pampas via massive immigration. While seemingly outlandish in conception, this idea would profoundly shape the course of Argentine history.

Since its publication, *Facundo* has served as a foundational text for understanding dictatorship in Latin America, although many rejected its ideas. Rosas was not the only Argentine who despised the book; even prominent liberals like Alberdi responded to its thesis (and author) with vitriol: "The gaucho whom Sarmiento labels 'barbarian' . . . is a better representative of European civilization than Sarmiento; the latter is a sterile, nonproductive worker who makes a pretense of being a lifetime employee of the state, which pays him to behave like a lackey to his boss."

NEW WORLD LEARNING

Sarmiento's relentless attacks on Rosas—including *Facundo*—led some senior Chilean officials to fear that Argentina might declare war on Chile. In part, this is what prompted Chilean minister Manuel Montt to dispatch Sarmiento on a two-year government-financed trip to Europe and North America to study their respective education systems, with hopes of bolstering the Chilean approach to pedagogy.

The Old World was on the whole a disappointing experience for Sarmiento. He talked with political figures and intellectuals in France concerned about Rosas's autocracy but was underwhelmed by Europe, given the inequities that plagued the continent. He held particular derision for France which, despite its supposed "high art" culture, was "still in a state of barbarism." He continued to England and then crossed the Atlantic to the United States, where he had a specific person he wanted to meet. Sarmiento had been mesmerized by New England educational theorist Horace Mann's unpromising-sounding *Seventh Report of the Secretary of the Massachusetts Board of Education*, and had vowed to meet his American counterpart in person: "when that important report came to my hands, I then had a fixed point where to go in the United States."

Once in the States, Sarmiento and Mann struck up a friendship, and Mann gave him a tour of the normal school he had founded in West Newton, Massachusetts. Sarmiento was astonished to learn that the state's schools employed seven thousand teachers; "a greater number than were soldiers in Chile." The Argentine observer was also impressed by girls and boys studying in the same classrooms—a revolutionary concept at the time—and women being trained in the sciences and physical education. And he was in awe of the level of literacy: "[It is] the only country in the world where the ability to read is universal, where writing is practiced by all in their daily lives. . . . Is there any country in the world which can compare with it in these respects?"

In addition to his deep esteem for US education, Sarmiento praised the so-called Puritan work ethic and the widespread representative democracy practiced across the nation, in town halls, city councils, and schools: "In the United States, every man has a natural right to a role in political affairs, and he exercises it." Mann and his wife Mary also introduced him to prominent Americans like essayist Ralph Waldo Emerson, poet Henry Longfellow, and abolitionist Wendell Phillips.

Sarmiento returned to Chile in early 1848 convinced that North and South America had much in common—and of his role in Argentina's future transformation. This sort of ambition is what Mary saw when the widowed activist corresponded with Sarmiento decades later, and breathlessly declared, "You are not a man but a nation."

A NATION IS REBORN—WITH IMPORTED EUROPEANS

By the late 1840s, Rosas's effective dominion included just about the entire Argentine Confederation (the name of the country during Rosas's rule). He now set out to annex Uruguay and Paraguay, but these advances were checked when Paris and London jointly conducted a naval blockade against the strongman. And things were about to get very much worse for Rosas. In February 1852, at the Battle of Caseros, Brazilian, Uruguayan, and insurrectionist provincial Argentines—around twenty-eight thousand soldiers in total—led by Justo José de Urquiza—defeated Rosas. When Urquiza entered Buenos Aires, his troops slaughtered hundreds of *rosistas* in cold blood, despite the fact Urquiza himself was an Argentine gaucho estanciero. Rosas sailed on a British ship to exile in England, where he spent the rest of his life as a planter before he died in 1877.

Rosas's removal opened the way for young activists to return home, including Alberdi whose book, *The Bases*, became the template for Argentina's new constitution, ratified in 1853, that remains in place today. Upon his own return, Sarmiento embarked on an ambitious series of substantial educational reforms, such as helping found dozens of new schools in the capital, editing the daily *El Nacional*, and launching a new journal. He also found the time and energy to serve as a congressman in the state of Buenos Aires and as the governor of San Juan province from 1862 to 1864.

But Sarmiento's new authority also revealed a dark side that brooked no opposition. Sarmiento's backing of economic and mining reforms was opposed by caudillo Ángel Vicente "Chacho" Peñaloza, who was then executed by the governor for being a subversive, despite the fact that he was a mere political rival. Alberdi and other prominent liberal thinkers heavily criticized Sarmiento's contention that Chacho was an outlaw, and Sarmiento resigned. In 1864, President Bartolomé Mitre aided the harried Sarmiento by giving him diplomatic postings in Santiago and Lima and then Washington, DC, where he was ambassador from 1865 to 1868.

Alongside his official duties, Sarmiento spent these years as a keen observer of US culture and institutions and traveled all over the country. He was taken back at how much the country had modernized (and industrialized) in the twenty years since he had last visited, in spite of the catastrophic war between the Union and the Confederacy. His estimation of the American way was so great that when Sarmiento founded a normal school in the Argentine city of Paraná, he brought over sixty female teachers from New York state and the Midwest to get the project off the ground. Ever productive, he published *Lincoln's Life* while in the capital and founded yet another journal, *Both Americas*, dedicated to literature, education, and agriculture.

Before he headed back to Buenos Aires at the end of his diplomatic stint, President Mitre urged him to attend the University of Michigan's commencement ceremony in Ann Arbor. To his complete surprise, he was awarded an honorary doctorate—a cherished feather in his cap for this avowed lover of all things scholastic.

"MAKE THE WHOLE REPUBLIC A SCHOOL"

While in the United States, Sarmiento had thrown his hat in the ring for the presidential elections back home, and en route to Argentina in port in Rio de Janeiro, he received news that he had won. He held the presidency from 1868 to 1874. During his administration, the number of students at schools more than tripled to one hundred thousand—the sort of gains that rightfully earned Sarmiento the title "the schoolmaster president." These swelling legions of students wore white uniforms, which became the standard in the country for decades.

Along with his fellow liberals, Sarmiento also pushed European immigration, technological innovations like the telegraph, agriculture modernizations, and increasingly, civil liberties, even if the country would not become a full participatory democracy for decades. He ordered the first national census and built the National Observatory—the first of its kind in South America. After leaving the presidency, Sarmiento spent considerable time on the beautification of Buenos Aires; the following decade, he served as the nation's school superintendent. He was an active public presence until just a few years before he died, on September 11, 1888.

Critics then and now have contended that Sarmiento, despite his undeniable and massive gains in education, was never able to smash the estanciero cattle barons to make for a more equitable country, rein in the Church's power, or anticipate the urban problems stemming from massive European immigration after the fall of Rosas. Some of his sociological views have also worn badly: in his later years, Sarmiento, writing in a never-completed sequel to *Facundo*, reasons against racial "mixing," clearly influenced by the spreading logic of Social Darwinism. But while his legacy is undoubtedly complex and various, his contribution to Argentina's development as a democratic nation is significant, especially when compared with the autocratic and divisive rule of his chief rival, Rosas.

10

Dom Pedro II
Brazil's Citizen Monarch

Handed the Brazilian empire from his father when he was just five, Pedro II served longer than any other nineteenth-century Latin American ruler. During his reign, he was influential in the development of the Brazilian economy (presciently promoting a shift from sugar to coffee production and export) and championed science, education, and culture. His leadership also witnessed Brazil making giant leaps in critical telegraph, railroad, and cable infrastructure that helped integrate the country both as a nation-state and into the modern world. Pedro II also recognized slavery as a moral evil and worked steadily to abolish it, although critics have argued too slowly, given that slavery endured until 1888. Always mindful of the need for stability, he peacefully went into exile after being toppled by a republican military coup in 1889, dying in Paris two years later.

EMPEROR OF THE FAIR

During its centennial commemoration of the Declaration of Independence in 1876, the United States hosted a rather curious head of state: Dom Pedro II of Brazil. Pedro II's coast-to-coast continental trip saw him, in three months, visit twenty-two states and four territories, and make a brief foray into Canada. "Whether he was traveling by steamship on the Mississippi River, or aboard a special Pullman railroad car in Cheyenne, San Francisco, or Baltimore," wrote historian Teresa Cribelli, "curious citizens gathered to greet the unusual visitor and his entourage at every stop." Dom Pedro II's relentless daily agenda included visits to "schools, factories, insane asylums, prisons, waterworks, government buildings, libraries, theaters, and religious institutions."

The dazzling dignitary was anomalous in numerous ways: yes, he was a Catholic who was a hereditary emperor with blood relations to most of the royal families of Europe. But he was a New World–born intellectual, who was emperor of an independent Brazil, not a venal Old World European country. The press fell in love with him: reporters such as the *New York Herald*'s James J. O'Kelley excited their readers with a glowing account of Brazil's "citizen monarch" who insisted on calling himself the humble moniker "Pedro de Alcântara." The editor of *Frank Leslie's Illustrated Newspaper* beamed about Dom Pedro's "peculiarly American qualities" of ingenuity and self-improvement.

The highlight of Pedro II's visit occurred on May 10 when he, along with empress Teresa Cristina, accompanied President Ulysses S. Grant to the opening ceremonies of the Centennial International Exposition at Fairmont Park, Philadelphia. The largest World's Fair at the time (involving thirty-seven exhibiting countries and drawing ten million visitors), the pageants celebrated cutting-edge work in science, industry, architecture, and the arts. Interestingly, Pedro II spent a bit of time at the fair interacting with Alexander Graham Bell, who proudly offered a trial of his latest gadget: the telephone. The monarch pledged to buy one as soon as it became available for sale: indeed, one of the earliest telephones was placed in Pedro's summer palace, Petrópolis, forty-something miles from Rio de Janeiro. Pedro II was also the first person to buy stocks of the inventor's company, the Bell Telephone Company.

While the exhibition provided the perfect opportunity for Pedro II to indulge his curiosity about the state of American innovation, industry, and ingenuity, it was also a venue to cut import and export deals; indeed, connections forged at these fairs could make or break a country's economic fortunes. Pedro II had a clear agenda, namely raising Brazil's exports of its most lucrative commodity: coffee. One of the Brazilian flyers printed for the exposition extolled Brazil's fertile soil, as well as its hard-working, peaceful, and intelligent people. Dom Pedro II was elated with the impression Brazil had made at the fair, "Our agricultural exhibit is an amazing sight," he penned in a dispatch to his beloved daughter, Isabel. And it was this unique combination of interests—the matters of the mind with the matters of the state—that made Pedro II such an extraordinary ruler.

New Nations of Latin America 1811–1839. (University of Wisconsin-Madison Cartography Lab)

A STEADY HAND

The Brazilian empire was a curious phenomenon in Latin American history. In stark contrast to the protracted, bloodthirsty independence wars in Spanish America, Brazil achieved independence from Portugal by pacific, albeit convoluted, means. Confronted with the imminent invasion of Napoleon's forces, in late 1807 Portuguese Emperor Dom João VI (grandfather of Pedro II) decided to relocate his court to its largest, most affluent colony, Brazil. All told, upward of fifteen thousand persons joined the exodus; the House of Bragança subsequently ruled for a dozen years, with Rio de Janeiro as the acting capital of the Portuguese Empire.

With Bonaparte vanquished by 1814, João returned to Portugal in 1821, leaving his son, Dom Pedro I, to rule in Brazil. But it soon became apparent that a return to the former status quo would be thorny. While crown officials in Lisbon believed that Brazil should revert to colonial status, Pedro I (who had arrived in the New World at age nine and felt more Brazilian than Portuguese) had other ideas. When his father ordered him to return home in 1822, Pedro I instead issued a declaration in September 1822 that unilaterally established the Brazilian empire. Just twenty-four years of age, Pedro I was crowned Brazil's first emperor, albeit a constitutional one. Brazilian elites—for example, enslaved sugar plantation and cattle ranchers of the Northeast; coffee growers of São Paulo—were thrilled with "independence," seeing as how it did not disrupt the social hierarchy of the few haves and countless have-nots.

But public mood soon soured on Pedro I, who abdicated in early 1831 and returned to Portugal, leaving his five-year-old son, Pedro II, to replace him. The child emperor was assigned adult guardians, or regents, who governed until he came of age. He spent much of his time alone or lonely in what was a dour childhood and early adolescence: his mother had passed away when he was a baby and his older sister died in 1833. A diagnosis of childhood epilepsy also led some court figures—self-servingly or otherwise—to question the boy's mental and physical acuity for ruling. Biographies have written that the interplay of his innate smarts and emotionally truncated youth paved the way for an adult ruler, who loathed social niceties and attempted to control those in his immediate orbit.

Confronted by a surge of revolts and counter-revolts, court conspiracies, and attempted coup d'états, the regency council expedited the youth's official "declaration of age" by a few years, enabling him to be sworn in at the age of

Dom Pedro II, Emperor of Brazil, 1876. *(Library of Congress Prints and Photographs Division, Washington, DC)*

fourteen on July 23, 1840, and crowned the following year. The regional disturbances continued for several more years, but the teen ruler's keen intellect and emerging deep affection for his subjects ultimately set the stage for stability, which became the touchstone of his reign.

As a constitutional monarch, his authority was necessarily limited, but he held tight to the prerogatives granted to him and pursued his ruling duties with intense concentration and seriousness. He also wielded a potent and amorphous *poder moderador* (moderating power) through which he could influence policies, even if not initiating them directly. Never endorsing the two main elite parties—the liberal and conservative—Pedro II ensured that neither faction became too powerful or entrenched. His oversight also ensured peaceful and legitimate transitions of power between elite (read, landholding oligarchy) elements.

This emphasis on stability, combined with his vigorous promotion of education, science, and culture, helped drive industrial and infrastructure dynamism and innovation in Brazil. The nation constructed Latin America's first stone-paved highway, the "União e Indústria" (Union and Industry) connecting the southern metropolises of Petrópolis and Juiz de Fora, which Pedro II inaugurated in 1861. Around this time, the country's first steam-engine locomotive commenced service between São Paulo and Santos. Communications infrastructure also developed at a rapid rate: in 1874 the Brazil–Europe submarine cable was laid and a telephone service started in 1877, the same year the nation's first postage stamp was issued. A telegraph network also helped unite the vast country.

Brazil's dynamism helped spur the arrival of European immigrants—actively encouraged by Pedro II's regime—wishing to leave behind poverty for opportunity and employment, while Pedro II's deft diplomacy ensured that Great Britain—then at its imperial peak—would be Brazil's most critical trading partner. Pedro II also cannily encouraged coffee cultivation and export over sugar. Indeed, coffee became for independent Brazil what sugar had been for the colonial period as the United States and parts of Europe picked up the addictive habit.

Aside from his efforts at national transformation, Pedro II was something of a hybrid: socially conservative and culturally liberal. Fluent in multiple languages (including Sanskrit and Hebrew as well as proficiency in Tupí-Guaraní, a South American indigenous dialect), the refined Pedro II preferred well-tailored suits that made him look like a scholar or banker and was at ease with some of the century's most influential thinkers. He was a regular correspondent with German naturalist Alexander von Humboldt and French novelist Victor Hugo, and forged friendships with Charles Darwin, Victor Hugo, Friedrich Nietzsche, Richard Wagner, Louis Pasteur, and Henry Wadsworth Longfellow, among others. His hobbies included astronomy and curating one of the most impressive libraries ever assembled in Latin America. As US citizen James Fletcher said in 1857, "It is very rare to find a monarch who combines all that the most scrupulous legitimist will exact, who is limited by all the checks that a constitutionalist would require, and yet who has the greatest claim for the respect of his subjects and the admiration of the world, in his native talent and in his acquisitions in science and literature. These rare combinations meet in Dom Pedro II."

Pedro II's scrupulous approach was not necessarily reflected in his attitude to his marriage. His father had agreed to marry Maria Leopoldina of Austria after apparently viewing a commanding portrait of her, only to be saddened when he saw her visage for real. Pedro II similarly agreed to wed someone, Teresa Cristina of the Kingdom of the Two Sicilies, whom he had never seen, and was likewise disappointed when he met Dona Teresa in Brazil. Yet, contrary to his philandering father, Pedro II was outwardly devoted to his wife through forty-six years of marriage even if he had multiple liaisons. When the strong-willed empress died in 1889, Pedro II was devastated.

WAR!

Pedro II also proved a steady hand both with regional revolts throughout Brazil and international crises and intrigue. Argentine dictator Juan Manuel de Rosas, for example, had been trying to capitalize on internal dissent in southern Brazil with a view to slicing off a province or two. (See Chapter 9, "Juan Manuel de Rosas and Domingo Sarmiento: The Struggle to Hatch Argentina.") Pedro II countered by joining up with a force of rebelling Argentine provinces and Uruguay in 1852, which then precipitated Rosas's overthrow.

But his fortunes began to take a downward turn with the calamitous Paraguayan War (1864–1870), which arose as a result of regional tariff and boundary disputes inherited from colonial times regarding the vital Rio de la Plata lifeline to the Atlantic Ocean, where Uruguay was located. At the center of it was Paraguayan caudillo Francisco Solano López, an ambitious and relentless egomaniac who ruled Paraguay with an iron fist and who had long eyed Brazil with deep suspicion. In late 1864, López launched an offensive into the Brazilian province of Matto Grosso, precipitating a war that pitted Paraguay against Brazil, Argentina, and Uruguay, the "triple alliance" that ultimately triumphed.

The war annihilated Paraguay's male population, which shrunk by 75 percent because of the war, in part due to López's unwillingness to concede defeat. However, Pedro II also bears significant responsibility for the scale of the casualties. In 1867 he dismissed Paraguay's pleas for peace, telling a royal confidant that "the war should be conducted as honor demands, cost what it cost." He insisted that López be totally vanquished, which occurred but took several further years of war. As biographer Roderick J. Barman wrote, "The mounting total of dead and wounded deterred him not at all. His cause, which was the cause of Brazil, was just and to the triumph of that case he was willing to sacrifice everything, even his throne."

The war also inflicted a heavy domestic cost on Brazil. Its vast expense cut into his state coffers in subsequent years, while Pedro's inconsistent support for his military during this protracted war undermined its support for him during an upswell in the 1880s of republican antimonarch sentiment. The war also foregrounded the powder keg issue of slavery in Brazil. The bitter irony that Brazilian enslaved people, purchased by the state from their owners to be enrolled as soldiers, were engaged in a war nominally being fought in the name of liberty (through deposing López) was not lost on many. (The emperor himself urged his military to enlist even more enslaved people: "Speed up the process of buying slaves and increase the numbers of our army by any means possible.") These enslaved people were freed after the war, but in the postconflict landscape, the issue of abolition took center stage. With slavery ended in the United States in the aftermath of the Union victory over the Confederacy, Brazil, and Madrid-controlled Cuba were the only countries in the Western Hemisphere in which slavery remained legal.

ABOLITION, EVENTUALLY

For three-and-a-half centuries, Brazil was at the core of the global enslaved-person trade, with 40 percent of the ten million Africans brought in chains to the Americas landed in Brazil. Enslaved people were also the fulcrum of Brazil's economy, with half of the approximately seven million persons in the country in 1850 being enslaved. One late nineteenth-century German resident in Brazil made this astute, sobering observation, "In this country, the Blacks occupy the main role. They are responsible for all the labor and produce all the wealth in this land. The white Brazilian just doesn't work."

Personally critical of slavery (he liberated his slaves, around three dozen, in 1840), Pedro II worked diligently to eradicate the practice in his country, even if this only entailed slowly whittling away at the scourge. With his inclination to stability, he believed that gradual abolition was the best way to preclude a violent backlash from landholders. Over the ensuing decades, a variety of piecemeal laws and policies moved Brazil, albeit with myriad setbacks, toward abolition. Himself frustrated by the glacial pace of the abolition campaign, Pedro II even established a program whereby freedom for enslaved people could be purchased; in fact, he once bought the freedom of an enslaved person he had encountered on a street. In 1871, the Brazilian Parliament passed the "Free Womb Law," meaning that offspring born to enslaved people were free. The catch was that the children were required to work for the owners of their parents until adulthood as financial compensation. It was also not uncommon for notaries—at times with at least the tacit awareness of priests—to make fake birth certificates so that they could claim the enslaved children had come into this world before the legislation had been enacted.

There were also notable retrograde steps. When the American Civil War was raging, the Brazilian legislature swiftly recognized the Confederate States of America. Following the Union victory in 1865, Pedro II asked Confederate cotton growers to relocate to Brazil (where slavery remained legal) as part of his effort to make Brazil a global cotton power. Between 1867 and 1871, no fewer than three thousand families decamped for southern Brazil. Many *confederados* eventually returned to the United States, although a single US settlement—Americana, established by Colonel William Hutchison Norris of Mobile, Alabama—remained. Into the twenty-first century, the confederado descendants (one in ten residents) of the city still spoke in Southern-accented English.

When Madrid ended slavery in Cuba in 1886, Brazil was the single outlier. By now, a solid section of Brazilians favored abolition, including many conservative circles. Through his campaigning and influential work *O Abolicionismo* (1883), attorney and tireless abolitionist leader Joaquim Nabuco had helped make the case of slavery being a moral sin and—in what he assumed would appeal to liberals like Pedro II—an obstacle to the nation's mantra of Progress. Another critical development was the development of technology and rural-to-urban migration that made slavery less fundamental to the Brazilian economy. On May 13, 1888, with Pedro II away in Europe, his daughter Princess Isabel of Bragança made Brazilian history when she signed Imperial Law #3,353. In fewer than two dozen words, the so-called Golden Law eradicated slavery in every form, without compensation to owners, thus granting freedom to the seven hundred thousand enslaved Brazilians. When Pedro got the news in Milan, Italy, he was overcome with emotion despite his wretched health.

All told, Brazil's emancipation struggle took almost seventy years. Keep in mind that emancipation did not markedly change the lives of most Afro-Brazilian citizens, who often remained detached from employment, educa-

Dom Pedro II and President Ulysses S. Grant. The print shows a large crowd around Ulysses Grant and Pedro II (Emperor of Brazil) who are starting a mighty Corliss steam engine during the American Centennial Exhibition in Philadelphia, May 27, 1876. *(Library of Congress Prints and Photographs Division, Washington, DC)*

tion, housing, or land opportunities. Out of desperation or ignorance, freed Blacks often fell into informal understandings with their former owners that resulted in effective slavery, which had endured in Brazil for three centuries. Subsequent Brazilian elites detested the notion that their country might hold a majority Afro-Brazilian population, which prompted an official policy of *branqueamento* (whitening) via white or Asian immigration.

DOWNFALL

Pedro II's grip on power began to slip following emancipation. Aging and out of touch, he lost the key support of the landowners who viewed the Golden Law as betrayal and surrender, while many liberals who had been focused on ending slavery now turned their sights on the monarchy. Many of these liberals were influenced by the philosophical movement known as positivism, which in its Latin American interpretation esteemed order and progress and criticized slavery, the monarchy and the church as impediments to national progress. (Notably, in Brazil the positivist concept of a modern republic was one governed by what we would call technocrats: it was not a democratic impetus.) These elites—from the plantations to the military barracks and city universities and cafes—hated the anachronistic monarchy as an institution, although many of them respected Pedro II personally. Pedro II, for his part, was not opposed to Brazil as a republic but simply wanted it to be a slow-moving transition, not unlike abolition.

Complicating matters, Pedro II's frequent, often prolonged trips abroad appeared to make him more detached from Brazilian politics and people—and vice versa. In a diary entry, he dismissed Brazil as a "desert," and bemoaned the fact he did not live in Europe. Writing in 1889, one Brazilian senator observed, "The emperor [is] everyday more forgetful of current matters and remote from political questions," and thus was ignorant of the gravity of the swelling antipathy against his teetering system. One newspaper editor noted the reappearance of "an old mania which is now his constant occupation: composing verses and charades."

Pedro II also might have erred in not reducing the swollen size of the armed forces in the aftermath of the Paraguayan War, with many veterans holding grievances about lack of adequate pay or too few opportunities for promotion. In November 1889 military officers carried out a bloodless coup—Pedro II accepted their ultimatum—that sent the Brazilian imperial court into exile to Portugal and later his beloved Paris.

Pedro II expressed little ill will at his ousting, writing from exile of his "ardent wishes for the greatness and prosperity of Brazil." On November 7, 1891, he wrote a revealing (and perhaps self-serving) piece in the Parisian daily *Le Figaro*: "During what is now a long life, I have applied all my forces and my devotion to assuring the progress and the prosperity of my people: it seems that I have not succeeded! . . . Because I have never loved power through personal ambition, I have never had any desire other than to promote the well-being of my country, and I have never wished to be anything other than *pastor populi* [shepherd of the people]."

When an exhausted Pedro II died in Paris a month later, he was only sixty-six but had been in office for fifty-eight years, which had aged him enormously. The French honored him with a state funeral that attracted thousands of mourners, but societal ambivalence about the institution of the monarchy in Brazil persisted, and it took until 1925 and two centenaries (Brazilian independence in 1822 and the emperor's birth in 1825) for the rehabilitation of Pedro II's legacy. This culminated in the return of the remains of Pedro II and Teresa Cristina to their final burial place in the metropolis named after him: Petrópolis.

From the vantage of history, Pedro II was a remarkable ruler because he wanted nothing to do with the trappings of the head of state, preferring to be in a classroom rather than the presidential palace. Although historians still debate the extent to which Pedro II deserves credit for accomplishments when, as a constitutional monarch, governance was shared between legislature and monarchy, he set the tone and provided an energetic and engaged figurehead for a period of progress that saw Brazil transition into a modern nation-state. Under his watch Brazil distinguished itself from its fellow Hispanic countries due to its institutions and customs that guarded political and civil rights and economic modernization and dynamism—all under a functional representative parliamentary democracy. Pedro II's accomplishments are even more impressive when we consider the chaos and violence that ravaged so much of ostensibly republican (read democratic and sovereign) Spanish America in these postindependence decades. Unlike many rulers who showered themselves with flattering titles, Dom Pedro II truly earned his sobriquet, "the Magnanimous."

11

José Martí

The Colossus of Cuba

[Upon learning of the need to defend his land, Nubia, against fierce, invading forces, the defiant warrior Abdala valiantly replies]

> Pues decirle al tirano que en la Nubia
> Hay un héroe por viente de sus lanzas: . . .
> Que la tierra compre su sangre:
> Que el agua ha de mezclarse con sus lágrimas.
>
> Well, tell the tyrant that in Nubia
> There is one hero to match twenty of their lances: . . .
> May the Earth consume their blood:
> May the water mix with their tears.
>
> —José Martí, "Abdala"

The annals of modern Latin American revolutions start with Cuba's José Martí, a masterful poet, bold and original writer, and original independence martyr for his still-shackled Caribbean island nation. But unlike most revolutionaries, Martí's most potent armament was his pen. His patriotism was absolute—"I live only for my country"—but he spent almost his entire adult life in exile, including New York City, the heart of the North American nation he both esteemed but also loathed: his "cup of poison."

As his political thinking evolved, he became not just a proponent of ending Spain's colonization of Cuba, but a staunch classical republican (read, democracy and the rule of law) who, like Argentina's Sarmiento, loathed tyranny and the cult of personality, so often manifested in Latin American in the shape of the caudillo. (See Chapter 9, "Juan Manuel de Rosas and Domingo Sarmiento:

The Struggle to Hatch Argentina.") But as with many of the figures in our story, his legacy is contested: after his battlefield death at the age of forty-two, his mantle as Cuba's most celebrated founder has been claimed by both pro and anti-Cuban Revolution propagandists and patriots.

THE FIRST EXILE

In the decades following the losses of its New World colonies in the 1810s and 1820s, Madrid clung onto the lucrative Cuba (the island was responsible for half of the world's sugar output, hence its sobriquet: *azucarera del mundo* "the world's sugar bowl") with remarkable doggedness. In this wealthy colony that Spain considered its "pearl of the Antilles," state repression of pro-independence civil society and media helped turn the island nation into a police state, which only served to fuel the revolutionary sentiment. Further, a small economic aristocracy controlled a disproportionate share of national wealth, which some idealistic rebels believed needed to be broken up after Spain departed.

In January 1853 in Havana, Cuba, José Julián Martí y Pérez was born in poverty to immigrants: his father, Mariano, was a sergeant in the Spanish Army's artillery corps, while Leonor was originally from the Canary Islands. Curious and brilliant, again like Sarmiento, José had only turned thirteen when he attempted to translate Hamlet and a Byron ode. The bright adolescent became very passionate about the revolutionary efforts to liberate Cuba from Spain, and therefore dedicated his life to fighting for Cuban independence. In 1869 and only sixteen years old, he founded his first newspaper, *The Free Homeland*, in which he used his writing to promote the independence movement. Incensed, the Spanish authorities threw the young Cuban rebel in prison where he was sentenced to six years of hard labor for his pro-independence agitation.

Yet in 1871 his confinement as a political prisoner ended early with a grant of clemency, and the youth departed for exile in Spain. It was here in the colonial mother country where he published details of the horrors of his imprisonment, as well as information on the incipient Cuban revolution, marshaling support among Spanish liberals, Cuban exiles, and all those who were allied or sympathized with Cuban independence from Spain. Then in 1873 Spain proclaimed itself a republic, which prompted Martí to demand that Cubans be granted the same rights that Spaniards now enjoyed.

During this initial period of exile, Martí also spent some years in Mexico, where he taught high school and wrote plays and political publications that got him in trouble for critiquing strongman Porfirio Díaz. He also spent time in Guatemala in 1877, where he taught foreign languages at an elite liberal (read, secular) normal school. With the end of the Ten Years' War in 1878—the first of three "wars" of anticolonial liberation (the other two being the Little War [1879–1880] and the Cuban War of Independence [1895–1898])—Martí returned to Cuba but was arrested and deported to Spain on anti-Spanish conspiracy charges. At this point, his once boundless ambitions had contracted, at least for now. "I'm going to be a lawyer, a farmer, a teacher; [in other words] a weaver of legal formulas, a producer of foodstuffs, a disseminator of muddled ideas—lost in the froth of the sea."

The emancipation of enslaved people was a looming question during each of the three wars of independence. Martí was opposed to slavery, which pitted him against Cuban planters who embraced an official role for Madrid but wanted some type of increased domestic autonomy—while others advocated for annexation to the United States. Also note that Cuba's colonialism was idiosyncratic: linked politically to Madrid, who got the lion's share of revenues, but economically to the United States, the country with which Cuba did most of its trading. Even before 1898, US investment in sugar plantations, banks, and railroads dwarfed Spain's.

By 1881, he had made his way to Venezuela, but, as had happened in Mexico, his writings offended sitting president Antonio Guzmán Blanco. Martí had to depart. At this point, while always a fervent and early proponent of Cuban liberty, Martí was shocked by the caudillo-like words and actions of pro-independence military leaders, both in Cuba and in exile. Critically, Martí disassociated himself, in 1884, from Antonio Maceo (known as the "Titan of Bronze" given his Afro-Cuban roots) and Máximo Gómez, loathing their fantasy of a military-run Cuba. Martí spent the next seven years teaching and publishing and planning his own kind of revolution, one predicated on democracy, social justice, and racial equality.

EL MONSTRUO

Upon spending extended stints in New York City, the restless Cuban exile now, as if on cue, took up writing as a correspondent for numerous Spanish-language Latin American newspapers. During his New York City tenure, Martí also helped establish and was an instructor at La Liga, a city school for Puerto Ricans and Afro-Cubans; a year later, he founded a branch campus in Tampa, Florida, where legions of Cubans lived.

José Martí. *(Library of Congress Prints and Photographs Division, Washington, DC)*

Referring to his intermittent time in New York, in a letter penned just days before his death, he said: "I have lived in the monster and I know its entrails; my sling is David's." Initially, however, Martí was full of praise for US democratic practices and the Constitution, just like Sarmiento; and he adored the work of Whitman and Emerson. Yet the country's "tradition of expansion [and] of some powerful [leaders]," as he wrote subsequently, complicated this love story. Over time, Martí's opinions on US imperial inclinations prompted some publishers to either highly edit or refrain from publishing these articles. Martí was also deeply concerned about the Colossus of the North annexing his beloved homeland, Cuba: Cuba should be for Cubans, not a New World nation with an insatiable "appetite for power or acquisitions or triumphs that are opposed to goodness and justice." Critics on the left and right have subsequently claimed, rather selectively, that Martí was either deeply jaundiced toward the United States or warmly open and appreciative, when in fact he was both. In the years close to his premature death, his outlook on the United States hardened into an outright disdain, warning of swapping one type of colonialism for another.

During his US exile, Martí penned what is now a seminal essay in the canon of Latin American nationalism—*Our America* (1891). Through its explicit and implicit rejection of US and European culture, Martí sought to articulate and identify that which was truly Latin American (or "Our America," in the title), positing a racially melodious, politically stalwart, unified, and self-confident community of countries. Published in serial form in two Hispanic papers, Martí began the work with a clarion call to his fellow Latins about the "[g]iants with seven-league boats," and the dangers of remaining in ignorant provincialism; Latins must see the world as it is, and resist the pernicious influence of North American acquisitiveness and interventionism and European dandyism.

Influenced by Sarmiento's *Facundo*, *Our America* describes the eternal fray between "the natural man" and "learned artificial men" as "not between civilization and barbarity, but between false erudition and Nature." Martí takes direct issue with Sarmiento's framing of life as a clash between civilization and barbarity in *Facundo*, instead positing that the true distinction is between "the natural man" and the "learned artificial man." Martí also upends the Europhilic stance of so many of his predecessors: "The natural man has triumphed over the imported book in América; natural men have triumphed over an artificial intelligentsia. The native mestizo has triumphed over the exotic criollo." For Martí, continental harmony was dependent on the inclusion of all peoples, and racism was utterly unconscionable: "Anyone who promotes and disseminates opposition or hatred among races is committing a sin against humanity."

He scorned the idea of governing on the US or French modes—"Our young men go out into the world wearing Yankee- or French-colored glasses, and aspire to govern by guesswork over a country about which they know nothing"— and suggested instead that it was necessary to develop a truly Latin American form of leadership based on a deep knowledge of the peoples and countries.

MARTYRDOM

In late 1891, Martí departed for Florida where he gave two addresses, first in Tampa and then in Key West, that sparked renewed passions in the hearts and minds of the local Cuban émigré population. Many of these Cubans, unlike those in New York who had departed for political reasons, had fled their native island looking for work but were still pro-independence. Tampa was home to thousands of exiled Cuban tobacco workers who were fervently anti-Spanish; Key West held the biggest Cuban population in the United States (seven thousand out of twenty-five thousand). In April of the following year, Martí was voted "Delegate" of the newly established Cuban Revolutionary Party. In the party's thinking, once "absolute independence" was achieved, Cuba would be a fraternity of dignified workers united to construct a democratic, just republic. Martí then spent the next two years touring the Caribbean and the United States to drum up support for a *Cuba libre*.

Then in mid-January 1895, having failed in a similar revolutionary campaign the prior year, Martí attempted to depart Florida to lead a more organized and potent anti-Spanish armed insurgency, but it was interdicted by US authorities, who seized the vessels and arms. The resolute Cuban insurgent leader then made it to the Dominican Republic, which allowed him to join forces with General Máximo Gómez, a former Spanish Army cavalry officer who subsequently joined the *insurrectos* (as Cuban insurgents were known). It was here that Martí and Gómez crafted and inked the Montecristi Manifesto, a declaration of independence of sorts for the embryonic yet idealistic movement.

From Hispaniola the next month, Martí, Gómez, and other exiles sailed to Cuba where they clandestinely linked up with a rebel force active on the island and took the fight to the colonists. The war would last three years, but Martí's involvement was over in little more than a month. In a never-finished May 18, 1895, missive to his friend Manuel Mercado, Martí contended that the war was not about defeating the hated Spanish but checking the annexation of the "nations of our America by the unruly and brutal North which despises them." Just hours later, Martí, charging valiantly directly into Spanish forces, was killed in one of the first battles in the war.

Martí had fallen, but the independence war continued without him, culminating in the Spanish-American War in 1898. The latter ended in a win for the invading Americans and an end to Spain's colonial possession. Then in 1902 the United States handed sovereignty over to the Cubans; as a condition of the transfer, though, the Cuban state included elements of the United States' Platt Amendment—several of its conditions restructured Cuban's sovereignty—into its new constitution. We will of course never know the answer, but it is worth pausing to wonder what Martí would have made of the US role in Cuba's freedom.

"APOSTLE OF INDEPENDENCE"

Before the communist Cuban Revolution in 1959, all Cubans celebrated the "Apostle of Independence" for sacrificing himself for their island nation's liberty. Indeed, José Martí was not only associated with Cuba but also with Latin American sovereignty and dignity. After Fidel Castro and company took power, though, his inheritance was claimed by Castroites, who emphasized his anti-Yankee side and claimed Martí as the ideological father of their communist revolution. (See Chapter 23, "Fidel Castro: A Rebel with a Cause.") And the equally passionate Cuban anti-Castroites, often from their exile in the United States, likewise claimed him as their own, seeing Martí through the pre-1959 lens as a prophet of freedom, peace, and national respect. They also held that Martí would have blasted the cult of personality that Fidel Castro maniacally cultivated over his roughly half-century of one-man rule.

Yet it might also be the case that while excoriating Fidel's heinous *caudillismo*, Martí, who was not a socialist but patently socially minded, would have welcomed the Revolution's social reform orientation. This disputed legacy was further politicized in the 1980s by the Reagan administration, which created *Radio Televisión Martí* and began broadcasting to the island (perhaps unaware of the irony of a US-funded station named after a vehement critic of the United States). Its mission? In its own words, to serve as "a contrast to Cuban media and provide its listeners with an uncensored view of current events"—and Havana naturally jammed the propaganda from Uncle Sam.

Contested as his legacy is, Martí is perhaps unique for being praised by both sides, and the evidence of his adoration is everywhere in Cuba. Today, visitors flying to Havana land at Aeropuerto José Martí; the national library is the Biblioteca José Martí; the martyr's image is on Cuban money and mail stamps; and his portrait is displayed in every schoolhouse; a bust in every town. In 2021, communist Cuba launched "Abdala" (the title of Martí's famous patriotic odes), its homemade COVID-19 candidate vaccine, the first manufactured in Latin America. Whichever way his name is claimed, Martí's pen has left an indelible mark on the country he loved.

bust of José Martí at Afro-Cuban Cultural Community Center, Callejón de Hamel (Hamel's Alley), 2018. A verse from the venerated poem, "Versos Sencillos," reads: "I am art among the arts, With the mountains I am one." *(Photograph by Angela Willis)*

III
FIRST HALF OF THE TWENTIETH CENTURY

12

José Enrique Rodó

Ariel *and a New Vision for Latin America*

I do not aspire to the 'Ivory Tower', I take pleasure in the type of literature which, in its own way, is militant.

—*José Enrique Rodó*

In 1900, prominent Uruguayan essayist, educator, and philosopher, José Enrique Rodó published his greatest book, *Ariel*, in the aftermath of the Spanish-American War of 1898. Inebriated from the total military defeat of Spain in both Cuba and the Philippines, the United States had reached unprecedented global stature, and many feared that it would impose a cultural and political hegemonic grip on its newly designated "backyard," Latin America. So Rodó's response, working off the insights of storied Nicaraguan poet and contemporary Rubén Darío, was to pen a moral discourse—*Ariel*—whose primary audience was Latin American youths. It would change the region's ideological trajectory for at least the next six decades, serving as a veritable moral bible for Latin America, especially its intellectuals and students.

This was a radical departure, bearing in mind that leading up to the fateful year of 1898, generations of liberals like Mexican Benito Juárez and Argentine Domingo Sarmiento had admired the United States as the north star of republicanism and democracy; the Argentine polymath even called himself "Franklincito." (See Chapter 8, "Benito Juárez: Mexico's Great Reformer" and Chapter 9, "Juan Manuel de Rosas and Domingo Sarmiento: The Struggle to Hatch Argentina.") Yet the US victory in Cuba, when combined with the earlier yanqui annexation of Texas (1836), the Mexican-American War (1846–

1848), and the private US citizen "filibuster" expeditions into Mexico, Cuba, and Central America (1830s–1850s) served as ample evidence to suggest a malevolent form of colonialism was unfolding in the New World.

Unlike Sarmiento, Juárez, and Cuban freedom fighter José Martí, Rodó never spent a day in the United States, and likely got his views about American inferiority and bawdiness from reading books such as Frenchman Paul Bourget's travel novel, *Outre Mer: Impressions of America*. Be that as it may, after *Ariel*, Latin American intellectualism became synonymous with anti-Americanism.

GRAND AMBITIONS

Contrary to what some historical sketches sometimes assume, Rodó, born in 1872 in the Uruguayan capital of Montevideo—then a swelling but still modest population of one hundred thousand, a majority of whom were immigrants from Europe—did not emerge from the Uruguayan upper class; rather, he was the son of an aristocratic mother who happened to marry a Catalan merchant of declining means. Their dwindling cash forced them to move their son from a private to a public school, which explains why so much of his subsequent and prodigious learning was self-taught. In the wake of his father's death, José Enrique was forced to work in a variety of odd jobs to help make family ends meet but continued to read and write voraciously.

By 1895, he had published essays on an assortment of artistic and literary topics; contributed to the founding of the National Review of Literature and Social Sciences; and was a professor at the University of the Republic in Montevideo, the country's oldest and largest public university. From this vantage point, Rodó headlined what would become known as the "Generation of 1900," the term for the country's literary and intellectual pantheon.

He was also becoming more politically engaged. In addition to the specter of emerging US military might in 1898, Rodó was strongly influenced by the chaos—and caudillismo—of the intermittent Uruguayan Civil War. Officially, this protracted postindependence civil war lasted from 1839 until 1851 between the *Blancos* (Whites) and *Colorados* (Reds); in fact, it started even earlier, in 1832, and was not fully settled until 1904, with the military defeat of the Blancos at the hands of the President José Battle y Ordóñez's (and thus Colorado) government. It was arguably this domestic instability, combined with the threat of northern influence, that catalyzed Rodo's famous *cri de coeur*.

José Enrique Rodó, 1901. *(Alamy Stock Photo)*

ARIEL

Ariel's premise is a tension between the collective spirit of Hispanic America (through the character Ariel in William Shakespeare's *The Tempest*) and Anglo-Saxon societies, especially the United States (Caliban, another character from the same Bard play). Ariel manifests the most noble elements of human nature while Caliban, the play's villain, is concerned solely with his material wishes. An extended sample from the legendary work:

> North American life, in fact, perfectly describes the vicious circle identified by Pascal: the fervent pursuit of well-being that has no object beyond itself. North American prosperity is as great as its inability to satisfy even an average concept of human destiny. In spite of its titanic accomplishments and the great force of will that those accomplishments represent, and in spite of its incomparable triumphs in all spheres of material success, it is nevertheless true that as an entity this civilization creates a singular impression of insufficiency and emptiness.

Unapologetic and passionate, *Ariel* elevated the cultural distinctions between these two divergent Anglo-Saxon and Latin camps and admonished Spanish Americans to be wary of North American might and materialism, which was ever poised to wrest away their own spiritual self-worth. Reminiscent of Bolívar's hope for a pan-regional confederation (see Chapter 6, "Simón Bolívar: The Great Liberator, Flawed Emancipator"), Rodó argued that a shared Latin American identity and solidarity was necessary to both remedy Latin America's inferiority complex and resist North American cultural imperialism. "I have always believed that in our America it was not possible to talk about many *patrias*, but only one great *patria* . . . the American *patria* transcends the national *patria*."

This emphasis on cultural distinction did not go against the fashionable philosophy of positivism: at its core, the Europe-hatched philosophy held that through scientific method, empirical observation, and rational thought, liberty could be integrated with "order and progress." Latin American elites who embraced positivism believed that such an approach was exactly the tonic their chaotic societies needed. The actual application of positivist policies revealed how intellectually incoherent the philosophy was—varying from public education systems to promote morality to free trade to anticlerical edicts to European immigration—in a hierarchical approach that overlapped with the era's ascendant Social Darwinism. In the turn-of-the-century milieu, positivism had overtaken liberalism in the region's intellectual pecking order. Amazingly, Rodó in effect was seeking to give positivism a new impetus, arguing that it was science that could help Latin America, but only if progress was measured according to the region's cultural identity, not that of North America's.

THE PLUNGE INTO POLITICS

Ariel granted Rodó immediate international esteem and financial security. It would also eventually bring him an invitation from the Colorados to enter the political fray, as "your name alone would adorn the electoral platform." And this is exactly what the laconic Uruguayan literary star did, and was elected as a Colorado deputy to the Uruguayan congress on multiple occasions, starting in 1902. In 1907, after declining an academic appointment to run for office again, he described the irresistible allure of politics for the thinker, citing "[the] inescapable fact of South American life that compels almost all of us who pick up a pen to go into politics. And I do not consider this to be

A stamp printed in Cuba shows the exotic plant, Cypella, and essayist José Enrique Rodó, series "Historia Latinoamericana," circa 1989. *(Alamy Stock Photo)*

an entirely bad thing." At a prior, more sullen moment when he thought his political career was over, he commented, "to say goodbye to politics would almost be like saying goodbye to the country, for our country and its politics are synonymous."

Then, for a whole set of political and personal reasons, Rodó and Battle, the Colorado reformer president who was, in this very age, bringing Latin America's first welfare state to Uruguay, had a falling out. Putting aside his decade-long political career, Rodó, in 1917, embarked for Europe, before falling ill with meningitis in Italy and dying at forty-five years old. When he had departed for Europe, crowds had gathered to bid their adored man of letters adieu. When his body returned to his native soil, the grieving country was in national mourning.

Rodó, like Sarmiento, viewed education as a transformative tool to spark national and regional modernity; he once led the National Library. His works influenced the so-called Latin American student reform movement—for example, more political autonomy for universities—throughout the region in the next few decades. Rodó's acolytes (*Arielistas*) and other intellectuals were inspired by his dissection of US culture, producing—from Mexico to Nicaragua to Peru to Argentina—a swelling political and intellectual support for left-wing policies (critically, economic nationalism, anti-imperialism, anti-dictatorship) over the ensuing decades. With his intellectual reputation largely based on *Ariel*, Rodó is held by many to be Latin America's greatest philosopher. While it is outside of our scope to settle this question, we can still be in awe at his insights and creativity that launched a century's worth of intellectual activity and mobilization.

13

José Vasconcelos

The Mexican Revolution's Cultural Caudillo

José Vasconcelos's extraordinary life encompassed a remarkable span of Mexican history: from the twilight of late nineteenth-century caudillo rule of Porfirio Díaz, through the rebellion to topple the hated dictator that led to a full-scale revolution from 1910–1920, and up to the consolidation of a civilian "revolutionary" government in the ensuing decade. First, as rector of the National Autonomous University and then minister of public education, Vasconcelos was a crucial pedagogical catalyst whose policies and ideas helped Mexico identify, implement, and celebrate the social values that the revolution was supposed to have fought for—and that would now modernize and democratize Mexico.

Vasconcelos's eclectic scholarship—much of it penned after he had left the government—still resonates into the twenty-first century. His many books were often brilliant and original, challenging white hegemony and promoting ideas of "Mexicanness," but were also highly contradictory, lacking the passion of his colossal reform agenda, and highly racialized, at least to modern eyes. There was also a sordid second act in the Teacher of America's towering career when he transformed from social reformist *par excellence* to a conservative Catholic nationalist who was a vocal champion of European fascism in the 1930s and 1940s. This complicated legacy has made him one of Mexico's most controversial historical figures.

COMING OF AGE IN A TURBULENT MEXICO

José Vasconcelos Calderón was born in the city of Oaxaca in 1882. His father was a government bureaucrat while his mother died when her son was a teenager. After relocating to the northern border town of Piedras Negras, the bright and studious José went to school in the US town of Eagle Pass, Texas, enabling him to become perfectly fluent in English and unusually comfortable in the Anglo realm.

By 1905 José was in Mexico City at one of the country's most elite high schools, the National Preparatory School. As was the case throughout late nineteenth-century Latin America, the deep influence of French positivism ensured that top Mexican schools were teaching science as part of a rational approach to societal organization. Positivism, as a counter to Iberian and Catholic values, promoted a rationally organized secular society predicated on the elevation of a scientific and technocratic elite. Its goal? Nothing less than modernity. Hatched by French philosopher Auguste Comte, this philosophy often had Social Darwinism (or the notion that individuals become powerful due to their innate abilities) sprinkled on top.

While studying law at university, Vasconcelos became involved in an underground political organization, the Youth Anthem. Its eclectic membership of students, teachers, and artists (including a young Diego Rivera) plotted against *el porfiriato*—the sclerotic, venal reign of Porfirio Díaz. Since first coming to power in 1876, Díaz had for three presidencies upheld a liberal platform of laissez-faire economics while failing to maintain an equally liberal (read, rule of law) political sphere.

The year 1910 was a watershed in Mexico's history. The porfiriato regime appeared as potent and entrenched as ever, but beneath the surface, dissent was reaching a fever pitch. Many hoped that a free and fair election would lead to Don Porfirio's departure, but others were less optimistic. Much of the anti-Díaz political opposition rallied around the cry of not permitting the strongman's getting *fraudulently* voted into office again—as he had been six times prior! Vasconcelos, who had started working for a law firm in Washington, DC, became a member of that city's local Anti-Reelection Club affiliated with presidential candidate Francisco I. Madero's Anti-Reelection Party. Returning to the Mexican capital, Vasconcelos escalated his political involvement when he started editing the opposition party's newspaper, *El Antireeleccionista*.

The opposition's efforts initially appeared to come to naught. As the midyear election neared, Madero's victory appeared likely—until he was arrested and jailed. The ensuing "vote" gave 98.93 percent to the octogenarian incumbent, and just 1.04 percent to Madero, but Díaz had fatally misjudged. Madero soon escaped from prison and from exile in Texas issued patriotic *cri de cœur*—the Plan of San Luis Potosí—that detailed the myriad reasons why

Díaz needed to be removed from office. His defiance inspired motley regional revolts led by the populist insurgent Francisco "Pancho" Villa in the north and, in the state of Morelos just south of the capital, by Emiliano Zapata. By May 1911, Díaz had been forced into exile in Paris, replaced by an interim government before Madero won a free and fair vote and took office.

Madero never intended to unleash widespread societal change but instead consolidate the nation's shift from a dictatorship into an electoral democracy—a stance that displeased both the left and right. Eventually, a rightist putsch led General Victoriano Huerta (the very commander Madero had depended upon to lead government forces) deposed Madero, who was later executed. Disconsolate but unwilling to give up, Vasconcelos joined the motley coalition of pro-Madero leaders (Venustiano Carranza, Villa, and Álvaro Obregón in the north and Zapata in the south) that had crystallized in the wake of Madero's murder. Vasconcelos's organizing resulted in his exile to Paris, where he befriended other Mexican activists. By mid-July 1914, Huerta had been removed, enabling Vasconcelos to return home.

But the situation in Mexico was far from stable. The once-formidable anti-Huerta alliance had fractured into rival factions with Carranza, leader of the so-called Constitutionalists, severing ties with Villa's populist movement and Zapata's agrarianism, and fierce fighting ensued. Vasconcelos backed the Constitutionalists, now the ruling faction, even becoming, albeit for only five weeks in late 1914, minister of public education. Legend has it that Vasconcelos worked so hard and was so successful that for his short tenure, he was the fledgling government's effective foreign and interior minister.

In 1915, Carranza's de facto government forces, led by his indispensable commander Obregón, defeated Villa's men. Under Carranza's tutelage, the Mexican Constitution of 1917 codified the broad outlines of a radically new state: universal male suffrage but also anticlerical provisions, subsoil rights, workers' rights, and land reform (including legalized expropriation).

But the revolution was far from over. In 1919, Carranza's agents murdered Zapata (who had refused to disarm his southern peasant army), then Carranza himself was ousted and killed in 1920 by a cohort of generals led by Obregón, marking the revolution's final successful coup. Late that same year Obregón won a fair election to become president of what was now post-revolutionary Mexico.

EDUCATION FOR THE NATION

As president, Obregón's goal was to implement through a civilian government all the revolutionary social reforms and policies while avoiding the savage, internecine violence of the immediate past. Although he had to go slowly, given the staggering payments to foreign individuals and companies, his government's first budget emphasized the funding of schools as well as the military. The 1917 Bolshevik revolution in Russia, once consolidated, also put wind in the sails of Mexico City's socialistic ideology.

In June 1920, Obregón appointed Vasconcelos (who had recently returned to Mexico after yet another exile) as rector of the National Autonomous University—a position that Vasconcelos held for sixteen months. From his secular pulpit, Vasconcelos sought to further the gospel of the revolution, elevating the notion that the country's essence could be achieved by rediscovering and celebrating its native residents. Echoing Uruguay's Rodó, what had to be resisted was the malign cultural and economic influence of North America (see Chapter 12, "José Enrique Rodó: *Ariel* and a New Vision for Latin America"). Outlined in messianic terms, Vasconcelos's platform and policies were awash with pro-Mexico nationalism to allow citizens to regain their identity and pride, but notably never deteriorated into xenophobia.

Vasconcelos became the most visible and inspiring leader of the so-called university reform movement that sought to pivot education away from porfiriato-tainted Positivism and adopt a humanist approach that would foster the development of a distinctly Mexican identity and redress past wrongs. Long-neglected social, economic, and political deficiencies would be addressed via the schoolhouse: in other words, mass emancipation through education. "I have not come to govern the University," he stated in his inaugural speech, "but to ask the University to work for the people." To this end, Vasconcelos hatched a massive literacy effort predicated on "honorary" (i.e., voluntary) teachers, and in 1921 convened the first Latin American student conference in Mexico City. Here is one of the university students on the rector's religion-like devotion:

> With dramatic gesture and inflammatory words Vasconcelos had pointed to the scars of illiteracy [and] he called upon us to fight against it with the same zeal and the same disinterestedness as the old Spanish missionary who went out to the most distant and humble dwelling places to save the pagan native's soul.

SPREADING THE REVOLUTIONARY WORD

On the heels of his bold accomplishments running the university, in 1921 Vasconcelos was appointed Secretary of Public Education, a newly organized and manifestly important agency. Building on his work as university rector, he put in motion ambitious plans to eradicate the national scourge of illiteracy: elementary enrolment was boosted by 50 percent through a frenetic campaign of school building and teacher training, while two million literary primers—often fused with the translations of classics—were printed. These were just a fraction of all the books and magazines being edited and published by Vasconcelos's ministry, which led the private publishing industry to complain that their profits were being squeezed by Vasconcelos's state monopoly, while others pointed out that Mexicans first needed to learn how to read before they could utilize all these books being published.

José Vasconcelos, 1914. *(Library of Congress Prints and Photographs Division, Washington, DC)*

But Vasconcelos had bigger concerns—nothing less than the inaugurating of a magnificent spiritual rebirth of Mexico. Pedagogy would be how the Mexican Revolution would be taught to citizens, creating a common foundational ideology that would bind the country together. Almost two thousand libraries were built across the country, often in rural hamlets which Vasconcelos would visit (to the great surprise of the locals). Practical skills were elevated: industrial and technical trades and pedagogies would be prioritized. "We would prefer to be the confectioner in the republic," Vasconcelos boasted, "than the worst lawyer in the village." The role of the instructor was paramount: "those teachers taking part in our work are convinced that they not only exercise a civil function but that they are also part of a modern crusade to elevate and liberate the minds and to improve the bodies of their fellow men."

Vasconcelos was also responsible for overseeing the Fine Arts wing of his ministry, which he did in signature spectacular form. The study of pre-Hispanic cultures and archeology were all energized, as were contemporary writers and artists, with Vasconcelos reconfiguring and relaunching arts institutions that had fallen by the wayside during the protracted revolution as well as during the porfiriato when Positivism reigned supreme: the San Carlos Academy of Fine Arts, the National Conservatory of Music, and the National Symphony Orchestra.

Vasconcelos also underwrote the nascent muralist movement in Mexican art, designed to transmit the doctrine of the revolution in a way any Mexican, even the illiterate, could understand and, crucially, act upon. Vasconcelos eagerly commissioned durable, didactic public murals across the nation, with the "Big Three"—Diego Rivera, Juan Clemente Orozco, and Davíd Alfaro Siquieros—becoming Vasconcelos's go-to artists. Vasconcelos even offered the walls of his own Public Education ministry to Rivera to paint a secular gospel of the Mexican Revolution—something he completed after several years of intensive work (see Chapter 14, "Diego Rivera and Frida Kahlo: Passion, Paint, and Politics"). Once again, "Mexican-ness" was a priority: Vasconcelos wanted to end the aesthetic and intellectual dependency on foreign methods in art and culture and return to indigenous modes of expression.

The results were astonishing: Vasconcelos's plan unleashed a golden age of Mexican art, with Rivera standing at the head of a group of astonishingly talented artists, some of whom seemed to emerge almost overnight. Máximo Pacheco, for example, was an indigenous fifteen-year-old who started out carrying paint buckets for Rivera but quickly was "painting amazingly intense and beautiful frescoes."

Vasconcelos's towering legacy in education has overshadowed the fact that during his years in the Mexican government he wasted few opportunities to publicly condemn tyranny, notably calling Venezuela's military dictator Juan Vicente Gómez "a human swine that dishonors our race." He also urged Mexican students to express solidarity with their forlorn counterparts in beleaguered Venezuela (which they did through mass protests), helped Venezuelan refugees secure employment in Mexico, and even persuaded President Obregón to sever diplomatic ties with the Gómez regime.

The Mexican titan then fired off a white-hot missive condemning the legions of Latin American intellectuals who reflexively bashed *yanqui* imperialism while overlooking caudillo tyranny closer to home: "It is the fashion nowadays in our part of America to protest loudly against the imperialism of the Yankees. Let us not forget however that in remaining under the heel of our local dictators we are admirably serving the schemes of our Northern neighbors."

Yet Vasconcelos's hope of becoming a "new Sarmiento" (the great Argentine reformer who constructed hundreds of schools and libraries, among other projects; see Chapter 9, "Juan Manuel de Rosas and Domingo Sarmiento: The Struggle to Hatch Argentina") was disappointed. Vasconcelos left the Education position in 1924 after only three years, in part because he loathed the heavy-handedness of soon-to-be inaugurated president, Plutarco Elías Calles.

After leaving office, Vasconcelos set about codifying his theories on the Mexican identity through 1925's *The Cosmic Race*, a fantastical manifesto that tackled the entrenched Social Darwinist ideologies that supported white supremacy—a prevalent view in intellectual circles across the Americas at the time. Radically, Vasconcelos argued that the Conquest and colonization had inexorably blended (*mestizaje*) the Iberian and the indigenous into a new race, the cosmic race, which would, in Vasconcelos's flights of fancy, go on to create its own Eden-like Amazonian civilization, Universópolis. The book gushes in celebration of ancient native peoples—an intentional contrast to the then-common valorization of the Spanish-influenced (i.e., religious) arts and cultures. Read today, *The Cosmic Race* appears exceptionally racialized, but it must be borne in mind that this was an era when the concept of mestizaje was at the core of Mexico's postrevolution nation-building, and that Vasconcelos was actually critiquing the influence of the dominant white culture.

PRESIDENTIAL TIMBER, FASCIST SYMPATHIZER?

Seeking a path back to political influence, Vasconcelos threw his hat into the ring for the governorship of Oaxaca, his native state, but after suffering a bitter setback, opted for self-exile. In 1928, Obregón won the presidential election but was assassinated before he could take office. By this point, Vasconcelos was back in Mexico and thus decided to run in the 1929 presidential election to select Obregón's replacement, but lost a lopsided and controversial vote against the candidate of the PRI (Institutional Revolutionary Party). Claiming electoral fraud, Vasconcelos hatched an armed insurrection, but it quickly flamed out.

A later crackdown on leftwing political opponents forced him into yet another self-imposed exile, this time in the United States and Europe, where over the next decade he penned no fewer than ten books, including weighty tomes on arcane academic topics (such as his volume *Positivism, Neo-positivism, and Phenomenology*). His masterpiece was a five-volume autobiography, a trenchant, brilliantly conceived, and written account of his life, published in abridged form as *A Mexican Ulysses*.

By 1940 Vasconcelos had returned to Mexico to take up an appointment as director of the National Library. Increasingly, however, Vasconcelos's thinking had become obsessed with dictators and dictatorships, especially Germany's Adolf Hitler and Italy's Benito Mussolini. With Europe on the cusp of war, Vasconcelos assented to edit *Rudder*, a publication financed by the German Embassy in Mexico City. Only a handful of issues were ever produced, but they were bursting with breathless anti-Semitic rants. Here is an excerpt from a Vasconcelos piece:

> Hitler's force does not come from the barracks but from the book [*Mein Kampf*] inspired by his intelligence. Hitler does not owe his power to soldiers, nor to battalions, but to his own speeches that won him power in democratic competition with the other leaders and aspiring leaders that Germany developed after the First World War.

Vasconcelos was also following an ultra-orthodox variant of Catholicism, becoming a Franciscan lay brother, and wrote supportive articles backing Spanish fascist dictator Francisco Franco, now that Adolf Hitler and Benito Mussolini had been defeated. He also had high praise for some of the most infamous Latin American strongmen of the age: Dominican Republic's Rafael Trujillo, Cuba's Fulgencio Batista, and Argentina's Juan Perón. (See Chapter 18, "Rafael Trujillo: 'Our S.O.B.'" and Chapter 20, "Juan and Eva Perón: Peronism's Dynamic Duo.") Later in his life, Vasconcelos would vehemently deny his fascistic leanings: "Me, a Nazi? I laugh at those who make that charge against me, because I am one of the few Mexicans who has struggled all his life against dictatorships."

Yet right up until the end, his writings suggested his sympathies had decidedly swung to the far right. Only a few years before he died in 1959, Vasconcelos wrote a fulsome introduction to a new edition of the book *Worldwide Defeat* by Mexican Nazi sympathizer and anti-Semitic conspiracy theorist Salvador Borrego Escalante. Another work, *Litanies of the Evening* (published posthumously) suggested that nuclear weapons might be necessary to combat global scourges.

TEACHER OF AMERICA

Before Latin America and the world had the example of the 1959 Cuban Revolution, the spirit and manifestation of the Mexican Revolution was a moral and ideological north star for many on the left—and José Vasconcelos played an outsize role in parlaying the zeitgeist into practical changes. He was a vital actor in the initial circa 1910–1911 "revolution" against Díaz before his extraordinary tenure as a minister in the nascent revolutionary government. As minister, he promoted massive shifts in literacy and education to refound the nation on civic, secular, and *indigenista* pillars—work that rightfully earned him the moniker "Teacher of the Youth of America" (often shortened to "Teacher of America"). Yet his political beliefs also ensured that he would spend a good chunk of his life in exile, while his later career after government saw an affection for strongmen in general and fascism in particular that formed a stark contradiction with his earlier views. In some ways, this tension is well captured by another of his monikers, that of Mexico's "cultural caudillo"—a man passionate about education, philosophy, art, and literature, but whose single-minded focus was also increasingly attracted by practitioners of absolute power.

14
Diego Rivera and Frida Kahlo
Passion, Paint, and Politics

Diego Rivera is widely considered the greatest muralist of twentieth-century Latin America. His sparkling murals were masterpieces of art and politics: defiantly didactic, they celebrated proletarian revolutionary fervor, blue-collar grit, and indigenous pride while villainizing industrialists, church leaders, and other rapacious deplorables. Rivera's artistic brilliance helped interpret the ideology of the Mexican Revolution—the world's first twentieth-century social revolution—to millions of his Mexican compatriots. But while Rivera's devotion to communism was deep, he was never a dyed-in-the-wool member and even accepted commissions from some of the world's greatest capitalists (although politics was often a bone of contention).

The art of Frida Kahlo was in the main more personal than that of her eventual husband Rivera, centering on intimate self-portraits that depict her abortion or mutilations—today in Mexico, she is known as *la heroína del dolor* (the heroine of the pain)—yet in several works, she also directly addressed political concerns and figures, including Joseph Stalin and Leon Trotsky. A study of her life reveals an iron-clad commitment to postrevolutionary Mexican nationalism as well as the overlapping global socialism and communism that formed an intriguing counterpoint with her husband's dalliance with capitalist commissions in the United States. Yet while Rivera's work now may appear inextricably linked to its historical moment, Kahlo's work has profoundly transcended it: by radically foregrounding the complexity of the female experience in a male-dominated milieu, she created a truly revolutionary body of work that has challenged and changed ideas of representation and gender across the world.

COMING OF AGE AND EUROPE

Diego Rivera was born in 1886 in Guanajuato, a provincial city north of Mexico City. Christened Diego María de la Concepción Juan Nepomuceno Estanislao de Rivera y Barrientos Acosta y Rodríguez, he came from Spanish, African, Jewish, Russian, Italian, and Portuguese stock. In a deeply devout country, Diego eventually learned that he came from *converso* blood, meaning that his family had compulsorily converted from Judaism to Catholicism in the fifteenth and sixteenth centuries. Throughout his life, he was tortured by issues of faith, although he was a professed atheist.

From the moment he could hold a pencil, Diego stood out for his habit of sketching and painting and was pushed by his well-to-do parents to pursue his artistic tendencies. When Diego was around seven, the family moved to Mexico City; before he was eleven, the precocious youth was studying full time at the San Carlos Academy, a prestigious art school where he earned a reputation as a very hard worker, bright student, and exceptional artist. During his teens, he fell in love with landscape painting depicting pastoral Mexico and its equally colorful peoples.

Winning a scholarship from Porfirio Díaz's autocratic government, in 1907, the aspiring young adult and painter—he had by then already sold some of his landscapes—moved to Spain and then, after four years, to Paris. It was in the City of Light—and critically the extended time spent in the gritty bohemian scene of Montparnasse—where he became enamored by the experiential artistic style of Cubism developed between 1907 and 1914 by painters Pablo Picasso and Georges Braque that was dedicated to "decomposing" realistic subjects into geometric shapes. Rivera even befriended fellow Catholic-raised Picasso, for whom he felt a "kind of organic sympathy." Rivera would later play up his Marxist revolutionary bona fides but, before and even during Europe, his political and artistic outlook was quite culturally conservative and politically agnostic.

REVOLUTION

After several dazzling years in the Old World, Rivera returned to Mexico, in 1910 in time for the hundredth-anniversary celebration of independence from Spain. The talented artist was eager to demonstrate what he had learned and produced during his extended stint abroad on the Díaz regime's coin and soon had the chance when none other than Carmen Romero Rubio de Díaz, spouse of Porfirio, opened the twenty-four-year-old's one-man exhibition in Mexico City.

But Mexico was soon to be thrown into turmoil after Díaz imprisoned opposition candidate Francisco I. Madero in the run-up to that year's presidential election, which Díaz eventually won with almost 99 percent of the vote. In response, a coalition of "anti-reelection" actors came together to challenge Díaz, eventually including militias led by Emiliano Zapata, Francisco "Pancho" Villa, and Pascual Orozco. By May 1911, Díaz had been forced from office, replaced by the legitimate Madero. A decade hence when he had become an in-house muralist for the post-Porfirian government in power, Rivera would claim that he had played an active fighting role in these early anti-Díaz campaigns, including becoming an expert in derailing trains while not harming the passengers.

Before 1911 was out, Rivera returned to Paris on yet another government-provided scholarship (this time funded by Madero's democratic administration), where he met and married Russian émigré, liberal (read anti-tsarist) thinker and artist, Angelina Beloff, with whom he had a child, Diego (who died young). His second spell in Paris also exposed the young Mexican artist to leftist ideology, namely communism. Finally, he decided to return to Mexico in 1921 after touring Italy for eighteen months and absorbing the magnificent Renaissance frescoes—an inspiring public medium that would shape Rivera's thinking about the purpose of art.

The Mexico that Diego returned to was very different from the country he had left a decade before. Madero's legitimate ascension in 1911 inspired hope of a more democratic and just society, but instead, the country had been wracked with what can best be described as a multifaceted civil war that left over a million dead and the economy in tatters. On December 1, 1920, having helped oust a sitting head of state in 1920, General Álvaro Obregón won a fair election to become president of what would become postrevolutionary Mexico.

Obregón appointed José Vasconcelos as minister for public education, with a mandate to do anything and everything to reinvigorate and reimagine Mexican culture and education (see Chapter 13, "José Vasconcelos: The Mexican Revolution's Cultural Caudillo"). In a country with high rates of illiteracy, art was one of Vasconcelos's most potent tools to spread the word about the new form of society being constructed and write the history of the revolution in ways that could be understood by all. The vehicle for this cultural transformation would be accessible, durable, (and highly didactic) muralism.

As if someone had turned on a switch, dazzling public murals appeared across the nation, with Rivera, José Clemente Orozco, and David Alfaro Siqueiros the "Big Three" contributing artists. The so-called Golden Age of Mexican muralism had begun. Rivera's first big government commission was a mural at the National Preparatory School which was finished in 1922. Vasconcelos then dispatched Rivera to Tehuantepec, an indigenous region nestled in the southeast part of Oaxaca state. During this research trip, Rivera began painting *The Bather of Tehuantepec* (1923), which portrayed a native woman naked from the waist up. The work marked a breakthrough in Rivera's style, where he finally found a way to fuse his talent with indigenous Mexican inspiration. As biographer Patrick Marnham put it, "the man who had returned to his country determined to endow it with a national art," eventually learned that "it was the Indian people of Mexico who were to endow him with a personal vision."

This new venture into revolutionary art was accompanied by increased political activism. In late 1922, Rivera was designated member #992 of the Mexican Communist Party, founded three years prior. The artist quickly became one of its leaders along with Siqueiros and Xavier Guerrero, a fellow muralist, and hosted Communist Party meetings along with his second wife Guadalupe Marín (married in 1922 after Rivera divorced Beloff the year before). The three communist muralists also founded the Union of Technical Workers, Painters and Sculptors in the same year and co-edited a new communistic mouthpiece, *El Machete*, with the strident motto:

> The Machete serves to cut the cane,
> To open paths in shadowed woods,
> To decapitate serpents, to cut down weeds,
> And to humble the pride of the impious rich.

The text included manifestoes on music and the arts, large engravings by Siqueiros and Guerrero, and whatever else from (as one scholar icily phrased it) the "self-appointed poets of the people." Ironically, *El Machete* sold for ten centavos an issue—far beyond the means of most working-class Mexicans when a full day's wage at a farm could be as pitiable as thirty centavos.

Rivera's reputation swelling, Vasconcelos pushed for him to paint the Public Education Ministry—the very institution that Vasconcelos ran. Begun in

March 1923 and completed in 1930 through an other-worldly work ethic—sixteen-hour days were routine—Rivera's colossal work encompassed around 125 fresco panels lining the walls of two courtyards over three floors. Besotted with workers' struggles and the Marxist imperative to throw down the chain that oppressed this class, Rivera's tale in his foundational mural was clear and simple. It started on the first floor—Mexicans are forced from their Eden-like agricultural community to become peons in dank mines owned by plutocrat foreigners. Rivera included a poem from radical writer Carlos Gutiérrez Cruz:

> Comrade miner,
> Bent under the weight of the earth,
> Your hand errs
> When it extracts metal for money.
> Make daggers
> With all the metals,
> And thus,
> You will see
> That the metals
> After all
> Are for you.

The second floor is centered on science and technology. Rivera returned to his communistic interpretations on the top level. After he finished it, Rivera explained his vision of the massive artwork: "I had the ambition to reflect the genuine essential elements of the land. I wanted my pictures to mirror the social life of Mexico as I see it."

But barely a year after Rivera began the commission, his patron Vasconcelos resigned as minister of public education in 1924. Late in the same year, reactionary candidate Plutarco Elías Calles won the presidency.

FROM STALIN TO SELLING OUT?

In 1927 Rivera finally achieved his long-held ambition of visiting the Soviet Union when he traveled as the official painter with the Mexican delegation to the Tenth Anniversary of the October Revolution. Rivera was given a warm welcome by his Russian hosts, including the General Secretary of the Communist Party, Joseph Stalin, who even signed Rivera's sketch of the Communist leader. There was some discussion of a Kremlin commission to do a fresco on the walls of the Red Army Officers' Club; it is not clear which party backed out first, but there is no doubt that Rivera was more than ready to return home, although the exact motives for this sentiment remain unclear.

Back in Mexico City, Rivera embarked on *The Arsenal* (1928), which depicted his fellow artist and love interest Frida Kahlo distributing arms beneath a Communist Party hammer-and-sickle banner while wearing a shirt with a red star (a traditional color and symbol of communism). But around this time Rivera also realized that he needed to diversify from murals, which might have brought public renown but paid poorly, especially given the time required for each commission. Rivera was also facing mounting bills stemming from his obligation to fund his three children (one with Beloff, two with Marín).

Rivera's solution was to sell the painting and sketches he did to prepare for the murals to rich collectors—an approach that outraged Communist hardliners, who also criticized Rivera accepting official projects from President Calles's administration, which had become far more conservative, even reactionary, compared to Obregón's "revolutionary" government. In 1929, one left-wing newspaper headline screamed "Diego Rivera Wants to be the Mussolini of the Artists"; one communist cuttingly quipped that the "People's Painter" had become the "Painter of Palaces." Then a ham-handed putsch against Calles sparked the president to lash out against his Communist enemies, banning the party and sending scores of members to be executed. *El Machete* was summarily closed, its printing presses demolished.

Just a few weeks after he had married his third wife, Frida Kahlo, Rivera was expelled by Communist Party in 1929, with Kahlo quitting in solidarity. (Over the next decades, his many reinstatement requests were rejected until a positive decision came in 1955, two years after the death of Stalin.) But one upside to his party ejection was that as a "former communist" Rivera could, unlike other now-banned communists, "legally" work on the official mural at the National Palace (completed in 1935) and other government-sponsored projects. Indeed, Rivera's post–Communist Party phase was when his international profile skyrocketed, with the artist becoming, in the words of biographer Gerry Souter, "the world's most famous muralist and most famous Communist west of the Soviet Union." He began to court some of America's most moneyed collectors, which continued to infuriate the orthodox communists while still making him even more famous State-side. In 1929 he was awarded the American Institute of Architect's prestigious Fine Arts Medal, with the citation claiming that "Mr. Rivera's work seems to embody an appreciation of the wall surface as the theme of his decoration which has hardly been surpassed since the days of Giotto."

His time in the United States was marked by a series of major commissions. In San Francisco, Rivera undertook two major murals at the Pacific Stock Exchange and the Art Institute. In Detroit in 1932, the Edsel B. Ford fund ultimately gave Rivera US$20,000 (US$380,000 in today's money) to do a series of industry-inspired frescoes at the Detroit Institute of Arts. Rivera was thrilled by the amount, even if this was before the sizable expenses. (Once again, communists back in Mexico were denouncing the erstwhile comrade as having become a "henchman of the Yankee millionaires.") Rivera spent three wondrous months visiting factories—vitally Ford's River Rouge Complex—to gain ideas and inspiration. The resulting work entailed twenty-seven paintings covering four walls—and nine months of intensive labor—all to create a geological, technological, and human history of Detroit. US President Franklin Roosevelt adored Rivera's Detroit works because the New Deal president thought the paintings provided searing scenes of American life, including worker solidarity. Close to one hundred thousand curious visitors ogled the walls in the first two weeks of the exhibition alone.

It was in New York City in 1933 where Rivera might have manifested his most singular political voice in his "Man at the Crossroads," and provided a riposte to his communist critics. From the outside, it seemed the most capitalist of commissions, when tycoon John D. Rockefeller Jr. asked Rivera to cover the lobby of the RCA building in the unfinished Rockefeller Center. The fee was once again $20,000, but so was the work, spanning over one thousand square feet.

The proposed themes were Rockefeller's, so to cover his *comunista* bona fides, Rivera decided to include a likeness of communist icon Vladimir Lenin in the mural. When Rockefeller officials discovered Lenin's face, they promptly disassembled Rivera's scaffolding, citing the fact that the Soviet figure had not been agreed upon in the contract. Hoping to salvage his commission, Rockefeller even sent Rivera a polite letter explaining how Lenin's image "might very easily seriously offend a great many people." It certainly went down badly among many New Yorkers: the *World Telegram*'s headline ran "Rivera Paints Scenes of Communist activity and John D. Jr. Foots the Bill."

Defying pressure to modify the work, Rivera retorted that he'd rather see the work demolished than altered. A good number of American artists came to their Mexican counterpart's defense, although some backed Rockefeller's stance. In a radio address over an American station, Rivera explained his intransigence. "The case of Diego Rivera is a small matter. I want to explain more clearly the principles involved. Let us take as an example an American millionaire who buys the Sistine Chapel, which contains the work of Michelangelo. . . . Would that millionaire have the right to destroy the Sistine Chapel?" But this is exactly what happened at midnight on February 9, 1934, when Rockefeller Center management ordered it demolished, having been never completed or displayed.

THE TROUBLED CHILDHOOD OF FRIDA KHALO

Magdalena Carmen Frida Kahlo y Calderón was born on July 6, 1907, in Coyoacán, a congenial suburb of the capital city. Her epileptic father, Guillermo Kahlo was of German-Jewish ancestry, and her mother, Matilde, Mexican-Spanish, had a diverse heritage that complicated Kahlo's later self-identification with the indigenous Mexican. A year before Kahlo's birth, Matilde saw her infant son die, a traumatic event that saw her fall into a periodic deep depression. This likely explains why, despite her privileged upbringing, Kahlo later described her earliest family years as "sad." Kahlo was also fiercely attached to her father, later stating that "I am in agreement with everything my father taught me and nothing my mother taught me." At the age of six or seven, Kahlo contracted polio, which worsened when her parents did not detect the pernicious malady and forced her to walk with iron supports, leading to her cruel nickname "peg leg" at school. The experience and lasting effects of the disease would profoundly shape her sense of self.

Aged fifteen, Kahlo was sent to the elite National Preparatory School, where she joined only a handful of girls among two thousand students. She planned to study medicine and become a physician, but in September 1925 fate intervened. She was riding across bucolic Coyoacán with her boyfriend in a creaky bus when it was rammed by a trolley. As the dust settled around the horrific wreckage, Frida had been impaled by a steel handrail that punctured her pelvis, producing three spinal fractures. It took two years of convalescence to recover from her horrific injuries, though she would never really be healed, as witnessed by the dozens of operations she endured over the remaining three decades of her remarkable life. Yet this was also the moment when Guillermo gave his adored oldest daughter boxes of paints and brushes. Frida Kahlo the artist had been born.

MARRIAGE AND MEXICANNESS

The most plausible version of how Frida and Diego met was through communist friends. By 1927, the two were in a passionate relationship and married in Mexico City two years later. They were an odd-matched couple in some ways, with Rivera two hundred pounds heavier, a foot taller, and two decades older, "gargantuan in both scale and appetite." Kahlo considered Rivera ugly

Diego Rivera watching his painter wife, Frida Kahlo, work on a self-portrait in Mexico City, 1940. *(Library of Congress Prints and Photographs Division, Washington, DC)*

but still found him irresistible, yet Rivera was also abusive with women, including Kahlo, although the specifics of the abuse remain foggy. Despite this tumult and betrayal, their marriage formalized an "obsessive, earthy, and doomed" union that would make them one of the most recognizable couples in the world art realm. Likely pregnant before she wed Rivera, Frida opted for an abortion after she learned that her gnarled pelvis from the tram accident prevented a safe birth. In a subsequent pregnancy, she carried a baby to term before a miscarriage.

Going forward, Frida and Diego would learn artistic habits and intuitions from each other. The synergy also reinforced and derived from the pair's swelling embrace of *mexicanidad* (Mexicanness), the postrevolutionary exaltation of indigenous cultures over malevolent colonial vestiges. While Diego had adopted such themes after his visit to Tehuantepec, it was Frida who most visibly embraced the movement by, say, dressing in the sublimely colorful intricately woven skirt-and-blouse outfits generically called Tehuana, for the indigenous women of Tehuantepec. Now Frida would publicly be "tricked out with silver and jade jewelry and ribbons woven into her plaited hair," and convinced Diego to grow only native plants in their yard in Coyoacán.

After their break with the Communist Party, Kahlo accompanied Rivera to the United States, where he landed several large commissions. For Kahlo, however, the exposure to North American society only deepened her commitment to political struggle: "I've learnt so much here," she wrote privately at the time, "and I'm more and more convinced it's only through communism we can become human."

THE TROTSKY AFFAIR

Yet communism at that time was dominated by two competing figures: Stalin and Trotsky, an intellectual architect of the Soviet Union who had been forced into exile in 1929 after Stalin's rise. Kahlo and Rivera had come to distance themselves from Stalinism and back Trotsky; it was Rivera who helped persuade sitting Mexican president Lázaro Cárdenas to grant the revolutionary icon and his spouse, Natalia Sedova, a refuge in Mexico in January 1937. (See Chapter 17, "Lázaro Cárdenas: Nuestro Petróleo.")

Kahlo was at the dock to welcome them, radiant in her Tehuana garb, and Frida and Diego loaned the Trotskys their residence *Casa Azul*, which was equipped with guards, reinforced windows, and alarms. In a letter to acquaintances, Sedova described "a blue house, a patio filled with plants, airy rooms, collections of Pre-Columbian art, paintings from all over: we were on a new planet, in Rivera's house."

On November 7, 1937—the Russian Revolution and Trotsky's birthday—Frida gave the Soviet refugee an intimate self-portrait: in the work Frida, her lips and cheeks rouged and abundant hair braided, wearing a startling skirt and embroidered shawl. The figure holds a letter reading: "To Leon Trotsky, with all my love. I dedicate this painting on 7th November 1937. Frida Kahlo in San Ángel, Mexico."

Leon proudly displayed Frida's gift in his office in a nearby building. By the end of the 1930s, though, Frida and Diego had soured on Trotsky as well as Trotskyism. This development has usually been explained as Diego's discovery of a Frida-Trotsky tryst—this was also the time when Rivera and Kahlo divorced—although more recent documents have challenged this interpretation. In any case, the Trotskys moved out of Casa Azul to a nearby house, but Leon was a marked man. In May 1940 a gang led by ultra-communist and fellow muralist Siqueiros fired almost two hundred bullets into Trotsky's residence but failed to hit the target. (Rivera was an initial suspect in the crime investigation since he had broken from Trotsky as well.) Trotsky's luck ran out that same August when Ramón Mercader, a secret agent of Stalin in Mexico, gruesomely assassinated Trotsky with an ice pick. Seeing as how Kahlo and Mercader had become acquaintances in Paris only the previous year, Mexican authorities brought her in for questioning as an accomplice in the barbarous political hit before releasing her after a day or two behind bars. Kahlo then met up with Rivera in San Francisco where they remarried in late 1940—his fifty-fourth birthday—before returning to their beloved Coyoacán.

THE TURN TO STALINISM

If Kahlo's brief jail stay affected her willingness to implant politics into her paintings, it did not show. The final roughly decade-and-a-half left in her life saw her art becoming "Stalinized" because her politics had become Stalinized. In 1950 she painted a large red hammer and sickle—the global symbol of proletariat solidarity—onto her plaster corset supporting her injured back, and in an entry from her private diary proclaimed "Viva Stalin/Viva Diego." Another entry outlined how she would render this increased political engagement in aesthetic terms:

I want to turn [my work] into something useful; until now I have managed simply an honest expression of my own self, but one which is unfortunately a long way from serving the Party. I must struggle with all my strength to ensure that the little positive that my health allows me to do also benefits the Revolution, the only real reason to live.

Sympathizers usually posit that, rather than ideology, it was Kahlo's mental and physical deterioration that made her embrace one of the twentieth century's most maniacal totalitarians whose regime was responsible for upward of twenty million deaths. Indeed, had she lived in the Soviet Union, she and Diego, as independent-minded artists, would have faced arrest, banishment, and death. But the conviction remained with her until the end; one of her final paintings was one of her final works, *Self Portrait with Stalin* (1954), which lacked her typically sharp detail—a deficiency likely caused by her potent painkillers.

That year also marked the overthrow of Guatemalan leftist Jacobo Árbenz in a Washington-hatched military coup (see Chapter 22, "Jacobo Árbenz: A Guatemalan Spring, Interrupted"). Kahlo and Rivera marched at a Mexico City demonstration against the naked act of imperialism, then on July 13, 1954, just days after the Árbenz protest, Kahlo died, likely by suicide through overdose. At her funeral, her coffin was draped with a shroud bearing the hammer and sickle device of communism. Almost exactly a year after her death, Rivera married Emma Hurtado, his agent for almost a decade, but died a couple of years later in bed in San Angel in 1957. His ashes mixed with Frida's, as he had requested.

THE COMPLICATED COUPLE

Throughout his career, Rivera considered himself a revolutionary painter. His life, however, paints a more nuanced picture, of a privileged childhood before long state-sponsored sojourns in Europe to study Old World art and mingle with the avant-garde; later, he commanded vast sums for American corporations and tycoons to deploy his revolutionary style on capitalist walls. His relationship with Communism was also complex and nuanced: while doubtlessly dedicated to the cause, he wavered in his affinity for Stalin. As an artist, he was singular, with his monumental murals broadcasting a strong contemporary political message defined in a new visual language that was unmistakably Mexican.

Kahlo likewise is a fascinatingly complex figure. Her art was predicated on her experience of life in all its hues—a radical political reimagining of the possibilities of art that has had an enduring and transformative influence on theories of representation and gender. Her absorption of the new aesthetic of Mexicanness was as profound as Rivera's, and perhaps more so, given the reinvention of her personal style to incorporate indigenous influence. But alongside this a larger, more overt relationship with Communism at large, from her disputed affair with Trotsky to her undeniable fascination with Stalin: a relationship which also permeated her work as she sought to join personal and political in her pair of self-portraits directed at the two opposing titans of Communism. From a modern vantage point, there is an unavoidable irony that this professed devotee of the Revolution has become a hot property in today's art market: in 2022, the very same plaster corset Kahlo had painted with the hammer and sickle was listed at an art auction house for US$3.8 million. Beyond the controversies, the power of Diego and Frida's art endures, infused by politics but also transcending them to present unique, and uniquely personal, visions of the world.

15

Berta Lutz

Brazil's Frog-Loving Feminist

Berta Lutz carried out world-renowned work in science and ecology but is now best remembered for her half-century-long and ultimately successful advocacy for women's rights in Brazil. She led the women's suffrage movement that won the right to vote in 1932 and was a protagonist in the so-called Pan-American feminist movement that championed a unified hemispheric movement to promote women's rights and world peace. Just the second woman to hold a high-level civil service job in Brazil, Lutz's reputation was so strong that she was picked to serve as a diplomat to represent Brazil in the United Nations Charter, which she signed after having successfully added "women" to the founding text. Yet Berta Lutz's feminist advocacy did have its moral and economic biases and blind spots, although this was far harder for her to discern than it is from our current perch.

TREE FROG

Berta Maria Júlia Lutz was born into a family driven by the idea of progress and improving the society around them. Her father Adolfo Lutz made monumental contributions to the emerging fields of tropical medicine and infectious diseases, or epidemiology. From Swiss stock but born in Río de Janeiro, Adolfo made breakthroughs in our understanding of how mosquitoes transmit yellow fever—work that eventually garnered him a nomination for a Nobel Prize for Medicine in 1938. His research also led to successful fights against yellow fever as well as other epidemics such as malaria and cholera that ravaged his nation. Lutz adorned Brazilian postage stamps and had two species of Brazilian snake and frog named after him. His British wife, Amy

Fowler Lutz, was a nurse who had worked at a leper colony in Hawaii and helped create Brazil's original school for abused boys.

In 1894, the São Paulo-based couple had a child, Berta. From an early age, Berta was fascinated by the natural world, reinforced by her experience of joining her father in his constant field research in the Brazilian rainforest. At some point, Berta became obsessed with the tree frog, a species she would study during her illustrious career as a scientist. (In fact, she outdid her father by having two species of Brazilian lizards and three species of Brazilian frogs named after her!)

Given her family's status and sizable financial means, Berta enjoyed opportunities for education, employment, and adventure that most of her fellow Brazilians lacked. This privilege is what allowed this ever-curious, dedicated adolescent to attend college at one of the most prestigious colleges in Europe, the Sorbonne at what was then the University of Paris. After seven years of study, in 1918 she picked up degrees in zoology and biology and returned home.

It was during her extended stay in the Old World that she came across feminist authors and writings about the British suffrage movement. Her emerging conception of feminism held that women were due equal access to education and a professional career. Once back in Brazil, Lutz started, albeit cautiously, writing appeals to women in glossy high-society Rio magazines, calling on them to form a new association not "of suffragettes who break windows in the streets, but a society of Brazilians who understand that that the woman should not live parasitically off [the prerogatives] of her sex, taking advantage of the animal instincts of man, but ought to be useful, educate herself and her children, and become capable of fulfilling the political duties that the future cannot but share with her."

At the time in Brazil, white-collar professions such as medicine, business, and law were dominated by men. Over the first two decades of the twentieth century, the situation was improved, albeit at a glacial pace. In 1919, in what made her the second woman to hold a high-level civil service post and itself a huge step for women, Lutz successfully secured an appointment as secretary of the National Museum of Rio de Janeiro, working both as a manager and scientist on amphibians. But the herpetologist's myriad responsibilities at the National Museum did not preclude Berta from continuing to cultivate her commitment to women's rights picked up in Paris. The same year that she began work at the National Museum, she joined the newly founded Brazilian Women's Legion, becoming an administrator for this agency that provided social services to Brazilian women. She also cofounded, with anarcho-feminist Maria Lacerda de Moura, the League for the Intellectual Emancipation of Women, an outfit that strived, initially, to open the sciences to women.

A WOMEN'S SUFFRAGE MOVEMENT

In 1922 the Brazilian government tapped Lutz to be its official delegate to the Pan American Conference of Women hosted in Baltimore, Maryland, and sponsored by the League of Women Voters of the United States. Suffrage had been achieved by US women in 1920 after more than eighty years of struggle and the Baltimore conference was called to spread the impetus of the US campaign to the rest of the Americas. It was attended by women across Latin America who would become principal leaders of feminist movements over the next twenty years. Remarkably, many Latin American feminists had not been focused on women's suffrage because, among other reasons, so many of their countries had little or no practice of even male suffrage!

It was at this seminal conference where Lutz consulted with US icon Carrie Chapman Catt and Uruguayan feminist Paulina Luisi on a strategy for change in Brazil. (Berta's scientific interests remained alive and well even when focusing on Pan-American women's rights; allegedly, while nearing a stream on a stroll with Chapman, Lutz shocked her American admirer by squatting near the freezing river to scoop up a "frog which she explained with absorbed scrutiny," having never seen the species before.)

Deeply influenced by what she had experienced in the United States, on August 19, 1922, Lutz founded a new umbrella organization, the Brazilian Federation for Feminine Progress (FBPF), which was linked to the International Women's Suffrage Alliance. Lutz's FBPF (which was Brazil's first suffragist society) began pushing for women's right to vote in Brazil, bolstered by the fact that, after studying Brazil's byzantine legal system, the FBPF found there was no law forbidding women from voting, despite the myriad occasions when women's registration drives had been stymied. The FBPF also pushed for greater women's-related educational reforms.

Their timing was perfect as 1922 was also the centennial year of Brazilian independence. Accordingly, ideas of nationalism and nativism were especially abundant in the intellectual milieu of the urban centers. Carrie Chapman Catt commenced her tour of South America by attending a conference hosted by FBPF, while a PR campaign was launched involving public interviews, forums, and manifestos. FBPF members backed politicians who supported their agenda while opposing others' views as reactionary. Lutz's outfit also forced the government to allow women to enroll in the prestigious public primary and secondary school, *Colégio Pedro II*, which had been the springboard for elite males into politics and other powerful professions. (See Chapter 10, "Dom Pedro II: Brazil's Citizen Monarch.") But the real breakthrough—women's suffrage—would have to wait a full decade.

O VOTO FEMININO NO BRASIL

The Constitutionalist Revolution of 1932 that erupted in and around São Paulo challenged the political supremacy of President Getúlio Vargas, who had come to national power in his own "revolution" two years prior. While this "Paulista" rebellion was vanquished, its reformist demands were granted by Vargas, including a new constitution. Lutz was tasked by the federal government to contribute to the document's language.

Her suggestions—known as the "13 Principles"—ensured that the ratified constitution finally granted women the right to vote (the fourth in the Americas to do so after Canada, the United States, and Ecuador) and promoted equality between men and women, including equal pay for equal work. Lutz had come to believe that women's liberation would come through wage labor: "Work is the most powerful instrument in the hand of a woman.... I consider that in Brazil the true 'leaders' of feminism, correctly understood, are the innumerable young women who work in industry, in commerce, in teaching, and in other spheres of human activity." Indeed, Lutz viewed women's suffrage as a manifestation of their innate value as well as a mechanism to ensure material and spiritual sustenance.

The early 1930s is also when the polymath enrolled at the then-called National Law School in Rio, leaving with a law degree. Under the auspices of the new constitution, Lutz threw her hat into the political arena, although she lost the congressional election. By 1936, though, she served in Congress after replacing an incumbent who died in office. Not surprisingly, Lutz founded the congressional committee "Statute of Women" to scrutinize the nation's laws to confirm that none discriminated against women. Lutz exhorted her fellow feminists to not erroneously conclude that women had entered, in her words, the "Promised Land," but instead had only reached the edges of a venal political system, or in her words "outskirts of a camp of gold seekers." One of the bitter ironies for Lutz's swelling, not successful movement is that, despite having just won the ballot, in subsequent years the rate of women registering to vote was pitiful, often tallying in the low double digits in percentage terms. For an overwhelming majority of Brazilian women, the daily preoccupation was bread, not the ballot box.

But Lutz's titanic achievements are not without complexity, at least for a modern audience. Lutz adhered to a "gendered" form of feminism that emerged in the late 1910s, believing that women were far more capable in, say, nursing or social welfare fields given their feminine (read, nurturing) instincts. To this end, Lutz's FBPF pushed gender equality but lobbied for preference in social services jobs where women's "patience, dedication, attention to detail, objectivity, thrift, and high moral sense" made them better equipped. For Lutz, this was a "female vocation," a phenomenon that she dreamed would someday take on "colossal proportions." The FBPF even advocated for a new female police squad tasked with handling women and children—as both victims and criminals—and that inmates in the country's women's prisons should be supervised by entirely female guards.

Modern scholars have observed that Lutz and other leading Brazilian feminists were not only upper-class but also had "patronizing attitudes about the lower classes"—including poor, usually illiterate women—a blind spot that included their domestic servants. Her notion of true empowerment was effectively restricted to the small middle- and upper-class women living in the cities. These women were the object of her push for increased access to higher education and coveted professions, not the millions upon millions of poor, rural Brazilian sisters who lacked literacy and faced significant discrimination.

At the same time, Lutz's defenders counter that, despite her undeniable social superiority, Lutz—and by extension the FBPF—eventually embraced the cooperation and inclusion of women of various regions and socioeconomic classes. Indeed, the organization passed a resolution that manifested its class-based advocacy: "Considering the urgency of insuring legal protection for female labor, which has been subject to inhuman exploitation, reducing women to an inferior position in the competition for industrial and agricultural salaries, as well as in other activities of modern life, it has become necessary to call to the attention of political leaders the need to incorporate protective measures for women into our social legislation."

Ultimately, Berta Lutz sparked a suffrage movement that worked to reform rather than radicalize her country's political, economic, and social systems.

The photograph shows Berta Lutz, Brazilian zoologist, feminist, and diplomat, probably at the home of Carrie Chapman Catt in New Rochelle, New York, 1925. *(Library of Congress Prints and Photographs Division, Washington, DC)*

She and her movement wanted women to join the preexisting system and then make it better, not break it down. As so many of her forebearers did, she took on the anti-suffragists' anxieties head-on, asserting that women's equality and empowerment would make them better mothers, just in a "home" that is far more capacious. In a 1921 interview, the illustrious figure argued that "it is neither accurate nor logical to assert that when women acquire electoral rights they will abandon the place conferred on them by nature. . . . Women's domain, all feminists agree, is the home. But . . . nowadays the home no longer is just the space encompassed within four walls."

Then a political tsunami struck when, in 1937, Vargas shuttered Congress, outlawing elections, and promulgating his so-called New State dictatorship which strangled Brazil until 1945. After winning voting rights, there were no national elections in which Brazilian women could exercise such rights.

Never to be deterred, Lutz dedicated her professional life to the sciences and diplomacy, culminating in her vital role at the UN's seminal San Francisco Conference in 1945.

"EQUAL RIGHTS OF MEN AND WOMEN"

In the aftermath of World War II, delegates from fifty Allied countries convened at a conference in San Francisco in the spring of 1945, an effort that resulted in the drafting of the UN Charter, ratified and enacted before this remarkable year was out. Berta Lutz, a diplomatic envoy from Brazil, had been speedily dispatched to the conference. Her mission: advocate for gender equality in the UN founding document. Lutz, working in concert with Minerva Bernardino, another feminist who was also attending in her official capacity as a Dominican Republic delegate, faced stiff headwinds, given many at the male-dominated convention were annoyed with these "extremist" Latin American activists who "wanted the word 'women' everywhere."

Critically, the first draft of the preamble did not mention "women." In response, Lutz worked furiously to modify the final document, despite resistance from British and US female officials, and was ultimately successful, with the adopted draft reaffirming "the equal rights of men and women." She also urged the UN to establish the Commission on the Status of Women, which it formally did the following year, to examine the "legal status of women" across the globe. All told, Lutz's work directly led to the UN's mandate to monitor and ensure women's rights.

Lutz followed this triumph by serving as vice president of the Inter-American Commission of Women from 1953 to 1959. In 1964, Lutz resigned from the National Museum at the very time that a military regime seized power and would rule the nation for just over two decades. When the UN designated 1975 to be the "International Year of the Woman," the (military) government asked Lutz to be Brazil's delegate to the International Conference on Women in Mexico City. The Mexico City meeting wound up being Lutz's final public act in a half-century vocation committed to women's rights and feminism. In 1976, at age eighty-four, Lutz died in Rio de Janeiro, having left an indelible mark on improving the lot of women not just in Brazil, but the world over.

16

Augusto Sandino versus the United States

Augusto César Sandino was an epochal guerrilla revolutionary who fought against the United States during its occupation of Nicaragua while seeking to carve out a new vision of the state. During the 1920s, US Marines hunted him to no avail and amidst mounting pressure from back home; by the time the leathernecks pulled out in 1933, Sandino was still at large, but what the United States couldn't achieve his countryfolk did, capturing and executing the revolutionary in 1934. But in death, Sandino achieved folklore status, inspiring Che Guevara and Fidel Castro and a new Nicaraguan revolutionary movement in the early 1960s, the Sandinista National Liberation Front (known as the Sandinistas) who would finally bring to end the hated Somoza dynastic dictatorship in 1979.

Starting at the beginning of the twentieth century, Nicaragua experienced a protracted period of political turmoil between the anti-American Liberal Party and US-backed Conservative Party, with arguments frequently erupting in violence. The United States intervened, both by supporting certain candidates in elections and sending in the Marines in 1910, who ended up staying for thirteen years. But political instability grew worse and threatened to escalate into civil war.

By April 1927, it appeared a breakthrough had been made. US officials had worked with President Adolfo Díaz to produce an accord with the Liberal rebel forces that were known as the *Espino Negro* agreement. Under the terms of the accord, Díaz would remain as president until US-supervised voting took place in 1928, while the Liberal generals would cease their insurrection and participate in a general amnesty. Díaz's conservatives were generally supportive of the accord as it kept them in power—at least for the moment. More vital, though, was the support Liberal General José María Moncada lent to the agreement. Eleven of Moncada's military lieutenants also agreed to abide by the terms of the accord and lay down their guns, but one rebel commander, Augusto Sandino, did not cooperate.

Espino Negro incensed Sandino, who saw Moncada, especially, as a traitor and he decided to form a rebellion. In a mountainous Nueva Segovia town—so the legend goes—Sandino laid a bullet on a board and demanded that his men pick sides. "From here to there: Yankees; from here to there: Sandino. All those who want to follow me, raise your hand." Ninety percent of his men fled, leaving only around thirty souls to join his rebellion. Writing to Moncada, his once commander, he painted a picture of total defiance: "I don't know why you keep ordering me around. Indubitably, you know my temperament and you know that I am unyielding ... I DO NOT SELL OUT, I DO NOT SURRENDER, you must defeat me."

A YOUNG RADICAL

Sandino was likely born in the pueblo of Niquinohomo, twenty-five miles south of Managua, in 1895. Sandino's coffee merchant father, Gregorio, was a Liberal, attesting to the fact that, in Nicaragua (as in Colombia) political allegiance owed as much to family history as conviction. Unlike his half-brother Sócrates, Augusto was illegitimate, having been the result of conjugation between Gregorio and his indigenous maid, Margarita. His being a "love child" might explain why Gregorio's spouse, América, chafed at having the lad around the house, relegating Augusto to a condition of penury despite being born into relative privilege. The future icon would later reflect that his exclusion from his own family engendered a loathing of "misery and impotence." Before he was five, the rambunctious boy was working picking coffee and corn, skipping school with abandon, and pinching food for his family. As a teen, Augusto's goal was to become a landowner like his *papá*.

After he shot a man in 1920, Sandino fled his native country and took a series of blue-collar jobs across Central America that would help shape his political development, most critically a stint in Honduras with US fruit and sugar behemoths and a job in Guatemala with the notorious United Fruit Company. Landing in Mexico in 1923, Sandino tapped into the residual spirit of the Mexican Revolution that had formally ended in 1920, discovering the potency of nationalism, anti-imperialism, and anticlericism, as well as leftist thinking—all of which he would eventually bring home. In 1923, while working in the mightily capitalist Standard Oil refineries in the states of Veracruz and Tampico—sort of the Mexican version of Louisiana—he embraced militant labor syndicalism, then the most prominent leftist ideology in Mexico (and would use the movement's red and black colors for his future flag).

Sandino returned to native soil in 1926 with a few thousand dollars in his pocket and set about creating his army. Its personnel came from disaffected workers at the US-owned San Albino gold mine (whom Sandino radicalized by exhorting them to demand cash payments instead of company scrip redeemable exclusively at company shops), while weapons were brought in from nearby Honduras. Coordinating with Moncada, Sandino's army linked up with the Liberal campaign until the May 4, 1927, inking of Espino Negro, when Moncada's perceived betrayal led Sandino to strike out alone.

By now, Sandino, aged thirty-two or thirty-three, had come to see the American occupiers as the real enemies to Nicaragua's sovereignty, though he also was adamant that loathed Conservative President Díaz be replaced. His father urged him to commit himself fully to the cause: "If you are ready to sacrifice yourself, you must do it with utmost honor. After firing the first bullet against the invader you should expect nothing less than death or victory. ... Better you commit suicide than to fall into shameful surrender."

On July 1, 1927, Sandino declared his willingness to die for his crusade, which nominally combined nationalism with the burning indigenous ideology known throughout the Americas as *indigenismo*. "I am a Nicaraguan and I am proud because in my veins flows above all the blood of the Indian race, which by some atavism encompasses the mystery of being patriotic, loyal, and sincere." In part, however, this was political opportunism: himself a *mestizo* (mixed indigenous and Iberian blood), Sandino was in fact at best apathetic about indigenous peoples themselves.

The scope of Sandino's vision quickly expanded to Bolivarian proportions, informed by a dream of regional unity. Bolívar himself was a self-acknowledged inspiration to the insurgent commander, as he explained in a 1928 press interview. "At the beginning of my campaign I thought only of Nicaragua. Afterward my ambition grew. I thought of the Central American Republic whose coat of arms has been sketched by one of my comrades. Tell Hispano-America that as long as Sandino breathes, the independence of Central America will have a defender. I shall never betray my cause. That is why I am the son of Bolívar." (See Chapter 6, "Simón Bolívar: The Great Liberator, Flawed Emancipator.") Sandino also located his movement in more contemporary regional dynamics, again drawing on his nomadic experience in exile: in 1930 he told a Mexican reporter that "our struggle in Nicaragua . . . is nothing more than the daughter of the Mexican Revolution." Perhaps the defining feature of Sandino's movement was its combination of various ideologies with an increasingly strong cult of personality. As historian Allen Wells teaches us, Sandino's political thought was replete with "messianic overtones and mysterious sounding spiritual bromides," making it "so amorphous" that contemporary readers can be forgiven for being flummoxed.

MARINES MEET THEIR MATCH

Whatever his ideological aspirations, the main target of Sandino's ire was undoubtedly clear: the US Marines ambling across his beloved homeland. "Come, morphine addicts," he goaded them, "come and kill us in our own land. I await you before my patriotic soldiers, feet firmly set, not worried about how many of you there may be. But keep in mind that when this happens the Capitol Building in Washington will shake with the destruction of your greatness, and our blood will redden the white dome of your famous White House, the cavern where you concoct your crimes."

Tensions rose in July 1927, when the US Marines and National Guard troops occupied the town of Ocotal, deep inside Sandino's mountain bastion of Nueva Segovia, sparking the first major confrontation. Marine Captain G. D. Hatfield sent a note to Sandino indicating that he was an "individual outside the law" and that "Nicaragua has had its last revolution." He added that Sandino had two days to give up or the Marines would "finish with you and your forces once and for all." Sandino sent an insolent note to Hatfield declining the offer, signing it "Your obedient servant, who wishes to put you in a handsome tomb with Soldiers." Hatfield responded, "Bravo, General. If words were bullets and phrases were soldiers, you would be a field marshal instead of a mule thief."

In the early hours of July 16, having plundered the San Albino mine for dynamite, the "Sandinistas" sneaked into the town where the force of forty-eight Marines and a slightly smaller number of National Guard were posted. After a day of fighting, a guerrilla approached the Marines with a flag of truce and a message from Sandino. In the note, Sandino complimented Hatfield on his "brave fight," but stated that the Marines and Guard needed to surrender within an hour or they would be destroyed. Hatfield responded that Marines "did not know how to surrender."

Map of Nicaragua. *(Andrew Rhodes)*

The subsequent fighting lasted sixteen hours and resulted in the death of an estimated fifty Sandinistas (although the Americans claimed they had killed three hundred). Marine and Guard losses together were one dead and five wounded. When daylight broke, the Marines deployed five DH-4 biplanes, each one outfitted with two machine guns and four twenty-five-pound bombs. In history's first instance of air support for ground troops, these planes dive-bombed the dumbfounded Sandinista troops, sending them scattering in terror. In a fascinating footnote of history, German war planners studied the Marine action at Ocotal carefully; the Nazi Luftwaffe subsequently used dive-bombing to devastating success during World War II.

While Sandino demonstrated that he could hold his own against Marine and Guardia forces, the battle of Ocotal was a bruising setback for the insurgency, made worse by the fact that the Marines routed the Sandinistas again only nine days later. Realizing that he could not continue to send his finite number of fighters head-to-head against well-defended positions, Sandino adopted the age-old guerrilla strategy of hit-and-run.

Later in that same year of 1927, the Marines reckoned Sandino was operating out of a clandestine base known as *El Chipote* somewhere in Nueva Segovia. To find the site, American commanders dispatched hundreds of Marines and Guard troops in small patrols, which became targets for Sandinista ambushes and raids. In a dramatic development, the Sandinistas shot down an American surveillance plane that was part of the effort to locate the elusive rebel forces. The Marines sent out a search party to locate the downed fliers, but they were stopped short by an insurgent ambush. The captured pilots were placed on trial and executed by Sandino's men. By November, Marine pilots had located El Chipote, east of the San Albino mine, and had started bombing it daily, though it reportedly transpired they had been bombing straw-stuffed dummies of Sandinistas. By the time a Marine-led ground force reached El Chipote, the slippery Sandino had already fled.

All told, Sandino proved to be an elusive foe for the next five years— something that deeply frustrated the American troops. According to one US reporter following the story, "The wily Sandino is a maddening problem for the Marine because of his swift shifting, and many officers declare earnestly they would give a year's pay only once to come to grips with him." With military efforts yielding little, US officials in Managua launched a public relations campaign that attempted to downplay Sandino's significance. Marine General Logan Feland, the commanding officer in Nicaragua, discredited Sandino as

United States Marines with the captured flag of Nicaraguan revolutionary leader Augusto César Sandino. *(Library of Congress Prints and Photographs Division, Washington, DC)*

nothing more than an ordinary bandit and declared the rebellion over. But the reality was very different: Sandino was proving to be a resilient guerrilla fighter and not just a simple "cattle thief."

DOMESTIC DISCORD

Between 1927 and 1932, US forces hunted for Sandino and his loyal forces to no avail, prompting increasing scrutiny of the entire American effort back home. Senator Burton K. Wheeler of Montana blasted President Calvin Coolidge for instituting a "dishonorable program of brutal bluff and bully." He added, "What right have we to send our boys into a foreign country to stamp out banditry? If we are to ask them to stamp out banditry, let's send them to Chicago to stamp it out there. As far as I'm concerned, I wouldn't sacrifice the lifeblood of one American boy for all the damn Nicaraguans." The noted satirist Will Rogers reflected the skeptical sense of many Americans with this pithy aphorism: "Why are we in Nicaragua and what the Hell are we doing there?"

Despite his brutal attacks on Marines, Sandino fared surprisingly well in the North American media, in part because he realized that he could sell his resistance as an American-style republican campaign. The itinerant journalist Carleton Beals was the first US newspaperman to interview Sandino, holed up in the rugged northern mountains, and enabled Sandino to address the US public directly in terms that would resonate:

> "Let me repeat," declared the General [Sandino]. "We are no more bandits than was [George] Washington. If the American public had not become calloused to justice and to the elemental rights of mankind, it would not so easily forget its own past when a handful of ragged soldiers marched through the snow leaving blood-tracks behind them to win liberty and independence. If their consciences had not become dulled by their scramble for wealth, Americans would not so easily forget the lesson that, sooner or later, every nation, however weak, achieves freedom, and that every abuse of power hastens the destruction of the one who wields it."

Such pronouncements were part of a conscious, effective public-relations strategy, with Sandino himself commenting that "we learned the tremendous value of publicity in terms of world opinion." An acolyte of the guerrilla leader explained it this way: "Every time there is a battle, every time marines are killed, the attention of the United States and the world is drawn to what is going on in Nicaragua."

This strategy began to generate serious pressure on the US intervention and helped establish Sandino as a shining knight for the anti-imperialist, anticapitalist ideological left in the United States and around the globe. In 1928, activists assembled near the White House to protest the occupation. Personal letters sent to Marines sailing for Nicaragua urged them not to fight and instead join Sandino's forces. Sandino's half brother, Sócrates, made anti-US campaign speeches across the United States. Some newspapers and magazines solicited funds for medical supplies or implored readers to "Enlist with Sandino" and "Defeat the War against Nicaragua." Senator J. Thomas Heflin of Alabama compared Sandino to the Founding Fathers: "Sandino crying for liberty, begging for the deliverance of his country from the invader, sounds like the cries of our fathers made in the days of the Revolution," he argued. "We are seeking this man out to kill him for fighting for principles that we fought for in 1776."

Opposition to US involvement was also predicated on the belief that US forces were prosecuting an inhumane war. In one account, the Coolidge administration had "used the armed forces of the United States to destroy human life, to burn villages, to bomb innocent women and children from the air." In truth, savagery was committed on both sides. In one episode, Sandino insisted upon an assortment of sentences for Nicaraguans caught collaborating with the Marines or the National Guard. One punishment was the *corte de chaleco* (the "vest cut"), whereby victims' heads and arms were cut off and sword markings were carved on their chests. A Sandinista ode extolled beheadings and other forms of maiming; Sandino's seal, used on his letters and forged coins, featured a Sandinista beheading a Marine. Not long before he was killed, Sandino expressed qualified remorse for the brutal approach: "It is a terrible thing to take a man's head . . . but those dogs forced us into that kind of tactic."

President Coolidge sent Brigadier General Frank McCoy, "one of these iron-willed, super logical, single-track types whose stern jaw carried not an ounce of compromise," to oversee the key 1928 presidential election agreed in the Espino Negro accord. To preempt fraud and smooth the way for the much-desired US departure, just under a thousand Marines and sailors observed the voting. Sandino wanted nothing to do with what he considered sham elections (in reality the freest and fairest in the country's history), but he was not in a position to prevent the vote from taking place. Remarkably, the Liberal former rebel general José María Moncada won the vote, and soon after, Sandino returned to Mexico to plot his next moves.

REENERGIZED IN MEXICO

Feeling the heat, Sandino fled to Mexico in 1929, which granted him asylum. Over the next year, Sandino's rather eclectic spiritualism came into full bloom. He joined the Magnetic Spiritual School of the Universal Commune (calling its founder, Joaquín Trincado Mateo, "one of the great contemporary philosophers") and embraced yoga, vegetarianism, seances, and a belief in reincarnation.

He brought these new inclinations back to Nicaragua when he returned to continue the struggle in 1930, insisting that his men refer to each other as "brother" and renaming a rebel camp "Joaquín Trincado." Sandino meditated each day and used Western medicine only for malaria, opting for homeopathic

Augusto Sandino, January 1930 *(standing, front)*. *(Library of Congress Prints and Photographs Division, Washington, DC)*

cures for other ailments. Booze on duty was forbidden. Rape was severely punished, with one of his generals put to death for the crime. He bragged that homosexuality and other "urban degenerations" were absent in his army.

His cult of personality also intensified. Often wearing silk underwear, Sandino rode a gleaming white horse with a glistening saddle; Charles Butters, an American who had been the rebel commander's captive, painted him as "exceptionally neat and clean [in] appearance, with highly polished boots and well-groomed clothes, always shaved and washed, an unusual trait in the Nicaraguan wilderness." Nicaraguan *campesinas* (peasant women) were believed to keep in their possession any item he might have put his hand on.

Sandino also embarked on his most robust efforts to establish a Sandinista state. From his secure base in mountainous Segovia, he named judges, minted gold coins (with, of course, his gruesome seal), and established agriculture and education departments, the latter to address the nation's ninety percent illiteracy rate. The great general also considered that, after ending his insurgency, he would found a Nationalist Party to compete electorally with the Conservatives and Liberals.

But before that time, there was first the issue of the Marines. In late December 1930 Sandinistas attacked a Marine patrol outside the same Ocotal, killing eight leathernecks.

The guerrilla attacks only increased pressure on the United States, and President Herbert Hoover decided on a phased withdrawal in the run-up to the November 6, 1932, Nicaraguan election as part of his "good neighbor" policy to improve relations with Latin American countries. (Hoover had witnessed firsthand the level of anti-American animosity—and support for Sandino—during a 1928 tour of ten Latin American countries as president-elect). The Liberal Juan Sacasa and the Conservative Adolfo Díaz competed yet again, and Sacasa won. US troops finally pulled out in 1933, this time for good.

Sacasa picked Anastasio "Tacho" Somoza García to be the new first commander of the National Guard, which following the American departure was the main force engaged in clashes with Sandino's guerrillas. Although the rebel commander despised Somoza, calling him the "penguin" for his rotund figure, he nevertheless agreed to a peace accord, driven to the negotiating table by a critical lack of cash and manpower. This agreement led to a February 3, 1933, pact that outlined the "gradual" disarmament of his insurgency in return for jobs for his men, infrastructure projects, and other guarantees, with Sandino telling his forces: "Men, I will accept peace, but I will embark on another revolution . . . this revolution will not be with rifles or weapons, it will be a political revolution." There were more than a few Nicaraguans who urged Sandino to run for president in the 1936 election.

On February 21, 1934, Sandino was in the capital to continue the pacification process with President Sacasa. After a "farewell" dinner with Somoza and the Nicaraguan head of state, Sandino was picked up by National Guard soldiers and, per Somoza's instructions, executed at a military airstrip along with two fellow insurgency leaders. At the same time, another squad of Guard troops murdered Sócrates, along with his son-in-law and ten-year-old servant.

With the death of their vaunted commander, Sandino's guerrilla insurgency collapsed. In 1936 Somoza seized power, initiating a nearly four-decade period of iron-fisted rule. Far from being a pillar of the rule of law in Nicaragua, the Guard soon became the Somoza family's personal shock troops, giving it the wherewithal to remain in power. But the United States refused to intervene in Nicaraguan politics to remove the new dictator, despite the requests of three former Nicaraguan presidents. Three decades of unpopular interventions had taken their toll on the American appetite for foreign adventure, in large part due to the efforts of Augusto César Sandino.

SANDINO LIVES

In death, Sandino became an even greater legend in his native country, an emblem of nationalism, anti-imperialism, and pride. In 1979, a movement under the Sandinista banner (though more inspired by Marxism and liberation theology than Sandino's rather eclectic political ideology) vanquished the Somoza tyranny and assumed power, with former guerrilla Daniel Ortega as president. (See Chapter 46, "Daniel Ortega and Rosario Murillo: Nicaragua's Toxic Power Couple.") During the 1980s, Ortega changed the name of Managua International Airport to Augusto C. Sandino International Airport. In 2001, after Ortega was voted out of power in 1990, anti-Sandinista President Arnoldo Alemán changed it back to Managua International. Six years later, having won the presidency back, Ortega reversed the nomenclature once more to honor Nicaragua's hero.

Today, Nicaraguans and foreign tourists can visit a towering Sandino steel-plate statue, with a signature outsized cowboy hat, which overlooks the capital from the spot where he was likely martyred. Now part of a national park and museum, the statue is one of Managua's most discernible landmarks. Yet if Sandino were to look down on his beloved Nicaragua in, say, 2018 and witnessed Ortega's bastardization of Sandinismo, he probably would have wept. But being Sandino, he would have also picked up a rifle and taken to the streets.

17

Lázaro Cárdenas

"Nuestro Petróleo"

Today, just as seven decades ago, oil is the patrimony for all Mexicans, a symbol of our sovereignty and an emblem of nationalism.
—*Felipe Calderón, president of Mexico, 2008*

When Lázaro Cárdenas assumed the presidency in the 1930s, Mexico was still reeling from the calamitous revolution that had begun in 1910, with violence persisting until 1920. He also faced the grim reality that the country's most valuable asset—petroleum—was largely controlled by foreign companies, who were glutting themselves on vast oil profits and sharing precious little of the cash with locals. For Cárdenas, who had a strong reformist streak, the situation was clearly egregious, and he supported unions striking for a better deal. The fractious events that followed resulted in a scarcely believable shift in the balance of power when, frustrated at the failure of the oil companies to come to terms, Cárdenas moved to nationalize US- and European-controlled petroleum assets inside the country.

LAND OF OIL—AND OIL COMPANIES

Mexico's decade of a chaotic, destructive revolution overlapped with an oil boom in the so-called Golden Belt near Tampico. Edward L. Doheny was the first to discover Mexican "black gold," reportedly offering five pesos to any local who could successfully steer him to the tar pits, as every prospector worth his salt knew that pits meant oil. Here is one of Doheny's reflections: "We found a small conical-shaped hill . . . where bubbled a spring of oil, the sight of which caused us to forget all about the dreaded climate—its hot, humid atmosphere, its apparently incessant rains . . . the dense forest jungle which seems to grow up as fast as cut down." He drilled his first hole, in 1901, and changed the face of the nation's economy.

By the mid-1920s, and despite the nation's ongoing political and social turmoil, Mexico was the world's second-largest oil producer and held the largest reserves in Latin America. Still predominantly an agrarian country, almost all the oil was sold to foreign markets, including the US, where in the early 1920s Mexican crude served one-fifth of the domestic market. During this time the Mexican Eagle Oil Company, owned by Royal Dutch/Shell after 1919, emerged in Mexico under the British industrialist and engineer Weetman Pearson. Pearson had a long connection with Mexico, going back to 1889 when the engineer had been enlisted by strongman President Porfirio Díaz to construct the Tehuantepec Railway linking the Pacific and Atlantic coasts. This railway ended up supporting key US-owned interests, including Standard Oil Company of New Jersey (today's ExxonMobil) and Standard Oil Company of California (today's Chevron). During the 1920s more than one hundred foreign-owned outfits were responsible for producing and selling over 90 percent of Mexico's nonrenewable natural resources.

Fine and dandy as it was for foreigners to exploit the rails and make a killing, the rub remained that Article 27 of Mexico's Constitution of 1917 explicitly gave ownership of subsoil to the nation. In the late 1920s, the Mexican government and corporations backed by the government caved into the might of Big Oil and allowed the foreign entities to maintain their rights in fields controlled before the 1917 promulgation. Predictably, such a position was not popular amid the heightened nationalism of postrevolutionary Mexico, and foreign corporations became the target of labor organizations and strikes starting in the mid-1920s, plaguing the refineries owned by the Mexican Eagle Oil Company in particular. Factor in the Great Depression in the 1930s and a dampened international demand for petroleum—which, not surprisingly, depressed Mexico's production—and doing business in Mexico looked anything but enticing. Despite this, the foreign entities held on grimly to their assets.

The situation was even worse for the locals who lived in the shadow of Big Oil. Lieutenant Colonel Lázaro Cárdenas, born on May 21, 1895, in the state of Michoacán, spent a few years in Tampico during the war and witnessed paramilitaries organized by the oil company terrorizing the local population. Years later he asked his Mexican compatriots, "In how many of the villages bordering on the oil fields is there a hospital, or school or social center, or a sanitary water supply, or an athletic field, or even an electric plant fed by the millions of cubic meters of natural gas allowed to go to waste?" Cárdenas would long hold a grudge about foreign oil companies who had "powerful friends," and operated as though they were on "conquered territory." Cárdenas's political mentor was Plutarco Calles, who had been a polarizing president between 1924 and 1928 and, in 1929, founded a new political party (eventually known as the Institutional Revolutionary Party, or PRI) that would hold national power for the next seventy-one years. Cárdenas was tapped by Calles to be the party's presidential candidate and, in 1934, facing token opposition, walked home with 98.2 percent of the vote.

TAKING BACK CONTROL

Cárdenas wasted no time in making sweeping changes. His policies confiscated millions of hectares of privately held holdings, including massive estates and foreign-owned properties, which were then given to the landless as *ejidos*, or communal land plots. What separated Cárdenas from his revolutionary predecessors was that the ejido was not just about social justice, but was also a potent tool for sweeping economic modernization, putting an end to the once-mighty class of *hacienda* (plantation) owners. During his six-year term, Cárdenas handed out 18,352,275 hectares of land to slightly over one million peasants. But the *ejiditarios* never actually owned the land held by the state and governed by its increasingly bureaucratic rules. Ironically, and largely unwittingly, the state became a form of hacienda ruler!

On the oil and labor front, by August 1935, with the full backing of Cárdenas's government, almost two dozen disparate labor syndicates organized into the National Petroleum Workers Syndicate. Oil workers, now in a better negotiating position vis-à-vis the mighty oil firms, went on strike in 1937 until Cárdenas brokered a deal to address the impasse. The Mexican labor bureau set a deadline of March 7, 1938, for foreign outfits to conform to the higher pay advocated by the militant unions, a decision upheld by the Mexican Supreme Court.

When the multinational companies dismissed the terms and the deadline passed, Cárdenas took matters into his own hands. Terrified that the oil sector might disintegrate, on March 18 Cárdenas declared the expropriation of almost all the private- and foreign-owned petroleum corporations active in

"For Sale, Gracias!" In 1938 President Lázaro Cárdenas nationalized the assets of foreign oil companies. Many countries, including the United States and Great Britain, retaliated by boycotting Mexican oil, but the onset of World War II resulted in the abandonment of the boycotts and an agreement by Mexico to provide compensation. *(Library of Congress Prints and Photographs Division, Washington, DC)*

Mexico, in effect nationalizing Mexico's oil. In the president's words, "It is the sovereignty of the nation which is thwarted through the maneuvers of foreign capitalists who, forgetting they have formed themselves into Mexican companies, now attempt to elude the mandates and avoid the obligations placed upon them by the authorities of this country." The headline in the influential newspaper *El Nacional* read, "OIL COMPANIES REFUSE TO ABIDE BY SUPREME COURT DECISION, THE GOVERNMENT WILL FOLLOW THE PATH OF THE LAW." Cárdenas also created the new state-run *Petróleos Mexicanos*, or PEMEX. Two hundred thousand ecstatic Mexicans flooded the capital's *Zócalo* (main plaza) to celebrate. *Corridos* were hastily written and belted out in the streets:

> On the eighteenth of March, the day of the great sensation!
> He nationalized the oil then! The Chief of our Nation! . . .
> And so Mexico is giving the world its greatest lesson!
> History is being redeemed through our Revolution!
> They wanted to make a joke of the laws of our free nation
> Without nothing how they were born from the roar of cannon!

To placate the foreign oil companies, Cárdenas emphasized that expropriation entailed not confiscation but compensation. To help fund the nationalization, Mexicans of all social classes rushed to donate money, jewelry, "even homely domestic objects, chickens, turkeys, and pigs," by lining up at the Palace of Fine Arts. Here was Cárdenas's encouragement: "I ask the nation to furnish the necessary moral and material support to face the consequences of a decision which we, of our own free will, would neither have sought nor desired." March 18 is now one of the nation's most unusual holidays: Oil Expropriation Day.

MEXICAN STANDOFF

Unsurprisingly, the oil companies did not want to play ball with Cárdenas, demanding levels of compensation far above what Cárdenas was either able or willing to offer and then summarily boycotting the now-nationalized Mexican crude in international markets. In another attempt to build pressure and force *el señor presidente* to reverse his move, they began planning to take their Mexico-based assets with them as they hastily departed. The companies also worked to influence public perception, urging a boycott of US tourists heading south, which cut the foreign visitor trade by a third. Standard Oil of New Jersey took to the papers, disseminating editorial cartoons depicting Cárdenas's gambit as entirely anti-American. But despite the corporations' many efforts, ordinary Americans never quite felt the fervor. The notion that expropriation was a serious offense—the foundation of the anti-Mexico effort—failed to catch hold.

Thwarted in their efforts to persuade the public to back their anti-Cárdenas case, oil firms turned to Washington, where Cárdenas's move had sent alarm bells ringing. For some in Washington, the loss of control over relatively nearby sources of oil was a national security calamity that would only escalate if other Latin American countries followed suit. As one US diplomat explained to Secretary of State Cordell Hull and President Roosevelt, "Should the government of Venezuela follow the government of Mexico and expropriate the foreign owned oil properties . . . without adequate payment therefor, the proper interpretation of the Monroe Doctrine [President James Monroe's 1823 eponymous address that warned foreign powers about interfering in the Western Hemisphere] add will become the gravest problem the State Department will have to face." Hull appeared convinced, and initially backed a more aggressive stance on the Mexican compensation issue. Cárdenas's negotiating maneuvers had convinced the top US diplomat on "the need to punish Mexico economically to gain its respect for American business" before the bilateral relationship could be healed. Hull even sent a note to Cárdenas raising the notion that the United States could stop purchases of Mexican silver.

But Hull's State Department lost the bureaucratic fight to the Interior and Treasury departments, which were inclined to caution due to the Roosevelt administration's self-proclaimed "Good Neighbor Policy" spirit and the worry that the oil boycott could plunge Mexico into chaos, the hands of the Axis powers, or to a communist revolution—none of which were desirable outcomes. US Secretary of the Interior Harold Ickes drafted a note: "If bad feelings should result in Central and South America as a result of the oil situation that exists just now with Mexico, it would be more expensive for us than the cost of all the oil in Mexico." Tellingly, in 1937 Bolivia expropriated the assets of Standard Oil, and while the amount of US investment at stake was a fraction of that in Mexico, FDR declined to intervene.

FDR's team finally came up with the policy of continuing to back the US private claim while not opposing Cárdenas's right to take over the assets. In April 1938 FDR used a folksy example from the Little White House in Warm Springs, Georgia, to expose Big Oil's exaggerated indemnification numbers. "If I have a piece of land at Warm Springs that is worth $5,000, and the Government, or the state of Georgia wants to take it over, I ought to get $5,000 out of it," the commander-in-chief said. "I ought not to be able to say, 'In a few years this is going to be worth $20,000, so you have got to pay me $20,000.'" Keep in mind that in the late 1930s oil companies were increasingly unpopular in the United States. The Teapot Dome scandal, involving the corrupt leasing of federal oil reserve lands in the 1920s, had presented the corporations as rapacious; FDR loathed them. So letting Big Oil suffer was not as unpopular or risky a move as it might have otherwise appeared.

Over the next few years, the oil firms continued to demand large compensation sums—each time dismissed by Cárdenas. But when World War II broke out and national interests outweighed whatever fidelity FDR's administration felt to the private companies, the US government pressed assertively to have the matter done and dusted. In April 1942, Mexico granted $29 million ($540 million in 2018) to the participating US firms (whose demands were far higher). Also in 1942 Mexican production finally returned to its pre-1938 levels, with Roosevelt dispatching engineers to help ensure that the Mexican crude flowed straight into the Allied war-making machine.

SAINT LÁZARO

On December 1, 1940, the very day his PRI presidential successor, the steady Manuel Ávila Camacho, was sworn in, Cárdenas confided to his diary: "I put my effort into serving my country and I gave my greatest commitment to the people most in need. I eliminated many privileges and in good measure I distributed the wealth that had been in the hands of the few." At least for historian Enrique Krauze, "word for word he was telling the truth." Still only forty-five when his presidency ended, the indefatigable Cárdenas spent a good share of his time with common people. He was more than willing to, say, solve a conflict between ejiditarios or help found a new school. In some instances, his arrival in his Jeep marked the first time an automobile had entered the said remote locale. Locals would plead, "Bring us the fire that doesn't burn, Tata," referring to electricity and using an affectionate term for granddad. At his home in Mexico City, he provided shelter for eighteen children.

Somehow Cárdenas had managed to both instigate and channel revolutionary rhetoric and unity, but never developed venality and the desire for self-enrichment. Critically, he institutionalized the revolution, mainly by establishing massive unions or confederations that were obligated to the state for resources: peasants, workers, and teachers, for example, were all consolidated into what was the forerunner of the juggernaut political party, the PRI.

Birthed by Cárdenas, PEMEX's principal role was to subsidize Mexico's industrialization. Subsidized oil also underpinned the "Mexican Miracle," a period of consistent economic growth from the 1940s to the 1960s. The overwhelming share of this oil produced was used for domestic purposes up until the late 1970s. PEMEX's production tripled from 1976 to 1982, driven by new finds in the state of Tabasco and Chiapas and a massive new oil field in the Bay of Campeche in the Gulf of Mexico. This is also when Mexico began exporting abroad more significantly. At its height, PEMEX was one of the world's largest petroleum entities, pumping 3.5 million barrels a day and providing up to one-third of the government's budget.

Yet as the twenty-first century dawned, these once-prosperous fields went into decline, and money that might have been put into exploration continued to fund broader state spending (some of which was undeniably very effective). Another complicating factor was the constitution's prohibitions on foreign entities that might have provided sorely needed financial or technological investments. Output sagged, which in turn hit government revenues. Various Mexican presidents attempted to open up the oil colossus to competition, on the assumption that this would mean greater investments and discoveries (and thus more money!), even if this was not especially popular with the Mexican public, from an early age in school, steeped in the sentimental lore of Cardenas's anti-gringo PEMEX birthing.

Arguably the most problematic aspect of Cárdenas's legacy was how oil money warped Mexico's political vitality. While providing undeniable social benefits to a growing Mexican population, PEMEX wound up bankrolling the PRI as it consolidated its increasingly autocratic grip on power. It was only dislodged in 2000 when the major conservative opposition party won the election.

A CUBA CODA

In an interesting coda, in June 1956 Cárdenas secured the release from a Mexico City jail of a twenty-nine-year-old Cuban exile named Fidel Castro, along with twenty other Cuban exiles, including brother Raúl and an Argentine Ernesto Guevara. (See Chapter 23, "Fidel Castro: A Rebel with a Cause" and Chapter 24, "Ernesto Guevara: Becoming Che.") Since arriving in Mexico in 1955, the Cubans had been organizing and training to overthrow their nation's hated strongman Fulgencio Batista. Around two dozen revolutionaries had been arrested in a raid weeks earlier at a ranch not far from the capital city. Cárdenas had been impressed with the restless, loquacious Cuban leader, calling Fidel "a young intellectual with a vehement temperament and the blood of a fighter." Two years hence, when Fidel was leading his rebel forces in the inhospitable Sierra Maestra range, he wrote to Lázaro to show his "external gratitude for the incredibly noble support you provided when we were persecuted in Mexico, thanks which we are now fulfilling our duty in Cuba."

After seizing power in January 1959, Mexico's Fidel Castro–led government issued the first Agrarian Reform Law, which paved the way for the expropriation of upward of twelve thousand large estates, including numerous American-owned holdings. That late July, and at the warm invitation of his comrade Fidel, Cárdenas gave a roaring address in Havana. While defiantly pro-Cuban Revolution, Cárdenas did not fail to quote the "illustrious" President Franklin Delano Roosevelt who in 1941 told the hemisphere, "So long as the nations of the Western Hemisphere continue to profess mutual respect, each and every one of them, without exception, has the right and the capacity to live freely and independently, without intervention or even without any officious advice from us." This late in his remarkable vocation, Cárdenas was still being Cárdenas: courageous, silver-tongued, patriotic, and consequential.

18

Rafael Trujillo
"Our S.O.B."

Rafael Leonidas Trujillo Molina, perhaps the archetypal Latin American dictator, ruled the Dominican Republic from 1930 to 1961 and served as Washington's man in the period leading up to World War II and after. Although portraying himself as an antifascist and anticommunist (as required) reformer of the country, he was also a brutal despot who tyrannized his people and build a personality cult around himself. After a period in the sun, Trujillo finally wound up on the wrong end of US policy preferences, and ultimately the CIA conspired in his assassination, bringing to an end his three-decade rule of terror.

A RAPID RISE THROUGH THE RANKS

The career of Rafael Leonidas Trujillo Molina is inextricably linked with the story of US involvement in and with the Dominican Republic. The United States militarily occupied the country from 1916 to 1924 as a result of Dominican defaults on loans; a subsequent Yankee justification and objective was to quell a brutal guerrilla insurgency in the eastern provinces of El Seibo and Marcorí. In the initial years of the occupation, many of the key US diplomatic appointments on the island were held by political appointees who often had only a rudimentary understanding of the country's culture and language. Complicating matters, the Dominican National Guard, created by the United States in 1917 and responsible for counterinsurgency and stability after an American withdrawal, was an unmitigated disaster, becoming a lethal tool for strongmen to wield against their people, as turned out to be the case with Trujillo.

Trujillo joined the newly formed Guard in 1918 in his late twenties and quickly capitalized on the social mobility that such an affiliation granted a mulatto, or mixed-blood Dominican, like himself. Ingratiating himself with US officers, he maneuvered his way up the career ladder: in 1924, on the eve of the US departure, he was promoted to major, being described by a US official as "calm, even-tempered, forceful, active, bold, and painstaking . . . one of the best in the service." In December of that year Horacio Vásquez, the newly elected democratic president, promoted Trujillo to lieutenant colonel and chief of staff of the national police. It took Trujillo less than a year to become the commander of the force.

By the end of the decade, the Dominican Republic had a newly constituted army and secret police—and Rafael Trujillo was in charge of both. It was time for him to turn his power against his benefactor. In February 1930, just a few months before the elections for which Vásquez had declared his candidacy, an uprising against his increasingly autocratic rule broke out in the city of Santiago de los Caballeros. US diplomats in Santo Domingo mediated between the insurgents and the national government and brought a stop to hostilities, and Vásquez agreed to step down. Rafael Estrella Ureña, a leader of the revolt, was named provisional president before the scheduled elections and was quickly recognized by Washington.

The cagey Trujillo had initially supported Estrella Ureña's revolt, anticipating that it would loosen Vásquez's grasp on power, but once that threat had been neutralized, he wasted no time pushing Estrella Ureña aside. Running for the presidency, Trujillo won the May 16, 1930, vote by the overwhelming—and highly fraudulent—margin of 223,731 to 1,883.

Although US officials were aware of Trujillo's electoral malfeasance, pretending that Trujillo had been democratically elected was preferable to get involved in the Dominican Republic again, especially as there was no guarantee that Trujillo's hypothetical replacement would be an improvement. In August, President Herbert Hoover cabled his recognition, commemorating the "auspicious occasion of your [Trujillo's] elevation to the high office of President of the Dominican Republic" and sending "best wishes" for "the happiness of the people of the Republic under your wise administration." The decision to recognize Trujillo was not an isolated instance. In 1930 alone the Hoover administration recognized seven military or personal dictatorships that overturned democratic governments.

SUPERFICIAL CHARM

Perhaps sensing the need to counterbalance his antidemocratic seizure of power with a diplomatic charm offensive, Trujillo, once in office, focused the Caribbean nation's policies on winning US favor through trade pacts and greater US investment. Over the ensuing decades, Trujillo spent vast sums of money employing top-level political lobbyists in Washington and entertaining the endless procession of US congressional delegations that came to Santo Domingo to view the "Trujilloist Miracle" of a dirt-poor nation modernizing into a Caribbean power. By renegotiating the Dominican Republic's sovereign debt, Trujillo was able to direct money toward long-overdue public works projects as well as his military and won acclaim by creating a favorable investment environment for foreign capital. The *New York Times* went so far as to say that Trujillo was on par with "the President of the United States as an economist and reformer."

Not everyone was convinced. Journalist Carleton Beals, who had written the seminal "With Sandino in Nicaragua," called the Trujillo regime "one of the most frightful tyrannies in the history of the Americas or the world." In his assessment, the United States deserved at least some part of the blame for Trujillo, given that the Dominican head of state was a "product of gangsterism, banditry, militarism, and our own marine occupation." Those inside the country who backed the strongman were "waste bending adulators" and Trujillo's scattered, terrified opposition "totaled several thousand dead, among them some of the finest men of Dominican literary and professional life."

Privately, the United States was also under no illusions as to the man they had backed. There is an apocryphal story of President Franklin Roosevelt or his Secretary of State Cordell Hull defending Trujillo despite his manifest flaws: "Sure, he's a son of a bitch, but he's *our* son of a bitch." (In some tellings the "son of a bitch" refers to Nicaragua's Anastasio Somoza García or General Francisco Franco of Spain). Even though the story might not be true, Roosevelt's administration privately understood that it could not jettison even the most unsavory actors if they might have a utility in the looming broader antifascist struggle and regional security imperatives. This was Realpolitik 101.

With such powerful external backers, Trujillo had free rein to shape the country as he pleased. Almost all political opposition was banned, and the Dominican Republic was transformed into a despotic, conspiratorial society. Relying on an intricate espionage network, Trujillo set out to consolidate his rule throughout the cities and countryside. The regime used violence, fear, and terror as ends in themselves, including overseas.

In one particularly heinous episode, in early October 1937, Trujillo ordered his military to massacre the Haitians, including Dominicans of Haitian descent, who lived along the binational border. These killings, carried out over roughly a week, were executed by machete "in order to sell the regime's official account that the massacre was a spontaneous uprising of patriotic Dominican farmers against Haitian cattle thieves." Estimates of the number killed in what is known as the Parsley Massacre range from ten thousand to thirty thousand. According to popular folklore, it gained its name since the Dominican troops pinned sprigs of parsley to their uniforms, asking locals to say the Spanish word for the herb—"perejil"—which Haitian Creole speakers pronounced differently.

Amid the subsequent international outcry, Trujillo sought to reaffirm his anti-Axis bona fides with Washington as the threat of European fascism grew ever more potent before erupting into World War II. In a remarkable step of both humanitarianism and self-preservation, Trujillo offered a haven for up to one hundred thousand European Jewish refugees on the run from Hitler's tyranny, although ultimately only seven hundred German Jews resettled at a seaside experimental agricultural colony Sosúa. There were also racial overtones to Trujillo's plan: by giving Jews land and livestock, Trujillo not only hoped they would tame the Dominican jungle through the plow but also to whiten the population. (His racism toward the overwhelmingly Black population was evident in his remark to Juan Perón when the Argentine leader was staying in the Dominican Republic: "The Negroes cannot be helped by social projects because they immediately destroy them.")

Throughout the thirties, forties, and fifties Trujillo continued to be either reelected or supposedly succeeded by a puppet president, but he was never content to be merely another venal strongman. There were significant advances in literacy rates and public works; it may have been the case that had free and fair elections taken place, the former Guard officer might have won them, at least until his last years of rule.

A true totalitarian in the ilk of Argentina's Juan Manuel de Rosas, he wanted to forge the country in his image through the establishment of a personality cult. A province was soon named after him, and the congress passed a resolution declaring him "Benefactor of the Fatherland." (All in all, Trujillo held over forty different titles, including Genius of Peace, Father of the New Fatherland, Protector of Fine Arts and Letters, and The First and Greatest of Dominican Chiefs of State.) In 1936 Santo Domingo, the oldest of European capitals in the Caribbean and named by Christopher Columbus in honor of Spain's patron saint, was renamed Ciudad Trujillo, and one figure put monuments to Benefactor in Ciudad Trujillo at eighteen hundred.

Alongside this social and political sway, the Trujillo family also aggregated vast economic power and was estimated to hold nearly two-thirds of the national wealth. All economic roads led to Trujillo, from state-run enterprises to small businesses, who had to pay political and monetary feasance to the Benefactor.

COMMUNIST CUBA CHANGES EVERYTHING

Initially, Trujillo was able to successfully pivot from being an anti-Axis S.O.B. to an anticommunist one when the Cold War began in the late 1940s. Most visibly, in 1947 he outlawed the Dominican Communist Party. After Vice President Richard Nixon toured the country in 1955, he extolled the national president: "[Trujillo is] one of the hemisphere's foremost spokesmen against the Communist movement."

But Trujillo's image deteriorated during the latter half of the 1950s. One egregious incident involved the March 12, 1956, kidnapping of Jesús Galíndez, a Spanish scholar and Columbia University law professor who had published a book scathingly critical of the strongman, who was snatched off the streets of New York City, taken by air to the Dominican Republic, and murdered. The body was never found. Then in early December of that same year, a Ford automobile belonging to Gerald Murphy, a young Oregonian pilot who had flown the plane carrying Galíndez, was discovered near the ocean in Ciudad Trujillo. To provide a cover story for the disappearance, Trujillo's men imprisoned and tortured a Dominican pilot and acquaintance of Murphy, Octavio de la Maza; in fact, Dominican officials even pointed to a note in which Maza detailed the murder of his friend.

These sorts of brazen incidents presented a dilemma for President Dwight Eisenhower and his foreign policy team, who were ostensibly committed to spreading liberty among the global communist oppressors. In 1956 Colonel Johnny Abbes García, a "violently anti-American, anti-clerical thug," became head of the secret police and the "principal confidant" of Trujillo, who was then in his mid-sixties and "whose behavior was increasingly erratic."

General Rafael Trujillo was accorded a luncheon at the US Capitol by Senator Theodore Green of Rhode Island. Avidly talking to the general, who spoke no English, are senators Green and Guy Gillette while Minister Andrés Pastoriza rapidly interprets. *(Left to right) Trujillo, Green, Pastoriza, Gillette. July 7, 1939. (Library of Congress Prints and Photographs Division, Washington, DC)*

Moreover, the Trujillo regime's method of rallying US congressmen—supplying prostitutes and over $5 million in bribes—became increasingly known, resulting in a public relations nightmare for the Eisenhower administration. After his ill-fated trip to Latin America in 1958—during which anti-American activists pelted him with "rocks, bottles, eggs, and oranges" in Peru and a mob tried to overturn his car in Caracas—Nixon came to see the US relationship with regional despots as counterproductive and that addressing poverty should be the real focus of US policy. Immediately after the trip, Nixon told the National Security Council that the US government "must be dedicated to raising the standard of living of the masses," and offer only a "cool handshake" to strongmen (advice which was mocked by moderates and leftists alike throughout the region), and champion democratic leaders. Eisenhower's team began talking with democratic reformers such as Costa Rica's José Figueres and Venezuela's Rómulo Betancourt. (See Chapter 21, "Rómulo Betancourt: Titan of Democracy.") In turn, these reformers urged Washington to distance itself from strongmen, above all, Trujillo.

Then, in 1959, when Fidel Castro and his motley band of bearded revolutionaries came to power, Trujillo was suddenly faced with an ideological and regional rival. It was admittedly a difficult start for the two in that the former Cuban strongman Fulgencio Batista had fled into exile in Trujillo's Dominican Republic, but things got worse when in June 1959 Castro ordered an invasion of the Dominican Republic by groups of insurgents of various nationalities. Trujillo's forces soon apprehended the invaders and killed them in what Trujillo labeled a "rabbit hunt." Insurgents who were not immediately killed were taken to the San Isidro Air Base, where Trujillo's son Ramfis tortured them. Only five guerrillas survived the invasion. Although he easily stomped Castro's plot, Trujillo didn't miss an opportunity to play up the threat of a Communist insurrection to his wavering US backers.

In 1960 it was Trujillo's turn to attempt regime change by backing a plot to assassinate his longtime regional rival, Venezuela's Betancourt. But Betancourt was only wounded in the bombing of his vehicle. In response, the multilateral Organization of American States supported by the Dwight Eisenhower administration slapped sanctions on Trujillo, including suspending diplomatic ties. Trujillo reacted through a series of diplomatic about-faces that highlighted just how conditional his political ideology was, easing tensions with Castro's Havana, reaching out to once-despised Moscow, and legalizing the Dominican Communist Party. Highlighting his capacity for doublethink, Trujillo also unleashed his propaganda network on the United States by "[taking] out advertisements in newspapers and planted stories with friendly journalists." These stories sought to reinforce Trujillo's anticommunist stance in the minds of American readers. However, they did little to return Trujillo to the good graces of the US government, which had had enough of the shocking abuses of power on the island.

That same year an exasperated Eisenhower approved a State Department paper on policies to be enacted "in the event of the flight, assassination, death, or overthrow of Trujillo" to prevent a Castro-type government or one sympathetic to Castro. Mooted options included sending a US naval force or even devising an armed intervention. On orders from the White House, former ambassador to Peru and Brazil William Pawley reported that his conversation with Trujillo resulted the same defiant line "You can come in here with the

Marines, and you can come in here with the Army, and you can come in here with the Navy or even the atomic bomb, but I'll never go out of here unless I go out on a stretcher."

All told, Washington's policy pivot away from Trujillo in 1960 and 1961 was linked far less to Trujillo's pitiable human rights record—which after all had been in plain view since the 1930s—and more to the Cuban Revolution. The Eisenhower and Kennedy teams believed that to get other Latin American nations to support anti-Havana diplomatic and economic positions, they needed to oust Trujillo first. And the shift became even more essential after Trujillo's brazen attempt to kill Betancourt.

REGIME CHANGE

Between September 1960 and May 1961 State Department and CIA officials labored over the question of whether and how to get rid of Trujillo via covert means. Eisenhower's thinking was that Washington would never be able to garner hemispheric diplomatic support for the (still secret and soon-to-be calamitous Bay of Pigs) anti-Castro invasion if Trujillo was still in power. There were also hesitations about a power vacuum in the Dominican Republic after Trujillo was dead. Here is Under Secretary of State C. Douglas Dillon to Eisenhower in October 1960: "We do not want to take concrete moves against the Dominican Republic just at present, since no successor to Trujillo is ready to take power, and the result might be to bring an individual of the Castro stripe into power there."

Per Eisenhower's request, US Ambassador in Santo Domingo, Joseph S. Farland, contacted Dominican anti-Trujillistas interested in removing the dictator, and the putative insurgents requested twelve sniper rifles. Farland's tenure as ambassador came to an end in 1960, but he introduced his successor, Henry Dearborn, who was very much left alone to run the operation, as some CIA personnel departed the Dominican Republic following Eisenhower's suspension of diplomatic relations with the Caribbean nation in 1960. Negotiations over the operation dragged on as the dissidents consistently changed their requests, from firearms to antitank and even certain chemical weapons that would kill the dictator with a mere handshake. It was likely this indecisiveness and disorganization that led Dearborn to cable Washington that the dissidents were "in no way ready to carry out any type of revolutionary activity in the foreseeable future, except the assassination of their principal enemy [Trujillo]."

As 1960 came to an end, the reins of operation were passed from Eisenhower to the newly elected president, John F. Kennedy. Under the inexperienced Kennedy, in early 1961 a supply of pistols and carbines was delivered to the Dominican dissidents via Dearborn. Shortly thereafter the world witnessed a CIA catastrophe: the April 1961 Bay of Pigs invasion. Kennedy's attempt to oust Castro from Cuba was such a disaster that the president reached out to Dearborn in the Dominican Republic to call off the assassination of Trujillo, but with arms already in the hands of the dissidents it was too late to change tack.

On May 30, 1961, after the sun had set, Antonio Imbert Barrera and Antonio de la Maza, both former military loyalists, prepared to confront the dictator. As Trujillo rode in his Chevrolet along an abandoned strip of road between Santo Domingo and San Cristóbal (the locale where he regularly met with a mistress), the assassins blocked his way and, in the ensuing gunfire, emptied twenty-seven rounds into his body.

After Trujillo's death, Kennedy forced out the remaining Trujillos, including Ramfis, through various saber-rattling measures, but then removed the United States significantly from the situation, pulling Dearborn from Santo Domingo, partly to save face: how would it look if the CIA was outed as being involved in the Dominican plot only weeks or months after Kennedy's covert Cuba operation had blown up in his face? It was only in the mid-1970s that a congressional investigation into secret CIA programs—known as the Church Committee after the chairman, Democratic Senator Frank Church of Idaho—concluded that the CIA had provided "material support" to the Dominican plotters who killed Trujillo, and the covert program, as the Ohio Democratic representative James V. Stanton put it, represented a "successful assassination attempt."

That said, many Dominican voices dispute the accounts depicting consequential CIA involvement in Trujillo's murder. Given how much suffering and political and social retardation had occurred under Trujillo's rule, it was a point of pride for many that Dominicans alone had been able to kill their tormentor. Antonio Imbert Berreras, the only plotter out of the seven who survived the initial post-Trujillo retribution phase, described the Church Committee's assessment as "a cowboy picture without any basis in reality. . . . The men who participated in that historic act did not need help. We had our own arms, we had our own cars, we had our own reasons. My friend, I challenge anybody to find the aid of any foreign organization in what we did."

SIN TRUJILLO

In the aftermath of the assassination, the Caribbean nation fell into disarray, but the broad drift of *trujillismo* endured even though Trujillo was no longer in power—an era often shamefully referred to on the island republic as "trujillismo sin Trujillo" (Trujillism without Trujillo). Trujillo's totalitarianism was so potent and insidious that the nation continued to act as if *el jefe* (the Chief) was still alive.

This sense of the persisting power of Trujillo is well captured in Mario Vargas Llosa's 2000 political novel *The Feast of the Goat*, which while aimed at then-Peruvian president Alberto Fujimori, takes its plot from Trujillo's brutal rule and assassination. (The title comes from the Dominican merengue number "Mataron al chivo, "They've Killed the Goat," referencing the assassination plotters who covertly referred to the strongman as "the Goat.") Although there are many horrific episodes during the rule of the Goat, some of the most disturbing depictions of *trujillismo* in the novel come *after* the assassination, when the reader might have assumed that the de-Trujillo-ing would have commenced with a vengeance.

In the novel, "The Professor" is a stand-in for Trujillo's token minister and puppet president Joaquín Balaguer. In real life, Balaguer served two lengthy stints as president in the post-Trujillo era, between 1966 and 1978 and 1986 and 1996. While not nearly as repressive, paranoid, or megalomaniacal as Trujillo, Balaguer, "short, shrewd and indomitable," and in his later years, blind, dominated Dominican society; under his watch, an array of human rights abuses and dubious elections continued to plague the Dominican social and political landscape. The trauma of trujillismo had become embedded in the national psyche and warped governance to such an extent that it would take decades to undo.

19

José Carlos Mariátegui and Victor Raúl Haya de la Torre

Peru's Long Revolution

Peru's political development in the twentieth century was greatly influenced by two leftist political figures: José Carlos Mariátegui and Victor Raúl Haya de La Torre. Bitter rivals, the duo would each hatch a towering legacy of ideas and movements that would transform Peru and inspire imitators and adherents across the Americas. Mariátegui became a champion of *indigenismo*, or the fusion of socialism and indigenous rights, while Haya's contribution came through the hugely influential political movement called *aprismo*, which eventually assumed power when the silver-tongued populist Alan García won the presidency in 1985.

MARIÁTEGUI, THE YOUNG RADICAL

Born in Moquegua, a small southern Peru city in 1894 and abandoned by his father at a young age, José Carlos Mariátegui was the sixth child of a poor family. Suffering acute medical conditions for much of his life, he would die prematurely two months before his thirty-fifth birthday from an incapacitating bone condition. But during his brief time, he had a remarkable intellectual and political influence on his native Peru, and Latin America more broadly. This achievement is especially notable because, like Argentina's iconic Domingo Sarmiento, he did not receive a decent education (see Chapter 9, "Juan Manuel de Rosas and Domingo Sarmiento: The Struggle to Hatch Argentina"). Following a terrible accident at eight years of age, José Carlos convalesced for four years in Lima, which although it kept him out of the classroom, did give him endless time to read. The budding polymath wrote poetry, often about loneliness, pain, and need, and never attended university.

Lima at that time had become something of a backwater, long eclipsed by Buenos Aires as a cultural metropolis. (In 1904 the Argentine city had just under one million residents while Lima, in 1903, had only around one hundred thousand) Lima's "latticed balconies, narrow winding streets, and the religiosity of its inhabitants" all suggested a city and people looking back to its glorious colonial past as the capital of a viceroyalty that spanned from Patagonia to Panama, yet modernization was underway. Right around the time the afflicted young boy moved there for convalescence, Lima's first electric tram network began to replace the oxen-pulled streetcars. This first decade of the century was also when the first permanent movie houses were constructed. Newspapers, who had been nothing more than mouthpieces for the political outfits that owned them, started imagining their work as noble providers of objective facts and information. The renowned *La Prensa*, established in 1903, is where the dirt-poor fifteen-year-old José Carlos would get his start as an apprentice

José Carlos Mariátegui. *(Alamy Stock Photo)*

typesetter before, some years later, moving to a "style corrector" and then a veritable essayist with a distinct bohemian flair. Mariátegui covered subjects ranging from horse races to indigenous land rights in the face of landowner repression and state neglect, but quickly realized that the media in Lima was too conservative for his voice and ideas, and so—while still only in his mid-twenties—founded a new leftist journal in around 1918. Scholars like Claudio Lomnitz reckon that Mariátegui's demonstrated talent as a journalist was even better than the legendary Cuban nationalist, José Martí. (See Chapter 11, "José Martí: The Colossus of Cuba.")

The political situation in Peru, however, was rapidly deteriorating. In 1919, Augusto B. Leguía came to power in a military coup and established himself as dictator. With the space for political expression increasingly restricted, especially for one of his iconoclastic ideas, by 1920 Mariátegui relocated to Europe. Over the next few years, the young radical would visit France and Italy, where he developed strong ties with key socialist and/or communist intellectuals, including Russian and Soviet writer Maxim Gorky, French novelist Henri Barbusse, and Italian philosopher Antonio Gramsci. One seminal moment for the exiled Peruvian was observing the founding of the Communist Party of Italy in 1921, a year before Mussolini's fascist regime came to power. "Until then, Marxism had been for me a rather confused, boring cold theory," Mariátegui reflected, but seeing the Italian communists construct a political body in the face of ascendant fascism allowed him to see the "revolutionary potential" of communism.

SEVEN ESSAYS

Mariátegui returned to Peru in 1923, where he began what would be a ferocious stream of writings spanning the history of the Incan cosmology to Surrealism, while increasingly pushing a Marxist interpretation that elevated native land rights. An admired lecturer, he lambasted European and North American hegemony in educational systems. It was during these years that he also became an avid backer of the anti-imperialist American Popular Revolutionary Alliance (APRA), founded by Victor Raúl Haya de la Torre. During this time, Mariátegui's wretched health issues worsened, causing him to lose a leg and be confined to a wheelchair, but not any of his resolve to found socialism in his native country. In 1927 Mariátegui founded *Amauta* (Quechua word meaning teacher and sage), a wildly innovative, influential politics, culture, art, literature, and science publication with a (decided!) Marxist angle.

In June 1927, Leguía, having unleashed a fresh wave of anti-leftist repression, jailed the intellectual for communist subversion.

Among his profile output, it was his 1928 *Seven Interpretive Essays on Peruvian Reality* that became one of the towering works of Latin American intellectual and literary history. In these essays, Mariátegui argued that the indigenous Peru, of the Aymaras and Incas, was authentic, and excoriated the racist and imperialist notion that the Peruvian indigenous peoples had to become "educated" to be freed from poverty and neglect. As such, what was wrong was nothing less than the whole social system: "Peru is a semi-feudal and semi-colonial country at the same time. Though this may seem like a paradox, this is a fact and has to be changed."

For Mariátegui, Marxism was the answer, but it could not simply be a facsimile imported from Europe. Instead, Peruvian Marxism had to evolve organically on home soil to create a fusion of socialism and indigenous rights (a theory that Mariátegui would develop as *indigenismo*). There were also pragmatic reasons for the divergence from European Marxism: because Peru lacked industry, revolution would have to be achieved through the rural peasantry, not the industrial working class (who were the target audience of European Marxism). Education of these rural classes was of crucial revolutionary import to Mariátegui, who interestingly viewed it in industrial terms. According to historian Fernando Iwasaki, Mariátegui "conceived of the university as a factory, and the students its workers. The object of the academic classrooms was to collaborate with the workers' unions, acquire experience of battle against conservative forces and practice autocriticism to maintain the vanguard of the ideological orientation."

Mariátegui's influential ideas would receive a violent reinterpretation in the late 1960s, when Abimael Guzmán, a philosophy professor who praised *Seven Interpretive Essays* as being an "unshakable document" that was "very much alive," used Mariátegui's expression *sendero luminoso al futuro* ("the Shining Path to the future") for the name of his terrorist guerrilla group, Shining Path, who would go on to wreak havoc in Peru in the 1980s and 1990s.

MAKING HAYA

Born just eight months after Mariátegui in a northern provincial city (Trujillo), Haya, like his compatriot, was a precocious student, learning French and German and taking a keen interest in Nietzsche. "Tall, elegant, of aristocratic lineage," Haya would go on to study at Lima's National University of San Marcos, where he was a student leader pushing, among other issues, for greater access to higher education. Critically, in 1921, Haya and other student leaders founded the González Prada Popular Universities for workers to study at San Marcos in 1921. The plan? In the spirit of the Latin America–wide university reform movement, exposing the working classes (who were often illiterate) to culture and education. (Invited by Haya, Mariátegui taught numerous classes at these "popular universities" before they were shut down in 1927 by Leguía.)

In 1923, Haya helped direct a massive protest against President Leguía's move to hold a religious ceremony in which the state and the church would be intertwined. Haya was arrested and deported, finally landing—after stops in Uruguay, Argentina, the Soviet Union, and elsewhere—in Mexico City, where he was very much influenced by the Mexican Revolution that had ended just a few years earlier.

While in Mexico in 1924, he and colleagues founded the movement that would later be called the American Popular Revolutionary Alliance (APRA). At its core APRA would be both anti-imperialist and embrace revolutionary nationalism. It would be, in the spirit of continentalists Simón Bolívar and José Martí, "Pan-American," crossing national frontiers to form a united hemispheric political party, the first of its kind in the region. On the economic front, Haya's APRA would also strive to promote what was called "State Capitalism," whereby the government would play an outsized role in managing both labor and production. As Latin Americans turned their backs on North American and European cultural hegemony, the homegrown APRA purported to provide Latin American remedies to Latin American ills.

Spending time in the Soviet Union and Germany in the late 1920s and early 1930s also impressed the awesome power of the personality cult in both fascist and communist parties upon Haya, which resulted in a strange political hybrid, as described by Peruvian novelist Mario Vargas Llosa: "the APRA, whose doctrine of state control is socialist, owes its hierarchical structure to fascism." Critics like writer Luis Alberto Sánchez, himself a storied APRA official, blasted Haya's "mixture of human solidarity and caudillo arrogance."

That Haya gained mythical status in the estimation of his *aprista* supporters—who called him *El Jefe* (chief) or, more affectionately, *El Viejo* (the old one)—only reinforced the messianic element of the entire political project. Haya biographer Iñigo García-Bryce recalled visiting the abode of an older aprista militant involved in the party from the outset, who put together an altar to Haya inside her home, "complete with numerous images and candles."

Victor Raúl Haya de la Torre, 1931. *(Alamy Stock Photo)*

Peruvians, in half-jest, would state that even in the most out-of-the-way pueblo, there would be a police station and an APRA party headquarters. Indeed, the party's rock-solid organization entailed even block-by-block organizing to spread literature, or what opponents blasted as propaganda.

By 1926, "apristas" had established Leninist-style "cells" (a gleaning from Haya's time in the Soviet Union) in Mexico City, Havana, and Buenos Aires; there were even ones in New York and Paris. But the focus quickly became overwhelming domestic: in 1927, Haya publicly severed ties to global communism during a conference in Belgium, and in 1928, APRA became a Peruvian political party.

SCHISMS AND ASSASSINATIONS

Mariátegui supported APRA for all its socialism—and there was a lot about APRA that was socialistic—but was less enthusiastic about Haya's push for uniting the lower and middle classes. Haya, far more impatient than his intellectual sparring partner, also thought that Peru did not have to wait for a full-scale workers' revolution (like Russia's in 1917) but instead could mobilize a multi-class coalition to topple the hated Leguía. Mariátegui disagreed, thinking the idea of a popular front hopelessly naïve, and pushed instead for full-scale communism—even if one interwoven with Peru's Incan ways. It was this divergence, combined with Mariátegui's belief that aprismo had become a cult of Haya—that led Mariátegui to leave APRA in 1928 to form the Socialist Party of Peru.

In 1930, the Peruvian Socialist Party would change its name to the Peruvian Communist Party, but that would also be the same year as Mariátegui's death. His burial procession, in Lima, brought thousands of grief-stricken workers out onto the streets, some holding waving communist and Marxist banners in honor of their literary hero. Here is how his beloved *Amauta* announced the fatality. "The greatest mind in Latin America has ceased forever to work." (By the end of the twentieth century, *Seven Essays on Peruvian Reality* had sold over two million copies, a prodigious total for a heady intellectual synthesis.)

This was also a searing time for Peruvian electoral politics, seeing as how in August 1930 Leguía was removed in a coup led by Colonel Sánchez Cerro. Just under a year later Haya returned from exile to a rapturous welcome. At an event on August 22 at the Plaza de Toros de Acho, the venerable bull-fighting coliseum, upward of forty thousand apristas came together to hear their hero deliver what became of his most legendary addresses:

> *Aprismo*, then, is not just a political banner. In all ways it is a force that answers a national yearning. It is a force that answers an old wound in Peru. *Aprismo* means a new Peru arising, one wanting its proper place, to "Peruvianize," as our national motto attests. *Aprimso* means the mobilization of all those who have remained at the margins of the business of the state and who now demanded their rights and that their rights be respected. ONLY APRISMO CAN SAVE US!

Haya was now bent on running as the aprista candidate for the 1931 presidential vote, which took place on October 11. His opponent Sánchez Cerro only just garnered a majority, despite the consolidated backing of the oligarchy, church, and armed forces, and was inaugurated that December. Now a politically marked man, Haya was arrested in early 1932, convicted without a trial and briefly sentenced to solitary confinement.

The apristas soon took their revenge, though it came at a heavy cost. That July up in the coastal city of Trujillo, Haya's native city, apristas attacked a military garrison, which prompted Sánchez Cerro to order his forces to retake the city, resulting in scores of aprista deaths. Then on April 30, 1933, an APRA militant assassinated Sánchez Cerro while the president was observing a military parade. The fallout from Cerro's assassination saw APRA banned and drove Haya underground between 1934 and 1945, though he continued to publish and organize, attempting to extend APRA's influence into teacher, miner, and sugar plantation syndicates.

BRUSHES WITH POWER

In 1945, at long last unbanned, APRA threw its weight behind the democratic José Luis Bustamante y Rivero, who won the presidency. In a turbulent period, Bustamante removed the apristas from his government before himself being removed in 1948 by General Manuel Odría. Haya sought asylum in the Colombian embassy in Lima, where he was forced to remain until 1954. After a brief interlude in Mexico, Haya returned to Peru in 1957 after Odría unexpectedly opened the political space.

The 1962 presidential election witnessed Haya running against Odría and Fernando Belaúnde Terry in an especially bitter campaign. Haya lost out to Belaúnde, but APRA did win a sizable share of legislature seats. Five years later, Haya appeared well placed to assume the supreme office, but the military deposed Belaúnde in the final months of 1968 and would hold power for the next dozen years, during which time they proscribed political parties, including, of course, APRA. The military finally authorized Peru's 1980 democratic election, but it was too late for Haya. The octogenarian was APRA's candidate once again but died in 1979 before the vote.

Despite never donning the presidential sash, Haya had nonetheless become one of Latin America's political juggernauts. Writing for the *New Yorker* in 2019, Daniel Alarcón explained APRA's legacy: "In a country where most parties have been weakened to the point of irrelevance and political alliances are often little more than marriages of convenience arranged for a specific election, the APRA, which was founded ninety-five years ago, is different, as much a cultural institution as a political party." For generation upon generation, Alarcón added, to be an aprista was to assume an "inherited identity." Militant youths might join the party because their parents had, and their grandparents before that. As one APRA elite told Alarcón, "Aprismo is a feeling. A brotherhood. It's like you're part of a big family."

ALAN GARCÍA: APRA TAKES CHARGE

Only six years after Haya's death, APRA finally achieved its great ambition. Hailed as "Latin America's Kennedy," APRA leader Alan García was only thirty-six years old when he took the presidency of Peru amidst economic and political chaos in 1985. It was also the first hand-off from one democratically elected president to another in almost four decades.

Yet García's dashing figure and political talents could not hide the fact that Peru went from bad to worse under his watch. Economically, his tenure was a disaster, in part due to García's decision to limit Peru's punishing debt payments to foreign creditors like the International Monetary Fund (IMF) and refusing to follow IMF prescriptions. Hyperinflation reached almost 8,000 percent per year in 1990, his last year in office. Slightly over 40 percent of Peruvians were impoverished when he took office, a rate that spiked to 55 percent by 1991.

Making matters far worse, Shining Path guerrillas took advantage of the economic catastrophe to increase their clandestine operations in Lima and elsewhere. Fighting fire with fire, García responded by unleashing the Peruvian military to conduct a scorched-earth counterinsurgency against suspected Shining Path operatives and sympathizers—overwhelmingly in the impoverished, Indian-majority highlands. By the time he vacated the presidency in 1990 amid charges of corruption, his position as the "bright young hope of the Latin American left" had evaporated.

Yet almost two decades later, he was to experience an improbable political resurgence, together with an almost equally improbable ideological reinvention. Again president after winning 2006's free and fair elections, in April 2007, García met with Republican US president George W. Bush to discuss their shared conservative views, both fiscal and political, and García mooted a free trade agreement between Peru and the United States. In 2010, García again visited the Oval Office to meet with Bush's successor, Barack Obama. During the roughly half-hour meeting, García warned his American counterpart about the dangers of leftist Venezuelan President Hugo Chávez. "When I was young, I was just like Chávez." He explained. "But now I've grown up." (See Chapter 40, "Hugo Chávez: The Richest Revolutionary in the World.")

Back in Peru and buoyed by soaring global prices for minerals, García oversaw part of the longest economic expansion in Peru's history, with economic policies the opposite of his first term. When he left office, Peru's poverty rate was about 27 percent—a reduction that entailed millions of citizens moving up to a lower-middle or middle-class existence. García ran for president once more in 2016, but this time only garnered a pitiful 5.8 percent share of the first-round ballot. With police on the verge of arresting him, in April 2019 García committed suicide rather than face a judicial prosecution related to a massive corruption scandal during his second administration. "I never asked for money or sold public works," he had just prior relayed via Twitter. "Those who accused me are the true corrupt. I believe in history."

García's death was the culmination of a decades-long process of political deterioration that ultimately rendered the once-dominant aprismo movement a shadow of its former self. At the 2020 parliamentary election, APRA took a miserable 2.7 percent of the vote and failed to win congressional representation for the first time in six decades. Sensing another electoral humiliation was on the cards, APRA's presidential candidate withdrew before the first round of voting at the 2021 presidential election. APRA, it appeared, had at long last died, although its outsized influence may yet live on.

IV
COLD WAR

20

Juan and Eva Perón

Peronism's Dynamic Duo

Juan Perón and his wife Eva reshaped Argentina in the mid-twentieth century. Their political movement *peronismo* sought to revolutionize labor rights and establish a more just nation. Yet although peronismo mobilized massive public support, the dream quickly fell apart due to Evita's early death and Perón's increasingly authoritarian ways. Several decades in exile ended with an ill-fated return to the presidency and marriage to Isabel, who would go on to become Argentina's first female president after Perón's death. But the evocative appeal of Perón and Eva persists today as a couple who reshaped how politics could connect with the people, despite their manifold failings.

FASCISM: "A TRUE SOCIAL DEMOCRACY"

Juan Domingo Perón was born in 1895 into the lower middle class in the province of Buenos Aires. The youth went to boarding school in Buenos Aires before becoming a cadet at the National Military College at the age of sixteen, after which he joined the officer ranks. Six feet tall and svelte, Perón would be the army's top fencer and was also a skilled boxer and skier. Early on in his military service, he helped mediate a fight between labor and management, presaging his deep involvement in labor issues throughout his political career.

He came to the attention of General José Féliz Uriburu, who sought Perón's participation in his plot against aging President Hipólito Yrigoyen. The aspiring officer declined and instead became involved in a separate plot led by another general, but he had backed the wrong horse: Uriburu ousted Yrigoyen in 1930 and Perón was ostracized to a remote outpost in the country's northwest while a conservative electoral alliance ruled via a succession of presidents from 1931 to 1943—an era Argentines call the "Infamous Decade."

Undeterred, Perón set about rebuilding his career in the wings, becoming a respected instructor and author of military history and political philosophy. His stamina, athletic build, and meticulous grooming ensured that he "cut a dashing figure" in his military uniform. His only defect was a reddened face—a symptom of his psoriasis, a skin disorder. He served as military attaché at the Argentine Embassy in Santiago from 1936–1938. On September 10, 1938, his wife of thirteen years, Aurelia Tizón, died from uterine cancer.

Around this time Perón was dispatched to Europe, visiting France, Spain, Germany, and Italy, the last of which left the deepest impression (he even spent a semester at the University of Turin). He was enthralled with the rhetoric and panache of Benito Mussolini's fascism and venerated the Italian ruler's political economy. In Perón's assessment, "Italian fascism led popular organizations to an effective national life, which had always been denied the people. Until the rise of Mussolini to power, the nation was going one way and the worker another, and the latter had no participation in the former."

Perón was similarly effusive about the Nazis' transformative effect: "The exact same phenomenon happened in Germany . . . a state organized for a perfectly ordered community, for a people perfectly ordered as well; a community where the state was an instrument of that people, whose representation was, in my judgment, effective. I thought that such had to be the political form of the future, that is to say, true popular democracy, true social democracy." Some say that Perón avidly read *Mein Kampf* (My Struggle), Hitler's 1925 anti-Semitic autobiography that detailed his political and economic designs for Germany.

As Perón wrote in his *Notes about Military History*, this idea of "social democracy" had the potential to serve as a true alternative to liberal democracy (which he saw as a veneer for oligarch rule). Armed with this political philosophy, he began to harbor serious political ambitions, with an eye on the ultimate prize: the presidency.

POWER AND *PERONISMO*

Perón returned to Argentina in 1941 and worked as a military ski instructor in the Andean mountain province of Mendoza. Now a colonel, he also joined the clandestine United Officers Group, which in 1943 deposed conservative civilian president Ramón Castillo, ending the Infamous Decade and oligarchy prerogatives. Owed a favor from the military regime, Perón merely asked to run the lower-profile labor ministry, but it proved a canny long-term move:

as labor secretary, Perón pushed through a variety of pro-worker policies that won him enormous support from workers. By 1944, as the protégé of the head of state, General Edelmiro J. Farrell, he had added the minister of war and vice president to his swelling portfolio—and power.

In early October 1945, an insurrection by rival officers forced Perón to resign from his senior positions in the military government, after which he was jailed. Yet within days, labor unions had mobilized to assemble the workers of greater Buenos Aires to push for their hero's release, while his paramour and radio actress, Eva Duarte, rallied support among the working classes. Perón was freed on October 17, a date later commemorated as Loyalty Day. Although no one quite realized it at the time, a new political movement, peronismo, had been born.

That same night, Perón spoke from the presidential palace balcony to an estimated three hundred thousand jubilant followers assembled in the capital, while those unable to see their hero listened to him on the radio. His promise to the nation? That as a candidate in the upcoming election he would finish his necessary revolution in labor rights and, more broadly, establish a more just nation. Less than a week later, he married "Evita."

Running as a Labor Party candidate, Perón swept to power in the June 1946 election, winning 56 percent of the vote (the last in which only males were enfranchised). The election was largely democratic, despite irregularities and strong-arm tactics, and was the first in an astonishing run of success. Starting with the 1946 election, "peronistas" won ten out of the thirteen presidential elections in which they were not banned.

Neither truly a liberal or conservative, revolutionary or reactionary, Perón's political philosophy lacked ideological cohesion, which may have explained its success: there was something for everyone, blue and white collar alike. His rhetoric, while not always his policies, were stridently anti-*yanqui* and anti-British; he touted the righteousness of *justicialismo*—a supposedly original but murky Peronist doctrine of social justice located in a morally superior "third position" between capitalism and communism. He was not a democrat, but neither did he aggregate power in the manner of a dictator. Perón and Evita criticized the oligarchy, but their government did not confiscate their property. As author Robert J. Alexander writes, "Perón at different times appealed to military elitism, disdain for militarism, working-class syndicalism, social Catholicism, [and] anticlericalism," among myriad others. Perhaps the one constant was Argentine nationalism, but even so, Perón cannot be described as a nationalist alone.

Above all, Perón was ultimately pragmatic and did whatever it took to improve the social and economic condition of his political base, embracing everything from expanding unions to wide-scale industrialization, often involving significant state intervention. Perón nationalized vital utilities like the British railways (a monumental disaster), instituted a government agency that managed key commodity exports like cattle and wheat and financed massive public works and services.

By the early 1950s, the country had at least four large-scale hydroelectric projects, compared to one or two back in the 1930s. By the end of the 1940s, Argentina had started its own steel and iron industries, and the manufacturing of farm equipment, ships, and autos was growing. His reforms included social security being made universal, collective bargaining, labor courts, expanding free public education, low-income housing, medical care for employees, pre- and postnatal maternal care, and paid leave. One slogan, "more wages, cheaper beef," encapsulates the kitchen table appeal of Perón, who proved fantastically effective at retaining support among his working-class base.

The General Confederation of Labor (CGT)—founded by communists and socialists in 1930—became the strongest Peronist union, giving the president a massive political base. The number of union workers during Perón's watch soared from just over five hundred thousand to 2.5 million, almost all belonging to the CGT or related syndicates. It was a great time to be a worker in Argentina—wages grew by 50 percent!—but part of peronism effectively entailed the unions not being able to strike without the state's permission. In a stroke of brilliance, Perón understood the massive but disparate labor movement that, if controlled correctly, would guarantee his power. Or as he put it in a later book, "to make rabbit stew, the first thing you have to have is the rabbit."

HEAVY HAND

In his quest to cement his platform, Perón fired political opponents—including non-Peronist far-left labor groups—from government positions and shut down opposition daily *La Prensa*. Perón also rooted out dissent in the supreme court, where four of the five justices were conservatives who opposed his agenda (and one even called the president a fascist). Citing improprieties and exploiting an arcane constitutional clause referencing "malfeasance,"

Perón's backers impeached three of the members (a fourth resigned). Perón subsequently appointed four new ones, all loyal to his rule. He sometimes even illegally imprisoned "enemy" journalists and politicians, including leaders of the Radicals, the main democratic party. In 1949, Radical leader Ricardo Balbín was expelled from Congress and tossed into a provincial penitentiary for "disrespecting" Perón. The prominent lawyer and politician appealed to the supreme court—where of course he hit a brick wall given Perón's packing. Several prominent opponents fled into exile.

Critics then and subsequently have contended that Perón's illiberal or unlawful moves were proof positive that he was not a Southern Cone FDR but a Latin American fascist. In one infamous episode, renowned Argentine author Jorge Luis Borges was "promoted" (read, fired) from his job at a Buenos Aires public library to a position as, in his inimitable phrasing, an "inspectorship of poultry and rabbits"—which he declined to take, leaving him unemployed for months. In the aftermath of the chicken inspector scandal, he savaged Perón's rule in an invited speech in 1946: "Dictatorships breed oppression, dictatorships breed servility, dictatorships breed cruelty; more loathsome still is the fact that they breed idiocy. Bellboys babbling orders, portraits of caudillos, prearranged cheers or insults, walls covered with names, unanimous ceremonies, mere discipline usurping the place of clear thinking. . . . Fighting these sad monotonies is one of the duties of a writer."

"WHAT I WANT IS TO PASS INTO HISTORY"—EVA PERÓN

María Eva Duarte—better known as Evita—was crucial in generating the popular support enjoyed by Perón during his first presidency, but her early life gave little indication of the outsize role she would play in her country's history. Born in 1919, she was an illegitimate child who left home at fifteen for greater Buenos Aires with barely any formal education. She moved from job to job and tried to fulfill her ambition of becoming an actress, but what she lacked in money or education she more than made up for with a keen natural intelligence, a burning ambition, and photogenic looks. (Some accounts describe her as a natural blond, others that after bleaching her hair blonde for a film role, she decided to stick with the more upper-class look.)

She met Perón at an event in 1944 to raise money for the victims of a devastating earthquake in the provincial city of San Juan that killed ten thousand. The pair married the next year, and she became First Lady after Perón's successful run for the presidency in 1946. And it was here that she came to the fore:

blessed with a powerful oratorical gift—"capable of impromptu eloquence and an emotional empathy that ran through crowds like an electric discharge"—she was adored by millions of supporters, known as *los decamisados* (the shirtless ones), and rarely missed an opportunity to lavish praise on Perón: "Sometimes I think Perón is no longer a man like the others; that he is an ideal incarnate."

But she was no mere cheerleader: the populist phenomenon of peronism was at heart the dyad of Evita and Perón: according to Enrique Krauze, the pair "heaved like a single and only legitimate lord and master of Argentina." Evita was actively involved as the president's liaison to organized labor and the poor, although she was never a member of Perón's cabinet nor voted into any public position. She also led the María Eva Duarte de Perón Foundation, created in July 1948, and the Female Peronist Party. Established by Evita in July 1949, the new organization enjoyed the fruits of the massive registration of women (it doubled to over eight hundred thousand in Buenos Aires alone) following the granting of suffrage in 1947. By 1952, Evita's party had over five hundred thousand members across over 3,500 branches across Argentina. She also led, on an unofficial basis, the Social Welfare ministry.

In her variety of capacities, official or otherwise, her notoriously frenetic daily schedule began early, about 7 a.m. Wearing informal clothing (she only dressed up for public events), she would host maybe a dozen or two delegations before touring a school, hospital, or factory. During Christmas in 1947, she distributed millions of toys to children across the country; that same year, the government announced that the first lady had given away $4 million ($12 million today) of donations in eleven months. She received on average twelve thousand letters each day—each read by personal assistants selected by Evita for their experiences of scarcity. She dedicated one day a week to hosting labor delegates who desired to talk with her, always with an eye on strengthening peronism's grip on power (by 1951, she had enacted an almost-total purge of the labor union leadership). These efforts might be followed by a gala event at night, where she donned the finest and most expensive fashions.

Sparking more emotion and controversy than just about any other figure in the nation's history, her admirers saw her as selfless and defiant. But given the machismo of the era, many in the government, especially the traditionalist armed forces, were vehemently opposed to a woman playing a prominent role in the national political discourse, not to mention her effective role as copresident. The upper classes and conservatives hated her for being an upstart, and off-color jokes during her era called her "la gran puta" (the great whore).

Her María Eva Duarte de Perón Foundation was a particular source of concern. Established by a congressional act but handed, with no oversight, to the first lady, it became a vast and wealthy enterprise. In addition to its congressional appropriations, the foundation relied upon a variety of revenue sources. An unusual one was that in each new collective bargaining accord anywhere in Argentina, the first month's wage was "donated" to the foundation. Business owners came to realize that they should also "donate" lest they get hit with, say a tax audit or health inspection. In just a few years, her foundation had fourteen thousand full-time employees and assets of $200 million ($600 million today), its influence surpassing most government ministries.

Eva Perón labeled her policy toward the descamisados "direct social control," which involved her meeting a variety of visitors and requests: a youth asking for an orthopedic leg; a poor woman needing a sewing machine. She would handle each of these cases personally and decide immediately, literally handing out cash or devices like sewing machines to desperate citizens. (Here is a sample of what it obtained to be handed out to the poor for the whole span: two hundred thousand cooking pots, four hundred thousand shoe pairs, five hundred thousand sewing machines.) Evita would also, one

Eva and Juan Perón wave to citizens from a balcony, October 23, 1950. *(Alamy Stock Photo)*

afternoon each week, "hold court" to counsel or console, whether it was marital troubles, an imperious boss, or an inability to make next month's rent payment. Invariably, Evita was joined by aides, to whom she would turn to see that the issue was addressed one way or another, often involving the provision of foundation funds.

Make no mistake, the foundation did all sorts of socially beneficial things, in addition to the basic distribution of goods: twelve hospitals with new equipment, orphan asylums, one thousand new schools, student cities, and a shelter for girls who had come to the capital in search of employment. There was a *Barrio Presidente Perón* not far outside Buenos Aires with six hundred new residences; Evita City, a planned community, had fifteen thousand. But so much of this was on a personalist basis, which ensured that political patronage and corruption were rife. It also served as effective propaganda for peronism: for scholar Robert B. Crassweller, "The names of Peron and Evita were everywhere, as were their pictures, their initials, and the reminders of their virtues. No wall of any foundation building was too small for a Peronist message of some kind, and no shirt too shoddy for a Peronist inscription." She quickly garnered new titles: The Lady of Hope, The Mother of the Innocents, The Workers' Plenipotentiary, and The Bridge of Love; Krauze equates her image in the minds of the predominantly Catholic Argentine people to that of the "Virgin Mary."

On May 7, 1952, her thirty-third birthday, Congress gave Evita the sobriquet "Spiritual Leader of the Nation." A week before, stricken by ovarian cancer, she had, for the last time, addressed the descamisados from the *Casa Rosada* (office of the President of Argentina). At 8:25 p.m. on July 26 and now down to eighty pounds, she succumbed to the disease, despite being the first Argentine to undergo chemotherapy. Within hours of the announcement of her passing, flower shops across the capital were selling out; the nation went into "immediate and total" mourning. "Everything stopped as of the moment of the announcement: movies, restaurant service, theatrical plays in progress, shops, even the usual street and store lights that contended with the darkness."

On Sunday, August 9, streets in and around were jammed with crestfallen citizens for a mile in each direction as the cortege with her casket inched its way to the labor ministry, where her body was placed on public display (leading to lines of mourners that backed up thirty blocks as they waited to pay their respects). That night, laid onto a carriage, the casket was taken to Congress for a state funeral despite her not holding elected office. Millions attended. As he witnessed the scene, Perón uttered to an aide, "I never knew they loved her so much."

The following day, as author Robert Crassweller described it, the "gun carriage resumed its slow pace through dark streets under lowering skies, past the street lamps shrouded with crepe, while Chopin's funeral march sounded and 17,000 soldiers held back the pressing multitudes, delivering the body to the headquarters of the [national trade union] CGT," where the permanent embalming would be performed. The embalmed body remained at the CGT headquarters, with the idea that her final internment would be in a massive mausoleum or next to a statue of her and descamisados. But in 1956, after Perón had fallen, the coffin holding the corpse vanished. In 1971 the remains were discovered in a tomb in Milan, Italy, and the corpse was returned to her exiled husband in Spain. (Perón and his new wife Isabel apparently kept the body on a platform inside their residence!)

International media reported that at the time of her death, Evita was believed to own 1,200 gold and silver brooches, hundreds of pairs of shoes, and almost two thousand diamonds, among other precious items, all of which amounted to tens of millions of dollars. Evita never felt any real contradiction between her riches and her relentless advocacy for the neglected and a "martyr of labor," and neither, it seems, did Argentine workers, who saw her as Saint Evita. After her death, the pope was overwhelmed by thousands of letters requesting her elevation to sainthood, and school books were edited to commemorate her, with this example taken from first-grade material:

> Evita!
> Friend of the poor,
> of the aged and children,
> Who helps them all,
> And brings them your comfort,
> what a loving mother,
> receive this rose:
> that of my love!

ELECTION, COUP, EXILE

Riding high on a first term of massive social reforms, public works, and buoyed commodity prices, Perón was reelected in late 1951, besting Radical candidate Balbín by a far greater share (2-1) than even his comfortable margin in 1946. It was also the first presidential election to include women.

Most histories, however, describe Perón's second term as the beginning of his troubles, even if critics would contend that his illiberalism had been around earlier. Commodity prices pushed up by World War II-era demand had dipped, and the economy lost steam. Evita's tragic death in 1952 further complicated Perón's ability to cultivate and rely upon the masses, given her brilliance and cunning on this front. Censorship and repression increased, which further antagonized his opponents, critically the upper but also middle classes. Perón's efforts on the separation of church and state and legalization of prostitution and divorce also sparked a backlash from conservative church elements, and the head of state was excommunicated in June 1955. Meanwhile, the state-driven glorification of the great leader increased. An elementary school textbook extolled him:

> Perón is the leader.
> Everybody loves Perón.
> Everybody sings "Viva Perón"!

It was far from true, and military and civilian plotting was afoot. On September 19, 1955, the army and navy officers who could not tolerate the corruption and demagoguery rebelled in a coup that killed hundreds, forcing Perón to flee to neighboring Paraguay, where dictator Alfredo Stroessner was in power. As General Eduardo Lonardi justified his coup, he called Perón "the secondary tyranny," with the nation's first tyranny being caudillo Juan Manuel de Rosas—a damning indictment. (See Chapter 9, "Juan Manuel de Rosas and Domingo Sarmiento: The Struggle to Hatch Argentina.") Peronist organizations were banned.

But not all were feeling the sense of triumph. Up in the mountain city of Salta, near Bolivia, author Ernesto Sabato was celebrating Perón's downfall, yet he retained empathy for those who had a completely different reaction, namely the lower classes:

> The September night in 1955, while we doctors, farm-owners and writers were noisily rejoicing in the living room over the fall of the tyrant, in a corner of the kitchen I saw how the two Indian women who worked there had their eyes drenched with tears. And although in all those years I had meditated upon the

tragic duality that divided the Argentine people, at that moment it appeared to me in its most moving form. . . . Many millions of dispossessed people and workers were shedding tears at that instant, for them a hard and sober moment. Great multitudes of their humble compatriots were symbolized by those two Indian girls who wept in a kitchen in Salta.

After Stroessner's Paraguay, Perón spent time in the rightist strongman Marcos Pérez Jiménez's Venezuela and Trujillo's Dominican Republic. (See Chapter 18, "Rafael Trujillo: 'Our S.O.B.'") Arriving in Trujillo's tyranny, Perón remarked later, "I breathed freely when I arrived in Ciudad Trujillo because I felt I was on friendly soil." The pair frequently met for dinner. In one conversation, Perón suggested that his Dominican host do more on the social front. Trujillo replied that he could not carry out what Perón had accomplished since Argentina's population was white, while 80 percent of Dominicans were Black. "The Negroes cannot be helped by social projects because they immediately destroy them." And therefore the Dominican ruler had to be "paternal," an explanation that Perón told him was "very wise."

In 1960, he settled in Franco's Spain, where the following year he married his third wife, María Estela (Isabel) Martínez, an Argentine dancer. Despite being thousands of miles away, Perón remained peronism's "leader-in-exile," and political figures often traveled to Spain to seek his wisdom and support. Argentina was riven by political and social tumult—military and civilian governments ruled precariously, but the Peronists were not allowed to hold national power (and indeed, peronism itself was fracturing into left-wing and right-wing factions). This state of affairs, when combined over time, made millions of Peronists pine for the halcyon days with strong wages and better life under *el presidente* and Evita.

HE'S BACK!

Assuming power in 1971, a military regime led by General Alejandro Lanusse committed to an eventual return to constitutional democracy, something that could entail the legalization of the Justicialist Party (the party founded by Juan Domingo and Eva which superseded the Labor Party). In the presidential election of 1973, left-wing Peronist Héctor José Cámpora triumphed, paving the way for Perón to return home for good after almost two decades in the wilderness, where he was greeted by an estimated one million compatriots. However, in a chilling harbinger of the movement's ongoing political fracture, right-wing Peronists opened fire on the leftist Peronist Youth militants on June 20, 1973, in a shoot-out that left at least a dozen dead and hundreds wounded. The incident came to be known as the Ezeiza Massacre, for the proximity to the international airport where Perón arrived.

Following a special vote in October, the seventy-eight-year-old Perón was sworn in for his third term by Isabel Perón—who, controversially, would become vice president—and handed the white-and-blue presidential sash "in the same pink mansion he was forced to abandon" in 1955. But his moment of redemption was short-lived: Perón succumbed to cancer the following July, leaving "Isabelita" to inherit the presidency, with the country riven by inflation and labor disputes, and her being resented by millions of Argentines forever nostalgic for Juan Domingo's second wife.

Under the hapless Isabelita's watch—her desperate slogan was "Isabel is Perón"—the vitriol between the rightist and leftist Peronist sects only worsened. Starting in the early 1970s, both factions ended up with armed elements, most infamously the radical urban guerrilla *Montoneros*, whose destructive operations were at times terroristic, leading Isabel Perón in late 1975 to call on the military to restore order. It was a fateful appeal: on March 24, 1976, the military yet again terminated a Perón presidency, removing her from office and installing a right-wing, anticommunist military junta. The ensuing period of military rule between 1976 and 1982 is known as the Dirty War in which tens of thousands were killed at the hands of the Argentine state bent on brutally cleansing the fatherland from communist subversion, real and imagined.

As one biographer, Joseph A. Page, has put it, there is so much to dislike in Perón from the twenty-first-century perch. His "cynicism, the utter disdain for the truth, the lack of principle, the selfishness, the irresponsibility. His willingness to condone violence, his distorting of truth beyond recognition, and his rejection of accountability set sorry examples." Yet this is also the revolutionary who, elected by wide margins in 1946, 1951, and 1973, provided workers with an "enduring self-awareness and cohesiveness," carried social services to them, and, together with Evita, embraced women's role in the political arena, even if his pro-working-class ideals far outweighed his accomplishments. Ultimately, his tenure as a reformer of Argentina was dominated by his and his wife's direct connection with their supporters, which superseded all other political considerations: as Perón himself said in a speech in 1948, "Peronism is a question of the heart rather than of the head." It was a passionate love affair that turned sour, but nevertheless left a deep, if divisive, impression on Argentina that persists to this day. In 2020, over a third of the population identified as Peronists, while the inimitable pair's image can be seen across present-day Buenos Aires. A giant Evita mural graces the Ministry of Public Works, while Juan and Evita's faces appear on t-shirts, bars, and cafes and even tattoos on a generation who never experienced peronism. They have become part of the iconography and cultural history of Argentina, as much for what people want them to represent as for what they actually did.

21
Rómulo Betancourt
Titan of Democracy

Rómulo Betancourt is considered the "Founding Father of Venezuelan Democracy," being the first Venezuelan president to hand over power through popular election. To get a sense of quite how ground-breaking an achievement this was, it helps to know that in the 113 preceding years before he became president, Venezuela had witnessed only 114 *months* led by civilian governments—and even these "civilian" regimes were often only the puppets of military men. Almost equally startling, Betancourt stepped down with less personal wealth than when he started, declaring "the only wealth that I have left is my honor." His upstanding conduct as a public servant led some to consider him a "miracle in Latin American politics." Detail-oriented and what today we call a workaholic (his presidential days started at 5 a.m. with a frantic perusal of domestic and international dailies), Betancourt would, over four decades, assume the Herculean (some would have said Sisyphean) burden of ridding his native nation of its chronic postindependence inclination to caudillismo and transforming it into a modern, even dynamic South American democracy.

COMING OF AGE

Betancourt was born on February 22, 1908, in the tranquil provincial town of Guatire, where verdant coffee bushes dotted the hillsides, just twenty-five miles or so east of Caracas, although at that time the capital was a bumpy three-hour trip by car, longer by horse. Betancourt's lower middle-class family consisted of two surviving siblings and loving parents, an accountant and poet. The teenager attended a private school before relocating to Caracas to attend high school.

In 1927, the bright student enrolled at law school at Central University of Venezuela in the capital, where his political activism sparked into life, specifically as part of the "Generation of '28" student movement. Betancourt and his fellow students began to plot against the despised Juan Vicente Gómez, the "tyrant of the Andes" who liked to be called *The Meritorious*. In early February 1928, authorities arrested the youthful leaders and hauled Rómulo into prison, where he spent his twentieth birthday. In an act of spontaneous solidarity, over two hundred students descended upon police stations demanding to be arrested, and Betancourt was released after less than two weeks behind bars. Betancourt and other student leaders then joined a military conspiracy that failed to oust the dictator, forcing Rómulo into his first exile.

The student activist first traveled to the nearby Dutch island colony of Curaçao (where he was briefly a member of the Venezuelan Communist Party on the island, before finding it too dogmatic), and then the Dominican Republic, where he participated in an insurrection against the hated Venezuelan tyrant. The vessel, though, was not seaworthy, stymieing the anti-Gómez revolution. He then started his first of multiple exiles in Colombia. His mission in exile was to travel, write, and speak to organize opposition to the tyranny at home. His nascent pro-democracy movement was also anti-US foreign oil investment (which they believed Gómez had been too soft on) and soon became a credible threat to Gómez's iron-fisted rule.

At this early stage in his political life, Betancourt was so leftwing that during his time in Costa Rica in the 1930s he became involved in Costa Rica's "cell" of the ascendant APRA, the anti-imperialist movement hatched by Peru's master orator Victor Raúl Haya de la Torre. (See Chapter 19, "José Carlos Mariátegui and Victor Raúl Haya de la Torre: Peru's Long Revolution.") Writing in 1930 in the Costa Rican outlet, Betancourt lauded Haya as one whose illustrious reputation is "tied to every effort in these times for Latin American emancipation." The following year, the Venezuelan added that the Peruvian duo of Haya and Marxist José Carlos Mariátegui "embodied the thought of a new generation."

But Rómulo's romance with *aprismo* soon faded, in no small part due to his belief that Haya's movement was too conciliatory with the United States. Betancourt was unequivocally no fan of the northern behemoth: "The Yankee government is not 'democratic' nor is it 'great.' It is an oligarchy of Quakers and adventurous and unscrupulous Jews which has committed, is currently committing, and is disposed to commit at every moment, the worst acts of banditry against our disorganized Latin American peoples."

In addition to his failed flirtation with APRA, Betancourt also helped found the Costa Rican Communist Party and edited its journal, *Work*. But despite his Communist Party membership card, he was, quietly, more Trotskyite—meaning that he still believed in communism but was critical of Stalin's totalitarianism. Professor Steven Schwartzberg gives us an insight into the young revolutionary's burgeoning sense of destiny: "While he never publicly glorified totalitarian social control as Trotsky did, and never showed anything like Lenin's tremendous private contempt for human life, he did for a time agree with their fantastic vision of themselves as the leaders of a Soviet Union in the vanguard of a progressive and historically necessary global transformation." Years later Betancourt confessed that his involvement in the undemocratic party had been beyond deplorable but also salutary for his political development—"a youthful attack of smallpox that left me immune to the disease."

In 1935, General Gómez died, creating political and social breathing room inside Venezuela, even if power was swiftly transferred to another military officer. Returning home in 1936, Betancourt emerged as a vital leader among the pro-democracy elements. By now, Betancourt's enthusiasm for communism or Marxism had softened (around this time he severed ties with the Venezuelan Communist Party), with his politics becoming more democratic.

Yet traces of his Communist past remained. He demanded strict discipline among the ranks of the party he founded that was the forerunner of Venezuela's most dominant twentieth-century political party, Democratic Action (AD), and placed organization and mass participation at the heart of his political vision.

In one of his first stump speeches in March 1936, the young, articulate politico stated that unlike previous civilian efforts (which had been dominated by rapacious, untrustworthy politicians), his movement would be "now and forever a movement rooted in the people. . . . We are the vanguard of the Venezuelan people, technically and politically organized within a great liberating movement." His campaign, he stressed, was about the bread-and-butter issues that really mattered, such as "the profound economic crisis annihilating the people . . . the tragic problem that its economy is intervened by a sector which has been criticized as the most unscrupulous and audacious in international finance . . . the problem of illiteracy, the problem of endemic illnesses, the problem of alcoholism, which here constitutes a terrible social curse."

Due to relentless persecution by the sitting military regime, Betancourt went underground within Venezuela between 1937 and 1939. Ironically, the military's antipathy toward Betancourt also served to enhance his reputation. One communist intellectual Manuel Caballero concluded that, for Betancourt, these years represented "the very brilliant beginning of his public career."

At the end of 1939, Betancourt was again exiled, this time to Chile. Unlike his first experience, he did not depart his native country as a naïve activist but as a far more seasoned organizer and Venezuela's most well-known democratic figure, as well as a key figure in the emerging "democratic left" across Latin America. Later in life, Betancourt revealed that, of all his time in exile, his year in Santiago was the best as it was the most normal; he lived as a parent and husband, not a man on the run.

RISE TO POWER

Returning home once again in February 1941, Betancourt founded (along with other Venezuelan exiles) AD, which described itself as a noncommunist, democratic, and socially just political party. It became the major civilian opposition to General Isaías Medina Angarita, who had recently assumed the presidency. After Medina backtracked on his support for a presidential election to pick his successor, AD joined the bloody military coup, led by disgruntled officers, on October 18, 1945, that turned over power to a "revolutionary junta" with three dissident officers and four civilians. A majority of the junta members were AD, and Betancourt was named head of the junta. Given he had been leading a democratic movement, it was highly ironic that Betancourt's ascension to power came through illiberal means.

Regardless of his path to power, Betancourt's actual administration turned out to be democratic, advocating an economic populism not unlike that of Mexico's Lázaro Cárdenas, Argentina's Juan Perón, and Brazil's Getúlio Vargas. (See Chapter 17, "Lázaro Cárdenas: 'Nuestro Petróleo'" and Chapter 20, "Juan and Eva Perón: Peronism's Dynamic Duo.") Betancourt undertook dramatic reforms, instating universal suffrage, rent control, and profit-sharing between workers and owners, launched a new constitution and land reform, and encouraged labor and peasants unions to organize. He also increased (by upward of 50 percent) foreign oil royalties through a novel "fifty-fifty" formula split of petroleum revenues between the oil corporations and the Venezuelan state, which funded the new Venezuelan Development Corporation and its related public works. There was also the opening of the country's borders to World War

II refugees, which resulted in the influx of tens of thousands of desperate souls. Under Betancourt, AD called itself the "party of the *choludos*" ("those who wear sandals") to cement its link with the poor classes, but it also had much broader societal appeal. A contemporary CIA intelligence analysis offered a glowing appraisal of the administration, concluding that AD was a useful bulwark against regional Communism: "the AD does not deserve the Communist label its enemies have sought to fix on it. In fact, the great popular support won by the party in the December elections is another indication that, in the special conditions of Latin American politics, an active non-Communist progressive party constitutes one of the best guarantees against a strong Communist movement."

The feeling was mutual. Having formerly been publicly critical of US influence, Betancourt now emphasized his predisposition to strong relations with the United States. Time and again, Betancourt reassured his North American counterparts he was on their side and a firm opponent of global communism, including its foray into the Western Hemisphere. Interestingly, he was receptive to the idea of US influence in the region. Regarding a circa 1945 US backing of a Uruguayan call for collective action to bolster democracy, Betancourt stated, "If intervention is collective, then there is no danger whatever in it." Indeed, he now believed that the region's dictatorships needed to be actively addressed, urging the Truman administration to crack down on the Somoza dynasty in Nicaragua and Rafael Trujillo in the Dominican Republic to refute the widespread hemispheric view that Washington coddled its "SOBs." (See Chapter 18, "Rafael Trujillo: 'Our S.O.B.'") In a speech in Panama, Betancourt warned his audience: "As long as there is a single government in America which does not guarantee the free competition of political parties; which does not guarantee freedom of the press and the free spoken and written expression of all ideological currents; as long as there is a government which does not guarantee the Four Freedoms of Franklin Roosevelt, the freedom of the entire Continent will be threatened."

If democracy could only come about through direct action, so be it. And he was a man of his word: in 1947, he, along with other Latin American reformers like Guatemala's Juan José Arévalo and Costa Rica's José Figueres, provided cash and arms to anti-Trujillo fighters in the Dominican Republic. The Dominican dictator responded in kind by backing rightist forces attempting to topple the AD-run government in Caracas.

There was sometimes a canny domestic angle to this international alignment. In one national television address in December 1945, Betancourt told the Venezuelan people that General Douglas MacArthur had abolished the Japanese landed estates. If someone as conservative as MacArthur was doing it in Japan, then certainly the same lingering issue could be boldly addressed in Venezuela, especially since it included the vast holding of erstwhile dictator, Gómez.

A NOBLE DEPARTURE FROM POWER

Betancourt's first term of office, as head of junta, ended in the wake of the 1947 presidential election, the country's first to be considered free and fair now under the newly promulgated constitution. The winner? AD's Rómulo Gallegos, one of the country's most illustrious poets and novelists, but also a spirited politician who won the vote handily and assumed the presidency. Before he left office, the departing president publicly responded to his critics who questioned his legitimacy as president: "The essential question, of a dramatic nature which the country asks us—us, responsible for having come to power by an insurrection—is this: Is the revolutionary event of October 18, 1945 justified historically by what has been so far and what will be done tomorrow? . . . With decisive emphasis we answer this question affirmatively, two long years after that violent event."

As he prepared to cede power, Betancourt dutifully followed the anticorruption laws his administration had implemented. His net worth? According to his sworn statement, it was a paltry 1,143.60 *bolívares* ($1,566 today), a plunge from 7,500 *bolívares* when he came into office. Impressed, a US Embassy cable reported that the departing head of state lived in a simple residence, using the presidential palace only for official events, though noted that "he may reasonably depend on being supported in his old age by the government, provided that all goes well."

But less than a year later, on November 24, 1948, Gallegos, who had pushed the AD social reform angle hard, was overthrown by a cabal of military officers—including Army Chief of Staff Marcos Pérez Jiménez, from the Andean state of Táchira—who were distressed by AD's perceived radical leftism. Many of the same officers whose coup had brought AD to power now felt a coup was the only way to get AD out of power. But the November 1948 coup was also a consequence of the broader disaffection with the AD across society, from the oligarchy and military to the Church and communists.

The military putsch forced Betancourt into another exile, this one protracted and forlorn, taking him over nine years to Cuba, Puerto Rico, Costa

Rica, New York, and Washington. From abroad, the Venezuelan patriot condemned the brutal dictatorship of Pérez Jiménez, which, by 1953, had also become a very well-funded dictatorship, due to a surge in oil revenue from higher global prices. Venezuelans enjoyed the benefits of flush capital flows and petro-funded dams, bridges, and roads, but also the sprawling university system, public plazas, and even a mountain-side cable car in Caracas. This was all part of Pérez Jiménez's New National Ideal for Venezuela, out of which derived the "Doctrine for the National Good," a mishmash of putative ideals covering everything from immigrants and foreign investment to public infrastructure projects. The Dwight E. Eisenhower administration also backed the Jiménez regime, perceiving it to be a reliable source of foreign oil and a government that advocated "a suitably militant brand of anti-communism."

But there was a very dark side to life under the dictator. Corruption was rampant, and the feared and loathed secret police, Directory of National Security, surveilled suspected political opponents, many of whom wound up in prison. The Venezuelan media was not allowed to even mention Betancourt's name, but the former president nonetheless remained an influential figure in Venezuelan politics. By the end of the 1950s, the Pérez Jiménez "miracle" had lost its luster. Under growing pressure from swelling public protests, in late January 1958 Pérez Jiménez himself was ousted in a coup led by aggrieved officers and fled to Trujillo's Dominican Republic and then Miami before resettlement in a Spain ruled by rightist caudillo Francisco Franco.

The long dictatorship over, Betancourt triumphantly returned to Venezuela to put AD back in order, including healing AD's self-inflicted wounds that led to the 1948 coup. The party joined up with the country's other major parties, the "Christian democratic" (influenced by Catholic social doctrine) COPEI, and the smaller Democratic Republican Union. Since all Venezuela's attempts at upholding an electoral democracy since independence in 1830 had failed miserably, these party leaders signed a formal agreement—the so-called *Pact of Punto Fijo*—in which the participating parties committed that each one would respect the vote of the subsequent presidential elections to forestall the possibility of another Pérez Jiménez–type regime coming to power. Betancourt duly won the general election on December 7, 1958, and once again took the top job.

THE BENEFACTOR STRIKES!

On the morning of June 24, 1960, only a few months after suppressing an army rebellion, President Betancourt was heading to an Army Day ceremony in the capital in his limousine when an incendiary bomb inside a nearby parked car detonated. The blast left Betancourt with first-degree burns and killed both his aide-de-camp, Colonel Ramón Armas Pérez, and his chauffeur, Luis Elpidio. All told, eight individuals died, and his minister of defense was injured. Betancourt was whisked away to hospital, where from his bed he addressed a shocked nation via radio and laid the blame for the abominable act squarely on his old nemesis, the Dominican Generalissimo Trujillo. Some Betancourt administration officials alleged, as proof positive of Santo Domingo's involvement and guilt, that Dominican media outlets were announcing the Venezuelan president's death at almost the same time as the attack. Before the dust settled, over one hundred suspects were rounded up in a search for the assassins.

As we saw earlier, certainly there was a history between the pair. Trujillo had applauded Gallegos's ouster in the 1948 coup, embracing Pérez Jiménez's autocracy. In addition, right-wing Venezuelans antithetical to democracy and Betancourt were welcomed in his dictatorship, and his state propaganda outlets repeatedly made personal attacks against his Venezuelan adversary. Most damningly, Trujillo had backed plots to remove Betancourt. Conversely, Betancourt had excoriated Trujillo's tyranny during his first term as president, which infuriated the strongman, while Dominican exiles fleeing *trujillismo* had found sanctuary in Betancourt's Venezuela (Betancourt even provided materiel to exiles hoping to return to their island nation to topple the dictator). At the diplomatic level, Caracas had also cut ties with Santo Domingo in 1959.

Trujillo's attempted assassination elevated Betancourt in the eyes of domestic and world public opinion, as well as further isolating the Dominican despot. It also helped Washington realize that Latin America would not follow the United States' lead in isolating Castro's Cuba if Trujillo had not been addressed. In concert with Costa Rica and Honduras, Betancourt mobilized this new Trujillo antipathy to persuade the regional diplomatic shop, the Organization of American States (OAS) to slap sanctions on Santo Domingo. But in 1961, Dominican dissidents backed by the CIA took care of Betancourt's Trujillo problem by assassinating The Benefactor. For the Eisenhower administration, the cost of being a "friend and supporter" of the strongman had risen too high.

In the years following the failed car bomb plot, Betancourt emerged as arguably the Latin American head of state most committed to democracy, even beyond his position during his first presidency. The so-called Betancourt Doctrine entailed rejecting dictatorships on principle and urged that democracies across the hemisphere stand together lest new Trujillos emerge and somehow gain (de facto or official) acceptance. And the best weapon, he posited, was to swiftly cut ties with autocrats, which was not an easy task seeing as how Latin America was full of these very regimes. Building democracy at home was crucial, he thought, but so was the hemispheric-wide need for solidarity among democracies. True to his word, Betancourt severed relations with all dictatorships in the region, creating a *"cordon sanitaire"* against tyrants, as he put it.

In particular, he took the fight to the new darling of regional Communism: Cuba's Fidel Castro. Back in 1959, Castro, just weeks into holding power, had visited Betancourt in Venezuela, asking his South American counterpart for a $300 million ($2.15 billion in today's money) loan and a discount on oil, emboldened perhaps by the fact Betancourt (thinking Castro a reformer) had previously given the anti-Batista rebels aid. Betancourt came away from their talks thinking that Castro was naïve and in over his head, but, within a few

Venezuelan President Rómulo Betancourt and First Lady Carmen Valverde de Betancourt greet their US counterparts, John F. Kennedy and Jacqueline Kennedy, at an airport just outside of Caracas, December 16, 1961. *(Library of Congress Prints and Photographs Division, Washington, DC)*

years, came to see the Cuban leader as a true threat to regional democracy, in large part due to the money, weapons, and advisors that Castro dispatched to the nascent Venezuelan guerrillas. Betancourt severed ties with Havana in 1961, followed by a successful effort the following year to expel Cuba from the OAS, because Castro's regime represented a "serious and immediate danger" to hemispheric security.

During the October 1962 missile crisis, Betancourt resoundingly stood with the United States, even contributing two naval vessels to the blockade of Cuba. Kennedy repaid the favor, toasting his Venezuelan counterpart at a February 1963 state dinner in Washington: "We wish the United States to be identified with leaders such as you." Betancourt's pro-US stance brought significant rewards, with Kennedy's Alliance for Progress effort (a pro-democracy, pro-modernization initiative) making Venezuela one of its biggest and most strategic recipients of hundreds of millions of dollars in aid.

In 1964, Betancourt finished his term, the first elected president to do so in the country's history. Four years later when AD was defeated in the electoral arena by its Christian Democratic foes, the former president, at his modest home, reassured the nation fearful that the change in administrations would usher in instability. "The democratic game is a little like baseball. The pitches keep on coming."

22
Jacobo Árbenz
A Guatemalan Spring, Interrupted

Elected in 1950, Jacobo Árbenz was one of the leading lights of Guatemala's so called Ten Years of Spring, an unprecedented period of democracy and social reform after decades of strongman rule and oligarchic control of the economy. He pushed through a program of reforms that broke the grip of the colossal US banana entity, United Fruit Company, over both land ownership and the economy. Unfortunately for Árbenz, United Fruit was well established in Washington circles, with the Eisenhower administration keen to protect big business. In an event that would have seismic repercussions, Árbenz was overthrown in 1954 by a CIA-backed coup. With the momentum of the progressive movement fatally undermined, the country slid into chaos, becoming a notorious example of US interventionism that influenced a certain young Argentine physician, Ernesto Guevara, who witnessed the coup firsthand, among many others. (See Chapter 24, "Ernesto Guevara: Becoming Che.")

A DEMOCRATIC SPRING

Guatemala's Ten Years of Spring was inaugurated by a coup against the repressive dictator Jorge Ubico in the summer of 1944 that was quickly followed by the "October Revolution" and an election to choose the next president. The intellectual Juan José Arévalo returned from exile to win the freest vote in Guatemala's history, citing Franklin Roosevelt's New Deal and the Four Freedoms—freedom of speech and religion and freedom from want and fear—as the inspiration for his administration in Guatemala. His March 15, 1945, inaugural address has a very FDR-like tone: "There has in the past been a fundamental lack of sympathy for the working man, and the faintest cry for justice was avoided and punished as if one were trying to eradicate the beginnings of

233

a frightful epidemic. Now we are going to begin a new period of sympathy for the man who works in the fields, in the shops, on the military bases, in small businesses. We are going to add justice and humanity to order, because order based on injustice and humiliation is good for nothing."

Arévalo's new constitution kick-started his agenda, greatly expanding enfranchisement (but still excluding illiterate women) and banning military officials from holding office. While banning the Guatemalan Communist Party (PGT), Arévalo's government also gave new liberties to labor unions, allowed freedom of the press, and promoted literacy campaigns, especially in the mountain highlands dominated by the indigenous Maya people. But despite his unprecedented social reforms, Arévalo was unable to meet many of the expectations surrounding his historic presidency. Furthermore, with the Iron Curtain coming down hard in postwar Europe, the US press was beginning to worry that there were Reds in the progressive Guatemalan government, bringing the Communist threat into the United States' proverbial backyard.

US anxiety levels rose further following the 1950 election of Jacobo Árbenz, a quiet, bright army colonel who won 65 percent of the vote and succeeded Arévalo. Born in the provincial western highland city of Quetzaltenango—his father a Swiss German pharmacist riddled with drug addiction and his mother a *ladino* (mixed blood) from the city's relatively prosperous merchant class—Árbenz was educated at the *Politécnica*, the country's military academy, where he was a top cadet (attaining the highest rank of "first sergeant") and boxing champion.

After graduating, he met María Vilanova, the daughter of a prestigious El Salvador family who would go on to become a major influence on her husband's political ideology. Despite their pronounced differences—she was a gregarious, well-traveled, and highly cultured member of the elite; he was reserved and relatively poor, and at that point had only lived in Guatemala—they found common ground in their mutual passion for reform. Despite her family's strong disapproval of the match, they married in 1939. During his administration, she became, like Argentina's Evita, an influential public figure with mass appeal. (See Chapter 20, "Juan and Eva Perón: Peronism's Dynamic Duo.")

After leading the storming of the presidential palace as part of the 1944 putsch, Árbenz served as Arévalo's defense minister and helped the new president face down numerous coup attempts during his administration. Following Árbenz's own election and now backed by the army and leftist parties, including the PGT, the patriotic, thirty-seven-year-old Árbenz unapologetically promised to "convert Guatemala from a backward country with a predominantly feudal economy into a modern capitalist state." María and Árbenz's communist education was greatly influenced by a friend and communist, José Manuel Fortuny, who discussed such matters late into the night with Árbenz while he was defense minister, and who ultimately ended up drafting the landmark agrarian reform and even writing Árbenz's speeches.

Árbenz's sweeping Agrarian Reform was approved by the national assembly and launched the year after he took office—the first attempt at land reform in the region's history. The Guatemalan head of state's urgency was understandable: even by Latin America's historically skewed standards, land distribution in Guatemala was highly unequal: 2 percent of owners held three-quarters of all arable land, while more than half of all farmland was locked in large plantations (of over 1,100 acres), much of it fallow. The vast majority of

Jacobo Árbenz addresses supporters, 1954. *(Library of Congress Prints and Photographs Division, Washington, DC)*

Guatemalans were Mayan peasants who, in the words of Peru's Mario Vargas Llosa, "worked for white and mestizo landowners for miserable wages, while the large estate landholders lived like colonizers in the days of the encomiendas, enjoying all the benefits of modernity."

The reforms initiated by Árbenz in his Decree 900 impacted unused land larger than 223 acres in area. Compensation was provided in interest-bearing bonds based on the land's declared tax value. In only two years, a million acres were distributed to roughly one hundred thousand families, and by 1954, the Árbenz government had expropriated roughly 1.5 million acres. But it is worth bearing in mind that, despite its massive scale, Árbenz's land reform was not radical, certainly compared to what was occurring in Mexico or Bolivia. Its focus was on giving plots to smallholders, not establishing state-run cooperatives, but for some of those targeted by the reforms, this distinction was moot. He also insisted that foreign entities pay more taxes.

At the top of the list of irate opponents to the reform was the United Fruit Company, the largest landholder in the country and known as the Octopus, because it had tentacles everywhere. Árbenz had called for the expropriation of roughly four hundred thousand acres of United Fruit land, around 40 percent of its holdings (one-fifth of total arable land) in Guatemala. Almost 85 percent of this land was fallow, ostensibly to hedge against Panama disease (a blight that hits banana plantations) and natural disasters. Boldly, Árbenz's government offered compensation of only up to what United Fruit had previously listed the holdings' value at $1.2 million; defiant, United Fruit now maintained the assets were worth a whopping $20 million.

"WALKS LIKE A COMMUNIST..."

With approval from the Truman administration, United Fruit officials collaborated with the CIA in an operation to plot a coup against Árbenz in 1952. However, upon learning of the conspiracy, Secretary of State Dean Acheson put a stop to the plot out of concern that it would damage the US image as a member of the newly formed Organization of American States (OAS). United Fruit would have to wait for the election of Eisenhower, who came to office in 1953 and who was far more anxious about the potential communist threat in Latin America (and Árbenz's leanings in particular).

He had some cause. Although Árbenz always claimed he was not a communist, he was undeniably influenced by communist ideology, and key members of Guatemala's communist party had entered his government. He was also surrounded by a "kitchen cabinet" of influential communists acting as informal advisors, who grew increasingly influential, while his wife reported that by 1952, "Jacobo was convinced that the triumph of communism in the world was inevitable and desirable. The march of history was toward communism. Capitalism was doomed." After Árbenz legalized the country's communist party, its membership grew from one hundred in 1950 to five thousand in 1954; it even won a mayoral race in a provincial city in 1953.

For the Eisenhower administration, Árbenz's formal administration alone reinforced the fear that Guatemala could become a Soviet colony. And the sentiment was widely shared in the United States: just months before the overthrow, the *New York Times* asserted that Árbenz was simply a "prisoner of the embrace he so long ago gave the Communists."

Big Business threw its weight behind the growing anticommunist sentiment and United Fruit, once again exerting considerable pressure on Washington to act. The banana giant had extremely close contacts with the Eisenhower administration: the brothers Allen and John Foster Dulles, for instance, were the director of the CIA and the secretary of state, respectively, and both had close ties with United Fruit through their work with the Sullivan & Cromwell law firm, who had brokered the 1936 deal that allowed United Fruit to build the railway to the Caribbean coast. Moreover, the family of the State Department's top diplomat for Latin America, John Moors Cabot, owned shares in United Fruit, and brother Thomas had been the corporation's president. Another relative, Massachusetts congressman Henry Cabot Lodge, was such a strident defender of United Fruit's interests that he earned the moniker "the senator from United Fruit." Ann Whitman, Eisenhower's personal secretary, was the spouse of the company's public relations director, who had produced the film *Why the Kremlin Hates Bananas*. The author Stephen Kinzer sums it up: "No American company has ever been so well connected to the White House."

With such machinations going on behind the scenes, the central question surrounding the Guatemala episode is to what extent Eisenhower and the Dulles brothers truly saw Árbenz as an ideological threat, or whether he was simply used as a pretext to protect United Fruit's bottom line. Many leading scholars, including Richard Immerman, argue persuasively that the US government's main reason for opposing Árbenz was genuinely rooted in concern about the spread of communism into the Americas. The Eisenhower administration held no truck with the notion that Árbenz could not be a communist while being surrounded by communists and enacting communist-style land expropriations. In 1950 Richard Patterson, the US ambassador to Guatemala, restated the question of Árbenz's communist leanings in terms of the infamous "duck test." "This bird wears no label that says 'duck.' But the bird certainly looks like a duck. Also he goes to the pond and you notice he swims like a duck. Then he opens his beak and quacks like a duck. Well, by this time you have probably reached the conclusion that the bird is a duck, whether he's wearing a label or not." Therefore, as the historian Stephen Streeter states, "Because Árbenz talked, thought, and acted like a Communist, he had to be one."

Some US officials, however, dissented from the Eisenhower team's rigid interpretation. One foreign service officer suggested that Árbenz might in fact be a domestic nationalist and reformer, not an agent doing Moscow's bidding. The senior diplomat Walter Bedell Smith and, from 1950 to 1953, head of the CIA, dismissed those who claimed Árbenz was not a communist. "You don't know what you're talking about," he told his subordinate. "Forget those stupid ideas and let's get on with our work."

WASHINGTON'S GREEN LIGHT FOR REGIME CHANGE

By the end of 1953, tensions between Washington and Guatemala City had not only escalated dramatically but also evolved into a multinational affair. Leaders in Guatemala's neighboring states—including the pro-US strongman Anastasio Somoza in Nicaragua and the civilian president Juan Manuel Gálvez in Honduras—were now also concerned about communist infiltrations into their countries.

Given authorization by Eisenhower in August 1953, the CIA prepared a covert operation to address the threat in Guatemala, and by January 1954 the operation had a code name: PBSUCCESS. An undistinguished Guatemala ex-army colonel and furniture salesman named Castillo Armas was picked to lead the anti-Árbenz Liberation Army, and his paramilitary force began training in Somoza's Nicaragua. Before launching the coup attempt, Castillo Armas was given housing and food on United Fruit property in Honduras; this was also where the invading troops assembled.

Washington dispatched a new ambassador to Guatemala City, John Peurifoy, who had been selected to coordinate PBSUCCESS on the ground. The fiercely anticommunist Peurifoy had worked in Greece in the late 1940s during the successful effort to support the anticommunist regime in Athens. This time, though, it would entail removing a pro-communist government rather than, as in Greece, keeping communists from overthrowing an American-backed government. The Eisenhower administration was optimistic about the plan, buoyed by the "success" of the 1953 CIA-involved coup that had elected Iranian nationalist prime minister, Mohammad Mossadegh.

Once again there were dissenters within the US intelligence community against the idea of launching a coup. The CIA's Latin America hand, Colonel J. C. King, feared a long-term backlash, arguing that the United States would "be starting a civil war in the middle of Central America!" Assistant Secretary of State for International Organization Affairs Robert Murphy got wind of the covert plot by happenstance and wrote a blistering memo to his boss, John Foster Dulles, stating that it was wrong and likely to be "very expensive in the long term." The CIA chief Allen Dulles, by contrast, had this instruction to the intelligence agency's top operational man in the plot, "You've got the green light!"—and this meant direct approval and support from the White House.

US officials continued to deny the veracity of published reports of secret armies and unfolding plots. Then, in March 1954, at a meeting of the OAS in Caracas, Venezuela, John Foster Dulles invoked the Monroe Doctrine and was able to obtain a majority resolution that effectively justified armed intervention in any member state that was "dominated by Communism" and was therefore a "hemispheric threat." With its diplomatic backing enhanced, the CIA proceeded with the training of Armas's paramilitary force in Nicaragua. Soviet-issue weapons were purchased, to be planted in Guatemala as purported evidence of Árbenz's strong ties with global communism. In April Eisenhower used aggressive language in an address to Congress, warning that the Reds were already in power in Guatemala and were now eager to spread their "tentacles" to other Central American republics.

Soon after, Árbenz's government accepted delivery of a cache of arms from communist Czechoslovakia. The clandestine shipment, intended to circumvent the Washington-imposed arms embargo in place since 1948, had originated in the Polish port of Szczecin, packed inside the Swedish freighter *Alfhem*. It arrived in Guatemala's Atlantic port of Puerto Barrios on May 15, 1954. For the CIA, which had tracked the freighter as it crossed the Atlantic, altering its course repeatedly, the delivery was proof positive of Árbenz's communist bona fides. Allen Dulles quickly convened senior administration officials and was supported in his plan to set the invasion date for the following month.

Over the ensuing weeks the CIA placed alarmist articles in newspapers across the region and handed out booklets warning of the growing communist threat in Guatemala. On June 2 a coup against Árbenz was foiled, but as the pressure continued Árbenz suspended constitutional guarantees for thirty days. Later that month US mercenaries began bombing missions over Guatemala, and Castillo Armas soon led his 480-man army across the Honduran border into the country.

At first it appeared as though Árbenz would be able to repel the invading forces, as his army largely remained loyal and fought back against the invaders. Castillo Armas managed to enter the city of Esquipulas, but he had difficulties elsewhere. As his advisors grew concerned about the possibility of failure, Eisenhower authorized the use of two more fighter bombers to strike targets throughout the country.

At the same time, psychological and propaganda efforts made the revolt appear to be much more widespread than it was. The CIA filmed anti-Árbenz propaganda in a studio in Miami and then broadcast it from Nicaragua after falsely claiming that the studio was located "deep into the jungle." Castillo Armas's planes buzzed over Guatemala City dropping leaflets intended to convince army troops to defect to the rebel side. Written on the pamphlets were such slogans as "Struggle against Communist atheism, Communist intervention, Communist oppression. Struggle with your patriotic brothers! Struggle with Castillo Armas!" Richard Bissell, a CIA official, hatched the inventive ploy of using a small, ragtag air force to drop relatively harmless Coca-Cola bottles over Guatemala City, which sounded like artillery shells when they exploded. The psychological operations were highly effective in spreading fear and uncertainty throughout the country.

On June 25, having seized the town of Chiquimula, Castillo Armas proclaimed it the capital of his "provisional government," and the momentum shifted away from Árbenz. Further sealing the Guatemalan president's fate, Washington won a United Nations vote five to four against an official inquiry into the events unfolding in the Central American country, delaying a UN investigation until after Castillo Armas's dictatorship had been installed.

It's important to note that this CIA-hatched episode of regime change never sparked a wide-scale insurrection against Árbenz, and neither did Castillo Armas's excuse of an "army" have a snowball's chance in hell of toppling the

Guatemalan military. The CIA was aware of this, hence why they employed the backdoor tactic of using cold hard cash to bribe the members of the high command—a tactic which worked brilliantly, with some of Árbenz's seemingly most loyal officers switching sides. The military brass also worried that there might be a gringo invasion if the campaign to oust Árbenz failed, further undermining the president's support.

Less than two weeks after the commencement of US bombings and Armas's invasion, Árbenz was unable to rely on his military's loyalty, forcing the Guatemalan president—after spending almost three months inside the Mexican Embassy—to flee into exile in Mexico in late June, where he was received by former president, Lázaro Cárdenas. (See Chapter 17, "Lázaro Cárdenas: Nuestro Petróleo.") Nothing exemplified his fall from power more than the fact he was forced to strip naked and be photographed at the airport while leaving the country, to ensure he was not carrying any valuables. But Árbenz did not leave without getting in one last word about the United States and its investors. The former president fearlessly gave his final thoughts on the coup in his resignation speech: "In the name of what do they [the United States] do these things? We all know what. They have taken the pretext of communism. The truth is elsewhere—in the financial interests of the United Fruit Company and other US firms that have invested much in Guatemala."

Just a few weeks after the operation President Eisenhower attended a reception for senior CIA officials and commented, "Thanks to all of you. You've averted a Soviet beachhead in our hemisphere." But while the ouster had been a success, what followed was chaotic and deeply troubling. Castillo Armas assumed the interim presidency and within a matter of days outlawed political parties and peasant and labor cooperatives and suspended the agrarian reform law. In the following months, police, military, and ad hoc vigilante militias killed three thousand to five thousand *Arbencistas*, while the prisons were filled with supposed "subversives," from unionists and teachers to journalists and students. There was a mass burning of books, newspapers, and pamphlets. Several months later his regime was endorsed in a dubious plebiscite in which he won 99 percent of the vote: 485,531 to 393. Within three years the share of Guatemala's lands that had been redistributed during Árbenz's tenure had all been taken away from the beneficiaries. For the next three decades, military generals and their civilian lackeys or allies maintained power in Guatemala.

Diego Rivera's traveling mural *Glorious Victory* (1954) depicts the US-hatched coup against President Jacobo Árbenz. Rivera is believed to have gifted the piece to the Soviet Union. The mural commenced touring Eastern Europe in 1956 when it abruptly vanished. In 2007, the Russian government loaned it to Guatemala's National Palace of Culture, so it could headline a temporary exhibition on this searing piece of political art. *(Mark Vallen/Art for a Change)*

The Ten Years of Spring Guatemala experienced from 1944 to 1954 were over, yet Washington's lesson from Árbenz's Guatemala was that targeted covert operations could help check communism in the hemisphere without the deep commitment or risk of putting American boots on the ground. Regionally, there were democratic political figures like Costa Rica's sitting president José Figueres who might have disagreed with Washington's strategy but felt that Árbenz had been deluded by communists and thus needed to be removed, although preferably by a multilateral force.

But Washington paid a high price in public esteem throughout Latin America for its blatant involvement in the ouster, as shown by protests outside US embassies in several Latin American capitals. The ouster also was an outstanding example of policy blowback, reinforcing the appeal of—and, in some eyes, the necessity for—communism: Che Guevara took firsthand notes of the coup, and Fidel Castro realized that efforts at reform in Cuba (which had been his Moncada-era aim) would be doomed without protection from yanqui interference—protection that only the Soviet Union could provide. What is also ironic about Eisenhower's stance against Árbenz is that, given the realization of how potent land reform could be as a tonic to communism, within several years Washington would be promoting the very type of land reform throughout Latin America and Asia that it had condemned as communism in Guatemala.

A PRESIDENT WITHOUT A COUNTRY

In the next few years, the figure once known as the "Red Colonel" for his leftwing policies lived in France, Switzerland, and Czechoslovakia. (Remarkably, CIA's own declassified files reveal that the agency considered ways to plant stories in the European and Guatemalan press discrediting the Europe-traveling Guatemalan as a stooge of global communism.) During a 1955 conversation in Prague with a *New York Times* correspondent, Árbenz pondered what he might have done differently: "I am completely sure that my government was following the correct path. Its program was not invented by any politician. It was an anti-feudal anti-imperialist program, good not only for Guatemala but for all of Latin America because it corresponded to the interests of the people of Latin America."

By 1957 he was in Uruguay and then Cuba, before, in 1970, returning to Mexico, where he was granted political asylum. On January 27, 1971, the foiled, forsaken reformer, aged fifty-seven, drowned while stepping into his scalding bathtub at his Mexico City residence. In one of his last public comments two months before death, he denounced the US role in his downfall and said that his political days were over. "All I want is to be left alone and die in Mexico." In late October 2011 during a solemn ceremony at the presidential palace, Guatemalan President Álvaro Colom formally apologized on behalf of the Guatemalan nation to Árbenz's family for the violation of its human rights during the searing events of 1954. A symbolic and healing step, to be sure, but the case of Jacobo Árbenz will continue to fascinate and perplex those attempting to understand the anxiety of the early Cold War period in Latin America.

23

Fidel Castro

A Rebel with a Cause

I began revolution with 82 men. If I had to do it again, I would do it with ten or fifteen men and absolute faith. It does not matter how small you are if you have faith and a plan of action.

—*Fidel Castro*

It is no exaggeration to say that Fidel Castro had a seismic influence not only on twentieth-century Cuba but also on the world at large. Together with a rough and ready band of supporters, Castro overthrew General Fulgencio Batista to establish a socialist government on the island. In the subsequent years, Cuba became a focal point for US Cold War anxiety, from the calamitous Bay of Pigs invasion to the Cuban Missile Crisis, when it seemed the world stood on the brink of nuclear war. Despite being heavily sanctioned and isolated, Castro's regime persisted through the collapse of the Soviet Union, becoming increasingly impoverished and anachronistic in a globalized world where bearded guerrillas were no longer feted as the vanguard of freedom.

AN UNLIKELY REVOLUTIONARY

Fidel Castro had an unlikely childhood for a future revolutionary. His father, Ángel Castro, had made a small fortune in the volatile sugarcane market, in part by diversifying his crop portfolio, which allowed him to withstand the economic gyrations that ruined many of his fellow growers. With this wealth, the patriarch of the Castro clan could provide his children with a stable upbringing that largely insulated them from the poverty of their peers. To be sure, Fidel was not ignorant of Cuba's political and economic maladies when growing up, but he would later admit that his home life made him one of the world's least likely revolutionaries. As a young man, his focus was "playing sports, exploring the countryside, climbing mountains, chasing girls, [and] riding horses high into the hills to go hunting."

As a youngster, Fidel had a stubborn, irascible nature that drew him into conflict with his stoic, hardworking father, and he was sent off to boarding school for remediation. After stints living with and being tutored by the Feliú family in Santiago de Cuba—a time of "hunger and ennui"—and attending the boarding school *De La Salle* (where his time was cut short on account of his bad behavior), Castro finally landed at the provincial city's *Dolores*— then one of the most prestigious secondary institutions in Cuba. It became evident that Fidel was an exceptionally gifted child: one who excelled in the classroom, competed fiercely on the basketball court and baseball diamond, and won over his peers with his easygoing, charismatic demeanor. Despite his petulance as a youth, upon graduation from Dolores, there was no doubt that Fidel had a bright future ahead of him.

In 1945, Fidel began his studies at the University of Havana, where he quickly developed a keen political awareness. According to a biographer, the university played host to an "alphabet soup of gangs" that sought money and influence. With weapons stashed all over campus, the university was as much a battleground as a place of learning, and it was in this turbulent setting that Castro honed his skills as a political leader. In the middle of his studies, he also made a (thwarted) attempt to join an expeditionary party to overthrow Dominican dictator Rafael Trujillo, and got married. (See Chapter 18, "Rafael Trujillo: 'Our S.O.B.'") In 1948, he and Mirta Díaz-Balart, scion of a wealthy Cuban family, went on a near-three-month honeymoon in New York, where they stayed in the leafy Upper West Side of Manhattan. Fidel used his extended stay to study English, read Karl Marx's *Das Kapital*, and, in a decidedly capitalist manner, motor around New York in a Lincoln convertible. He thought about applying to study law at Columbia University, but in the end, he decided to return to Cuba, where he earned his degree in 1950.

He appeared primed for a rapid ascension in Cuban politics after graduation. For a time he worked as a lawyer with a special devotion to the downtrodden and the overlooked, and in 1952, threw his hat into the electoral ring, hoping to win a seat in Cuba's national assembly as a member of the leftist Orthodox Party. The election did not go ahead, however, because of a coup, in March 1952, led by the Army-backed Batista, who suspended the voting along with the country's constitution.

Ever the man of action, Fidel did not sit idly in the wake of Batista's takeover and enlisted 160 members of the leftist Orthodox Party (of which he had been a high-profile member during his university days) to assault the Moncada barracks in the eastern end of the island. In a foretaste of things to come, the fighters were poorly equipped, and the plan of attack promptly fell apart when the assault began. Some Orthodox Party members were killed in the heat of battle; scores were captured and later executed by the Moncada soldiers. Fidel was captured and thrown into a notorious prison, but he was spared execution. Instead, he was sentenced to fifteen years imprisonment, along with twenty-five of his fellow soldiers. Determined to make the best of the situation, Fidel and his cohort used the long hours of prison life to further their education, with Fidel instructing the group in philosophy and history, among other subjects. Determined to expand his horizons, Fidel, according to biographer Tony Perrottet, "read voraciously, giving himself virtual PhDs in Western literature and political science."

Letters written between Fidel and his lover, Naty Revuelta, chart the imprisoned man's political development. Fidel read Immanuel Kant's *Critique of Pure Reason*, which made him think hard about questions of individual experience and the relativity of knowledge. Marx's "The Eighteenth Brumaire of Louis Napoleon" and "The Civil War in France," Lenin's *State and Revolution*, and Rousseau's *Discourse on Inequality* all helped Fidel to grapple with issues of revolution, wealth distribution, and nationalism. For a revolutionary who would eventually have to determine whether to appropriate Batista's state apparatus, the questions Marx raised in *The Communist Manifesto* were especially pertinent.

Mounting public pressure induced Batista to release the Moncada prisoners on May 6, 1955. However, granting Fidel amnesty did little to placate him, and within six weeks of his release, he was in Mexico planning another attempt to overthrow the Cuban strongman. Fidel's group—now calling itself the *26th of July Movement* (M-26-7) to commemorate the supposedly storied attack at Moncada—was able to establish itself in Mexico City, which was generally hospitable to leftist groups. (President Lázaro Cárdenas himself intervened to have Castro and supporters released from prison in June 1956, although Batista continued to pressure Mexican police to harass the group.) (See Chapter 17, "Lázaro Cárdenas: 'Nuestro Petróleo.'")

Castro's group began to amass weapons, cash, and more members who, although lacking military experience, made for an interesting cast of characters.

These included Argentinian doctor Ernesto "Che" Guevara and Fidel's brother, Raúl. (See Chapter 24, "Ernesto Guevara: Becoming Che.") With an infusion of cash from sympathizers in the United States, the addition of new recruits, and an ascetic training regimen, the group started to look more like a fighting force—albeit one that still seemed to stand no chance against a battalion of Batista's seasoned troops. Ultimately, a raid by Mexican authorities precipitated the Cubans' operation. Although they were released from custody (due to an intervention from former president Lázaro Cárdenas), staying in Mexico would have risked their being arrested again, and possibly extradited. They had no choice but to make their move: it was time for revolution.

REVOLUTION!

In the early morning of November 25, Fidel and eighty-one fellow revolutionaries set sail from Tuxpan, Mexico: destination Cuba. The two-thousand-kilometer crossing was supposed to take five days, and their arrival was timed to coincide with coordinated attacks across Cuba on November 30. However, Fidel's "invasion craft," a dilapidated pleasure yacht named *Granma*, did not reach Cuba until December 2. Since there had been no way to inform the co-conspirators on land of the Granma's delay, their attacks had been unsuccessfully carried out two days prior, doing little except to heighten government awareness of rebel activity in *El Oriente* (the eastern tip of Cuba).

On the morning of December 2, the *Granma* nearly ran out of fuel, forcing the vessel to land at the edge of a mangrove swamp. Some members of the expedition questioned whether the landing site was Cuba at all, and Fidel had to be reassured that they were not in Jamaica. With the planned landing site nowhere to be found, the hapless revolutionaries were forced to disembark in waist-deep water and stagger through a hellish thicket of mangroves. In the words of Che Guevara, "It was less an invasion than a shipwreck." After trudging for hours through the swamp, the revolutionaries were greeted by dry land and a not-inconsiderable number of military intelligence officers, soon joined by army regulars, who had orders to destroy Fidel and the rebels. The fortunes of the fledgling insurgency further deteriorated as seventeen of their number were captured and more than a dozen were executed while attempting to surrender. The only saving grace was that the landing party had divided into smaller groups by the time it arrived in Cuba, meaning not all were lost in one fell swoop. For five days, Fidel and two other M-26-7 comrades, who

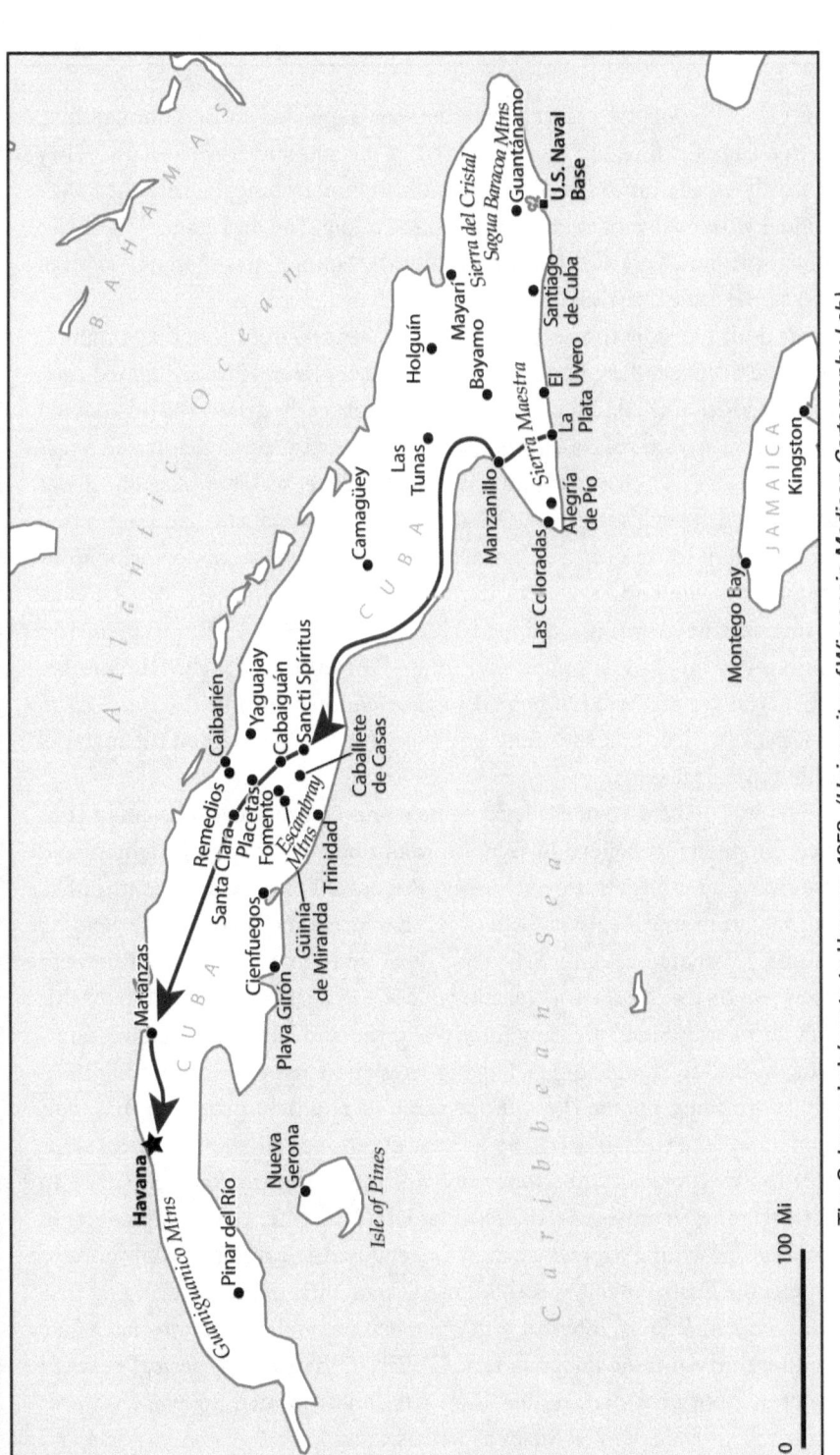

The Cuban rebels' route to Havana, 1958. (*University of Wisconsin-Madison Cartography Lab*)

were cut off from the contingent Fidel was supposed to be commanding, hid in a cane field, where they sweltered in the sun and froze at night. They eventually escaped into the *Sierra Maestra* mountain range, where they were reunited with twelve of their comrades, including Che and Raúl. Still, it was an inauspicious start: only two weeks after the landing, less than one-sixth of the original force remained.

The odds faced by the remaining fighters were so poor that they might as well have been stepping up to a roulette table at one of Havana's famed casinos. But Fidel and company learned from their early disasters and adapted accordingly. As a result, skill gradually supplanted luck as the decisive factor for M-26-7. Their mountain base, for instance, was well chosen: it was still isolated from the rest of Cuba, meaning that Batista had committed few resources to its defense. Besides Moncada, there were no major military bases in the region, and isolated outposts made for easy attacks, even for inexperienced and ill-equipped M-26-7 forces. Still, the movement was running low on men, supplies, and funds. The efforts of Celia Sánchez, an early organizer for M-26-7, helped to alleviate shortages in the short term, but it became clear that she alone would not be able to summon the materiel needed to defeat Batista.

Fidel was perceptive of the local context and realized that if he could convince the public to believe in him, he would be able to recruit fighters and raise funds on a large scale. Achieving this would require some deft public relations, so in mid-February 1956, less than three months after his landing in Cuba, he invited veteran *New York Times* journalist Herbert Matthews to interview him during the first meeting of M-26-7's national leadership. At this point in the war, Fidel's fighting force was green and hardly impressive, numbering in the low double digits. Fidel ordered these men to dress up in different uniforms and parade through the camp to give the impression that their numbers were in the hundreds. Some have questioned whether this ridiculous deception took place, as the topography of the camp was not well suited to such a scheme. In any event, the reporter left Cuba with a lofty impression of the rebels, informing his readers that "General Batista cannot possibly hope to suppress the Castro revolt." Fidel followed up on this success by bringing *CBS* correspondent Robert Taber to film the rebels a couple of months later. The resulting thirty-minute documentary, "Rebels of the Sierra Maestra," reached tens of millions of American television sets and drummed up broad support for the rebels in the United States as well as Cuba.

Batista sent ten thousand soldiers into the Sierra Maestra, covered by air support and naval long guns, to search for and destroy the rebel army's 280 members. At one point, the rebels found themselves confined to an area measuring only ten square kilometers. Still, the Sierra Maestra's harsh terrain and vegetation shielded them while slowing the advance of Batista's forces. The rebels' harassing sniper fire and psychological warfare eroded the morale of the conventional forces. Castro's kidnapping of Americans (including twenty-eight Marines and sailors returning to the US naval station at Guantanamo Bay) also negated the conventional forces' air superiority: Batista could not risk killing citizens of the country that was supplying his aircraft and bombs.

Emboldened by Batista's failed siege on their mountainous refuge, the revolutionaries started conducting operations in the plains of the eastern lands and later ventured farther west. Fidel's forces, while still badly outnumbered by Batista's, achieved unexpected victories that sapped the opposition's will to fight. Eventually realizing that his regime was doomed, Batista fled the country on January 1, 1959. The rebels whose mission had seemed so impossible two years earlier claimed their improbable victory.

FIDELMANIA

Three months into his world-rattling revolution, Castro, seeking to gin up positive press coverage, paid an informal eleven-day visit to the United States. There he was to meet with a mixed reception. President Dwight Eisenhower chose to go golfing when Castro visited Washington, DC, on April 19, but Vice President Richard M. Nixon, a noted anticommunist, spent a couple of hours with the "somewhat nervous and tense" Cuban leader.

After the meeting, Nixon wrote a memo to Eisenhower, Secretary of State Christian Herter, and CIA Director Allen Dulles in which he observed that Castro "has those undefinable qualities which make him a leader of men," and that "whatever we may think of him he is going to be a great factor in the development of Cuba and very possibly in Latin American affairs generally." Nixon assessed that Castro was "either incredibly naïve about Communism or under Communist discipline—my guess is the former." For now, Nixon concluded, Washington had "no choice but at least to try and orient him in the right direction."

Two days later, Castro, attired in his trademark olive-green fatigues, arrived in New York for four frenetic days, during which time his charisma

Fidel Castro arriving in Washington, DC, April 15, 1959. *(Library of Congress Prints and Photographs Division, Washington, DC)*

and personal story proved irresistible to many Americans. The Cuban leader walked the floor of the New York Stock Exchange, ate hot dogs and ice cream, lobbed peanuts to elephants at the Bronx Zoo, met Black baseball legend Jackie Robinson, and told tens of thousands of Cuban Americans in a Central Park speech that the revolution was "Bread with Liberty."

Arthur Schlesinger Jr., who would later play a role in the Kennedy administration's handling of the Cuban Missile Crisis, watched as Castro gave a ninety-minute address to thousands of awed students and Bostonians at Harvard's football stadium on April 25, 1959. Schlesinger noted Castro's ability to connect with idealistic, liberal, middle-class students, and citizens:

> The [Harvard] undergraduates saw in him, I think, the hipster who in the era of the Organization Man had joyfully defied the system, summoned a dozen good friends and overturned a government of wicked old men.

But Castro was also courting the Soviets, and in February 1960 inked a deal for "oil, goods, and technical assistance for sugar" with Moscow. Havana then nationalized US oil refineries after they refused to refine Soviet crude. In retaliation, Eisenhower cut sugar quotas. With only a year left before their two-term tenure at the White House would be over, Eisenhower and Nixon elected to give up on Castro's revolutionary government, which itself had effectively done the same in reverse. Eisenhower's senior advisers convened classified meetings, as Dulles put it, to figure out if "covert contingency planning to accomplish the fall of the Castro government might be in order."

British prime minister Harold Macmillan tried both empathy and admonishment in a letter to his American counterpart on July 25, 1960: "We fully share your concern at the way in which Castro has allowed his country to become even more open to communist and Soviet influence," he wrote, conceding that a communist Cuba would represent an "obvious menace." But he also warned that if the United States applied too much pressure, "many Cubans who might otherwise have gradually drifted into opposition to Castro will instead be inclined to regard him—and themselves—as martyrs." A better path forward, according to Macmillan, would simply be to "let the yeast rise of its own accord." It would also "help if we had a rather clearer understanding of your purpose—the unseating of Castro and his replacement by a more suitable regime—but I am not very clear how you really mean to achieve this aim." He finished by raising the still-sensitive topic of London's failed 1956 gambit to remove Egypt's Gamal Abdel Nasser: "We have been through it all ourselves and know the difficulties and dangers."

Soviet premier Nikita Khrushchev himself was explicit about what those dangers might be. He had initially been doubtful of Castro's bona fides, but by July 1960 Khrushchev was publicly threatening that if "aggressive forces in the Pentagon" dared to launch an intervention against Cuba, then "Soviet artillerymen" would back the Cuban nation "with rocket fire." Setting British caution and Soviet threats aside, Eisenhower eventually gave the green light for regime change. His plan was inherited and endorsed by his fresh-faced Democratic successor, John F. Kennedy, and was put into action in April 1961 in what would become known as the Bay of Pigs invasion. Before that happened, however, Castro visited New York one more time.

A NOT-SO-UNITED NATIONS

A sense of revolutionary change was very much in the air in September 1960 as the 15th UN General Assembly opened in New York City. The preceding months had been exceptionally tense in the aftermath of the diplomatic crisis that had arisen after the Soviets shot down an American U-2 spy plane on a "photographic-reconnaissance mission" deep within Soviet territory on May 1. Worse, pilot Francis Gary Powers had been taken captive—a development that forced Eisenhower to admit that the CIA had been running the covert mission for a good while.

Joining the long list of heads of state, prime ministers, and foreign ministers who were converging on New York in 1960 was Castro, and the Americans didn't exactly roll out the red carpet. Indeed, the mood in New York was overtly hostile, although African American activists still backed Castro for his stated goal of tackling racial inequality in Cuba. US officials tasked with providing security for Castro's visit reckoned that two hundred thousand Americans would assassinate him "if given half a chance." Staten Island residents burned the Cuban leader in effigy. To further spite the visiting dignitary, Secretary of State Herter ordered that Castro not be allowed to venture anywhere off Manhattan Island. Said CBS journalist Taber in the run-up to Castro's arrival: "When he descends from the plane at the international airport in New York...Fidel will enter an atmosphere more poisonous than that which the Cubans breathed in the hellish Havana of the days of Batista."

While in New York, Castro received two eminent visitors at his modest Harlem hotel. First was civil rights activist Malcolm X, with whom the Cuban commander smoked cigars and discussed the problem of racism. Castro's take was that African Americans had "more political consciousness, more vision than anyone else," while X praised the Cuban leader for "denounc[ing] racial discrimination in Cuba," adding that "usually when one sees a man whom the United States is against, there is something good in that man." Castro rejoined that "only the people in power in the United States are against him [X], not the masses."

Next to visit was Khrushchev, who, like Castro, had initially been met with a hostile reception when "anti-communist longshoremen" shouted expletives at his ship, the *Baltika*, as it docked in the East River. Their meeting lasted less than a half hour, but the significance was immense. Speaking before the press, the Soviet premier heaped acclaim upon Castro, calling him a "heroic man" who had fearlessly freed his country from "the tyranny of Batista" and "provided a better life for his people." The meeting was a major publicity coup for Castro: Eisenhower may have snubbed him the year before, but now the Soviet premier was coming to him.

Castro also made his mark at the UN General Assembly, where, after promising to be brief, he spoke for four-and-a-half hours (still a record). Khrushchev's address was also markedly idiosyncratic, with the Soviet premier taking off his shoe and waving it "menacingly" at speaker Lorenzo Sumulong of the Philippines, who had just mentioned Soviet machinations behind the Iron Curtain.

In the end, Castro's time in New York elevated the global south to become part of the Cold War agenda. Equally significant is that the fast relationship that developed between Castro and Khrushchev all but guaranteed a "decisive and fateful rupture" between Washington and Havana, and the disastrous Bay of Pigs invasion would only strengthen the Castro–Khrushchev compact.

BAY OF PIGS

Among the myriad other briefings that president elect Kennedy received in November 1960 was the CIA blueprint for an invasion of Cuba. Earlier that year, Eisenhower had commissioned the CIA to replicate some of its 1954 magic, when it had organized a successful coup against Guatemalan president Jacobo Árbenz (see Chapter 22, "Jacobo Árbenz: A Guatemalan Spring, Interrupted") and it had come up with a plan. (Ironically, Castro may have known about US intentions before Kennedy did, having become aware of US training camps in Guatemala in October.) Shortly after his inauguration, Kennedy authorized the invasion to go ahead.

On Saturday, April 15, 1961, the secret operation to overthrow Castro's regime was launched from "Happy Valley," the CIA code name assigned to a village on Nicaragua's Atlantic coast. Under the glow of floodlights, eight Douglas B-26 Invaders lined up for take-off. (One of the American pilots, Albert C. Persons, reportedly asked, "Is that all?" after counting the aircraft as the plans had originally called for sixteen.) The planes had recently been acquired from a US Air Force "bone-yard" near Tucson, Arizona, and then refurbished and painted to resemble the B-26s in Castro's air force, down to the FAR ("Fuerza Aérea Revolucionaria") markings on their fuselages. The idea was that the disguised planes would enter Cuban airspace and sow confusion as the defending forces mistook the "B-26s" for friendly forces.

Two days later, in the early hours of April 17, an assortment of 1,400 men, mostly Cuban exiles, attempted to invade their homeland and oust Castro. Operation Zapata had identified three landing points adjacent to the Bay of Pigs, the most important of which was *Playa Girón*, or "Blue Beach" in the circle of CIA planners. Despite the now-apocryphal narrative that Operation Zapata plotted a complete military takeover, the goal was instead to simply use the 1,400-man force to occupy part of Cuban territory long enough to permit the eruption of a nationwide anti-Castro uprising. Unbeknownst to the CIA, however, was the dearth of native Castro naysayers to foment revolution, since most were already in prison.

Things quickly started to go wrong. A day into the invasion, landed forces had done their part by gaining a foothold on the beach but were running out of ammunition: a consequence of their maritime supply chain coming under attack by Castro's planes. McGeorge Bundy, the US National Security Advisor at the time of the invasion, briefed Kennedy that "The Cuban armed forces are stronger, the popular response is weaker, and our tactical position is feebler than we had hoped." A mere three days after landing on the island, the CIA-trained task force was in tatters, with over one thousand survivors quickly captured by Castro's celebrating forces. In only five days, the CIA operation blew through $46 million and was responsible for the loss of over one hundred lives (some of whom were US citizens).

In the heat of battle, President Kennedy's advisors prescribed increased military force to the decaying original plans, but although Kennedy did approve limited, highly restricted military operations over the Cuban beaches, he effectively opted to accept the initial blunder and cut US losses. Secretary of State Dean Rusk alluded to the White House's miscalculation when he commented, "It doesn't take Price Waterhouse to figure out that fifteen hundred Cubans aren't as good as twenty-five thousand." Yet although it is easy to critique Kennedy for his seemingly prosperous idea of approving a 1,400-man insurgency to usurp Fidel, it's worth remembering that Castro himself achieved much more with far fewer men and far fewer resources. The difference was that Castro intimately understood the situation in the country, while the CIA did not.

All in all, the Bay of Pigs episode was another publicity coup for Castro and a disaster for Washington. The Kennedy administration's initial denial of the United States' involvement—not only had Washington organized and backed the operation but both the Joint Chiefs of Staff and White House officials had approved the plan—meant they were known liars. Even more humiliating for Washington was the open defeat they suffered at the hands of an infinitely weaker communist foe. In the words of historian Theodore Draper, it was "a perfect failure," but the lessons learned during the Bay of Pigs may have contributed to the successful resolution of another situation in which the stakes were far higher: the Cuban Missile Crisis.

THE MISSILES OF OCTOBER

On the morning of October 14, 1962, an American U-2 plane flying high above Cuba took a series of photographs that would, within a matter of days, lead the CIA's National Photographic Interpretation Center to confirm the presence on Cuban soil of at least two medium-range ballistic missiles capable of hitting American cities east of the Mississippi River with nuclear payloads.

Kennedy convened a group of senior advisers known as "ExComm" (Executive Committee) to determine how the United States should respond. While the internal ExComm deliberations are well known, Kennedy also pursued a "complicated clandestine" approach to Castro through Brazilian intermediaries. Kennedy approved sending Castro a message disguised as a Brazilian communiqué, asking Brazil's Ambassador in Havana to transmit the message as if it were a Brazilian initiative. This veiled message was to have told Castro that the presence of the Soviets' offensive nuclear missiles had put the Cuban nation in extreme danger. The Brazilians would then offer the diplomatic carrot of warmer ties with Washington if Castro would kick out the Russians and stop supporting revolutionary movements in Latin America. However, overshadowed by the Washington-Moscow bilateral correspondences over the missile issue, this simultaneous Washington-Havana (via Brazil) track went nowhere.

After the bitter experience of the Bay of Pigs, Kennedy resisted his Joint Chiefs of Staff's riskier call for aerial bombing and subsequent ground invasion of Cuba and instead opted for a naval quarantine of the island nation and the demand that the Soviets remove the missiles. After thirteen days of existential angst in which the world seemed poised on the brink of a nuclear holocaust, Kennedy and Khrushchev found a way through. The Soviets would remove their nuclear missiles (but not their conventional armaments) from Cuba, while in a deal that remained secret for a quarter-century, the United States agreed to remove their nuclear missiles from Turkey.

The incident marked a sea change in Kennedy's formerly antagonistic stance toward the Cold War in general and Castro in particular. Only a few days before his assassination, on November 18, 1963, Kennedy gave a speech in Miami in which he claimed that Cuba had become "a weapon in an effort dictated by external powers to subvert the other American republics. This and

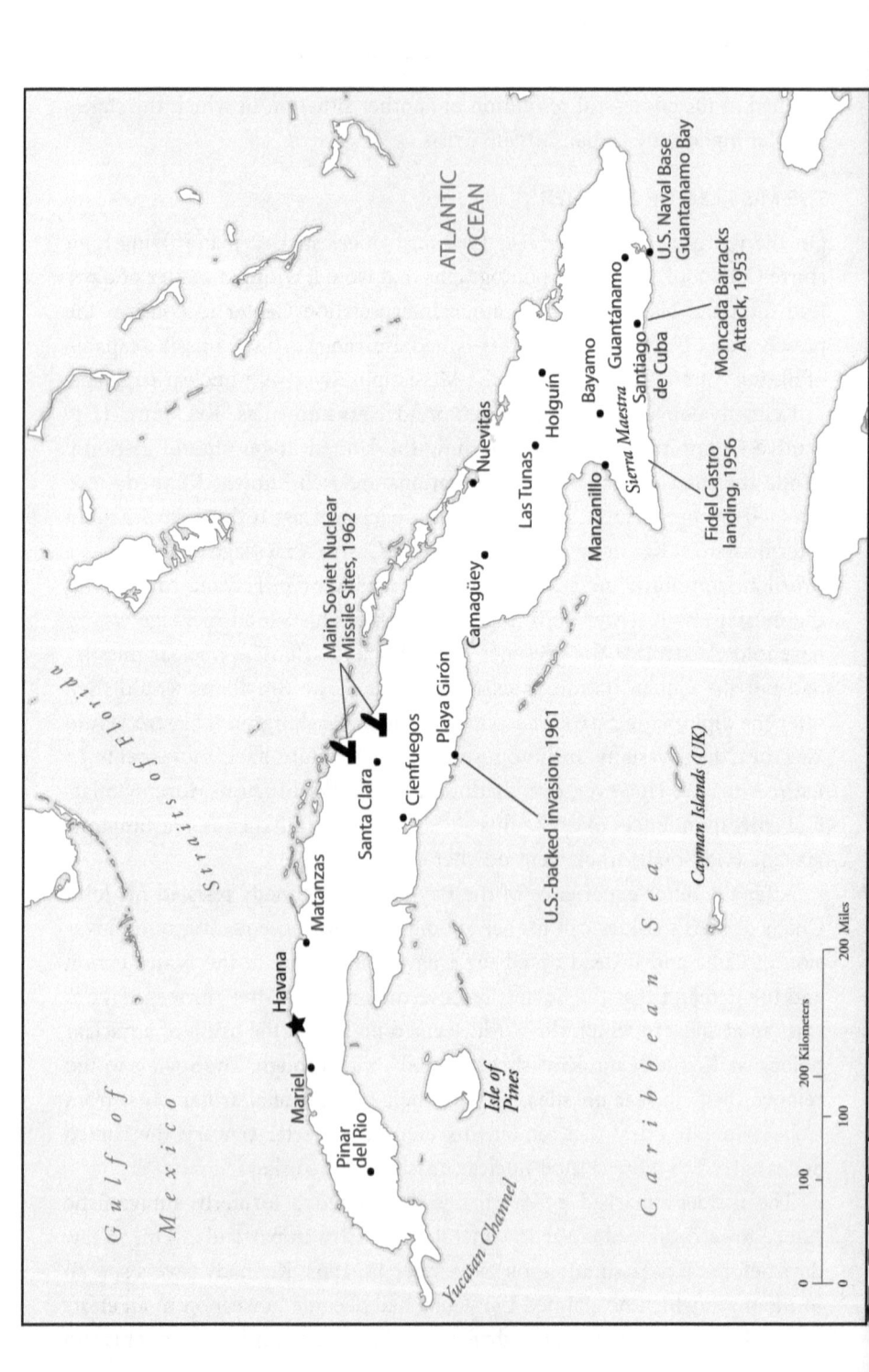

this alone divides us. As long as this is true, nothing is possible. Without it, everything is possible." Kennedy's trusted White House aide, Arthur Schlesinger Jr., helped draft the speech and later claimed that its language was intended to show Castro that normalization was possible. Yet this putative olive branch was so well disguised that the following day the *Los Angeles Times* ran a headline reading, "Kennedy Urges Cuban Revolt."

Around this time Kennedy also met privately with French journalist Jean Daniel, who was en route to Havana. More explicitly than in his Miami speech, Kennedy told Daniel that he was willing to lift the trade embargo—first enacted back in the last year of the Eisenhower administration (1960)—if Castro would cut support for revolutionary movements in the region. According to Daniel, Kennedy also expressed some empathy for Castro's virulent anti-Americanism, stating that Washington had committed a "number of sins" in Cuba, not least having turned the island into "the whorehouse of the U.S." After conveying Kennedy's message to Castro a few days later, Daniel reflected that both leaders "seemed ready to make peace." But Kennedy's assassination would abruptly cancel the promising rapprochement between the two.

GLOBAL REVOLUTION TO GLOBAL ISOLATION

The span between the Cuban Missile Crisis and the end of the Cold War in 1991 witnessed Fidel Castro becoming a regional figurehead for revolution, critically in Latin America. He solidified his standing as a world "revolutionary" icon in the 1960s and 1970s via his trademark combat fatigues, cigars, and beard. But despite Castro's best efforts, only one Cuba-styled Marxist revolution was successful: that of Daniel Ortega's Sandinistas in Nicaragua. (See Chapter 46, "Daniel Ortega and Rosario Murillo: Nicaragua's Toxic Power Couple.") Eager to promote global communist solidarity as well as demonstrate that Cuba was not a vassal of Moscow, Fidel, in two separate operations, dispatched his expeditionary military force to Africa, from 1975 to the end of the 1980s. This involved backing anti-imperialist forces in Angola and Ethiopia, further sealing Castro's position as head of the "nonaligned countries," even if he remained linked to the Soviet Union.

Domestically, Castro set about transforming the country along radical lines. From the early 1960s, Havana started pushing forward sweeping literacy and land reform campaigns. Cuba developed surging numbers of doctors and literacy rates massively improved, but Castro's economic reforms also critically impaired standards of living generally. This was in part alleviated by Soviet yearly subsidies which ran to the tune of between $4 billion to $6 billion, but this all changed in 1991, when Russia imported 80 percent of the island's sugar harvest.

But the end of the Cold War proved catastrophic for Castro's Cuba, not least of which was the overnight evaporation of $4 to $5 billion in Soviet subsidies. Havana's main export market since the US embargo commenced under JFK in 1962—you guessed it, was Moscow, including vital sugar where 80 percent of the harvest went to Russia. Cuba had run out of other people's money. The loss of export income sparked a "tsunami of shortages," including critical inputs like oil to keep electricity plants humming. Flush out of cash, Cuba suddenly lacked the means to import enough (80 percent) foodstuffs to prevent its people from starving. And this was a nation that before 1959 produced 80 percent of the food it ingested. Overnight, vegetables were as unavailable as meat.

The crisis without precedent, Fidel, in September 1990, told his compatriots that the patria had commenced—in one of history's great euphemisms—a "Special Period in Time of Peace," asking them, "What are we going to do? Give up? Never. Renounce socialism? Renounce independence? Never. What we have to do is resist and fight. We must resist, fight, and, of course, win." Life in Cuba, the ostensible socialist Eden was reduced to the basic imperatives of locating enough to eat three meals each day, or even just two in the worst moments of the crisis. Before it was over by 1995 (some experts contend it lasted another five years), Cuba's economy had shrunk by a third. Gasoline rationing and a total dearth of spare parts meant that buses, trucks, and even the circa 1950s American classics were sidelined, replaced by Chinese-imported bicycles with curious names like Flying Pigeon and Follow Me. (An estimated three hundred thousand *habaneros* alone out of a city of two million were issued bikes, which led to unwelcomed further weight loss but also a surge in accidents.) As the crisis deteriorated further into 1994, the Castro regime made the sanction for killing a cow without state authorization a felony equal to killing a human. Power blackouts became so frequent and so long that residents rejoiced when the electricity came back on. But as it had done even since 1959, Havana used the threat of potential American invasion as the smokescreen for its deficiencies to provide for its people.

As its communist comrades China and Vietnam slowly accepted once-noxious but now-necessary capitalism to bolster and ensure its forever grip on political power, Fidel's Cuba stubbornly held onto an anachronistic model of centralized planning and state ownership into the twenty-first century. With Soviet subsidies an increasingly distant memory, Fidel Castro turned to Hugo Chávez's Venezuela for external support and solidarity. The premise of the Havana-Caracas axis was Cuban doctors and intelligence officers in exchange for subsidized Venezuelan crude.

In 2011, for health reasons, Fidel stepped aside as secretary-general of the Cuban Communist Party, replaced by his brother Raúl. In late 2016, a remarkable ninety-years-old after ruling for more than half of that, Fidel Castro died of natural causes. It was a peaceful end for a man who had caught the attention of the world through his revolutionary zeal, personal charm, and brutally autocratic interpretation of communism. Ultimately, he was a communist who endured the demise of communism: a fact that by the time of his death, had rendered him both an icon and a relic of a world that had long since passed.

24

Ernesto Guevara

Becoming Che

There might not be a single twentieth-century Latin American figure who has captured the world spotlight as a revolutionary symbol more than Ernesto "Che" Guevara. *Time* magazine called him one of the "icons of the century," and there are legions of admirers, even today, who revere the Argentine-born Che for his preternatural courage and vision in the face of mighty Western economic imperialism, as well as his swashbuckling guerrilla style. Yet his role in the Cuba revolution also highlighted a ruthlessness that is often overlooked, and his final doomed attempt to foster a revolution in Bolivia was marked by blunders and a failure to connect with the peasant base.

ON THE ROAD TO COMMUNISM

Born in Rosario, Argentina, on June 14, 1928, Ernesto Guevara de la Serna came from a long aristocratic line of Spanish and Irish blood, even if his parents had struggled to fund their elevated social status. When Ernesto was still young, his father relocated the family to the mountain spa town of Alta Gracia to provide the boy, who was asthmatic, with a more salubrious climate. There, Ernesto's doggedness was apparent to his friends and family: to test himself, in addition to golf and shooting, he took up the oxygen-depleting sport of rugby, the cherished game of the "Anglophone upper classes of Argentina." Ernesto even wrote for the country's first publication chronicling the novel sport, *Tackle*.

Acquaintances considered Ernesto to be an "attractive oddball" bohemian iconoclast, but without any apparent political inclinations—certainly not

Marxism, which was prevalent in Latin American universities and cities at the time. However, like many apolitical Argentines, he nevertheless held a deep antipathy for the United States. As recalled by his friend Dolores Moyano, a scion of an especially rich and privileged bloodline, "In his eyes, the twin evils in Latin America were the native oligarchies and the United States. The only thing he liked about his country were its poets and novelists; I never heard him say one good thing about anything else." Yet his life would soon be unrecognizable from its privileged beginnings. Between late December 1951 through June 1952, Guevara embarked on an epic trip across Argentina, Chile, Peru, Colombia, Venezuela, and the United States with his friend Alberto Granado. The first part of the trip was on Granado's adored Norton 500cc motorbike *Poderosa II*—hence the title of Ernesto's famous *Motorcycle Diaries* (first called *Travel Notes*).

On the road, Ernesto witnessed countless examples of injustices and the excesses of US-led capitalism. Roughly halfway through their voyage, the Argentine pair found themselves in Valparaiso, Chile, when Ernesto saw an elderly asthmatic woman: "The poor thing was in a pitiful state, breathing the acrid smell of concentrated sweat and dirty feet that filled her room, mixed with the dust from a couple of armchairs, the only luxury items in her house. On top of her asthma, she had a heart condition." A week later the pair reached the Chuquicamata (or "Chuqui"), a gargantuan US-owned mine in Chile's northern desert region. Ernesto observed that "cold efficiency and impotent resentment go hand in hand in the big mine, linked despite the hatred by a common necessity to live, on the one hand, and to speculate on the other."

These experiences, and others like it, led the civilian Ernesto, at the time training to be a physician, to begin his ideological metamorphosis into communist Che, although there may have been some other interesting political shades along the way. Cuban poet Cinio Vitier cites an episode from Ernesto and Alberto's visit to a leper colony in the Peruvian Amazon where "Che spoke in a style reminiscent of [Simón] Bolívar and [José] Martí" and quotes Ernesto giving a toast for his Peruvian hosts: "We constitute a single mestizo race, which from Mexico to the Magellan Straits bears notable ethnographic similarities." Was Ernesto manifesting a Latin American nationalism or chauvinism, as was very much the case for Bolívar and Martí? (See Chapter 6,

Ernesto Guevara's first Latin America journey as recounted in *The Motorcycle Diaries*, January–July 1952. *(University of Wisconsin-Madison Cartography Lab)*

"Simón Bolívar: The Great Liberator, Flawed Emancipator" and Chapter 11, "José Martí: The Colossus of Cuba.")

Whatever the journey, the change was clear. For the author himself, the episode caused a complete break with his former self: "The person who wrote these notes passed away the moment his feet touched Argentine soil again. The person who reorganizes and polishes them, me, is no longer, at least I'm not the person I once was. All this wandering around 'Our America with a capital A' [a reference to Martí's *Our América*] has changed me more than I thought." Or as famed Uruguayan essayist Eduardo Galeano put it, "On this journey of journeys, solitude found solidarity, 'I' turned into 'we.'" In a previous edition, Che's second wife and fellow Cuban revolutionary icon, Aleida March, similarly lauded the diary's power. "The reader can witness the extraordinary change which takes place in him as he discovers Latin America, gets right to its very heart and develops a growing sense of Latin American identity, ultimately making him a precursor for the new history of America." There were also darker inklings of what was to come. In one famous passage, Ernesto writes: "My nostrils dilate while savoring the acrid odor of gunpowder and blood. Crazy with fury I will stain my rifle red while slaughtering any *vencido* [vanquished person] that falls in my hands!"

In August 1952, Ernesto returned to his family in the provincial city of Córdoba; he got his degree in medicine and surgery the following year. Only four decades later would his diary and typewritten notes be organized and published as the memoir by Che's daughter Aleida and other members of Che's family. In a *New York Times* opinion piece published in 2004, Aleida explained that while she immediately identified with the protagonist in this disorganized assembly of papers, she only later came to realize that the chronicler was her dad. Some, however, saw a more calculating design. In *Che's Afterlife*, Michael Casey claimed that *Motorcycle Diaries* was not "a diary at all but rather a deliberately constructed memoir that the young Ernesto fashioned and embellished."

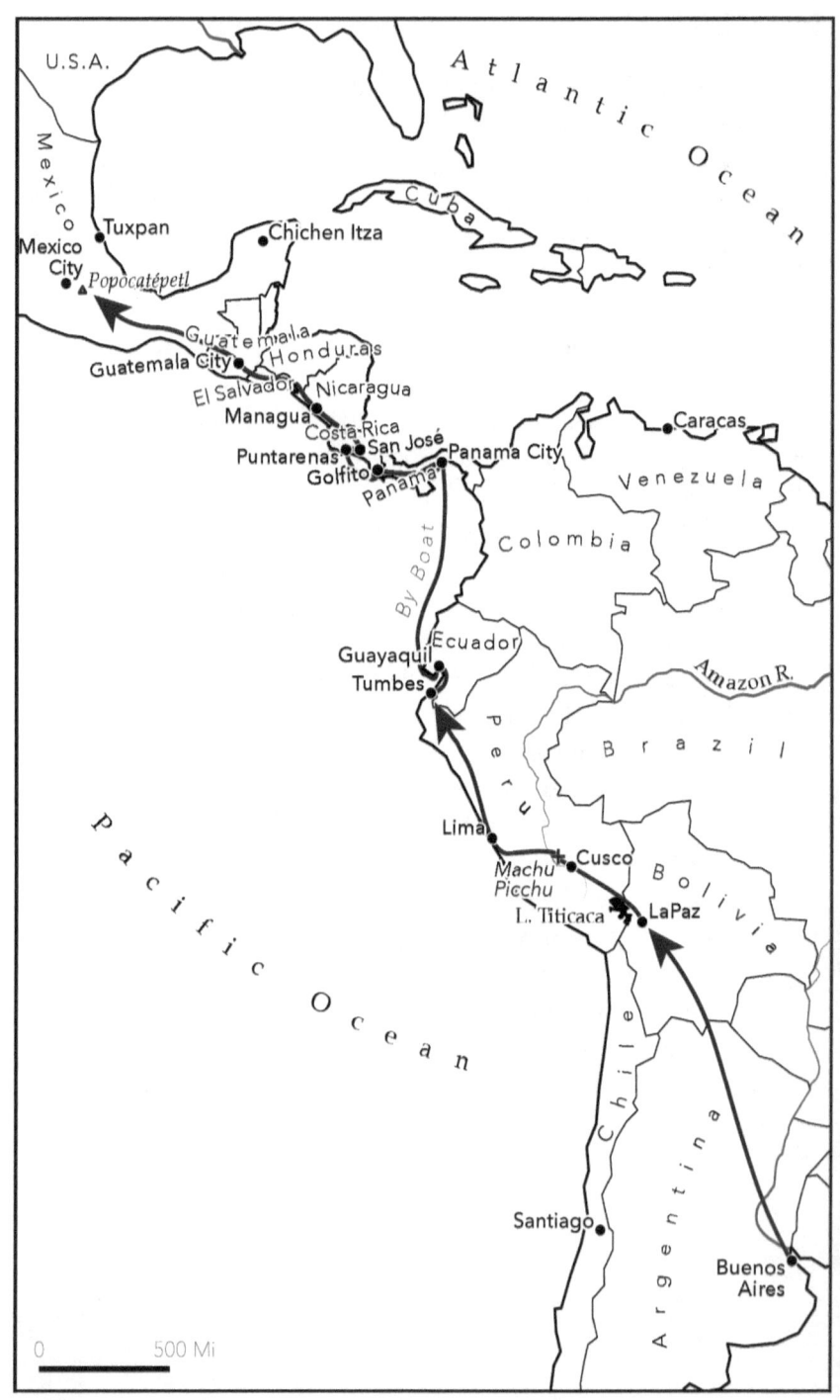

Ernesto Guevara's Latin America second journey as recounted in *Back on the Road*, 1953–1956. *(University of Wisconsin-Madison Cartography Lab)*

WITNESS TO A COUP

In 1953, Ernesto set out on another continental voyage, meeting with political parties and organizations from Bolivia and Ecuador to Panama, Costa Rica, and, most fatefully, Guatemala. In Guatemala, President Jacobo Árbenz was attempting to deepen the still-embryonic reformist path put in place by his civilian predecessor, Juan José Arévalo. (See Chapter 22, "Jacobo Árbenz: A Guatemalan Spring, Interrupted.") In 1952, Árbenz's government enacted a sweeping land reform program intended to break up the nation's notorious *latifundios* (large estates) as well as massive agrarian holdings by the US multinational United Fruit Company. For Ernesto, these bold policies gave the otherwise-impoverished Central American country "the most democratic air" in the region.

Joining Ernesto in Árbenz's Guatemala were legions of Latin American leftists, including Hilda Gadea, a "short, plump" Peruvian three years older than Ernesto who was active in the anti-imperialist party known as American Popular Revolutionary Alliance and sent into exile. Like Ernesto, but with far more political experience from her Peru activism, she held a position in the Guatemalan government, hoping to make a small difference in this noble cause. Here is Ernesto writing from Guatemala to his mother in April 1954: "I'm carrying on interminable discussions with Comrade Hilda Gadea, an aprista girl. With my characteristic tact, I've been trying to convince her to abandon that shit-eating party." As one Guevara biographer observed, their union was founded on an "intellectual and political comradeship," even if Ernesto was headed (if not there already) to communism while Gadea worshipped her Aprista (but quietly anticommunist) icon, Victor Raúl Haya de la Torre. (See Chapter 19, "José Carlos Mariátegui and Victor Raúl Haya de la Torre: Peru's Long Revolution.") There were also several visible Cubans in Guatemala, including some who had actually fought a revolution and were thus in exile from strongman Fulgencio Batista's regime. These *moncadistas* (for the Moncada Barracks that they famously attacked in July 1953) had considerable cache among the Marxist circles as veteran fighters but were nonetheless without their vital leader, Fidel Castro, who remained in prison after a judge gave him a fifteen-year sentence for the failed raid. (See Chapter 23, "Fidel Castro: A Rebel with a Cause.")

Ernesto was still in Guatemala when the CIA unleashed the most active phase of its attempt to oust Árbenz in mid-June. Ernesto breathlessly chronicled the fast-moving events filled with "gunfire and bombs" and treated wounded government supporters. In the words of Guevara biographer Jon Lee Anderson, "The invasion had begun, and with it so did Ernesto Guevara's future." By early July and roughly a week after Árbenz had gone into exile in Mexico, Castillo Armas was in the capital city, accompanied by the hardline US ambassador, John Peurifoy.

Ernesto now saw Guatemala as the first battle of what was destined to be a global conflagration between capitalism and communism. Developing a much more rigid and orthodox pro-Moscow ideology-driven "more by emotion than knowledge," Ernesto was becoming an outright Stalinist—in favor of rapid industrialization, totalitarian politics, collectivized agriculture, and a cult of party and central leader. He reflected on an earlier 1953 visit to Costa Rica, writing to his family, "I had the opportunity to pass through the dominions of United Fruit, convincing me yet one more time of how terrible those capitalist octopuses are. I have taken an oath before a picture of the old and lamented comrade Stalin not to rest until [I see them] destroyed."

And, make no mistake, he had an unshakable sense of who was responsible for the myriad injustices and repression in Guatemala and elsewhere: Uncle Sam, "the blond and efficient administrators, the Yankee masters," he wrote. He was now done with "the way in which the gringos have been treating Latin America," and that "someday the dark forces that oppress the subjugated, colonial world will be defeated." Ernesto, Hilda, and scores of other leftists would follow Árbenz to exile in Mexico.

A FATEFUL MEETING IN MEXICO

Upon arriving in Mexico City, Ernesto found work as a freelance photographer, including weddings and birthday celebrations. He also found time to assist as an allergist at a city medical clinic, but he was clearly pining for adventure. One scholar describes his wanderlust during those days: "He climbs volcanoes, visits the Maya country, dreams about Paris, where he intends to go 'swimming, if need be.' He is a 'knight errant,' a 'pilgrim,' 'an anarchic spirit,' a 'total vagrant,' a man 'ambitious for horizons.'" Mexico is also where Ernesto was reunited with Hilda, whom he married in 1955. Ernesto and Hilda had a daughter but then divorced in 1959, around which time Ernesto married his new romantic interest, Cuban rebel Aleida March.

Ernesto used these months and years to read up on Marxism and communism and supported the Soviet invasion of Hungary in 1956. He developed a professional relationship with Nikolai Lenov, a Soviet citizen who was later found to be a KGB agent assigned to Mexico City. But much more fatefully, Mexico is where Ernesto first met Fidel Castro in 1954. (Hilda liked to say that she was responsible for introducing her spouse to Fidel and Raúl Castro, but as a result, lost her husband to the revolution.) At *tertulias* (chats) he met other Cuban revolutionaries who represented what was only a few dozen individuals directly involved in the anti-Batista plot. This is where the Cubans started calling Ernesto "Che" (after an Argentine mannerism of interjecting "che"), who was given the job of being the insurrection's in-house doctor. In the early 1970s, Fidel Castro explained what led to Che joining this unbelievably risky and improbable Cuba revolution:

> [Because] of the extremely bitter experiences he lived through [in Guatemala]—that cowardly aggression against the country, the interruption of a process that had awakened the hopes of the people—because of his revolutionary vocation [calling], his spirit of struggle, we can't say it took hours, we can say that in a matter of minutes Che decided to join the small group of Cubans who were ... organizing a new phase of the struggle in our country.

CHE GOES TO CUBA

Soon after midnight on November 25, 1956, the revolutionaries struck out for Cuba aboard the rickety *Granma*. Ferocious bailing was required to keep the vessel from sinking. Unfortunately for Che, he left his asthma medicine in Mexico and suffered heavy seasickness. After a chaotic landing, Che and the Castro brothers, along with a handful of others, managed to reach the Sierra Maestra mountain range, where they set up base. Over the ensuing months, fresh and usually quite idealistic men and women journeyed to the Sierra Maestra to join up with the insurrection. Che was in charge of vetting these individuals, looking for spies or otherwise unsavory elements. He also taught literacy and political courses in these mountain lairs.

Similar to Guatemala, Che's correspondences here are revealing. In a letter to Hilda in January 1957, he described his situation as: "Here in the Cuban jungle, alive and bloodthirsty." For critics, this kind of thought demonstrated Che's transformation not into just a communist but a cold-blooded killer. It was indeed the case that during the two years in the mountains before Batista's downfall, Che personally executed or oversaw the execution of scores of individuals: "proven enemies, suspected enemies, and those who happened to be in the wrong place at the wrong time." That same month of January 1957, he shot Eutímio Guerra in the back of the head for allegedly being a *chivito*, or spy: "I ended the problem with a .32 caliber pistol, in the right side of his brain.... His belongings were now mine." In some instances, Che would fake an execution to enact psychological terror. At least one biographer thought that part of Che's extremism in carrying out rebel justice was linked to a "Calvinistic zeal" in condemning those who had fallen off the "right path." Indeed, writes Jon Lee Anderson, "He had wholeheartedly embraced the '*la revolución*' as the ultimate embodiment of history's lessons and the correct path to the future." Here are Che's reflections on the Sierra Maestra days, "[The situation] called for an iron first. We were obliged to inflict ... punishment [as a warning to others] in order to curb all violations of discipline and to eliminate the seeds of anarchy [lawlessness], which sprang up in areas lacking a stable government." There could be no shades of gray, and Che instructed his revolutionary subordinates to follow one simple rule: "If in doubt, kill him."

In July 1957, Che distinguished himself in a firefight with government forces, prompting Fidel to promote his subordinate to the position of *comandante*—the highest rank in the guerrilla army. The following year, Che led the seizure of the city of Sancti Spiritus, where he then tried and failed to impose a communistic version of *sharia* (Islamic canonical law), as journalist Álvaro Vargas Llosa writes, "regulating relations between men and women, the use of alcohol, and informal gambling—a puritanism that did not exactly characterize his own way of life." Che even tasked his soldiers to rob banks in this vicinity, which he justified in correspondence to another revolutionary leader: "The struggling masses agree to robbing banks because none of them has a penny in them."

At the tail end of 1958, Che performed a vital role in inflicting several military defeats on the government across the eastern and central regions of the island. At the battle of Santa Clara in December, Che's men destroyed roads and railways, which prevented a Cuban army effort to hold the last crucial city before Havana. After a train carrying materiel and soldiers derailed, the guerrillas moved in for the kill, making the most of their basic weaponry: "[The men] in the armored train had been dislodged by our Molotov cocktails; in spite of their excellent protection they were prepared to fight only at long range, from comfortable positions, and against a virtually unarmed enemy. . . . Harassed by our men who ... were hurling bottles of flaming gasoline, the train—thanks to its armor-plate—became a veritable oven for its soldiers."

Within days of the Santa Clara setback, Batista fled the country with friends and family for Trujillo's Dominican Republic and left the government in the hands of military subordinates like General Eulogio Cantillo. On January 8, rebels led by Castro triumphantly entered Havana to declare a revolutionary victory in front of jubilant, flag-waving crowds. The most fulsome Cuban praise was reserved for Fidel, but Che was also celebrated. One of Cuba's most-read poets, Nicolás Guillén, exiled in Argentina at the time, penned an ode titled "Che Guevara":

> As if San Martín's pure hand,
> Were extended to fight his brother, Martí,
> And the plant-banked Plata streamed through the sea,
> To join the Cauto's love-swept overture
>
> Thus, Guevara, strong-voiced gaucho, moved to assure
> His guerrilla blood to Fidel
> And his broad hand was most comradely
> When our night was blackest, most obscure
>
> Death retreated, Of its shadows impure,
> Of the dagger, poison, and of beasts,
> Only savage memories endure.
>
> Focused from two, a single soul shines,
> As if San Martín's pure hand,
> Were extended to his brother, Martí

COMRADE CHE: RUTHLESS AND IDEALISTIC

One of Fidel's first tasks for Comandante Che Guevara was to lead the military tribunals for accused Batista officials or supplicants. The setting was the notorious San Carlos de La Cabaña, an eighteenth-century citadel built to defend colonial Spain from English pirates. For the first half of 1959, Che's role as "supreme prosecutor" of the "purifying commission" was to make the final decision in such tribunals, yet for Vargas Llosa, Che's execution of anywhere between fifty and five hundred individuals was further evidence of the guerrilla's lust for homicide, citing the eyewitness account of former Basque Catholic priest Javier Arzuaga, who reported:

> There were about eight hundred prisoners in a space fit for no more than three hundred: former Batista military and police personnel, some journalists, a few businessmen and merchants. The revolutionary tribunal was made of militiamen. Che Guevara presided over the appellate court. He never overturned a

sentence. I would visit those on death row at the *galera de la muerte* (death gallery). A rumor went around that I hypnotized prisoners because many remained calm, so Che ordered that I be present at the executions. After I left in May, they executed many more, but I personally witnessed fifty-five executions. . . . I pleaded many times with Che on behalf of prisoners. I remember especially the case of Ariel Lima, a young boy. Che did not budge . . . I became so traumatized that at the end of May 1959 I was ordered to leave the parish of Casa Blanca, where La Cabaña was located and where I had held Mass for three years. I went to Mexico for treatment. The day I left, Che told me we had both tried to bring one another to each other's side and had failed. His last words were: "When we take our masks off, we will be enemies."

But Che also had much bigger ambitions than a mere purge of traitors and dissidents and pushed for a total transfiguration of Cuban society. To this end, he assumed several high-level positions, at times simultaneously, at the National Institute of Agrarian Reform, the National Bank, and, in 1961, the Ministry of Industry, all the while not relinquishing his affiliations with revolutionary militias tasked to stymie a gringo invasion.

Che with Cigar. *(Library of Congress Prints and Photographs Division, Washington, DC)*

Che's work ethic and ascetic lifestyle were legendary, from around-the-clock hosting of foreign dignitaries to the basest manual labor, designed to highlight the revolution's egalitarian ethos and principle of self-sacrifice for the collective good. Che also held that a true revolution had to immediately and permanently eliminate capitalism, especially private enterprise. He oversaw the confiscation of US-owned property—incensing these *yanqui* landholders—claiming "the only way to carry out an agrarian revolution is to take land first and worry about compensation later." Che also advocated for gains in literacy, to which end Havana deemed 1961 the "year of education" entailing hundreds of thousands of volunteers heading to the *campo* (countryside) in "illiteracy brigades," which brought the literacy rate up to almost one hundred percent from around 75 percent, although the teaching materials were deeply politicized. (History usually does not remember that the pre-1959 rate was one of the highest in Latin America.)

Che is also credited with having established Cuba's close economic ties with the Communist bloc, which started with the Soviet Union. Time and again, Moscow's willingness to purchase Cuban exports served to underwrite the Caribbean island's teetering economy. After Washington ended the remaining quota of seven hundred thousand tons of Cuban sugar in 1960, the Soviets stepped in to buy the same amount. Critics, however, point out that Che's greatest influence in the Cuban economy coincided with the island nation's economic near-collapse, though supporters cite the hardening US embargo, first hatched in 1960, that laid waste to any potential for Che's collectivization to succeed. Whatever the case, by the mid-1960s Cuba's dreams of economic independence and industrialization had been dashed, replaced by a grudging dependence on foreign powers—just this time it was Red Moscow instead of Uncle Sam.

A CALL FOR REGIONAL REVOLUTION

In 1960, Che penned the short but widely influential tome, *Guerrilla Warfare*, in which he outlines how communist revolutionaries around the world can repeat the Cuban magic. In what is almost a facsimile of Mao's 1937 work, *On Guerrilla Warfare*, Che drives home that "popular forces" can indeed beat a superior force. But Che departed from the Maoist by contending that a committed *foco* (armed nucleus of revolutionary fighters practicing rural armed insurgency) can bring about the revolution even faster than otherwise would be required. The trick for the weaker insurgent fighters is to win the so-called hearts and minds of the rural population, who then become a potent military asset. As Che describes, the hard life of these rural peasants makes them prime candidates for revolutionary conversion: "[This] great mass earns its livelihood by working as peons [servants] on the plantations for the most miserable wages, or they work the soil under conditions of exploitation indistinguishable from those of the Middle Ages.... These are the circumstances which determine that the poor population of the countryside constitutes a tremendous potential revolutionary force."

Critically for Che, the *focos* could not show any weakness against their imperial foes. In a seminal 1960 address to the First Latin American Youth Congress, Guevara said that weakness had been the downfall of Jacobo Árbenz's Guatemala (who was in the audience now that he was living in revolutionary Cuba). The Cubans, by contrast, had decapitated in one stroke those in power, resisting calls for moderation. "'Moderation' is another one of the terms colonial agents like to use," Che contended. "All those who are afraid, or who are considering some form of treason, are moderates.... [But] the people are by no means moderate."

Che also further developed the idea that Cuba's revolution could be replicated via the foco method in other areas of Latin America—a hypothesis that did not go unnoticed by the United States. In February 1959, the acting US ambassador Daniel Bradock issued a report titled, "Cuba as a Base for Revolutionary Operations against Other Latin American Governments," which stated: "A number of leaders of the successful revolutionary movement in Cuba consider that efforts should now be undertaken to 'free' the people of some other Latin American nations from their 'dictatorial' governments. While Ernesto 'Che' GUEVARA Serna is generally regarded as the principal force behind such thinking, and is indeed active in the planning, he is far from alone. Fidel CASTRO has reportedly made remarks along such lines, particularly during his recent visit to Venezuela."

With Fidel's green light, Che convened "prospective revolutionaries" from across the hemisphere eager for Cuban training (and funding) to precipitate their own insurgencies. In some of these cases, the countries targeted by Che's *foquista* plots—like Bolivia, Argentina, Colombia, and especially Venezuela— either had (albeit imperfect) electoral democracies or had experienced widespread agrarian reform, or sometimes both, but for Che, such middle-of-the-roadways fell short: only a communist utopia was acceptable.

In the case of his native Argentina, Che sent a foco contingency led by the former Argentine journalist Jorge Ricardo Masetti right about the time the country was experiencing a wave of democratic reform via the ballot box. In less than a year, Masetti—who had increasingly turned into a madman—had disappeared, and his Che-inspired foco revolution had turned into an unmitigated disaster. Historian Enrique Krauze chronicles the unbelievable collateral damage of these focos, including the myriad of counterinsurgencies who emerged to crush them: "The thousands of young men and women who took to the mountains in emulation of him, to create 'the new man' or meet death as martyrs; the sequel of desolation and slaughter left by the guerrilla wars and their suppression from Mexico to Argentina."

As history would prove, Che's foco strategy was fatally flawed. Other than the Sandinistas in Nicaragua in the late 1970s, every single Che-inspired revolution failed, at the cost of many lives and significant destruction. Che's blind spot just might have been that he did not realize how relatively easy a regime he faced with the almost universally loathed Batista, whose army, according to Álvaro Vargas Llosa, "was not an army, but a corrupt bunch of thugs with no motivation and not much organization."

CHE'S LAST ADVENTURES

Perhaps surprisingly, Che's first attempt at putting his foco strategy into practice was not in Latin America, but in Africa. In late April 1965 Che and a band of Afro-Caribbean Cubans dismounted on the shores of Lake Tanganyika to aid the political heirs of the murdered Congolese nationalist Patrice Lumumba, but their mission was doomed almost from the start. For one, the Africans did not take to a didactic outsider, and Cuban lectures were ill-received. Guevara lamented to Fidel: "The soldiers are of peasant stock and completely raw, for whom the main attraction is to have a rifle and a uniform, sometimes even shoes and a certain authority in the area. . . . Lazy and undisciplined, they are without any spirit of combat or self-sacrifice."

Che abandoned his African adventure and returned to Cuba in 1966 to refocus his energies on Latin America, especially Bolivia. Like the Congo case, however, in many aspects Bolivia didn't fit the archetypal model of a country ready for a foco-led revolution. Moreover, any desire for a leftist revolution had most likely already been exploited in the 1952 revolution, which had at least partially addressed common demands like land redistribution.

Nonetheless, Che and his gang of guerrillas marched into Bolivia but were seriously hindered by their poor preparation. Lacking an equipped base camp in the Andean mountains, the guerrillas (numbering at this point only a few dozen Cubans, Bolivians, and several Peruvians and other foreigners) were forced to carry their revolution east to the country's underpopulated and inhospitable Gran Chaco region, where revolutionary fervor was underwhelming. Matters were not helped by the fact that Che's guerrillas had received instruction in the Quechua language, but locals in the new region spoke Guaraní. As a result, the insurgents were barely able to communicate with the locals and were unable to sway them toward the cause, resulting in a lack of material support and solidarity. The region's peasants even labeled the insurgents as gringos because of their peculiar speech and thick beards. The revolutionary hopefuls were alone, isolated both physically and ideologically.

Despite everything, Che did manage to lead a successful expedition against the Bolivian government in spring 1967, albeit at a price. The topography was a greater adversary than the government, with thick jungle and roaring rivers making Cuba's Sierra Maestra look like a bucolic summer camp. Not having accurate maps, the guerrillas squandered supplies and, more important, morale during their misguided expeditions. A fruitful ambush of an army patrol offered vital weapons and supplies, yet gave away the rebels' position to spotter planes and helicopters.

When the tide began to turn against them, the insurgents found they couldn't shake the bloodhound Bolivian military, no matter how deep into the jungle they fled. Their cover was soon blown, too, when the Bolivian strongman René Barrientos condemned the rebels as agents of "Castro Communism." With the nation against them, the rebels grew increasingly dispirited under their crestfallen leader. The guerrillas' ranks dwindled as men were either captured or killed. In April Che summarized the bleak situation facing the group: "[Our] isolation appears to be complete, sickness has undermined the health of some comrades, forcing us to divide forces, which has greatly diminished our effectiveness.... The peasant base has not yet been developed."

In August 1967, a US Special Forces Mobile Training Team consisting of sixteen Green Berets under Major Ralph "Pappy" Shelton came to help Barrientos in his hunt for Che. Shelton repurposed a former sugar plantation and trained four hundred Bolivian conscripts who were to be tasked with taking down Che's battered foco, and by September 1967 a Bolivian Ranger force was

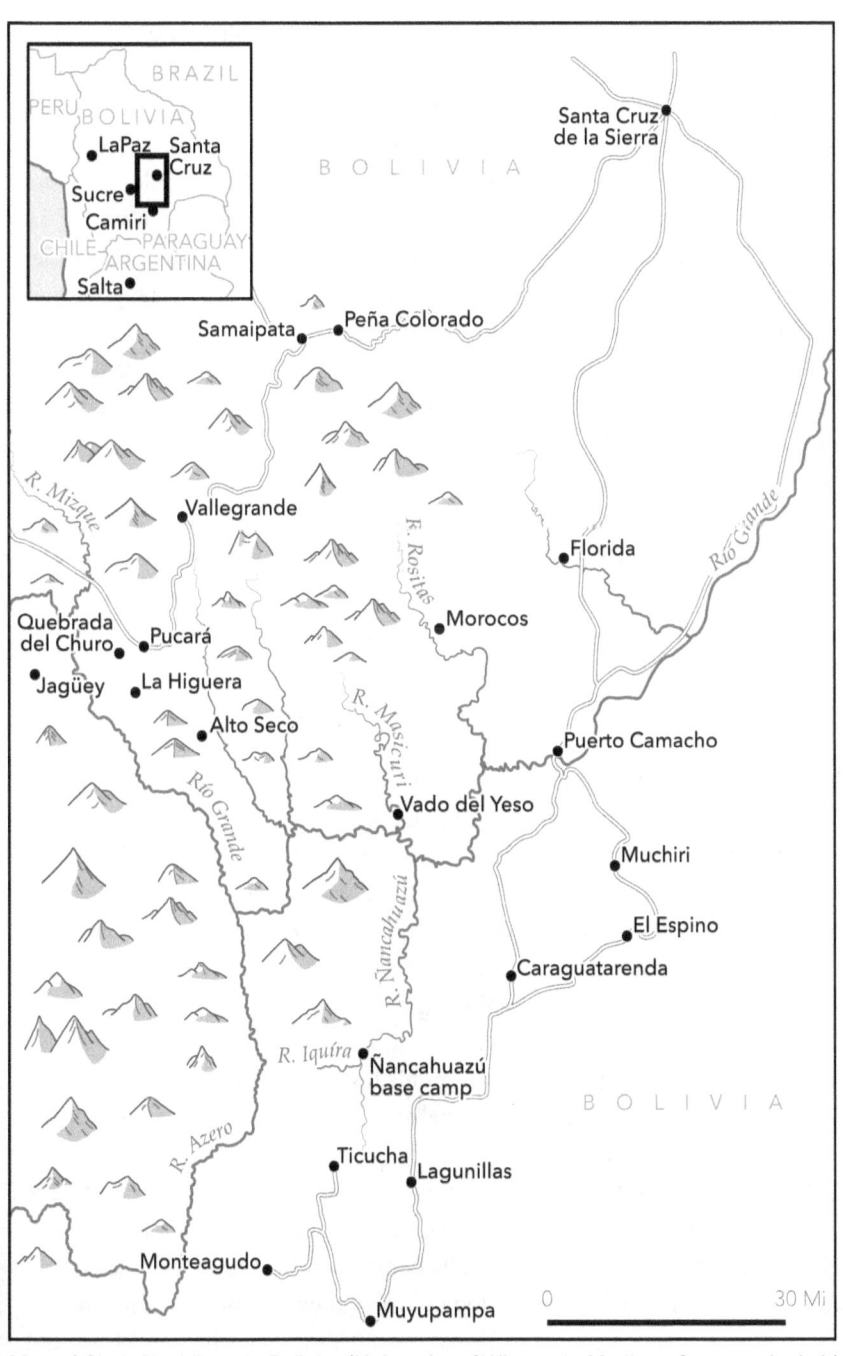

Map of Che's Final Days in Bolivia. *(University of Wisconsin-Madison Cartography Lab)*

ready to deploy. For good measure, the CIA also scrambled its operatives to create another Bolivian unit. Among the agents recruited was a young Cuban American paramilitary operative named Félix Rodríguez, who had earned Washington's admiration by leading a communications unit of CIA-funded anti-Castro commandos out of Nicaragua since 1963. Meanwhile, Che and his battered band of guerrillas set their sights on the remote town of La Higuera. Notably, during this final leg of Che's Bolivia campaign, the leader contradicted nearly all of the major rules of foco insurgency strategy, such as avoiding roads and sticking to the cover of forests.

The end was not long in coming: by early October, the US-trained 2nd Ranger Battalion had surrounded Che's men at La Higuera and taken the wounded Che prisoner. Rodríguez soon arrived by helicopter and documented the dilapidated state of the distinguished revolutionary: "He was a mess.... Hair matted, clothes ragged and torn." Despite Rodríguez's alleged effort to take him alive, on October 9 Che Guevara, thirty-nine years old, was executed by gunshot by a bitter Bolivian army sergeant eager to avenge the casualties of his fellow soldiers in the pursuit of a communist icon. The insurrection was over.

AFTERMATH

Paradoxically, it seemed that Che in death had won more supporters in Washington's patio than in the US backyard. On October 21, 1967, twelve days after Guevara's death, an estimated fifty thousand Americans stood in silence at the Lincoln Memorial. Faces of Che dotted the crowd as demonstrators carried signs with his image. Even more perplexing were the cool reactions from Moscow and Beijing, who were not only disinterested in the communist icon's death but even critical of his final escapades. A poignant indication of how Cuban-style focos had fallen out of favor in non-Western communist realms, public Soviet channels poured scorn on his taste for "adventurism," while the Chinese press criticized the Argentine for allowing the gun to control the party and not vice versa.

With the death of Che the revolutionary came the acceleration of Che the icon, which has led to an interesting paradox. More than a few Marxist guerrillas in Central America in the 1980s considered Che to be their guardian angel, and he is part of the mythology of revolutionary and resistance movements from Central America to Nepal, East Timor, Palestine, and Iran. But he is now also a recognizable "brand" whose famous 1960 photograph adorns products the world over. His face is worn by people who may have no idea of his struggle and history, other than that he represents something "counter" to the mainstream—failing to realize that his mass-produced image is now very much *of* the mainstream.

Perhaps nothing captures better the perplexing and contradictory ways Che has been interpreted than an episode in 2008, when Colombian commandos dressed in Che t-shirts to fool hostage-holding guerrillas into thinking that the rescuers were sympathetic Marxist revolutionaries. The captors did not for a minute doubt the rescuers' rebel bona fides. More than almost anyone else, Che's image carries the aura of revolutionary leftist authority, but in today's hyper-capitalist world, that is just another commodity for sale.

25

Manuel Marulanda
Founding Father of the FARC

In May 2008, readers around the world learned about the death of septuagenarian Pedro Antonio Marín, far better known as the mythical Manuel Marulanda Vélez—the Colombian peasant who rose to the highest rung of Latin America's most formidable Marxist guerrilla insurgency, the Revolutionary Armed Forces of Colombia (FARC). At the height of its powers, Marulanda's FARC was an exceptionally well-armed, highly lethal fighting force of seventeen thousand men, women, and children which effectively controlled over 40 percent of the country. But right up until his death, the guerrilla figure maintained the traits of a Colombian campesino: "cautious, stubborn, resilient and distrustful" of the urban denizens, which helps explain why the FARC never took off in the cities, where most Colombians resided. And, similar to the guerrilla Shining Path in Peru (See Chapter 35, "Abimael Guzmán and Shining Path: The Philosophy of Terror"), his communist revolutionary army never won the hearts and minds of the rural population either—the very key to a successful insurgent strategy. The group's longevity was instead a result of its military potency, and, later, the huge volumes of cash generated by Colombia's cocaine boom.

A COMMUNIST GUERRILLERO IS BORN

Pedro Antonio Marín's early life was profoundly shaped by the schism between Colombia's two leading political parties, the Conservatives and Liberals. Indeed, the Andean nation experienced eight civil wars and more than a dozen provincial rebellions in its first century of existence, and the instability persisted into the twentieth century. Exacerbated by the assassination of a populist firebrand Liberal politician, Jorge Eliécer Gaitán, on April 9, 1948, the period of civil strife known as La Violencia led to the deaths of hundreds of thousands of Colombians and the displacement of many more.

Gaitán's killing had an immediate impact on teenage Pedro Antonio: that April, Conservative forces went door to door in his home pueblo of Génova looking for Liberals to eliminate. Being a loyal Liberal, he picked up a gun and began organizing a rag-tag "self-defense" force, later explaining "In those days, to take up arms was the only way to survive." (The future guerrilla legend recalled being an eyewitness to one grisly slaughter in a far-flung pueblo that left almost three hundred Liberal adherents dead, their bodies consumed as carrion.) By the early 1950s, however, he had abandoned the Liberal Party for communism and assumed the *nom de guerre* Manuel Marulanda Vélez, in honor of a slain communist labor organizer.

La Violencia lasted until 1957 when the Liberal and Conservative elites brokered a power-sharing agreement they called the National Front. But if the civil war was winding down, Marulanda's war was just getting started, spurred in part by the new government's eagerness to get rid of communist groups after Fidel Castro seized power in Cuba in 1959. Marulanda, for his part, blasted the National Front as a thinly veiled rapacious oligarchy. After creating a new guerrilla unit, he helped establish an "independent republic" of Marquetalia, a remote hamlet to the east of where he had grown up. In 1964, the Colombian military razed Marquetalia and almost captured Marulanda and his comrades (perhaps forty in total).

Marulanda became convinced that only armed revolution could overthrow the central government and install a Marxist state. Using Marquetalia exiles, Marulanda formally founded the FARC in 1966 and was named a member of its general staff. While communist, the embryonic guerrilla group claimed that it was not part of the Colombian Communist Party. "We're independent," said one leader, "we don't depend on them nor are we going to dissolve the day they say, 'FARC, dissolve.'" The sui generis *guerrillero* commander also took dressing in trademark campesino garb: long-sleeved plaid tops, white t-shirts, pants tucked into high rubber boots, a white towel over one shoulder, and machete and pistol holstered around the waist. Marulanda was an extraordinary military tactician, while his skill as a rifleman earned him his nickname, Sureshot.

Manuel Marulanda. *(Marcelo Salinas)*

In these early years, the FARC still only had several hundred poorly armed men and women in its ranks. They fought a typical guerrilla war in the mountains and jungles, operating according to a "Strategic Plan" that emphasized the need to control key segments of the rural population. This they accomplished through a tremendous dispersal of guerrilla forces into regional "fronts" and "blocs" across Colombia's vast and often inhospitable territory. Once established, the insurgents deployed propaganda to indoctrinate the rural poor and selectively threatened and killed members of the propertied class—mostly large-scale farmers and cattle ranchers. One FARC tactic that was a particular source of consternation was "miracle fishing." Insurgents would set up roadblocks throughout the country and demand national identity cards from motorists they saw. When they hooked a "big fish"—anyone who appeared to have financial means—they kidnapped him or her and demanded a ransom.

By the end of the 1970s, FARC guerrillas held dominion over the sprawling, sweltering Middle Magdalena valley, but the FARC leadership deduced that total victory in Colombia would ultimately require developing a serious political force to seize power in the cities as well—part of a strategy known as "the combination of all forms of struggle." As part of a series of peace talks that ultimately foundered in the early 1980s, the FARC created a legally constituted political party, the Patriotic Union (UP). Between 1984 and 1988, when support for the party was at its peak, the FARC added around a dozen new military fronts, doubling in size. Not coincidentally, a large number of these new fronts arose around cities where the UP held the mayor's office, with some reckoning that municipal funds were making their way into rebel coffers to finance the new units. It also happened that many UP strongholds were also bastions of coca production.

FARCLANDIA

During the cocaine frenzy of the late 1970s and early 1980s, the Pablo Escobar-led Medellín Cartel discovered that the raw coca leaves they were shipped in from Peru and Bolivia also grew exceptionally well in Colombian soil. (See Chapter 38, "Pablo Escobar: The First Drug Lord.") The cartel's operatives in rural agricultural regions in the Amazonia region encouraged farmers to increase their plantings. Soon enough, a poor peasant could raise his paltry income by a factor of ten by switching from licit crops to coca. Cultivation soared and cash piled up in these hitherto desperately poor regions.

The Cali and Medellín cartels controlled this domestic coca-growing industry, dictating the terms of trade and sending buyers into jungles to purchase semi-refined paste. But, beginning in the 1980s, the FARC began to establish a more forceful presence in these areas. Ironically, for much of its existence, Marulanda and the senior command had considered the drug business counter-revolutionary and feared that drug money would corrupt its adherents. Yet, with money always in short supply, the FARC leadership finally changed course in 1982 and began taxing drug producers and smugglers, starting at 10 percent per kilogram of coca base. The rebels also collected fees for every drug flight that left the areas under their control. As the FARC gained a foothold in other parts of the country, they extended the tax to marijuana and opium poppy growers. When they took the southeast, the FARC levied a fee on coca plantings. This virtually limitless revenue source fueled a two-decades-long military expansion.

Once the Medellín and Cali cartels were decapitated by the Colombian state in the 1990s, the FARC was the only major player left standing. They enjoyed effective dominion over the first stages of the cocaine production chain, and the atomized organizations that emerged in the cartels' absence turned to the guerrillas for security. At the same time, the relative success of US-supported crackdowns in Peru and Bolivia drove the illicit agricultural production over the border into rural Colombia; coca production in Colombia surpassed that of Bolivia in 1995 and Peru in 1997, much of it in the FARC-controlled eastern plains and Amazon basin, making the nation the world's largest supplier of coca leaves. Once covering only a few thousand acres, Colombia's coca plantings spiked to four hundred thousand acres annually by 2000, producing upward of 680 tons of cocaine. For the FARC, this was a gift made in white gold. The insurgency was at one point believed to reap USD$500 million a year from the drug business.

Swollen with these revenues, in the mid-1990s Marulanda launched a vicious new stage of its revolutionary war. In August 1996, guerrillas attacked and destroyed a military base in the remote jungle region of Putumayo. Fifty-four Colombian soldiers were killed, seventeen were wounded, and sixty were taken prisoner. In late December 1997, the FARC bombed a military intelligence base, taking eighteen soldiers captive and once again embarrassing the political elite and military brass in Bogotá. Then, in a stunning move, in March 1998 the FARC decimated an entire elite army unit in Caquetá department after villagers relayed the soldiers' whereabouts to guerrilla spies. Within forty-eight hours, 154 soldiers were killed.

Emboldened by this success, Marulanda imagined seizing larger cities, including Bogotá, and from there, the entire country. To strike fear in the Colombian nation, the guerrillas started bombing electrical towers to cut off electricity in Bogotá. The situation was so dire that in 1998 the US Defense Intelligence Agency secretly estimated that the FARC and its drug-trafficking allies would be able to overthrow the central government and convert Colombia into a "narco-state." While this scenario was unlikely, the important thing for the FARC leadership was that the Colombian people believe such a proposition was possible.

With the nation paralyzed by the offensives, Conservative presidential candidate Andrés Pastrana campaigned in 1998 on a platform of peace, promising to negotiate an end to the conflict with the FARC. In May, his Liberal opponent, Horacio Serpa, won a plurality, but not a clear majority, and a second round was scheduled for June. A few days before the decisive national election, media outlets were abuzz with the image of Pastrana's peace advisor meeting Marulanda, providing compelling evidence that the FARC had decided which of the two candidates it would make peace with. Less than a week later, on June 21, 1998, the Colombian people elected Pastrana with a strong majority.

Pastrana's and the electorate's bet that the FARC wanted peace was not unreasonable given so many believed that Marulanda's insurgency had maximized its military gains and now wanted to get out of the business of war, but it soon became clear that the cost of downing guns would be very high. As a precondition to peace talks, the FARC made an unbelievable demand: a demilitarized zone of over sixteen thousand square miles, about the size of Switzerland. Pastrana granted the request, much to the outrage of his political opposition in Bogotá. The official easing zone was often referred to as "El Caguán," given its location in the Caguán River basin. Others called it *el despeje*, or the clearing. But the most popular and enduring name for this state-within-a-state by far was simply *Farclandia*.

In January 1999, Pastrana took the risky step of traveling to a FARC stronghold in the eastern part of the Andes to inaugurate peace talks with Marulanda. It was an astonishing inversion of precedent: the newly elected head of state, in effect, was being received by a belligerent force in its own territory. But the FARC leader failed to appear despite the "home court" locale, and a humiliated Pastrana was left sitting next to an empty chair. Formal peace talks did finally kick off two days later, but the FARC suspended them again, noting that rightist paramilitaries had increased their offensive maneuvers. That May, Pastrana decided to reauthorize the despeje, against the advice of his defense minister, who promptly resigned, and the seventeen generals and two hundred colonels who threatened to follow him.

Pastrana's increasingly impotent administration repeatedly returned to the despeje to negotiate, while the FARC launched brazen attacks across the country. In July 1999, over four thousand FARC troops left El Caguán to assault military bases and isolated towns in five regions. The following year, FARC commandos killed Diego Turbay, head of the Congressional Peace Committee. As the months dragged on, and a deal receded further out of sight, it became increasingly evident that the FARC was not interested in peace. It had used the negotiations to buy time while they exploited the despeje for a massive expansion of coca growing and cocaine processing. Meanwhile, they invited luminaries, including the CEOs of AOL and the New York Stock Exchange, to observe a carefully curated selection of the FARC's activities in the region and to pressure Bogotá into ending the war on favorable terms. In other parts of the autonomous zone, it later became clear, bomb-making experts from the Irish Republic Army were teaching FARC operatives how to make crude gas cylinder bombs. The FARC was also busy deepening ties with Mexico's

Tijuana Cartel and Brazilian cocaine smugglers. In 2001, an incarcerated Brazilian drug trafficker, Luiz Fernando Da Costa, revealed to Colombian agents that the FARC had assisted him in smuggling more than two hundred tons of cocaine to Brazil the previous year, levying a "revolutionary tax" of $500 per kilo and $15,000 per drug flight.

PLAN COLOMBIA AND URIBE'S "WAR FIRST" POLICY

But during the late 1990s and early 2000s, the balance of power was slowly beginning to shift, in part due to the Clinton administration's multibillion-dollar military and economic aid package known as Plan Colombia, designed to combat the US crack cocaine scourge at the root. US policy in Colombia in the two decades before Plan Colombia was already centered on interdiction, but despite a few high-profile successes, the explosion in coca production and a concomitant surge in violence had the Colombian state on the ropes. Plan Colombia attempted to save the country by drastically escalating the drug war methodology and did produce results. After 2000, Colombia's military (with US assistance) managed to gain some control, and security improved.

Another factor in the turning tide was President Álvaro Uribe, a former governor of the Antioquia department who claimed that in 1982 the FARC had killed his father in a botched kidnapping attempt. Uribe was elected in 2002 on the promise to establish security in all areas of the country, a platform notably supported by Colombian elites (predominantly of European descent and 37 percent of the population) who, having been generally insulated from the country's misery, had begun to be affected by the insurgent violence as it encroached into the cities. Uribe quickly capitalized on the support of this influential power base, imposing a one-time war tax on wealthy citizens (1.2 percent of liquid assets) that raised over $1 billion.

With the security forces swelling in numbers, materiel, and lethal capability, Colombian military convoys now began opening up key highways by placing an armed soldier every kilometer or so. Enhanced air mobility allowed the security forces to chase FARC bands across high, craggy mountain ranges and thick jungles. Not surprisingly, Uribe's hardline approach was controversial. Critics believed that it simply used violence to fight violence. Yet for many Colombians, who had seen the embarrassing failure of Pastrana's peace-building effort during the previous four years, Uribe's "war first, peace later" approach was exactly what was required.

And it appeared to be working. Operations during the presidencies of Uribe and his successor, Juan Manuel Santos began to inflict heavy casualties

Map of Colombia. *(University of Wisconsin-Madison Cartography Lab)*

on FARC's ideological leadership, especially with the use of precision-guided missiles. This began in March 2008, when the military attacked a FARC jungle camp just over the border in Ecuador. The raid was controversial in that it violated Ecuador's sovereignty, but it killed Raúl Reyes, the FARC's second-in-command. The raid also recovered FARC laptop computers full of incriminating information—most sensationally, the group's clandestine relationship with Venezuela's President Hugo Chávez. The FARC sustained another heavy blow a few weeks later without a shot being fired when Marulanda died of a heart attack.

In September 2010, the Colombian military unleashed a ferocious raid against the second-in-command and chief military strategist of the FARC, Victor Julio Suárez, known universally by his second nom de guerre, Mono Jojoy. Employing thirty planes, twenty-seven helicopters, and more than thirty tons of explosives (including fifty precision-guided munitions), Operation Sodom ended in the death of the most feared man in the country, wanted for over one hundred separate crimes. President Santos ebulliently called the strike a "turning point" and "the beginning of the end for the FARC."

FARC soldiers, most of whom were forcibly recruited into the guerrilla ranks in the first place, began fleeing. Deserters reported that hunger was often what drove them to flee, even though they faced certain death if the FARC captured them. At times, the military debriefed deserters and then reinserted them into FARC ranks without the guerrilla commanders' even noticing they had left in the first place. These "plants" provided critical on-the-ground intelligence to the Colombian security forces. Illicit trade revenues also plummeted. By 2015, the FARC could wreak only a fraction of the havoc it had only a few years ago, and at last, decided to enter into a peace process with the state. The 2016 peace deal between ten FARC guerrilla groups and Bogotá represented a major step toward bringing the fifty-year internal conflict to an end, although the smaller National Liberation Army did not sign the deal, and there had been further episodes of violence.

The insurgency that Marulanda helped found had morphed into a very different beast by 2016, one whose Marxist ideology was increasingly compromised by the group's ties to drug trafficking and allegations of human rights violations (though the Colombian state was not immune from such violations either). Over the intervening fifty-odd years, Marulanda was often a shadowy figure, leaving little in the way of written or spoken communique, yet in his shrewd duplicitous handling of Pastrana, he perhaps helped the group achieve the acme of its power—as well as sowing the seeds of its downfall.

26

Salvador Allende

"All Things to All Men"

Chilean democracy is a conquest by all of its people.
—*Salvador Allende*

It's that son of a bitch Allende. We're going to smash him.
—*Richard Nixon*

The story of Salvador Allende is one of idealism and political moxie that took him to the heights of power in Chile's constitutional democracy, yet his socialist tendencies won him powerful Cold War enemies, not least the United States, which supported efforts to prevent him from winning in a democratic election in the 1960s. He eventually overcame the odds in a stunning 1970 electoral victory and assumed office despite Washington's covert machinations to prevent him from taking the presidential sash. An avowed Marxist, his socialist program preached a radical but democratic, nonviolent "transition to socialism," but soon ran into difficulties, exacerbated by US support for the Chilean president's critics and opponents, internal and external. Without having completed three full years in power, he was deposed in a coup led by General Augusto Pinochet (see Chapter 27, "Augusto Pinochet: The Unlikely Model Dictator"), and rather than surrender or flee, he chose to commit suicide. His short but dramatic tenure as president has been poured over by historians, searching for the truth amid the competing narratives, together with the question of what might have been had he stayed in power.

"I AM GOING TO BE PRESIDENT OF CHILE"

Born in 1908 into an upper-middle-class family with leftist political instincts and allegiances, Salvador Allende came of age and attended school in the gritty port city of Valparaíso. A precocious and curious teenager, Salvador was certainly not plagued with self-doubt, declaring "I am going to be President of Chile." As one biographer put it, his "ambition and self-confidence border[ed] on arrogance." He smoothed this over with self-deprecating quips and spontaneous jokes but his temper could be ferocious. The stylish dresser and lithe athlete was an inveterate womanizer (a trait shared with his father). Picking up his medical degree from the University of Chile in 1933—he chose medicine over law since he thought it would help serve "the most poor and needy"—the twenty-something physician embraced Marxist ideology and politics.

Allende's early life and political career overlapped with an especially heady time for politics, ideology, and debate in Chile, with the country riding a wave of reform. Chile's seminal modern constitution, approved in 1925 in a plebiscite by 134,421 voters, in addition to upholding the separation of church and state, created an institutional framework for a variety of social sectors—such as peasants and urban workers—that the old oligarchic system had ignored or excluded.

In 1932 and with the economy flagging in the aftermath of the Wall Street crash of 1929, socialist plotters enacted a coup d'état, which forced the sitting president to resign and dissolve Congress. Jubilant revolutionaries then proclaimed the Socialist Republic of Chile, which barely lasted one hundred days, but the regime's forty-point program—which included five hundred thousand free meals for the jobless; foreign bank deposits seized by the state; amnesty for political prisoners; and establishing diplomatic ties with the Soviet Union—showed socialists and other leftists, including Allende, what could be accomplished.

The following year, Allende became a founding member of the Socialist Party of Chile, two decades after its both rival and ally, the Communist Party of Chile was established. The Socialist Party was a motley assortment of social democrats, anti-imperialists, Trotskyists, and former Communists who had rejected the Communist Party's submission to the doctrinaire Soviet Union. In 1937, Allende won a spot in the Chamber of Deputies, before serving as health minister in a leftist government. Then in 1945 he became a senator, a position he would hold until 1970. And it was in the Senate where he became an activist for the left-wing issues dear to him: workers' rights; a wider social safety net; and the nationalization of US-owned copper mines.

In the decades following World War II, Chile enacted a series of reforms to open the political and electoral space: female enfranchisement in 1949; the secret ballot in 1958 ("a devastating blow," author Barry Gewen writes, "to the landowners in the countryside, who previously had been able to keep a close eye on cowed tenants"); compulsory voter registration in 1962; the elimination of the literacy prerequisite in 1964; and lowering of the voting age to eighteen. Consequently, the registered voter rate soared from a sorry 13.7 percent to 44 percent between 1950 and 1973; in 1970, over eight out of ten eligible voters were registered to vote. Chile in this period had become the most democratic country in Latin America.

Yet Chile's democratic awakening occurred simultaneously with a plunge in economic conditions: rural and city jobs grew scarcer, and in the countryside, wages plunged almost a quarter from the mid-1950s to the mid-1960s. Seasoned foreign visitors who had come to admire Chile's outsized political gains were aghast at this society on the precipice of economic and social chaos; despite a more civic, broadly prosperous democracy and economy the country had splintered into haves and have-nots. Professor Frederick B. Pike, an astute contemporary observer, fretfully concluded: "The profound consequences of the social problem have created in Chile two distinct modes of existence separated by well-nigh unbreachable barriers." He went on to warn of the possibility of "a devastating social revolution."

COZYING WITH CASTRO

Into this heady political milieu came Salvador Allende: in Gewen's words, "compassionate, romantic, unbending, undisciplined, manipulative, hedonistic, naïve, theatrical." Régis Debray labeled him an "immaculate socialist militant." Seasoned US ambassador Nathaniel Davis called him "all things to all men." But even his most ardent supporters would acknowledge that he did not hold the sharpest intellect. The US envoy Edward Korry once quipped that "economically, he was almost an illiterate." Allende fancied his variant of socialism as mild, "with the savor of empanadas and red wine."

Allende encountered a very different kind of leftist politics during a visit to Cuba in 1959, where he met Communist firebrand Fidel Castro. (See Chapter 23, "Fidel Castro: A Rebel with a Cause.") It was a bit of a culture shock for the

Chilean bon vivant: "There were peasants playing chess and cards, lying on the floor, machine guns and all"—all a far cry from Allende's buttoned-down parliamentary environs. Fidel and Salvador would strike up a personal amity that would last under the latter's death, and Allende returned to his native homeland more committed to a Cuba-style path of economic "revolution" (although not necessarily Che Guevara–like guerrilla insurgency), while his connections with Havana bolstered his revolutionary bona fides on the radical, revolutionary left.

Soon after the 1959 successful ouster of Cuban strongman Batista, Castro returned the courtesy and visited Chile, where Allende told him that "the Chilean people have been aroused and deeply moved by the Cuban revolution," and that although each nation might have its own means, all were "marching toward a common goal." Raising alarm bells in Washington, Allende stated that "Cuba in the Caribbean and a Socialist Chile in the Southern Cone will make the revolution in Latin America."

It is important to remember that for all his solidarity with Castro, Allende wasn't a Communist naïf. The Soviets, who had long-standing ties to the Chilean communists, had worked with Allende and the socialists since the early 1950s, with the KGB, eager to poke Uncle Sam in the eye in its hemisphere, ready to "provide any necessary assistance." Yet Allende—a Socialist and not a Communist—by no means took his command from the Russians. Not unlike Castro in Cuba after 1959, Allende could often be a "problematic and unpredictable" ally of Moscow, a fact demonstrated by his opposition to the Soviet crushing of the tanks of the 1956 Hungarian Revolution. In the end, Moscow might have given cash to Allende, but it couldn't buy the affirmed but stubbornly independent Marxist. For their part, Moscow never considered Allende's Chile to hold the strategic value of Castro's Cuba: a fact reflected in the respective amounts of Soviet aid; while Cuba was showered with $4.1 billion in economic aid between 1967 and 1972, one estimate puts Moscow's outlay to Allende at $183 million between 1971 and 1973, with an additional $110 million from the Eastern Bloc and $65 million from Mao's China.

Such distinctions were arguably lost on Washington, with both the John F. Kennedy and Lyndon B. Johnson administrations viewing the prospect of Allende in power as anathema to US national security interests. In 1964 Foreign Service Officer wrote a cautionary memo to Kennedy's national security advisor, McGeorge Bundy: "Another 'Castro' in the hemisphere, particularly one who achieved power through the democratic process . . .

would be awfully tough to handle from both the international and domestic standpoints. This would clearly be a case where one and one totaled much more than two and the consequences throughout the hemisphere of a second Castro would be serious."

PRESIDENT ALLENDE, FINALLY

Allende first threw his hat into the presidential ring for the 1952 election but came away with a minuscule 5.5 percent of the vote. His performance improved dramatically in the 1958 election, now backed by the Communist Party, and he got exceptionally close to winning, garnering 29 percent versus winner Jorge Alessandri, a moderate conservative, who received 31.2 percent. If it hadn't been for the fact that rightist parties had given cash to an outlying candidate, whose 3 percent share could have easily gone to Allende, he could have won.

It was all getting a little close for Washington's comfort, but the rise of the Christian Democratic Party (PDC), founded in 1957 for Eduardo Frei Montalvo's presidential bid, offered a useful vehicle for anti-Allende influence. By 1963, the PDC was Chile's largest political party, with a swelling appeal to the recently enfranchised mass sectors. The party, of which Frei was on the moderate side of the moderate wing of this heterogeneous party that ranged from centrist to left-wing, cared about the poor and downtrodden as the Marxists and communists did but lacked their atheism or anticapitalist and class warfare element. They called their approach "communitarianism," or sometimes "Communitarian Socialism," which emphasized the connection between an individual and the community and that the government should play a role in overcoming societal injustices and ruptures.

This sounded good to a lot of Chilean citizens in the 1960s who were torn, as Gewen writes, between "looking for ways to reconcile economic growth with social justice or political protest with traditional values." And for an anxious Washington, the Frei/PDC rise could not have come a moment too soon, with the 1964 election looming. Washington's involvement started with covert (or "nonattributable," in CIA parlance) assistance to the PDC in 1962, but then expanded greatly, involving "incredible sums of money" as election day 1964 neared: cash for campaign publicity, cash for aligned labor and women's syndicates and groups, and cash for bribes. A White House aide reflected in July 1964, just two months before the September 4 vote: "We can't afford to lose this one, so I don't think there should be any economy shaving in this instance. . . . Let's pour it on and in."

And pour it did, with half the PDC's budget coming from the CIA. (This was the conclusion of the so-called Church Committee, a 1975 Senate inquiry into US covert operations that included the assassination of Dominican caudillo Trujillo and anti-Allende actions.) (See Chapter 18, "Rafael Trujillo: 'Our S.O.B.'") But it didn't stop there: according to the Church Committee, the CIA "mounted a massive anti-Communist propaganda campaign. Extensive use was made of the press, radio, films, pamphlets, posters, leaflets, direct mailings, paper streamers and wall painting." In one week in June 1964 alone, the agency cranked out scores of daily radio ads; longer "news updates" were aired several times a day on three separate capital city stations.

All in all, the CIA spent $3 million to influence the outcome of the election, and it paid off. In an effective two-person race, Frei bested Allende by a handy seventeen-point margin, fifty-six to thirty-nine, in a two-candidate race as the Conservative Party did not run a candidate that year. Critically, women voted for Frei over Allende, two to one. Frei thanked the United States for the support, but even the PDC leader had no notion of its extent, while the CIA patted itself on the back for being one of the "indispensable ingredients in Frei's success." (The extent to which Moscow and Havana were backing Allende in this same election is not fully clear, but there was support.)

After the victory, the United States was keen to keep the momentum going, pouring over $500 million in direct loans, aid, and grants during Frei's term, making Chile the highest per capita recipient of Washington's (anticommunist) largesse in Latin America. As for Allende, after losing three elections on the bounce, he jokingly claimed that his epitaph would read, "Here lies the next President of Chile."

Often left out of history is that despite his US backing, there was a lot that was revolutionary, socialistic, and even Marxist impetus in Frei's presidency between 1964 and 1970. Once in office, Frei moved to enact (as promised) a sweeping reformist agenda, his "revolution in liberty": land reform benefiting peasants; the Chilean state gaining a majority stake in the US-owned copper mines; a wealth tax and more progressive taxation system (which almost doubled taxes as a percentage of GDP, from 13 to 21 percent); soaring investment in primary care clinics and hospitals; housing projects for the poor, backed by a 70 percent raise in public construction funding; and a doubling in education spending, helping the nation's secondary school enrollment to hit 49 percent in 1970 (from 18 percent in the early 1960s). By 1970, the number of Chileans

Chilean President Salvador Allende at the United Nations in New York City, December 4, 1972. *(Library of Congress Prints and Photographs Division, Washington, DC)*

in unions swelled to half a million; Frei even established diplomatic ties with Moscow and the Eastern Bloc.

But despite these beneficial gains, Frei ended up losing support. His revolution in liberty was too radical for Chile's conservatives and too timid for the Marxists. For example, Frei wanted to buy the US mining companies using a process he labeled "Chileanization," while the far-left wanted full-scale confiscation. Allende damningly dismissed Frei as a rightist "reformer." By 1970, the left, right, and middle of Chilean politics were all disgruntled. Frei's "Third Way" had not succeeded sufficiently to usher in a new centrist-leftist political movement. What's more, the right and left were both energized and radicalized. Six years prior, conservatives had supported Frei's Christian Democrats to stymie an Allende win. This time around, though, the right would not play ball, instead supporting former president Alessandri, the 1958 victor. Christian Democrats were unable to renominate Frei given it was banned by the constitution, instead tapping the vapid Radomiro Tomic, who was further to the left than Frei.

Allende was determined to run again in the September 4, 1970 election and supported by the Communist Party under the banner of the Popular Unity (UP) coalition, further stoking Washington's anxieties about the prospect of a winning paradigm for communism through the ballot box. In July 1968, six months before Republican Richard M. Nixon took office, the CIA hatched a "modest covert program," placing anti-Marxist propaganda in the media to back nonleftist "individual electoral factions." By subtly helping build a congressional majority, the CIA hoped to stymie the radical political agenda of a possible Allende presidency. As the CIA's official history put it, "The objective was to divide the left and create conditions for a non-Marxist candidate to win the elections. . . . The plan was to alert the Chilean people to the dangers of a Marxist regime under Allende."

But the CIA's plotting could not check Allende's growing popularity. On election day, the veteran campaigner won a plurality of the vote (36 percent), just ahead of Alessandri (35 percent), while Tomic came in third with 28 percent. While subsequently giving him precious little assistance, the Soviets hailed Allende's stunning victory as being "second only to the Cuban Revolution in the magnitude of its significance as a revolutionary blow to the imperialist system in Latin America." And unlike Castro, Allende had won power in a democratic election in a constitutional system, the first Marxist to do so, even if he had garnered a lower percentage of the electorate than in 1964, The big difference is that the 1970 election had three major candidates, not two, allowing Allende to squeak out a constitutional win! "He called himself a Marxist, but a democrat as well." Nothing was more disturbing for Washington than the prospect of an elected Marxist with a popular mandate—and they were keen to do something about it.

OFF TRACK

Nixon loathed the prospect of an Allende presidency. In mid-September he met with National Security Advisor Henry Kissinger, CIA Director Richard Helms, and other top foreign policy officials to consider what to do. Kissinger supported his boss's view: "I don't see why we need to stand by and watch a country go communist due to the irresponsibility of its people. The issues are much too important for the Chilean voters to be left to decide for themselves." Helms later recalled that Nixon pledged to "save Chile" from Allende's destruction via a preventive coup, "even if the chances [were] one in ten" of such a plot succeeding.

There was a window of opportunity. As no candidate had won a majority, tradition stipulated that the election be decided via a congressional vote held on October 24, giving the Nixon administration ample time to "open its bag of dirty tricks," and two anti-Allende plans were born. The State Department and the CIA drew up a scheme for Chile called Track I, a secret diplomatic effort to have the Chilean congress refuse to endorse Allende's win and instead confirm the runner-up, Alessandri, as president. Nixon also ordered the CIA to initiate a second secret program, Track II, which coordinated with three rebel military groups, including the extreme rightist paramilitary group Homeland and Liberty, who were plotting pre-inauguration coups to keep Allende out of office. Track II was so confidential that not even the US ambassador in Santiago was briefed on it. Langley, the headquarters of the CIA, sent instructions to the CIA station in Santiago on October 16: "It is firm and continuing policy that Allende be overthrown by a coup. . . . We are to continue to generate maximum pressure toward this end, utilizing every appropriate resource. It is imperative that these actions be implemented clandestinely and securely so that USG and American hand be well hidden." The CIA did warn the executive branch that this was going to be a dicey effort: "You have asked us to provoke chaos in Chile. . . . We provide you with a formula for chaos which is unlikely to be bloodless. To dissimulate the U.S. involvement will be clearly impossible."

The CIA quickly discovered that the idea of a military-led coup was out of the question due to the Chilean military's respect for constitutional democracy, even if the high brass had supported a coup in 1924. (Ironically, the chief obstacle to a victorious military coup in Chile was the military!) Most emblematic of this constitutionalism was the deep opposition to a revolt of the Chilean army commander-in-chief, General René Schneider. As the conservative scholar Mark Falcoff put it, "His view, simply stated, was that since the politicians had gotten the country into the mess in which it found itself, the politicians would have to find a way out."

The CIA hastily tried to identify willing Chilean military personnel, like the retired general Roberto Viaux, a vain and mercurial retired officer who had links to Homeland and Liberty, to remove Schneider and clear the way for a military coup. But Kissinger reportedly wasn't enamored of Viaux's plot, claiming in his memoirs that he had told Nixon he'd "turned it off." Critics counter, however, that there is no record of Kissinger making such remarks in the meeting's minutes. Meanwhile, the CIA kept working on possible alternatives. According to declassified CIA documents, on October 19 the agency delivered tens of thousands of dollars and guns to one of the rebel groups (which one is not clear) to keep the covert plot against Schneider "financially lubricated." The CIA also delivered three submachine guns to a group led by General Camilo Valenzuela, who, after failing to convince General Schneider to join him in a coup attempt, wanted Schneider sent out of the country. However, Valenzuela's men would never get the opportunity to put the CIA-supplied weapons to use, as Viaux's group struck first.

On October 22 Homeland and Liberty officers attempted to hit the military hard by kidnapping Schneider while he was heading to work in the morning but wound up killing him—the first political assassination in Chile in at least a century and a half. Only hours after Schneider had been shot, Langley sent a congratulatory cable to the Santiago office: "The station has done [an] excellent job of guiding [the] Chileans to [the] point today where a military solution is at least an option for them." (For "military solution," read a putsch against Allende.) Showing how one hand of US policy worked while the other was blind, Ambassador Korry sent repeated cables to Foggy Bottom reporting that his embassy did not have any contact with Patria y Libertad, yet Korry was ignorant of the fact that the military attachés under his command had orders to engage this shady quasi-fascist group. Even one observer sympathetic to the US involvement acknowledged, "What is beyond debate is that the U.S. government, despite a lack of any operational control, was inextricably linked with the plot, to its eternal shame."

Almost everyone who has closely studied Track II has concluded that it was an unmitigated failure in terms of Nixon's desire to forestall Allende's inauguration. The Schneider killing led to the appointment of his fellow constitutionalist General Carlos Prats on October 22. Prats also believed in the legitimacy of Allende's election and opposed a military coup, and his appointment ultimately "discredited right-wing cabals both inside the army and out." Chileans lined up behind Allende, or at least the notion of him being the legitimate president-elect, even if they disagreed with him politically. There was no longer any appetite by Chilean brass, no matter how radical, for a Track II–style pre-inauguration coup.

On October 24, 1970, two days after the assassination of Schneider, the Chilean assembly formally endorsed Allende as president-elect, 153–35. While Allende's plurality may have been razor thin, such "minority" vote leaders (that is, lacking an absolute majority) had been features of the nation's democratic fabric for over a century, and the Chilean assembly was maintaining the democratic norm. Less than two weeks after Schneider's assassination, Allende was sworn into power.

ALLENDE'S SOCIALIST EXPERIMENT TURNS SOUR

As he settled into the highest office, Allende wasted little time in moving forward on an aggressive leftist economic agenda. During his first twelve months in office, Allende nationalized the mining sector (a good share of it US-owned), over three-quarters of the banks, and the textile and fishing sectors, among others. In November 1971, he declared a moratorium on foreign debt repayments. Allende also obtained control of the nation's phone entity, in which the US corporation International Telephone and Telegraph Corporation (ITT) had a majority stake. ITT would months later privately deliver a detailed plan to topple Allende to the White House, but the Nixon administration did not act on it.

Allende's "distributive" policies, as economists call them, helped jumpstart the anemic economy: gross national product surged by 8 percent, industrial production by 12 percent. They also massively increased state control over the economy, with one study estimating that the state oversaw 90 percent of the gross domestic product. Some of the radicalism was done legislatively—the copper nationalization, for example, was done through a congressional bill that passed unanimously—but there were also instances of more strongarmed tactics. Allende's Chilean Road to Socialism was also burning through reserves. After taking power, his UP government exhausted almost all the $500 million Frei's team had left in the treasury coffers; total foreign debt roughly doubled to $4 billion.

On the social side of policy, one noteworthy and controversial reform was the administration's push to infuse the "values of socialist humanism" into public and private school curricula. The education minister got the idea from the East German education system, sparking fury among domestic opponents, including a Catholic Church official who warned that it would ensure Chile's pedagogy was dictated "by a partisan ideology." The education issue represented one of the first times the church had publicly opposed Allende.

Another issue during the Allende era was freedom of the press. For some socialists, news sources had to be used to usher in a "new culture and a new man." Radio, television, and newspapers felt as though Allende had it out for them, especially the staunchly anti-Allende *El Mercurio*, the country's largest daily. The president allegedly limited its access to newsprint and forced a wage hike to smash the paper's coffers, but Washington ensured that would not happen, sending the paper between $1.5–$2 million out of the $7 million in secret aid spent between 1970 and 1973.

But Allende had far bigger problems than bad press. As intended, Allende's policies benefited Chile's poorest: health care became more widely available and infant mortality decreased; land expropriations, predicated on Frei's 1967 agrarian reform law, increased vastly. In the first phase of his presidency, the unemployment rate halved and was at a record low of 8 percent, while food consumption moved up by a quarter. Here is one historical take in praise of these developments, "In many a modest Chilean family . . . the Allende years will be remembered as the time when the first school was built . . . or when the poorly fed children of the family suddenly began to receive medical attention and half a litre of milk a day." (Some forty-eight million liters of milk were distributed in 1971 alone.)

The rub was that outside of Allende's not-insignificant base of the poor, Chileans were feeling squeezed by inflation: a 20 percent rate in 1971, rising to 78 percent the next year, and 353 percent in 1973—the highest rate in the world at that moment. The distributive policies, as intended, had put pesos in the hands of the poor, who then spent them—which was great for them but not great for the inflation rate, which was effectively a cut in purchasing power, or wages. Having scared off foreign investors (some scared off by Washington), Allende's UP government lacked foreign exchange reserves, and without a majority in congress, the UP also couldn't use legislation to raise taxes, so it simply printed more money—again making inflation worse. Allende's use of price controls to check the rampant inflation sparked shortages of basic goods, with Chileans queuing to purchase tea and toilet paper.

Inflation hit the middle class (and even parts of the working class) particularly hard. In early December 1971, as many as thirty thousand mostly middle- and upper-class women took to the streets for the first consequential protest against Allende's government. Later called the March of the Empty Pots, protestors banged empty pots and pans, chanting, "There is no meat; there is nothing." Some protestors were even pelted with stones or worse, leading to a curfew and state of emergency. Allende's backers called them spoiled brats, and the Secretary-General of the Chilean Communist Party, Luis Corvalán, struck a baleful tone, "The workers of Chile are determined not to permit the Fascist hordes to control the streets again;" Corvalán urged Marxist organizations in the cities and countryside to "mobilize" militia forces. In May 1972, the CIA was reporting that Allende was arming his supporters throughout the country. Shadowy rightist paramilitary outfits were setting off bombs.

With inflation and scarcity surging, anti-Allende protests and strikes increased in 1972. That August, store owners declared a twenty-four-hour strike that became unruly, precipitating another state of emergency. Then in October 1972, the country's truck drivers' union embarked on a twenty-six-day strike protesting what they perceived as the government's attempt to nationalize the transport industry. The strike was a disaster for the Allende administration, paralyzing the county and costing the economy some $200 million. Many have subsequently seen evidence of shady North American dealings, namely that US operatives compensated the truckers so that they would strike and paralyze the long, thin country's economy, which relied overwhelmingly on road transportation. A month before another truck strike commenced in August 1973 the truck drivers' union reached out to the US for assistance. The 40 Committee, the high-level executive branch team responsible for the issue, did not approve direct aid but, in the words of one US official, funds "could have filtered [down]" to the striking truck drivers via local field operatives in receipt of CIA cash. In April 1973, copper miners—ceased working, a strike that lasted about eight weeks. Seeing as how the miners were the aristocracy of the Chilean working class given they were paid higher wages, their walk-off was an especially significant and unexpected development. (A good share of Chile's workers were rapid supporters of Allende's UP.) That same year, middle-class professionals and taxi drivers did so as well.

A CONTESTED COUP

In a 2014 *Foreign Affairs* piece, Jack Devine, a former CIA operative, recalled the polarized political climate inside Chile he found after being assigned to Santiago: "Rumors of a military coup against the socialist Chilean president, Salvador Allende, had been swirling for months. There had already been one attempt [in June 1973, by junior military officers and quickly suppressed by their constitutionalist superiors]. Allende's opponents were taking to the streets; rightist paramilitary groups were being established. Labor strikes and economic disarray made basic necessities difficult to find. Occasionally, bombs rocked the capital. The whole country seemed exhausted and tense." Despite the fraught domestic climate, the March 1973 midterm saw the UP *increasing* its share of the vote to 40 percent, up four points from 1970. So even months before the coup, the president enjoyed considerable popular support.

In a momentous move, on August 22 the Christian Democratic-chaired Chamber of Deputies voted eighty-one to forty-five in favor of a resolution stating that Allende's government was unconstitutional for its overreach. On September 9, Devine sent a cable marked CRITIC, the highest priority, to Langley: "A coup attempt will be initiated on 11 September. . . . All three branches of the armed forces and the *carabiñeros* [national police] are involved in this action." Devine argues that this is "how the U.S. government learned of the coup in Chile."

That same August, General Prats was pushed aside by the high command; the *golpistas* (anti-Allende coup plotters) now controlled the military. The military revolt was led by the president's newly installed top military commander, General Augusto Pinochet, who quickly took control. By midafternoon on September 11, the Allende-led resistance had been quelled. The president committed suicide before he could be killed or captured. Pinochet established a military junta. The Christian Democrat Frei, now a senator, welcomed the coup, arguing that Allende had been taking the country toward a dictatorship.

To what extent the United States was responsible for the coup has been hotly contested. In Devine's analysis, "The Chilean military moved against Allende not because the United States wanted it to do so but because the country was in disarray. . . . The generals decided to take charge of the coup plotting to maintain discipline in Chile's military institutions and to preserve stability." The longtime Allende coup researcher Peter Kornbluh offered a fierce rebuttal (also in *Foreign Affairs*) of Devine's interpretation of events, but he concurs with Devine that Washington "did not directly participate in the coup." To Kornbluh, the far more crucial question is the extent to which Washington sought to bring down Allende by fomenting conditions "in which a collapse or overthrow may be feasible," and how much the CIA's programs "influenced the political environment and contributed to Allende's downfall."

Kissinger's and Nixon's assessment of the US role is ambiguous yet suggestive. "In the Eisenhower period we would be heroes," Kissinger said in a September 16, 1973, telephone chat with his boss, referring to the operation by Eisenhower and the Dulles brothers that toppled Guatemala's Jacobo Árbenz.

(See Chapter 22, "Jacobo Árbenz: A Guatemalan Spring, Interrupted.") Nixon added, "Our hand doesn't show on this one though." Kissinger clarified, "We didn't do it, I mean we helped them. [Word omitted] created the conditions as great as possible." Kornbluh for one finds Kissinger's comment alone proof positive of "what really happened in Chile," while Devine counters that a statement from Nixon or Kissinger about Chile "doesn't make it true," given that it is "hardly uncommon" for politicians to "take excessive credit for developments they see as positive"—or vice versa.

Interestingly, Devine concedes Kornbluh's take on the CIA's role in fomenting coup conditions: "Against all odds, the Santiago station had helped create a

Chile! The September 20, 1973, cartoon by artist Oliver Wendell Harrington shows Richard Nixon as an executioner, wearing nothing but a loincloth labeled "CIA," standing beside a guillotine. The body of a beheaded woman labeled "Democracy" lies on the guillotine. In addition to his celebrated cartoons, the multiracial Harrington was a prominent civil rights activist. *(Library of Congress Prints and Photographs Division, Washington, DC)*

climate for the coup without tainting the effort by becoming directly involved. In the heady days immediately following, we took pride in having helped thwart the development of Cuban-style socialism in Chile and having prevented the country's drift into the Soviet orbit." The vital historical unknown, of course, is whether the coup plotters would have acted without US coup conditioning. With 300 percent inflation, rampant strikes, food shortages, and the plotters' iron-clad sense that Marxist cancer had metastasized inside the Chilean body politic, the answer is a qualified yes. As historian Peter Winn argues in his splendid work *Weavers of Revolution*, Allende's revolution from above was far too cautious for the legions of UP militants who wanted a radical revolution from below. It is also important to keep in mind that the solid share of Chileans who backed the anti-Allende coup did so under the not-preposterous assumption that the armed forces would restore order and call for fresh elections.

PINOCHET: DICTATOR

Like many Chileans, the CIA believed that Pinochet's new junta would rule temporarily before calling elections and thus return the country to democracy. Instead, Pinochet's dictatorship lasted for seventeen years and tortured and killed thousands of its citizens: 1,200 in the first months following the coup and a total of around 3,100.

The horrific course of Chile's post-Allende history gives rise to the burning counterfactual question as to how Allende's presidency would have turned out had Nixon not initiated Track II or fostered coup conditions. The scholar Kenneth Maxwell argues that "left to their own devices, the Chileans might just have found the good sense to resolve their own deep-seated problems. Allende might have fallen by his own weight, victim of his own incompetence, and not become a tragic martyr to a lost cause." But while apologists for the CIA's actions in Allende's Chile readily acknowledge that the agency's operations succeeded in "reducing support for Allende," they also emphasize that the "fierce opposition" to Allende came from within the country—particularly when the sitting president's "flawed economic policies" that initially stimulated the economy began to falter.

Ultimately, the overthrow of Allende in 1973 can be thought of as a Cold War Rorschach Test, where both sides tend to see what they want to see. That the United States was involved, albeit indirectly, is uncontestable; how directly efficacious its fostering of "coup conditions" were in leading to the overthrow of the Allende administration is perhaps still open to debate.

27

Augusto Pinochet

The Unlikely Model Dictator

History teaches you that dictators never end up well.

—*Augusto Pinochet, 1998*

Augusto Pinochet is one of the twentieth century's most infamous figures. As one foreign correspondent put it, "He looked the archetype of a Cold War Latin America dictator, with sunglasses, small moustache, and defiant stare." He ruled Chile with an iron fist for close to two decades, a period in which tens of thousands of regime opponents were tortured and another three thousand murdered or "disappeared."

But he was in many ways an unlikely candidate for the role of dictator, having spent decades in obscurity and providing no indication that he harbored burning political ambition. Indeed, he seemed a status quo figure, which convinced President Salvador Allende to appoint him as commander-in-chief of the army (see Chapter 26, "Salvador Allende: 'All Things to All Men'"). But in 1973 he betrayed Allende and took power in a dramatic coup, promising to eradicate communism from the country and revive the country's economy. Deeply influenced by his wife Lucía Hiriart, he brutally repressed opposition and adopted radical free market policies. Defeated in a landmark 1988 referendum, he nevertheless had sufficient influence to resist all efforts to prosecute him before he died in 2006.

"ASSASSINS, FASCISTS!"

On September 21, 1976, an especially sultry morning in Washington, Orlando Letelier, the forty-four-year-old former Chilean ambassador to the United

States under socialist Salvador Allende's democratic government, was driving to work at the Institute for Policy Studies, a left-leaning policy think tank. An economist who was sent to multiple detention camps after the 1973 coup, Letelier was also the most influential Chilean exile living in the United States. Riding alongside was his twenty-five-year-old work colleague Ronni Moffitt and her husband, Michael.

As he sped down Massachusetts Avenue, a remote-controlled explosive hidden underneath the car detonated. The burning vehicle skidded to a stop near the Romanian embassy. In a commemorative piece marking the fortieth anniversary of the attack, the *Washington Post* painted a graphic picture of the carnage: "There was blood and debris everywhere and a human foot in the roadway. A fatally wounded man lay on the pavement; his legs were missing from above the knees."

The man was Letelier, who would live only a few more minutes, shouting, "Assassins, fascists!" before he died. Ronni Moffitt drowned in her own blood from a shrapnel cut to her throat. Miraculously, Michael was uninjured. In the *Post*'s account, Letelier and Moffitt were victims of a "brazen, perhaps unprecedented" state-sponsored terrorist plot on American soil to assassinate Letelier, orchestrated by one of the United States' principal anticommunist allies in Latin America: General Augusto Pinochet of Chile.

TOY SOLDIERS

Augusto José Ramón Pinochet Ugarte was born in the coastal port city of Valparaiso on November 25, 1915, the son of disciplinarians Augusto Pinochet Vera, a customs agent of Basque and French Breton blood, and Avelina Ugarte Martínez, a pious Catholic. The family lived in the countryside for a few years before Augusto returned to Valparaiso with his parents, while his siblings stayed put. One interpretation of this development is that Augusto simply could not tolerate the notion of being separated from his mother, who was a driving force in his life and enrolled him in 1928 in one of the oldest private schools in Latin America, the Catholic Sacred Hearts. A mediocre student with a disposition for painting but no aptitude for athletics, Augusto's braying laugh earned him the nickname "Donkey," although it also could have been due to his reputation for being dim-witted.

His step-grandfather of French descent might have been responsible for getting the youth fascinated with French emperor Napoleon Bonaparte—and thus an early interest in pursuing a military career. Augusto endlessly played with toy soldiers and watched in awe the military parades that would pass by his home, later lauding "the uniforms and martial nature" and the "way they treated people according to his rank." Despite his father wanting him to study medicine, it was therefore unsurprising that, despite his mother's wishes, Augusto opted for the Military Academy in Santiago, although he was rejected twice before finally being accepted in 1933. And it was here where one of his teachers gave him the advice that he appeared to dutifully follow for four decades: "Never to be outstanding in your career because you will be envied by others; also don't be the last. To progress in the military career, keep just in the middle, in the anonymous masses."

In 1937, the cadet graduated with the rank of second lieutenant in the infantry. In 1943, he married Lucía Hiriart, ten years younger at twenty-eight and a redoubtable individual and daughter of an influential politician congressman and an antimilitarist. Sick and tired of feeling socially inferior because of the military marriage, Lucía convinced her husband to resign from the army and join her father's private sector firm, but Augusto missed the rigid military culture and within half a year had returned to his vocation. Frustrated in her plan, Lucía nevertheless resolved to make the best of the situation and henceforth became deeply involved in her husband's career, relentlessly exhorting him to gain the couple more influence and status—and, in the manner of Lady Macbeth, reminding him that great ends might require unpleasant means.

AN UNLIKELY ELEVATION

Pinochet embarked on a steady but no means meteoric rise through the infantry ranks, attaining the rank of major by 1953. There were stints teaching at the War Academy and he authored an unmemorable book or two. Revealing his singular carelessness and intellectual mediocrity, Pinochet wrote a report for the Army War Academy that included a map of the Southern Cone with such appalling errors that it had to be recalled lest it jeopardizes some of Chile's long-standing territorial claims. In 1968, Pinochet (now a colonel) published a volume, *Geopolitical*, that included a map of North America that showed the US capital on the Pacific Coast, suggesting that the officer had confused Washington state and Washington, DC. By 1971 and at the age of fifty-five he was a general, although there was nothing special about him to set him apart from other career officers.

Crucially, however, he was awarded the post of commander of the Santiago army garrison in 1971, a position of significant power as the capital became the epicenter of domestic political turbulence. President Allende had run into serious political headwinds by the end of 1971: bare store shelves and skyrocketing inflation were sapping the president's popular support, while the CIA was providing covert support to antiregime operatives and organizations. At the end of 1972, a general strike froze the capital, leading Allende to call upon Pinochet to restore order through a curfew and targeted arrests of both leftist and rightist agitators. This was the first encounter ordinary Chileans had with the "tall, broad-shouldered" military commander with a "brush mustache on his unsmiling face." And Pinochet's steely message to the citizenry: "I will not tolerate agents of chaos no matter what their political ideology."

Pinochet's stock rose even further in June 1973 during an attempted military coup known as the *Tanquetazo* (as they utilized tanks in their attack on the presidential palace, La Moneda). Although the coup attempt failed almost im-

General Augusto Pinochet (*right*) and Fidel Castro stand next to each other in Santiago during, in late 1971, the Cuban leader's controversial twenty-three-day state visit. *(Alamy Stock Photo)*

mediately, Pinochet was literally at Allende's side through some tense moments, which only served to reinforce the president's trust in his subordinate. Other developments also paved the way for Pinochet's dramatic rise. Commander-in-Chief General Prats, a pro-Allende constitutionalist who believed in the separation of the political and military realms, was under pressure from anti-Allende military brass; in fact, on August 21, 1973, the wives of military officers noisily demonstrated in front of his residence to humiliate him into stepping down. Two days later, a beleaguered Prats resigned. His recommendation for a putatively loyal constitutionalist replacement? Yes, Pinochet, who was promoted immediately. According to Prats, "I believed that if General Pinochet succeeded me—having so much loyalty toward me—there was a possibility that the critical situation of the country would tend to unwind."

The reaction to the news was mixed. A right-wing magazine, *PEC*, predicted that the inept Pinochet would last just weeks or months as the top army chief, saying that his reputation was as "a man with a loud voice toward those below him, but with zero voice regarding those above him." When Pinochet told Lucía that Allende had appointed him commander-in-chief, she assumed he was joking.

PINOCHET TAKES CONTROL

Pinochet's apparent loyalty to Allende and the Chilean constitution meant that he was initially excluded from discussions within the military over a new coup attempt, but then, just seventy-two hours before the coup was slated to commence, Pinochet received an ultimatum from the commanders-in-chief of the navy and air force to participate or be treated as an enemy. Pinochet later revealed that his wife beseeched him to join the plotters, lest he be left out of power in the post-coup climate. "She turned to me and said, 'They [our grandchildren] will be slaves because you haven't been able to make a decision.'"

Just eighteen days after he had been promoted by Allende, Pinochet led the early morning September 11, 1973 coup against Allende. As the British-made Hawker Hunter fighters rained bombs on *La Moneda* palace, Allende, now in battle dress, worried about the fate of his supposedly loyal army chief: "What have they done to poor Pinochet?" But unknown to his president, Pinochet was taking control of the coup. A civilian aide reflected years later, "He realized what had dropped into his lap and had no alternative but to follow it through." At one point during the radio-transmitted negotiations with Allende to secure the beleaguered president's capitulation, Pinochet chillingly quipped that they should probably just go ahead and allow Allende to depart the country in a plane but then shoot it out of the sky. "Kill the bitch and you finish the spawn," he said. But President Allende refused to surrender, instead committing suicide in La Moneda with the Kalashnikov gifted to him by Fidel Castro.

In the aftermath of the coup, the four leaders of the armed forces branches—army, air force, navy, and police—agreed to alternate the top position of the junta's governing council; astutely, Hiriart urged her husband to be the first leader. Right after the coup, General Prats fled to Buenos Aires. A year later, he and his wife were assassinated in a car bomb attack personally ordered by Pinochet.

THE JUNTA CRACKS DOWN

It is worth noting that at the time a good share of both Chile's assembly and population supported the putsch, believing it would end the Allende chaos and pave the way for fresh elections and a quick and permanent return to constitutional democracy. But the reality was very different. The junta's initial crackdown on leftist opponents was ruthless, with tens of thousands arrested within the first weeks and months, scores of whom were tortured or killed. Of the 3,200 officially killed during his rule, half were murdered in the first year, including hundreds at the National Stadium. Up and down the country, scores of concentration camps were created. The Caravan of Death, a Chilean army death squad that flew across the country in the aftermath of the coup, killed over seventy-five victims. In some instances, the victims were drugged before being pushed out of helicopters over the Pacific Ocean, stomachs sliced so the bodies would not float.

By 1974, boldly pushing aside the other junta generals, Pinochet had consolidated his position as the sole leader of the country. He suspended political parties, censored media, shuttered Congress, proscribed workers' unions and strikes, and voided the constitution. The rank of captain-general, previously only given to the nation's founder Bernardo O'Higgins, was resurrected for Pinochet. The cult of Pinochet had been born, etching in the public imagination the story of a figure led by the "mysterious hand of God" who had striven to ensure that Chile was "the only country in history to have broken free from the yoke of communism."

Some observers contend that Pinochet's deft manipulation of the regime's power and privileges allowed it to avoid the factionalism and drama of other regions' myriad other military dictatorships. Also relevant is that the Chilean army, trained by nineteenth-century Prussian officers, was traditionally one of the most hierarchical and disciplined in the Americas, which facilitated its otherwise inexplicable personal fidelity to Pinochet. And once again, the guiding hand of his wife was also significant. Whether it was appointing or dismissing government ministers or military officers, Hiriart came to have a well-earned reputation for wielding outsized power in La Moneda.

Keen to expand the military's footprint to tackle communism, Pinochet appointed retired military personnel as deans of universities, who then conducted purges of suspected leftists. In a crucial move, he merged rival intelligence outfits into the feared National Intelligence Directorate (DINA), placing the obscure Army colonel Manuel Contreras in charge. DINA became the primary vehicle for tracking, apprehending, and killing subversives at clandestine detention facilities, sometimes in other countries. Osvaldo Romo, an infamous torturer, years later provided horrifying testimony about his work: among myriad heinous methods was the "electric grill" that saw nude prisoners strapped to a metal bedframe and tortured with electrical shocks to the hands, feet, and genitals.

Tens of thousands of Chileans fled into exile, including Michelle Bachelet, who would go on to become president of Chile in the twenty-first century, and her mother. (See Chapter 42, "Michelle Bachelet: Healing Chile.") But just because they had fled didn't mean that Pinochet forgot about them: a communist was a communist, no matter where they lived. By the end of 1975 DINA had hatched Operation Condor, which formalized the web of rightist military intelligence agencies that "tracked, abducted, and assassinated" tens of thousands of suspected leftist activists, politicians, intellectuals, and other putative subversives throughout the region. Under Condor, DINA would provide, say, its Brazilian counterpart intelligence on certain Brazil dissidents living in Chile—and vice versa. The assassination of Orlando Letelier highlighted that there was nowhere beyond Pinochet's reach, even the streets of the US capital.

LOS CHICAGO BOYS

Pinochet could have political prisoners disappeared at will, but far more vexing was how to address the wretched domestic economy, with inflation and unemployment both soaring in early 1975. Pinochet and his coterie of young, ideological civilian advisors known as the Chicago Boys (for the University of Chicago, where they studied with economist Milton Friedman and colleague Arnold Harberger) believed that a hyper-free market economy would address the countless ills of Allende-era socialism. In a meeting with Pinochet, Friedman convinced the strongman that massive cuts in public spending could cure Chile's economic cancer.

Pinochet gave free rein to the Chicago Boys to put the plan into action, and the early signs were promising. Despite the widespread initial contraction, by late 1976 even some of the regime's fiercest critics inside and outside Chile had come to acknowledge that the economy had stabilized and then surged, with 1977 witnessing a growth rate of 8.7 percent. The sweeping privatizations of key industries (which notably, however, did not encompass the lucrative copper mines) balanced budgets and free trade ensued. By 1981, the Chicago Boys were bragging about Chile's "economic miracle."

A temporary but sharp setback occurred in the shape of the 1982 banking crisis, which saw unemployment soar to 30 percent, but by the end of the 1980s the Chilean economy was growing by leaps and bounds (although Chile now had the highest levels of inequality in the Americas, which endured for decades). Yet the banking crisis had other, more long-lasting consequences. As the banking crisis-related recession ravaged Chileans (especially the poor), there were repeated strikes and protests, often hatched by fledgling trade syndicates. The radical armed opposition inside the Southern Cone country never believed that it could defeat the mighty Chilean military; instead, its strategy was predicated on these sorts of continued social disturbances that might lead some in the security forces to switch sides. The protests also had the effect of increasing pressure on the regime, which responded to the disruption not only with batons and water cannons but also with political reforms.

Further complicating the political landscape was Fidel Castro's decision, spurred by the level of anti-Pinochet agitation, to provide arms to pro-Havana guerrillas inside Chile. From August through September 1986, the Chilean military intercepted "thousands of pounds of rocket launchers, automatic rifles, grenades and ammunition" in ten caches along the country's northern Atacama Desert coastline. Some of the smuggled arms were used in a failed attempt to assassinate Pinochet on September 7 of the same year, although many opponents of the Pinochet dictatorship dismissed the Cuban weapon delivery as a regime ploy to justify more repression.

PRESSURE GROWS

Throughout these years, Pinochet did not seem unsettled by allegations of human rights violations—when questioned about a mass grave of leftists, he sardonically joked that it was an "efficient" burial option—but international attention was increasing. Pope John Paul II emerged as a fierce critic, his April 1987 visit firing controversy even before his jetliner landed, as he told reporters on board that Pinochet's regime was "dictatorial" and that he backed the Chilean Catholic Church's nonviolent civic opposition efforts. Pinochet fired back that "it would be better if [clergy] spent 90 percent of their time praying." Unintimated by the bluster, the Pope's response was categorical: "There are those who tell us, 'Stay in the sacristy and do nothing else, yes, yes, do nothing else, do nothing else.' Because they say it is politics, but it is not politics. That is what we are."

Even President Ronald W. Reagan's administration, which was more supportive of Pinochet's rule (due to the Chilean's fierce anticommunism) than Jimmy E. Carter's, was searching for ways to broker the dictator's departure. The Reagan White House feared that the Castro-backed Chilean radical left's agenda—and the more generalized and swelling antiregime sentiment—might propel the nation into a full-blown civil war, a consideration that led it to contemplate offering political asylum to the Chilean dictator. One declassified document described how the offer would provide "an honorable departure for President [Pinochet], who would be received as a guest of our [US] government." The eventual Reagan stance was two-track: on one hand, nudging Pinochet with a "mix of quiet diplomacy, public criticism and largely symbolic economic pressures," while on the other working with moderate opposition organizations.

The opportunity for change came in the shape of the 1988 referendum. Back in 1980, Pinochet had put forward a new constitution that was "approved" by the citizenry in a referendum and granted Pinochet an eight-year term as president. When this term expired, Pinochet decided to hold another to win a fresh eight-year term. If he was rejected in the nationwide vote, then presidential elections would be conducted within a short amount of time. In short, the vote was quite simple: "No" for elections, "Yes" for a continuation of military rule.

It remains a visceral debate inside Chile as to why, despite banning almost all meaningful political opposition for years, the dictator preceded to hold the vote. The most likely explanation is that getting all incessant glowing assessments about his population from supplicant aides, *el general* never believed victory to be in doubt. If so, his intelligence was deeply flawed: by the mid-1980s, various opposition groups (ranging from former Allende ministers to centrist Christian Democrats to *pinochetistas* who had fallen out with the regime) had signed a pact committing members to remove the caudillo from power. By the time of the long-awaited 1988 referendum, there was considerably more anti-Pinochet unity than met the eye.

The opposition was further boosted by Washington's providing somewhere upward of $1 million to support the democratic opposition's efforts, such as get-out-the-vote drives in Santiago shantytowns and helping citizens obtain the photographs they needed for ID cards. With only months to go before the referendum, pro-regime newspapers like *El Mercurio* blasted Washington's subversive involvement in Chile's internal matters, claiming that funding the opposition as not a "neutral and impartial option to promote democracy."

A month before the plebiscite, both the No and Yes camps were allotted fifteen minutes of gratis media exposure each day (at 11 p.m.), per regime rules, but Pinochet made an acute error by underestimating these weekly segments. Before this development, the No movement had never had any reach into television—and they made the most of the unexpected opportunity. In conjunction with Washington-financed Madison Avenue consultants, the No side employed a deft media campaign for the weekly slot, including a catchy musical tune, "Joy is coming," and a rainbow symbol, painting a radiant vision of life without Pinochet.

NO!

On the night of the referendum, as he was given preliminary results indicating a significant lead for "No," Pinochet was apoplectic: "It's a big lie, a big lie. Here there are only traitors and liars!" He then commanded his subordinates to cease publishing results and summoned his ministers to an immediate meeting. Credible accounts of the fateful conversation contend that Pinochet requested his cabinet grant him emergency powers to address the chaos provoked by the "No" victory, but Defense Minister Fernando Mattei and other top officers refused to sign the decree. Rebuffed by his own regime, Pinochet grudgingly accepted the results: "We follow the constitution." Hours after the meeting, Matthei told the media gaggle waiting anxiously outside the palace, "It seems to me that the No have really won." (The official tabulation had No winning 56 percent to 44 percent.)

The result paved the way for the country's first general elections in almost twenty years, which were won by centrist Christian Democrat opposition leader, Patricio Aylwin, in December 1989. In March 1990, a somber Pinochet handed the presidential sash over to Aylwn in a ceremony in Valparaiso. Pinochet himself remained commander in chief of the Chilean Army until 1998, and wielded his remaining power to stymie any attempt to prosecute members of his security forces for *dictadura*-era abuses: "The day they touch one of my men, the rule of law ends."

In March 1998, Pinochet became senator-for-life, which gave him immunity from prosecution—but not criticism. On his first official day as a senator, Pinochet entered the assembly flanked by rightist parliamentarians, to be confronted by leftist politicians defiantly displaying photographs of Allende, General Prats, Letelier, and other martyrs on their desks. Other assembly members entered the room wearing black arms bands while holding pictures of *los desaparecidos* (the disappeared). Protestors shouted and banged pots outside the building, while police answered with tear gas and water cannons. Yet despite this, Pinochet retained a significant level of popularity among some Chileans: in a 1998 profile for the *New Yorker*, Jon Lee Anderson said that Pinochet had become "rarest of creatures, a successful former dictator."

DOWNFALL

In 1998, Pinochet traveled to London—one of his favorite cities, in part due to his close connection with Conservative Prime Minister Margaret Thatcher—for back surgery. Arriving on September 22, Pinochet checked in at the high-end InterContinental Hotel on Park Lane and went to eat at a restaurant, where an employee who was also a Chilean exile recognized the former dictator and alerted lawyers at Amnesty International. On October 16, Pinochet was arrested on an order from a Spanish magistrate that included an extradition request. (Among the charges was the murder of Spanish citizens living in Chile—crimes that fell into Spanish jurisdiction.) Prominent voices in the UK supported the extradition to Spain: *The Economist* for example ran an editorial supporting the extradition to Spain since "former dictators are not immune." Thatcher's support remained constant although her influence had dimmed, especially given the comprehensive defeat of the Conservative Party at the 1997 British general elections.

In Santiago, thousands took to the streets to either celebrate—"It's a carnival, the dictator's in jail"—or, in the tony upper-class districts, to castigate the detainment: "English pirates, return our granddad!" The daily *La Tercera* noted the deep irony that "this time the protestors throwing rocks were not students or militants of some leftist party, but ladies with high heels and hand-

Murderer! A poster condemning Chilean General Augusto Pinochet for the Washington, DC, killing of Chilean dissident Orlando Letelier and his twenty-six-year-old US aide, Ronni Moffitt. *(Library of Congress Prints and Photographs Division, Washington, DC)*

bags." Chilean president Eduardo Frei, a centrist, publicly contended that, no matter how terrible Pinochet's crimes might have been, the arrest violated Chile's sovereignty and the principle of diplomatic immunity linked to the senator-for-life designation.

British authorities held Pinochet, now eighty-three, for a year and a half before releasing him in March 2000 on the humanitarian grounds of impaired health. Controversy flared almost the minute he landed in Chile on March: after departing the aircraft while seated in a wheelchair, he then abruptly stood up and walked sprightly before speaking to the press and cheering supporters.

Pinochet may have thought that he was safe and sound, but he could not have been more mistaken. Over the subsequent years, the Chilean courts worked to strip the general of his parliamentary immunity and ordered him to stand trial. Some three hundred criminal charges against him were brought for numerous human rights abuses. The publication of numerous independent reports was also starting to give ordinary Chileans an idea of the true scale of the abuses committed under Pinochet. Indeed, the effort to bring those responsible to account was already underway. In 1993 DINA chief Miguel Contreras received a seven-year prison sentence for his involvement in the Letelier–Moffitt murders, and in subsequent years more than 1,300 officers and soldiers—including some of Pinochet's closest collaborators—were tried and in some cases convicted.

Revelations regarding Pinochet's (and the First Lady's) personal corruption also tarnished his image, especially given the long-held belief on the right that while Pinochet might have ruled with a *mano dura* (iron fist), he never stole a peso. An official US investigation discovered that the dictator had opened over a hundred bank accounts, through which he laundered no less than $15–$27 million. Chileans also learned that Pinochet possessed numerous false passports. Contreras, an unreliable witness at the least, would allege Pinochet knew that cocaine and weapons sales to foreign buyers represented the bulk of the illicit income.

When he died on December 10, 2006, at age ninety-nine, in the Military Hospital of Santiago, some of his few remaining supporters openly cried and chanted, "Viva Pinochet!" Despite all the court proceedings, Pinochet was never convicted of the numerous crimes of which he was accused, although he was under house arrest in the period leading up to his death. Hiriart, who died in December 2021 at age ninety-nine, never expressed public regret regarding her husband's blood-soaked legacy. Justice was ultimately denied for countless Chileans, both in the country and abroad, whose lives were torn asunder by the Pinochet regime—a sobering indication of the power of a dictator who remained seemingly untouchable until the very end.

28

Eduardo Galeano

Poet of History

I'm a writer obsessed with remembering . . . with remembering the past of America above all, and above all that of Latin America, intimate land condemned to forgetfulness.

—*Eduardo Galeano*

During the April 2009 *Summit of the Americas* in Trinidad and Tobago, Venezuelan president Hugo Chávez approached the newly inaugurated US president Barack Obama, patted his shoulder, and, with a firm handshake, handed his hemispheric counterpart a gift: a paperback copy of *Open Veins of Latin America*. Obama graciously received the book, telling the press soon after, "I thought it was one of Chávez's books. I was going to give him one of mine."

While perhaps relatively unfamiliar to the general public, *Open Veins* has been widely read since its 1971 publication not only by Latin American, US, and European students of Latin American history but also by scholars of anthropology, economics, and geography. Readers learned from the myriad breathless blurbs that it was the canonical anticapitalist, anti-imperialist, and antigringo text that, at its zenith, had a profound influence throughout Latin American university campuses and opinion-generating intellectual circles, and, critically, their North American and Western Europe equivalents. Indeed, by the 2010s, *Open Veins* was into its eighty-fourth impression, having sold more than a million copies, and been translated into more than a dozen languages.

The book's author, Eduardo Galeano, was considered one of Latin America's most magisterial authors and public intellectuals whose sui generis books shed light on the history and politics of the continent. In 2014, a year before his death, *The Economist* concluded that, apart from Gabriel García Márquez, no Latin American author had "done more to shape the mental image that both locals and outsiders have" of the region than Galeano.

A WORLD UPSIDE DOWN

As a youth in post–World War II in Uruguay, Eduardo, like so many of his peers, dreamed of being a professional soccer player, despite not being especially talented at the sport that is almost a religion in his native country. Born in Montevideo in 1940 to a middle-class Roman Catholic family, Eduardo came to realize that he needed an alternative to the soccer pitch. "I was going to do with my hands what I never could accomplish with my feet," he revealed in a later book, *Soccer in Sun and Shadow*. As a teen, the intellectually intrigued boy sketched political cartoons for the weekly Uruguayan Socialist Party magazine, *El Sol*. In an indication of how even at this adolescent age he was moving in leftist political and intellectual circles, he occasionally created the illustrations for articles by Raúl Sendic (a labor organizer who would go on to found the Tupamaro Marxist guerrilla group).

Not unlike Peru's José Carlos Mariátegui some decades before, Galeano soon became a brilliant and respected newspaper and magazine editor, poet, and vaunted social commentator. (See Chapter 19, "José Carlos Mariátegui and Victor Raúl Haya de la Torre: Peru's Long Revolution.") Along with many of his youthful compatriots, Eduardo was buoyed by the cultural and political headiness of the Cuban Revolution in 1959. Around twenty, he scored a plum position as the managing editor for *Marcha*, a prestigious and widely read political weekly; before he was thirty, he was editing, for a short while, the leftist daily *Época*—one of the country's most visible newspapers. With his ferocious work ethic and cavernous memory for political history, Eduardo was making a mark for himself in the emerging milieu of what came to be known as the "Latin American Boom" circa 1960s generation—Argentina's Julio Cortázar, Peru's Mario Vargas Llosa, Colombia's Gabriel García Márquez, Mexico's Carlos Fuentes, to name some of the most illustrious members—that placed Latin American fiction on top of the world literary standing.

In the middle of that searing decade, Galeano left Montevideo for Guatemala, where he observed up close a Cuban-inspired Marxist guerrilla insurgency in the Sierra de las Minas, as well as a rightist counterinsurgency. By that time, the term "disappeared" was being used in Guatemala in relation to those citizens—usually leftists or rebels or at least perceived leftists or rebels—

who were seized by state authorities and never seen again. The Uruguayan polymath recounted his experiences in the book, *Guatemala: Occupied Country*, published in 1969.

PATH TO *LAS VEINAS ABIERTAS*

The era of Galeano's youth, post-1945 and into the early 1960s, was the apex of what came to be called "dependency theory," a school profoundly influenced by the work of Argentine economist Raúl Prebisch who, between 1950 and 1963, ran the United Nations Economic Commission for Latin America headquartered in Santiago. Critically, *dependentistas* influenced by Prebisch were deeply troubled by the perceived destructive consequences of the rapacious "core" (read, rich Western countries) penetration into the so-called periphery—that is, underdeveloped Latin American economies.

The dependentistas turned this notion upside down, arguing that the existence of this prosperous core depended upon the existence of a poor and subjugated periphery. A hallmark tenet of *dependencia* was the concept of "unequal exchange," or that vulnerable Latin American underdeveloped periphery had to continuously export *more and more* primary goods only importing the *same* amount of manufactured wares from wealthy, Western capitalist cores. Perniciously, this capitalistic system *by intent* enriched the former at the expense of the latter, in what economists called a zero-sum game.

Galeano had long been concerned with the history of Western influence in Latin America and what had brought the continent to this juncture, and in 1970, he decided to put pen to paper. While keeping up his already-prodigious daytime workload of editing magazines and books and a position at a university, Galeano, working feverishly at night, scribed *Open Veins* in just three months. Written in "powerful prose, with intoxicating passion," as one review put it, Galeano's anti-imperialist, anticapitalist thesis was that of a five-hundred-year struggle between the rapacious West (North America and Europe, namely) and a violent, impoverished, and inequitable Latin America. The subtitle says it all: *Five Centuries of the Pillage of a Continent*. The extraction of the continent's natural resource wealth (e.g., gold, silver, sugar, coffee) during the Iberian colonization and imperialist dominion of the peoples of the Americas had paved the way for an equally malevolent modern system of exploitation—in his parlance, "the contemporary structure of plunder."

And it was this structure of plunder that had caused the region's chronic ills, not least of which was underdevelopment. As Galeano phrased it, "Underdevelopment isn't a stage of development, but its consequence." And here is one of the book's most famous lines: "Our defeat was always implicit in the victory of others; our wealth has always generated our poverty by nourishing the prosperity of others." The opening of the book states his dependency-influenced political position clearly and starkly, but it also shows Galeano's extraordinary style and use of imagery:

> The division of labor among nations is that some specialize in winning and others in losing. Our part of the world, known today as Latin America, was precocious: it has specialized in losing ever since those remote times when Renaissance Europeans ventured across the ocean and buried their teeth in the throats of the Indian civilizations. Centuries passed, and Latin America perfected its role. We are no longer in the era of marvels when face surpassed fable and imagination was shamed by the trophies of conquest—the lodes of gold, the mountains of silver. But our region still works as a menial.

The publication of *Open Veins* made Galeano an instant cultural celebrity at home and abroad, even if he had been well known in literary circles before. Also helpful to the book's status was the fact that the military juntas across the Southern Cone quickly banned the subversive tome. Much later, Galeano said that *Open Veins* "had the good fortune of earning high praise from several military dictatorships, which banned it. The truth is, that's what gave the book prestige."

In her foreword to the twenty-fifth-anniversary edition in 1997, renowned Chilean novelist Isabel Allende explained to her readers how, upon first encountering the book in the early 1970s, she had "devoured in two days with such emotion that I had to read it again a couple more times to absorb all its meaning." For her, that work demonstrated beyond question that "there were no safe islands in our region, we all shared 500 years of exploitation and colonization, we were all linked by a common fate, we all belonged to the same race of the oppressed." When she fled into exile in Venezuela following Pinochet's coup against Salvador Allende (her father was the president's first cousin), *Open Veins* was only one of two books she took, together with "some clothes, family pictures, [and] a small bag with dirt from my garden." As was the case with Che Guevara's *Guerrilla Warfare*, *Open Veins* inspired youth, including rousing them to join leftist revolutionary groups (see Chapter 24, "Ernesto Guevara: Becoming Che").

EXILE!

A couple of years later, *Open Veins* also made Galeano persona non grata in his own country, which had turned actively hostile to leftists. After a 1973 coup ushered in a military dictatorship, independent media outlets were restricted and political opponents and guerrillas were ruthlessly targeted, all under the guise of protecting the homeland from communist subversion. The country imprisoned one out of every fifty people for political reasons—the world's highest such rate—and hundreds of people "disappeared." Some 10 percent of the population fled into exile: a huge loss to a county of just three million.

Predictably given his political leanings, Galeanos did not escape the junta's dragnet. Arrested in the capital, he described what followed: "They put me in a car. . . . They moved me and locked me in a cell. I scratched my name on the wall. At night I heard screams." He had no idea whether his incarceration would last days, months, or years; fortunately for him, it wound up being days. "I've always been lucky," the author reflected.

Soon after his release, Galeano went into exile in Argentina and put his prodigious energies into managing the prestigious weekly journal *Crisis*, whose contributors included some of the most distinguished writers in Latin America pages. Yet after the rightist military coup against Isabel Perón in 1976, the military junta shuttered *Crisis*, forcing Galeano back into exile, eventually settling in Barcelona.

In Spain, Galeano went beyond the political economy of *Open Veins* to a more holistic and idiosyncratic rendering of history. In *Memory of Fire*—an epic three-volume history of the Americas relayed year by year in a chain of riveting anecdotes—he covered hundreds of different topics, many only a page or two long. As well as being fascinated by the major currents of history, Galeano was keen to include a multitude of voices and also had a sharp eye for the surreal and quirky. Here, for example, is a delectable nugget about how the Mexican revolutionary Pancho Villa learned to read while in jail by reading Don Quixote:

> A small blackboard and a few books arrive. Pancho Villa knows how to read people, but not letters. Magaña [a fellow prisoner] teaches him, and together they enter, word by word, sword-thrust by sword-thrust, the castles of *The Three Musketeers*. Then they start the journey through Don Quixote de la Mancha, crazy roads of old Spain; and Pancho Villa, fierce warrior of the desert, strokes the pages with the hand of a lover.
>
> Magaña tells him: "This book . . . you know? A jailbird wrote it. One of us."

Published in Madrid in 1982, the first volume *Genesis* spanned pre-Columbian history to the end of the seventeenth century, while *Faces and Masks* (1984) addressed the subsequent two centuries. The last volume, *Century of the Wind*, published after he returned to a newly democratized Uruguay (the military had been defeated in a plebiscite in 1985), took his legions of avid readers to the current era. *Century* is widely believed to be the best of the three or even the best of all his books.

COUNTERPOINT

Despite the huge influence of *Open Veins*, the book's argument has come in for heavy criticism over the years. In 1996, a trio of libertarian Latin American intellectuals—Peruvian author Álvaro Vargas Llosa (son of Mario Vargas Llosa), Colombian journalist and envoy Plinio Apuleyo Mendoza, and exiled Cuban Carlos Alberto Montaner—wrote a much-discussed book, *Guide to the Perfect Latin American Idiot*. A revisionist approach intended to unsettle what they believed were entrenched Marxist orthodoxies, the book dedicated one chapter to responding to Galeano's *Open Veins*, which they sardonically called the "idiot's bible." The *New York Times* reported that the authors had boiled down the thesis of *Open Veins* into a single pithy maxim: "We're poor; it's their fault." In a later article, Montaner argued that Galeano's theory was myopic: "Galeano had never stopped to think why other poor societies—such as South Korea, Taiwan, Estonia, Singapore, and Hong Kong—had emerged from misery without being stopped by anyone.... The truth is that economic progress and prosperity are elective."

In his 2007 book *The Forgotten Continent*, Michael Reid examined *Open Veins*' accuracy and legacy. Acknowledging that Galeano was a "writer of brilliance and passion," the author nevertheless finds the author's history is that of "the propagandist, a mix of selective truths, exaggeration and falsehood, caricature and conspiracy theory." Reid believes that Galeano is far too sweeping in including under his "agents of plunder" such diverse actors as "the caravelled conquistadors and the jet-propelled technocrats; Hernan Cortés and the [US] Marines; the agents of the Spanish Crown and the International Monetary Fund missions; the dividends from the trade of enslaved people and the profits from General Motors." According to Reid, Galeano "seems to reject all possibility of reform," in the sense of a Sarmiento, Juárez, Betancourt or JFK's Alliance for Progress. (See Chapter 8, "Benino Juárez: Mexico's Great Reformer" and Chapter 9, "Juan Manuel de Rosas and Domingo Sarmiento:

Uruguayan writer Eduardo Galeano (*right*) hugs Nobel Peace prize Rigoberta Menchú during peace culture conference in Montevideo, April 14, 2000. *(Alamy Stock Photo)*

The Struggle to Hatch Argentina.") For Galeano, (as Reid would write several years later), "Cuban communism offers the only route to Salvation."

And toward the end of his life, it appeared that the author agreed with at least some of the criticism. At a book fair event in Brazil in April 2014, Galeano—to a blindsided audience—disavowed his book during a questions and answers session. "I wouldn't be capable of reading this book again; I'd keel over. For me, this prose of the traditional left is extremely leaden, and my physique can't tolerate it." The seventy-three-year-old Uruguayan added that he intended *Open Veins* to be a "book of political economy" but at the time he "didn't yet have the necessary training or preparation."

For Galeano, the book "belonged to a past era. . . . Reality has changed a lot, and I have changed a lot. . . . Reality is much more complex precisely because the human condition is diverse. Some political sectors close to me thought such diversity was a heresy. Even today, there are some survivors of this type who think that all diversity is a threat. Fortunately, it is not." Speaking more broadly than the book, he conceded that the left sometimes "commits grave errors in power," a rebuke that many observers took to mean communist Cuba and Hugo Chávez's Venezuela. (Chávez had died the year before Galeano's revelations.)

His comments unleashed a spirited conversation across the Americas, with conservatives gloating and the left, in the words of the *New York Times*, "clinging to a dogged defensiveness." In a brashly titled blog post, "The Idiots Lose Their Religion," in the conservative US magazine, *National Review*, Carlos Alberto Montaner rejoiced at Galeano's volte-face. An unsigned, cheeky editorial in *The Economist* said that Galenao's change in direction was "almost as if Jesus's disciples had admitted that the New Testament was a big misunderstanding." More seriously, the Brazilian polemicist Rodrigo Constantino, author of *The Caviar Left*, claimed that Galeano's political economy was one of the causes of many of the region's woes: "He should feel really guilty for the damage he caused."

Despite his shifted perspective on his work, Galeano remained an intellectual of the left up until his death, in Montevideo, from lung cancer in 2015. He applauded, for instance, the democratic progressive (more socialistic than outright socialist) administrations—sometimes called "social democracy"—in Brazil, Chile, and his own Uruguay in the 2010s. (See Chapter 45, "Luiz Inácio Lula da Silva: Brazil's First Working-Class President.") Perhaps most notably, *Open Veins* remains on college syllabi, both inside and outside Latin America. Its thesis that Latins are impoverished because "multinationals, local capitalists, or the United States" have robbed their riches continues to resonate; to quote one North American professor, the book will still be read "because it still captures the essence of the emotional memory of being colonized." Perhaps one small irony is that just hours after the media reported on the Chávez gift copy to Obama, *Open Veins* surged into Amazon's Top 10 paperback sales (to the sixth place), albeit for a short while. Those capitalist laws of supply and demand would have entailed a tidy royalty to Galeano, but maybe that's something that the new Galeano would not be so upset about.

29

Gabriel García Márquez
Magical versus Social Realism

If you and Fidel could sit down face to face, there wouldn't be any problem left.
—*Gabriel García Márquez to US President Bill Clinton, 1996*

Gabriel García Márquez is "the greatest Colombian who ever lived," according to former Colombia president Juan Manuel Santos. He was a pioneer of so-called magical realism, a literary style encapsulated in the fantastical 1967 novel, *One Hundred Years of Solitude* and its inimitable setting of the pueblo of Macondo. *One Hundred Years* brought García Márquez global fame, selling approximately fifty million copies and being translated into forty-four languages—the most of any Spanish-language novel after *Don Quixote*. An acclaimed journalist long before his novelistic breakthrough, his writings all shared a common theme: the acquisition and usage of power, including its potential to corrupt. Like his Peruvian counterpart, Mario Vargas Llosa (See Chapter 37, "Mario Vargas Llosa: Cartographies of Power"), Gabo wasted few opportunities to excoriate dictators and their lackeys, although Fidel Castro was an exception. (When Gabo won the Nobel Prize for Literature in 1982, Comandante Fidel sent him a case of Cuban rum.)

García Márquez's life transected several searing episodes of Colombian history, each of which left its mark on his thought and work. When he was one, he was within a stone's throw of a 1928 massacre of striking workers near his *costeño* (coastal) hometown; twenty years later, a twenty-year-old Gabo was staying at a Bogotá pension just a few blocks from where one of the nation's most consequential political assassinations took place, plunging the country into a decade of brutal civil war. Many of the events depicted in *One Hundred*

Years and other books draw their inspiration from these seminal economic and political developments, but García Márquez also had a keen eye for how Colombia was changing: in the last stages of his storied vocation, his attention shifted to the nation's newest scourge—drug trafficking—culminating in the chilling book *News of a Kidnapping*, which told the stories of ten prominent Colombians kidnapped by Medellín kingpin Pablo Escobar.

BOOM TOWN

Gabo was born in 1927 in Aracataca, a small river town near Colombia's Caribbean coast, where his mother's parents lived. The new parents soon decamped to the nearby mid-sized port city of Barranquilla for work, leaving Gabo behind in Aracataca to be raised by his maternal grandfather, Colonel Nicolás Ricardo Márquez Mejía. The colonel was a colorful veteran who had served under Liberal General Rafael Uribe Uribe in the War of a Thousand Days—the bloody civil war between Liberals and Conservatives (centralists versus federalists) that broke out 1899 and killed eighty thousand out of a population of only four million. Day and night, he would regale "Gabito" with stories of heroic ventures during the civil wars; much later on, General Uribe Uribe would become the model for the character Aureliano Buendía in García Márquez's *One Hundred Years of Solitude*.

Gabo spent the first eight years of his life in his grandfather's "big house" along with a motley assortment of siblings and relatives. It was a heady time to be in Aracataca. Colonel Márquez had moved his family to sweltering, banana-rich Aracataca in 1910 amid the "Banana Boom," spearheaded by the US-based United Fruit Company, that was transforming a somnolent pueblo of a few hundred to upward of ten thousand residents by 1920. In his best-selling memoir, *Living to Tell the Tale*, Gabo describes Aracataca in the banana years as a "Wild West boom town," a veritable "forbidden city" where the "Biblical curse of the gringos with their slow blue lawns with peacocks and quail, the houses with red roofs and screens on the windows and little tables with folding chairs for eating, among palm trees and dusty rose bushes. . . . These were fleeting visions of a remote and unlikely world that was off limits to us mortals."

What García Márquez omits in his memoirs is that Colonel Márquez's family directly benefited from the United Fruit investment in Aracataca and the surrounding zone. The "big house" was bigger than almost any other in town, with its tennis court. Decades hence, García Márquez acknowledged that his mother Luisa (Ursula in *One Hundred Years*) "yearned for the golden age of the banana company" as they were her years as a "rich girl."

There was also a darker side to the banana boom. In 1928 United Fruit officials pressured the Colombian federal troops to crack down on a labor strike of upward of thirty thousand field workers in the coastal settlement of Ciénaga. In the ensuing cold-blooded massacre between four hundred and one thousand died, the pueblo's central plaza was soaked in blood. Some survivors fled to nearby Aracataca where they were also executed, infant Gabito within hearing distance. Maybe in a fit of "expressionistic hyperbole," when he recreated this historical 1928 Banana massacre in *One Hundred Years*, García Marquez put the number murdered at three thousand, a figure that most readers have no reason to assume is not accurate.

When Colonel Márquez died in 1937, the family moved to Barranquilla, then to the Magdalena River-delta town of Sucre. In 1940, Gabo returned to Barranquilla to study at the Jesuit San José school, where he inked his first stories, which appeared in the *Youth* magazine.

LOVE IN THE TIME OF VAPORES

In 1943, at the age of sixteen, García Márquez took the first of his eleven riverboat trips from his home along the mighty Magdalena up to Bogotá (experiences which would later play into his 1985 prize-winning novel, *Love in the Time of Cholera*). Author Wade Davis sets the scene:

> As an orchestra welcomed the passengers and the ship made ready to sail, García Márquez rushed to the highest deck and watched as the lights of the town of Magangué slowly receded in the darkness. Tears filled his eyes, and he remained, as he later recalled, in a state of ecstasy throughout the entire night and, indeed, the entire journey. It took six days to reach Puerto Salgar, where he caught the train for Bogotá. A boy from the coast who had never stood higher than the hood of a truck found himself climbing into the Andes, whistling and wheezing like a struggling *arriero* gasping for air.

Damp, gray, cold, high up, Bogotá—where he'd been sent for schooling and employment opportunities—came as a shock to García Márquez. He ached for his familiar costeño customs—and heat. As he settled into his new urban environs, García Márquez won a prestigious scholarship at an innovative institution, the National College for Boys in Zipaquirá, around thirty miles from the capital. Inspired by the iconic Mexican reformer Jose

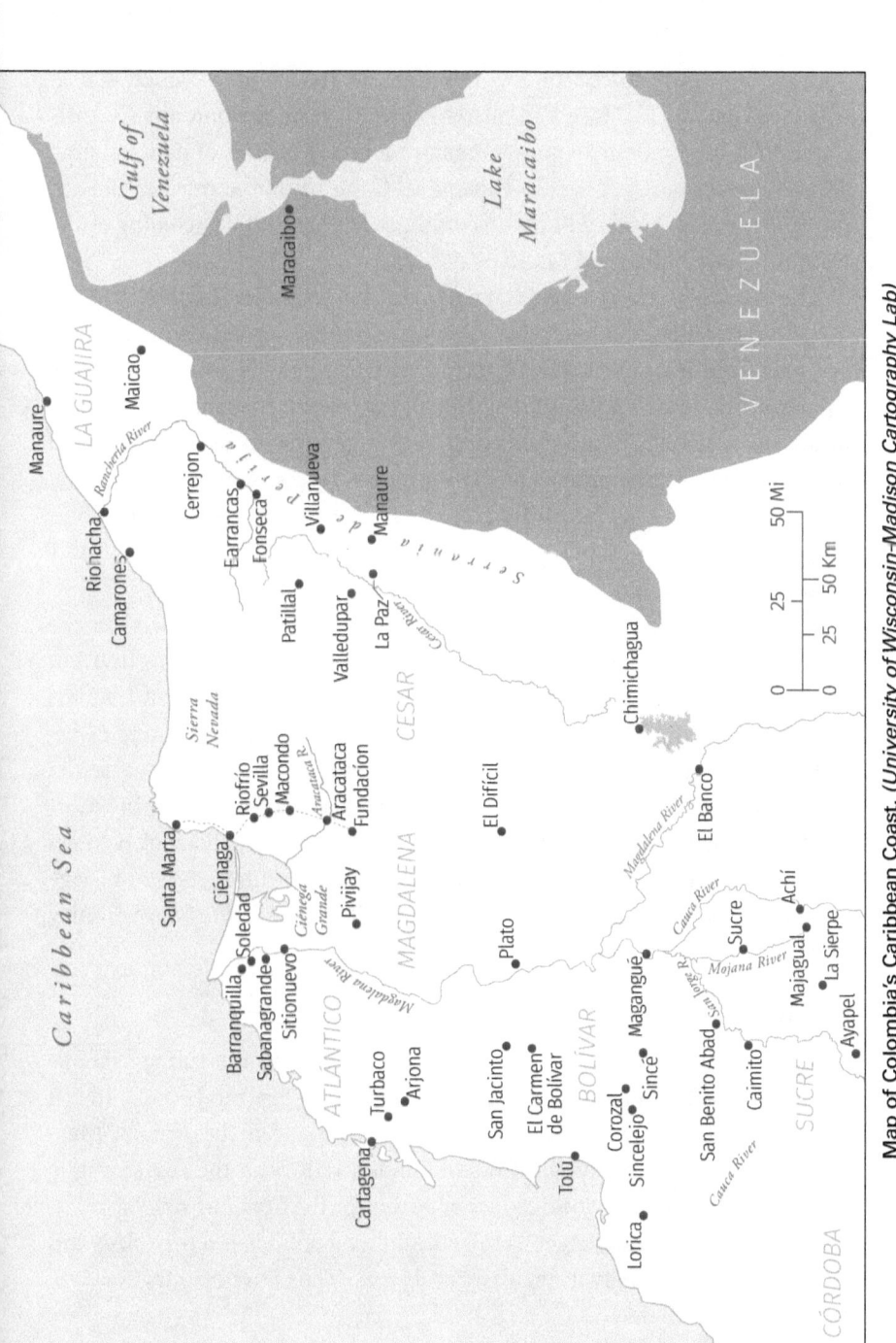

Map of Colombia's Caribbean Coast. (*University of Wisconsin-Madison Cartography Lab*)

Vasconcelos's push to consolidate the Mexican Revolution through education (see Chapter 13, "José Vasconcelos: The Mexican Revolution's Cultural Caudillo"), the Colombian government established a series of national high schools, with the first being in Zipaquirá. Gabo made the most of the opportunity, inhaling every book he could get his hands on, including Pablo Neruda, Franz Kafka, and Mark Twain.

The Zipaquirá era is when García Márquez manifested his first inclinations toward leftist politics—which was unsurprising, given that many of his National College teachers were Marxists. As Gabo told his dear friend Plinio Apuleyo Mendoza, "At the school, the algebra teacher taught us about the history of materialism; the chemistry teacher gave us books on Lenin; and the history teacher lectured us on class struggle. By the time I got out of that dungeon, I didn't know north from south, but I had two strong convictions: that good novels should be a poetic translation of reality, and that humanity's destiny in the near future was socialism."

The teenager and his friends also frequented "sinister brothels" in the seedier reaches of Bogotá, where we would "drain away our gloomy bouts of drunkenness." But these hormone-fueled escapades did not affect his productivity. In late 1944, the venerable daily *El Tiempo* published one of his poems in its literary addendum—a foreshadowing of big things to come. By 1946, García Márquez was studying law at the National University, the most prestigious pedagogical institution of law in this most legalistic of Andean nations. One of the few close acquaintances he made with *bogotano*s his age was the studious, socially empathetic Camilo Torres, a figure who will play into our story shortly.

THE *BOGOTAZO*

There was a major political development in 1946 when the ruling Liberals produced two candidates for the presidential vote—one moderate, and the radical populist Jorge Gaitán who routinely referenced the Banana Massacre. This split the party faithful and handed victory to the Conservative candidate. Having been excluded from power for the previous sixteen years, Conservatives were now eager to roll back Liberal politics and privileges and enact revenge, especially in the vast rural areas. The entire country was in a state of boiling anxiety.

On February 7, 1948, García Márquez attended his first-ever political event, a raucous rally led by Gaitán, now the uncontested leader of the Liberal Party. Gaitán's impassioned oratory was revelatory, his use of the terms "oligarchy," "exploitation," and "disenfranchisement" effectively "inventing a lingua franca" for the country's masses, according to Gabo.

Six weeks later, the Ninth Pan-American Conference commenced in Bogotá, with its main objective being to usher in the Washington-backed Organization of American States (OAS). A twenty-one-year-old University of Havana law student leader by the name of Fidel Castro was in the Andean capital as a delegate to a hemispheric youth congress intended to contrast with the imperialist OAS. On April 7, Castro met with his hero Gaitán in the Liberal leader's downtown office: Gaitán was so impressed by his Cuban interlocutor that he scheduled another one-on-one meeting two days later. But history intervened.

On April 9, 1948, García Márquez was sitting down to lunch with some friends at his downtown low-budget boarding house. An acquaintance entered the dining room in a breathless panic: "The country's fucked," he told Gabo. "They just killed Gaitán in front of El Gato Negro [a café]." And indeed, just a block or two away, as Gaitán was walking from his office, an unemployed worker, Juan Roa Serra, ran out from the café and fired three or four times at point-blank range. Gabo raced over to the scene but Gaitán had already been taken to the Central Clinic, where he died. (It is almost certain that García Márquez and Castro were, unknown to them, within a hundred yards or so of each other in these frantic, history-altering moments.)

Bogota's Liberals took it as fact that the Conservatives were behind the killing to forestall the social revolution Gaitán had so eloquently argued for. Consistent with Colombian political history, they took to solving their political problems through retribution and violence. Within hours, leaders of Liberal militias were urging their rank and file to take revenge.

Known as the *Bogotazo*, riots erupted in the center of the capital city, including torched buses used as spontaneous barricades and bands going house to house to execute adversaries. The downtown became a veritable war zone, leaving three thousand dead in a single day! Although the riots quickly fizzled out, the trauma of Bogotazo further fueled the widespread inter-party violence that escalated into the ten-year civil war known as *La Violencia*, which left between six hundred thousand and eight hundred thousand dead.

With the National University shuttered in the aftermath of Bogotazo, García Márquez was forced to flee the capital. He wound up at the University of Cartagena, where administrators graciously allowed Gabo to transfer

Map of Colombia. *(University of Wisconsin-Madison Cartography Lab)*

credits despite his lousy grades from Bogotá. But with La Violencia ravaging the country, García Márquez realized that books and newsprint, not law, was his vocation. Make no mistake, this was absolutely the worst time to be getting into the news business given the extent of state censorship, but García Márquez was undeterred and landed a job as a cub reporter for a new Liberal daily, *El Universal*, whose managing editor had by chance read one of Gabo's short stories. Over the next two years, the news novice penned 343 articles, about half unsigned. It was not a lucrative career, and Gabo was evicted from his pension for failing to make rent. He routinely slept on park benches, in friends' apartments, and, most memorably and literally, on the newsprint rolls in the *El Universal* office that stayed open around the clock.

TO THE IRON CURTAIN AND BACK

In 1954, García Márquez moved back to Bogotá, this time to work for the renowned newspaper *El Espectador*, which soon sent him to cover Cold War diplomacy in Europe. By December 1955, after a stint in Rome, he was living in Paris, frequenting the locale favored by Latin American intellectuals during that time: the Latin Quarter's Hôtel de Flandre at 16 Rue Cujas. The hotel was right in front of the stately Grand Hôtel Saint-Michel, also a popular spot for his fellow brethren from the New World. It was at the haggard but hospitable hotel where the Colombian correspondent befriended Afro-Cuban Nicolás Guillén, one of the many Latin American intellectuals exiled from the hemisphere's steely dictatorships. Guillén was the leading figure of one of García Márquez's most cherished anecdotes from his Paris years:

> It was when Perón ruled Argentina, Odría Peru and Rojas Pinilla in my country; the time of Somoza [Nicaragua], Batista [Cuba], Trujillo [Dominican Republic], Pérez Jiménez [Venezuela], Stroessner [Paraguay]; in fact, Latin America was paved with dictators. Nicolás Guillén used to get up at five in the morning as he read the newspapers over a couple of coffee, then he'd open the window and shout so he could be heard in both hotels, which were full of Latin Americans, just as if he was in a patio in Camagüey. One day he opened his window and said, "the man has fallen!" and everyone—Argentinians, Paraguayans, Dominicans, Peruvians—thought it was their man. I heard him too and thought, "Shit, Rojas Pinilla's gone!" Later he told me it was Perón.

Given his hardening socialist sympathies, García Márquez harbored a desire to explore behind the iron curtain. To his dismay, he found much of East

Germany—his first destination—despondent, though he argued that this was in part due to the construction in non-Soviet bloc West Berlin, which in his estimation was a cynical ploy to make Eastern Europe look decrepit: "West Berlin is an enormous capitalist propaganda agency." Following an exhausting three-day train ride he arrived in Moscow, a city he immediately dubbed the "largest village in the world." In the capital city on invitation from the Kremlin to attend a Youth Festival, García Márquez rubbed elbows with some of Latin America's most famous leftist literary figures, including Pablo Neruda.

García Márquez was relatively impressed with the Soviet experiment, although he did presciently wonder how a system that could put on such a dazzling festival and launch Sputnik into orbit could not provide its nation with even the most basic of consumer goods. Upon a state-directed visit to a collective farm, Gabo observed that its director acted like "a socialized feudal lord." After Moscow's ruthless, controversial invasion to quash a popular uprising in Hungary in November 1956, García Márquez was again at the scene. He visited Budapest where he scored an interview with János Kádár, the Soviet puppet who replaced Imre Nagy as head of Hungary. Less generous scholars believe this instance from Gabo's life reveals his intoxication with direct access to leftist power, whether it be in Budapest or Havana.

The end of Gabo's time in Paris was frantic as due to a solvency issue he had been let go by his Colombian newspaper. Penniless with only a rusting typewriter to his name, he had no option but to head home, but before moving back he became a correspondent in Venezuela in the late 1950s. Spending time in Caracas where General Marcos Pérez Jiménez led a dictatorship, García Márquez repeatedly heard everyday Venezuelans holding this despot in high esteem. What, Gabo asked himself, made the masses so smitten with this strongman? He then commented to a friend that he was playing around with the idea of writing a novel about this very topic, which he would do in the shape of *Autumn of the Patriarch* (1975).

Finally back at home, on March 31, 1958, Garcia Márquez wed his lifelong love and costeña confidant, Mercedes Barcha, in the Colombian capital. As Gabo recounts it, she became enamored of her future husband at the age of nine, when the fourteen-year-old Gabo was writing informally for a local newspaper. Gabo even claims to have proposed marriage at this adolescent stage.

In late August 1959, Mercedes gave birth to a son, Rodrigo. For the baptism, Gabo thought of his dear friend from National University law school days, Camilo Torres, who was now a priest active in the many marginalized barrios of Bogotá and increasingly removed from orthodox Church dogma. One of Gabo and Mercedes's friends joked during the baptism, "We're going to make this boy into a great guerrilla fighter." Torres gently responded, "Yes, but a guerrilla fighter for God." Around five years later, Torres joined the guerrilla insurgency called the National Liberation Army but was killed in his first combat mission on February 5, 1966. García Márquez writes fondly about Camilo's personal evolution but never mentions whether he supported his friend's decision to pick up arms. Yet there was one revolutionary he was very much in favor of: Fidel Castro.

COVERING THE CUBAN REVOLUTION

In Paris, Nicolás Guillén had regaled García Márquez with tales about the intrepid Fidel Castro, leader of the 26 of July Movement then fighting in the Sierra Maestra against Batista's forces. Gabo was even more impressed when, after interviewing Fidel's sister Emma, he grasped Fidel's connection to the Bogotazo. Over the next years and decades, García Márquez would become a vocal advocate of the Cuban Revolution, or more accurately Fidel Castro's Cuban Revolution. "Fidel Castro was one of the few things in which he was ever able to believe," wrote astute biographer Gerald Martin. (See Chapter 23, "Fidel Castro: A Rebel with a Cause.")

After Castro's forces had shocked the world by seizing Havana and forcing Batista from power in early 1959, García Márquez raced to the Cuban capital to cover history being made, although the narrative was hotly contested. The revolutionary authorities invited Gabo and other foreign journalists to cover "Operation Truth" where Batista regime defendants were put on trial (to demonstrate to the world that these were not kangaroo courts), while US dailies were breathlessly depicting a bloodbath in Havana. García Márquez, who spent six euphoric months on the island, came away feeling as though the hundreds of "revolutionary executions" were warranted given the systematic repression that led to the revolution in the first place. Argentine journalist Jorge Ricardo Masetti was also covering events in Cuba and persuaded Che Guevara to establish an official Cuban state press agency—*Latin Press*—which quickly hired Gabo as a political correspondent in Colombia.

Working for *Latin Press*, García Márquez spent much of the 1960s reporting on and living in revolutionary Cuba. He even agreed to be the news agency's correspondent in the heart of the *yanqui* capitalist empire, New York City—an assignment that entailed bringing his young family stateside, but after the catastrophic failure of the Kennedy administration–hatched April 1961 invasion of Cuba at the Bay of Pigs, decided to relocate to Mexico City, where they arrived after a series of bus rides from the Big Apple.

Their two-week journey on a Greyhound bus took them through the American South, in no small part because Gabo was infatuated with William Faulkner and the world he crafted with his fiction. It was on this *gringolandia* adventure that Gabo came to loath the "cardboard hamburgers" and "sawdust hotdogs," and they also experienced firsthand the scourge of Jim Crow racism and segregation when they were denied a reservation from a motel that did not rent rooms to "dirty Mexicans."

FAME, A SCANDAL, AND A PERSONAL RUPTURE

It was in the Mexican capital where, in 1965, Gabo started working on *One Hundred Years of Solitude*, with its setting of the magical "Macondo" inspired by his childhood experiences in Aracataca. Having worked full time as a reporter for around a decade by then, he now did nothing but write the book. He told Apuleyo Mendoza, "I'll have a big hit with this one or I'll lose my mind." Money was extremely tight by the time he finished: his wife had to pawn her blow dryer and blender for Gabo to send the manuscript to his editor in Buenos Aires. The novel that man would call a South American Genesis—"an intricate stew of truths and mirages," as the author put it—sold only eight thousand copies in its first printing in 1967, but then turned into a hit beyond Gabo's wildest dreams. He won the prestigious Rómulo Gallegos Prize and became *the* face of what literary critics were calling the "Latin American Boom" cohort, which included Cuba's Alejo Carpentier, Peru's Mario Vargas Llosa, Mexico's Carlos Fuentes, and Argentina's Julio Cortázar.

But any ideas this literacy cohort was united on political grounds were soon dispelled by a scandal over a poet in which Gabo took a controversial stance. In the late summer of 1968, it became apparent to Cuban authorities that "counterrevolutionary" poet Heberto Padilla was going to be awarded the poetry prize. The authorities summarily sequestered the prize's jury members for a few weeks, but the jury refused to change its decision, so Cuban officials put "health warnings" on Padilla's book when it came out. In 1971, having been interrogated for a month by security operatives, Padilla—a man who had "mildly satirized" the Cuban leader in some of his work—was thrown into prison and was forced to read a trumped-up statement of his "demented" acts of betrayal "against the morals of the true intellectual" and, what is worse, "against the revolution itself."

A petition signed by prominent figures such as Simone de Beauvoir, Jean-Paul Sartre, and Susan Sontag expressed outrage at Padilla's ill-treatment. Gabo did not sign. One jury member, Spanish poet Juan Marsé Carbó recounted how Gabo reacted to the Spaniard's anti-Havana stance: "He said that I was an idiot, that I didn't understand anything about literature and even less about politics. Politics always came first. It didn't matter if they hanged us writers. Padilla was a bastard who worked for the CIA and we should never have given them the prize to him." The Padilla Affair, as it came to be called, marked the end of the Boom as any form of literary/political element.

THE PATRIARCH

On September 11, 1973, García Márquez turned on the television to witness the searing scenes of the General Augusto Pinochet-led military coup attacking the government palace in Santiago, where democratic Marxist president Salvador Allende was holed up. (See Chapter 27, "Augusto Pinochet: The Unlikely Model Dictator.") Within hours, Allende would be dead.

For García Márquez, the decimation of Allende's lofty "socialism with liberty" was a catastrophic setback in the hemispheric march toward justice, respect, and development. The coup reinforced his identification with and commitment to radical politics, militant journalism, and the Cuban Revolution. Pinochet's ascent was also a creative catalyst, driving García Márquez to work on his long-simmering book on dictators, *Autumn of the Patriarch*, which came out in 1975. In a later interview, the author described the work as "a poem about the solitude of power," describing that he "always believed that absolute power is the highest and most complete realization of being human." García Márquez undertook extensive research for the novel and was fascinated by Julius Caesar. He read and reread Thornton Wilder's iconic *The Ides of March*, which for the Colombian novelist was a "dazzling look into the agonies and ecstasies of power."

Everything in the novel occurs through the consciousness of the patriarch who is an "obsessive, solitary dictator." The protagonist, the General (his specific rank is General of the Universe who lived between 107 and 232 years, and sires thousands of children, all bastards) is a composite of many different strongmen. Here is how one book reviewer, writing in 1976, reacted:

> There is nothing to celebrate in the General's long and tortured life. He is given endless opportunity to persuade us that his anguish and grief and bafflement

are real. But we are never persuaded. He is not even pitiable. He is a spectacle, the embodiment of egocentric evil, maniacally violent, cosmically worthless and, despite pretensions to eternity, as devoid of meaning as anything else in an absurd world. His main contribution to life, finally, is fear; but fear such as thunder, cancer or madness may provoke, fear based on irrational possibility, on the oblique ravages of a diabolical deity.

After reading the novel, Panamanian populist strongman Omar Torrijos is purported to have told his friend Gabo, "It's true, it's us. That's what we're like."

García Márquez's regard for power was complex. He admired Torrijos and Castro—caudillos with social(ist) agendas but considered others like Pinochet the devil incarnate. Yet despite his affection for Castro, there is a hint of the Cuban leader in the novel's portrait of the dictator obsessed with agrarian customs who also loved sports: "He built the largest baseball stadium in the Caribbean and imparted to our team the motto of victory and death." At another point, the Americans snatch away the Caribbean Sea, a metaphor for the gringo blockade, leading the Patriarch to reflect "I had to bear the weight of the punishment alone . . . no one knows better . . . that it's better to be left without the sea than to allow a landing of marines."

A FELLOW TRAVELER

The mid-1970s through early 80s was an active time for García Márquez, with committed involvement in hemispheric leftwing solidarity and activism. Of the countless guests to Gabo and Mercedes's Mexico City residence, Sandinista founder Tomás Borge was a reliable visitor. García Márquez helped broker the agreement that brought together three distinct Nicaraguan revolutionary groups to create the Sandinista National Liberation Front that ultimately toppled the Somoza dynasty. In 1978, a group of Sandinista commandos led by Edén Pastor seized the National Palace in Managua, taking around two dozen legislators as hostages. They then flew to Panama with scores of freed political prisoners from Somoza's dungeons and a residual number of hostages, later freed. García Márquez called his friend Torrijos to gain the green light to travel to Panama to cover the perpetrators' remarkable feat, and the Colombian believed that his subsequent report on the escapade helped turn the Carter administration against the Somoza dictatorship.

In 1978, García founded a human rights foundation, *Habeaus*, that focused on cases of political prisoners held in military dictatorships across the Ameri-

Cuban President Fidel Castro chats with Colombian Nobel Prize–winning author Gabriel García Márquez (*right*) during a gala dinner marking the Cuban Cigars Festival in Havana. The dinner was held before an auction of humidors filled with Habanos (premium Cuban cigars) signed by Castro, March 4, 2000. *(Rafael Pérez/Alamy)*

cas. Board members included outspoken radical Catholic priest, Ernesto Cardenal, and Danilo Bartulín, a friend of Gabo and physician to Chile's Salvador Allende who was at the embattled president's side in the terrifying last hours of Allende's life. Cuba was not a target of the foundation, despite an estimated one hundred political prisoners on the island. Mexican novelist Octavio Paz wasn't buying Gabo's objectivity in this realm, claiming that he switched out "magical realism for socialist realism." However, García Márquez later said that he privately pleaded with Fidel in at least a few cases that led to the freeing of scores of important writers, artists, and other political prisoners.

In an interview with the *New York Times*, the storied writer said that despite his constant trips and extended stays to the island, "I could not live in Cuba because I haven't been through the process. It would be very difficult to arrive now and adapt myself to the conditions. I'd miss too many things. I couldn't live with the lack of information. I'm a voracious reader of newspapers and magazines from around the world." This stance came under withering attack in a 1980 article by Cuban dissident Reinaldo Arenas titled "Gabriel García Márquez: Ass or an Asshole?":

That a writer like Señor García Márquez, who has lived and written in the West, where his work has had an immense impact and reception which has guaranteed him a lifestyle and intellectual prestige, that such a writer, protected by the freedom and opportunities that such a world affords him, should use them to produce apologies for totalitarian communism, which turns intellectuals into policemen and policemen into criminals, is simply outrageous.

García Márquez defended himself: "There is no contradiction between being rich and being revolutionary, as long as you are sincere about being a revolutionary and not sincere about being a rich man." And he stuck to his path, continuing to visit Fidel in Cuba annually into the 1990s.

The moral balancing act grew even more difficult when the highly decorated Cuban army officer, General Arnaldo Ochoa, "Hero of the Revolution," was arrested for drug trafficking and corruption—charges which many believed were a cover for the Castro regime's involvement in drug trafficking. Also thrown in jail were fellow officers Colonel Tony de la Guardia, a friend of García Márquez, and his twin brother, Patricio. (Gabo had recently dedicated his recently published novel, *The General in His Labyrinth*, to Tony.) After what critics said was a show trial, all the defendants were convicted and Ochoa and Tony were executed in July 1989, while Patricio was sentenced to thirty years in prison. García Márquez intervened with Castro on behalf of Tony de la Guardia's family but Castro insisted to Gabo that he did not have the authority to alter the sentence. García Márquez told the French President that the dispute was a "quarrel among officers" and that he had "good information" the charges were legitimate.

In *The General in His Labyrinth* (1989), the author included a scene that appeared to foreshadow the tensions in the Ochoa/Guardia affair. In the scene, a hallucinating Bolívar is tortured by the memory of his summary order thirteen years earlier to execute the valiant mulatto General Manuel Piar, who was crucial to defeating the Spanish and adored by the masses, over and above the exhortations of his subordinates. "It was the most savage use of power in his life," García Márquez wrote. "But the most opportune as well, for with it he consolidated his authority, unified his command, and cleared the way to glory." At the end of the chapter, Bolívar states to his aide that he "would do it again." (See Chapter 6, "Simón Bolívar: The Great Liberator, Flawed Emancipator.")

At the 2003 Bogotá Book Fair, Mario Vargas Llosa blasted his erstwhile best friend as a "writer who is a courtesan of Fidel Castro, whom the dictatorship holds up as an intellectual alibi, and he so far has come to accept very well all the abuses, the trampling of human rights that the Cuban dictatorship has committed, saying that secretly he helps political prisoners released. It is no secret to anyone that Fidel Castro hands over some political prisoners to his courtesans once in a while. That is how he keeps his conscience clean. To me it seems more like repugnant cynicism. Writers are how they are, and each assumes a responsibility with that kind of conduct. I have never read an article or essay by García Márquez that explains in moral and civic terms this systematic alignment that seems religiously devout, because intellectually he should explain it and he hasn't so far, and I doubt very much that he ever will."

A TITAN OF LITERATURE

But his ideological sympathies did not diminish his literary standing, and in 1982 García Márquez was awarded the Nobel Prize for Literature. His acceptance was quite remarkable for laying out the heartache of the continent in the past decades but also challenged the tendency of Europe to look down on Latin America and forget its millennia of bloody history.

In the latter part of his career, García Márquez turned his attention to the new challenge facing Colombia: drugs. In *News of a Kidnapping*, Gabo was in vintage reporting form through his intimate portrayals of Medellin's Escobar (see Chapter 38, "Pablo Escobar: The First Drug Lord") and his myriad captives from the most rarefied of the country's social and cultural circles.

García Márquez, succumbing to Alzheimer's disease, died at the age of eighty-seven in 2014. He left behind an extraordinary and groundbreaking body of work that fused history, fiction, and biography to create highly imaginative yet trenchant portrayals of his country and Latin America as a whole. His friendship with Castro won him many enemies, but García Márquez also occupied a unique position as one of the few people who could criticize Fidel to his face, and argue for clemency on behalf of others. His comment to US President Bill Clinton in 1996—"If you and Fidel could sit down face to face, there wouldn't be any problem left"—demonstrates his enduring (some would say naïve) belief in the possibility of human connection to overcome deep division (of which his early life had much experience). This he achieved profoundly in his fiction, which continues to be read across the world by people of all manner of political persuasion and background.

30
Óscar Romero
Priest, Saint, Revolutionary

The violence we preach is not the violence of the sword, the violence of hatred. It is the violence of love, of brotherhood, the violence that wills to beat weapons into sickles for work.

—Óscar Romero, *The Violence of Love*

Óscar Romero was a transformational figure in El Salvador's modern history. After he was appointed archbishop in 1977, he began to speak out against the iniquities of society, influenced by the Catholic Church's new emphasis on social justice, or what came to be known as "liberation theology" in Latin America. This stance brought him into confrontation with the rightwing militarists and oligarchs, who perceived the priest's outspoken criticism as fomenting revolution. In 1980, Romero was assassinated while celebrating mass, sparking outrage. Tensions in the country dramatically escalated, eventually culminating in the outbreak of a brutal civil war. In death, Romero became a symbol of courage and unflinching commitment to social justice and was canonized by the Vatican in 2018.

RISE OF LIBERATION THEOLOGY

After the Second Vatican Convention (1962–1965, also known as Vatican II), the Catholic Church began to increase its focus on human rights and social justice. In Latin America, this shift gave rise to what Peruvian priest Gustavo Gutiérrez called liberation theology, whose advocates contended that Latin American society was highly unequal and exploitative, and that lasting justice could come only through radical social and economic change. The notion of structures of sin or sinful structures became influential in Catholic social teaching: faced with the structural "sin" of social inequality, redemption had to begin here and now.

In El Salvador, the transformation of the church took root in the 1960s with the establishment throughout the countryside of a variety of community-level organizations, or base communities, dedicated to economic and social welfare. Working in the countryside and shantytowns of cities, energized theologians promoted the "conscientization" of the masses—a clear notification that their hunger, underemployment, and desperation were not "God's will or the result of their own failures." Sister Joan Petrik was a North American Maryknoll nun who worked in El Salvador in the 1970s; as she recalled, "When I first arrived in [rural coffee-harvesting community of] Tamanique, every time a child died the family would say, 'It's the will of God.' But after the people became involved in the Christian communities, that attitude began to change.... They began to say, 'The system caused this.'" In the eyes of some conservative factions, this kind of thinking was Marxism dressed up as religion and led some to view priests as partners in crime with leftist guerrillas.

Yet despite this surge of liberation theology in El Salvador, Archbishop Óscar Romero's advocacy of social justice came as a surprise to many. His appointment as archbishop in 1977, succeeding the progressive Luis Chávez y González, had been generally attributed to his doctrinal conservatism, a view that was reinforced when the military government applauded the appointment while leftists and Marxists expressed deep dissatisfaction. A classified US government communication reported the consensus thinking, which was that Romero would prove docile toward the oligarchy and military. One journalist described the unassuming Romero as "a diminutive, shy-looking man who was 60 when he assumed the archbishop's post, [and] looked and acted like the last person in the world who would be a burr in the blanket of the military or aristocracy."

MAKING OF A "TROUBLESOME PRIEST"

Born in a small town in the province of San Miguel in eastern El Salvador in 1917, Romero was the son of a telegraph operator. After attending seminary in San Miguel, Romero became a priest in his local region. "I could have been called a conservative," he reflected. "But I followed the principles of Vatican II with considerable interest and noted the changes we were being asked to make."

Romero then became secretary to the bishops' conference in San Salvador and then bishop in the village of Santiago de María from 1974 to 1976. He described living a "very private life—anonymous, you might say." But it was in Santiago de María where Romero "became close to the problems of the campesinos [peasants] and the repression their organizing efforts aroused." It is important to note that Vatican II also resulted in a reformulation of responsibility in Latin America that gave bishops a greater role in their local areas.

Yet where the liberation theology saw a moral imperative to "sanctify the world"—building the Kingdom of God here and now—the regime saw church-led agitation. After the (fraudulent) election in 1977 of strongman General Carlos Humberto Romero (no relation to Óscar Romero), the regime began a series of attacks against the church. Concluding that priests were overseeing the intellectual formation of a "new generation of Communist youth" in the Jesuit-run Central American University, the right targeted "subversives" like priests, nuns, the archbishop himself, and "anyone associated with the left wing of the Church." Foreign priests belonging to the Jesuit, Maryknoll, and Benedictine orders were arrested and expelled. Around this time a "death squad," the White Warriors Union, issued the flyer "Be Patriotic—Kill a Priest." The group also presented to the press its "War Bulletin #6" in which it accused forty-six Jesuits of "terrorism" and ordered them to depart the country within a month; after that date, their death would be "immediate and systematic."

In March 1977, liberation theology proponent Father Rutilio Grande was brutally murdered by an assassin who used a type of bullet only issued to the armed forces. The murder of his trusted colleague shook Romero to his core and became a moment of revelation that convinced him of the urgent need to act. He suspended all Sunday masses for a month except for the National Cathedral, and along with fellow bishops, also boycotted the "inauguration" of General Romero on July 1, 1977. The violence also drew foreign attention, particularly in US Catholic communities.

Rattled by the negative press reports, dictator General Romero ordered a reduction in anti-church operations; he even placed soldiers in Jesuit residences and made an ostentatious pledge for their safety. General Romero seemed to understand that El Salvador was becoming known for killing priests, which, as a contemporary writer observed, was "the only country in the world named after Christ."

Archbishop Romero, however, was firmly launched on his path and began to speak out publicly against rightist violence and social inequality. In August 1979, he spoke of the need for a discussion on social reform that could transcend the fraught battle of Cold War political ideologies: "Fear of Marxism . . . keeps many from confronting the oppressive reality of liberal capitalism. Before the danger of a system clearly marked by sin, they forget to denounce and combat the reality implanted by another system equally marked by sin."

The church-operated YSAX radio station became Romero's main avenue for broadcasting his Sunday homilies and propagating his message to the masses. Forty-seven percent of the urban population and 73 percent in the countryside tuned in to hear the archbishop, creating one of the largest audiences for any broadcast in El Salvador, save for soccer matches. A *Washington Post* article described the role of YSAX in El Salvador as a channel for unvarnished news: "While government-controlled stations transmit official communiques, station YSAX, owned and operated by the Archdiocese of San Salvador, digs out the news." The influence of Romero's sermons made the station a target for the extreme right. There were at least four attempted bombings of the station before it was finally destroyed on September 20, 1980.

In addition to hostility and violence from the right and security forces, Romero also faced divisions within the church hierarchy. While a strong majority of parish priests supported Romero, four of the other five bishops in the country were inclined to characterize his position as "encouragement to communist elements bent on manipulating the church and overthrowing our constitutional government." Such a split over liberation theology was common in Latin America at the time, but Romero himself was keen to avoid the impression of a divided church, commenting that "I would rather say there is pluralism within the church."

In May 1979, Romero traveled to the Vatican to provide the pope with seven dossiers filled with reports and documents regarding El Salvador's horrifying condition. Romero subsequently returned to El Salvador where he continued to call for social justice and an end to violence, although he was increasingly aware that his activism was putting him in danger. Almost a year later, he told a journalist, "You can tell the people that if they succeed in killing me, that I forgive and bless those who do it. Hopefully, they will realize they are wasting their time. A bishop will die, but the church of God, which is the people, will never perish."

Romero's increased visibility abroad likely helped lead to his nomination in 1978 for the Nobel Peace Prize. Among those nominating him were twenty-three members of the US Congress who in their letter to the Nobel committee wrote: "An individual of unsurpassed courage and integrity, Romero has not allowed government prosecutors to frighten him into silence or submission. He has remained a forthright and compelling advocate of human rights, nonviolence and social progress—setting a standard in defense of human liberty which can be applied not only in Latin America but throughout the world." Romero also received the Peace Prize of the Swedish Free Churches and honorary doctorates from two Catholic universities, Georgetown in Washington, DC, and Louvain in Belgium.

A LETTER TO CARTER, AND AN ORDER TO EL SALVADOR'S SOLDIERS

In early 1980, and only weeks after two key civilians had resigned from the junta that had ousted General Romero late the previous year, Archbishop Romero asked President Jimmy E. Carter in a letter to halt even nonlethal military aid that was "being used to repress my people." Unlike the junta and Washington, Romero insisted that the "popular organizations" (either formally or otherwise linked to the guerrillas) must be recognized in any negotiation to the country's conflagration. "It is beyond doubt that the people are rising to the times, each day becoming increasingly conscious and more organized, and beginning to summon the ability to direct, to take charge of the future of El Salvador." The archbishop subsequently publicly announced that the ruling junta did not effectively govern the country.

Secretary of State Cyrus Vance responded in Carter's name to the letter. Vance wrote that Romero and the president both embraced the "advancement of human rights," but that the United States believed the junta's reform program "offers the best prospect for peaceful change toward a more just society." Vance added, "We understand your concerns about the dangers of providing military assistance given the unfortunate role which some elements of the security forces occasionally have played in the past." Given the intensity of repression at the time, critics jumped on the use of the qualifying language of "some" and "occasionally."

Undaunted, Romero's stance against the government's abuses grew harder—in some eyes, bordering on revolutionary. On March 7, 1980, he gave an interview with the Havana-run *Latin Press*, in which he argued that the oppressive conditions made certain forms of violence acceptable: "Christians are not afraid of combat; they know how to fight, but they prefer the language of peace. However, when a dictatorship seriously violates human rights and attacks the common good of the nation, when it becomes unbearable and closes all channels of dialogue, when this happens, the Church speaks of the legitimate right of insurrectional violence."

In his Lenten homily on March 23, 1980, the archbishop bypassed politics and spoke directly to those perpetrating the violence:

> I would like to appeal in a special way to the men of the army, and in particular to the troops of the National Guard, the Police, and the garrisons. Brothers, you belong to our own people. You kill your own brother peasants; and in the face of an order to kill that is given by a man, the law of God should prevail that says: Do not kill! No soldier is obliged to obey an order counter to the law of God. No one has to comply with an immoral law. It is time now that you recover your conscience and obey its dictates rather than the command of sin. The Church, defender of the rights of God, of the law of God, of the dignity of the human person, cannot remain silent before so much abomination. We want the government to seriously consider that reforms mean nothing when they come bathed in so much blood. Therefore, in the name of God, and in the name of this long-suffering people, whose laments rise to heaven every day more tumultuous, I beseech you, I beg you, I order you, in the name of God, to stop the repression!

"MAY GOD HAVE MERCY ON THE ASSASSINS"

The next day, Archbishop Romero was assassinated while celebrating mass at the small chapel of the Divine Providence Hospital where he lived. A professional assassin fired a single .22 caliber bullet from a red Volkswagen. The bullet hit the archbishop, causing death from severe bleeding from the ruptured aorta. Romero's last words were reported to be, "May God have mercy on the assassins."

In response to the assassination, Vance stated, "We are deeply shocked by this deplorable criminal act," calling Romero "a man who embodies the basic principles of compassion and concern for all the citizens of El Salvador." A week after his murder, tens of thousands of Salvadorans attended Romero's funeral at the National Cathedral. Here is an observation by an American Catholic priest, one of the fifty foreign guests who were present:

> The day of the funeral ceremony—Palm Sunday—ushered with it glimpses of keen expectation as we made our way to the Cathedral through streets

overflowing with people.... It was obvious that most were peasant families, some of them having walked overnight to render homage to their beloved pastor. There was a distinct mood of sober joy in the air. "We have had six days to weep," a priest told us. "Now we anticipate the Resurrection Day." The square in front of the Cathedral throbbed with people, 80,000 of the faithful. They were singing, waving palm branches and holding up little pictures of the Archbishop snapped up from enterprising street children. Cool water was served, gratis, by the Baptists, in the shade of large umbrellas.

But the procession turned chaotic when unidentified gunmen opened fire on the mourners, killing and wounding dozens. The government and security forces claimed it was the protestors who instigated the violence to provoke a backlash. The images of unarmed demonstrators and mourners being gunned down on the steps of the National Cathedral had a large impact abroad, especially in the United States, where Congress was debating the Carter administration's request for $5.7 million in nonlethal military aid to the Salvadoran armed forces—the very aid Romero had objected to in his letter to Carter.

This sparse funding quickly became a test of Carter's El Salvador policy. Critics said that even this symbolic amount of nonlethal aid was counterproductive since it would "legitimate what has become dictatorial violence." A leading Catholic spokesman stated: "Any military aid to El Salvador . . . ends up in the hands of the military and paramilitary rightist groups who are themselves at the root of the problems of the country." To influence the congressional vote, Protestant and Catholic Church organizations "overwhelmed congressional offices" with letters, telegrams, and visits. They had one imperative: stop military aid.

Yet even congressional Democrats had reservations about stopping the aid. Florida representative William Lehman lamented, "We have seen in other countries that one form of violence, repression, tyranny, can too often be succeeded by even worse violence and repression and tyranny. . . . I dread the alternative that can come out of the left." Representative Matthew McHugh said, "If this junta falls, the repressive elements of the government will be in control[;] that will be followed by a civil war, and I do not see how that benefits the El Salvadorean [sic] people." (McHugh later revealed that his yes vote on the Salvador aid was the toughest of his career.) Two weeks after Romero's death, Congress approved the assistance.

Salvadoran Óscar Romero depicted in an alley mural in Los Angeles, 2016. *(Library of Congress Prints and Photographs Division, Washington, DC)*

THE MAN BEHIND THE MURDER

Soon after Romero's murder, Roberto D'Aubuisson, a former national guard major, made a speech in which he indicated that he was pleased with the killing, even though he denied his involvement. (Shortly before his assassination, Romero had publicly denounced D'Aubuisson as a "liar, torturer, and murderer.") A few months later, D'Aubuisson was arrested along with at least a dozen active and retired military personnel and a similar number of civilians, who were all accused of plotting to overthrow the government through a coup. The raid uncovered weapons and documents that implicated the group in death squad activity, including Romero's killing.

The most sensational item recovered was the diary of former military captain Álvaro Rafael Saravia, which contained information on the Romero assassination. The "Saravia diary" referenced the purchase and delivery of arms and munitions, some of which were the same as the ones used in the Romero assassination. Another key document was titled "General Framework for the Organization of the Anti-Marxist Struggle in El Salvador" and reflected the views of those meeting at the estate. The manifesto included the goal of seizing power in El Salvador and the need for "direct action," including "attacks on selected individuals." Finally, in April 2010,

Saravia revealed in an interview with the Salvadoran newspaper *El Faro* that D'Aubuisson had given the order to murder Romero.

D'Aubuisson also likely ordered the same men to murder Atilio Ramírez Amaya, the judge investigating the archbishop's murder who had involved himself deeply in the case. Aided by a team of doctors, Judge Ramírez used plastic bags to recover evidence extracted from the archbishop's body; Ramírez was also the only person to inspect the body from head to toe. A few days after the murder, junta chief Colonel Adolfo Majano announced on television that the perpetrators would be apprehended and that INTERPOL had given his government their names, information which would be delivered to the investigating judge—that is, Ramírez.

This publicity quickly resulted in death threats being sent to Ramírez and his family; shortly thereafter, armed assassins entered his house to murder the investigating judge. They failed in their attempt and fled, but Ramírez's maid was killed in the process. While he was engaged in a firefight with the killers, Ramírez thought to himself, "Shit, they're going to kill me like they killed Mario Zamora," referring to the junta government's murdered attorney general. The next day when he asked for special protection from the Supreme Court of Justice, Ramírez was told dismissively, "Don't invent ghosts, Atilio." On Sunday, March 29, just a week after Romero's assassination, Ramírez fled to Costa Rica.

D'Aubuisson—the "godfather of the politics of hate" as journalist James Lemoyne called him—escaped sanction for Romero's murder and continued to conduct both death squad work and politics, founding the rightist ARENA party in late 1981. That same year, he openly promoted the need to kill two hundred thousand to three hundred thousand people to restore peace in El Salvador. To his supporters, he was simply the single most effective leader to prevent a leftwing takeover of El Salvador—an outcome that many in the oligarchy found unacceptable. In December 1984, roughly a dozen archconservative co-organizations honored D'Aubuisson in Washington with a plaque and dinner attended by 120 guests at the Capitol Hill Club. The plaque expressed appreciation for D'Aubuisson's "continuing efforts for freedom in the face of communist aggression which is an inspiration to freedom-loving people everywhere." (In late February 1992, at the age of forty-eight, D'Aubuisson died after a long bout with throat cancer, including medical trips to the United States. In a clandestine radio broadcast, the Marxist guerrillas rejoiced in his death, saying that it "seems to be an act of divine justice.")

CIVIL WAR

The Romero assassination became one of the contributing factors to El Salvador's "irredeemable horror" that was the internal war. Romero's brutal murder galvanized many on the left to join the nascent Farabundo Martí National Liberation Front (FMLN) after concluding that the archbishop's message could only be realized through the barrel of a gun. Former guerrilla leader Gerson Martínez commented in a 2008 interview that "this assassination was the consecration of the civil war."

Whatever the starting point, El Salvador's violence intensified after Romero's assassination and endured until 1992, claiming roughly seventy-five thousand lives and displacing more than a million people in a country of only five million. Notably, the oppression of the church continued: from 1980 until 1992, death squads killed at least seventeen priests and nuns. Unwilling to tolerate an advance of apparent Soviet and Cuban-backed communism in its geopolitical backyard in what turned out to be the last phase of the Cold War, three successive US presidential administrations (Democrat Carter and Republicans Ronald W. Reagan and George H. W. Bush) delivered over $6 billion in military and economic aid to the Salvadoran government. Finally, on January 16, 1992, after a couple of years of exhausting and sporadic UN-led negotiations, the Salvadoran government signed a peace deal with the Marxist rebels at a nineteenth-century castle in Mexico City. The FMLN would soon transition into a political party, one that would compete with ARENA in the electoral realm, not on the battlefield.

In San Salvador in January 1992, foreign correspondents described the theretofore-unimaginable sight of a sea of black-and-red guerrilla flags and supporters filling the main plaza in front of the Metropolitan Cathedral to celebrate the peace accord. The cathedral itself was "adorned with an enormous banner" of Romero.

"FOR ME, ROMERO IS A MAN OF GOD"

In the decades following the war, Romero remained the most revered man in El Salvador. His international reputation was cemented when he was posthumously awarded the Nobel Peace Prize in 1981 and continued to grow. Most significantly, in 2005, the Vatican opened the plodding beatification process, the final step toward canonization. The campaign had strong but not universal support. Some conservative Latin American clerics still said he was murdered

Political graffiti, mural paintings, and portraits of Cold War Latin American leftist icons: (left to right) Colombian Camilo Torres, Salvadoran Óscar Romero, and Chilean Salvador Allende. Panama City, March 2018. (Alamy Stock Photo)

not for his Catholic faith but for his political ideology. (In fact, while he was still alive some critical bishops began telling the Vatican quietly that Romero was "politicizing the Church.") But for a sizable number of people, the church's formal approval was considered largely incidental: as Dr. Juan Romagoza, a former guerrilla and founder of a public clinic, commented: "For many Salvadorans, Latin Americans and people throughout the world, he is already a saint. He is Saint Romero of America."

On the days leading up to the thirty-first anniversary of the assassination in March 2011, President Barack Obama visited Romero's grave. The civilian president Mauricio Funes, a member of the FMLN political party, recognized the powerful symbolism of this visit in a letter to the White House: "The archbishop is the spiritual guide of this nation, and the visit that you are going to carry out to the tomb of the archbishop implies for us a recognition of a leader, an international leader like President Obama."

At the same time, a member of the ARENA party commented that "half of Salvadorans do not believe Romero is worthy of sanctification" and that Obama "should also go to the grave of Major Roberto D'Aubuisson." A former ARENA presidential aide, Luis López Portillo, contended that the civilian

FMLN had appropriated Romero's legacy. "The former rebels, the FMLN ... were saying this is *our* saint, this is the left's saint. ... It's a terrible contamination of something religious by politics." He added:

> [For those on the right] Romero is also seen as a *guerrillero* dressed as a priest, a pastor who took sides with kidnappers, hid outlaws in his chapel, or told the poor that they should take what they could from the rich. ... I have a friend whose father was kidnapped in 1978, and when the guerrillas finally got the ransom, freed him, Romero was with the ones that handed him back. My friend says, "I can't take it that this man [who] participated with the guerrillas ... is becoming a saint."

During an August 2014 in-flight press conference after a trip to South Korea, Pope Francis told reporters that Romero's beatification process needed to "move in haste" and that "for me, Romero is a man of God. ... But there has to be the process, and the Lord will have to give his sign [of approval]. But if He wishes, He will do so!"

And it appeared he did. Romero was officially beatified in San Salvador on May 23, 2015, and on a bright morning of October 14, 2018, at St. Peter's Square in the Vatican, Pope Francis donned the "blood-stained rope belt" that Romero had worn on the day of his assassination and elevated him to sainthood.

31

The Mothers and Grandmothers of the Plaza de Mayo

Despair, Resistance, and Remembrance

Of course we were mad. Mad with grief, with impotence. They took a woman's most precious gift, her child.
—*Taty Almeida, mother of son Horacio, a biology student who "disappeared" in August 1976*

The Madres de Plaza Mayo were a group of mothers (with the *Abuelas* representing grandmothers) who began gathering in the Plaza de Mayo, Buenos Aires, in 1977, in protest at their "disappeared" relatives who had been snatched away by the military regime during Argentina's "Dirty War." Over thousands of marches and many years, the movement swelled in size and influence, forcing the issue onto the national and international stage. After the disastrous Falklands War led to the implosion of the junta, several high-level junta members (including three former presidents) were successfully prosecuted for human rights abuses, yet for many of the Madres and Abuelas, the fate of their lost loved ones remains a heart-rending mystery to the present day.

ARGENTINA'S DIRTY WAR

On March 23, 1976, a right-wing coup ousted Argentina's president Isabel Perón (Juan Perón's third wife), who was replaced by a triumvirate military junta led by Lieutenant General Jorge Rafael Videla. (See Chapter 20, "Juan and Eva Perón: Peronism's Dynamic Duo.") The military's ensuing Process of National Reorganization, or often simply, *El Proceso*, was the name the military leaders used to describe their iron-fisted rule, which involved shuttering the National Congress, putting regional governments under military authority, and outlawing labor unions and left-wing peronism. As a term,

"The Process" implied social and political order and obedience, but the era became known to the world as the *Dirty War*, characterized by secret terror and homicide to annihilate a secret, revolutionary enemy.

In reality, El Proceso targeted not only suspected militants and dissidents, but also students, intellectuals, journalists, priests, and artists, with estimates of the total number of victims varying between nine thousand and thirty thousand killed. Most were picked up at school, work, getting off a bus, or buying up the newspaper. Once kidnapped, the victims were taken to clandestine detention camps where they were often tortured, raped, and killed. Legions died in unspeakable ways: some were drugged and then thrown, unconscious but still alive, out of military aircraft into the Atlantic Ocean. These were the "disappeared," the civilians who vanished without a trace, victims of a deliberate government strategy to pretend they never existed.

The junta's brutal tactics must be seen in the context of the emergence of leftist revolutionary guerrillas in Argentina in the late 1960s and early 1970s who perpetrated a spate of bombings, kidnappings, and brazen daylight assassinations of businessmen and generals. The return of the Peróns in 1973 did nothing to calm the waters, with far-right death squads murdering union leaders, leftist Peronists, and leftist guerrillas (who might be also Peronists, given the movements split into Marxist and conservative factions). In late 1975, Isabel Perón fatefully called on the military to "eliminate" crime, chaos, and subversion.

Thus, well before the 1976 coup, Argentina was already a fraught, riven country with a military well-versed in terror tactics, but the junta's brutal methods would make the situation inestimably worse. In such conditions, resistance of any kind was a dangerous endeavor, but one group of civilians would make a stand that would win the world's admiration: the Mothers of the Plaza de Mayo.

A MOVEMENT IS BORN

On November 24, 1976, upward of over one hundred soldiers attacked the home of a young economist Daniel Mariani and his wife Diana Terrugi, along with their child, Clara Anahí, born just three months prior, in the small, tranquil city of La Plata, just south of Buenos Aires. The couple were both members of the underground *Montoneros* urban guerrillas and operated a printing press in the basement, cranking out copies of the clandestine publication *Evita*. Daniel had made a trip to the capital just before the attack, so was not present, but Diana and three other militants inside the home refused to surrender. Before being killed by troops storming the house, Diana likely hid Clara Anahí in the bathroom, where the baby was later discovered by a soldier who handed her over to two police officers.

Daniel's mother, María Isabel Chrobik de Mariani (known as Chicha), lived nearby and, by the following day, came to realize Clara Anahí had been inside during the attack and had somehow vanished. Over frantic and fruitless weeks and months, Mariani contacted police stations, churches, schools, and the court system to ascertain her granddaughter's whereabouts, but no one would help. Some of her closest neighbors now refused to talk to her; some said she was a "terrorist." But one juvenile protection official took pity: "You're very alone, Señora," he said, and recommended that she get in contact with other women trying to locate the whereabouts of their missing children. (Mariani's son, Daniel, refused to forsake his revolutionary ways; less than a year after Diana had been shot, he was also gunned down.)

Mariani got in touch with Alicia de la Cuadra, whose pregnant daughter had also disappeared, and this is when Mariani learned about the Mothers of the Plaza de Mayo who were protesting in front of the iconic *Casa Rosada*, the executive palace and political heart of the entire nation. This movement was spontaneously hatched when fourteen women came together on April 30, 1977, to shame a regime that had snatched their sons and daughters. (The women had to march two-by-two in the square since, following a junta edict, meetings of more than this number were banned.) Pointedly, the mothers first walked around a single structure within the plaza, the Pyramid de Mayo, which references the date (May 25, 1810) that Argentina became independent from Spain. Indeed, the "independence" motif was significant for the women who were making a statement that they could not be controlled by the regime, which was implicitly being compared to Argentina's erstwhile colonial oppressions.

Despite their tragedy, the women found scant support among the general population. In a 2011 press interview Haydeé Gastelú, then eighty-eight years old, recalled that "people were scared. . . . If I talked about my kidnapped son at the hairdresser or supermarket they would run away. Even listening was dangerous. But I couldn't keep quiet. We needed everyone to know, even if nobody believed us. That's probably why they called us the Mad Mothers at first." Undeterred, the women of the disappeared began assembling every Thursday at 3:30 p.m., wearing what came to be iconic, tyranny-defying white scarves, with their children's and grandchildren's names and sometimes the date of disappearance sewn on them. Mariani and de la Cuadra and around a dozen other grandmothers who demanded information about their missing grandchildren came to be called the *Abuelas de Plaza de Mayo*.

These women were the first public representatives of an unfolding tragedy that was affecting thousands of women and children in Argentina, whose fate was frequently horrific. In total, some 30 percent of the disappeared were women; if the abductee was pregnant (around 3 percent of the cases) or impregnated by a guard or torturer, they would be kept alive until the baby arrived, before being disappeared. Scholar Marguerite Feitlowitz wrote that the junta's "depravity reached its outer limit with pregnant detainees." One surviving female captive reported that "our bodies were a source of special fascination. They said my swollen nipples invited the 'prod' [the electric cattle prod]. They presented a truly sickening combination—the curiosity of little boys, the intense arousal of twisted men."

The babies could be given up for "adoption" to military families and others intimate with the junta, and it is estimated that there were four hundred such illegal adoptions into military families during the war. Decades hence, hundreds upon hundreds of "children of the disappeared" were now adults, or even middle-aged, having no idea that their adopted parents were complicit (or worse) in the murder of their biological ones.

Several noted the horrific parallels with recent history, often citing firsthand experience. Sara Rus had survived Auschwitz and then, after liberation, ended up in the Southern Cone nation, only to have her son killed by the military in 1977: "The Argentine military took lessons from the Nazis," said the Madre.

JUSTICE FOR THE JUNTA, EVENTUALLY

The junta initially imposed a brutal punishment on some of the mothers—in December 1977, three Madres were rounded up and killed via a "death flight"—and tried to delegitimize them by calling them "*las locas*" (the madwomen). But fearing an outcry from the general population, the regime never found a surefire way to deal with these sui generis protestors. Emboldened, the women increasingly adopted more public tactics, marching during the 1978 World Cup hosted by Argentina and, in 1981, launching a twenty-four-hour-long "March of Resistance," which turned into a yearly congregation.

By 1978 the Dirty War was effectively over, and the left was decimated. Within just a few years, however, the victors were on the back foot. Successive juntas (there were three in all, the first being responsible for the majority of the oppression) failed to arrest a sense of terminal decline, driven by chronic mismanagement of the economy and rising corruption, while opposition civil society groups were becoming more active. To deflect criticism and rally the Argentine nation around the flag, new junta leader Lieutenant General Leopoldo Galtieri authorized the invasion of the Falkland Islands (which Argentina claimed as sovereign territory) on April 2, 1982. But in a fierce seventy-four-day war, the British inflicted a humiliating defeat on their South American foe. This led the now-largely despised military to yield power, leading to democratic elections that witnessed the Radical Civic Union's Raúl Alfonsín entering the presidential palace in 1983.

In the same year he took office, Alfonsín created the first inquiry into the disappearances, called the National Commission on the Disappearances of Persons, which, after conducting a wide investigation involving the voices of thousands of victims and family members, issued the historic book, *Never Again*. The Never Again approach became the gold standard for other Latin American countries dealing with what is called "transitional justice." The report also, stunningly, led to the trials, between April and September 1985, of the nine most senior junta members, including former president Jorge Rafael Videla and two other former presidents. Videla was convicted and given a life sentence.

But feeling the heat from military brass and rank-and-file, Alfonsín then supported two amnesty laws: "Full Stop" in 1986 that put an end to prosecutions relating to El Proceso–era political violence; and, the following year, "Due Obedience," declaring that individuals could not be held accountable for crimes they were ordered to do by supervisors. But despite the partial amnesties, pro-military mutinies broke out—most notoriously the so-called Painted Faces between 1987 and 1990—over Dirty War–linked prosecutions but also grievances about poor pay and equipment.

In 1990, Alfonsín's democratic successor, Carlos Menen, pardoned several military officers behind bars, including Videla, leading a despondent Alfonsín to declare, "This is the saddest day in Argentine history." An overwhelming majority of Argentines were likewise dismayed with Menem's executive order. Here is Francisco Goldman's exquisite take on the excruciating reality that ensued for victims:

> Argentines, officially free of the dictatorship, were nevertheless forced to live in passive accommodation with its crimes and its criminals. Some of the junta's most notorious sadists roamed Buenos Aires with defiant smirks and told their stories on television. Women ran into their torturers and rapists in supermar-

kets. Veteran officers hosted their old comrades for *parrilladas* [cookouts] at their country chalets, toasting one another as heroes who had saved the nation from Communism.

In 2005, however, in a 7-1 vote with one abstention, the Argentine Supreme Court voided the two controversial amnesty laws that protected military officers from prosecution, ushering in a slew of convictions of hundreds for crimes against humanity and genocide. It was one of the first acts of Néstor Kirchner's administration, which was bent on justice for crimes committed in the Dirty War.

One high-profile case in 2006 saw Miguel Etchecolatz sentenced to life for commanding secret detention centers during his tenure as provincial police chief for Buenos Aires during El Proceso. Back in 1986, Etchecolatz had been sentenced to twenty-three years for his role in the disappearances but gained freedom following the amnesty. The 2006 three-month-long trial involved dozens of witnesses, including former president Alfonsín, who in his testimony defended his support for amnesty as essential to forestalling a military revolt. Etchecolatz himself claimed to be a political prisoner of war. "I know that you will convict me. I also know you aren't ashamed of convicting a sick, poor, powerless old man. I was part of a war that we won with weapons but we lost politically."

Hundreds of jubilant family members and human rights activists anxiously waiting outside La Plata's courtroom erupted in celebration when the

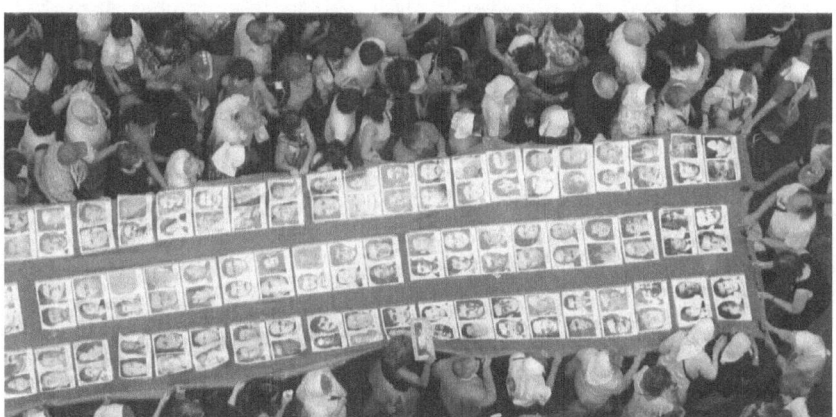

Members of the human rights group Madres de Plaza de Mayo carry a banner with pictures of people who disappeared during Argentina's Dirty War, March 24, 2006. *(Marcos Brindicci/Alamy)*

sentence was read. Chicha Mariani told the press. "I don't think 'satisfied' is the right word, but this is what this man deserves and finally justice is done." (In 2020, this "enigmatic figure of adduction, torture, and murder" received his eighth life sentence.)

General Videla—sometimes known as the "Hitler of the Pampa"—also received a new trial, leading to a late December 2010 conviction in which he was again given a life sentence. It was this same year that he assumed full responsibility for his involvement in the Dirty War. "I accept my responsibility as the highest military authority during the internal war. My subordinates followed my orders." Two years later, he received a fifty-year sentence for the network of abductions of children during his rule. He died in 2013 when he fell in a prison shower.

JUSTICE

In 1986, the Mothers of Plaza de Mayo split into two associations. The redoubtable, politically savvy Hebe de Bonafini ran the more prominent and at times controversial faction known as the Mothers of the Plaza de Mayo Association (the other was known as the Mothers of the Plaza de Mayo Founding Line). At various points in time, critics contended that Bonafini placed politics and (far-left) ideology over truth-seeking. She was certainly close to President Néstor Kirchner, who routinely appeared at public events with the Madres and Abuelas—and more specifically, with the powerful Bonafini—declaring, "We are all children of the Madres and Abuelas de Plaza de Mayo." In 2006, Bonafini said that they would cease their weekly marches since there was "no longer an enemy in the Casa Rosada," though the marches continued. Kirchner's government was also providing Bonafini's organization—now moving into social justice and antipoverty—with tens of millions of dollars to construct social housing.

The tight collaboration between the presidency and Bonafini and the Mothers continued when Cristina Fernández de Kirchner—a prominent Peronist senator and her husband's presidential aide—successfully ran for the top job after her husband decided to step down in 2007. As one foreign correspondent put it. "Few political rallies are complete without a white headscarf appearing prominently next to the president, who has staked much of her public reputation on championing human rights."

Such political proximity was perhaps bound to lead to scandal sooner or later. In the middle of 2011, there was a scandal that charged Sergio

Schoklender, who was the top aide in Bonafini's outfit, with the misuse of government funds for the housing projects for the destitute, including money laundering that allowed him to acquire a mansion, sports car, and yacht. The Association fired Schoklender and Bonafini denied any wrongdoing, calling Sergio a "traitor" and a "scammer." Nevertheless, some visible trade union leaders and human rights leaders demanded that judicial officials investigate Bonafini's misdeeds.

Nevertheless, the mothers remained the nation's moral conscience regarding a tragic period in its history. Praised by Pope Francis, former UN secretary-general Ban Ki-moon, and other global luminaries, they became one of the globe's most recognizable, awarded, and influential human rights organizations. In 2000, the Mothers founded an eponymous university that taught human rights, among other related fields. In terms of justice, more than one thousand of the regime's officials had been tried as of 2016, with seven hundred convicted.

Their search for their children and grandchildren never ceased and evolved to include the latest scientific technology. American geneticist Mary-Claire King began collaborating with the Abuelas in 1984, which involved testing the grandmothers' mitochondrial DNA—inherited exclusively from mothers—to assist in finding a match with grandchildren, even if the mothers had disappeared. (King told a journalist, "The grandmothers like to say that this proves that God is a woman because she put mitochondrial DNA on earth specifically for the use of the Abuelas.") That same decade the grandmothers advocated for a national genetic database that would preserve blood samples from grandparents. By 2019, these tools had helped trace the birth identities of 130 forced adoptees.

Alongside her work with Las Abuelas (of which she was also a president), Mariani committed her life to remaining in La Plata and locating Clara Anahí. She created a nonprofit named after her granddaughter and even turned Daniel's home into a museum, "its bombed rubble enclosed by Plexiglass," as writer Francisco Goldman put it. In 2012 Mariani, now eighty-two, was vocal about the personal cost of her quest, telling Goldman: "I'm alone in the world. I was always expecting to find Clara Anahí. Every morning I wake and think, I don't want to, I don't want to go on. After a while, I think, but if I don't move, what will happen? And I get up and go out to search for her." In her last interview not long before she died in 2018, she said, "I never lost hope. There is always hope."

32

Becoming Pope Francis

Jorge Mario Bergoglio and the Dirty War

Jorge Mario Bergoglio was an Argentinian priest who became Pope Francis—the first pope from Latin America—in 2013. It was a controversial choice due to Bergoglio's leadership of the Jesuits during the 1970s when the country was ruled by a right-wing military junta. Emerging from a period of deep reflection, Bergoglio underwent a startling transformation, becoming a staunch defender of the poor and oppressed. As pope, he actively sought to raise issues of human rights and draw attention to official abuses, including by canonizing the murdered Archbishop Óscar Romero (see Chapter 30, "Óscar Romero: Priest, Saint, Revolutionary").

THE PATH TO LIBERATION THEOLOGY

Like millions of others who came to call Argentina home, Jorge Mario Bergoglio, born in Buenos Aires in 1936, was the child (the first of five) of Italian immigrants to Argentina. In his teen years, he studied chemistry at a vocational school, which led him to a job at a laboratory in the capital. His supervisor happened to be a communism-sympathizing Paraguayan woman whose indefatigable work ethic and equanimity had an outsized influence on the impressionable youth. "I had an extraordinary boss there," he reflected. His mother was a devout Catholic, but, ironically, did not push him toward the priesthood. Someone who did help along this path was none other than his friend Jorge Luis Borges, the Argentine literary titan; Borges recalled that Bergoglio was "an agnostic who said the Our Father every night because he had made a promise to his mother."

Bergoglio entered the Jesuit novitiate in 1958, the first step in an especially demanding intellectual and spiritual training for the priesthood that often takes over twelve years to complete. Ignatius Loyola, the Jesuit founder, was a military man before he found God, and a military hierarchy is one of the order's hallmarks. Bergoglio was ordained a priest in 1969 and took his final Jesuit vows in 1973, the same year that he was named (the youngest ever in the history of the order) Provincial Superior (chief) of the Jesuit province of Argentina and Uruguay, which he ran, by his own admission in later years, as a strict disciplinarian until 1979.

Bergoglio, like so many others of his generation, studied Catholic theology at the very moment the Second Vatican Council (1962–1965; more widely known as Vatican II) reexamined the church's understanding of itself and its relationship with the world. One prominent idea to emerge from this time of reexamination was that of liberation theology, which placed increased emphasis on the sinfulness of socioeconomic and political structures that resulted in inequality and oppression. Its solution was the scripture-driven imperative for "the preferential option for the poor."

Up and down Latin America, these Vatican II-inspired priests, nuns, lay workers, and grassroots "base communities" took on the church hierarchy, which was perceived as being joined at the hip to dictators and oligarchs. As American author James Carroll put it, "Theology left the classroom, and clergy left the sacristy for the street." Interestingly, however, Bergoglio appears to have been either modestly or vehemently opposed to liberation theology. He even served as the spiritual mentor to the Iron Guard, a right-wing Peronist outfit.

ACCUSATIONS OF COMPLICITY DURING THE DIRTY WAR

The tension between the left and right during the 1960s in Argentina saw Catholics pitted on both sides, pitting pro-Vatican II progressives against conservatives, even within the nation's Jesuit order itself. More than a few Catholic leftists sympathized with or outright joined the nascent guerrilla groups, including the potent leftist *Montoneros*, born out of peronism in the late 1960s. (See Chapter 20, "Juan and Eva Perón: Peronism's Dynamic Duo.") Indeed, Mario Firmenich, a founder of the Montoneros, had earlier studied to be a priest and served as president of the Catholic Action Youth Group. On the other side, the Argentine Catholic Church in Argentina tolerated or more actively backed the anticommunist (and oligarchy) elements, even after the junta took over in 1976.

The "queasily intimate" relationship between the dictatorship and top layers of church national hierarchy—which, despite being head of the Jesuits,

Bergoglio was not part of—was an indelible element of the country's so-called Dirty War. Priests had close relations with security officers, even making lists of the "subversive" priests who then were stalked by the security forces. Military chaplains might have even literally blessed "death flights" (in which drugged but still-alive prisoners were thrown out of aircraft flying at altitude into the River Plate and Atlantic Ocean), while not supporting the killing of infants or unborn children. Juan Carlos Aramburu, who had become archbishop of Buenos Aires in 1976, backed the military regime-promoted philosophy of the necessity of purging the "anti-systemic" enemy. Regarding the allegations of mass graves being located with unidentified bodies, he contended:

> In Argentina there are no common graves. . . . Everything was recorded in the regular fashion in the books. The common graves belong to people who died without the authorities being able to identify them. Disappeared? Let's not confuse things. You know that there are "disappeared people" who live quietly in Europe.

At best, the leadership of the Argentine Catholic Church remained silent about what was occurring; at worst, it was complicit. In 2007, Christian von Vernich, police chaplain of the Buenos Aires Province Police, was convicted on charges implicating him in seven killings, forty-two kidnappings, and thirty-two instances of torture. Handed down a life term in prison, the judge described his actions as constituting crimes against humanity. The nation's church leaders released a statement expressing dismay caused "by the pain of a priest's participation in these very grave crimes." Six years later, the Argentine judicial branch issued a ruling that the church was complicit in the crimes, and that the institution had not fully investigated those culpable.

One incident during the Dirty War had life-changing consequences for Bergoglio. In 1976, Jesuit priests Orlando Yorio and Francisco Jalics were living among the poor in a Buenos Aires slum called Bajo Flores. But this seemingly innocuous choice of residence put them in the crosshairs of the military regime that had seized power that March, who saw such activity as communist subversion ingeniously veiled as religious outreach. In May, security forces apprehended the pair and took them to the Naval Mechanics School, which had been converted into the country's biggest and most infamous secret detention facility for political prisoners. The blindfolded pair were kept in a dank cell and tortured ferociously, but unlike so many who entered the facility, after five months Father Yorio and Father Jalics were released, left in an open field outside the capital.

As early as 1977, rumors grew that Bergoglio was complicit in the abduction. In this telling of the tale, Bergoglio, still relatively young at thirty-nine, had told the two activist priests that they needed to leave Bajo Flores as the regime and allied conservative sectors of the church considered their work subversive. The priests declined, after which Bergoglio indicated that they would be kicked out of the order—which would, in effect, make them sitting ducks for the junta's anticommunist purge. After they were seized, Bergoglio reportedly did not do anything to win their release. (Another assertion to emerge is that Bergoglio provided the military with the names of priests.) Shortly before his death in 2000, Yorio said that "I don't have any reason to think that [Bergoglio] did anything for our freedom." He added scathingly that the Jesuit leader did not want to rattle his cozy ties with the junta: "He didn't wait for me to come out alive."

In 2005, a human rights attorney filed a lawsuit against Bergoglio—now Archbishop of Buenos Aires—over the episode, indicting him with "complicity" in the priests' kidnapping, but the case was eventually dismissed. But the episode came back to haunt him again in 2010 when Archbishop Bergoglio was called as a formal noncriminal witness in a trial of eighteen officers at the Naval Mechanics School, and thus related to Yorio and Jalics's abduction. This time, Bergoglio was keen to put his side of events across. Invoking his clerical privilege, Bergoglio's four-plus hours of testimony were not confidential; he even held the interview from his official office. In his account, "every priest that worked with the poor was a target for suspicion and accusation from some sectors," yet as a "Jesuit brother" of the priests, he wanted them to "continue working." He said that he worked immediately and furiously to get them released. "The very night I learned that they had been kidnapped, I set the ball rolling." He also personally pleaded with the authorities to have the pair freed, but to no avail, although he acknowledged that he did not submit a formal judicial complaint about the missing men. His supporters pointed out that the fact that Jalics and Yori were indeed freed (and not killed like all the others picked up in that night's raid) might have been due to Bergoglio's exhortations.

That same year, Bergoglio testified in a separate case on "stolen babies," in which mothers were killed and the infants given to "suitable" police and military families. The case involved Elena de la Cuadra who in 1977, at five months pregnant, was made to disappear. Her mother, Alicia Zubasnabar de De la Cuadra (or "Licha") was one of a handful of founding *Abuelas* (Grandmothers looking for their grandchildren) of the Plaza de Mayo (see Chapter 31, "The Mothers and Grandmothers of the Plaza de Mayo: Despair, Resistance, and Remembrance"). The family stated that they had reached out, via letters, to Father Bergoglio to help them locate and save Elena. Her sibling, Estela, added, "He gave my dad a handwritten note with the name of a bishop who could give us information on our missing relatives. When my father met the bishop, he was informed that his granddaughter was 'now with a good family.'"

The archbishop contended that he only became aware of the "baby stealing" well after democracy was returned in 1983; Estela countered that his handwritten letters contradicted this version. Elena was never seen again, nor was her baby's identity ever discovered. In a separate interview that same year, Bergoglio added that he did what he could on behalf of others, including keeping them hidden in seminary or, for another forlorn soul, having him use a priest's garb and identification to cross over the border into Brazil.

A TIME OF REFLECTION AND REORIENTATION

According to one of his fellow Jesuits, Bergoglio's experience during the Dirty War was "searing," although it is not clear if he was traumatized by it or whether the two priests had a huge impact on him. After leaving his Jesuit leadership post, he spent some time praying and working on his doctoral thesis at a Jesuit residence in the provincial city of Córdoba, which was, as one friend put it, "for Bergoglio, a place of humility and humiliation." Or as Paul Vallely, the author of *Pope Francis: The Struggle for the Soul of Catholicism* put it, "In Córdoba, Bergoglio had had two long years to reflect on his divisive leadership of the Jesuits in Argentina and on what he had done wrong or inadequately during the Dirty War." Later, he discussed his shortcomings during his stint leading the country's Jesuits:

> I don't want to mislead anyone—the truth is that I'm a sinner.... From a young age, life pushed me into leadership roles—as soon as I was ordained a priest, I was designated as a master of novices, and two and a half years later, leader of the province—and I had to learn from my errors along the way because, to tell the truth, I made hundreds of errors. Errors and sins.

In 1992, Bergoglio went home to Buenos Aires where, first as auxiliary bishop and, after 1998, as archbishop, he embraced a far less controlling approach to leadership, and began to open all his meetings by asking the others to pray for his soul. Bergoglio also began campaigning against inhumane and unjust modern global capitalist structures and set about forging a deep connection with the poor, including joining his priests for mass in the slums. His approach was relaxed and informal: according to Paul Vallely, "he would just turn up, wander the alleyways, chat with the locals and drink *mate* herbal tea." On his first Maundy Thursday as archbishop, he swapped the cathedral for the hospital, where he washed the feet of patients stricken with AIDS. The next year, he took public transportation to wash the feet of prisoners. Some more critical voices add that this is also when Bergoglio began to cagily cultivate the Argentina media. In October 1999, during a solemn ceremony for the interment of a priest killed for his left-wing beliefs, Bergoglio apologized for the church's stance during the Dirty War: "Let us pray for Fr. Carlos's assassins, and the ideologues who lay behind it, but also for the complicit silence of most of society and of the church."

Yet despite his pro-poor instincts and actions, in Argentina, he was a "doctrinal conservative," opposing hot-button social issues like gay marriage and gay adoption, as well abortion and the ordination of women. On some occasions his outspoken orthodox theology put him at odds with populist Peronist President Néstor Kirchner and his spouse and successor, Cristina Fernández de Kirchner. In 2010, Bergoglio excoriated a same-sex marriage law backed by Fernández de Kircher, calling it a "maneuver by the devil," to which the sitting president fired back, "Bergoglio's position is medieval." She also painted the archbishop as a rightist ideologue who had backed the junta—an accusation that would once again rear its head when Bergoglio became pope.

BECOMING FRANCIS

On March 13, 2013, with clouds of white smoke pluming from the Sistine Chapel's chimney, Cardinal Bergoglio, seventy-six, was elected pope—the infallible leader of the globe's over one billion Roman Catholics—becoming the first pontiff from the Western Hemisphere, Latin America, or the Jesuits.

Francis (the name he chose) quickly garnered overwhelmingly positive media attention for his modest lifestyle, including riding the bus to work rather than being chauffeured in a limousine. Just months after his election, his first

Estela de la Cuadra, who is seeking her missing family members during Argentina's Dirty War, shows a photo of her sister Elena and a handwritten letter from then Jesuit leader Jorge Bergoglio, subsequently Pope Francis, in Buenos Aires, March 15, 2013. *(Agustin Marcarian/Alamy)*

official trip, in July 2013, was to Brazil where he spent time inside a notorious Rio de Janeiro *favela* (slum), leading some to start calling him the "slum pope." But once again, the Dirty War–related accusations resurfaced, forcing the Vatican to publicly reject them. As Jon Lee Anderson put it, "Francis the Humble, as he perhaps would like to be known, is an Argentine with a cloudy past." Estela de la Cuadra, seventy-seven in 2013, was withering: "He is a good actor." Graciela Yorio, sister of Orlando Yorio, said "I see a lot of joy and celebration for Pope Francis, but I'm living his election with a lot of pain."

But there were also defenders, most notably Adolfo Pérez Esquivel, the dissident who was awarded the Nobel Peace Prize in 1980, who told the nation, "Bergoglio was not an accomplice of the dictatorship. . . . There were bishops who were accomplices of the Argentine dictatorship, but not Bergoglio." A devout Catholic, Esquivel specifically referenced the long-simmering debate over the facts and culpability of the Yorio and Jalics case. "He is being accused of not doing enough to get the two priests out of prison, but I know personally that there were many bishops who asked the military junta for the release of certain prisoners and were also refused." Backed by an outpouring of patriotism following his election, a solid majority of Argentines seemed willing to let Bergoglio's possible sins slide into the past.

And Bergoglio had changed greatly since those days too. By the time he became pope, the former conservative disciplinarian had become one of the most outspoken proponents of liberation theology. During his first week in the Vatican, he proclaimed, "How I would like a Church which is poor and for the poor." A few weeks after that, he broke the papal tradition of only washing men's feet by washing the feet of women and Muslims in a detention center in Rome.

And he made strenuous public efforts to recognize liberation theologists who, as Jon Lee Anderson puts it, "having been largely abandoned by the Vatican, fell victims to the anticommunist witch hunt that took place in the

Residents pray during a mass to celebrate the election of Argentine Cardinal Jorge Mario Bergoglio as Pope, in the Virgin of Caacupé chapel, where Bergoglio used to give mass, in the Barracas neighborhood of Buenos Aires, March 14, 2013. *(Enrique Marcarian/Alamy)*

region during the nineteen-seventies and eighties." During a July 2015 official trip to Bolivia, Pope Francis stopped his "popemobile" to pray at the place where the body of Jesuit priest and filmmaker Father Luis Espinal had been discovered. On the orders of a right-wing military dictatorship ruling Bolivia at the time, Espinal had been abducted in March 1980 on his way back from a movie house in La Paz, Bolivia, then brutally tortured and murdered by a death squad, Bridegrooms of Death. After praying, Pope Francis said that the Jesuit had been "the victim of those who did not want him to fight for freedom in Bolivia." (Bolivian President Evo Morales caused a stir when he presented Pope Francis with a crucifix mounted upon a wooden hammer and sickle, which commentators interpreted as a political gambit, although it later emerged that the cross was a replica of one used by Espinal.) Francis was also instrumental in securing the 2018 canonization of Archbishop Óscar Romero, the liberation theology priest who was assassinated in 1980 in El Salvador while celebrating mass—a hit ordered by the founder of the country's leading right-wing political party, ARENA.

But he also made strident efforts to reconcile opposing parties. Perhaps most notably, he facilitated the secret negotiations that led to a diplomatic thaw between the United States and Cuba in 2014. The following year, having met Francis in Rome, Cuban President Raúl Castro proclaimed "if the Pope continues to speak like this, sooner or later I will start praying again and I will return to the Catholic Church—and I'm not saying this jokingly." Through his passionate commitment to the poor, Pope Francis was changing the perceived ideas of how a spiritual leader should act, a process that had started decades ago in those reflective years as Father Bergoglio.

33

Efraín Ríos Montt

From God to Genocide

We have no scorched-earth policy. We have a policy of scorched Communists.
—*Ríos Montt*

During the Cold War, Guatemalan generals were infamous for their cruelty and thirst for power. And General Efraín Ríos Montt fits the mold perfectly, ruling Guatemala with an iron fist in the early 1980s at the height of the country's decades-long internal war. Yet this general, who chillingly unleashed a ferocious counterinsurgency campaign that killed tens of thousands of civilians, actually began his public life as a civilian centrist reformer before becoming a teetotal evangelical minister "with a mission to save the country—even the continent—for Jesus."

From our twenty-first-century perch, it can seem inconceivable that any Guatemalan would find anything redeeming about this savage monster. Back in his time, though, the climate was different: while millions of Guatemalans— and not to mention human rights activists outside the country—loathed this "born-again butcher," there was perhaps an equal share who believed his *mano dura* (iron fist) and *corazón grande* (big heart) were the only things between them and a catastrophic communist revolution. Even after he was ousted in a coup, Ríos Montt remained an influential and popular figure for decades, until the end of his political career and increasing awareness of the scale of atrocities under his rule led to him becoming the first former head of state to be convicted (albeit quickly annulled) of genocide by their national court.

OFFICER MATERIAL

Ríos Montt was born in 1926 into a large family in the provincial highland department of Huehuetenango. His father was a store owner and his mother a seamstress, who instilled a strong work ethic in the young boy. By his teens, Efraín had opted for a vocation in the military, while his younger sibling, Mario, opted for the Catholic priesthood. (Mario would later chair the church's human rights committee looking into abuses during his brother's rule.)

One story has it that a colonel was taken by Efrain's steely bearing and helped him enter the military academy in Guatemala City, but whatever the case, Ríos Montt joined the army around the time long-time dictator Jorge Ubico was ousted in 1944, an event which ushered in the democratic and socially reformist Ten Years of Spring. This exultant era came to a polarizing end with the CIA-crafted right-wing overthrow of leftist president Jacobo Árbenz

Efraín Ríos Montt. *(Library of Congress Prints and Photographs Division, Washington, DC)*

in 1954, by which time Ríos Montt was an officer. (See Chapter 22, "Jacobo Árbenz: A Guatemalan Spring, Interrupted.") The army brass had already identified him as being less conservative and potentially more subversive than other ascendant elements in the officer ranks, yet Ríos Montt chose to not join those officers who in the early 1960s broke away to start the country's first wave of guerrilla groups. Instead, the ambitious and charismatic Ríos Montt chose to work his way up through the military ranks.

Like many of his era, the distinguished officer cut his teeth with US instruction and training, namely in the Panama Canal Zone and Fort Bragg, North Carolina, and also spent a stint at the Army School of War in Italy. By the early 1970s he was a brigadier general and the army's chief of staff, but resigned his commission in 1974 to run for president, heading an alliance led by the center-left Christian Democrats against the candidate handpicked by the sitting military regime. Unwilling to be voted out of power (least of all by a former officer), the military resorted to fraud to ensure that their candidate, General Kjell Laugerud, won. Ríos Montt, rushed back into active service, was sent into thinly veiled exile in Spain, where he worked as the military attaché for the next four years.

Then came a Damascene conversion. In early February 1976, a calamitous earthquake hit Guatemala. As part of the international relief response, Gospel Outreach, a California-based evangelical Protestant missionary organization, set up operations in the country. In common with many US evangelical missions at the time, the organization was also fiercely anticommunist, which immediately politicized its work in Marxist insurgency-riddled Guatemala. Returning from Madrid, Ríos Montt, undergoing a personal crisis of faith, foreswore his Catholicism and joined up with Gospel Outreach's local affiliate Church of the Word, where he would become a preacher, and a charismatic one at that. This religious reinvention also included forming friendships with prominent US evangelicals such as Pat Robertson and Jerry Falwell, who shared the Guatemalan minister's love for Jesus and equally rabid anticommunism.

FROM PREACHER TO PRESIDENT

By 1981 the Sandinistas had taken over in Nicaragua and El Salvador appeared to be headed in a similar direction, with its potent Marxist insurgency declaring a "Final Offensive" in late 1980. Guatemala's guerrilla groups had also escalated their attacks, including on the capital. In response, Guatemalan regime chief General Fernando Romeo Lucas García signed off on a brutal counterinsurgency strategy, displacing hundreds of thousands—many to neighboring Mexico—and killing thousands more, almost entirely citizens of Maya descent.

Yet some within the military were anxious that Lucas García's excesses could make a Marxist takeover more likely, citing how Somoza's despotism had paved the way for a Sandinista revolution. Tensions rose further when official party candidate General Ángel Aníbal Guevara was declared the winner in the March 1982 presidential election, despite the opposition's cries of electoral foul play. A group of young reformist officers decided the time had come to act, and two weeks later launched a coup ousting Lucas García and preventing his successor from taking office.

Like Augusto Pinochet, Ríos Montt was not a party to the scheming behind the putsch. (See Chapter 27, "Augusto Pinochet: The Unlikely Model Dictator.") One story has it that he was either preaching or just sweeping the floor in his church when the junior officers asked him to be a leader in the new government. He might have even driven over to the National Palace in a Volkswagen in civilian garb, only to emerge that night dressed in camouflage to address the television cameras. When one TV viewer saw him halfway through his first evening address, he "thought he was a comedian doing a parody of General Ríos Montt." For the young soldiers, Ríos Montt's "slicked-back hair, bushy mustache, charismatic speaking style and reputation for personal rectitude," as his *New York Times* obituary styles him, as well as his civilian role in the stolen 1974 elections, made him the perfect candidate. One foreign diplomat described the enigmatic figure this way: "[He] is not your average banana republic military general. He's a complex man. He believes in discipline, and military hierarchy. But he's neither a figurehead nor a manipulator of the coup."

That said, Ríos Montt was not averse to the idea of power and soon proved himself hungry for more. His three-man junta quickly proscribed political parties, suspended congress, and annulled the constitution. By June, pushing aside the other junta members, Ríos Montt had declared himself commander-in-chief and president who ruled by decree after announcing a "state of siege." Now the officer-cum-preacher-cum-president would "moralize national life from the top down."

"I DON'T STEAL, I DON'T LIE, I DON'T ABUSE"

Despite his undemocratic ascension, Ríos Montt seemed to be implementing a reformist shift. For example, immediately after the March 1982 coup he disbanded the infamous Detectives Corps of the National Police, initiated a smattering of human rights reforms, and garnered support from the Guatemalan population through anticorruption campaigns—including one that mandated government officials to wear pins that said, "I don't steal, I don't lie, I don't abuse." In a progressive move, he also appointed several indigenous politicians. Many Guatemalans, fatigued by two decades of war, saw him as a beacon of stability. His catchy slogan "Education, Nationalism, and End to Want and Hunger, and a sense of civic pride" did not hurt the general's cause either.

The moderate Christian Democratic movement, which had seen 130 of the party's leaders and activists assassinated in the previous two years under Lucas García's rule, also applauded Ríos Montt's actions. Frederic Chapin, the top American envoy in Guatemala City, stated publicly that the seemingly progressive nature of the junta warranted the resumption of US assistance: "No question they're better. No question. The killings have stopped. This is light years ahead from what we had before. The Guatemalan government has come out of the darkness and into the light." In 1983, President Ronald W. Reagan lifted the arms embargo that had been imposed by the Jimmy E. Carter administration due to human rights violations.

This diplomatic warming came in the context of increasing communist influence in Central America, but it was not solely US hawks who were inclined to give the new government the benefit of the doubt. Even outspoken critics of Reagan's Central America policies, such as the Democrat congressman Michael Barnes, echoed the sense of a new, less homicidal climate under Ríos Montt. "I think it's clear that there's been a change in Guatemala," Barnes asserted in January 1983. "The reports I've received are still mixed—some quite encouraging, some still quite pessimistic—but everyone concedes that the Government of Ríos Montt seems to be operating in a way that's very different from that of Lucas García in trying to deal with the problems facing the country."

Nongovernmental actors also sensed an improved human rights climate. According to one Catholic Church source in the countryside, "Massacres are down in the sense that we have not heard in the past two months of those of the size that we had been hearing before that.... The basic rule in the campo [countryside] now is control—it doesn't seem to be killing anymore." Predictably, Ríos Montt's Christianist anticommunism was also well received by the likes of Robertson and Falwell: he was, in their estimation, the perfect solution to the regional curse of the "oppression of corrupt oligarchies and the tyranny of Russian-backed Communist totalitarianism." Yet as subsequent months would prove, these assessments of a more pacific political climate were fatally wide of the mark.

RIFLES, BEANS, AND SCORCHED COMMUNISTS

Just a few months into his rule Ríos Montt touted a "beans and rifles" initiative that combined civic action programs, religious outreach, and antiguerrilla military units to win the hearts and minds of the crucial rural Maya population. In a July 1982 article, *New York Times* correspondent Raymond Bonner explained how the program was being realized in a rural hamlet in the mountainous and rebel-populated department of Quiché: "Church, state and army had gathered in this tranquil, isolated mountain village to deliver a message: a union of God, the army and the people can defeat 'the subversives.'"

Participation in the initiative, however, was far from voluntary, with Ríos Montt giving the Guatemalan peasants a stark choice: "If you are with us, we will feed you. If not, we will kill you." A fundamental element of the program required all adult males in the communities to join the civilian militias, which often entailed being "corralled into model villages" in return for political allegiance. In some instances, the so-called civilian self-defense patrols were led by members of the Church of the Word. "A Christian should carry his bible and his machine-gun," Ríos Montt once quipped.

This mobilizing of civilians spoke to the real purpose of the initiative: counterinsurgency. The four major guerrilla groups, now collectively numbering thirty thousand men, had joined forces under the Guatemala National Revolutionary Unity umbrella and were occupying villages and towns throughout rural Guatemala. These guerrillas would often flee before the approaching army forces, leading Ríos Montt to devise a cold-blooded strategy: "if you can't catch the fish," he said, "you must drain the sea." Hundreds of Maya villages simply vanished; beheadings, garrotting, immolation, and summary massacres were conducted throughout the alleged guerrilla strongholds. In 1982 Amnesty International estimated that ten thousand peasants were killed in just the first five months of Ríos Montt's rule, and as many as seventeen thousand during his seventeen months in charge.

To Ríos Montt, the conflict was total and victory would come at any cost: "I must do what I must. . . . We here are fighting the Third World War." In late 1982 he famously denied accusations that his government was conducting a

Forensic anthropologists exhume the remains from a mass grave at a former Guatemalan military base near Comalapa, September 7, 2003. *(Victor J. Blue)*

dirty war: "We have no scorched-earth policy; we have a policy of scorched Communists." Criticism within and outside the country abounded. One former foreign minister concluded that Ríos Montt's Guatemala was "like Cambodia under Pol Pot."

COUP

Surprisingly, it wasn't the criticism of atrocities that spelled the end for Ríos Montt, but petty politics. On August 8, 1983, Ríos Montt was ousted in a military coup by rival officers, led by his former defense minister Óscar Humberto Mejía Víctores, who was unhappy about the president's lack of clarity over stepping down, as well as his habit of promoting Church of the Word officers over more deserving candidates. Some military hardliners were elated that the coup meant the end of Ríos Montt's sui generis style: now they could dispense with piety and concentrate on guns. "Guatemala does not need any more prayers," Mejía Víctores was quoted as saying, "just more executions."

By 1985 there was a new constitution, ushering in elections won by the Christian Democrat Vinicio Cerezo, the country's first civilian president in sixteen years. The military still held an outsized share of power, however, and although mass murders diminished, extrajudicial killings and other forms of abuse continued. To the dismay of many human rights activists and families of victims, Cerezo granted an amnesty to members of the army that gave them immunity from prosecution for historical human rights abuses. In total, approximately two hundred thousand people were killed in the protracted internal war from 1960 to 1996, overwhelmingly at the hands of state forces.

Ríos Montt himself was by no means finished. In 1989 he started a new populist political alliance, later known as the Guatemalan Republican Front, emphasizing citizen security and individual responsibility. The former resonated with many Guatemalans who felt that, despite the war's welcome end, the endemic ills of urban crime and political corruption were still rampant—and needed a Ríos Montt-like mano dura to fix it.

And this is what effectively happened. Ríos Montt was elected to Congress in 1990, and ultimately became president of the legislature, despite the Maya rights activist Rigoberta Menchú-led effort to have him face charges of genocide in a Spanish court. (See Chapter 34, "Rigoberta Menchú: Voice for the Voiceless.") The general was constitutionally banned from running for president due to his participation in a military coup, but the polls indicated that if allowed to run, he would have been the favorite. In 1991, anthropologist David Stoll described the population's deep connection to Ríos Montt: "The authoritarianism which foreigners so hold against Ríos Montt appeals to the many Guatemalans ... who, shaking their heads at the latest outrage, are willing to say: 'We need a strongman to control us.' Here is, they say, a just military man, even as they fear and despise the army for all the killing it has done."

Paradoxically, a significant share of his backing came from the very Maya lands "that had been ravaged by his troops." For organized crime scholar Steven Dudley, the locals' stance was incomprehensible:

> When I first went to Guatemala in 1991, I traveled to the embattled department of Quiché, in the northwestern highlands. There, in Santa Cruz del Quiché's central plaza in front of the town's shorn-white Catholic church, a flag supporting the political party of the former General Efraín Ríos Montt fluttered in the wind.
>
> The flag—which had a blue hand with its two forefingers and a thumb raised—baffled me. I could not fathom why anyone would support a general who after overthrowing the government had piloted a scorched earth campaign in this, the epicenter of the northwestern highlands. The campaign was as short as Ríos Montt's time in office—15 months—but it left thousands dead, disappeared and displaced, and forever divided this country.

In 1991, evangelical Protestant civilian Jorge Serrano Elias took office, although the open secret was that Ríos Montt would have been the victor if allowed to stand. In 2000, Ríos Montt remained unable to run, leaving politician Alfonso Portillo to run in his stead, but even Portillo acknowledged that Ríos Montt was "Guatemala's real leader." Yet several corruption scandals, including Portillo's conviction on money laundering and Ríos Montt's son in a different pilfering episode, tarnished the former general's theretofore-spotless reputation for honesty.

In July 2003, now aged seventy-seven, Ríos Montt was able to overcome the ban to stand as a presidential candidate in the November elections of that year. Many human rights advocates like Miguel Ángel Sandoval were aghast. "[He] should not be standing as a candidate for the presidency, he should be on trial in The Hague alongside former Serbian ruler Slobodan Milosevic." Many accused him of being behind a massive rampage in Guatemala City on July 24, 2003, when three thousand supporters, wielding machetes and guns, demanded that Ríos Montt be allowed to run after the Supreme Court blocked his campaign. The violence of Black Thursday, as the day became known, ended only after a journalist covering the riots died of a heart attack while being pursued by Ríos Montt supporters. Although the Supreme Court's ruling was swiftly overturned by the Constitutional Court, enabling Ríos Montt to run, his law-and-order image had been irreversibly damaged. He came in third place in the November polls, with just under one in five voters backing him. He ran and lost again in 2006 in an election marked by the killings of politically active citizens.

"I AM INNOCENT"

Ríos Montt once again returned to elected office by winning a seat in Congress, which gave him immunity from prosecution over his alleged war crimes, but by 2012 his term had concluded and protection expired. Just weeks after he had retired from the legislature, the former dictator appeared in person before a Guatemalan court for his indictment for crimes against humanity and genocide. It is important to understand that by this time Guatemalans—especially through the UN and Church-sponsored "truth commissions"—gave the nation a much better sense of the reprehensible level of killing. Most telling was the fact that the disproportionate share of the deaths (83 percent) were of Maya, meaning that the mass murder amounted to a "genocide," or the deliberate targeting of a significant number

General Efraín Ríos Montt on trial for genocide, Guatemala City, Guatemala, March 19, 2013. *(Hiroko Tanaka/Alamy)*

of a particular ethnicity, religion, or nationality. A declining Ríos Montt was tried and, on May 10, 2013, convicted for being aware of but not stopping the widespread slaughter of civilians in the dozen or so mountain hamlets in the so-called Ixil triangle of El Quiché department, where 1,771 Maya women, men, and children were killed. Ríos Montt became the first former head of state to be tried (and convicted) for genocide inside his own country.

During the trial, the former strongman, eighty-six, was largely mute but did speak some words right before the trial concluded: "I am innocent. I never had the intent to destroy any national race, religion, or ethnic group." He contended that his "mission as head of state was to reclaim order, because Guatemala was in ruins," as opposed to actively managing the counterinsurgency war. Well over one hundred witnesses testified for the prosecution, describing atrocities against the Ixil ethnic group that he was accused of ordering or being aware of. Chief judge Yassmín Barríos stated that she was "completely convinced" of the general's guilt and that he had "full knowledge of everything that was happening and did not stop it." After the verdict was delivered, relatives of some of the killed, many dressed in their traditional vibrant garments, erupted into celebration, cheering "Justice!" and "Yes, it was genocide!"

One foreign scholar, American Jo-Marie Burt, said the historical court case "broke ground that these people are no longer untouchable. . . . The Ríos Montt trial was another example of Latin America leading the way in showing that it is possible to bring war criminals to trial and to bring some measure of reparation to the victims, and to rewrite the historical record so that it's a more accurate reflection of what happened and who was responsible."

Yet it was to be a short-lived victory. Less than two weeks later, Guatemala's constitutional court—citing a technicality—ruled against the conviction, and Ríos Montt's eighty-year prison sentence was rendered void. Five years later, as he was being retried in absentia (although due to his dementia he would not be sentenced if convicted), Ríos Montt succumbed to a heart attack, age ninety-one, on April 1, 2018. The next day his obituary in the *New York Times* painted the strongman's brutal legacy: "In the panoply of commanders who turned much of Central America into a killing field in the 1980s, General Ríos Montt was one of the most murderous."

And yet for many Guatemalans, he continued to have a strong political appeal right into his later years. The perplexing paradox of Ríos Montt's reputation in Guatemala is well characterized by David Stoll: "Consider the thousands of unarmed men, women and children killed by the army while he sermonized about morality, and he is a monster. Consider the hopes invested in him by many Guatemalans, including poverty-stricken Catholic peasants, and he becomes a hero of mythic proportions." Steven Dudley remained baffled, but keenly saw that a figure such as Ríos Montt might continue to have a lasting appeal, highlighting Guatemalans' complex relationship with power: "Heroic general, military dictator, victim of voter fraud, perpetrator of genocide, populist president of congress, apocalyptic predicator, father of corrupt networks—and I will never fully understand why he was popular in Quiché, the epicenter of some of his cruelest military policies and the ultimate manifestation of his political-religious machismo. But I can guarantee that his flag, or one like it, still flutters in Santa Cruz del Quiché's central plaza."

34

Rigoberta Menchú

A Voice for the Voiceless

Only together can we move forward, so that there is light and hope for all women on the planet.

—*Rigoberta Menchú*

Through her writings and activism, Rigoberta Menchú shone a spotlight on oppression in Guatemala and helped bring the issue of indigenous rights to a global audience. The landmark book, *I, Rigoberta Menchú: An Indian Woman in Guatemala*, evocatively portrayed the horrors and hardships of life under the military regime. Awarded the Nobel Peace Prize when she was just thirty-three, she used her elevated standing in the newly democratic Guatemala to push for justice against the perpetrators of human rights abuses, including requesting the extradition of two former presidents for trial on charges of genocide. She also broke new ground by setting up Guatemala's first indigenous political party and becoming the first Maya woman to even run for the presidency.

COMING OF AGE

Like so many indigenous youths in Guatemala's northcentral highlands, Rigoberta Menchú Tum's early years were far from privileged. Born into an impoverished peasant family on January 9, 1959, in the tiny, remote cloud-shrouded pueblo of Chimel, around two hundred miles north of Guatemala City, the capital, she was raised within the K'iche' (formerly written Quiché), one of the subgroups of Maya people who made up roughly half of the nation's population of eleven million. Rigoberta was almost in her twenties before she learned Spanish in addition to K'iche'.

From the age of eight, the girl started accompanying her siblings and parents to look for seasonal work on the country's crop plantations near the southern coast, as the family's farming plot was insufficient to sustain them. Conditions were generally brutal and working on the plantations resulted in the death of two of Menchú's brothers from malnourishment and pesticide poisoning respectively.

Rigoberta's coming-of-age took place against the backdrop of the internal war that broke out in Guatemala in the early 1960s. This war had its roots in the US-hatched overthrow of democratic leftist president Jacobo Árbenz in 1954, which ushered in a period of military rule (see Chapter 22, "Jacobo Árbenz: A Guatemalan Spring, Interrupted"); opposing the military regime were a motley assortment of Marxist guerrilla insurgencies inspired by the 1959 Cuban Revolution. Marxist ideology and activism also found an outlet through community, regional, and national organizations, including liberation theology-inspired efforts to push for radical social and economic change.

Rigoberta's father, Vicente, was one of those arguing for change. He traveled between rural *indígena* communities, exhorting villagers to organize. Following in her father's footsteps, an adolescent Rigoberta became involved with Church-linked women's rights groups to protest the state's oppression and injustices. For the nation's military, however, this sort of organizing was subversive. That a guerrilla group became active in Menchú's region only further blurred the line between reformers and revolutionaries for those landowners and military officers already inclined to "see Red."

Due to his labor-organizing work, Vicente was suspected of being a *guerrillero* and thrown into jail, where he was tortured for allegedly executing a local *hacendado*, or plantation owner. Following his release, Vicente joined the Peasant Unity Committee (CUC), which had been established in 1978 to advocate for land protections for vulnerable peasants. In 1979, Rigoberta joined the CUC and began teaching herself Spanish—the language of the Spanish conquerors and twentieth-century oligarchy—as well as other indigenous tongues, and was quickly put in charge of organizing the nation's almost two dozen indigenous groups to contest repression, exploitation, and exclusion.

But as one biographical account put it, the Menchú clan's "activism came at a great cost." In 1979 her brother was picked up, tortured, and killed by the security forces or an anticommunist death squad, while in 1980 her mother was abducted, raped, and killed by troops. That same year, her father was part of a pacific protest that involved the occupation of the Spanish Embassy in the capital. The army's operation to recapture the compound sparked a fire, killing thirty-nine inside, including Vicente. Desperate and vengeful, two of her sisters joined the guerrilla ranks, but Rigoberta remained committed to the activist cause, playing a leading role in a CUC-backed labor strike on haciendas on the Pacific coast, where years earlier she had been an effective peon.

EXILE ... AND STARDOM

Due to the threat against her life, Menchú, only twenty-one, went into exile in Chiapas, Mexico, where a Catholic organization provided succor. From this sanctuary, Menchú worked to raise international awareness—including via a United Nations working group on indigenous peoples—of the situation in Guatemala. In 1982, she, along with other prominent Guatemalan leftist exiles, founded the multifaceted opposition organization.

In 1983, during a trip to Paris to push her mission, she told her life story in Spanish (despite having learned it only three years before) to Venezuelan anthropologist Elisabeth Burgos Debray. The resulting book, *I, Rigoberta Menchú: An Indian Woman in Guatemala*, made a huge impact. It was translated into a dozen languages, sold five hundred thousand copies and was awarded a host of global prizes. As well as describing the experience of life as one of Guatemala's downtrodden working class (such as her time as a maid for a rich family in Guatemala City, where the pets were treated better than her), Menchú also harrowingly portrayed her family's persecution by the state. Here is the author describing her mother's killing: "They left her there dying for four or five days, enduring the sun, the rain and the night. My mother was covered in worms, because in the mountains there is a fly which gets straight into any wound." She detailed the kidnapping of her teenage brother, Petrocinio, who was snatched on his way to a market. Falsely accused of being a *guerrillero*, he was burnt alive in front of local villagers, who were forced to watch. (She quoted one of the perpetrating troops as saying, "This is what we've done with the subversives we catch because they have to die by violence.")

The book held up a picture of Guatemala's internal strife—including grisly massacres of Maya villagers at the hands of the military—to a horrified world community hitherto largely ignorant of the scale of the atrocities and injustices. Almost overnight, Menchú became the most prominent and visible spokesperson for indigenous peoples' rights and representations across the world. According to Peter Canby, "The horrifying experiences Rigoberta recounted were made all the more vivid by her small size, her open smile, and the fact that she always appeared in the colorful dress of her region."

By the late 1980s, Menchú was attempting to return to her native soil, but this resulted in her incarceration or being threatened with death; subsequently, she spent only short stints in Guatemala. She happened to be in the Central American country in October 1992, the five hundredth anniversary of Columbus's arrival, when (still only thirty-three) she learned that she had been awarded the Nobel Peace Prize for (in the committee's words): "her struggle for *social justice* and *ethno-cultural reconciliation based* on *respect* for the *rights* of *indigenous peoples*." She used the money to establish the pro-indigenous Rigoberta Menchú Tum Foundation, and in her acceptance speech cited the inspiring example of Argentine revolutionary Che Guevara (see Chapter 24, "Ernesto Guevara: Becoming Che"):

> In the harshest of times across this long struggle for respect for human rights and as indigenous peoples, the image of Che has embodied our conscience, and the determination to be faithful unto death to the ideas in which we believe.

The Guatemalan Civil War ended with the peace accord in 1996, which saw the guerrilla groups disarm (although most had already been devastated by the military's counterinsurgency campaigns). The Central American nation's internal conflagration had resulted in upward of two hundred thousand deaths—around 90 percent of which were at the hands of the security forces, not the guerrillas—while five times that number had been displaced. In total, four hundred and fifty Mayan pueblos had been wiped off the face of the earth. Later, the country's democratic president asked her to serve as Presidential Goodwill Ambassador for the historic peace agreement.

While Menchú endorsed the internal war's formal cessation, she nevertheless advocated tirelessly for some of the country's most powerful political and military officials to be tried for civil war–era crimes in Spanish courtrooms. Yet these efforts were stymied by the Spanish courts' determination that these sorts of plaintiff efforts had to be first exhausted in Guatemala. Despite these legal barriers, Madrid requested the extradition of several former regime members who had ruled the country in the early to mid-1980s, such as Efraín Ríos Montt and Óscar Mejía, to face charges of genocide and torture. In subsequent years, Menchú's Foundation played a vital role in advocating for just outcomes in several prominent domestic court cases, such as the 2013 trial of

Ríos Montt and the 2015 trial over the 1980 Spanish Embassy conflagration, which had claimed the life of Menchú's father.

AN INACCURATE TESTIMONY?

In 1999 controversy broke out over the veracity of Menchú's wrenching personal account. US anthropologist David Stoll had conducted in-person research and interviews and published his findings in *Rigoberta Menchú and the Story of All Poor Guatemalans*, which concluded that some aspects of Menchú's account were inaccurate and "cannot be the eyewitness account it purports to be" since it describes "experiences she did not have herself." Following up on Stoll's work, a *New York Times* reporter conducted interviews with those who knew Menchú who claimed that "A younger brother whom Ms. Menchú says she saw die of starvation never existed, while a second, whose suffering she says she and her parents were forced to watch as he was being burned alive by army troops, was killed in entirely different circumstances when the family was not present."

Stoll also discovered that, despite her describing a childhood without education, Rigoberta had studied at convent schools in Guatemala City and the provincial city of Huehuetenango. And being in school, Stoll concluded, would have made it impossible for her to work as a maid to a wealthy family, or to have worked on an inhospitable coastal plantation.

As would be expected, Professor Stoll's research and allegations sparked a spirited debate within the field of anthropology. Some applauded his intellectual valor and independence, no matter how distressing for the Nobel Prize winner and human rights titan; others blasted Stoll for attacking a long-excluded voice, although interestingly Stoll did not disagree with the decision to award Menchú the peace prize. A committee member from the Norwegian Nobel Committee took a similar standing, contending that her selection was "not based exclusively or primarily on the autobiography," and thus there was no need to rescind the award.

Despite this setback, Menchú continued her advocacy, which had, over the years, expanded from human and indigenous rights to condemning the evils of "globalization"—that is, the nefarious "neoliberal" (free market) enslaving people around the world. She was among the most celebrated speakers at the much-covered 2002 World Social Forum in Brazil, where she blasted the George W. Bush administration's "war on terror."

Nobel laureates (*left to right*): Shirin Ebadi, Jody Williams, Tawakkol Karman, Rigoberta Menchú arriving in Belfast, Ireland to attend the fourth biennial conference of the Nobel Women's Initiative, 27 April 2013. *(Paul Faith/Alamy)*

In 2007, Menchú formed Guatemala's first indigenous political party, WINAQ, and threw her hat into the presidential ring, becoming the first Maya female ever to run for the top job, although she lost in the first round, taking a scant 3 percent of the vote. (She also lost decisively in a 2011 national election as well, with an almost identical vote count.) In 2013, Menchú received the news that the Autonomous National University of Mexico had designated her as a Special Investigator for its Multicultural Nation campaign. All told, Menchú bravely opened up new political and cultural space for indigenous communities, most critically those of her own Guatemala.

35

Abimael Guzmán and Shining Path

The Philosophy of Terror

Abimael Guzmán was the "maximum leader" of the clandestine Maoist revolutionary sect known as *Sendero Luminoso* (Shining Path), which between 1980 and the early 1990s waged a brutal and traumatic insurgency that, together with the counterinsurgency, led to the deaths of seventy thousand Peruvians, displaced another six hundred thousand, and destroyed $2 billion worth of property. For decades a mysterious figure glimpsed only in a 1978 mugshot and a few videos, Guzmán was eventually brought to justice in September 1992, aged fifty-seven, and exhibited before the media in his striped prison uniform, the nation's tyrannizer finally brought behind bars. And there he would stay, give or take a retrial or two, until his death on September 11, 2021. For Peru, however, the scars of his bloody revolutionary campaign will last much longer.

AN UNCERTAIN CHILDHOOD

Manuel Rubén Abimael Guzmán Reynoso was born on December 3, 1934, in Mollendo, a city on Peru's remote southern coast. Like Sor Juana three centuries prior (see Chapter 3, "Sor Juana Inés de la Cruz: Latin America's First Feminist"), Abimael was an "hijo natural" (the euphemistic term for an illegitimate child), in this case, the result of a romance between his father, a conservative and imperious man with an aristocratic streak, and Berenice Reynoso. (Many accounts have it that Berenice died while Abimael was still a child, but a more likely story is that she simply abandoned the boy in 1942 as she didn't want the burden of parenting while also trying to attract a rich husband. That year, Abimael was sent hundreds of miles north to live with an uncle in the gritty port city of Callao, next to Lima.

In 1945, Abimael was catapulted into an entirely different world when his father and his father's legal wife requested that the boy relocate, once again, to live with them in their especially storied colonial mansion in the major provincial city of Arequipa, near Mollendo. Guzmán's father also enrolled his son in the prestigious private high school, *La Salle*, but the boy's illegitimate status (he was the first hijo natural to ever be enrolled in the school) made it a testing experience, with his classmates frequently ridiculing him for being a bastard. (Such abuse was not confined to the classroom: even his grandmother taunted him by asking, "Do you know who your mother is?") Although the shy but eager Abimael thrived in the classroom, especially in history, logic, and ethics, the biographer Santiago Roncagliolo reckons that his bastard condition might be the critical variable to explain why this otherwise privileged child did not follow the more conventional path of Arequipan elites, instead opting for "rebellion" in the form of communist revolution.

In 1953, Abimael enrolled at the National University of Saint Augustine (UNSA) in Arequipa. A half-century later, in only two public interviews ever given, Guzmán reflected that while the UNSA did not have many Marxist professors or Marxist texts, it did have legions of peers with whom he could discuss politics and theory. Guzmán's assessment of his university days is somewhat at odds with those who knew him, however. His academic mentor Miguel Ángel Rodríguez considered Abimael to be brilliant (according to Rodríguez, Guzmán's defense of his thesis on the German philosopher Immanuel Kant in front of a panel of academics lasted an unbelievable six hours) but in no way inclined toward agitation or organizing. Some of Abimael's UNSA peers later recalled that Abimael was more interested in culture and a boozy social life than Marxism; he also pursued myriad sexual relationships, including with a young widow who was a close friend of the Guzmán family's maid and sporadically frequented a high-class brothel. But the youthful Abimael was certainly interested in Marxism enough to try to join the Peruvian Communist Party, although he was rejected for not being the son of a worker.

FIRST BLOOD

Upon graduation, Guzmán was not able to score a teaching position at his alma mater, and in 1962, then just under thirty years old, left Arequipa to take up a philosophy professorship at the San Cristóbal de Huamanga University in the highlands city of Ayacucho. In this isolated mountain community, where there were no telephones, only one movie theater, and a population of less than thirty thousand, he expected to finally experience the "deep Peru"—what anthropologist Orin Starn and historian Miguel La Serna describe in their chilling biography of Shining Path as "the Andean heartland in its wrenching poverty and indigenous traditions." Indeed, Ayacucho had been a zone of desperation, resistance, and conflict for centuries. During La Conquista, local indigenous populations such as the Wari and Chankas had allied with the Spanish to liberate themselves from the imperial Incas who had long subjugated them. During the protracted Spanish viceroyalty, the city had been a hotspot of resistance first in the shape of Túpac Amaru I in 1580 and, two centuries later, Túpac Amaru II. (See Chapter 4, "Túpac Amaru II and the Great Andean Rebellion.")

The university where Guzmán was to teach was revolutionary in its approach to education. San Cristóbal was the country's second oldest institution of higher learning but had been shuttered for over one hundred years before reopening in 1958 with the expectation that it would be Ayacucho's cultural and intellectual epicenter. It quickly became a source of pride for *ayacuchanos* that in the university's classrooms the children of hacienda owners were sitting next to the sons and daughters of campesinos, bridging a divide that had characterized Peruvian society for centuries. This heady social mix proved naturally receptive to the fertile ideological environment of the late 1960s when the influence of Che Guevara and Fidel Castro in Cuba, and North Vietnam's Ho Chi Minh loomed large. (See Chapter 23, "Fidel Castro: A Rebel with a Cause" and Chapter 24, "Ernesto Guevara: Becoming Che.")

Guzmán quickly gained a reputation as a dynamic instructor at the university, with students signing up for his classes in droves. (Some called him "Dr. Shampoo" for his supposed ability to wash young brains.) His leftist political ideology was also developing apace—and made the poster boys of global communism look like moderates. Years later, Carlos Tapia, a San Cristóbal faculty colleague, recalled an illustrative episode from October 1967. A few days after Che Guevara's death, Tapia dedicated his lecture to discussing the Argentine revolutionary's legacy. Following the class, a student approached him in the cafeteria to invite him to repeat his remarks to a different student audience. Happy to oblige, Tapia was then met with a shock when he entered an auditorium packed with two hundred students sat in sepulchral silence. The walls were plastered with red flags emblazed with hammers and sickles; no one invited Tapia to speak. Then suddenly Guzmán started addressing the students, announcing that it had come to his attention that a professor was praising that "punk" Che Guevara. Guzmán proceeded to blast Fidel Castro's Cuba as no better than an "advanced bourgeois state" and not a paradigm of the popular revolution. Tapia then walked out of the room.

Having decided that only Mao Zedong was upholding true communist ideology—he dismissed Soviet premier Nikita Khrushchev as "sinister"— Guzmán made several extensive trips to China in the mid-1960s to study "political-military" strategy while in the provincial city of Nanking, accompanied by at least one visit by his wife Augusta La Torre. Guzmán was in China just as Mao's Cultural Revolution—which would ultimately leave as many as two million dead and untold numbers of ruined family and individual lives—was beginning. It is an open question as to whether Guzmán witnessed some of the Cultural Revolution's ruthlessness and liked what he saw; others surmise that Chinese officials might have kept their guests ignorant. In any event, Guzmán's experience helped cement his belief that he could bring Maoism (and its elevation of peasant insurgency over urban/industrial-driven revolution) to the Peruvian highlands. If Mao's communists could use the remote Yan'an area as their base of operations, could not the soaring peaks around the historically rebellious Ayacucho "become the stronghold for a Peruvian people's war?"

After returning to Peru, Guzmán founded Shining Path in 1970. The Maoist group, like many of its leftist revolutionary brethren, set out to reform a highly unequal and impoverished country via communist revolution (the group took its name from José Carlos Mariátegui's slogan "Marxism-Leninism will open the shining path to revolution" [see Chapter 19, "José Carlos Mariátegui and Victor Raúl Haya de la Torre: Peru's Long Revolution"]). Guzmán and La Torre would be joined by Elena Iparraguirre to make up a revolutionary troika; indeed, it was notable that women comprised a large share of Shining Path members and leadership when compared to most Cold War armed leftist insurgencies. Fresh recruits had to sign a loyalty pledge to Shining Path but also to Guzmán himself, who now adopted the nom de guerre "Comrade Gonzalo." His guerrilla acolytes celebrated their leader as the "Fourth Sword" of communist ideology, after Marx, Lenin, and Mao.

The three Shining Path revolutionaries rented safe houses in Lima's toniest neighborhoods—Miraflores, San Borja, San Isidro—reasoning that the authorities would never think to look for communist leaders there. When they did leave the capital, they usually relocated to equally pacific locations such as tranquil, apolitical Arequipa, rather than violent Ayacucho. (The higher elevation there also aggravated Guzmán's debilitating polycythemia, a rare blood disease, and in any case, he liked his creature comforts.) This choice of neighborhoods highlighted an ideological oddity about Shining Path: what many inside and outside Peru later came to believe was a rural, indigenous revolution that was run by fair-skinned Peruvians from Lima's diplomatic and political barrios.

But although Guzmán, La Torre, and Iparraguirre had come from the petite bourgeoisie, their rebellion's foot soldiers mostly came from humbler, Quechua-speaking communities: the children of peasants, construction workers, and craftsmen. According to Peru expert Robin Kirk, "By joining Abimael's movement, young people became better than white; they went instantly from the bottom to the top of the social pyramid."

THE MAOISTS MAKE THEIR MOVE

The revolution began on May 17, 1980, when half a dozen armed and hooded insurgents burned ballots for an imminent presidential election—the first such election after twelve years of military rule—and seized a clerk in an Ayacucho village. In what would become a signature move, the fighters raised hammer-and-sickle flags over the town. By June they were in Lima, where they blew up power lines. As the city lay in darkness, the rebels lit torches, sometimes arranged to form a hammer and sickle, on nearby hills.

New president Fernando Belaúnde Terry, elected the day after the first Shining Path attack, quickly came under pressure to do something about the Maoist bandits, even if they only effectively controlled Ayacucho. Given that the military could not be fully trusted to stay out of politics, Belaúnde's preference was to call on Peru's anti-terrorism police to hunt down the guerrillas in their remote mountain lairs. It was, as Starn and La Serna describe, the beginning of the "dirty war": "Soldiers broke down doors to search for weapons and propaganda. . . . Whispered stories described nighttime executions, gang rapes, and target practice with live prisoners." Many detainees were never seen again. "Someone from Ayacucho has disappeared," lamented a song from this period, "Where could she be?" Things only escalated after the military intervened in 1983. In 1985, newly elected president Alan García promised to stop fighting "barbarism with barbarism," yet the abuses continued to pile up.

Shining Path was also wreaking havoc; the revolution had failed to win many hearts and minds. Shining Path's anachronistic Maoist caricatures of nefarious landlords and suffering serfs did not translate well in the Andes.

Peru in the 1980s was not China in the 1920s: in fact, the Peruvian military regime that ruled after 1968 implemented a far-reaching, albeit checkered, left-wing agrarian reform program that eliminated most of the large, landed estates. And any support Shining Path may have initially garnered in poor communities quickly withered under the group's brutal rule, which also drove the formation of so-called *rondas campesinas* (peasant militias whose members were called *ronderos*). These poor Andean villagers, often using only the most rudimentary of arms, such as rusted Winchester rifles, were remarkably effective at beating back the Shining Path thugs terrorizing their pueblos with impunity. Yet such resistance often came at an unbearable high price. In March 1983, ronderos executed a Shining Path commander in the Andean village of Lucanamarca. In revenge, on April 3, 1983, Shining Path revolutionaries marched into the village and executed sixty-nine civilians, including women and children. The Lucanamarca massacre set the pattern for the years of extreme violence that was to come. On July 16, 1984, 117 people were killed in the village of Soros, in Ayacucho.

By the late 1980s, Shining Path's original strategy of winning over the rural population had flopped in the face of *rondero* resistance. Guzmán's Plan B was to relocate the war from the Andean highlands to Lima, where destitute rural migrants who had fled the violence became a source of recruits. ("Ayacucho is the cradle," Guzmán was fond of uttering, "but Lima is the catapult.") The guerrillas were also aided by hyperinflation and economic contraction that was threatening to turn Peru into a failed state. The urban phase of Guzmán's rebellion involved car bombs and more blackouts—there were over one thousand attacks in Lima in 1989 alone—as well as the targeting of civil-society actors whom the Maoists considered threats.

But any vestige of support for Shining Path evaporated in 1992 after the group assassinated María Elena Moyano, president of the Villa Women's Federation and a community activist who was hugely popular. Shining Path wanted to take control of the federation and its twenty thousand members, accusing Moyano of "suffocate[ing] the revolutionary struggle of the masses," but the assassination (and the subsequent brutal destruction of Moyano's body with dynamite) prompted a massive popular backlash against Shining Path, with some three hundred thousand people attending Moyano's funeral.

By that time, the group was already firmly on the back foot. President Alberto Fujimori, elected in 1990, had placed the rondas at the center of his counter-insurgency strategy, but by the early 1990s, it had become clear to the

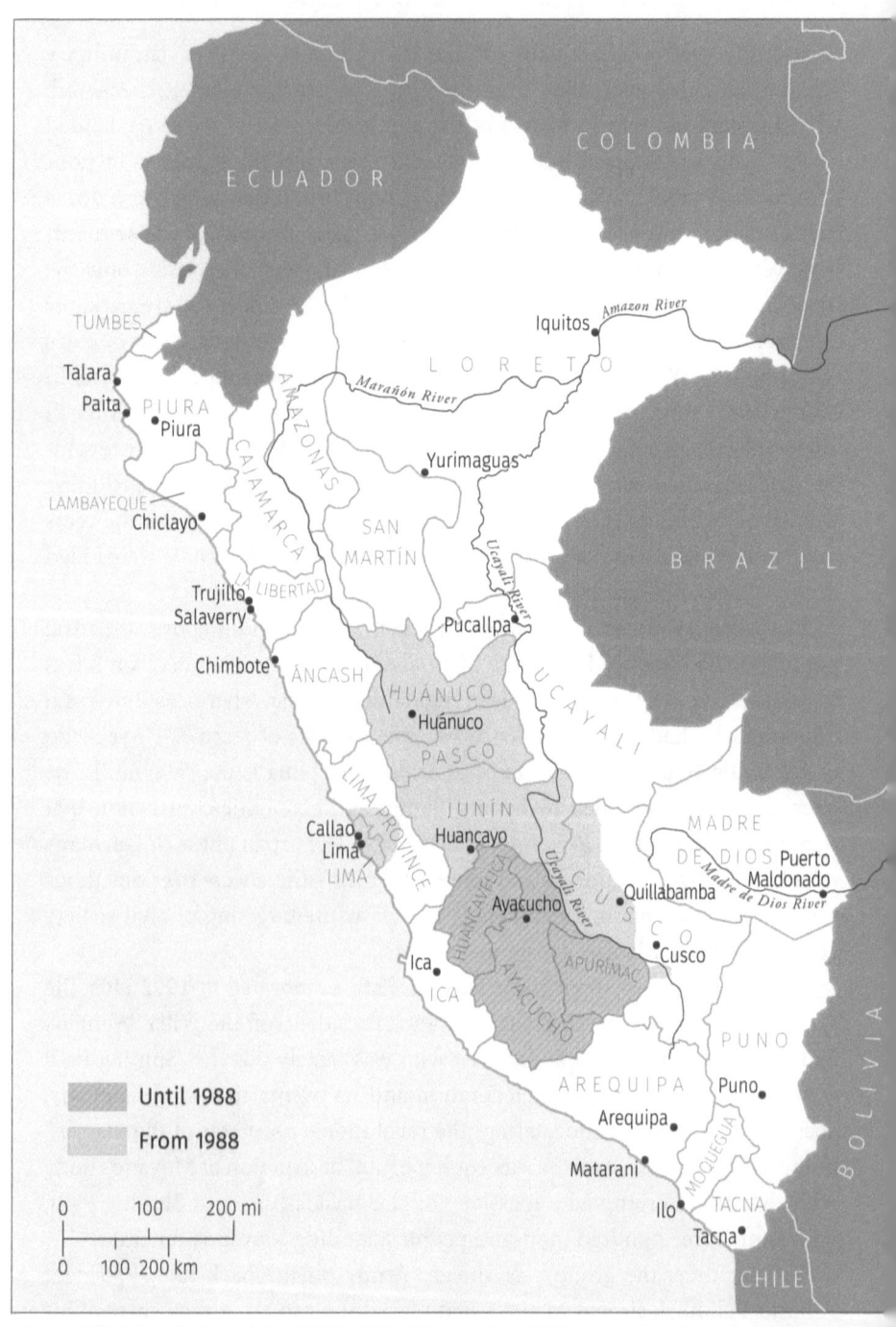

Map of Shining Path Activity, 1980–1992. *(University of Wisconsin-Madison Cartography Lab)*

Peruvian authorities that efforts by the military and the *ronderos* would not be decisive—the only way to defeat the Shining Path insurgency would be to decapitate it. A new government intelligence unit was formed to track down the troika and key subordinates, and its agents carried out a relentless investigation, eventually retrieving cigarette butts—Guzmán preferred Winstons—and polycythemia medicine from trash bins. ("Garbage speaks an eloquent language," quipped one officer, in reference to Umberto Eco's lasting novel, *The Name of the Rose*.) This evidence led to the remarkably low-key arrest of Guzmán and Iparraguirre in September 1992 (La Torre had died in 1988 in mysterious circumstances).

The nation's most notorious terrorist was held in a purpose-built prison that was the most secure in the world, making Alcatraz seem positively lax. To escape, Guzmán would have to get past walls of reinforced concrete, seven guarded metal doors, and a minefield. The prison was surrounded by a swamp, and then the ocean. Swimming across the ocean would bring him to the Callao Naval Base. His cell measured just two by three meters.

A TALE OF TWO TRIALS

After a ten-day military trial in October 1992, Guzmán was convicted of treason and sentenced to life in prison by a judge who wore a hood to protect his identity. Iparraguirre and eight other Shining Path commanders were also sentenced to life imprisonment at other trials. Life sentences for terrorists, military trials, and judicial anonymity were all recent innovations passed by Fujimori to prosecute Shining Path leaders, but the proceedings were criticized by Guzmán's lawyer, who said he had been unable to call any witnesses and only been able to meet his client twice, for ten minutes at a time.

Criticisms of the judicial process mounted, leading to the 1992 convictions being thrown out by Peru's constitutional court in 2003. The first retrial in 2004, now in a civilian court, saw Guzmán shouting communist slogs to the live television cameras and was abandoned after eight days. The next attempt lasted a whole year, culminating in 2006 when Guzmán, then aged seventy-one, received multiple life sentences from a judge who took more than five hours to read the verdict. Elena Iparraguirre, then aged fifty-nine, again received a life sentence. Guzmán reacted to the verdict with a fist-banging tirade replete with revolutionary slogans, but it would be his last opportunity for such grandstanding. He was led away to prison, where

Shining Path founder Abimael Guzmán attends trial at Ancon prison in Callao, Peru, June 6, 2017. On the left is his wife, Elena Iparraguirre, herself a senior leader of the Maoist insurgency. *(Mariana Bazo/Alamy)*

he would remain until his death in 2021, although in 2010 he was allowed to marry his long-time partner Iparraguirre.

Estimates of the damage done by Shining Path under Guzmán's leadership vary, but in 2003 Peru's Truth and Reconciliation Committee issued a report stating that 37,800 of the estimated 70,000 deaths in Peru's twenty-year insurgency conflict were caused by Shining Path guerrillas led by Guzmán. The Shining Path's terrorist activities also seriously disrupted the country's economy. It is also indisputable that the military is responsible for many deaths during that period: the Truth and Reconciliation Commission attributed roughly half of all deaths to Shining Path, 30 percent to the government, and the remainder to the *rondas*. Yet many Peruvians who lived through the war years draw a clear moral distinction between the instigating Shining Path and the reacting Peruvian military. It is not that they are eager to whitewash the latter's myriad abuses, but rather that they perceive the military as a highly imperfect but legitimate instrument of state power possessing a monopoly over the use of lethal force. Others, however, argue that the security forces committed crimes against humanity during the internal conflict, including the notorious 1991 Barrios Altos massacre, at which fifteen people, including an eight-year-old boy, were killed in cold blood at a barbeque by a death squad, who were reputedly looking for Shining Path members. The massacre was part of the charges of human rights violations brought against Fujimori, who was eventually sentenced in 2009 to twenty-five years imprisonment.

A DIMINISHED BUT STILL LETHAL FORCE

With Guzmán no longer at the helm, Shining Path splintered, with a rebel faction based in the Apurímac, Ene and Mantaro River Valley (VRAEM) region labeling Guzmán a traitor, while the main group remained loyal. Yet the general trajectory of both was of decline. In July 1999, the main group's new leader Óscar Ramírez Durand, aka Comrade Feliciano, was captured and sentenced to life imprisonment. (His sentence was reduced in the 2006 retrial to twenty-four years.) In 2011, new leader Comrade Artemio finally admitted the main group's defeat in 2011, a reality that was sealed by his capture in 2012 and sentence of life imprisonment in 2013.

Yet the VRAEM rebel faction—now calling itself the Militarized Communist Party of Peru (MPCP) insurgency—continued the struggle, funded by its ties with drug trafficking groups in Peru. In 2015, the Peruvian army rescued fifty people from the VRAEM area who had been kidnapped by Shining Path up to twenty-five years ago; among the rescued were children who had been conceived when the original victims were raped. In May 2021, the MPCP faction killed sixteen civilians, including two children, in an attack on the village of San Miguel del Ene. Pamphlets scattered about warned people not to vote in the upcoming presidential elections.

The legacy of the original Shining Path also reared its head in another, more unforeseen quarter in 2021. The presidential elections that year were won by Pedro Castillo, a hard-left teacher, farmer, and unionist who had never previously held political office, beating rightist Keiko Fujimori (daughter of former president Alberto Fujimori) by just forty-four thousand votes out of 17.5 million cast in total. The new president's honeymoon period came to an abrupt end after he appointed his first Cabinet, naming Guido Bellido, who has been accused of being a Shining Path sympathizer, as prime minister and chief of cabinet. In addition, Castillo's nomination for minister of labor allegedly had ties with a pro-Shining Path organization. Facing a wave of discontent from Peruvians over these connections with the terrorist group, in November 2021 Bellido resigned and Castillo appointed a new, more moderate cabinet.

The year 2021 also witnessed a dispute over what to do with Guzmán's body. His imprisoned partner Iparraguirre demanded that the body be handed over to her for burial, but officials resisted for fear the grave would become a symbolic place for would-be revolutionaries and terrorists. A change in law was hastily rushed through, empowering the state with the authority to cremate Guzmán and scatter the ashes, which it duly did on September 24, although it did not reveal what would be done with the ashes.

Guzmán the man was finally gone, but the former philosophy professor's career of terror has left an indelible mark on Peru and its people. The purest of ideologues—even Mao came to realize that he was getting it wrong—Guzmán pursued his path with all the maniacal focus of a philosophy professor who thought he had truly seen the light.

36

Chico Mendes and Marina Silva

Defenders of the Amazon

At first I thought I was fighting to save rubber trees. Then I thought I was fighting to save the Amazon rainforest. Now I realize I am fighting for humanity.

—*Chico Mendes, 1987*

Chico Mendes was a rubber tapper in Acre, Brazil's least developed state, whose experience of the destruction of the natural environment through rapacious business set him on the path to becoming a world-famous environmental activist. Through steely determination and an unflagging work ethic, he became a rural workers' union leader who courageously defended his fellow tappers as well as local indigenous against the landholding powers in Acre, using strikes and other pressure tactics to stem the tide of Amazonian deforestation and expanding cattle ranches. For Mendes, human rights and the earth's rights were inextricably linked through sustainable economic exploitation, leading to his development of the idea of "extractive reserves," which eventually became part of Brazil's legislation.

His assassination at the age of forty-four marked a blow to Brazil's environmental movement, but his work was continued and institutionalized by another tapper, Marina Silva. Her origins tale is one of Brazil's most compelling: a humble girl who overcame fatal maladies and unspeakable poverty to become a juggernaut in Brazil's notoriously rough-and-tumble political arena. Their mutual legacy is one of a country in which areas of the Amazon gained critical legal protection from deforestation, although rates of destruction remained worryingly high.

LAND OF RUBBER

Born near Xapuri in 1944, Francisco Alves Mendes Filho—universally known as Chico Mendes—was one of seventeen children (although only six lived into adulthood) and grew up in the forest. Like virtually everyone else born into poverty in the Brazilian state Acre in this time, he did not receive a formal education; he did not learn to read until he was close to twenty. Instead, before he turned ten, he started working as a rubber tapper, work which involved harvesting latex from a rubber tree through a cut in the bark (which does not significantly damage the tree).

This milky tree sap (roughly 30 percent of the sap is rubber) had long been harvested by indigenous groups in South America and used to make balls for a game they called *ollama*, but it was also a key part of Brazil's rubber bonanza, driven by the industrializing world's insatiable demand for products that could be made better and cheaper with natural rubber: hoses, tires, industrial bands. In 1839, Charles Goodyear accidentally discovered that the properties of rubber could be greatly enhanced by cooking the latex with a small amount of sulfur and other materials, even soot—a process he named vulcanization. The vulcanized rubber rage only surged after the invention of the automobile in the late nineteenth century, closely followed by John Dunlop's invention of tires and Henry Ford's pioneering of the mass production of autos. Tens of thousands of men—*seringueiros*, or rubber tree tappers—were drawn to these far-flung jungle locales that were heretofore populated by indigenous peoples.

By the turn of the twentieth century, Acre state (where Xapuri is located) had emerged as a central player in Brazil's rubber industry, but the good times were about to end. By the 1910s, Brazil had lost its long-held monopoly of natural rubber—until then exclusively located and cultivated in the Amazon basin—to global competitors, crucially British colonies in Africa and Asia. The world price collapsed, but there was a second boom during World War II after the Japanese takeover of the western Pacific resulted in the Allies losing access to virtually its entire source of rubber. A US-Brazil military agreement jumpstarted expanded rubber production by forcibly relocating over fifty thousand workers, dubbed the "Rubber Army" by the government of President Getúlio Vargas, from other parts of the country to the Amazon. Tens of thousands of these men came from the desperately poor northeast, including Chico Mendes's father, Francisco Mendes, who migrated from Ceará. When the war ended and with it the rubber emergency, many of these Rubber Soldiers were isolated or missing.

Over the ensuing post–World War II decades, construction of a highway continued to open the once-remote region—and, as scholar Kenneth Maxwell describes, "the inexorable Brazilian process of settlement, land grabbing, ranching, and social conflict soon followed." As the global price of rubber sagged, the hardscrabble *seringueiros* were increasingly being evicted from their tapping locations, the land was then sold, deforested, and scorched to make way for cattle pastures. Financial entities bought up entire rubber estates and converted them to pasture; Catholic Church officials estimated that ten thousand rubber tappers had been displaced.

The young Chico was on the front line of these social earthquakes, which gave rise to a febrile atmosphere of activism. During his adolescence Chico Mendes met local priests with an activist bent, but perhaps his most seismic encounter was at eighteen with Euclides Fernandes Távora, a dedicated Communist and erstwhile military officer on the run from authorities. In addition to most likely teaching Mendes to read and write, Távora introduced Mendes to liberation theology and Marxism, and instructed his young charge on how to stand up for his beliefs. According to Mendes, "[Távora] gave me a lot of advice about how to organize in the trade union movement. . . . Despite the defeats, humiliations, and massacres, the roots of the movement were always there, he said. The plants would always germinate again sooner or later, however much they were attacked."

A UNION OF TAPPERS

Chico Mendes moved to the town of Xapuri in 1971 and continued his intellectual awakening. By 1975, Mendes was taking classes in syndicate creation and leadership conducted by elements of the state-run Brazilian Confederation of Agricultural Workers. Change seemed to be in the air: during the late 1970s, the Catholic Church—once a stalwart of the landed aristocracy—supported the aggressive placement of more priests who followed liberation theology and pushed for greater community organizing so-called base communities and, before long, numbered into the tens of thousands.

But there was still the issue that the ranchers held all the financial resources and means of violence. Mendes's response was novel: in 1977, he unionized the tappers as the Xapuri Rural Workers Union, of which he later became president. Through the union, Mendes and his fellow activists (including women and children) devised a new tool of resistance, the *empate* (standoff). A deliberate showdown between rubber tappers and the pitiably paid work crews dispatched by the ranching barons to slash the forest, the empate involved forming human barricades (often entire families) to block tractors or chainsaw crews. Proponents contended that the empate was legal as Brazilian law permitted an individual to "maintain or reinstate his claim through his own force, provided he do so immediately." Despite what some observers assumed, the tactic was "not a form of Gandhian passive resistance," but a form of pressure and persuasion. According to author Augusta Dwyer, the empate "was first an attempt to bring these fellow workers around to the other side, to make them understand that they were taking the food from the mouths of their comrades. It was also a statement, one that said to everyone: 'You will have to kill us to get us out of here.'" And it initially appeared to work, with the union pushing out from Acre two of the region's most powerful ranchers, Rubens Adrade de Carvalho (the "King of Cattle") and Geraldo Bordon, who ran the country's largest meat-processing companies.

Mendes built on this success by founding the Acre wing of the Workers' Party (PT), an antimilitary regime party formed in 1978 and led by the "burly, bearded, charismatic" unionist Luiz Inácio Lula da Silva (see Chapter 45, "Luiz Inácio Lula da Silva: Brazil's First Working-Class President"). Within a few years, the PT was the country's fourth-largest political party, fighting for better job conditions and higher pay in the cities and, in the hinterlands, land reform. Mendes successfully pushed the party to include a plank on environmentalism in its national electoral platform, but with the tappers just one interest among many in the PT, Mendes launched a national *seringueiros* union, which started to give these otherwise anonymous Brazilian agents some international attention, albeit limited to the environmental movement. In the mid-1980, Mendes threw his hat into the political ring, although his candidacy as a PT member for the Acre assembly failed.

Throughout the 1980s, Mendes's affability and aggressive but nonviolent tactics garnered him increasing admiration and support from international environmentalists. As Maxwell put it, "He spoke the lingua franca of visiting anthropologists from Berkeley and Paris, European TV producers, and Washington environmental lobbyists." He accepted invitations to speak in numerous locales, including a crucial 1987 visit to Washington, DC, where he spoke with hosts at the World Bank, Inter-American Development Bank (IADB), and Capitol Hill about the need to sever international support for road construction that allowed the nefarious cattle industry to expand even more deeply into the virgin Amazon, a massive region larger than Western Europe.

At the First National Rubber Tappers' Congress in Brasilia in 1985, Chico Mendes and his seringueiros compatriots posed the idea of the "extractive reserves" where locals, including indigenous, would have the right to harvest ecologically desirable forest products (e.g., rubber tapping and nut harvesting) from public lands while destructive practices would be proscribed. Pressured by Mendes's advocacy, both the IADB and World Bank backed his extractive reserves notion, which became a landmark of the global environmental movement. In 1984, the UN granted Mendes its Global 500 award for his environmental courage in the face of pronounced political, social, and logistical hurdles. Mendes never personally profited from the swelling recognition and awards, giving any external payments to his beloved seringueiros' union. As another tapper organizer, Gomercindo Rodrigues, put it, "He led a very simple, almost poverty-stricken life." In 1986, his wife, Ilzamar, came close to death while giving birth to twins—one of the babies was stillborn—and Chico was despondent that he did not have enough money to cover the hospital costs. But his commitment to the cause never wavered: he named the surviving twin "Sandino" in honor of the Nicaraguan anti-imperialist rebel (see Chapter 16, "Augusto César Sandino versus the United States"). Daughter Elenira was named after a famed Marxist guerrilla who harassed the security forces in the Amazon state of Pará in the early 1970s when the country was still under a military dictatorship. His spouse was fully aware of Chico's obsession with his vocation. "My work is not play," he would tell her time and again. Ilzamar reckoned that she had not spent over a week with Chico between 1986 and 1988.

POWERFUL ENEMIES

Chico Mendes's activism also earned him the hostility of powerful landowners, who were apoplectic over Mendes's militant anti-logging protests against the lucrative business model of clearing virgin rainforests for pastures. The long-simmering, sometimes violent dispute between the unionists and ranchers in Acre came to a boil with the 1980 murder of Wilson Pinheiro, an adored syndicate leader who was killed in his own union's building. The assassins might have been trying to get Mendes but settled for shooting his mentor. The *seringueiros* lawlessly killed a rancher they believed was complicit in Pinheiro's death.

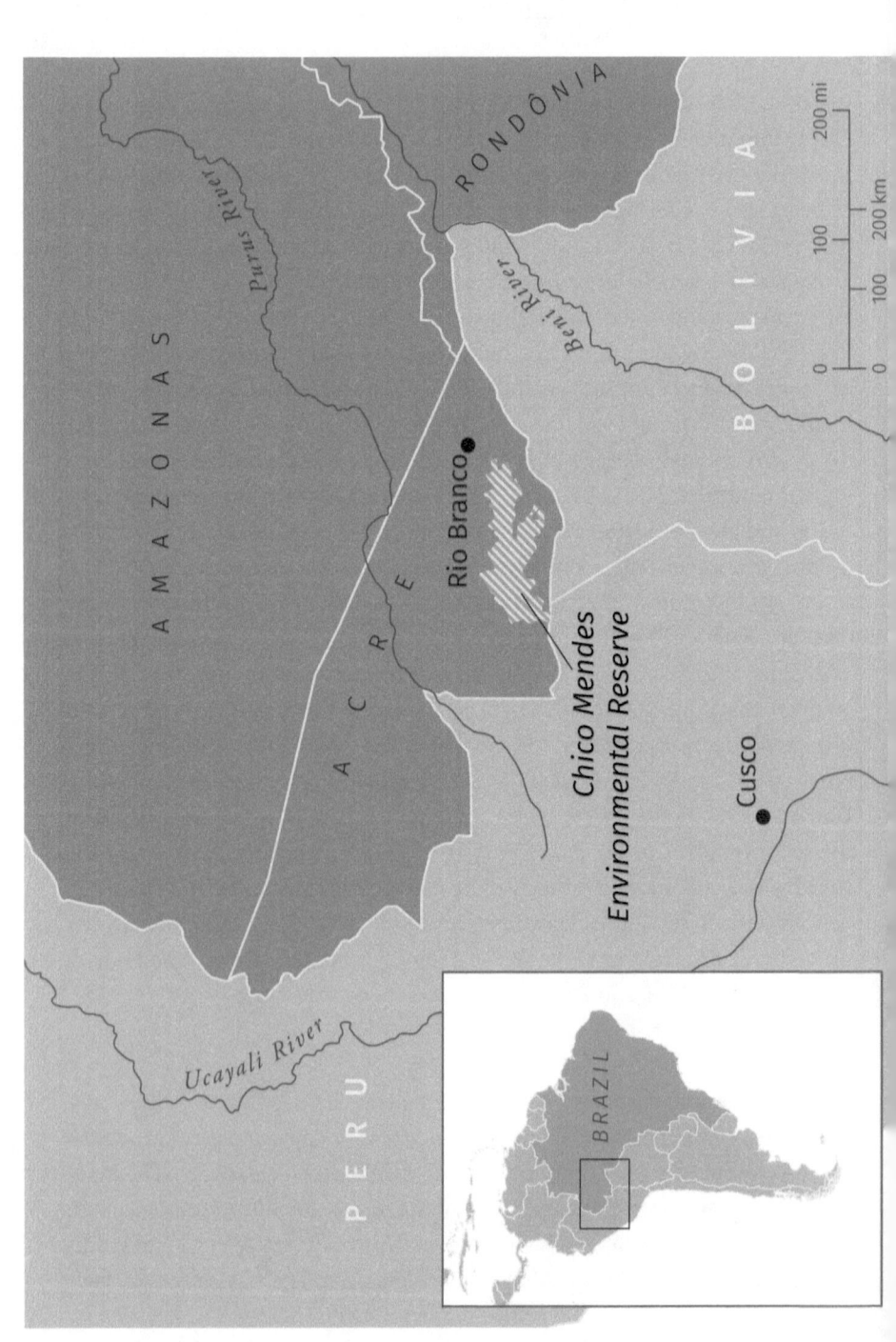

Around the time that Brazil returned to democracy in the mid-1980s, the cattle ranchers established the Rural Democratic Union to stymie reforms and intimidate activists and leaders like Mendes. Vigilantism swelled in this part of Brazil that many deemed its Wild West. Tensions rose even further in the late 1980s when the government declared that a sixty-one thousand-acre land expanse near Xapuri into an "extractive reserve," meaning that the rainforest could be not felled and that it had to be exploited sustainably. As well as the announcement being a direct result of Chico Mendes's proposal at the 1985 First National Rubber Tappers' Congress, this land was also where Mendes had spent his childhood and his first years as a seringueiro. It was a landmark in the history of global environmentalism.

On December 22, 1988, Mendes was sitting at the kitchen table in Xapuri playing dominos with the two bodyguards assigned after the labor leader had received scores of credible death threats and been subject to six failed murder attempts. When Mendes walked to the back patio to shower, two men approached. One fired a single blast from a 12-gauge shotgun, killing Mendes instantaneously.

The two assailants were Darly Alves da Silva and his son, Darci, who pulled the trigger, members of a local cattle-ranching clan who lived on a ten-thousand-acre ranch. Captured, convicted, and sentenced to nineteen years in prison in 1990, the pair escaped from a regional detention facility but were recaptured and sent to a federal prison.

Yet the very reason for their crime—to silence Chico Mendes—backfired dramatically, as the Brazilian's legend and power only swelled. One of his aides Gomercindo Rodrigues asserted, "Those who killed Chico got it wrong. They thought by killing him, the tappers' movement would be demobilized, but they made him immortal." Or as one journalistic account written years later put it: "It was the end of a man who had won global acclaim for championing the sanctity of the forest and the rights of compatriots who eked out a living by extracting latex from rubber trees."

AN INSPIRING LEGACY: MARINA SILVA

One of those inspired by Mendes's life and work was his Acre colleague and daughter of a rubber tapper, Marina Silva. Born on February 8, 1958, Maria Osmarina da Silva grew up in the small Acre community of Seringal Bagaço, an especially impoverished and remote section of the state. Of Portuguese and Black African ancestry, her parents were rubber tappers and had eleven children, including Marina, although three died before adulthood.

As a child, Marina passed her days hunting and fishing as well as, starting at eleven, tapping rubber to provide income for what her website describes as a family living in semi-slavery. In her press interviews conducted a half-century later, she described a typical day as entailing leaving her modest abode before 5 a.m., only to return home after dark, having walked over nine miles. Their closest neighbor was an hour-long hike away through the rainforest. The state capital, Rio Branco, was less than fifty miles away but a bus trip could take up to a week to reach the city during the rainy season.

Disease was ubiquitous in the jungle; Marina's mother died when Marina was only eleven and two younger sisters were felled by malaria and measles. Marina herself survived five bouts with malaria, but illness also helped Marina shape a new life for herself: after catching hepatitis at sixteen, she was brought to Rio Branco where she was treated by nuns and stayed on to receive a Catholic education (she was illiterate until then but learned to read and write in two weeks), and also receive an introduction to liberation theology.

And this was just the start of her insatiable quest to become educated. In 1975 Marina, took a course on rural union leadership taught by Clodovis Boff, a liberation theologian, and Chico Mendes. Having given up her ambitions to become a nun after she had graduated from high school, in her mid-twenties she earned, after just two years of furious studying, a history degree at the Federal University of Acre, where she also joined the Revolutionary Communist Party, an underground outfit linked to the PT that was dedicated to fighting the country's military regime.

Silva dedicated herself to labor organization in Acre in the mid-1980s, working for Mendes's workers' movement committed to empates. Silva herself led dozens of empates, which prevented hundreds of thousands of acres of virgin tropical forest from being razed and enabled tappers to continue their work. Refusing to be intimated by Chico's murder, Silva continued advocating for the establishment of extractive reserves.

Union organizing whetted Silva's appetite for politics. In 1990 she was elected a councilwoman in Rio Branco, followed by a state legislator two years later. In 1994, she was elected as a federal senator (representing Acre) in 1994, becoming the youngest Brazilian to ever hold this high office, where she remained until 2011. From her senate seat in Brasilia, this indigenous Amazonian (and first rubber tapper in this federal body) accrued a well-earned

Brazilian Senator Marina Silva poses beside a banner of renowned environmentalist Chico Mendes in Brasilia, December 11, 2002. *(Jamil Battar/Alamy)*

reputation for sustainable development and social justice in the rainforest. Throughout and following her senate career, Silva was plagued with chronic health issues, some resulting from exposure to heavy metals over her lifetime, which at times entailed extended hospital stays, but her star continued to rise. In 1997, she was one of the six geographical winners of the Goldman Environmental Prize (also called the Green Nobel). In 2007, the British newspaper *The Guardian* listed her as one of fifty people who would save the planet.

In 2002, President Luíz Inácio Lula da Silva appointed Silva to join his PT administration as Minister of the Environment. Silva put together a national campaign to battle deforestation, which included an indigenous reservation two times the size of Texas. All told, under Silva's watch deforestation decreased by almost two-thirds between 2004 and 2007. Having grown wary of the bureaucratic inertia and her growing sense that her party of three decades, the PT (and thus by definition presumably the party of workers and unions) had yielded to rancher and investor bullying on the rainforest, Silva resigned as minister and switched to the Green Party, becoming in 2010 "the first black woman of poor origins" (her words) to run for president. Silva did not win the presidency, but she did shock the nation's political establishment by garnering 19 percent—enough for a third-place finish that forced a second round of voting, eventually won by the PT's Dilma Rouseff. It was around this time that Silva became a Pentecostal Christian as part of the massive Assemblies of God. (As a candidate, she opposed gay marriage and abortion, as dictated by her religion.)

In early 2013, Silva unveiled a new party, Sustainability Network, and planned to be its presidential contender. But following a legal decision that terminated the party's official status, she jumped ship to the Socialist Party, where she agreed to be its vice presidential candidate along with her running mate, the young Eduardo Campos. When Campos died tragically in a plane crash on a campaign stump, Silva was catapulted to the top of the ticket. House money was on President Dilma winning an easy reelection, but Silva started surging and even became the frontrunner, even though Campos had only polled around 10 percent. At one point in the campaign, Dilma contended that only supporting her would guarantee that the nation's beloved antipoverty program, Bolsa Família (thirty million beneficiaries out of a population of 140 million) would be continued. Yet Silva's televised response revealed her deeply personal investment in her political mission:

> We are going to keep the Bolsa Família. Do you know why? Because I was born in the Seringal Bagaço, and I know what it is to go hungry. All that my mother used to have for eight children was an egg and a bit of flour and salt, and some chopped onion. I remember looking at my father and mother and asking: Are you not going to eat? And my mother answered . . . my mother answered: We are not hungry.
>
> And a child believed that. But afterwards, I understood that for yet another day, they had nothing to eat. Someone who has lived through that will never end the Bolsa Familia. This is not a speech. It is a life.

But Silva failed to make it to the runoff with Dilma, taking just 20 percent of the vote. Part of her failure was due to her profound lack of finances compared to the flush coffers of Dilma and Aecio Neves, the two who made it to the second round. In the 2018 presidential election, she ran again, this time as the Sustainability Network's candidate but drew only 1 percent, taking eighth place.

Yet while Marina Silva's presidential fortunes appeared to be over, her example and influence continued. At the time of writing, extractive reserves in Acre encompassed around five million acres, overseen by the very persons and communities that will lead lives of dignity and balance that were unimaginable before Chico Mendes and Marina Silva started their reformist paths. Silva herself paid tribute to Mendes's world-changing contribution in the preface to Gomercindo Rodrigues's memoir about the influential unionist:

> He organized a resistance movement that established pioneering links between environmentalists and unionists, Indians, and extractivists, political parties, civic organizations, Amazonian people and the world. Most important he put together environment and social justice issues in practice, not just in theory.

After he won, in October 2022, a bitter but victorious presidential campaign against incumbent right-wing populist Jair Bolsonaro, President-elect Lula announced that Silva would join his administration as environmental minister. The struggle would go on.

POSTMODERN AGE

37

Mario Vargas Llosa

Cartographies of Power

Mario Vargas Llosa was one of the leading lights of the so-called Latin American Boom cohort of the 1960s and 1970s and over subsequent decades has become a giant of world literature. Born in Peru, Vargas Llosa lived much of his adult life in Europe—the only place that he felt could provide him the freedom he needed to become a great writer. His relationship with his homeland was thus complicated (he once wrote "I often loathe it"). In his estimation, his calling was to be "cosmopolitan and an expatriate who has always detested nationalism," a posture he carried through many novels that took as their subject, in the words of Michael Greenberg, "fanaticism, social desperation, power, and sex." A pioneering stylist, his often-autobiographical works ranged widely in approach and ambition, from his socially excoriating début blockbuster *The Hero in Time* and comic *Aunt Julia and the Screenwriter* to the high-modernist *Conversation in the Cathedral* about his leftist-leaning university days.

An early supporter of Fidel Castro's 1959 revolution, he broke with the left and gravitated toward free-market economic principles—a stance that motivated his stunning return to Peru in the late 1980s to run for president, with the country in the grip of an economic catastrophe under leftist President Alan García (see Chapter 19, "José Carlos Mariátegui and Victor Raúl Haya de la Torre: Peru's Long Revolution"). After being trounced by political neophyte Alberto Fujimori, he wrote *A Fish in the Water*, a bittersweet but wise memoir reflecting on his direct experience of the political universe, and returned to fiction. But he kept a keen eye on the increasingly autocratic tendencies of Fujimori, which fed into the towering novel about Dominican dictator Rafael Trujillo (*The Feast of the Goat*) as well as (more directly) *The Neighbourhood*. A staunch advocate for the importance of literature, he heaped scorn on an entertainment industry that, in his estimation, was nurturing not art but a culture of "banalization, frivolization, and superficiality," just days before accepting the Nobel Prize in December 2010. For Vargas Llosa, art had a higher calling: "Good literature always ends up showing those who read it . . . the inevitable limitation of all power to fulfill human aspirations and desires."

THE TIME OF THE HERO

Vargas Llosa, an only child, was born in 1936 in the majestic colonial-era city of Arequipa in southern Peru. When he was a year old he moved with his mother to Bolivia, then to the northern desert city of Piura, before settling in Lima at the age of eleven. Vargas Llosa initially believed that his father, Ernesto Vargas, had died when in reality he had ditched the family soon after Mario was born. The return of the father to the family home when Mario was ten was not, for the boy, a happy reunion, and Vargas Llosa's later opposition to strongmen may have had its psychological template in the tempestuous paternal relationship. From Ernesto's perspective, his son was worthy of ridicule and contempt for his bookish, "eccentric, bohemian" ways. The only thing worse—and this could have meant Mario's banishment—was if Mario had been gay. (He wasn't.)

With the family now living in a middle-class barrio in Lima, Ernesto sent Mario, then aged fourteen, to the Leoncio Prado Military Academy. While he only lasted two years, the military academy, whose intake was drawn from all manner of social and racial classes from across Peru, was a veritable school of life for Vargas Llosa and became the setting of his precocious first novel, *The Time of the Hero*. The plot revolves around a group of hormone-riddled cadets who combine to reject sadistic hazing rituals, institutional mindlessness, and their own indifference. Published in 1963, the book was so searing that the military ceremoniously torched hundreds of copies, an act which backfired, as it became an unexpected publicity boost for the budding novelist.

Vargas Llosa's post–Leoncio Prado adolescence included stints as a cub reporter for a Lima daily, where he covered the city's down-and-outs: whores, drunks, and grisly murders—all of which would appear years later in his fiction. Before he had hit the age of twenty, he was writing for Lima literary magazines. And, in what also became a novel—the rip-roaring *Aunt Julia and the Scriptwriter* (1977)—he started dating his "Aunt" Julia (in fact his uncle's sister-in-law), whom he eventually married when she was thirty-two and he was only nineteen.

POLITICAL FLIP-FLOP

In 1948, General Manuel Odría launched a coup and established himself as dictator of Peru, inaugurating eight brutal years that Peruvians call the "*ochenia de Odría*." Now a student at the University of San Marco, Vargas Llosa plunged into a cauldron of leftist politics, with Communist Party student recruiters feeding him a "diet of Marx, Engels, and Lenin" and inviting him to join the cause. While he opted to be a sympathizer rather than a member, he still had to pick a pseudonym and chose Comrade Alberto. These subversive experiences would later inform Vargas Llosa's 1969 opus *Conversation in the Cathedral*, set in the ochenia and featuring the memorable second line, "At what precise moment had Peru fucked itself up?" Weaving a tangled web of arcane historical mentions and furtive tales, Vargas Llosa deconstructs the cerebral and moral levers that determine power and those who yield it. It examines a lack of personal and societal agency and can scar a citizen—or a nation.

Yet his communist sympathies could never compete with his towering ambition to become a great writer, and this, he knew, required leaving his native land for Europe. There was practically no way in which an intellectual of a country such as Peru was able to work, to earn his living, to publish without rendering homage to the socialist ideology and demonstrating by his public acts—his writing and his civic activities—that he belonged to the left. Vargas Llosa determined that he could not become "the cut-rate intellectual" and still live with himself.

At some point during his time in Europe, where he taught Spanish, did translation work, and wrote numerous novels, Vargas Llosa stopped believing in communism. A good part of this was due to his frustration with the stilted, incestuous intellectual life back in Lima. Then came the highly public break from numerous other Latin American and Western intellectuals over Fidel Castro's persecution of Cuban poet Heberto Padilla, who had "mildly satirized" the Cuban leader in some of his work. (See Chapter 29, "Gabriel García Márquez: Magical versus Social Realism.")

While he had been an enthusiastic supporter of Castro's leftist revolution in 1959, Vargas Llosa was dismayed by what happened to Padilla. For Vargas Llosa, that Padilla believed in the revolution and intended his art to help mend its errant ways was categorical proof that Castro's regime was verging on tyranny:

To force comrades, with methods repugnant to human dignity, to accuse themselves of imaginary betrayals and sign letters in which even the syntax seems to be that of the police, is the negation of everything that made me embrace, from the first day, the cause of the Cuban revolution: its decision to fight for justice without losing respect for individuals.

Colombian heavyweight author Gabriel García Márquez, by contrast, justified Havana's actions as necessary measures in the face of relentless North American imperialism, which contributed to the antipathy Vargas Llosa felt toward his former best friend.

After breaking with the orthodox global literary leftover Castro, within a decade Vargas Llosa had become an advocate of free market economics along the lines of British Prime Minister Margaret Thatcher. But he was no longer content to take a purely theoretical stance. From his vantage in Europe, Vargas Llosa was deeply disturbed by the trajectory of his native Peru, and rather than writing about it, decided to throw his hat into the political ring.

FROM PAGE TO POLITICS

Known as the Lost Decade, the 1980s was a horrific time for Latin America's hyperinflationary economies. Perhaps no country epitomized the economic Armageddon more than Peru, and no year could compete in terms of ignominy with 1987. In a 1994 piece for the *New York Review of Books*, Alma Guillermoprieto vividly described a situation in which unemployment soared beyond 50 percent and poverty was about 40 percent, with extreme poverty hitting a quarter of the population. Inflation was running around 8,000 percent on an annual basis and gross domestic product (GDP) growth for the year was negative 15 percent. A "huge and inept bureaucracy gobbled up whatever small proportion of the government budget was not devoured by graft and interest payments" on foreign debt payments that totaled almost half of the country's GDP. Peru's president at the time was Alan García, a brilliant orator whom the adoring press called the "Kennedy of Latin America" for his youth (thirty-six when he took office), but his economic policy was a disaster, as epitomized by his 1987 nationalization of the banking sector, a move that further undermined investor confidence. And as if the country needed another threat, the Shining Path Maoist guerrilla insurgency, led by Abimael Guzmán, had expanded its dominion in the Andean countryside, and there were fears it might eventually seize Lima itself (see Chapter 35, "Abimael Guzmán and Shining Path: The Philosophy of Terror").

For Vargas Llosa, García's incompetent demagoguery was too much. Soon thereafter, Vargas Llosa made a political speech—his first—that resonated with many Peruvians and led to his becoming a presidential candidate in the 1990 election (despite Mexican novelist Octavio Paz warning him that novelists should stick to writing novels). For Vargas Llosa, the "Peru of my childhood was a poor and backward country," but now under Garcia's watch it had become "poorer still and in many regions wretchedly poverty-stricken, a country that was going to inhuman patterns of existence."

The tonic to García's economic statism was, according to Vargas Llosa, hyper-libertarianism packaged as "radical liberalism"—the free market with a happy face. Vargas Llosa's manifesto declared his intention to dismantle "privileges, government handouts, protectionism, and state control, opening up the world and creating a free society in which everyone would have access to the market and live under the protection of the law."

But entering the political arena brought intense scrutiny. Vargas Llosa was targeted for his putative atheism (one television spot asked viewers, "Do you want an atheist in the office of president of Peru?") among various other political and personal shenanigans and indignities. As Thomas Mallon describes, these included:

> lies about his finances, threats to his life, and attacks on the supposed depravity of his books: [His erotic novel] *In Praise of the Stepmother* was read, one chapter per day, during prime time on government-run television. Slender and elegant, the author-candidate looked more patrician than he actually was, and couldn't overcome a cool, Kennedyesque refusal to be carried on his supporters' shoulders, [in Vargas Llosa's words] "a ridiculous custom of Peruvian politicians in imitation of bullfighters."

Enjoying a solid lead for almost the entire campaign, Vargas Llosa's momentum was fatally undermined by Alberto Fujimori just weeks before the first round of voting. A political unknown who had been rector of the Agrarian University of Peru, Fujimori cannily exploited an electoral legal quirk that allowed someone approved for the senate election to file simultaneously for the presidential election. Despite having barely a cent in political funding, Fujimori had a seemingly limitless supply of personal moxie that allowed him to wage a tireless campaign. He was also the inadvertent beneficiary of attacks from upper-class media, which mercilessly mocked *El Chino*—a generic term for Asians—as well as his slogan of "Honesty, Technology, and Work." A majority of Peruvian voters, who were either ethnically or culturally mestizo or Indian (and not of the minority Asian immigrant community), were turned off by the racist onslaught aimed at Fujimori and developed an affection for him. (The visceral bigotry and racism of some of his moneyed elite supporters also deeply unsettled Vargas Llosa.)

By the April 8 first-round vote, García's ruling APRA party had lined up behind El Chino, making Fujimori's embryonic campaign penniless no more. Vargas Llosa beat Fujimori in the first round—28 to 25 percent—but the head-to-head second-round outcome was now effectively cemented, given that many minor parties would now be supporting Fujimori. Only dire warnings from friends and advisers that dropping out might spark a military putsch dissuaded Vargas Llosa from skipping the second round. On June 10, 1990, as expected, Fujimori won the second round with an almost twenty-four-point landslide over Vargas Llosa.

The Peruvian novelist's venture into politics was over. Reeling from a bruising campaign, Vargas Llosa found refuge in books, writing, and returning to the Old World. Many assumed that the searing presidential gambit would result in a novel, but what emerged was a memoir, *A Fish in the Water*, a tome that is a superb primer on how politics works and whose analysis of power neatly describes the career of many a figure in our study:

> I made a depressing discovery ... that real politics, not the kind that one reads and writes about, thinks about and imagines (the only sort I was acquainted with) but politics as lived and practiced day by day, has little to do with ideas, values, and imagination, with teleological visions—the ideal society we would like to create—and, to put it bluntly, little to do with generosity, solidarity, and idealism. It consists almost exclusively of maneuvers, intrigues, plots, paranoias, betrayals, a great deal of calculation, no little cynicism, and every variety of con game. Because what really gets the professional politician, whether of the center, the left, or the right, moving, what excites him and keeps him going is power, attaining it, remaining in it, or returning to it as soon as possible. There are exceptions, of course, but they are just that: exceptions. Many politicians begin their careers impelled by altruistic sentiments-changing society, attaining justice, fostering development, bringing morality into public

life. But along the way, in the petty, pedestrian practice of day-to-day politics, these fine objectives become, little by little, mere cliches of the speeches and statements of the public persona they acquire, which in the end makes them all but indistinguishable from each other.

PORTRAITS OF POWER

After his electoral defeat, Vargas Llosa returned to what he did best: capturing the mechanisms of power in fiction. Quite easily his best political novel, *The Feast of the Goat* (2000) chronicles the three-decade-long dictatorship of Dominican Republic strongman Rafael Trujillo (see Chapter 18, "Rafael Trujillo: 'Our S.O.B.'") and in so doing gives the reader a chilling sense of the physical and psychological power of "state terror when it is embodied in a single man." Domestic critics are imprisoned in the Goat's torture chambers while stealthy assassins ruthlessly take out Dominican civilian dissidents on the streets of faraway Manhattan. Yet even in what appears to be a work of historical fiction, Vargas Llosa was also shaping an allegory for what was happening in Peru, where Fujimori was demonstrating increasingly autocratic tendencies.

Vargas Llosa would confront the issue more directly in his nineteenth novel, *The Neighborhood*, which describes 1990s Peru under President Fujimori and his Rasputin-like palace adviser Vladimiro Montesinos. Lore has it that Montesinos used a dubious birth certificate to prove that Fujimori had been born in Peru, not Japan, thus making him eligible to run for president, as well as helping the candidate with a delicate tax fraud issue. After taking office in 1990, Fujimori brought Montesinos into his inner political circle, making him the effective chief of the military intelligence agency, a position which Montesinos used to persecute Fujimori's political and media adversaries.

In *The Neighborhood*, the character of El Doctor is unmistakably Montesinos (Fujimori is referred to by his actual name). In the novel, El Doctor instructs one of his compromised reporters how to do her job now that she was working for him: "I'll tell you whom to investigate, whom to defend, and, above all, whom to screw. To screw those who want to screw Peru."

Yet what marks Vargas Llosa out as a true literary titan is the fact that his fiction can range across the entire political spectrum and inhabit any number of perspectives. In 2018's *Harsh Times*, Vargas Llosa takes the readers back to the US-hatched coup of democratic leftist Guatemalan president Jacobo Árbenz in June 1954 (see Chapter 22: "Jacobo Árbenz: A Guatemalan Spring,

Peruvian Nobel laureate Mario Vargas Llosa arriving for a book signing at Bogota's 27th International Book Fair, April 30, 2014. Two Nobel laureates, the late Gabriel García Márquez of Colombia and Vargas Llosa, were honored during the literary celebrations. *(John Vizcaino/Alamy)*

Interrupted"). Vargas Llosa excoriates US motivations and methods (which were motivated by the commercial concerns of United Fruit, a major investor in Guatemala), and presents a nuanced and delicate portrait of Árbenz's political evolution. Despite his own *lassiez-faire* economic leanings, Vargas Llosa brilliantly evokes the political agenda of the new presidential couple in a line that could have been written by prominent leftist Noam Chomsky:

> They [the presidential husband and wife] would have to change the feudal structures that reigned in the countryside, where the peasants—the immense majority of Guatemalans—worked for white and mestizo landowners for miserable wages, while the large estate landholders lived like colonizers in the days of the encomiendas, enjoying all the benefits of modernity.

While there is much that the historian might refute or modify—Vargas Llosa arguably overstates Árbenz's virtues and reforms and Washington's and United Fruit's sins—*Harsh Times* marked yet another signpost in the author's literary journey of how power manifested in Latin America.

The ultimate literary recognition came in 2010 when Vargas Llosa was awarded the Nobel Prize for "cartography of structures of power and his trenchant images of the individual's resistance, revolt and defeat." Read by itself, his novels comprise a fascinating analysis of Latin America's political history, yet their significance is arguably heightened by the author's complicated relationship with Peru, not least his run for the presidency. Indeed, it may be this experience that allowed him to delve most deeply into the nature of power and perceive its singular appeal that, time and time again in Latin America, has warped ideologies and alliances in service of itself.

38

Pablo Escobar

The First Drug Lord

One day, I'm going to be president of the Republic of Colombia.
—*Pablo Escobar*

Pablo Escobar was Colombia's first cocaine kingpin who rewrote the rules for the global illicit drugs trade. Fabulously wealthy, he was for a period untouchable in Colombia, ensconced in his *Hacienda Nápoles* (complete with private zoo) and with law enforcement and politicians on the payroll. He also sought to forge a benevolent public persona through lavish gifts and initiatives aimed at the poor, including constructing a whole neighborhood. But increasing pressure from the United States combined with domestic outrage over criminal violence eventually forced him on the back foot. Facing overwhelming odds, he brokered a deal to surrender, but then went on the run, before a US-assisted search team finally tracked him down and executed him in 1993.

THE COCAINE TRADE IS BORN

Colombia's sweet-smelling cannabis was ubiquitous, from the countryside to interior cities, such as Medellín. In the early 1970s, the export-grade product became the global gold standard for pot. Savvy Colombian kingpins first shipped cannabis northward, sometimes using American pilots, who would land at remote airstrips to pick up hundreds of kilos at a time. Cocaine, by contrast, was at this point leaving Colombia only a kilo or two at a time. Brought across by paid (or, sometimes, unwitting) smugglers known as mules, imports of the white powder to the United States totaled maybe five hundred to six hundred kilos a year, according to US drug agencies' reckoning.

An oft-repeated but unconfirmed story describes how Colombian cocaine went from an almost incidental tag-along to cannabis to America's drug *du jour*. It began in the early 1970s, in the Federal Correctional Institution in Danbury, Connecticut, where Carlos Lehder Rivas, then a "humble automobile parts smuggler," shared a cell with a young pot dealer. As writer Robert Stone imagined, "The hippie kept holding forth on how grand and festive the day of his release would be. His girl would be there, his good buddies, some mellow sounds. And there would be coke, cocaine . . . and if God ever made anything better, He never let on. Except of course for heroin." Colombian journalist and author Gabriel García Márquez picks up the story: "Caramba!" says Lehder, "If cocaine is what you like, we have it lying around on the ground in my country.'" A business partnership was born: Lehder and the flower-child inmate "took to importing cocaine—and the rest is very, very bad history."

During the mid-1970s, pure cocaine bought for $2,000 a kilo in Colombia started selling for more than $55,000 stateside. These incredible profit margins attracted a motley assortment of characters. José Gonzalo Rodriguez Gacha was an emerald dealer before he got into the cocaine game. The Ochoa brothers—Fabio, Juan David, and Jorge Luis—owned a restaurant before setting up a "brutal, million-dollar business smuggling drugs" around the world. With Lehder running logistics, they formed a small price-fixing cartel based in Medellín. Another organization was formed in Bogotá, the nation's capital. And the Rodríguez Orijuela brothers—Jorge, Gilberto, and Miguel—busied themselves building the Cali cartel. But the Medellín was the clear market leader. At the height of Colombia's cocaine boom in the 1980s, as much as 80 percent of the cocaine in the United States could be traced back to one source: the Medellín cartel. And at the center of this storm of greed, violence, and excess, there was one man: Pablo Escobar.

PABLITO

The third of seven children, Pablo was born on December 1, 1949, in Rio Negro, less than thirty miles from Medellín. His mother was a teacher; his father worked on a farm. Escobar's maternal grandfather, foreshadowing his grandson's path, bootlegged moonshine, among other illicit goods. Escobar himself came of age during the horrific period of civil war between factions of Colombia's Liberal and Conservative parties known as *La Violencia*.

Fleeing the interparty violence in the countryside, the Escobar family relocated to the bucolic township of Envigado, next to Medellín. Pablo was a good student who loved playing soccer, but he eventually dropped out of high school. He started smoking marijuana daily as a teenager and slept late—habits he kept for the rest of his life—but he set his sights high: as he once told his cousin and friend, Gustavo Gaviria, "I want to be big."

Pablo Escobar's first arrest is believed to have occurred when he was twenty-four, on September 5, 1974, when Medellín police booked him for stealing an automobile. Just two years later, Colombian authorities arrested him and five associates for smuggling dozens of kilos of cocaine through Medellín hidden inside the gang's vehicle. Escobar had served only three months of his jail term when his arrest order was mysteriously withdrawn. Less than three months later, police arrested him again, but he was freed on bail within weeks.

At the time, Escobar was processing cocaine in a squalid apartment as a side hustle. He got to know another Medellín trafficker, Fabio Restrepo, who was running a few dozen kilos of cocaine northward annually. Escobar wanted in on Restrepo's lucrative business, but the seasoned player was unimpressed by the "small, soft-spoken man" and his minor drug operation. It proved to be a fatal underestimation: within a few months of their meeting, Restrepo was dead and it was clear to everyone that Pablo Escobar meant business.

Colombia's security service arrested Escobar in the aftermath of Restrepo's murder but Escobar was sprung within a few weeks after his associates made the appropriate payments. In his memoir, Roberto Escobar described his brother's plans for the two narcotics agents who had arrested him: "Pablo promised, 'I'm going to kill those motherfuckers myself'... I have heard from others that Pablo had them brought to a house, made them get down on their knees, then put a gun to their head and killed them." Whether or not Pablo executed the men himself or delegated the job to his hired guns is unknown, but shortly after his release, Medellín newspapers reported the discovery of the bodies of the two domestic intelligence agents riddled with bullets.

In 1975 Escobar organized a scheme in which he and his business partners used several French Renault sedans outfitted with secret storage containers to smuggle coca paste from Peru to Colombia. Escobar personally drove one of the cars. According to Kim MacQuarrie, within the year, Pablo, "who had once processed a single kilo of [unrefined base paste] in his own bathtub, was soon sending forty to sixty kilos of refined cocaine to Miami by small plane *per week* and earning roughly $8 million of profits per month." The preferred route was an established marijuana pathway: a short flight over the Caribbean

Sea to Florida, where packages were dropped into the Everglades, snagged by launches, and whisked over to Miami.

Within years, Escobar and the consolidating Medellín cartel were shipping multiple hundreds of kilos at a time, a fact confirmed by a Colombian police raid that uncovered six hundred kilos in a single aircraft. Even more innovative tactics emerged, such as radio-controlled "narco-subs" that could carry two thousand kilos of coke from Colombia's northern Pacific coast to a Caribbean rendezvous location. Men used scuba gear to locate the craft and remove the cargo, and then carried the shipment to southern Florida by boat.

Profits reached almost incomprehensible figures. Between 1976 and 1980, bank deposits in Colombia's three largest cities, Bogotá, Cali, and Medellín, roughly doubled. At the peak, Medellín was likely pulling in $60 million *every day*. There was so much cash that the cartel began burying it in secret

Mugshot of Colombian drug lord Pablo Escobar, Medellín, Colombia, 1976. *(Alamy Stock Photo)*

locations around the country. A 1988 story in *Fortune* magazine made waves when it estimated Colombian cocaine exports at more than $4 billion annually—more than the country's coffee and oil exports combined. *Fortune* marveled at the Medellín cartel's business acumen.

Escobar used these prodigious revenues to vertically integrate his business. He traveled to Peru, Bolivia, and Panama to establish direct business links with the initial growers and invested millions in protecting his intermediate processors and distributors. He built a cartel organization that set prices and funded its security, while largely operating as a franchise. Escobar commanded large percentages from his associates, charging his fellow runners not just for the cost of trafficking but also for what he called "my struggle."

The overheads of running a transnational drug trafficking organization were not insignificant, and bribes were the oil that lubricated the machine. The entity had customs agents, industrialists, bankers, ranchers, military brass, cops, and, not least, politicians playing along. Pablo established a hallmark way of dealing with local and federal officials: *plata o plomo*—you either took Escobar's *plata* (silver) or his *plomo* (lead). When people could not be bought—or when others betrayed them—Medellín called in the guns. By the mid-1980s, the cartel relied on multiple thousands of *sicarios* (hired killers who were often teenagers). The signature sicario execution was a motorcycle drive-by shooting. For his part, Escobar preferred that his men use two bullets to the forehead. "A person might survive *one* of those bullets, Escobar advised, but never *two*."

THE CARTELS ORGANIZE

By the end of the 1970s, Marxist guerrillas known as the Revolutionary Armed Forces of Colombia (FARC) held dominion over the Middle Magdalena Valley, but the country's drug lords and their private armies viewed the relatively stateless territory of the region as their dominion as well and started using their exorbitant profits to buy up cattle ranches and other rural properties. In the end, the Medellín and Cali cartels owned upwards of 2.5 million acres, or one-twelfth of Colombia's farmland, much of it in the Middle Magdalena. The investment allowed the traffickers to launder the cocaine money and gain a semblance of social status, which Colombia's old-money elites had not permitted them to share. Escobar's most extravagant contribution to the land grab was the sprawling seven-thousand-acre Hacienda Nápoles. The ranch boasted a palace that could house a hundred guests at a time, a zoo stocked with hippopotami and elephants, and—mounted "as if it were a national monument" in novelist Gabriel García Márquez's trenchant observation—the small plane used to smuggle the cartel's first cocaine load. By the mid-1980s Escobar and others were the richest "landowners" in the Andean nation's checkered history. Like the guerrillas, the narcos desired greater and greater isolation to operate the cocaine business.

Perhaps unsurprisingly, the guerrillas saw the newcomers as potential cash cows. In 1981, Manuel Marulanda's FARC kidnapped the father of a two-bit drug and emerald dealer named Fidel Castaño. (See Chapter 25, "Manuel Marulanda: Founding Father of the FARC.") It was an everyday operation for the Marxist rebels to finance their war machine, but it would have fateful consequences. According to writer Alma Guillermoprieto's account, Castaño's father, "who had been held to a tree by a long rope for many days, slammed his head against the tree trunk until he dropped to the ground and there was 'left to die' by the guerrillas, presumably of a heart attack." Then, on November 12, 1981, a smaller leftist guerrilla group known as M-19 kidnapped Marta Nieves Ochoa, the youngest sister of Jorge Ochoa and daughter of drug lord Don Fabio Ochoa. The guerrillas' demands included a ransom of $10 million to $15 million. Despite grave worry, the Ochoa family refused to cooperate with the captors.

Instead, in early December 1981, a small airplane circled above a stadium in Cali as soccer fans were gearing up for a match between local side *América* and a rival Medellín-based team. Just as the first half began, the plane dropped leaflets that described a recent "general assembly," in which a group of prominent Colombian businessmen, drug traffickers, and military officers agreed that they had had enough of the guerrillas. These men had each committed treasure and their reputations to establish a paramilitary death squad, *Muerte a Secuestradores* (MAS) (Death to Kidnappers). "The basic objective will be the public and immediate execution of all those involved in kidnappings beginning from the date of this communiqué." The guilty "will be hung from the trees in public parks or shot and marked with the sign of our group—MAS." Guerrilla kidnappers already in jail would be killed as well. If this failed, "our retribution will fall on their closest family members."

After scores of M-19 guerrillas and their family members had been killed, the chastened rebels made a pact with the traffickers never to kidnap them or their relatives again. Journalists covering Colombia's drug war at the time concluded that MAS represented a new era in Colombia's drug history, being the first time that the drug cartels took a coordinated public position on a particular matter. The original MAS soon unraveled but it had two broader effects. First, it galvanized the Medellín cartel to take a more active political stance. Second, it spawned a generation of paramilitary groups in the Middle Magdalena.

In 1983, the Castaño sons avenged their father's death. A group of men under orders from son Fidel descended on villages around Segovia, where Castaño *pater* had been held captive, and killed twenty-two villagers, "pulling babies out of their mothers' arms and shooting them, nailing a child to a plank, impaling a man on a bamboo pole, hacking a woman to pieces with a machete." The murders were but the first in what became a decades-long assassination campaign known as paramilitaries. The "paras" were exterminators, paid by the cartels or otherwise self-deputized to purify the Middle Magdalena of Marxist guerrillas and their suspected sympathizers. As Guillermoprieto writes, the paramilitaries "sprang up, like soldiers grown from dragons' teeth" and quickly found support in a familiar class of actors. Narco-landowners, including Escobar and the especially bloodthirsty José Gonzalo "El Mexicano" Rodríguez Gacha, funded the paras to make the FARC problem disappear.

PEAK PABLO

In a system in which the cartels owned or rented law enforcement, from those in the villages and barrios up to the military leadership, the bosses faced only one real threat: extradition. In 1979, under Presidents Jimmy Carter and Julio César Turbay, the United States and Colombia signed a treaty that proscribed international drug trafficking, which would henceforth constitute a crime against the United States; Colombian traffickers could now be extradited to the United States and, if convicted, imprisoned there. (Escobar predictably denounced the treaty, calling it an infringement of Colombian "national security.") US authorities were confident that the treaty, backed by $26 million in foreign aid, would usher in a lasting era of bilateral antidrug cooperation. This hope was set back when President Belisario Betancur, who took office in 1982, refused to extradite Colombian nationals as a matter of principle.

The *capos* (bosses) celebrated an apparent victory. For his part, Escobar exploited an especially nationalistic mood to run for national office as a Liberal Party candidate, and was elected an "alternate" congressman. Whenever his partner on the congressional ticket, Jairo Ortega, was absent, Escobar substituted for him in the Chamber of Representatives. The position came with automatic judicial immunity, so Escobar could no longer be prosecuted for crimes under Colombian law. He was also entitled to a diplomatic visa and diplomatic immunity, allowing him to travel to the United States. In May 1980, his family visited Disney World and Washington, DC, where he had a family picture taken in front of the White House. Meanwhile, Pablo's illicit cocaine continued to flow northward. His mules were coming back to Colombia with so many $100 bills that the Medellín accountants found it easier to weigh them than count them by hand.

With his status officially legitimized, Escobar funded the installation of floodlights at soccer fields, made countless public addresses, and dished out cash—a lot of cash. He started a social agency called *Medellín without Slums*, funded a radio show, *Civics on the March*, and made plans to construct the not-immodestly named Barrio Pablo Escobar, a massive apartment complex for the city's desperately poor. Thanks to these charitable efforts, Escobar and his colleagues enjoyed total impunity and even a certain social prestige. Don Pablo also employed a gaggle of publicists and paid reporters to burnish his public persona. For two or three years they did a reasonably good job casting Escobar as a philanthropist determined to give back to the poor barrios where he began. The conservative Catholic Church in Medellín supported Don Pablo's social programs. However, the Colombian police continued to eye him, suspecting that, whatever his political and social ambitions, he was still the same ruthless and vengeful enforcer he'd always been. More to Pablo's dismay, his quest for respectability was never accepted by "polite Colombian society." A blue-blood Medellín country club, *Club Campestre*, denied his application to join.

The congressional seat turned out to be the high-water mark of Escobar's political career. In August 1983 Colombia's young justice minister, an ambitious member of Luis Carlos Galán's reformist New Liberal movement, Rodrigo Lara Bonilla, revealed Escobar's not-so-well-kept secret. "Pablito" was no real estate tycoon, Bonilla told the nation, but the world's biggest cocaine trafficker. "The more I learn," Lara Bonilla said, "the more I know of the damage that the *narcos* are causing the country. I will never again refuse the extradition of one of these dogs." An embarrassed Bogotá promptly seized upward of one hundred of Pablo's exotic animals at Nápoles, citing illegal importation. Days later, the influential daily *El Espectador* ran new pieces touting Escobar's mid-1970s drug trafficking arrest, alongside the now-infamous police mug shot from the same arrest, with Pablo wearing a knowing smile. The New Liberals ejected the cocaine baron from the party, along with his seat, his immunity, and his diplomatic visa.

Lara Bonilla also authorized the US Drug Enforcement Agency (DEA)-assisted Colombian National Police's raid on March 10, 1984, on a massive cocaine-processing lab in the hamlet of Tranquilandia, on the Yarí River in the southern jungle. This sprawling facility consisted of nineteen scattered camps and utilized scores of laborers who lived in dorms. The security forces confiscated an astounding 12,250 kilos of cocaine. Marxist guerrillas were suspected to have served as guards. This so-called grandfather lab, the largest known to exist in Colombia at the time, was producing five thousand kilos of refined cocaine per week, at a street value of $1.2 billion.

With his licit cover blown and political aspirations extinguished, a humiliated Escobar no longer needed to pretend as though he was anything other than a ruthless criminal. In retaliation, Escobar declared war on the Colombian state. Political kidnappings, assassinations, and bombings surged. The key objective for the Medellín cocaine baron was to force Bogotá to rescind its extradition treaty with the United States. A summary phrase is often attributed to Escobar, "Better a tomb in Colombia than a jail cell in the United States."

Lara Bonilla became Escobar's obsession. Escobar first tried to smear him with outlandish accusations, which Lara Bonilla countered by denouncing Escobar in a congressional session. Terrified, Lara Bonilla accepted the US Embassy's offer to relocate his family to the United States under assumed names. On April 30, 1984, an ex-convict sicario on a red Yamaha motorcycle hit Lara Bonilla's car with a spray of bullets. Seven of them struck the justice minister.

Conservative President Betancur refused to jettison Lara Bonilla's "crusade" against the drug barons and the *gringo* aid that came with it. During Lara Bonilla's memorial, the Colombian president declared "war without cease-fire"; he declared a state of siege and ordered the National Police to seize the *capos*' estates and other illicit assets. Reversing his previous stance, he extradited jailed drug lords to the United States, thirteen in total from 1984 to mid-1987. Top DEA official in Bogotá, John Phelps, told the *New York Times* he was confident that Bentancur's swift measures would pay dividends: "If the campaign continues at this pace, it is going to have a major impact on trafficking in Colombia and to the United States and Europe." An increase in wholesale cocaine prices indeed seemed to indicate that the policies, including the bust of the mega-lab in Tranquilandia, were having the desired impact.

A DECADE OF LIVING DANGEROUSLY

Lara Bonilla's killing marked the onset of the nation's "decade of living dangerously." Pablo Escobar hastily departed from Medellín to Panama City, where his business partners Carlos Lehder, José Rodríguez Gacha, and the Ochoa brothers were already hiding out at a country club residence. From their headquarters-in-exile, the Medellín cartel waged a war of incredible intensity against the Colombian state and anyone else they perceived as threatening business. Medellín-dispatched sicarios tracked Lara Bonilla's successor, Enrique Parejo, all the way to Bupadest. One of the assassins shot the minister in the head, though not lethally. A federal judge, Tulio Manuel Castro Gil, was killed by sicarios in July 1985 while hailing a cab, soon after he had indicted Escobar and other Medellín cartel leaders as conspirators in Lara Bonilla's murder.

On November 6, 1985, M-19—the very same group that had kidnapped Marta Nieves Ochoa and spurred the "Death to Kidnappers" campaign—raided the Palace of Justice in the heart of Bogotá. Guerrillas held hostage the Colombian Supreme Court justice and aides and ritually placed President Betancur on trial for not having brokered peace. They also demanded that the government reverse the 1979 extradition treaty. Refusing to negotiate, Betancur ordered the military to storm the palace. After a fiery ten-hour battle, ninety-five people were confirmed dead, including eleven of twenty-five judges and Chief Justice Alfonso Reyes Echandía. The raid undermined Colombia's legal system and effectively terminated Betancur's peace moves with the FARC and M-19. Also believed to have been destroyed in the stand-off were thousands of criminal records, including the casework against Pablo Escobar. The unconfirmed theory is that Escobar and other kingpins paid the M-19 as much as a million US dollars to carry out the mission.

The decade's bloody toll made Bogotá more willing to accept American aid and training. President Virgilio Barco, elected in 1986, intensified the cartel war, first issuing a sweeping set of temporary but pervasive state-of-siege decrees that placed Colombia under martial law. The cartels responded with a spate of bombings in the capital and at least one commercial airline. On August 18, 1989, a *sicario* murdered pro-extradition presidential candidate Luis Carlos Galán. President Barco responded to the carnage by sending more than twenty suspected traffickers to the United States. He established three special operations police units, one of which, the Search Bloc, was assigned the single task of getting Escobar. Within two weeks of the Search Bloc's existence, more than two dozen of its men had fallen.

The violence also alarmed Washington, especially after cartel operatives were busted attempting to purchase over one hundred Stinger antiaircraft missiles in Florida. The Bush administration released a Justice Department opinion concluding that deploying US military personnel abroad to hunt narco lords would not violate the 1878 Posse Comitatus Act that restricted military involvement in civilian law enforcement matters. It was in this atmosphere that a new side of the supply of the US war on drugs emerged. Robert Bonner, a former federal prosecutor and judge, now head of the DEA, is credited with developing the "kingpin strategy," whose aim was to "decapitate" the cartels by targeting their leaders for execution or capture. In journalist Andrew Cockburn's assessment, the strategy assumed that the United States faced a "hierarchically structured threat that could be defeated by removing key leadership components."

President George H. W. Bush allocated $250 million in emergency enforcement assistance to combat drug operations in the Andes and deployed a Special Forces team to train their counterparts in the Colombian armed forces and national police. Within weeks of Galán's assassination, US materiel began to arrive in Colombia, including two C-130 transport planes, five UH1H helicopters, and eight A-37 Dragonfly light attack aircraft. In February 1990, Bush escalated the rhetoric during a visit to Colombia, declaring, "We have committed ourselves to the first common, comprehensive international drug control strategy." He backed the words with $2 billion in American aid over five years.

In 1990 Escobar began kidnapping prominent journalists and society scions—a shrewd political and psychological calculation given how close these individuals were to the ruling class. Among the victims was Maruja Pachón de Villamizar, sister-in-law of the assassinated presidential candidate Galán and wife of the prominent Liberal politician Alberto Villamizar, who had spearheaded the extradition legislation. Another was Marina Montoya, sister of politician Germán Montoya. Diana Turbay, a television executive and daughter of the former Liberal Party head, Julio César Turbay, was captured on the same day as Francisco Santos, editor-in-chief of the influential paper *El Tiempo*. Sadly, there was little the Colombian justice system could do to bring Escobar and his cadre to account. Judges and magistrates faced an awful dilemma: sell themselves to the traffickers or be killed, plata o plomo. Many of them chose death.

Meanwhile, a new president, César Gaviria, and his top aides and ministers were attempting to negotiate Escobar's surrender, an effort that was now tied up with the hostages. In late May 1991, Escobar indicated that he was ready to give himself up in exchange for lenient punishment and immunity from extradition. Impossibly, Gaviria dispatched Alberto Villamizar to Medellín to meet with Escobar to hammer out the details of his surrender and the release of the hostages. Villamizar was not only the husband of Escobar's highest-profile hostage but had also been the victim of at least one assassination attempt, allegedly at the hands of Escobar's sicarios. He revealed to one of Gaviria's national security aides, "Imagine how I feel. First he threatens me. Then he makes an attempt on my life, and it's a miracle I escape. He goes on threatening me. He assassinates Galán. He abducts my wife and my sister, and now he wants me to defend his rights."

Escobar held out until the constitutional assembly approved a prohibition on extradition—a move vehemently opposed by Washington. Then he turned himself in through a deal brokered between his lawyers and the government that included house arrest at a newly built "residence." At the time of his surrender, Escobar faced ten indictments for drug trafficking and murder in the United States. Escobar admitted to having been present at the meeting when the decision to kill Galán was made but denied ordering the politician's murder. "The fact is that everybody wanted to kill Dr. Galán," he said.

PABLO'S ESCAPE

As the *New York Times* told an incredulous global audience, Escobar's new home on a wooded hilltop on the edge of Envigado consisted of a "cluster of red-tiled bungalows with private baths and panoramic views of the Andes." Surrounding the perimeter was a menacing eighteen-foot-high electrified fence. Arguably, the prison, dubbed *La Catedral*, was designed more to keep Escobar's enemies out than to keep him and his crew in. The surrender contract even prohibited police and soldiers from entering the two-and-a-half-acre compound. But this was also the entire premise of the surrender deal: Escobar would never agree to give himself up if he could not count on his own security.

Escobar continued to run his empire from La Catedral, but Bogotá's efforts had disrupted Medellín's cocaine trafficking significantly. One report suggested that the "preeminence in the drug trade has passed to the quieter, more businesslike traffickers based in the city of Cali." But US officials at the Embassy were getting reports that Escobar was still collecting a $500,000 "war tax" from traffickers on the outside. There was also intelligence documenting lascivious parties with prostitutes and incessant unchecked visitors. In mid-1992, Escobar invited several of his former associates, including Fernando and Mario Galeano and brothers Gerardo and William Julio Moncada, to La Catedral, ostensibly for a business meeting. Instead, Escobar had them killed for hoarding millions of dollars they "did not feel like turning over to El Patrón."

Rattled and more than a little embarrassed by the revelations, Gaviria swiftly approved an operation to snag Escobar from his "prison" and move him to a higher-security facility. Escobar likely learned of Gaviria's plan on television news. Assuming that the government's real plan was either to kill him or to ship him in chains to the United States, he deduced it was time to find a safer locale. In July 1992, under the noses of the five hundred troops surrounding the compound in preparation for the emergency transfer, Escobar and his closest confidants walked out hours before the operation was slated to begin. The security forces they almost certainly encountered were either "too friendly or too intimidated" to stop them.

Now on the run, Escobar quickly realized the enormity of his miscalculation and pleaded with Gaviria to "repeat the favor of imprisoning him" through an unconditional surrender. Being Escobar, he matched this "carrot" with the stick of a ferocious terrorist bombing offensive. Gaviria ignored his proposals and an epic manhunt began.

Only days after Escobar fled La Catedral, Ambassador Morris Busby requested US military support from the US State Department, which passed the request along to the National Security Council. After consulting with Joint Chiefs Chairman Colin Powell, President Bush told Secretary of Defense Richard Cheney to give the US Embassy anything it wanted. With this green light from the Executive Branch's top officials, men and materiel were rushed to Colombia to aid the hunt.

The force included at least one elite US Army Delta Force unit (usually composed of a dozen operators) active in Bogotá and Medellín. The Air Force dispatched Boeing RC-135 reconnaissance jets, Lockheed C-130 Hercules cargo planes, Lockheed ultra-high altitude U-2 planes, and Lockheed SR-71 Blackbirds. The Navy sent Lockheed P-3 Orion maritime surveillance planes. In a precursor of the post-modern military and intelligence drone, the CIA dispatched a Schweizer SGM 2-37, a fixed-wing surveillance glider that could hover stealthily over a target for hours. The operation required ten C-130s just to deliver the contractors and maintenance staff for all of the equipment. At one point, seventeen American spy planes were in Medellín airspace at one time, so many that the Air Force had to put a Boeing E-3 Sentry in the air just to monitor them.

Despite the scale of the deployment, the greatest difficulty for Colombia's Search Bloc and its American counterparts proved to be simply finding Escobar. He was in his home territory, a city in the "center of terrorism." Colombian intelligence estimated that over two thousand individuals were working in the slums for Escobar. Even still, Pablo delegated little. He served as "his own military commander, his own head of security, intelligence, and counterintelligence, an unpredictable strategist, and an unparalleled purveyor of disinformation." Under especially intense pressure, he changed his eight-person team of bodyguards each day. He used state-of-the-art communications, wiretapping, and tracking devices. When law enforcement gave out two phone numbers for submitting information on his location, Escobar "hired whole schools of children" to create a wave of phone calls that would ensure the line remained busy. When Escobar realized that his phone calls were being tapped, he spoke into his radio phone: "Colonel, I'm going to kill you. I'm going to kill all of your family up to the third generation, and then I will dig up your grandparents and shoot them and bury them again. Do you *hear* me?"

LOS PEPES

In late January 1993, an explosion rocked Medellín, this time from a car bomb that demolished one of Escobar's family residences. A shadowy outfit calling itself People Persecuted by Pablo Escobar (or *Los Pepes*) claimed responsibility. It was the first of scores of operations. The Pepes located and killed attorneys working for Escobar, torched his antique car collection to "molten rubble," and "bombed and burned" several of his properties. On February 3, the corpse of Luis Isaza, a Medellín cartel member, was dropped off in a city neighborhood with a sign around his neck reading, "For working for the narco-terrorist baby-killer Pablo Escobar. For Colombia. Los Pepes." On April 16, police found the tortured body of Pablo's most prominent lawyer, Guido Parra, alongside his teenage son, Guido Andrés Parra, in the back of a vehicle near a Medellín social club. A stern message was painted nearby: "Through their profession, they initiated abductions for Pablo Escobar. Los Pepes." And as a postscript, "What do you think of the exchange for the bombs in Bogotá,

Pablo?" In June, Los Pepes kidnapped and shot one of Pablo's brothers-in-law. The reprisals were proving more effective in hunting the fugitive Escobar than the efforts of either the Colombian or the US government. This led journalist Alma Guillermoprieto to reflect, "If it weren't for Los Pepes, it is unlikely that the government could have Escobar so cornered today."

US officials were ebullient, believing that courageous civilians were finally fighting back. "We thought it was a citizen group that had finally reached the stage where they were going to straighten things up." But before long, US intelligence—and just about everyone else in Colombia—understood that the Pepes was a creation of the Cali cartel. US officials were further discouraged to learn that the Pepes were even paying Colombian police officers to kill Escobar's allies, effectively turning the force into "assassins for Cali interests." Said Joe Toft, DEA agent-in-charge in Bogotá, "We knew that Cali had a better game plan and were smarter, and that they would try to capitalize on Escobar's problems. But I don't think anyone understood how fully they were to take advantage of the situation until the process was well underway."

KILLING PABLO

By 1993, Pablo Escobar's world had changed. Allies who could have helped him now had little reason to do so. A fortune once estimated at $30 billion was largely lost to his protracted war. There was no place his family could live "where they would sleep without nightmares." Escobar himself could not spend more than six hours in a single location. Escobar continued offering to turn himself in, the last time in October 1993 in a message conveyed to the mayor of Medellín.

On December 2, 1993, Escobar "couldn't resist the temptation" of speaking on the telephone for several minutes with his son, Juan Pablo. This gave a team of Colombian and US specialists in a surveillance van in Medellín the necessary time to confirm Pablo's exact location in the middle-class Los Olivos neighborhood. US personnel were inside the van at the time Escobar's final call was traced. A little after three o'clock that afternoon, a team of twenty-three special plainclothes police cordoned off the immediate area and forced their way to the second floor.

Escobar spoke his last words to Juan Pablo: "I'm hanging up because something funny's going on here." Minutes later, Search Bloc officers shouted and called superiors. "Viva Colombia! We have just killed Pablo Escobar!" A chase that endured for sixteen months and involved six separate US agencies was over. In years hence, a rumor endured that a US Delta Force soldier had delivered the fatal shot, but evidence for this alternative scenario is scant.

POST-PABLO

Despite his bloody and brutal reign, Pablo's demise was not celebrated by all. For those who had been the beneficiaries of his lavish gifts, the drug lord was one of them made good, who had not forgotten his roots. Thousands of sobbing *paisas* mourned as his casket was drawn through the streets of Medellín before arriving in a "muddy hilltop cemetery." A *New York Times* headline encapsulated the scene: "A Drug Lord Is Buried as a Folk Hero." In the ensuing years, his grave became a tourist attraction—or for some a spiritual pilgrimage. Journalist Mark Bowden keenly observed, "A man of lesser ambition might still be alive, rich, powerful, and living well and openly in Medellín. But Pablo wasn't content to be just rich and powerful. He wanted to be admired. He wanted to be respected. He wanted to be loved." Escobar was not a populist in the ilk of Argentina's Juan Perón; crime, not politics, was his core. But he freely used the populist playbook—cash to the poor, violence, and manicured public persona—to pioneer a new form of power in Latin America.

39

Subcommander Marcos
The First Postmodern Guerrilla

At stake is what Subcomandante Marcos is, not who he was.
—*Subcomandante Marcos*

Subcommander Marcos was the enigmatic, and highly charismatic, spokesman of the Zapatista Army of National Liberation (EZLN), which emerged in the early 1990s in Mexico to champion the rights of the persecuted indigenous people of Chiapas. Marcos's trademark wit and eloquence were perfectly suited to the emerging mass media machine and won the Zapatistas outsized attention in Mexico and beyond. In the new post–Cold War context, Marcos also became a figurehead for the anticapitalist and antiglobalization movements across the world.

Although a light-skinned and middle-class university professor, Marcos had earned his revolutionary chops by spending more than a decade in the jungle with the locals building up the guerrilla group. But although he and the movement made a seismic impression, the reality of the ground did not change: the *San Andrés Accords* were meant to usher in a new understanding between Mexico City and the Chiapas but were not implemented according to the agreement. Still, EZLN had shown how a leftist insurrection was possible in the post–Cold War climate, with Marcos rewriting the guerrilla public-relations handbook.

A TOAST AND A TELEPHONE CALL

Very late in the night of December 31, 1993, Mexican president Carlos Salinas de Gortari, less than a year in his six-year term, had much to justify his ebullience as he toasted the New Year at Los Pinos, the Mexican version of the White House. The next day, the North American Free Trade Agreement would go into effect, an initiative that the technocratic, US-trained neoliberal economist had been a vital proponent of; the Aztec Nation was on the cusp of being admitted into the Organization for Economic Cooperation and Development, an exclusive club of supposedly stable and dynamic economies; and not long prior, *Time* magazine selected Salinas as its "International Newsmaker of the Year for Latin America." The smart money also favored him to be tapped as the head of the newly established World Trade Organization.

Salinas then received a breathless telephone call from his secretary of defense, informing him that an armed leftist revolutionary group had seized several localities in the forlorn, impoverished state of Chiapas (where Bartolomé de las Casas had once been bishop), including the cultural capital, San Cristóbal.

Mexico in 1994 was an unlikely spot for such an insurgency: the end of the Cold War precipitated the demise of El Salvador's Farabundo Martí National Liberation Front and Daniel Ortega's Sandinistas in Nicaragua, while Mexico's guerrilla organizations had been rendered impotent through President Luis Echeverría's 1970s strategy of "co-optation, infiltration, and brutal repression." Salinas's free-market reforms also appeared to have ushered in an unprecedented era of economic stability and dynamism. If bearded guerrillas were a "Third World phenomenon," then such revolutions were surely an impossibility in this seeming "First World country."

But the view from the center is always different from the periphery. Around four hundred miles to the south of Mexico City, Chiapas was another world of endemic, unspeakable poverty (over half of the population) and neglect. And these conditions had, with some deft guerrilla organizing, given rise to the EZLN, which effectively declared war on the Mexican state, promising in their December 31, 1993, manifesto that "we will not stop fighting until the basic demands of our people have been met by forming a government of our country that is free and democratic."

As dawn broke on January 1, 1994, the person soon to be known as Subcommander "Marcos" stepped to the balcony of picturesque San Cristóbal's city hall to speak to the four-hundred-odd residents assembled below, many of them bemused at the unfolding events. His role as spokesperson was more a case of circumstance than design. As biographer Nick Henck describes, "He wore a black poncho, black slacks, munition-filled bandoliers, and a revolver and an Ingram sub-machine gun tucked in his belt, a Rambo-style outfit," setting him apart from the red-and-white traditional attire of the Maya rebels flanking him.

But despite his classic guerrilla style, Marcos soon proved himself to be a very different kind of insurgent. Unsettled and anxious, a couple from Switzerland approached Marcos and inquired if they were free to go. "We have reservations to visit the ruins at Palenque," they informed him, referring to the Maya archaeological site popular with foreign tourists. Marcos quickly rejoined with his characteristic wit: "I apologize for the inconvenience, but this is a revolution." One woman in the audience asked him what was up with the black ski mask given that few others, if any, were wearing them; in response, he quipped, "Actually, only the most handsome of us are required to wear them, for our own protection." As Henck put it, "Marcos was evidently thoroughly enjoying being the center of attention," but in Marcos's mind, there was no doubt that this would be a "media war, not a guerrilla war." To this end, he told reporters on that same fateful first day, "We want to know what this event will provoke, what will move the national consciousness."

One writer summed up the effect of his badinage: "In the moment he pronounced these words the guerrilla captured his interlocutors: tourists, onlookers, local press, who scarcely a few hours after his first public appearance converted him into a star." By dusk, Subcommander Marcos had become the most famous guerrilla since Che Guevara (see Chapter 24, "Ernesto Guevara: Becoming Che"). But unlike his hero Che, "El Sub" as he was often referred to in his native country, quickly came to be an icon for the swelling global anticapitalism and antiglobalization movements, not orthodox Communism. This was a post-Soviet, postmodern leftist revolution, although still rooted in a narrative of oppression and poverty. Having marched into San Cristóbal, the guerrillas proceeded to torch the city hall's public files, which as Henck relates, "contained thousands of petitions for land and justice, filed but unresolved; property records, falsified and authentic; law suits pending; deeds and titles; and other such documents." Juan Bañuelos, himself a *chiapaneco* (those from the state) and an award-winning poet, put the events in context. "It was a symbolic act: the EZLN set fire to the lies, robbery, oppression, and cynicism of the system, as represented by City Hall. It was an act of purification." The next stop was a prison where they liberated just under two hundred prisoners. "Zapatista" roadblocks now controlled access into and out of the vital metropolis.

In the days, weeks, and months that followed, Marcos went on the publicity warpath to arouse the nation and world about the indigenous insurrection. Perhaps his most evocative and moving statement came in his written reply to Salinas's unilateral tender of a pardon that January:

> Why do we need to be pardoned? What are we to be pardoned for? For not dying of hunger? For not accepting our misery in silence? For not accepting humbly the historic burden of disdain and abandonment? For having risen up in arms after we found all other paths closed? For not heeding the Chiapas penal code, one of the most absurd and repressive in history? For showing the rest of the country and the whole world that human dignity still exists even among the world's poorest peoples? For having made careful preparations before we began our uprising? For bringing guns to battle instead of bows and arrows? For being Mexicans? For being mainly indigenous? For calling on the Mexican people to fight by whatever means possible for what belongs to them? For fighting for liberty, democracy and justice? For not following the example of previous guerrilla armies? For refusing to surrender? For refusing to sell ourselves out? Who should we ask for pardon, and who can grant it? Those who for many years glutted themselves at a table of plenty while we sat with death so often, we finally stopped fearing it? Those who filled our pockets and our souls with empty promises and words? Or should we ask pardon from the dead, our dead, who died "natural" deaths of "natural causes" like measles, whooping cough, breakbone fever, cholera, typhus, mononucleosis, tetanus, pneumonia, malaria and other lovely gastrointestinal and pulmonary diseases? Our dead, so very dead, so democratically dead from sorrow because no one did anything, because the dead, our dead, went just like that, with no one keeping count, with no one saying, "Enough!" which would at least have granted some meaning to their deaths, a meaning no one ever sought for them, the dead of all times, who are now dying once again, but now in order to live? Should we ask pardon from those who deny us the right and capacity to govern ourselves? From those who don't respect our customs and our culture and who ask us for identification papers and obedience to a law whose existence and moral basis we don't accept? From those who oppress us, torture us, assassinate us, disappear us for the grave "crime" of wanting a piece of land, not too big and not too small, but just a simple piece of land on which we can grow something to fill our stomachs? Who should ask for pardon, and who can grant it?

This missive's potency was sufficient to move even the eminent conservative intellectual and novelist Octavio Paz, who acknowledged: "The eloquent letter that Subcommander Marcos sent to various newspapers on 18 January truly moved me, even though it was sent by someone who has taken a course of action of which I disapprove. They, the Indians of Mexico, are not the ones who should ask for pardon. Rather, we are the ones who should ask for pardon."

Around two-thirds of the population were initially supportive of the Zapatistas—a number that went up to three-quarters after some of Marcos's most searing communique was broadcast over media airwaves. A "March for Peace" assembled over one hundred thousand citizens in Mexico City's storied Zócalo, or central plaza. Some of the myriad banners read were intended to ridicule Salinas, "First World, Ha, Ha, Ha!"

Mexico City's initial strategy was designed to appear placatory and even-handed. Less than two weeks after the onset, Salinas told the nation that he "taken the decision to suspend all military offensives in Chiapas," having "taken into account that the Mexican army has already achieved the prime objective of its constitutional mission to guarantee security in the region." But it was also engaging in more underhand tactics, using the state-controlled media to suggest that the Zapatista leader had been trained and financed by shadowy foreign actors and powers, that they were committing gross abuses, and were commanded by a "blond-haired, blue-eyed" (read, foreign!) soldier—and thus a far cry from patriotic but long-marginalized chiapanecos demanding justice. Attempting to isolate Marcos as the "gringo" mastermind behind this manipulation of well-intended but wayward *indios*, Salinas called him a "usurper and a traitor to this country" and a "professional of violence," to which Marcos calmly replied that he was actually "a professional of hope."

In a brilliant stroke of public relations, Marcos's Zapatistas intentionally elevated the likeness of the circa 1910s Mexican Revolution's martyred campesino hero, Emiliano Zapata—the very indigenous insurgent whose legacy the ruling PRI had sought to associate itself with. Salinas even had named one of his sons Carlos Emiliano, while the presidential jet got the moniker, Emiliano Zapata. Back in 1991 when Salinas announced a landmark reform to the 1917 Mexican Constitution's Article 27, he (and very much genuinely) did so in front of an image of Zapata to reinforce the notion that the liberalization of the communal lands, or *ejido* (enshrined in founding charter), was pro campesino and pro-Indian. But now somehow it was Marcos and the EZLN claiming to be the champions of landless campesinos! Its most visible and eloquent leader not only claimed inspiration from Zapata but also wore ammunition belts that unmistakably evoked the early twentieth-century revolutionary warrior's iconic uniform.

With foreign and domestic attention and pressure mounting, the Mexican government quickly realized that it would have to wait out the dexterous Zapatistas, eventually pouring large sums of money into the impoverished region to alleviate some of the sociopolitical symptoms that led residents to join the revolution.

THE MAN BEHIND THE MASK

Marcos's image and charm went viral in Mexico and internationally. A *Vanity Fair* writer told her readers that Marcos "looked the very stuff of myth" and extolled "his good features" and "his manner—one of palpable gentleness." Her conclusion: "There could never be a convincing imitation of this unique creature." Foreign correspondent Alma Guillermoprieto, who had spent considerable time with Marxist revolutionaries in Central America, came away convinced Marcos was "more articulate, cosmopolitan, humorous, and coquettishly manipulative than any guerrilla leader of El Salvador or Nicaragua who ever locked horns with the press." A female Mexican reporter took the adulation even further: "Why does this man motivate an almost irrational sexuality?" One male reporter who visited Marcos's Chiapas lair described the EZLN enigma "sprawling on one of the beds with his ski-mask on, puffing on his pipe, adoring women on every side, one under each arm."

But not everyone was charmed. French intellectual Régis Debray, who had interviewed Che and Chilean Marxist president Salvador Allende (see Chapter 26, "Salvador Allende: 'All Things to All Men'"), trekked to the forbidding Lancondón tropical rainforest, the Zapatistas' redoubt, and found Marcos egotistical as well as mendacious. Or take Oppenheimer's impression after a one-on-one session: "I had intended to ask him whether his name was one of about half a dozen that Interior Ministry intelligence officials were periodically leaking to the press, but I decided it would be of no use: he would have lied anyway. His standard response was that he had been born when he arrived in Chiapas ten years earlier, that his parents were the Indians who accepted him as one of them and that his real name was Marcos."

This perhaps fails to read between the lines of the purpose of the "Marcos" identity. In an interview with writer Gabriel García Márquez (see Chapter 29, "Gabriel García Márquez: Magical versus Social Realism"), the Mexican guerrilla said, "At stake is what Subcomandante Marcos is, not who he was"—

and in this sense, his "standard" response gains a deeper dimension: it was a persona created to serve a cause. Yet as the Zapatista insurgency played out, the question of Subcommander Marcos's real identity persisted, especially given the jarring anomaly of a white man acting as the spokesperson for an indigenous insurrection. Over the next several months, Salinas's one-party Institutional Revolutionary Party (PRI), via a media organ, falsely "reported" that the EZLN leader getting all the attention was in fact Father Pablo Romo, the head of the Fray Bartolomé de las Casas Human Rights Center in San Cristóbal. Finally, in the first part of 1995, the justice agency of the incoming PRI president Ernesto Zedillo publicly unmasked Subcommander Marcos (using intelligence provided by the turncoat rebel comrade Subcommander Daniel).

The man behind the mask was Rafael Sebastián Guillén Vicente, who had been a Mexico City university professor about a decade before he helped hatch the EZLN. To squelch Marcos's credibility as a person of and for the oppressed, Zedillo's administration ran photos of the urbane Guillén through the news cycle, including the nascent internet. Yet while Zedillo was lambasting Guillén as a "terrorist," the National Autonomous University of Mexico (UNAM), one of the most prominent public universities in the country, was giving its celebrated graduate an honorary degree.

THE MAKINGS OF A GUERRILLA

Born in the Gulf Coast city of Tampico on June 19, 1957, Guillén came into a privileged family considered "part of [Tampico] society though not high society." His father owned furniture stores, while his mother was a dedicated teacher who had strong views about the value of education (seven of her eight children went to university). Guillén's primary and secondary education was done at a strict Jesuit school in the port city, which not only pushed reading, writing, and mathematics but also character and spiritual development, including through experiential immersion in local slums, which very likely rubbed off on Guillén. As Marcos, he was asked what the roots of his "personal rebellion." His answer: "It's a process . . . you begin to take steps—first becoming interested in a situation, then understanding that there is injustice, then trying to understand the roots of this injustice. . . . You begin by helping out in small ways, taking logical steps." His sixth-grade teacher, Refugio Marín, recalled Rafael's awareness and compassion. "He always helped his compañeros, he always shared what he had, always, always, always. He saved his pocket money and any compañero who didn't have any money he would buy a cake or a drink. He was a good compañero. He always helped the needy." All of his teachers agreed that the precocious lad had formidable oratorical skills as well as a love for movies, plays, and (even if he wasn't especially good at it) basketball.

Like legions of young idealists across the world, the youthful Rafael fell madly in love with Che, even donning a beret and smoking a pipe, albeit unconvincingly affected. (Che is forever associated with Cuban cigars but often only had access to pipe tobacco on his guerrilla adventures.) "Che is closer to us than many people think," Marcos stated in 1997, "He is still around and alive thirty years on from his death . . . one way or another, all rebel movements in Latin America are the heirs to Che's rebellion." Fatefully, a literature teacher recalled Rafael, on the cusp of heading to Mexico City for his university studies, saying, "Now I am going to make the revolution."

In 1977, Rafael moved from somnolent Tampico to gargantuan, chaotic Mexico City to study humanities at UNAM. The young intellectual was in a paradise of used bookstores and literary and political salons fueled by black coffee and tequila, facilitated by the fact that strikes at UNAM meant fewer classes to attend, leaving him free, in his words, "to go to the theatre, the movies, to get good books, magazines like *Penthouse* and *Playboy*." But alongside the intellectual bonhomie, universities in the Mexican capital—and indeed Latin America—were also a breeding ground of leftist ideology. A year or two after arriving in the capital, Guillén likely started interacting with the clandestine National Liberation Forces (FLN), at the time a small outfit founded in 1969. Like their university-aged guerrilla counterparts from Managua to El Salvador to Peru, the FLN consisted of educated urbanites, in this case, some with organizing experience from the 1968 antigovernment student protests (which ultimately had been brutally suppressed in the Tlatelolco Plaza October massacre, in which hundreds of people were killed). A former student explained: "The majority of the members of this organization [the FLN] were from the middle class; university professors, professionals, engineers, medics," adding that, "It was a very, very small group: I am talking of ten or so, perhaps twenty people."

Concomitant with his entry into the FLN, Guillén started teaching at the recently founded university, the Autonomous Municipal University (UAM), which, overnight, had surpassed its more prestigious UNAM counterpart for radical politics and ideas and strikes—whether it was by administrators, faculty, or students, or some combination thereof. Ilan Stavans, a UAM student in this tumultuous time and later a literature professor at Amherst College in Massachusetts, relayed the circa late 1970s climate: "Our teachers were dissatisfied middle-class Mexican Leftists, exiled Argentine intellectuals, and other Latin American émigrés. Our idols were Che Guevara, and Herbert Marcuse. Wealthy professors urged us to agitate among peasants in the countryside."

This was an especially heady time for Marxist insurgency in the region, given that Cuba's revolution appeared fully consolidated and, in Nicaragua, the Sandinistas in July 1979 had scored a "Havana 1959" style ouster of their nation's strongman dynasty. (Contrary to what is often assumed, the Sandinistas were the only Marxist revolution group to in fact win "another Cuba".) Guillén may have ventured to Managua in the aftermath of the Sandinistas' triumph to soak up the atmosphere and figure out what needed to be done to replicate the magic potion in Mexico.

CHIAPAS CHAPTER

During his FLN activity, which ran alongside his UAM teaching duties, Guillén traveled to Chiapas on several occasions with the express intent of understanding how to live as an insurgent as well as helping construct, along with other UAM colleagues, the FLN's guerrilla Chiapas "frente" (front), which would become the EZLN. His final departure from Mexico City probably occurred in 1984, after which time the Lancondón region of Chiapas would be his and the nascent EZLN's base for the next decade. Of course, no aspiring Marxist guerrilla commander could go without a nom de guerre. Guillén's first was "Zacarías," and Zacarías was now in charge of a supposed "first aid" clinic that was the Zapatistas' poorly concealed guerrilla training.

The FLN leadership had not chosen Chiapas for their next guerrilla activity at random. Rather, the topography, remoteness, and endemic poverty and exploitation based on a semi-feudal land/labor systems (scholar Enrique Krauze scathingly called it the "Peru of Mexico") made it a propitious location for Che-inspired *foquismo* that aimed at organizing the rural masses to take up arms and usher in a new revolutionary era. British novelist Graham Greene harrowingly described the indigenous condition after visiting in 1938: "In bad years they say hundreds starve to death, but no one knows—they retire like wounded animals into the mountains and forests, eating berries, lasting as long as they can, seeking no pity." And the situation in Chiapas in 1979 or 1984 (or even 1994) was a little different, or even worse, than in Greene's era.

OVERCOMING THE GHOST OF CHE

Not surprisingly, the spartan guerrilla existence in Chiapas was exceptionally trying for Guillén, who said, "It was a nightmare . . . like landing on another planet. . . . Everything tells you: 'Leave. This is a mistake. You don't belong in this place.'" Another FLN leader, Rodrigo, "never imagined that Guillén could endure the jungle, he was too bourgeois, but he surprised everyone."

To many Mexican thinkers, both left and right, it was this protracted commitment to the Chiapas revolution that gave Marcos legitimacy. Krauze, for one, was dubious about Marcos but believed that "his commitment to altering the social reality of Chiapas and Mexico is authentic (his democratic convictions less certain) . . . it is a real and some would say admirable life choice." Novelist Elena Poniatowska had a similar reaction: "he has lived according to his ideas, which seems a lot to ask in our country . . . he stayed in the jungle for eleven years, he has shared and continues to share the Indian's living conditions."

But back then, the task before the would-be revolutionary was daunting. Marcos later admitted feeling haunted by the "ghost of Che," and in particular the "ghost of Ñancahuazú," which meant that he was terrified that his Chiapas insurgency would, like Che's in Bolivia, fail to enlist and motivate the support of local campesinos: the very essence of foquismo. In fact, in 1974 the FLN had hatched a Chiapas foco, which not only failed to win the hearts and minds of campesinos but was betrayed by these campesinos. Marcos realized a change in tactics was called for—"If we had continued with that form of organization we would still be deep in the rain forest with 15 or 20 guerrillas"—and subsequently amplified the importance of local (read, indigenous) allegiances: "We had to be in contact with the neighboring population, not only out of logistical considerations but also for political ones, because when it came to it we were seeking to be a revolutionary movement of all these people."

Complicating the task immensely was the fact that the Spanish-speaking Marxists were incomprehensible to the overwhelmingly indigenous locals, who spoke Maya languages. This posed manifold difficulties. Subcommander Elisa said: "Before going to the jungle I had intended to learn Tzotzil but I dropped it as a student. So, I spoke in Spanish and asked someone to translate for me. At times it wasn't easy. For example, they had no equivalent for the word Liberty."

The guerrilleros' arcane Marxist jargon made communication even more fraught. Marcos explained, "Imperialism, social crisis, the correlation of force with opportunity, these things were not understood. . . . They were very honest. You asked them, 'Do you understand?,' and they told you, 'No.'" This challenge humbled Marcos into adopting a language that would speak more clearly to the Chiapas context: "In order to survive we had to translate ourselves using a different code . . . this language constructed itself from the bottom upwards."

Despite these sorts of obstacles and setbacks, by the late 1980s the motley band of EZLN leaders had succeeded in recruiting enthusiastic and committed locals, including well-established militant labor and campesino syndicates like Unión de Unions led by Francisco López, a Ch'ol (Maya) from Sabanilla. For Marcos, the recruitment of committed soldiers sparked a virtuous cycle: "The indigenous of this intermediary group chatted with their families, who were also indigenous, Tzeltals, Tzotzils, Chols, Tojolobals, and these families decided to send their youngest sons and daughters to the mountains to become guerrillas. There we had this political-military group with an indigenous ingredient within it." In 1987, Marcos married a Tzotzil woman from Sabanilla, whose indigenous roots proved integral to the ongoing outreach.

But there were bumps in the road. Sometime in 1986, the FLN leadership reached out to El Salvador's potent Marxist insurgents for cash, training, and weapons, but although sympathetic, the Salvadoran counterparts declined, as the Mexican government had strong ties with them. Next, the Zapatistas tried Havana, where they were also politely turned down for the same reason (as a Cuban diplomat put it, getting crosswise of Mexico City would "amount to committing political hara-kari"). Then, at the start of 1989, there was a serious schism between the nascent Marxist revolutionaries and the Catholic Church led by Chiapas bishop Samuel Ruiz, whom right-wing landowners in the region called "the Red Bishop." If anything, the two groups had enjoyed a mutually productive relationship up to this point. Nick Henck explains that through the church, the guerrillas had gained ways "to politicize, organize, educate, and establish contact between the various communities living in the region." Some observers contended that Ruiz's network had started indigenous education and organization years before Marcos and company were even in high school. According to one local priest, "the Church was not behind the Zapatistas: it went before them." As Henck relates, Bishop Ruiz agreed, declaring that "these people have arrived to mount a saddled horse."

SOMETHING STRANGE HAPPENED ON THE WAY TO THE ELECTION

July 6, 1988, brought national elections, including the presidency, to Mexico, which if the PRI's past domination of the nation's "electoral democracy" was any indication, it would win. Part of what made the PRI's rule—the "perfect dictatorship" in Mario Vargas Llosa's brilliant phrasing (see Chapter 37, "Mario Vargas Llosa: Cartographies of Power")—is that the system had all the appearance of a free and fair democracy, when in fact the PRI's grip on power was hermetic.

But this time around things went far from smoothly. In what became one of the most infamous instances of outright fraud in a modern Latin American election—and that was saying something—initial televised public electoral returns had the leftist opposition candidate Cuauhtémoc Cárdenas (son of Lázaro, Mexico's FDR; see Chapter 17, "Lázaro Cárdenas: 'Nuestro Petróleo'") in the lead, before a "power outage" stopped the counting. When the electricity returned, the RPI's Salinas was magically in front and soon declared the winner.

Down in Chiapas, the PRI's approach would not have been out of place in the world's most totalitarian countries: in Ocosingo, the largest municipality, authorities reported 102,000 votes compared to 3,000 for the runner-up party, despite the entire population of the district is 110,000. The PRI's vote share in Chiapas overall was almost around 40 percent greater than the national average. This flagrant subversion of democracy would, however, prove a recruitment boon for the revolutionaries. As Marcos later recounted, "by means of the electoral fraud, president Salinas was imposed on us and with him the whole neo-liberal project. In these moments many people began to arrive, many compañeros, and the dream that the EZLN would become a regular army with great potential was realized." (The 1988 ballot box fraud in Chiapas recurred on a similar scale in the 1991 midterm elections, further facilitating the EZLN's recruitment of fed-up citizens.)

Yet the global situation was also turning against them. The November 1989 fall of the Berlin Wall was demoralizing enough for the committed Zapatistas, but the shocking electoral defeat, in March 1990, of the ruling Sandinistas was a gut punch for Marcos and company. None of these developments, however, convinced the EZLN to abandon its path to guerrilla insurgency. More bad news came in early 1992 when an amendment to Article 27 permitting the sale of ejido lands was passed. There was a glimmer of good news in October of that year when Guatemala's Rigoberta Menchú was awarded the Nobel Peace Prize. (See Chapter 34, "Rigoberta Menchú: A Voice for the Voiceless.")

MARCOS'S LAST LAP

By the middle of 1995, President Zedillo had called the military out of the Zapatistas' sphere of operations, which lowered tensions. Mexico City and the EZLN would, not without controversy and mutual acrimony, preside over peace negotiations, which led to the San Andrés Accords the following year, although the pact was never formalized. Marcos continued, often via the incipient internet, to pound away against his two favorite whipping horses—neoliberalism and globalization—and thus remaining popular with the global leftist audience receptive to this post–Cold War anti-West condemnation, while downplaying (consciously or otherwise) the insurgency's Marxist ideology.

Jump forward to 2000 and, with the electoral victory of conservative candidate Vicente Fox, Mexico had completed an admirable democratic transition. And this, many critics pointed out, made it harder to make sense of why Mexico City and the EZLN could not forge a way to formally end the insurgency. Others wondered why, in a democratic Mexico, Marcos simply didn't run for president or governor of Mexico. Be that as it may, the Zapatistas were more isolated than ever, public opinion sagging and the news cycle moving on. And for Marcos, to quote Krauze, the guerrillero was "clinging to his myth, until his myth begins to waver."

But being Marcos, the EZLN subcommander was not finished just yet. In late February 2001, in what was his first confirmed departure from the Lacandon jungle in years, he presided over a two-week, 1,800-mile caravan from Chiapas to Mexico City to promote indigenous peoples and rights in Mexico and pressure Congress to adopt the San Andrés Accords. Marcos's March for Indian Dignity (almost immediately dubbed the Zapatour by domestic and global outlets) saw upward of twenty thousand chiapanecos gathered to bid the delegation adios, which then stopped at dozens of indigenous communities as it followed the same path to the national capital as Emiliano Zapata when he vanquished Mexico City in 1914. When Red Cross support for the travelers fell through, an Italian anarchist outfit that called itself Ya Basta! (Enough is enough!, a Zapatista cry) provided security.

As the marchers closed in their stated final stop, the Zócalo, an estimated 140,000 capital city residents came out to welcome their compatriots.

Subcommander Marcos attends a meeting between his Zapatista National Liberation Army and indigenous organizations in a remote hamlet in Chiapas, Mexico, August 13, 2005. *(Alamy Stock Photo)*

International leftist celebrities, most notably film industry Americans Oliver Stone and Robert Redford and French activist Danielle Mitterrand, were in attendance. Marcos then went before members of Congress to implore them to back the capacious peace pact. The following month, Congress passed a revised accord, but this time it was the Zapatistas who resisted.

In his last public correspondence in 2014, Marcos announced that the personality of "Subcommander Marcos" was being retired: it had all along been a "hologram" and "that today [he] no longer exists." Yet if little changed during the Zapatistas' revolution—levels of poverty and desperation in Chiapis remained stubbornly high (as high in 2018 as in 1994!), despite Mexico City's promises of aid and development—Marcos had forged a new approach to fighting for justice, creating a persona "who seduced his audiences by combining the machos aura of a guerrilla leader with the self-deriding sense of humor of a sensitive male of the nineties."

40

Hugo Chávez

The Richest Revolutionary in the World

During the halcyon years of President Hugo Chávez and his "Bolivarian socialism" ideology, literacy rates soared, subsidized food and gas supported many poor Venezuelans, and an anti-*yanqui* and anti-imperialist fervor dominated the foreign-policy discourse. A former army officer who had inculcated Marxism and believed himself heir to Simón Bolivar's legacy, Chávez was a charismatic leader who had been elected as president in 1998 after failing to topple the government in a military coup and set about reforming Venezuela as a socialist paradise.

But there were worrying signs for those who cared to look: the growing cult of Chávez was steadily eroding Venezuela's institutional checks and balances, while corruption was running rampant. The economy ran well on the back of high oil prices (with oil mainly sold to the United States, an irony for a socialist regime), but when these prices fell, the good times ended abruptly. By the time of Chávez's death in 2013, political repression and economic recession were pushing Venezuela into crisis, a process that dramatically accelerated under Chávez's successor, Nicolás Maduro. Even so, Chávez remains an enduringly popular (if divisive) figure in Venezuela, a testament to his magnetic ability to connect with his base of poor Venezuelans, and despite his role in bringing the country to the brink of collapse.

BIOGRAPHY OF A BOLIVARIAN

Born in 1954, Hugo Rafael Chávez Frías first lived in a "dirt-floored abode house" in the poor, remote western plains town of Sabaneta before his family moved to the nearby provincial city of Barinas. A history buff who loved to play the great American pastime (read, *beísbol*), the young Chávez also worshiped Bolívar, learning the Great Liberator's speeches by heart; he even reenacted his hero's Hannibal-like march through the Andes (see Chapter 6, "Simón Bolívar: The Great Liberator, Flawed Emancipator"). "Instead of Superman, my hero was Bolívar," he told a journalist in the late 1990s.

After giving up his dream of pitching in the Major Leagues at Yankee Stadium, in his late teens Chávez enlisted as a junior cadet at the nation's military, where he also started reading leftist pamphlets and books. Upon graduating with a diploma, Chávez joined a counterinsurgency unit. One of his first operations was in September 1977, when he was sent as part of a task force to quell a Maoist insurgency, the Red Flag, in the state of Anzoátegui. It was, in Chávez's subsequent telling, a transformative encounter, marking the point when Chávez began to identify with the downtrodden and, even more critically, left-wing politics and sociology.

Another foundational moment occurred in 1977 when he read the 1898 opus *The Role of the Individual in History* by Georgi Plekhanov, the father of Russian Marxism who coined the term "dialectical materialism" and promoted the "great men in history" theory. "I read Plekhanov," Chávez later recounted, "when I belonged to an anti-guerrilla unit in the mountains . . . and it made a deep impression on me. I remember that it was a wonderful starry night in the mountains and I read it in my tent by the light of a flashlight." The young soldier read the tome over and over again, "in search of ideas [about] the role of the individual in historical processes." Decades later, Chávez boasted how that "little book that survived storms and the years; the same little book with the same little underlining a person makes, and the same little arrows and the same cover I used as camouflage so that my superiors wouldn't say 'what are you doing reading that?'"

For historian Enrique Krauze, Chavez's understanding of Plekhanov was, at best, "highly idiosyncratic," with the boy from Barinas using the Marxist's theories to justify a pro-caudillo ideology. "If they [the caudillos] develop a real awareness, they become removed from themselves and view the process from a distance," said Chávez. "If they devote their lives, their efforts, to use their 'mythical' power to collectivize . . . then the presence of the caudillo can be justified." Alfredo Garrido, a notable Venezuelan analyst, contended that Chavez was "perfectly convinced that he has a historic mission, which is to assume Bolívar's mantle." In a 1995 statement, Chávez revealed some other hints about what his political ideology was—and was not: "I don't know anything about Marxism, I never read *El Capital*, I'm not a Marxist or an anti-Marxist."

HUGO CHÁVEZ

A spray and stencil artwork, depicting Venezuelan president Hugo Chávez, appears on the street of Caracas, Venezuela. "Chávez is the people." March 2005. *(Jan Sochor/Alamy)*

This self-assessment needs to be taken with a grain of salt: there were most definitely Marxist currents of thought in Chávez, but these were fused with the big man history of Bolívar to create what might be termed "socialism with caudillo characteristics."

Chávez's political awakening in the 1970s took place against a heady backdrop of soaring petroleum prices that drove a period of economic growth which earned Venezuela the moniker "the Saudi Arabia of South America." Venezuela's putatively stable two-party political system—formed of the venerable COPEI (Christian Democratic) and the social-democratic Democratic Action (or AD)—traced their electoral supremacy back to the 1958 *Pact of Punto Fijo*, which had helped replace strongman Pérez Jiménez's dictatorship with democracy (see Chapter 21, "Rómulo Betancourt: Titan of Democracy"). Although *puntofijismo* effectively prevented any other political party from competition for power—and made state petroleum revenues a two-party monopoly—it was functional and therefore appealing in the times like the 1970s and early 1980s when oil prices were sky high.

By the latter half of the 1980s, though, the bottom had fallen out of the price of a barrel of oil. In 1988, AD's Carlos Andrés Pérez (or CAP as he was widely and often affectionately called) campaigned on a left-wing populist platform of returning Venezuela to its rightful place as a rich and upwardly mobile country as had been the case—or at least appeared to have been the case—under his presidency between 1974 and 1979. CAP freely bashed the World Bank as "genocide workers in the pay of economic totalitarianism" and the International Monetary Fund (IMF) as being "a neutron bomb that killed people, but left buildings standing." Only weeks after he took office in early 1989, though, CAP did a political 180-degree flip, embracing the IMF's neoliberal (read, laissez-faire) austerity program. The first steps of the new fiscal belt-tightening would be innocuous increases in the already well-subsidized public transportation fares and retail gasoline, but these seemingly uncontroversial measures precipitated a week of bloody anti-CAP protests and controversial countermeasures by the security forces. The unrest originated in Caracas's vertiginous slums before catching fire across the nation.

In the end, the so-called *Caracazo* rampage resulted in hundreds of millions of damage to property and untold numbers of killed and wounded (estimates range from a few hundred to a few thousand), deaths which were ascribed to the state response. Although Chávez did not play a part in suppressing the unrest, Caracazo cemented his feeling that he could no longer be a tool of the state. "I was just a simple soldier then," he told the *New Yorker*'s Jon Lee Anderson in a 2002 interview,

> But then I had to ask, "What do I do with this rifle, where do I point it?" It was a terrible crisis of conscience. Now that the hurricane is unleashed, what do I do? Do I throw my rifle on the ground and run off, and stop being a soldier, or do I point it at the miserable peasants? Or do I point it against those who have led the people to this situation? My comrades and I took the road of Bolívar, who said, "Damned be the soldier who turns his weapons against his people."

COUP!

Chavez and his ideologically aligned conspirators had been plotting ever since founding the clandestine Bolivarian Revolutionary Movement 200 (MRB-200; two hundred was the number of years between Bolívar's year of birth and their outfit's creation) in 1982—and the time finally seemed to be ripe to make their move. As far as Chávez was concerned, CAP's unwillingness to abandon his newly adopted neoliberal agenda was justification enough to remove him from office. On February 4, 1992, Chávez launched his coup d'état—which quickly failed, with loyal troops preventing CAP's capture (and almost certain

Cuba billboard of three heroes in revolutionary Cuban life—Hugo Chávez, Fidel Castro, and Nelson Mandela—near Trinidad, Cuba, circa 2000. The text reads "The Large Homeland That Grows." *(Bill Bachmann/Alamy)*

execution). With many of his compatriots shot dead and the situation hopeless, Chávez surrendered. All told, the February putsch took seventeen lives, including civilians caught in the crossfire.

Yet Chávez managed to snatch a PR victory from the jaws of defeat when Venezuelan authorities allowed Chávez to make a live televised statement from jail just hours after he had been caught. Dressed in the distinct red beret of the paratroopers, Chávez did call for his still-active comrades to give up the fight, yet the phrasing was suggestive that the struggle would resume before long: "Comrades, the objectives we set for ourselves have not been possible to achieve *por ahora* [for now] . . . but new possibilities will arise again, and the country will be able to move forward to a better future. . . . I alone take responsibility for this Bolivarian military uprising." As Anderson commented, the significance of the phrase "por ahora" was unmistakable. Defeated but undaunted, Chávez became a symbol of defiant resistance and a champion of the millions of Venezuelans who had come to despise everything about their rancid *puntofijista* ruling class.

After the dust settled, Chávez received a court marshal and was imprisoned at Yare prison on the outskirts of the capital. In an early media interview from inside the penitentiary, Chávez used language that reinforced his association with the Venezuelan icon, "Bolívar and I led a coup d'état. Bolívar and I want the country to change." While Chávez was incarcerated, a second, much bloodier pro-MBR 200 coup attempt took place in late November 1992. This also failed, but not before over one hundred lives were lost.

In December 1993, Chávez was visited in prison by young leftist radical activists, including one Nicolás Maduro (a figure who will enter our story in due course). Maduro later recounted how Chavez "started talking, fifty minutes without stopping. . . . About the forces gathering on the street, the popular forces gathering, the construction of . . . everything." The revolutionary fire still burned bright within the incarcerated leader: Maduro recalled, "He said, 'A new popular military insurrection.' And all of our hearts were beating faster." Before the protracted encounter had concluded, Maduro had his own code word, "Verde" (Green), and was also the effective commander of Chávez's political project. Over the next two decades, Maduro would become one of Chávez's most vital aides.

CITIZEN CHÁVEZ

Released from prison in 1994 and now a civilian, Chávez worked tirelessly to establish his political profile and platform. Within a few years, this resulted in the establishment of the Movement for the Fifth Republic, a democratic update of his earlier shadowy outfit, MRB-200. In 1998, Chávez won the presidency on the back of a campaign that blasted puntofijismo and "savage neoliberalism." Interestingly, many moderate politicians and governments outside of Venezuela were rooting for the incoming socially oriented Chávez to succeed, especially given how his successors had failed to translate prodigious oil revenues into widely shared prosperity. It is also worth noting how back then Chávez was "ideologically flexible," intrigued by US President Bill Clinton and British Prime Minister Tony Blair's more centrist "third-way" politics, as well as far-left ideologies. Echoing Fidel Castro's 1959 trip to the United States (see Chapter 23, "Fidel Castro: A Rebel with a Cause"), in January 1999 president-elect Chávez met with Clinton, presided over a New York Stock exchange session and, not unimportantly for the baseball-mad leader, tossed the first pitch at a Yankees game. Like his Cuban counterpart, Chávez seemed to have his eyes open to the world of possibilities and recognized the importance of powerful political friends. It would prove to be a false dawn.

In these initial years as a civilian presidential candidate and first-term head of state that the former paratrooper also began to embrace more fully the "myth of the hero." In Mexico in the 1990s, the insurgent Zapatistas elevated their martyr from the Mexican Revolution, and the circa 1970s Marxist anti-Somoza fighters embraced their fallen comrade, Augusto César Sandino, who fought US Marines a half-century prior. (See Chapter 16, "Augusto César Sandino versus the United States.") But "Bolívar" had a far deeper significance to Venezuelans than Zapata or Sandino did to their respective nations, and Chávez was well aware of its galvanizing power. "If the myth of Bolívar helps to get people and ideas moving," Chávez quipped, "that's good." As a part of his "national re-founding," in 1999, President Chávez officially changed the country's name to the Bolivarian Republic of Venezuela, and the new civilian-promulgated constitution would be "based on the doctrine of Bolívar." In Krauze's analysis, Chávez turned Bolívar into an omniscient, eternal, infallible figure, whom Chávez described as "Our infinite Father," "genius of America," "shining star," "shaper of republics," "truly great hero of our times," and "true owner of this process."

Despite Chávez's lofty Bolivarian rhetoric, his ability to implement a radical national agenda was initially limited by (relatively) pitiful oil revenues; at the time, a barrel on the world market fetched just $10, which meant a government budget of $7 billion. Just under a decade later, though, the price was nudging toward $150 and Chávez's budget swelled to $54 billion. Social spending (often through "Bolivarian missions" after 2003) soared to three times the initial amounts. Here is Jon Lee Anderson's succinct analysis from 2008: "Even though many of these 'missions,' as they're known, have foundered or have proved inadequate, the volume of revenues has meant an improvement in living standards for the country's poorest citizens, who are, unsurprisingly, Chávez's strongest supporters. It has also given him the means to buy influence with his neighbors, usually at the expense of the United States."

This was most evident in the closeness of relations between Venezuela and the United States' regional thorn, Cuba. In 2000, the ideologically aligned and personally close Chávez and Castro inked accords that, among other things, guaranteed the supply of fifty-three thousand barrels of petroleum a day at below world market prices, in effect providing a subsidy to Havana of a whopping $2.5 billion per year for the next decade. In return, Havana pledged twenty thousand Cuban medics, teachers, and other sorts of ostensibly socially oriented professionals. Over time, the amount of subsidized oil almost doubled, as did the number of such Cubans coming to the South American nation to staff urban slums and far-flung rural outposts. After one of the first batches of Cubans arrived, an ebullient Chávez described his sense of historical import: "Just as Cuba took its own revolutionary path, with its own characteristics, forty years ago, the Bolivarian revolution is taking its first steps today." Thousands of Venezuelans traveled to Cuba for education; over one hundred thousand received treatment for eye maladies alone. Less publicized but unquestionably part of the deal was Castro's provision of myriad intelligence, military, and security officials to Chavez's increasingly autocratic government.

Many observers believe that this relationship with Castro is what moved Chávez away from any sort of moderation toward what he came to call "socialism for the twenty-first century." Certainly, the ties between the two leaders went much deeper than the usual diplomatic declarations of affinity: "For me, Fidel is like a father. Like a beacon. Fidel is, I believe, irreplaceable," Chávez said in 2008. "He is a giant of the twentieth century, and, just as he entered its history, he has also entered into that of the twenty-first. And there he is, even now, doing everything he can to keep on fighting what he calls the battle of ideas, until his last breath." While at this point still a minority, millions of anti-Chávez citizens were not thrilled with what they saw as the Castro regime's stealthy manipulation of the fawning Chávez. Some would march holding signs such as "We Want Citizens, Not Militiamen," "Don't Mess with Our Kids," "No to Cubanization," and "Education Yes, Indoctrination No."

THE REVOLUTION HARDENS

Chávez's broad popularity (solidly over 50 percent his first decade in office) and frenetic political agenda allowed him to win multiple national referenda, including those that authorized reelection and longer terms (from five to seven years). He easily won reelection in 2000, garnering around 60 percent of the vote, but then came a shock. In April 2002, Chávez was briefly removed from power following a coup led by industry chief Pedro Carmona after months of labor and antigovernment tumult, most critically a massive labor strike in the vital oil sector. Chávez had initially agreed to step down with the assurance that he would be allowed to flee to exile in Cuba. Just under two days later, however, *el comandante* triumphantly returned, in no small part due to the organizing and actions of loyalist General Raúl Baduel, Commander of the 42nd Paratrooper Infantry Brigade.

Chávez immediately consolidated his hold on power, assuming full control of the heretofore strike-riddled and relatively autonomous state oil behemoth, PDVSA, throwing out almost one-third of its total—whom he replaced with loyalists. Now PDVSA would be an unapologetic tool of "Bolivarianism," as seen through the mission programs it funded across the country. The new *chavista* PDVSA chief, Rafael Ramírez, expanded on the goal of moving the country from an "oil sultanate to a productive society within a socialist framework."

On the social and security side, Chávez established new pro-regime organizations known as *colectivos*. To their supporters, these often motorcycle-riding militiamen were "knights of steel," committed to ensuring local enforcement of all things Bolivarian. These groups initially provided Chávez not only with a hedge against disloyalty from military ranks but also an "ability to rapidly concentrate political shock troops against opposition demonstrators." Within a decade, however, the colectivos would "look more like criminal gangs with immense social control," according to a global crime investigative organization.

In the aftermath of his decisive 2006 landslide reelection—"Nothing can stop the revolution!" in his words—Chávez launched a single united leftist political party, United Socialist Party of Venezuela, the undisputed legislative and municipal juggernaut for all things Bolivarian. (It would not lose its majority in Congress until 2015.) In 2009, a Chávez-backed referendum that included language on abolishing term limits won a narrow majority, and the Venezuelan leader indicated his desire to remain in office for at least another ten years. More political maneuverings, which ran roughshod over the nation's weakened checks and balances, tightened the Chavista grip over a packed Supreme Court and unicameral National Assembly. Lastly, Chavez used the post-coup years to entrench the "Cubanization" of the security forces.

The Caracas–Havana relationship also had regional aspirations. In 2004, Caracas and Havana jointly agreed to uphold Chávez's hemispheric Bolivarian Alliance for the Peoples of Our America (ALBA, which means "dawn" in Spanish), a putative rejoinder to the neoliberalism of the US Treasury and IMF's preferred Free Trade Area of the Americas. Within five years, leftist governments such as Bolivia, Nicaragua, Bolivia, and Honduras had joined up (in part due to the attractive petroleum deals offered by Venezuela). Leftist figures and political parties and organizations around the world became recipients of Chávez's oil-driven largesse, with the Venezuelan allocating an estimated US$16 billion to US$25 billion on foreign aid between 1999 and 2006. Jon Lee Anderson's keen 2008 observation highlights how this anti-US stance was ironically largely funded by US purchases of Venezuelan oil:

> Chávez's hemispheric ambitions have made him one of the most compelling, audacious, and polarizing figures in the world. . . . A generation ago, Castro sought to undermine United States authority by supporting armed guerrilla forces; Chávez has pursued that goal mainly by using money—thanks, in large measure, to U.S. oil purchases. Venezuela is the fifth-largest supplier of oil to the U.S., providing around a million barrels a day.

Here is Anderson's retrospective take on the Venezuelan president's role in this diplomatic petro-bonanza: "Chávez flew around the world on his Presidential jet, giving speeches, dispensing largesse, funding political campaigns, and promoting the idea of a multipolar world in which the United States was no longer the single hegemon. He befriended America's enemies, from Saddam Hussein to Vladimir Putin, Mahmoud Ahmadinejad, and Muammar Qaddafi, and delighted in taunting George W. Bush, whom he called Mr. Danger on his weekly television broadcasts."

Despite Chávez's outsized authority over Venezuela in this period, there were moments of significant opposition and protest. Take, for instance, the 2004 referendum in which opposition groups managed to get over 2.7 million (about 10 percent of the entire population) Venezuelans to request a recall of the head of state. Controversy erupted after pro-Chávez elements posted the confidential petition names online, which put these putative regime opponents into potentially delicate circumstances regarding, say, employment. Then in the ensuing national August referendum on Chávez's continued rule, an astounding seven in ten citizens went to the polling sites, with 59 percent of the turnout voting for Chávez to continue in power. The impartial and widely respected Carter Center certified the vote as clear and fair, which complicated the ability of other organizations to pursue what they believe were cases of vote manipulation or patent fraud.

Chávez took advantage of his unexpected but resounding anti-recall mandate to install what critics labeled "political apartheid," whereby the millions who voted against him in the August referendum were susceptible to all sorts of pressures or prosecution. The nation's sole independent television outlet, RCTV, was also targeted, closing down in 2007, and Chávez deployed his own formidable media resources—hundreds of radio stations, newspapers, and several television outlets in the crucial segment of Caracas—to push his Bolivarian message. The following year, he barred hundreds of potential politicians from running as opposition candidates in regional campaigns. Before one of the votes on Chávez's reelection, public sector workers distributed pamphlets saying "Chávez loves us, and you pay back love with love."

In an especially provocative, now infamous diplomatic gesture at the height of his petro-fueled Bolivarian Revolution, in his September 2006 speech to the UN General Assembly Chávez held a copy of globally recognized, left-wing American academic Noam Chomsky's book *Hegemony or Survival: America's Quest for Global Dominance* and told the audience full of diplomats and heads of states that "the devil [George W. Bush] came here yesterday. It still smells of sulfur today.... He came here talking as if he were the owner of the world." For anyone who had been following Chávez's actions over the preceding years, his comments about Bush were nothing new: alongside "Mr. Danger," "donkey," "drunkard," and "coward" were some of Chávez's less-than-flattering nicknames for the US president. While it usually tried to ignore the bombastic Venezuelan, the Bush administration periodically made public its views regarding Chávez. Over her tenure as secretary of state, Condoleezza Rice called Chávez a "negative force" in the hemisphere, criticized his ties to Cuba, and claimed that he was pursuing a "Latin American brand of populism that has taken countries down the drain."

Another notorious incident came at a Chile-hosted regional summit in 2007. Chávez repeatedly interrupted the Spanish Prime Minister, prompting Spanish king Juan Carlos to utter, "¿Por que no te callas?" ("Why don't you shut up?"), prompting millions of antiregime Venezuelans (many in exile in Spain, the United States, and the rest of Latin America) to cheer that someone had put the rhetorical bully in his place. Also in 2007, Chávez suffered a rare defeat over his referendum proposing sixty-nine amendments to the 1999 constitution, including one on indefinite reelection, which might have meant Chávez in power for life given how unfair these votes were becoming, as well as amendments curtailing rights for media and citizens detained in states of emergencies. Somewhat surprisingly, Chávez honored this stinging and narrow defeat (a 51 to 49 percent margin).

Yet other attempts to check the charismatic leader were less successful. In mid-September 2008, the nongovernmental organization Human Rights Watch issued a report declaring that Chávez's government had "consolidated power by eliminating the independence of the judiciary, punishing critical news organizations and engaging in wide-ranging acts of political discrimination against opponents." One of the report's authors, Chilean José Miguel Vivanco, stated that Chávez's "demonization of opponents" had instilled an "environment of fear" within the country. Hours after the report was issued, armed men apprehended Vivanco and his Human Rights Watch colleague at their Caracas hotel room and drove them to the airport, where they were forced onto a commercial flight to Brazil. The Venezuelan government justified the move by saying the authors had violated the constitution "by attacking the institutions of the Venezuelan democracy and illegally meddling in our country's domestic affairs." Officials added that the two activists were conspiring on behalf of the George W. Bush administration.

The cult of Chávez became all-powerful, permeating every facet of Venezuelan life to the exclusion of all else: Here is Krauze's writing in 2009: "His takeover of the Bolivar myth is complete. All the fantastic strains of popular religiosity in Venezuela, its folk political theology, are now centered in him." And for Krauze, the media had been willing accomplices: "The key to Chávez's enthronement lies not in his erratic record of economic development or in the arguable success of his social programs, but in the press's handling of his colossal persona."

Chávez's behavior and policies—foreign and domestic alike—led his adversaries to claim he was turning into a "dictatorial caudillo" similar to Juan Perón or his beloved Fidel Castro (see Chapter 20, "Juan and Eva Perón: Peronism's Dynamic Duo"). These critics pointed to all sorts of public comments from the voluble Chávez as evidence of his autocratic ways. "Liberal democracy is no good, its time has passed, new models must be invented, new formulas. . . . Democracy is like a rotten mango: it has to be taken as seed and sowed." Or "the opposition will never return to power, by fair means or foul." Chavista supporters, by contrast, contended that his seeming excess was radicalism in the face of (US-backed) tyranny and injustice through the CIA or heartless international financial bodies, above all the IMF. Whatever the case, there is little question that Chávez's ability to dole out domestic and foreign largesse won him far more friends and allies than his words or policies alone, and this ability was inextricably linked to the price of oil: Chavismo peaked when prices were high and faded when they dropped.

CRACKS IN THE BOOM

The flood of revenues generated by oil selling at prices around US$125/barrel masked the dearth of needed infrastructure and exploration investment in the petrol sector. By 2008, the cracks had grown more obvious, production and

Cuba's President Fidel Castro (center) sits between Venezuela's President Hugo Chávez (left) and Bolivia's President Evo Morales during an event on Havana's Revolution Square, April 29, 2006. (Claudia Daut/Alamy)

exports down by just over one-third and one-half, respectively. But the Chávez regime was living in the moment and thought that the party would never stop (just as the nationalist CAP had assumed back in the heady circa 1970s oil boom days). One Chávez senior official boasted that it was "impossible" for the oil price to drop, while Chávez himself bragged that he had the fortitude to get the barrel price to over US$250. But his bluster was useless in the face of the sweeping global recession between 2007 and 2009. Crude oil—the very commodity so central to Chávez's Bolivarian revolution—plunged from US$177 a barrel to just under US$60. And alongside economic woes came ever-greater domestic repression. In 2010, Amnesty International excoriated Chávez for its persecution of government opponents. The same year, Organization of American States investigators were banned from entering Venezuela.

In October 2012, Chávez once again prevailed in a seemingly decisive head-to-head presidential vote, besting Henrique Capriles of the Democratic

Unity Roundtable by a margin of 54 to 44 percent. Within a few months of the vote, Venezuelans learned that their president would be treated for cancer in Cuba; Chávez declared that should he be unable to execute his office, his political heir Nicolás Maduro (who ran the National Assembly and was now vice president) would become president. By March 2013, amidst several months of turmoil due to Chávez's absence, Maduro told the nation that the nation's leader had died in Cuba, and blamed the United States for causing the malady: "The old enemies of our fatherland looked for a way to harm his health."

Hundreds of thousands of crestfallen chavistas, dressed in trademark revolutionary red, lined the route of the funeral procession as Chávez's flag-draped coffin inched its way across Caracas to the military academy. His death also sparked an outpouring of international sympathy: Iranian President Mahmoud Ahmadinejad praised the Venezuelan "martyr," while Ken Livingstone, a former mayor of London and longtime Chávez supporter, caught the mood of many of the global left. "Hugo Chávez showed there is an alternative to neo-liberalism and colonialism in Venezuela and worldwide," the socialist politician wrote. "He was a friend and comrade." US actor Sean Penn, also a stalwart backer of the Venezuelan revolutionary, put it this way. "Poor people around the world lost a champion. I lost a friend I was blessed to have."

INTO THE ABYSS UNDER MADURO

The shortcomings of Chavismo were already apparent by the end of Chávez's life, but the country plunged into the abyss under his successor Maduro, who defeated Carpriles in an election just weeks after Chávez's death by just 1.5 percentage points (51 percent to 49 percent). The brittle economy, which had run hot during the glory years of high oil prices, was shattered by the drop in those prices. Basic goods became increasingly restricted: in 2014, citizens were queuing for five hours a day on average for grocery stores that had already run out of toilet paper, flour, milk, and other staples. In 2017, just under 75 percent of Venezuelans lost an average of nineteen pounds due to the sustained food scarcity in what became known as the "Maduro diet." The UN estimated that between 2013 and 2018, 13 percent of the country's children suffered from malnourishment. A fifth of the population fled abroad, creating a refugee crisis comparable to those created by conflict.

Corruption and political mismanagement reached endemic proportions under Maduro, fueling the economic fire devastating the country. The country entered a protracted period of hyperinflation, peaking in 2018 when the annual inflation rate hit over 130,000 percent. Working families were plunged into abject poverty as savings and earnings became worthless. And as the regime's handouts to like-minded Latin American governments waned, its influence did too; it was not a coincidence that Havana's diplomatic outreach to the Barack Obama administration occurred right as subsidized crude oil and refined oil shipments from Venezuela plunged by roughly half.

Maduro was increasingly blatant in his manipulation of the Venezuelan system, issuing new executive decrees and cracking down in ways that cemented his control of the country. His statements and actions usurped what remained of democratic norms and the will of the Venezuelan people, whose frustration continued to grow. In December 2015, when the opposition coalition Democratic Union Table won a supermajority's worth of seats in the National Assembly, it seemed a huge opportunity to change the course of Venezuelan politics and a newfound check on Maduro's power. One of the opposition majority's first acts was to "ostentatiously remove" images of Chávez and Bolívar from inside the National Assembly. The opposition's celebratory feelings were short-lived, however, as the head of state quickly nullified the victories of a handful of legislators via a ruling by the Supreme Tribunal of Justice, an institution whose members were largely appointed by Maduro and adjudicated squarely under his thumb. In July, Maduro even threatened to do away with the National Assembly altogether, claiming that they had not served any useful purpose and should "say goodbye to history, because their time is up."

In the final analysis, Chavismo was a complex phenomenon. As the self-proclaimed champion of Venezuela's poor and the reincarnation of Bolívar, Hugo Chávez was adored by millions of chavistas at home and leftist devotees abroad. The massive swelling of oil revenues enabled an explosion of social spending that made a difference for many of Venezuela's citizens while giving the country renewed regional clout.

Yet as the years went by, the personality cult of Chávez gathered pace and the incessant rhetoric of anti-yanqui solidarity failed to mask what was, in reality, a kleptocratic and chaotic administration (one international crime outfit reckoned that, Chávez's net worth topped US$1 billion at the time of his death). As the country plunged further into crisis under Maduro, it became more and more difficult to avoid the conclusion that, for all his desire to emulate Bolívar and refound Venezuela, Chávez had presided over its unraveling.

41

Yoani Sánchez

Cuba's Underground Revolutionary

You have to believe that you are free and try to act like it.... Little by little, acting as though you are free can be contagious.
—*Yoani Sánchez*

Yoani Sánchez is a spirited independent Cuban journalist who, starting in 2007, gained global renown for her blog, which offered a trenchant window into everyday life beyond the communist regime's official propaganda. A confessed tech geek, "accidental blogger," and bibliophile (in a country where reading certain books could get you tossed into prison), Sánchez's defiance occurred *inside* Cuba, making her distinctive among her fellow antiregime bloggers who mainly operated in the relative safety of foreign exile.

"AN OVERDOSE OF PRIVACY"

Yoani María Sánchez Cordero was born in Havana on September 4, 1975, the child of a housewife and state railroad employee. As she once explained to foreign journalists, she attended primary school during the relatively ebullient 1970s, when billions of dollars of annual Soviet subsidies helped usher in a spirit of social utopia, in contrast to the voracious Western capitalism. Like so many of her peers, Yoani was a "pioneer": the Cuban equivalent of Boy Scouts. She dutifully recited its pledge: "I am a pioneer for Communism, I will be like Che!" (See Chapter 24, "Ernesto Guevara: Becoming Che.")

By the time she was in high school and college, the Revolution's wheels had fallen off after Moscow's largesse dissipated after the Soviet Union imploded in the early 1990s. In fact, Fidel Castro, in 1991, declared a "special period" of draconian cutbacks and commensurate scarcity (see Chapter 23, "Fidel Castro: A Rebel with a Cause"). Reduced food rations, to pick an example, severed daily caloric rate by almost half! Grapefruit rinds substituted as "meat" and, at least according to local lore, melted condoms replaced cheese on "pizza." A new term—"alumbrón"—was the word for the rare times when the electricity was on.

Sánchez's "revolutionary" rural high school—which had been established to acclimatize urban students to agriculture—was named for the Socialist Republic of Romania, even though, by her enrollment in 1990, the Eastern Bloc communist regime was no longer in power. Yoani recalled students hoarding food under their beds, which at night brought rodents. The lack of soap and sanitary napkins further scarred her as she grew into her body. She concluded the searing school experience made her covet privacy:

> I left high school in the countryside feeling that nothing belonged to me, not even my body. Living in shelters creates the sensation that your whole life, your privacy, your personal possessions and even your nakedness has become public property. "Sharing" is the obligatory word and it comes to seem normal not to be able—ever—to be alone. After years of mobilizations, agricultural camps, and a sad school. . . . I needed an overdose of privacy.

Having witnessed her parents' vertiginous plunge into economic ruin—which was so often the case for her generation—the special period ensured that Yoani had, along with countless others, moved from a dyed-in-the-wool revolutionary to a cynic.

Yoani ended up at the University of Havana for her college studies where she pursued Hispanic philology (the study of language), which facilitated her love for contemporary Latin American novelists. Yet Sánchez's budding academic career ran afoul of cultural authorities who saw her thesis—boldly titled: "Words under Pressure: A Study of the Literature of Dictatorships in Latin American"—as counterrevolutionary. "The thesis wasn't overly critical, but the mere act of defining what a dictatorship is in an academic paper made people really nervous, because the definition was a portrait of Cuba," she recalled. The dispiriting setback meant that she had to start working gigs in tourism, where at least the pay could be in US dollars and she could brush up on her German. But her frustration with the limitations imposed on her by the Castro regime only intensified.

In 1995 she had a son, Teo, with the independent-minded Reinaldo Escobar, a noted Cuban reporter. Sometime in the 1980s, Escobar had written critically of the regime, which resulted in his losing his journalist job and pursuing a new vocation teaching Spanish to tourists—including contacts in Germany and Switzerland. This is also when the ever-curious Sánchez started fiddling with computers, even building one out of spare parts.

NEVER A SLAVE

Fed up and desperate, in 2002 Sánchez, illegal as it was then and thanks to her European friends, departed for Switzerland, assuming she'd never set foot back on the island. Reinaldo and Teo soon joined her. This was an epoch when tens of thousands of Cubans were annually leaving their homeland, the overwhelming majority never to return. But despite the pleas of her relatives and friends to stay in Switzerland, within a couple of years, Sánchez's heart and head were telling her to go back to Cuba. She did, however, promise herself one thing regarding her post-return existence on the communist island: she would "live as a free person, and accept the consequences."

Fatefully, it was during her stint in Switzerland that Sánchez cultivated her newly discovered passion for computers and the nascent internet. And thus her budding political activism, nonconformity, witty pen, and tech-savviness were beginning to come together. The irony was that the impact and reach of her just-beginning online activism were minimal given that such a low percentage of Cubans were regular internet users, not to mention the fact that regime operatives monitored and harassed independent outlets. Despite this daunting reality, by 2007 Sánchez had founded her blog, *Generación Y*. (The name is linked to her "lost generation" who grew up with the romance of communism and solidarity but were then confronted with special period deprivations of even the most basic necessities.)

Unlike most of the practicing Cuban bloggers who operated anonymously from abroad, Sánchez displayed her photograph and biography on her website. After the Cuban operatives blocked her more conventional postings, the intrepid dissident's approach often involved emailing her blog entries to acquaintances outside the country who then translated them (into seventeen languages!) and posted them independently. To carry out this ploy, she often dressed up as a tourist and spoke in German so that she could slip into an internet café in one of the capital's high-end hotels, which otherwise proscribed ordinary Cubans. Here is a *Wall Street Journal* profile, "Dressed in gray surf shorts, T-shirt and lime-green espadrilles, she strode toward a guard at the hotel's threshold and flashed a wide smile. The guard, a towering man with a shaved head, stepped aside. . . . Once inside the cafe, she attached a flash memory drive to the hotel computer and, in quick, intense movements, uploaded her material. Time matters: The $3 she paid for a half-hour is nearly a week's wage for many Cubans."

Sánchez's writing addressed seemingly mundane issues and frustrations such as bread lines—except there was no bread to be had (the ration was one bun per day). The digital medium allowed her to, in her own words, put aside her "internal policeman" and "push the limits, to find the line where the internal limits end and the real limits begin." Here is an extended blog excerpt:

> On an island where acquiring cement, cinderblocks or steel is comparable to obtaining a bit of lunar dust, destroying in order to build has become a common practice. There are specialists in removing bricks of clay intact from the walls in which they have been embedded for 80 years; experts in disengaging blue ceramic tiles from demolished mansions; and skillful "deconstructors" who extract metal beams from heaps of rubble.
>
> They use what they have recovered to create their own living space, this in a country where no one can legally buy a house. The main "quarries" where they obtain their material are houses that have collapsed or workplaces that the state's inactivity has left abandoned for many years. They fall upon these with an efficiency in their plunder that one would wish to see in the lethargic bricklayers working for a salary.
>
> Some of these skillful recyclers have died when a roof collapses or when a wall too riddled with holes at its base falls. But sometimes luck smiles on them, and they find a toilet without cracks or an electrical outlet that the owners of the demolished house could not in their haste take with them. A kilometer from the looting site, a small house of tin and zinc slowly begins to change. They have added the tile pavement from a building that collapsed at the corner of Neptuno and Aguila, a piece of the exterior grating from an abandoned mansion on Linea Street and even a stained-glass window plucked from a convent in the old part of Havana. Within this home that is the fruit of looting, a family equally ravaged by life of dreams of the next factory to be dismantled and carried away on their shoulders.

The post also had a link to a video by Afro-Cuban artist, Amaury Pacheco, reading one of his poems, "Economic Plan":

Economy! We have fulfilled the annual plan:
1,100 street hustlers; 2,000 young prostitutes; 8,000 opportunists.
Plus, 300 non-mentally disabled and the syndrome of mediocrity.
Economy! In times of a Havana that is unrecognizable,
By sweeping the house, you cleanse the economy.
Strong legs for the rocky path,
Legs that are only for the percentages of economic shame.
Shameful economy! Economy of shame! Economy of shame!

Sánchez described the feeling of freedom in such writing. "Once you experience the flavor of saying what you think, of publishing it and signing it with your name, well, there's no turning back," she said. "One of the first things we have to do, a great way to begin to change, is to be more honest about saying what you think."

The one hundred-thousand-peso question was why the authorities did not summarily end her subversion. Some reckoned that, at least back in her earliest blogging days, Raúl Castro thought that allowing Sánchez's online presence made him appear more moderate than he really was. Whatever the case, Sánchez was perplexed by the skepticism. "It's funny, but it seems that the only way some people will believe I am authentic is if I am thrown in jail."

WORLD ATTENTION

Within two years, *Generación Y* was fetching an eye-popping fourteen million page views each month; thousands of readers left comments (given the lack of internet access on the communist island, most of the readership was outside Cuba). Accolades began to pour in, including *Time* magazine and Spain's *El País* both calling her one of the one hundred most influential persons in the world for 2009, aged only thirty-two years old. Here is *Time*: "Under the nose of a regime that has never tolerated dissent, Sánchez has practiced what paper-bound journalists in her country cannot: freedom of speech." In late 2009, US President Barack Obama—whom Sánchez interviewed—wrote that *Generación Y* "provides the world a unique window into the realities of daily life in Cuba" and lauded Sánchez's efforts to "empower fellow Cubans to express themselves through the use of technology." That same year, *El País* announced that the "Cuban journalist" would join its team as their Havana correspondent.

Cuba's best-known dissident blogger Yoani Sánchez takes a picture with her iPad after she delivered a speech to students of the Iberoamericana University in Mexico City, March 13, 2013. *(Henry Romero/Alamy)*

Perhaps it was this international attention that prompted regime officials to send a message. As Sánchez described the story, on a day in early November 2009, she and several colleagues were driving to an antiviolence march when they were picked up by security officers. On her blog, she called the detention a "kidnapping." Later that same month, Reinaldo, also blogging at this time, was also roughed up by Cuban agents as he contested the ill-treatment his wife had been given. As Escobar relayed the story, hundreds of pro-regime citizens came up to him and started shouting "Viva la Revolución." Over a dozen of his supporters then fired back with their own slogans. The fight was on. While not present, Sánchez supported her spouse via Twitter in this brazen move of intimidation. "Until when will the language of force, of intolerance and disrespect for the opinion of others be the one that prevails in my country?"

A group of Mexican pro-Cuba activists protest outside the Justice Committee of Senate as Cuba's best-known dissident blogger Yoani Sánchez holds a news conference inside, in Mexico City, March 12, 2013. The poster reads, "Yoani, CIA agent." *(Edgard Garrido/Alamy)*

Within hours of the melee, an official Cuban mouthpiece ran the headline, "The Cuban people are tired of Yoani Sánchez," clarifying that the agents had pulled aside Escobar so "he would not suffer the ire of a people that has tired of so many provocations."

In 2013, after being denied at least five times over several years by Cuban authorities, Sánchez was granted an exit visa, allowing the dissident blogger to venture abroad. But the state badly miscalculated, as its official approval inadvertently legalized what turned into a whirlwind eighty-day, ten-country public relations odyssey for Sánchez. In New York City, she was hosted by the Columbia University Graduate School of Journalism; while in Washington, DC, she met with congressional members. (Although in Mexico City and Miami she was confronted with pro-regime protestors who chanted and held up signs calling her a CIA spy.) Asked at one point whether she would return to Cuba if Havana attempted to block her. "It won't happen," she said, "And if [her being blocked] did, all that would change would be instead of returning legally through an airport, I would come back on a raft."

14.5

By 2014, this passionate free speech advocate had launched a digital newspaper, *14ymedio* (*14-and-a-half*, named for its founding year as well as its headquarters on the fourteenth floor of a Soviet-era Havana building), featuring exclusive political and cultural news and a commitment to upholding "liberty, truth, and human rights." Escobar was the managing editor. At this point Sánchez's Twitter following was over six hundred thousand—a rate ten times that of the official newspaper, *Granma*, and five times that of Raúl Castro. Yet, within hours of going live, *14ymedio* was hacked; readers in Cuba were redirected to an official blog—*Yoani$landia*, with the dollar sign being a state reference that she was in the digital criticism business to make big bucks from the US government and Cuban exiles. The blog declared that it had been founded by Cubans "tired of Yoani Sánchez presenting herself as the Mother Teresa of Calcutta of dissident Cubans," and that Sánchez is "probably the richest Cuban on the island."

Undaunted as ever, Sánchez fired back. "From #Cuba there is nothing as attractive as what is prohibited." Despite this inauspicious beginning, *14ymedio* ran provocative articles like one that called Castro's putative economic reforms overly timid. Echoing her blog, the embattled news outlet followed through on its commitment to provide facts rather than propaganda, publishing, for example, the prices of vegetables in various markets around the capital and even a weather update—hot and muggy! Just under thirty prominent authors, journalists, and political figures from across the globe—including Peru's Mario Vargas Llosa—signed a joint letter championing *14ymedio* (see Chapter 37, "Mario Vargas Llosa: Cartography of Power"). At the time of writing, Sánchez was continuing to write and publish, undaunted by the state.

42

Michelle Bachelet

Healing Chile

Verónica Michelle Bachelet's life stands as a testament both to the traumas that can be inflicted by political systems, and the power of politics to heal. As a young leftist, Bachelet's social conscience drove her to study medicine and become involved in the youth wing of the Socialist Party, but her life was thrown into tumult by the coup of 1973. General Augusto Pinochet's repressive military regime imprisoned and tortured her and her father and mother, before she and her mother escaped into exile. After a spell in Australia and East Berlin, she returned to Chile where, after the end of the Pinochet dictatorship (see Chapter 27, "Augusto Pinochet: The Unlikely Model Dictator"), she became involved in politics, first as minister of health and then defense. In 2006, she became the first female president of Chile—in itself a remarkable landmark, and especially so given the fact she was an avowed agnostic divorcée and mother of three children to two fathers in one of South America's most conservative Roman Catholic countries.

As president, she set in train a series of progressive reforms and made significant achievements in civil rights—momentum which she continued when she returned to the presidency for a second term in 2014, albeit with more mixed results. The psychological wounds she suffered during the Pinochet dictatorship unquestionably influenced her political career as a socialist, and her suffering was also a significant reason why untold numbers of Chileans, and especially women, identified with her. Her administrations were marked by a dedication to remembering the past and creating a better future, with Bachelet routinely asserting that politics was like medicine, just on a larger scale.

A CHILD OF THE LEFT

Verónica Michelle Bachelet Jeria enjoyed a stable and happy childhood, albeit a peripatetic one. Born in Santiago in 1951 to Ángela Jeria, a housewife and later archeologist, and Alberto Bachelet, a Chilean Air Force officer who ascended to the rank of brigadier general. In 1962, Alberto was assigned a plum two-year position as military attaché in the Chilean Embassy in Washington, DC, which meant relocating his family to the capital city's tony suburb of Bethesda, Maryland, where the children attended local schools for two years.

The United States left a strong impression on Michelle, who encountered a society riven with racial tension but also crucially, the morally uplifting civil rights movement led by the iconic Martin Luther King Jr. "It was a lovely experience, because I found a society with a democratic history, a rich diversity of thought, and which offered opportunities to its citizens," she recalled when president. "The idea of the melting pot was the biggest novelty to me, and I would say that all of that allowed me to acquire a political and cultural foundation that has been quite positive to my political performance." She also experienced politically aware folk music, and after returning from Washington in her late teens, Bachelet formed a traveling folk music duo called "Las Clap Clap" with her cousin Alicia Galdames, covering Bob Dylan and Joan Baez. The 1960s was a heady time to be in Chile: according to Galdames, "The seeds of her ideals were planted in this period."

In 1970, Bachelet was considering studying economics or sociology, but a visit to see a friend at a bustling public hospital, Posta Central, opened her eyes to the essential work of medicine in her native country, and she duly enrolled in medical school, a path not unlike Argentine Ernesto Guevara a few decades prior (see Chapter 24, "Ernesto Guevara: Becoming Che"). While a college student, Bachelet also became involved in the youth wing of the Socialist Party, led at the time by a young physician Carlos Lorca (who would later be "disappeared" by the Pinochet regime). The student group might have had "Socialist" in its name, but its ideology and politics were decidedly Marxist; indeed, the line between democratic leftists and armed Marxist revolutionaries was very thin, if it existed at all. Michelle's alias was "Commander Claudia," although she was known for being more moderate than most of her fellow members. One comrade reflected, "It was a time of black and white, but she managed to get along with everybody, no matter what their political persuasion. She wasn't the one to look for fights; she was the one who was tolerant, always looking for consensus."

Bachelet's family soon found itself at the forefront of the dramatic changes sweeping Chile. Her parents were both devoted supporters of Salvador Allende, who stunned the country with his 1970 presidential win (see Chapter 26, "Salvador Allende: 'All Things to All Men'"). In 1972, President Allende called on General Bachelet, a hyper-efficient manager and planner, to head up the revolutionary government's Food Distribution Office, a position Alberto loyally held until September 11, 1973, when Allende was ousted in a brutal coup by his commander-in-chief Pinochet. Having refused to support the *golpistas* (coup plotters) and rebuffed an offer of exile, General Bachelet was imprisoned and tortured by the security forces. He eventually succumbed to a fatal heart attack on March 12, 1974, while still in captivity.

The *pinochetista* coup and Alberto's torture and subsequent murder were a massive shock for Michelle and her family; on top of his tragic death, the family was now facing financial ruin. Decades hence, Michelle later told a foreign reporter how her family's "bank accounts had been blocked and they didn't let us take out money." She also described how pro-Pinochet neighbors acted toward her in this polarized, terrorized country. "When I walked down the street, people who had been very close to us crossed to the other side so as not to have to see us."

Despite this personal and national trauma, a defiant Michelle continued at medical school and also remained involved in leftist politics, which were now entirely clandestine. On January 10, 1975, two agents from DINA (the Pinochet-era secret police) arrived at the apartment where Michelle lived with Ángela and whisked the blindfolded pair to the Villa Grimaldi, the infamous concentration camp for political detainees, where they were both tortured for over a month. "They put a hood over my head, threatened me and hit me. But I was spared the grill [electrical shocks]," she later said. "There were others, even in my own cell who had it much worse than I did."

In a 2002 interview, she reflected on the legacy of this unspeakable period: "I haven't forgotten. It left pain. But I have tried to channel that pain into a constructive realm. I insist on the idea that what we experienced here in Chile was so painful, so terrible, that I wouldn't wish for anyone to live through our situation again."

EXILE AND RETURN

It is likely that a relative was able to secure the pair's release, after which they departed for exile in Australia, where Michelle's older brother was living. After just a few months, Michelle and her mother went to the communist German Democratic Republic (East Germany), which offered them political asylum along with thousands of other leftist exiles from Latin America. After acquiring sufficient command of the German language, Michelle studied pediatrics at the Humboldt University in East Berlin, where she once again became involved in political organizing. East Germany was also where she wed Jorge Dávalos, another Chilean political exile, and had her first of three children, Sebastián, born in 1978. Years later, Bachelet would state that her time in East Germany gave her a new sense of the value of persistence and of living in a foreign culture. At the time, she probably was not aware of the irony that having fled Pinochet's dictatorship, she was living in one of the most repressive societies in the Communist Bloc.

With her mother's residence proscription lifted, in 1979 Michelle's family returned to Santiago, and three years later she picked up her medical degree from the prestigious University of Chile. Her father's association with the Allende government limited her employment opportunities—regime authorities cited "political grounds" when they rejected her application to work as a public-sector doctor—but Bachelet did eventually find work at the clinical wing of a Swedish-funded nongovernmental organization where she treated traumatized youth of parents detained or disappeared by the regime. In 1984, Jorge and Michelle had another baby, Francisca. Two years later, the couple separated, this being a time when Chilean laws made divorce especially arduous. (Without the divorce, Bachelet could not marry the doctor with whom she had her third child in 1990.) Sometime between 1985 and 1987, Bachelet had a relationship with the engineer Alex Vojkovic Trier, who happened to be a senior member of the Manuel Rodríguez Patriotic Front, the armed guerrilla band that attempted to assassinate Pinochet in 1986. The issue came up occasionally during her first presidential run but fizzled out after she denied any support for Vojkovic's ideology or actions.

After the Pinochet dictatorship ended, Bachelet began a successful career as an aide in the Health Ministry and assumed various leadership positions within the Socialist Party. At some point during this period, Bachelet would regularly share an elevator ride with another resident of her apartment building whom she recognized as one of her torturers. Then one day she said to him, "I know who you are; I have not forgotten." Startled, the man did not respond. But each time that he subsequently came into contact with her, he averted his gaze. During this time, she also manifested an interest—in no small part derived from her father's vocation—in military affairs, which included a prestigious fellowship at the Inter-American Defense College in Washington, DC "Most of the people with my background feel a profound rejection towards anything that has to do with the military," she later told the press, "but I felt like I was recovering part of my being."

For the 2000 presidential election, Ricardo Lagos of the Socialist Party was the candidate for the so-called Coalition, a broad assembly of center and leftist parties founded in 1988 that had won every presidential election since the return to democracy. Lagos became the first socialist president since Allende. He tapped Bachelet—then a political unknown—to be minister of health, managing a sprawling bureaucracy filled with seventy thousand employees. Her deft handling of the agency, including her dramatic reduction of hospital wait times, aided her political ascent, and in 2002, she became the first woman in Latin American history to be appointed minister of defense. Under her careful guidance, Chile changed its laws about obligatory military service and provided increased equity for women within the military and police ranks. This former victim of state security violence was, however, unwilling to publicly utilize the term "reconciliation," preferring the more circumspect use of the phrase "re-encounter." A historic day occurred in 2003 when Chilean Army Commander-in-Chief Juan Emilio Cheyre declared that "never again" would the military topple democracy.

LA SEÑORA PRESIDENTA

In late 2005, Bachelet stepped down from Ministry of Defense position to focus on her political prospects, which culminated in her becoming the Coalition's presidential candidate the following year. Relying on her natural empathy with all Chileans, her campaign appealed to broad-based themes of "change with continuity" and "social inclusion," yet there was also the looming issue of her atheism and her now being a divorced mother of multiple children in a majority Catholic, male-dominated country. December 2005 first-round balloting did not give her an outright majority, which meant she would face conservative billionaire businessman Sebastián Piñera in the runoff, yet she emerged with a rock-solid victory, garnering 53 percent of the vote. "Violence ravaged my life," she told her exultant supporters on election night. "I was a victim of hatred, and I have dedicated my life to reversing that hatred."

Her first domestic crisis occurred right out of the gate. One month into her presidency, the country witnessed an unprecedented eruption of student-led protests and strikes—often called the Penguins' Revolution due to the high school students wearing black and white school uniforms. Students protested Chile's myriad deficiencies and inequalities in public education, not least of which was the Pinochet-era privatization of key components of the country's education system. Upward of eight hundred thousand students took part—an astonishing number in a country, at the time, of seventeen million—in the most visible and coordinated protest since the end of the Pinochet regime. On June 1, 2006, President Bachelet addressed the nation through radio and television to announce a litany of reforms—both big and small, from a reshuffling of the Ministry of Education to free transport tickets for poor students—that served to quell the student-generated social movement. Less than one year later, however, she was on the defense again. This time the country was stymied by commuter rage over the botched inauguration of a long-awaited new Santiago transit system, designed to alleviate pressure on the city's wretched bus network. "The inhabitants of Santiago, especially the poorest, deserve an apology from all of us," Bachelet declared.

Despite the rocky opening months, Bachelet was able to deliver much of what her campaign promised. Buoyed by a historically high price for copper—Chile's largest export—she presided over economic expansion; launched literacy and health campaigns; and bolstered pension support. In 2010, women gained the freedom to choose their preferred form of contraception, including the morning-after pill. Bachelet also inaugurated the Museum of Memory and Human Rights in Santiago, set up to document and preserve the experience of the military regime. Overall, her administration was characterized by moderation and compassion: "We believe strongly in a democracy that has a strong social tint, with social justice and solidarity. The state is important, but I also aspire to a warmer, more human society in which people help each other and struggle against all forms of inequality." Constitutionally prevented from seeking a consecutive term, Bachelet's presidency ended in March 2010, when she left office with a sky-high public approval rating of 84 percent.

A DIFFICULT SECOND TERM

Between 2010 and 2013, Bachelet was the head of UN Women, the newly created United Nations entity dedicated to female equity. But itching to don the presidential sash again, stood once again as the Coalition's candidate in the 2013 election, where she won the first ballot but again did not achieve an outright majority. This time, her run-off opponent was Evelyn Matthei, a

Former Chilean president Michelle Bachelet (*center*) and her mother Ángela Jeria (*second on the left*) hold up pictures of victims of human rights abuse during a ceremony commemorating forty years of the military coup at the "Parque Por La Paz" (Park for Peace), on the grounds of the former Villa Grimaldi torture center, in Santiago, September 10, 2013. *(Ivan Alvarado/Alamy)*

childhood friend and now candidate for the conservative coalition, Alliance. In a strange coincidence, Matthei and Bachelet were both daughters of military generals, yet their experience after the 1973 coup could not have been more different: General Bachelet's loyalty to Allende had led to his death, while Matthei's father had flourished under the Pinochet regime. Bachelet won the December 2013 run-off with a huge 62 percent of the vote, making her the country's first two-time head of state since the return to democracy.

Returning to La Moneda, the seat of the presidency, in March 2014, Bachelet had little reason to assume that her second term would be any less successful or significant than her first. Her campaign platform embraced economic growth and societal and state reforms, and she advocated thorny issues such as women's and gay and transgender rights, and abortion liberalization. Delivering on these promises would prove difficult, but Bachelet demonstrated her political tenacity by ending tuition fees and introducing legislation on legalizing same-sex adoption and gay marriage, which were legalized in 2022. Arguably her greatest achievement was in the case of abortion rights, which had long been a hot-button social issue in a country where some sixty thousand to two hundred thousand illegal abortions were carried out each year because of Chile's categorical ban on abortion (unique in South America). Bachelet faced powerful opponents in the shape of the Catholic Church and a right-wing coalition, Let's Go Chile, but won a stunning victory in August 2017 when the country's Constitutional Court upheld a new law partially lifting the abortion ban in cases of risk to the mother's life, fetus demonstrating a birth defect, or the pregnancy resulted from rape. An overwhelming 70 percent of Chileans supported the liberalization. Ebullient, the physician and former chief of UN Women, stated, "Today, women have won, democracy has won, all of Chile has won." Bachelet also used her feminist bona fides to help pass legislation that required political parties to select women in at least 40 percent of primary election candidates and public enterprise board seats—a far higher rate of female participation than existed theretofore.

Bachelet's second term also continued her focus on income inequality. While the economic envy of many South American neighbors (per capita income had soared from US$4,400 in 1990 to around US$22,000 in 2013), Chile exhibited some of the worst income inequality anywhere: the richest 5 percent of households held over half of the nation's wealth. Despite these palpable gains, Bachelet's once-gleaming image was tarnished by a stubborn economy, mixed results on employment, education, and tax reform, and, in an especially personal blow given her administration's rectitude, a protracted influence-selling scandal in which her son, Sebastián Dávalos, was the principal player. While she repeatedly denied any involvement, Bachelet never publicly condemned Sebastián. With plummeting public support for her government, Bachelet asked her entire cabinet to submit their resignations in May 2015; three of the ministers did not return to the reconstructed cabinet. But she maintained her progressive policies to the very end: weeks before leaving the presidency, this time for good, Bachelet apologized on behalf of the Chilean state for the exclusions and injustices inflicted upon the Mapuche people; she also unveiled new government efforts to ensure indigenous rights in Chile.

UN COMMISSIONER FOR HUMAN RIGHTS

In September 2018, Bachelet assumed the prestigious, vital position of UN High Commissioner for Human Rights. During her four-year term, she was vocal about many issues, including the erosion of abortion rights and the separation of migrant children from their families in the United States; the United Kingdom's amendments to its human rights law; and the killings of Palestinians by the Israeli security forces. However, she drew fierce criticism from other human rights organizations for her failure to condemn human rights abuses in China during and after her trip to the country in May 2022, leading to claims that she had walked into a propaganda trap for Beijing. A UN report detailing the persecution of Uyghur Muslims in Xinjiang was fiercely resisted by China, leading to publication being delayed until the very last minutes of her term, generating yet more criticism. Bachelet chose to not seek a second term, but stand down in August 2022 and return to her family in Chile.

Michelle Bachelet came of age as a revolutionary in a time of revolutionary fervent. She and her family suffered beyond comprehension in fidelity to these ideas, but once in power, she exhibited anything but animus. Instead, her presidential terms were defined by their commitment to harmony and greater inclusion, not division.

43

Evo Morales

Reclaiming Bolivia

This is coca leaf, this is not cocaine, this is part and parcel of a culture.
—*Evo Morales*

In December 2005, 1.5 million Bolivian voters proudly backed Evo Morales, a decidedly unconventional politician and indigenous Aymara Indian who had cut his political teeth in the late 1970s and 1980s as a coca growers' union boss in the vast eastern lowlands. He was the first member of the country's indigenous majority to ascend to the presidential palace and did so with an emphatic 54 percent of the vote—almost twice as much as his closest rival. Once in power, he pursued a revolutionary agenda that would set Bolivia on a completely new path. A new constitution was adopted that transformed Bolivia into a secular state, while lucrative natural resources were nationalized. Foreign policy was orientated away from the United States and toward other leftist regional governments, a move that would have particularly significant ramifications over the hot-button topic of coca, the main ingredient of cocaine.

Committed to improving indigenous communities and alleviating poverty, Morales's initial years were a domestic success, bringing much-needed stability to the country, but his tenure as president ended in ignominy. Allegations of fraud over his winning an already-controversial fourth term incited mass protests that the military refused to suppress, forcing Morales into temporary exile. Yet the party he founded once again secured power in the 2020 elections, hinting that Morales's political legacy may outlast his idiosyncratic career.

LLAMA HERDER TO PARTY LEADER

Born in a mining district in the *altiplano* (high Andean plain) western region of Oruro in 1959, Evo Morales came from a family of llama herders, an activity in which he also participated. After high school and military service, he moved with his family to the Chapare region, where they hoped to earn a better living growing traditional crops like cassava. But there was also another crop that offered far better returns: coca, which traditionally in Bolivia is chewed or brewed as a tea to help with altitude sickness, increase strength, and stave off feelings of hunger. It is also the core ingredient of cocaine.

During the early 1980s, the roaring global demand for cocaine sparked a coca boom in Bolivia, particularly in the scrappy and moist Chapare. Almost overnight, coca came to represent up to 4 percent of Bolivia's national income. Desperately poor, mostly indigenous Bolivians living in the highlands migrated to Chapare to take part in the "coca gold rush." An estimated 7 to 13 percent of Bolivia's workforce became involved in coca cultivation as annual production soared from five thousand to about forty thousand hectares per year, with growers of coca—the "cocaleros"—organizing into labor federations based on the model they had used for generations as miners in the Andes. While some of this production was used for legal, traditional purposes, the rest fed directly into the cocaine industry, at that time dominated by Pablo Escobar and his Medellín Cartel in Colombia, who transformed the processing and trafficking of cocaine to North America into a multibillion-dollar machine (see Chapter 38, "Pablo Escobar: The First Drug Lord").

Horrified by the scourge of crack cocaine ravaging its inner cities, the United States ratcheted up its "supply side" drug war in the Andes in the mid-1980s with programs like the semi-clandestine *Operation Blast Furnace* in July–October 1986, combining alternative-crop development programs, voluntary and forced coca-eradication drives, and the interdiction of processed cocaine. But crop eradication programs also affected the farmers growing the plant for legal purposes. Accordingly, in 1988 the Bolivian government ratified Law 1008, the Coca and Controlled Substance Law, which permitted coca intended for traditional use to be grown on twelve thousand hectares of the Yungas region, where the crop had a centuries-long cultural history. Coca intended for illicit derivatives was banned, and Law 1008 articulated brutal punishments for the consumption and possession of controlled substances—that is, cocaine. By making one rule for the Yungas region and another for

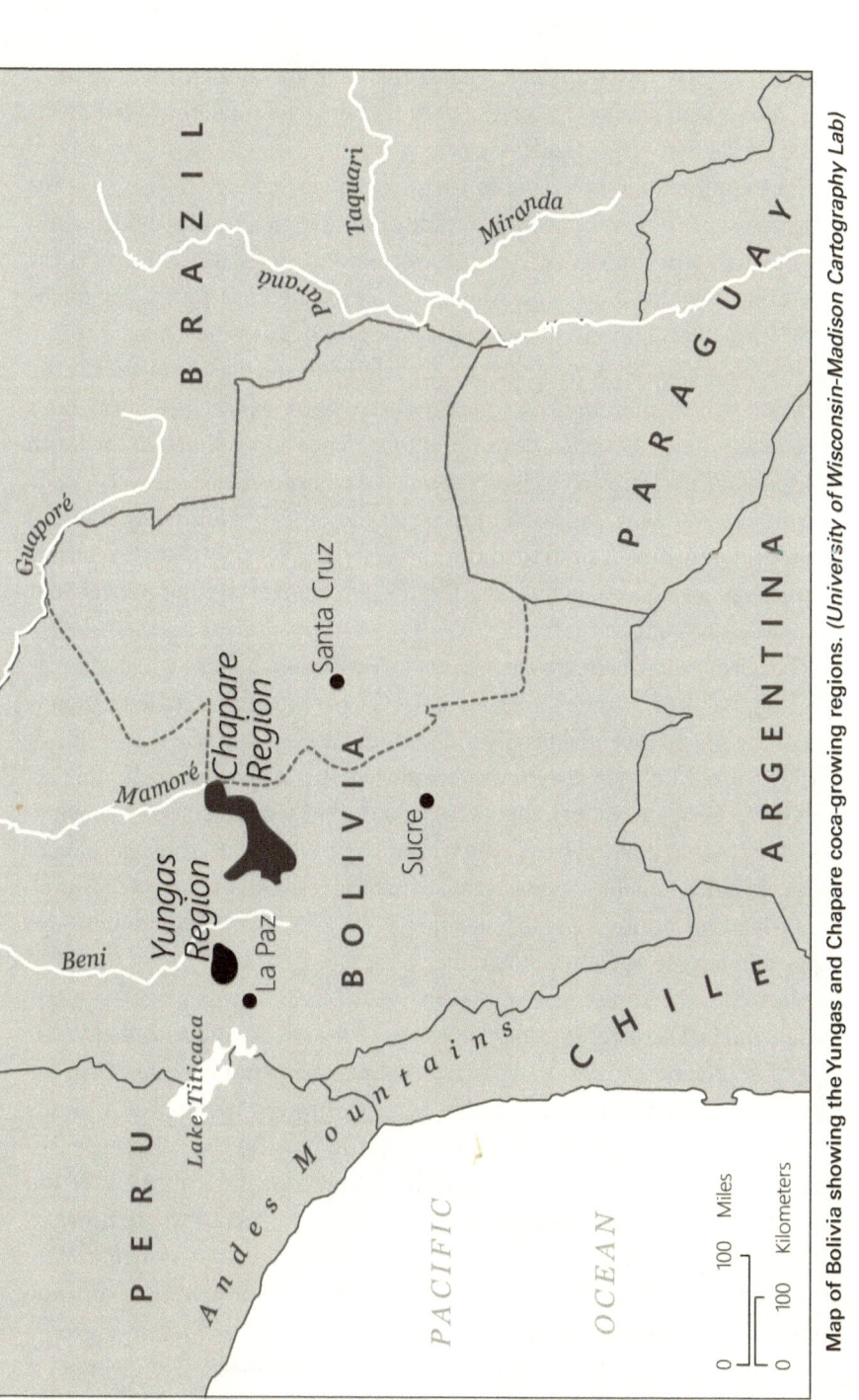

Map of Bolivia showing the Yungas and Chapare coca-growing regions. (University of Wisconsin-Madison Cartography Lab)

Chapare, the law discriminated against the Chapare cocaleros and sparked deep resentment among the wave of coca farmers who suddenly found themselves engaged in illegal trade.

Coca continued to be grown in Chapare, however, much to the ire of the Americans. In 1997, after nearly a decade of Washington's incessant demands, the Bolivian government agreed to accelerate its efforts in Chapare via the Operation Dignity Plan, which aimed to eradicate coca in the region by 2002. If successful, the zero-coca strategy would deprive the Chapare region of US$700 million in annual income. Cocaleros in the region staged a series of major strikes, fighting to save the industry upon which their livelihoods depended. The strikes often devolved into violence and resulted in the death of legions of cocaleros as well as several police officers. After several years of conflict, President Carlos Mesa resolved the crisis by informally allowing 3,200 hectares of coca production in the Chapare. Sensing that all available alternatives would be much worse, the US government did not publicly oppose the compromise.

The tensions in Chapare over coca made Morales—who through his deft organizing skills had become the leader of the Chapare coca growers' federation—one of the most influential people in the country. He was a vehement critic of the US-backed Bolivian government's antidrug operations and eradication efforts in the Chapare region in the 1990s, and in 1998 founded the Movement to Socialism (MAS) political party, which campaigned for the decriminalization of coca cultivation and the nationalization of natural resources. Crucially, however, he retained his position as the federation boss, which would bring him huge support in his attempt to break into the political mainstream.

Elected to the House of Deputies in 1997, Morales swiftly made a name for himself in a series of disputes over natural resources. The so-called Water War of 2000 emerged from a controversial plan to privatize water distribution in Cochabamba province, which Morales strongly opposed as a savage imposition by a foreign multinational consortium. After the federal government's "state of siege" failed to quell the tumult, the crisis eased after the foreign entity pulled the plug on the project, but the fallout would prove to be long-lasting, with many scholars convinced that the "anti-systemic" fury generated during and following the so-called water war contributed to the eventual overturning of Bolivia's entire political system. Morales's profile rose immeasurably, with his vocal opposition to privatization allowing him to connect with a broad political base beyond the coca federations. Ávila

Montaño, a Bolivian researcher, put it this way, "You cannot understand the rise to power of Morales without looking at the Water War. It was an event that changed Bolivian society."

Morales's increasing prominence in Bolivarian politics started attracting attention from further afield: in the run-up to the 2002 presidential election, Washington threatened to cut off aid to Bolivia if the pro-coca and antidrug-war candidate was elected. In the end, Morales lost, but only by a sliver, and his 21 percent share of the vote marked a dramatic change in fortunes for indigenous politics. That same year, Morales was removed from the national congress following rumors that he had been involved in the killings of three security forces officers during a cocalero protest.

Morales's star rose further in 2003 during the fierce debate over nationalizing natural gas deposits (the region's second largest, behind Venezuela), with Morales loudly calling for nationalization. By 2003 the "gas war" had led to the outbreak of violent strikes and protesters fighting street-to-street with security forces in La Paz, the nation's capital. The rioting was so bad that neoliberal President Gonzalo Sánchez de Lozada had to flee the presidential palace hidden in an ambulance to avoid being apprehended and likely killed by violent mobs, many directly or indirectly supported by Morales. Indeed, this period saw Morales both working within and against the political system: one day he was a candidate stumping La Paz for votes, the next he might be urging antineoliberal protestors to torch the presidential palace.

Yet while Morales may have been responsible for inciting unrest, it was certainly true that even without him the country was on the verge of chaos. Of Bolivia's five presidents between the 2000 water war and 2005, two were pushed out in violent popular revolts. By the time the December 2005 election rolled around, it was clear that people wanted change. Riding the so-called regional "pink tide"—the wave of popular support in much of Latin America for left-wing parties that in 2003 brought to power Luiz Inácio Lula da Silva in Brazil (see Chapter 45, "Luiz Inácio Lula da Silva: Brazil's First Working-Class President"), Néstor Kirchner in Argentina, among others—Morales was elected president by an emphatic margin.

THE POST-NEOLIBERAL PRESIDENT

Once in power Morales was quick to make changes, realigning Bolivia's foreign policy with other left-wing governments in Latin America and the Caribbean, including Argentina, Brazil, Cuba, and Venezuela, and away from the

United States. It was a broadly popular move, with many Bolivians who detested Morales for all sorts of alleged derelictions lauding the way Evo refused to defer to foreign counterparts, as had forever been the Bolivian custom. Domestically, Morales implemented an economic program that he promoted as "post-neoliberal," seeking to displace market mechanisms with state planning in some areas. On May 1, 2006 (Workers' Day, of course), he signed a decree nationalizing the country's natural gas reserves—"the state recovers ownership, possession and total and absolute control of these resources." He also boosted state involvement in telecommunications and mining.

Aided by the increase in global gas prices, over the next several years fiscal revenues soared, fueling Morales's aggressive social(ist) agenda. Morales also took advantage of his popularity to implement sweeping land reform and impose a ceiling on public sector salaries (including his own) of just under $3,000 a year. In early 2009, Bolivian voters overwhelmingly (61 percent) approved a new Morales-engineered constitution that, according to its proponents, "refounded" Bolivia as a "secular" (no longer Catholic) state, now officially called the Plurinational State of Bolivia. Among other bold

President Evo Morales Ayma greeting his supporters from the balcony of the government palace during his reelection ceremony, Vice President Álvaro García Linera on his left and the Nobel Peace Prize winner Rigoberta Menchú on his right, La Paz, Bolivia, January 22, 2010. *(Florian Kopp/Alamy)*

cultural, juridical, and linguistic reforms geared toward belated justice for the indigenous majority, the new founding charter (the nation's seventeenth) stated that natural resources were the exclusive holding of the citizens but operated by the state. Even more radical was Morales's unapologetic advocacy for indigenous Bolivians, which gave them something they never experienced before: dignity.

Morales's initial years were unquestionably "revolutionary," yet he did also show considerable pragmatism. Notwithstanding Morales's social programs and his anti-US rhetoric, his government never directly targeted the wealthy, and analysts have noted that some of Morales's economic policies were more friendly to markets and less orthodox socialist than his rhetoric would suggest. The landmark decree nationalizing Bolivia's gas resources made for a great soundbite, but in reality Morales knew that gas nationalization could not mean expropriation or confiscation: foreign companies were still the lynchpins of the sector, but now they would be made to pay more (a move which massively swelled Bolivia's revenues). The most distinctive parts of his and MAS's platform were those advancing the position of indigenous citizens in Bolivian society—for example, the primary beneficiary of the land reform was the indigenous population. Bolivia remained surprisingly capitalistic, as reflected by the private-sector construction boom in La Paz.

"COCA SÍ, COCAÍNA NO"

During his 2005 campaign, Morales promised that as president he would end the controversial practice of forced coca eradication. Calling his policy "coca sí, cocaína no," Morales contended that there was no reason that Bolivia could not cultivate copious volumes of coca for legal products and still successfully combat illegal cocaine trafficking. Indeed, Morales made legal coca the center of a new industry, with Bolivia manufacturing coca hemorrhoid cream, coca flour, and even coca wine, and raised the possibility of sending five hundred thousand tons of coca leaf to China for medicinal uses. Most experts, however, were dubious about the prospects for what the coca strategy that Evo dubbed *industrialización*: as one US official succinctly put it, "Coca flour costs three times as much as normal flour and it tastes like shit." Furthermore, many observers were convinced that, even if it were practical, developing new licit coca markets in the region would do little to reduce the amount of the crop supplied to cocaine producers. And despite Morales's protestations, the illegal trade was thriving: in 2008 and 2009, Bolivian coca was being used to produce between 160 and 200 metric tons of cocaine annually—a steep increase from prior years.

But there was little the United States could do. In 2008, Morales expelled the US ambassador and the US Drug Enforcement Administration, which had been working, with admittedly checkered results, for over twenty years in the country, and the entire US Agency for International Development mission five years later. Where once the United States could wield a punitive "stick"—human rights decertification or a withdrawal of development assistance, for example—Morales's increased hydrocarbon revenues and widespread popular support gave him the confidence and authority to resist Washington's influence.

But while Morales's belief that cocaine production could be kept in check attracted well-justified criticism, his arguments over the traditional role coca played in Bolivian society also merited serious consideration. In 2013, Bolivia gained a special exemption to the 1961 UN Single Convention on Narcotic Drugs, whereby Bolivia's indigenous people would be permitted to chew coca leaves, despite claims by the United States (which had voted against the exemption) that the exemption would only increase coca (and cocaine) production. It was a significant and hard-won victory for Morales, who had played

A billboard showing (left to right) Hugo Chávez, Fidel Castro, and Evo Morales in La Paz, Bolivia, on March 8, 2007. (Mark Pearson/Alamy)

hardball by withdrawing Bolivia from the Convention the year before, and demonstrated that he was not afraid to stand up to the might of the United States and United Nations. After the Barack Obama administration issued a report in 2016 stating that Bolivia had "failed demonstrably" to fight the drug war, Morales confidently declared that "the world knows that our counternarcotics model is better without the Americans."

MORALES'S WANING THIRD-TERM POPULARITY

Morales easily gained reelection for a second term in 2009 and third term (originally prohibited by the constitution) in 2014. His success was understandable, given that his social initiatives unquestionably made lives better for millions of Bolivians: poverty dropped by around 25 percent and extreme poverty by over 40 percent during his presidency.

By 2016, however, even Bolivia's 62 percent indigenous majority had grown wary of Morales's increasingly paranoid and autocratic governing style. The Bolivian intelligence and security apparatus, with the collaboration of Venezuelan and Cuban operatives, maintained close surveillance of political activity, while corruption was rampant. Public bids for government contracts virtually disappeared, falling from 76 percent in 2010 to 8 percent in 2013 to 1 percent in 2014, with the government transferring public funds to handpicked private companies—and these funds were no small change. Bolivian political analyst Diego Ayo estimated in 2016 that the government had spent upward of US$27 billion in public works since Morales took office, most for big-ticket, high-visibility "presidential projects" that created "an illusion of prosperity" with relatively minor long-term benefits.

Personal scandal also tainted Morales's image. In February 2016, reports emerged that he had fathered a child with Gabriela Zapata, a former girlfriend whom he started seeing in 2005 when she was eighteen. Morales initially denied fathering the child and claimed he had not seen Zapata in five years, attributing the rumors to a US government conspiracy, but social media images quickly surfaced showing Morales and Zapata at a fiesta the previous year. Vice President García Linera threatened to jail the journalists responsible, whom he called liars. Morales then claimed the child—Ernesto Fidel—had died soon after birth, which Zapata said was untrue. Even more infuriating to the Bolivian public was the fact that Zapata had worked as an "executive" for a Chinese firm and had facilitated it being awarded public contracts totaling over US$500 million. Morales denied that his administration had engaged in any untoward conduct and had Zapata arrested on charges of corruption, money laundering, and influence-peddling. From jail, Zapata told the press that Morales had gone from saint to sinner in the time they were together.

Much of the Zapata story broke right before a referendum in late February 2016 on whether Morales could stand for an unprecedented fourth term, from 2020–2025. During the run-up to the vote, Morales behaved like a populist demagogue, profusely praising himself and warning that the opposition would sell the country's resources to the highest bidder and govern like an oligarchy. Despite the scare tactics he still lost, albeit by the narrowest of margins (51 percent to 49 percent). Morales initially refused to endorse the outcome but eventually backed down while implying that he would try again to extend his time in office. And so it came to pass: a year later, Bolivia's Constitutional Court annulled the result of the election based on the defamatory campaign over Morales's supposed paternity of Ernesto Fidel and cleared the way for him to run for an unprecedented fourth term, a decision validated by the Supreme Electoral Council in 2018. But Morales's long winning streak would soon come to an end.

CIVIC COUP?

On election day, October 20, 2019, Morales once again was on the ballot for president, pitted against opposition candidate Carlos Mesa, a centrist former president. Morales's goal was to avoid a runoff that he would almost certainly have lost, meaning he needed to beat Mesa in the first round by over 10 percent. But just as media reports began indicating that a second round was on the cards, the reporting ceased for an entire day, only to resume with the news that Evo had won by a margin just over the vital 10 percent threshold. Opposition figures cried foul, including many who once supported Morales but now saw nothing more than a power grab. An October 30 Organization of American States report affirmed that "intentional manipulation and serious irregularities" made it "impossible to validate" the results (though its audit methodology has itself been called into question).

With anti-Morales protests and violence continuing for close to three weeks after the dubious vote, the military called on Morales to resign, which he duly did on November 10 before fleeing to exile in Mexico the next day, claiming that he was the victim of a "civic coup." Other prominent voices, like the British Labour Party leader Jeremy Corbyn, also claimed a nefarious coup and one more instance of the reactionary right getting its way in Latin

America. President Donald Trump, by contrast, countered that the protests and Morales's subsequent resignation were a win for democracy: "The United States applauds the Bolivian people for demanding freedom and the Bolivian military for abiding by its oath to protect not just a single person, but Bolivia's constitution." After MAS government ministers in the line of succession resigned in protest at the involvement of the armed forces, a little-known conservative senator from the opposition, Jeanine Áñez, assumed the presidency on an interim basis until new elections could be organized. Her new interior minister swiftly charged the absent Morales with terrorism and sedition.

Bruised as it was by Morales's expulsion from the political scene, MAS nevertheless roused itself sufficiently to win an astonishing victory at the rerun of the general election in October 2020, with its candidate Luis Arce, a former finance minister under Morales, winning 55 percent of the vote. In an act of revenge, Acre would later jail Áñez on charges of staging a coup (as well as sedition, terrorism, genocide, and conspiracy), and cleared Morales of all criminal charges, paving the way for the former president to return to Bolivia in November 2020, although Arce made it clear the former president would not be involved in the new administration.

Morales's fourteen years of power have left an indelible legacy in Bolivia, transforming the country not only through this elevation of indigenous identity and liberal reforms but also through hard negotiating with the world's largest hydrocarbon companies and the United Nations. As with many of the figures profiled in this book, the deployment of his singular political identity gradually morphed into autocracy and a reluctance to cede power, while his protection of the coca industry from US interference granted cocaine traffickers much more freedom to do business. Yet tainted as his legacy is, his ascent and ambition remain matchless: an indigenous rural boy who faced down a mountain of odds to become president of his country, a revolutionary who won power through the ballot box. Mobilizing a unique blend of populism and pragmatism, he crafted a more inclusive and confident vision of Bolivia and its place in the world.

44

José "Pepe" Mujica

From Communism to Chrysanthemums

I would say that social democracy was invented in Uruguay.
—*José Mujica*

José Alberto Mujica Cordano (known as "Pepe" Mujica) was in many ways the most unlikely of presidents—and the most humble. A former leftist guerrilla leader who was jailed by the police for fourteen years (ten in solitary confinement), Mujica entered mainstream politics after his release and was elected president in 2009. After taking office in 2010, he promptly donated 90 percent of his salary to a housing charity, leaving him only around $1,250/month. He continued to live with his wife (also an ex-guerrilla, Lucía Topolansky) in a tiny house they had occupied for years, not in the opulent presidential palace that required almost fifty staff to maintain. In their modest abode, the presidential couple did not have servants and used their tiny farming plot to grow chrysanthemums to sell in the nearby market, while the security "entourage" consisted of two unarmed and nonuniformed police officers. Upon taking office, Mujica reported a net worth of $1,800—approximately the value of his circa 1987 Volkswagen Beetle. Mujica also pursued a political agenda that turned Uruguay into one of the most liberal countries in Latin America. Under Mujica's watch, Uruguay became the first country in the world to legalize the cultivation, sale, and use of recreational marijuana. It also became the first in South America to legalize on-demand abortion and was a pioneer in same-sex marriage and renewable energy.

Through his spartan lifestyle and progressive politics, Mujica became an immensely powerful image of political humility and helped burnish his nation's reputation around the world. US President Barack Obama extolled his Uruguayan counterpart's "extraordinary credibility when it comes to issues of democracy and human rights," putting the seal on a remarkable transformation for this erstwhile guerrilla.

COLD WAR SKELETONS

Born in Montevideo on May 20, 1935, into a small-scale farming family, Pepe grew up in a family of modest means. His father, Demetrio Mujica, came from Spanish Basque stock, while his mother, Lucía Cordona, was born to Italian immigrants. Before Pepe was five, his father had died, apparently bankrupt. The death was a crushing blow for the entire family, especially his youngest sister, Maria Eudosia, who suffered from schizophrenia. The family's precarious financial situation meant that Pepe's formal education was limited, but he was a solid student. Biographers don't fail to add that even as a boy, Pepe was fascinated by politics in large part because politics and history were the topics of conversation at seemingly every meal. His maternal uncle, Ángel Cordano, a notorious nationalist, regaled the youth with tales about epic political battles between the *Colorados* (Reds) and *Blancos* (Whites)—the dominant parties of the era whose animosity arguably catalyzed José Enrique Rodó's famous treatise *Ariel* (see Chapter 12, "José Enrique Rodó: *Ariel* and a New Vision for Latin America"). Pepe's youth also coincided with Uruguay's entry into an enviable period of economic prosperity and political institutionalism. In Mujica's words: "I belong to a young country that in the 1920s and 1930s had a per capita income that rivaled France or Belgium, a country that came to be called the Switzerland of America. It is the country that I understood, that I was born into."

Likely through his mother's connections, Pepe was introduced to Blanco officials and quickly became the leader of the party's youth wing. By 1958 Mujica had tied his fortunes to Blanco star Enrique Erro. Soon Erro, working with Mujica, left the party to found a new party, Popular Union, which then linked up with the Socialist Party of Uruguay and other smaller entities, but the new challenger fared poorly at the polls, with its candidate for the 1966 presidential election taking home a pitiable 3 percent of the vote.

This failed venture into democratic politics may have hardened Mujica's commitment to exploring other paths to power, which he had started even before becoming involved in national politics. By the mid-1960s, Mujica had joined the Tupamaro revolutionary group with plans to overthrow the Uruguayan state and usher in Castro-style communism. Named after the legendary colonial-era rebel Túpac Amaru II (see Chapter 4, "Túpac Amaru II and the Great Andean Rebellion") and led by the Marxist labor syndicate lawyer, Raúl Sendic, the Tupamaros numbered around two thousand combatants plus auxiliary elements by the early 1970s—a remarkable number given the country's population of only 2.9 million and its twelve-thousand-strong military.

Part of the reason for the group's strength was the backing of Cuba. According to historian Hal Brands, Fidel Castro was hoping to spark another Cuban revolution and to that end provided guerrilla-warfare training to around 1,500 Uruguayan *compañeros*; the Cubans also provided at least US$180,000 to fund the Tupamaros' clandestine and military activities. For Castro, this sort of revolutionary involvement was part of Cuba's unwavering commitment to "never renounce her right and duty to collaborate with those who wish to change society when that is found to be impossible by the democratic method." (See Chapter 23, "Fidel Castro: A Rebel with a Cause.")

This Cuban aid allowed the Tupamaros to become a formidable fighting force that pursued increasingly aggressive operations, including bank robberies and kidnappings. In mid-1968, in response to increasing labor and rebel tumult, President Jorge Pacheco declared a state of emergency and suspended constitutional protections. In response, the Tupamaros went on the offensive, with notorious landmarks of their bloody campaign including the October 1969 seizure of the pueblo of Pando, outside the capital; the July 1970 kidnapping and execution of US government agent Dan Mitrione (later revealed to have been a CIA interrogation advisor who possibly instructed Uruguayan counterparts on torture methods); the September 29, 1970, bombing of the Carrasco Bowling Club; the January 1971 kidnapping of British Ambassador Geoffrey Jackson; and the lethal hit on peasant Ramón Pascasio Báez (who accidentally discovered one of their hideouts) by sodium pentothal injection. The group also widely utilized their own Cárcel del Pueblos (People's Prison), including by publicly interviewing their high-profile hostages—or, as they put it, political prisoners.

And Mujica was very much in the vanguard. In the 1969 short-lived Pando occupation, Mujica led a squad of guerrillas tasked with seizing the telephone system, which they did successfully. In March 1970, police discovered Mujica at a Montevideo dining spot, shooting him six times (only intensive medical attention prevented his death). He then participated in the September 1971

Punta Carretas prison break in which more than a hundred incarcerated Tupamaros escaped by digging a tunnel that led them to a nearby residence, although Mujica was apprehended just weeks later. In April 1972, Mujica again broke out of prison, this time joining around twelve fellow inmates in escaping through a tunnel. Recaptured again that same year, Mujica, along with several other Tupamaros (including the leader Sendic), would spend the next fourteen years in prison, including a decade in solitary confinement. Two especially wretched years consisted of being confined to the "bottom of a well with only ants and rats for company."

Suffering from a host of maladies, it was a veritable miracle that Mujica did not die or go insane behind bars. While generally hesitant to speak specifically about this era, he once reflected on the impact of this protracted, often inhumane confinement: "A lot of what came afterwards was the fruit of how much I thought, thought and rewound," he explained. "I wouldn't have developed the political persona that I have if I hadn't lived such tough years."

Yet contrary to how it is often portrayed in sympathetic histories, it is worth reflecting that the target of the Tupamaros' revolutionary efforts was a *democratic* government. The guerrillas' prowess helped turn the normally peaceful Uruguay into a nightmare. Far from guerrillas galvanizing grassroots backing, as was the aim of Che's *foco* strategy, public support for the Tupamaros dissipated rapidly in the face of the group's violent tactics: one poll taken in the aftermath of the Dan Mitrione episode indicated that over 50 percent believed the revolutionary group was "illegitimate." (At the same time, public confidence in the government also plummeted and foreign investment poured out of the country—exactly what the guerrillas wanted.)

The Tupamaros' campaign of bloody terror ultimately resulted in massive blowback for the guerrillas by creating the perfect conditions for an anticommunist rightist military regime to seize power in 1973. The regime swiftly outlawed the group and turned the country into the "torture chamber of Latin America" with an outsize share of political prisoners (many tortured), "disappeared," and exiles (the latter amounting to 10 percent of the population). By the late 1970s, after suffering severe repression at the hands of the security forces, all the assorted revolutionary groups had been systematically wiped out in Uruguay; the Tupamaros had effectively disappeared by the middle of the decade. The military dictatorship would rule the country for twelve long years until it was finally replaced in 1985 by a democratic government. That same year, as part of an amnesty pact for political crimes, Mujica was freed.

In the years after the 1985 transition to democracy, Mujica, along with scores of former guerrilleros, joined a leftist political party, the Movement of Popular Participation (MPP). The party was subsequently integrated into the Broad Front (FA) coalition, itself originally founded in 1971. In the early 1990s Mujica won a seat as a deputy, followed by another win for senator in 1999, shocking "the parking attendants at Parliament by arriving on a Vespa." By 2004, Mujica's MPP had emerged as the largest bloc in the FA, which won the presidency for its candidate, Tabaré Vásquez, that year. Vásquez appointed Mujica as Minister of Livestock, Agriculture, and Fisheries. Continuing his political ascent, he became the FA's 2009 presidential candidate and, running on a platform of FA continuity despite being a former terrorist, won the election against former president Luis Alberto Lacalle.

A REMARKABLE PRESIDENCY

Victory did little to change Mujica's low-key approach to public life; he resisted the traditional trappings of the presidency, continuing to live on his smallholding and driving to work in his antiquated Beetle. In part, such a story was only possible in Uruguay, as described in a 2013 profile by *New York Times* correspondent Simon Romero: "Indeed, if there is any country in South America where a president can drive a Beetle and get by without a large entourage of bodyguards, it might be Uruguay, which consistently ranks among the region's least corrupt and least unequal nations. . . . Uruguay remains a contender for the region's safest country." His outward appearance belied the authority he now wielded, with *The Economist* describing the unorthodox South American head of state in 2014 as "gruff but with a twinkle in his gimlet eyes. . . . He was dressed in a beige fleece, brown tracksuit bottoms, leather sandals and black socks."

As well as resisting the stylings of power, Mujica's presidency was also remarkable, given his guerrilla background, for its lack of anything that could be interpreted as revolutionary, at least in the Marxist sense. He largely maintained the generally capitalist macroeconomic policies of his predecessor and worked within the democratic rules of the game. But Mujica's presidency was certainly revolutionary in other ways, helping make Uruguay the region's standard-bearer on progressive policies, such as the drive toward green energy. While started in 2005 under FA predecessor Tabaré Vásquez, Mujica's Uruguay oversaw a dramatic increase in the generation of renewable energy,

José Mujica visits the Socialist Party Congress in Montevideo, Uruguay, on December 11, 2011. *(Alamy Stock Photo)*

from basically nothing to 98 percent of all electricity from solar, wind, and hydropower over a decade, all without subsidies or higher consumer costs.

Civil rights were a major area of focus, underpinned by Mujica's belief that social liberalism and progress were part of his nation's "long tradition of secularism and social democracy" going back to his early twentieth-century predecessor, José Battle y Ordóñez, who oversaw the creation of the nation's welfare state. In 2012 abortion was legalized, followed by same-sex marriage in 2013 (making Uruguay the first country to do so in South America). In 2018, Mujica spoke out in favor of the campaign—ultimately successful—to legalize abortion in neighboring Argentina, adding that it was imperative for "men to remain silent" during the debate.

One of the most eye-catching and controversial moves was the legalization of marijuana in 2013. On December 10, 2013, Uruguay's Senate voted

16–13 to establish state regulation (and effective legalization) of marijuana. Calling the marijuana law an "intellectual experiment," Mujica framed it as a sober anticrime measure, not a radical rethinking of a failed puritanical drug war. According to the country's drug czar, the approach was intended to take marijuana smokers "out of the dark alleyways" where they are tempted to purchase more dangerous drugs and allow police to focus on more serious illicit drugs like cocaine and its wicked cousin, base cocaine—the highly addictive crack-like drug. With Uruguayans spending hundreds of millions on illicit marijuana each year, Mujica's government also saw a lucrative revenue source.

The success of the experiment was mixed. Despite the legions of Uruguayans who feared a spike in crime and drug availability, usage only increased by 5 percent from 2013 to 2018. Still, in 2018 only one in three cannabis users bought their product from the regulated market, suggesting that the illicit pot market had not vanished as legalization adherents had predicted.

A PEACEFUL TRANSFER OF POWER

In September 2013, Mujica made a powerful address at the UN General Assembly in New York, exhorting the international community to preserve the planet for future generations and reconsider the economic system based on consumption and ever-increasing production. "Perhaps our world needs fewer global organizations, organized forums and conferences, which serve only to aid hotel chains and airlines; perhaps no one really benefits from their decisions anyway. We must return to what is old and eternal in human life." He urged people to shift their focus to a radical simplicity of sorts, prioritizing love, kindness, solidarity, family, and human interactions, rather than money and consumption.

Constitutionally prevented from running for immediate reelection, in March 2015 Mujica was succeeded by electoral victor Tabaré Vásquez, representing another FA victory and a fifteen-year (democratic!) hold on the presidency. *The Economist* reckoned that this peaceful transition of power represented a "backhanded tribute to the guerrilla turned popular philosopher of democracy." (Note this was an era of the early 2010s when leftist governments and rulers from Nicaragua to Ecuador to Venezuela and Cuba were ruling dictatorially or at best illiberally.)

Despite his seemingly unblemished record as president, some in Uruguay were irked that Mujica did not hold grudges against his former enemies or captors, while his critics highlighted that he never publicly apologized for his revolutionary actions against a democratic government. Yet given the incredible amount he suffered, perhaps a good majority of the nation's citizens believed he had been more than punished for any crimes. He will always be remembered for his sage social and political insights and aphorisms, such as "Republics entered the world to affirm that men are basically equal," or "If democracy means representing the majority, as a symbol I think that those with the highest responsibilities should live like the majority do, not the minority." Despite keeping a photo of Castro in his study, he was a wholehearted proponent of democracy and its goal of "peaceful coexistence."

The scale of his transformation was perhaps best described in 2021, when Argentine intellectual Eduardo Sanguinetti scribed an editorial in the Uruguayan daily, *La República*, urging Mujica's nomination for the Nobel Peace Prize. Pepe Mujica might have adopted armed revolution early in his political formation, but he ended up becoming one of Uruguay's most democratic, electoral, institutional, and, indeed, humane leaders. His presidency's social progressiveness and inclusivity helped the nation's political healing, addressing the wounds inflicted back when Pepe had taken up arms as a youth and demonstrating the ability of ballots over violence to effect change.

45

Luiz Inácio Lula da Silva

Brazil's First Working-Class President

(BY BRITTA H. CRANDALL)

I arrived at the presidency to do the things that needed to be done and that many presidents before me were cowards and didn't have the courage to do.
—*Luiz Inácio Lula da Silva, 2003*

Born into poverty to illiterate, sharecropping parents, and rising to become one of Brazil's most popular presidents, perhaps no other leader in Brazil's history embodies the ideals of upward mobility more than Luiz Inácio Lula da Silva, known universally as Lula. After coming of age in the unions and participating in a series of massive strikes, the deeply charismatic Lula helped create the Workers' Party (PT) in 1980—the first class-based political party under Brazil's then-ailing military regime. After several near misses, he was elected president in 2002 after vowing to diminish hunger, poverty, and income inequality—and largely fulfilled those promises, with the help of a healthy trade surplus and the prudent financial policies of his predecessor.

But beloved as he was—he finished his second term with a scarcely believable approval rating of 87 percent—his tenure was also dogged by scandal. Lula managed to avoid the fallout of a bribes-for-votes investigation but was imprisoned after being caught up in the massive anticorruption drive known as Operation Car Wash. Yet incredibly, it did not spell the end: after being exonerated due to judicial irregularities, Lula once again stood as the PT's presidential candidate in the 2022 election and won by a razor-thin margin over his ultra-right incumbent opponent, Jair Bolsonaro. If there ever was a phoenix rising from the ashes in Latin American politics, it is Lula.

THE VIEW FROM THE FACTORY FLOOR

Born in 1945, the seventh of eight children in the state of Pernambuco in Brazil's poverty-ridden northeast, Lula was effectively left fatherless soon after birth. Aristides Inácio da Silva, Lula's father, moved to the metropolis of São Paulo with the cousin of his wife Euridice to seek work when Lula was just two weeks old. It wasn't until 1952 that Euridice and her children joined him in the big city. Traveling on the back of a truck covered by a canvas top for thirteen days, the motley crew was part of a mass rural-to-urban migration that began in Brazil in the 1950s and fueled the country's rapid industrialization. But their arrival to São Paulo was not a picture-perfect family reunion. Aristides had begun a second family with Euridice's cousin and had fathered three new children. Thus began a tense transition to São Paulo, with the forced integration of these two families, until Euridice and her children finally left her unfaithful and increasingly abusive husband.

While tumultuous, the move to São Paulo opened up a world of freedom and opportunity for Lula. As historian Richard Bourne describes, "This was the point at which he ceased to be a rather ignorant country child and began to grow up as a streetwise kid, close to Brazil's industrial heartland." Lula helped make ends meet for his now-single mother by dropping out of school in elementary school to earn money delivering laundry and working as a shoeshine boy. When he was a teen, he was accepted into a two-year industrial training program and became a lathe operator. It was a life-changing experience in more ways than one. Being a skilled worker opened the door for several factory jobs for Lula—including one in which he famously lost the pinky finger of his left hand in an accident—but these jobs also revealed to him the lack of worker rights in a country that since 1964 was governed by a military regime. In the late 1960s, Lula became increasingly involved in campaigns for higher wages and started serving in various roles for the metalworkers' union. It didn't take long for him to rise in the ranks of union leadership.

During this time, he met and fell in love with Maria de Lourdes Ribeiro. They married in 1969, and she was pregnant the next year. But their marriage was short-lived; when eight months pregnant, Lourdes contracted hepatitis. Rushing to a São Paulo hospital in great pain, she and her unborn baby died. Their sudden and unexpected death had a profound impact on Lula, making him a widow at just twenty-six years old. Believing their deaths the result of substandard care and an initially incorrect diagnosis, he took up championing healthcare and social services for the poor, who made up the majority of Brazil's citizens.

GOING NATIONAL

After Lourdes's death, Lula became increasingly involved in labor politics, and by 1975, he was elected president of the São Bernardo metalworkers' union. Under his leadership, the union took a more aggressive stance toward worker wages, culminating in a wave of strikes in 1978 and 1979—strikes which were at that time illegal under Brazil's military government. But Lula had picked his moment well: with an ailing economy and ever-declining legitimacy, Brazil's military leaders hoped to dictate the terms of their exit and thus began a deliberate strategy of political *abertura* (opening), and decided to allow the strikes to go forward. Upward of eighty thousand workers refused to work, forcing companies to negotiate. The result was a 34 percent wage hike for workers, bolstered by a World Bank report that revealed the government had several years prior falsified the inflation rate used to determine wages. The strikes were a resounding success for Lula and the unions and galvanized the working class in Brazil.

Lula gained crucial exposure in these widespread strikes. Famously, when he was speaking at a soccer stadium during a general strike in 1979, it began to rain and the sound system failed. Although fearful of public speaking at this relatively early point in his career, Lula commanded an audience of an estimated ninety thousand people for four hours, yelling to be heard as listeners passed his words back through the crowd. His profile was growing rapidly: in 1978 Lula was on the cover of the prominent weekly magazine *This Is*, and in 1981, the *New York Times* referred to him as Brazil's Lech Wałęsa, the iconic leader of the Solidarity labor movement in Poland.

Now thirty-five years old, Lula was respected by workers from different political affiliations for his straightforward and honest approach to negotiation; many strikers even carried signs comparing him to Jesus. (The holy connotation would persist through later decades: Lilia Schwarcz, an anthropology professor at the University of São Paulo, said in 2010 that because of his "seductive rhetoric, his command of populist language and his personal charisma, Lula . . . is sometimes compared to saints and miracle-workers.")

It was only a matter of time before Lula would harness his enormous success in worker empowerment and pivot to the realm of national politics—but the time had to be right. He often claimed that he would never join either of the two parties allowed by the military regime (party critics icily dubbed "Yes" and "Yes Sir"), as neither represented the working class. He was skeptical of political parties organized from the top down and believed that neither would effectively challenge military rule. Hence, Lula and other labor leaders advocated for the labor movement to develop a new workers' political party, and once again the regime obliged. Given the abertura and military regime's desire for a soft exit, the military sanctioned the creation of new political parties, and in 1980 the Workers' Party was born. This was a significant milestone in Brazilian politics—never had a class-based party existed—but the creation of the PT also divided Brazil's opposition to the waning military regime, with some more traditional Marxist groups holding that the PT lacked sufficient ideology.

Notably, the PT was an early supporter of the pivotal *Diretas Já* (Direct [Elections] Now) campaign that took place in 1983 1984. This massive grassroots movement, ultimately backed by Brazil's principal opposition political parties, involved popular protests unprecedented in size that demanded direct elections of the president. (At that point, the president—always drawn from the armed forces—was elected indirectly by an electoral college.) The civil movement brought together broad swathes of Brazilian society, including political parties, celebrities, soccer teams, and even the Catholic church, to push Congress to act. While the two-thirds congressional majority needed to approve the constitutional amendment was narrowly missed, a Pandora's box had been opened. By 1985, given the unexpected death of a congressionally elected president Tancredo Neves, Congress voted to allow direct elections, giving millions of Brazilians the ability to elect their president for the first time.

PRESIDENTIAL ASPIRATIONS

Lula ran three unsuccessful campaigns for president in 1989, 1994, and 1998. He came incredibly close in 1989, losing by a small margin to the charismatic Fernando Collor de Mello. In 1994, he was defeated by the revered Fernando Henrique Cardoso, who had slayed the beast of hyperinflation with his *Real Plan* as finance minister in 1994. And in 1998, Lula lost again to Cardoso, still lacking the broad political appeal required to unseat the incumbent. But the stars finally aligned for Lula in 2002.

On the one hand, Brazil had changed: no longer wracked by hyperinflation or a repressive military regime, it had finally reached a state of relative political and economic stability. But Lula had changed as well. Knowing he needed to broaden his support base, he adopted a more conservative appearance, donning a business suit instead of his standard work clothes and getting his teeth polished and beard trimmed. He also moderated his pro-worker, anti-establishment message. Celso Furtado, a left-leaning Brazilian economist, allegedly advised Lula to "never give up on your radicals. They give vitality to the party, and more important, show you the path you shouldn't follow." Lula chose a center-right running mate and wrote a "Letter to the Brazilian People" vowing to honor financial commitments and stay the economic course of Cardoso. The strategy succeeded. Lula ended up receiving an overwhelming 61 percent of the vote to his opponent's 38 percent in the second round of voting.

"God has publicly admitted he is Brazilian," stated Lula when campaigning on behalf of a PT local candidate in 2008. Measuring by the bulk of Lula's two presidencies, one would be hard-pressed to disagree. His commitment to his predecessor's economic policies when first taking office, including prudent fiscal and monetary policy, meant that initially skittish markets quickly adapted to a leftist president of Brazil, and the value of the stock market and currency did not plummet as feared. His administration surpassed the primary fiscal surplus it had pledged to the International Monetary Fund and began to reduce the national debt. At the same time, his government succeeded in raising the minimum wage and revamped a preexisting conditional cash transfer program, naming it *Bolsa Família* (Family Purse), which provided monthly payments to lower-income families contingent upon a commitment to keep their children vaccinated and to stay in school. Lula claimed that he would judge his presidency as a success if every Brazilian could eat three meals a day, and his policies proved that he meant it. Under Lula's watch, economic growth increased from less than 2 percent annually to over 5 percent, which combined with his social programs pulled millions out of poverty. What was one secret to the miracle? Quite simply the insatiable Chinese demand for Brazil's core exports, principally soy, iron ore, and petroleum. Buoyed by economic growth and rising export receipts, the Lula administration could both increase social spending as well as maintain fiscal balance.

Lula was reelected in 2006 (against center-right Geraldo Alckmin, then governor of São Paulo, who coincidentally would become Lula's running mate in 2022). Lula's good fortune continued into his second term. Petrobras, Brazil's national oil company, discovered massive oil reserves off the coast of Rio de Janeiro in October 2006, an event that Lula described as "the second independence of Brazil." (Highlighting his significant sense of self-regard, several years after the discovery he changed the name of these reserves from the "Tupi" to the "Lula" oil fields.) In 2007 Brazil won hosting rights for the 2014 World Cup, and in October 2009, after heavy personal lobbying by Lula himself, São Paulo won the bid for the 2016 Summer Olympics, beating Chicago, among other cities. In preparation for the events, the administration proudly boasted the country's ability to quickly build twelve new football stadiums (to the tune of over US$3 billion).

As popular as Lula was domestically, he was also respected and admired abroad. President Barack Obama once described him as "one of the most popular politicians on earth." President George W. Bush extolled his virtues, as did the head of the World Bank, James Wolfensohn, who described Lula as "one of the great world leaders." But Lula was no Western lackey: his administration refused to back the US effort to topple Saddam Hussein and focused on fostering diplomatic ties between and among the developing economies of the world instead of with the United States. This "south–south" foreign policy worked toward stronger relations among the BRIC nations (Brazil, Russia, India, and China), as well as expanding economic and political connections with Africa. Lula's administration flexed its economic clout as well, winning a World Trade Organization dispute against the United States in a case opposing US government subsidies to domestic cotton growers.

A TALE OF TWO CORRUPTION SCANDALS

Lula finished his second term at the end of 2010 with an astonishing 83 percent approval rating, but there had been rocky moments during his presidency. The summer of 2005 brought the so-called *mensalão* ("big monthly payout") scandal when authorities unveiled that the PT had been exchanging money for political support in Congress. This "tradition" of buying votes to gain approval for pending legislation—involving an estimated monthly stipend of $12,000 paid to individual representatives—explained at least part of Lula's success in getting his reform agenda passed.

Several in his cabinet were forced to resign, including his hyper-powerful chief of staff José Dirceu, who was convicted of running the scheme (Dirceu has a fascinating back story of his own. He forged strong ties with Lula through their resistance to the military regime in the 1960s. The military arrested him in 1968, but he was freed the next year in a prisoner exchange for US Ambassador Charles Elbrick, who had been kidnapped by a leftist guerrilla group. Exiled to Cuba, Dirceu underwent extensive plastic surgery to disguise his identity before secretly returning to Brazil. Given that warrants were still out for his arrest, he took on the role of a Jewish grocer and even married and had a child under his assumed identity. Only when political amnesty was declared in 1979 did he return to politics after restoring his original facial features in Cuba).

Ultimately, Lula was able to deflect the blame for the mensalão scandal. He denied any knowledge of the payments and emerged relatively unscathed, easily securing his second term. This was an astonishing escape act from what was the largest political corruption scandal ever uncovered in Brazil, with high-level political figures put on trial and sentenced to prison terms for the first time in the country's history. But the subsequent corruption scandal, which dwarfed mensalão in terms of money involved and complexity, proved more difficult for Lula to evade.

In 2014, a relatively standard operation was launched to investigate money laundering using a gas station in Brasilia, the nation's capital, but the investigation soon exposed a much larger web of official corruption at

Women kiss a photograph of former Brazilian president Luiz Inácio Lula da Silva, in Fortaleza, Brazil, October 7, 2018. *(Alamy)*

the highest levels of Brazil's government. Dubbed Operation Carwash for its origins, the investigation revealed that senior officials at Petrobras were accepting bribes from the country's largest construction companies in exchange for inflated contracts. By the time of the probe's termination in 2021, it had recovered illegal payments of more than $4.3 billion and had secured the convictions of over 270 people, including presidents from several other Latin American countries.

One of these presidents was Lula, who was imprisoned in April 2018 for illegal enrichment, barred from the 2018 election, and sentenced to twelve years in prison. The irony was not lost on him that he was to be imprisoned in the very same police building that he had inaugurated as president, but he remained defiant. "I'm going to prove that the thieves are the ones who arrested me," Lula vowed to a crowd of thousands before starting his prison sentence, declaring his determination to carry on fighting for the rights of the poor.

> A long time ago, I dreamt it was possible to rule this country by including millions and millions of poor people in the economy, including millions of people in universities, creating millions and millions of jobs in this country.... If the charges are for these crimes, for including the poor in universities, black people in universities, poor people to eat meat, poor people to buy cars, poor people to travel by plane, poor people to have their small farm, have a small business, have their own home: if that is the crime I've committed, then I'd like to say I am going to continue to be a criminal in this country, because I am going to do so much more. I am going to do so much more.

The last sentence of this impassioned speech was prophetic, "I will leave with my head held high and my chest out, because I will prove my innocence." Five hundred eighty days later, he was released, welcomed by an ecstatic crowd waving red PT flags and posters with his image. By 2022, Lula was on the cusp of pulling off one of his biggest comebacks ever, having been fully exonerated and once again nominated as the PT's presidential candidate. (His freedom was secured after leaked text messages revealed that the judge who spearheaded the Car Wash campaign and determined Lula's sentence, Sergio Moro, had counseled the prosecution during two years of the trial.) His margin of victory over the incumbent Jair Bolsonaro was 51 to 49 percent, roughly two million votes.

It is difficult to exaggerate Lula's significance and impact on Brazil's political and economic trajectory. He accomplished what no other Brazilian president ever had in narrowing the gap between the rich and poor. He was Brazil's first working-class president, a boy from the *humilde* class who rose to the highest echelons of Brazilian power. Lula embodied the hopes of the disenfranchised of Brazil, both the nonrich as well as the nonwhite. And as he became a globally admired president, these hopes expanded to encompass those of an entire nation as Lula launched Brazil closer to developed economy status and put the country in the global eye by hosting landmark sporting events. At the same time, one undeniable legacy of Lula as well as his PT was the unprecedented scale and depth of official corruption. While vowing to profoundly change the "patrimonial" nature of politics, in which elite politicians simply look out for themselves and their own, Lula's presidency revealed that alongside his great reforms, money still oiled the wheels of power and business in Brazil.

46

Daniel Ortega and Rosario Murillo

Nicaragua's Toxic Power Couple

Conditions are ripe for triumph. We will win. And we will wield great power here.

—*Daniel Ortega, 2006*

Daniel Ortega and Rosario Murillo are Nicaragua's comeback couple. After Ortega's leftist Sandinista regime was ousted (democratically) from power in 1990, Murillo helped Ortega reinvent himself as a Church-going, private-sector-friendly leader with a focus on social initiatives—a dramatic about-turn for this former revolutionary. Aided by Murillo's deft New Age public relations strategy (and some dubious constitutional tinkering), Ortega returned to power via the ballot box in 2006.

At first, times appeared to be good—Nicaragua's economy enjoyed a honeymoon period fueled by Venezuelan petrodollars, while Ortega cracked down on crime and improved social benefits. But authoritarian cracks soon showed in the façade: Ortega reshaped the constitution to allow him to secure multiple consecutive terms (via rigged elections), while Murillo became the unelected arbiter of official policy, creating a powerful family dynasty that for many recalled the loathed Somoza family dynasty that ruled mid-century Nicaragua with an iron fist. Rampant corruption, family scandal (including Ortega's alleged rape of his step-daughter when she was a child), and harsh repression of Nicaragua's citizens further tarnished the couple's image. Aided and abetted by Murillo, Ortega has completed the transformation from Cold War guerrilla to postmodern strongman, holding no value so dear as that of power.

DANIEL ORTEGA: FROM PRISON TO PRESIDENT

José Daniel Ortega Saavedra was born on November 11, 1945, in La Libertad, Nicaragua; Humberto, his younger brother, was born two years later. They were the offspring of a merchant who had fought with Sandino's campesino army against the US Marines. (See Chapter 16, "Augusto Sandino versus the United States.") In the mid-1950s, the father, who instilled his feisty anti-establishment inclination in his children, moved the family to a blue-collar barrio. Daniel did a stint at the capital's Central American University, but by 1963, he had abandoned his study of law to join the clandestine Sandinista National Liberation Front (FSLN). More commonly referred to as the Sandinistas, the FSLN purported to be the formal political expression of Sandino's eclectic ideological mix of nationalism, anti-imperialism, and principles of radical social change along Marxist lines. Despite backing from Havana, the Sandinistas had not hitherto posed a serious threat to the dynastic Somoza regime that had ruled Nicaragua since 1936, but Ortega was about to change all that.

By 1967, the FSLN had tapped him to join the group's urban campaign against Anastasio "Tachito" Somoza Debayle, who had assumed power in Nicaragua that year. Within months, Ortega was arrested for participating in a robbery of a bank and subsequently spent seven years in prison, where he was tortured. He was released with other revolutionary prisoners in 1974, in exchange for "Somocista" hostages held by the FSLN, but had been radicalized by the experience. Daniel found sanctuary—and guerrilla warfare training for several months—in Cuba, before covertly returning home.

In 1975, the Ortega brothers, with a few others, founded the moderate Sandinista faction known as the Third Way. It was a canny move, for the faction's political positioning made them indispensable mediators to the motley bunch of feuding FSLN groups, as well as helping the brothers forge alliances with civil society and the private sector. By 1978, the faction had become the dominant revolutionary group both militarily and politically—and Daniel and Humberto were more influential than ever.

They were helped by the fact that hostility to the regime was rising. After a catastrophic earthquake hit Managua on December 23, 1972, the Somozas and their cronies stole humanitarian aid while the mounds of rubble remained untouched, heightening the nation's ire. Then on the morning of January 10, 1978, Pedro Joaquín Chamorro, editor of *La Prensa* (the only opposition paper in Nicaragua), was gunned down by two assassins in Managua on his way to work. Tachito contended that pro-Chamorro groups had perpetrated the murder to embarrass his government, but the Nicaraguan population was having none of it. Many laid the blame at the feet of Tachito and his despised *somocista* National Guard; youth spontaneously rioted across the nation, throwing Molotov cocktails; and the crucial business class embraced the notion of a national strike to demand justice. By May 1978, a coalition of anti-Somoza political parties, unions, and social organizations had founded the Broad Opposition Front. As Somoza's popularity inside and outside Nicaragua continued to plummet, one US congressional delegation came away terrified that the ruler was becoming the Idi Amin of Latin America, in reference to the bloodthirsty Ugandan strongman of this period. Ultimately, President Jimmy Carter concluded that supporting Somoza was no longer politically viable. He cut military aid and, within months, slapped sanctions on Managua. And all the while, in the shadows, more and more people were joining the Sandinistas.

In May 1979 the guerrillas made their move, launching a final offensive, or the "hour of the overthrow," to borrow the language of its radio programming. Sandinista units attacked Guard outposts all over the country as a general strike began to take a severe toll on the economy. By now the Sandinistas were

Daniel Ortega at the United Nations, 1986. *(Library of Congress Prints and Photographs Division, Washington, DC)*

calling the city of León their provincial capital, but Managua was in the rebels' crosshairs. Some of the attacks against the Guard were perpetrated by parties other than the Sandinistas, strengthening the impression that resistance to Somoza was broad and diverse. Indeed, it is highly unlikely that the Sandinistas could have seized power had a strong majority of Nicaraguans not actively opposed the regime, just as a broad consensus of Cubans had opposed Batista. In July 1979, Somoza fled the country, ultimately ending up in Paraguay, where he was assassinated the following year.

Now a new, five-person junta comprising both Sandinista and non-Sandinista opposition figures was in charge and benefited from almost universal international and domestic support. Within days of the July overthrow, however, senior US intelligence officials predicted that "the hard-core Marxists in the regime will quickly begin trying to neutralize the influence of the junta's more moderate members and seize control." Carter policy makers attempted to get more non-Sandinistas (read, more moderates) into the junta, but this task was complicated by Washington's crisis of credibility, given how long it had taken the Americans to abandon Somoza.

Washington's prognosis proved grimly accurate. The Sandinistas pushed out the more moderate members of the junta and consolidated their revolution. By 1981, Daniel had installed himself as the head of the new "revolutionary government" (he would be elected president in 1984 in a vote that the Reagan administration would criticize as being not fully free), while Humberto, a brilliant military strategist, was named minister of defense. Much as Fidel Castro and his younger brother Raúl had done in Cuba, the two Ortega brothers became the figureheads of the new Nicaragua, yet unlike Fidel, Daniel was not an especially charismatic revolutionary leader nor the most devout Marxist among his comrades. In marked contrast to his later career, Daniel at this period was pragmatic, inclined toward compromise.

REGIME CHANGE AT THE BALLOT BOX

There was now great pressure on the Sandinistas to legitimize their rule. They were confident that they would win any popular vote handily, and they set presidential elections for early 1990. In September 1989 the new George H. W. Bush administration began efforts to provide funding for the elections. Officials insisted that the aid would be used for "non-partisan technical support of the elections process," but the funding went almost exclusively to the anti-Sandinista opposition known as the Nicaragua

Opposition Union, whose presidential candidate, Violeta Chamorro, was the widow of the assassinated journalist.

There were an estimated seven hundred official observers of the elections on February 25, 1990. That night the UN team's "quick count" of less than 10 percent of the vote showed Chamorro winning a decisive victory. Stunned, the Sandinista Directorate called a hasty meeting to decide its next moves. Within hours, an official from the Supreme Electoral Council read the initial results aloud, further indicating a major upset. When the dust had settled and all the votes were counted Chamorro had taken 55 percent to Ortega's 41 percent. Indeed, Nicaraguans of all walks of life had given the Sandinistas a clear mandate: it was time to go. The Sandinista revolution was over, killed in the end by the ballot box.

The Sandinistas, however, quickly began preparing to fight another day. Right before Daniel Ortega stepped down, his government nationalized state assets and seized private property, an event that was quickly labeled "La Piñata," for the ubiquitous children's game where a papier-mâché container is beaten to unleash the candy. Mansions and beach houses went to party leaders—Daniel himself got a grouping of luxury residences in central Managua—but thousands upon thousands of acres of state-owned properties were also doled out to poor farmers and urban residents, whose gratitude the Sandinistas would later call upon. Daniel also succeeded in keeping Humberto as commander-in-chief of the military, then called the Sandinista Popular Army. In 1995 it was renamed the Nicaraguan Army with a new commander, who was a committed Sandinista.

Daniel Ortega passed the following sixteen years "governing from below," as he called it, keeping his grip on the Sandinista party and relying upon Humberto's control of the military to bolster his political power despite being out of office. In both 1996 and 2001, Ortega ran unsuccessfully for president as the FSLN candidate, taking a not insignificant 42 percent of the vote in the latter.

Pivotal to Ortega's eventual comeback was the dubious accord from the year 2000—known officially (and euphemistically) as the "Government Agreement" and infamously as "The Pact"—between him and corrupt sitting president Arnoldo Alemán of the Constitutionalist Liberal Party. The Pact ensured that, now in exchange for giving immunity to the venal Alemán, a candidate only required as little as 35 percent to win in the first round. Ortega had never managed to garner support beyond his core base of Sandinista voters, maybe 35–40 percent, so in a stunning display of political chutzpah, he lowered the bar to this minoritarian level! And there was another factor that also helped propel Daniel back to power in 2006: his long-time partner, Rosario Murillo.

"COMRADE ROSARIO"

Rosario María Murillo Zambrana was born in Managua in 1951 to an agrarian father and a mother who was a poet and niece of Sandino. The relatively privileged Rosario attended high school in a small city in southwest England, followed by a well-regarded art institute in Switzerland. Back home and still a teenager, Murillo had her first child, Zoilamérica, in 1967.

Like so many of her generation, before she was twenty, the bright polyglot (fluent in Spanish, English, Italian, and French) joined up with the Sandinistas, although she continued her day job as a secretary at Pedro Joaquín Chamorro's *La Prensa*. Murillo's guerrilla activities landed her in a regime prison in 1976; following her release she fled, along with Zoilámerica, first to Panama and then Venezuela, before settling at a Sandinista safe house in Costa Rica in 1977. This was also the year when Rosario met Daniel. An amorous relationship ensued, producing numerous children.

In 1998, Zoilamérica publicly alleged that Daniel Ortega had started molesting her when she was eleven in Costa Rica; after they had returned to Nicaragua and she turned fifteen, Ortega began to rape her, which endured until 1990, when Daniel was no longer president of Nicaragua. It was the shame of having her adopted father (a legal process that occurred in her teens) committing these barbarities that prevented her from telling her mother. Confronted with the allegations, Ortega blasted Zoilamérica for breeding "a real conspiracy" against him, while Murillo not only backed her husband but was the public face of the patent denial, calling her daughter a deranged fabulist at a press conference surrounded by her adult offspring—all of whom backed their mother, forging a dynastic family "ring of steel" around Daniel Ortega. Ultimately, the judicial proceeding ended because Ortega enjoyed parliamentary immunity, at least initially. Since 2013, Zoilamérica was relegated to life in Costa Rica where she continued to revile Ortega but also her mother for morale cowardice by opting for power and fame over her family and the truth. The number of trusted aides did shrink in the aftermath of the rape scandal. And over the ensuing two decades this core faction would constrict even more.

Near the end of 2005 Ortega and Rosario Murillo officially remarried, this time in a Roman Catholic service, and the couple would go on to define the next chapter of power in Nicaragua. Indeed, according to the *New York Times*, "Murillo cleverly reshaped [Ortega's] image after he ran in two more elections and lost. Her New Age ideas appeared in symbols of peace and love and banners painted with psychedelic colors. Rather conveniently, Mr. Ortega and his wife metamorphosed into devout Catholics after decades of revolutionary atheism. To further win over the Catholic Church, Mr. Ortega's nemesis in the '80s, he agreed to back a complete ban on abortion."

BACK IN POWER

Aided by the amended thresholds under The Pact and his new public image, Daniel Ortega won the presidential election in 2006 with 39 percent, defeating conservative opponent Eduardo Montealegre. Ortega started his fresh term in January 2007 by pursuing a host of widely applauded policies, such as those focused on reducing levels of hunger and illiteracy, with many crediting Murillo for the initiatives. Murillo's influence was enshrined in her role as the president's "communicator-in-chief," which meant that other ministers had to get her green light before making public comments. According to a Reuters 2007 article, many Nicaraguans perceived her as the true power behind the throne.

Nicaragua's President Daniel Ortega (*center*), Bolivia's President Evo Morales (*left*), and Venezuela's President Hugo Chávez raise their fists at a square in Managua after Ortega was sworn in on January 10, 2007. *(Daniel Leclair/Alamy)*

Surprisingly, Daniel Ortega also backed a free trade pact with the United States and called on the domestic and foreign private sectors to increase hiring and investment. The Sandinista-led security forces brought crime and drug gangs under control (in stark contrast to the soaring citizen insecurity crises in Honduras, El Salvador, and Guatemala). The Nicaraguan economy grew at an impressive clip (4–6 percent annually) for the next decade, social spending on the poor swelled, national debt eased, trade relations were warm, and Ortega was reasonably popular. As the *Washington Post* described him, in this period "Ortega was seen as an aging, but not entirely benign, leftist who had warmed to capitalism and kept gang violence at bay."

Another boosting factor was the so-called Pink Tide of leftism in the early 2000s, funded by Hugo Chávez's petroleum revenue largesse (see Chapter 40, "Hugo Chávez: The Richest Revolutionary in the World"). Indeed, there is little question that the hundreds of billions of dollars loaned to Ortega's government by Hugo Chavez's eighteen-nation *PetroCaribe* alliance gave the Nicaraguan head of state a massive additional source of fiscal revenue—and by extension social spending. Over a give-or-take-a-decade period ending in 2017, the poverty rate in the country fell from 27 to 10 percent.

Yet even when he was initially relatively popular, there were signs of Ortega's autocratic inclinations. His regime's "ruthless survival strategy" was state control of the media, the politicization of the military and national police, cooptation of the judiciary, and a highly complicit private sector that, long ago embraced a modus vivendi with his "socialist" government. In July 2009—the thirtieth anniversary of the anti-Somoza Nicaraguan revolution—Ortega declared that he would amend the constitution to permit reelection, in his case for a second, consecutive term. Three months later, the Nicaraguan Supreme Court ended the constitution proscription on consecutive re-election, paving the way for the former *guerrillero* to "constitutionally" contest the 2011 national vote, which he won with 60 percent of the vote. The FSLN also claimed sixty-two of ninety National Assembly seats, giving the party a "supermajority" that enabled it to pursue its legislative priorities without hindrance.

Ortega didn't stop there, and by 2014, Sandinista allies had pushed through a constitutional amendment to abolish presidential term limits altogether, allowing Ortega to run for a third consecutive term. For the 2016 general election, a regime-dominated electoral force succeeded in removing sixteen opposition legislators from their positions in the assembly and banning election-observation missions. The Ortega-compliant Supreme Court prevented the main opposition candidate, Eduardo Montealegre, from running against the incumbent, while Ortega also managed to have officials permit Murillo to run for vice president. Given the certainty he'd win the 2016 election, this was tantamount to an appointment, thus sealing a family dynasty that rivaled the Somoza dictatorship. Murillo, sixty-five, now had her hands in all aspects of running the Ortega's administration. Said reporter Frances Robles in a 2016 profile, "She is the one who gives daily news briefings about the latest earthquake or damage from an industrial fire. If a child has Zika [a mosquito-borne virus], Ms. Murillo knows the boy's name and might just call the parents herself. She meets regularly with municipal leaders and makes it clear that decisions cannot be made without her approval."

Outside the ruling dyad, the Ortega/Murillo siblings also wielded vast influence, holding the rank of "presidential advisors" and controlling all sorts of lucrative businesses, from petroleum distribution and almost all TV stations to advertising firms holding lucrative media deals with the same Ortega government!

THE CRISIS OF 2018

To no one's great surprise, Ortega was the overwhelming victor in the 2016 presidential contest, capturing over 72 percent of the vote in an election in which there were widespread boycotts and no official international observers. By now it was clear that Ortega and his co-president Murillo, together a loyal coterie of family and loyalists, were increasingly running the country as a personality cult, echoing the Perón–Evita partnership in Argentina a half-century before (see Chapter 20, "Juan and Eva Perón: Peronism's Dynamic Duo"). According to the *Washington Post*, "Together they fostered an image on billboards and government broadcasts as beneficent parents of the nation."

But by 2018, the world had changed. The Venezuelan lifeline of petrodollars was no more, given the South American nation's economic implosion, a change that forced the Ortega/Murillo regime to cut the pension benefits, which in turn sparked widespread protests. Images of geriatric protestors being roughed up by pro-government activists unleashed a wave of student-led marches and rallies, including university takeovers, no longer just in Managua but also in provincial cities and even pueblos. The wave grew, with hundreds of thousands calling for the first couple's summary resignation.

In response, Ortega unleashed security forces and militias to crack down on the protestors. Joshua Partlow vividly captured the early clashes: "Chaotic

Commuters travel in a bus along a street in Managua, Nicaragua, June 25, 2018. The graffiti on the bus reads: "Go out Daniel [Ortega] and you Chayo [Rosario Murillo]." *(Andrés Martínez Casares/Alamy)*

scenes broke out as police fired into crowds in downtown Managua. Masked gunmen apparently affiliated with the government set fire to a dissident radio station. Police and assailants entered the Metropolitan Cathedral grounds and fired on hundreds of students huddled inside."

Unexpectedly, Ortega then ended the modifications to the pension system and entered into negotiations (overseen by the Catholic Church) with protestors, civil society, and the private sector. This dialogue, however, proved fruitless, and any fleeting hope that the regime might attempt to find a diplomatic solution was almost immediately dashed. Opposition leaders and other protestors were hunted down in their hundreds, leading to, throughout the months-long crisis, between five hundred deaths and an equal number incarcerated (a significant share of these political prisoners) and even as high as a hundred thousand more in exile (a huge share fleeing to neighboring Costa Rica). Two dozen security officers were killed. The economy sank, forcing even more citizens to flee their homeland. The Interdisciplinary Group of Independent Experts—a body of the Organization of American States—noted gross human rights abuses that met the definition of "crimes against humanity." (Furious, Ortega ejected them from the country, along with the Inter-

American Commission on Human Rights Special Monitoring Mechanism for Nicaragua). Notably, key Catholic priests such as Padre Edwin Román took up high-profile functions in the opposition movement and used phrases like "dictatorship" to describe the regime. Rodolfo López, a priest beaten up by government-launched counter-protestors, put it starkly: "We are living in a country without rules. We're talking about a situation here where people deliberately, freely, offer their souls to the devil," referring to Ortega and Murillo.

ORTEGA, FOREVER?

As the crisis unfolded, some of the keenest Nicaragua watchers concluded that Ortega's ouster was simply a matter of time, the opposition being too large and too united, not to mention the faltering economy, mass emigration, and denunciations and sanctions against the inner circles from the Trump administration. Yet Ortega and Murillo merely tightened their grip further. In the run-up to the November 2021 elections, the regime jailed five presidential candidates and many opposition figures, including former revolutionary comrades-in-arms such as Dora María Téllez (the only woman who was present at the 1978 raid on the National Palace), Hugo Torres (who in 1974 once helped capture Somocista hostages to swap with Daniel Ortega), and Victor Hugo Tinoco (former Sandinista deputy foreign minister). According to the Supreme Electoral Council, Ortega won the presidential race with 75 percent of the vote, clearing the way for his fourth consecutive term. The council claimed a 65 percent turnout, but Open Ballot Boxes, a civil society group, countered by saying the turnout was more like 19 percent. US President Joe Biden blasted the process as a "pantomime election that was neither free nor fair," while the European Union said the elections "complete the conversion of Nicaragua into an autocratic regime."

At the heart of this conversion has been the profound change in Ortega himself. Ruiz, a fellow Sandinista guerrillero, said "The Ortega of today is not recognizable to anyone who knew him." Another former Sandinista historian, "For a majority of people, he is an assassin, he is a torturer." Having fought against the dynastic, corrupt, and autocratic Somozas, Ortega has created a new regime that parallels them in many respects. This circular history was neatly captured during the 2018 protests in the popular chant "Ortega y Somoza, son la misma cosa" ("Ortega and Somoza are the same thing"). Yet Somoza was always what he appeared to be; Ortega, by contrast, has in the eyes of many betrayed the revolutionary promise in the pursuit of absolute power.

47

Berta Cáceres

The Guardian of the River

Defending human rights in Honduras is a crime. . . . They are criminalizing the right to our identity and to our sense of self.
—*Berta Cáceres*

Berta Cáceres was Honduras' most "famous and fearless" indigenous leader in the Central American country's uneven modern history. A member of the Lenca indigenous community (the largest in Honduras), Cáceres's outsized impact spanned two tumultuous decades in which this community organizer and activist defended the rights of her fellow indigenous peoples and lands, although some critics lambasted her tactics as militant.

Cáceres's most resounding triumph came in the 2010s when she spearheaded a campaign opposing the construction of a Chinese-financed private hydroelectric dam project on sacred Lenca *tierra*. Defying all domestic and foreign prognostications, her success on the dam question brought her instant global recognition, including one of the world's most prestigious environmental prizes in 2015. But she paid the highest price for her advocacy: in 2016, she was assassinated aged forty-four, leaving behind four children. That said, those who knew her well would counter that she had been born to make this total sacrifice.

THE HOPE

Berta Isabel Cáceres Flores was born in 1971 into a notable Lenca family in mountainous western Honduras, where the Lenca people live. Although Honduras was relatively peaceful, the revolutionary insurrections and counterrevolutionary terror in neighboring El Salvador and Guatemala during the 1970s and 1980s meant that Berta grew up in a tumultuous geopolitical climate. Her mother, Austra Berta Flores, was a social worker, politician (twice mayor), and midwife who routinely welcomed Salvadoran refugees streaming across the nearby border into their spartan but dignified home in the market pueblo of La Esperanza. These and other acts of daily solidarity made a deep impression on the young girl, the youngest of twelve. "Berta grew up with struggle. She saw it every day," Flores later told an interviewer. "It was her schooling. I knew she would be important. I was always pushing her to become what she became."

By her early twenties, Berta had opted for student activism, leading to, in 1993, her cofounding the National Council of Popular and Indigenous Organizations of Honduras (COPINH), whose principal mission was to counter the myriad threats to the Lenca community—not least of which was illegal logging. COPINH's antipatriarchy and anti-imperialist orientation was predicated on the Lenca's respect for and immersion in the natural environment, and Berta was its indisputable leader: "Berta was COPINH and COPINH was Berta," said Canadian researcher Karen Spring. Cáceres showed indefatigable energy and organizing capacity, setting up a training center (called Utopia), a chain of radio stations called *La Voz Lenca* (The Lenca Voice), and a council of sage elders. One seventy-five-year-old elder, Pascualita Vásquez, in a 2017 interview, described how Cáceres resurrected cultural rituals which in turn instilled pride and awareness. "Before Berta, our ceremonies were being forgotten. I remembered them as a child, but we no longer did them," she said. "But Berta emphasized for us how important it was to rescue our traditions, and to hold ceremonies before discussions of current issues like dams. We revere our ancestors, and now that Berta is dead, we see her as an ancestor, too."

In the wild aftermath of the June 2009 coup that removed democratic president Manuel "Mel" Zelaya, Cáceres increased her social activism and profile for all things related to leftist causes. Later that same year she ran as a vice presidential candidate on an independent ticket under a venerable labor leader, although the pair withdrew as a form of protest against numerous election irregularities.

THE DAM BREAKS

In 2010 Honduran Congress enacted legislation that resulted in contracts being awarded to private entities to construct scores of dams across the country.

One went to a joint project of the Honduran construction outfit, known as DESA, and the massive Chinese state-owned Sinohydro. The contract envisioned the construction of four dams on the Gualcarque River, twenty-five miles outside of La Esperanza, to be collectively known as the Agua Zarca Dam. Fatefully, the Agua Zarca's location also happened to be home to one decidedly defiant Lenca village called Río Blanco.

According to Cáceres and her activist colleagues, Río Blanco residents only became aware that a dam was planned when they started seeing bulldozers and other construction equipment in the vicinity. And this was even though the Honduran government, under international law, was obligated to consult indigenous communities before signing off on the new projects that would, by definition, affect their lands. The dam would do environmental harm to the water and food and impede Lenca access to their land and thus livelihoods, to be sure. But far more vitally, the construction and continued existence of the dams would violate the Gualcarque, their sacred river. At the very least, they argued, prior consent from local Lenca would be needed before the engineering project could be considered legitimate.

Desperate, Río Blanco community members went to COPINH for guidance, and Cáceres was more than willing to help them. Bracing herself for a long fight, Cáceres started with small, cautious steps, such as having Río Blanco members formally vote against the dam, filing complaints with government agencies, and taking community members on fact-finding or testimony trips to Tegucigalpa, the capital. After such efforts bore little fruit, Cáceres upped the ante by engaging international and regional bodies and actors. Among other actions, she and COPINH brought the case to the Inter-American Human Rights Commission and placed an objection before the project's financial backers, the International Finance Corporation (IFC), the World Bank's private sector wing. Her strategy also entailed establishing robust links with global solidarity groups, most critically in the United States and Western Europe.

Yet none of these international tactic moves seemed to convince (or pressure!) DESA to budge. Cáceres thus opted for escalation in 2013: protracted and multifaceted civic actions were engaged, including using human blockades to impede access to the construction site. Domestic opponents accused her of gratuitous rabble-rousing; Aline Flores, president of the Honduran Council for Private Business, quipped that the ignorant individuals and organizations under Cáceres's self-aggrandizing leadership were "boycotting, invading and making Honduras look bad internationally."

On July 15, things took a turn for the worse when, as part of a mission where Honduran security forces arrested protestors in Río Blanco en masse, a soldier fatally shot beloved COPINH leader Tomás García, while several others were wounded. (The soldier did face a court trial but was acquitted after arguing that he had fired in self-defense.)

While Cáceres was likely not fully aware of her country's deterioration, the toxic cocktail of corruption, global corporate bottom lines, landholding estates, paramilitary thuggery, and judicial impunity led to, between 2010 to 2014, over one hundred human rights and environmental actors killed. Honduras now had the dubious distinction, on a per capita basis, of being the world's most dangerous country for environmental activists.

By the end of 2013, at least three of Cáceres's colleagues had been murdered in retaliation for their anti-Agua Zarca organizing. Cáceres's four children were directly threatened, leading three to flee the country, and Berta herself was forced into internal exile, albeit briefly. Complicating matters, DESA hatched what morphed into a criminal case against her linked to her alleged possession of an unlicensed firearm (she countered that it had been planted by government agents at a roadblock) and subsequently accused her of "engendering the security of the Honduran state." The charges were eventually dropped in early 2014, but the stress on the Honduran was undeniable, not least because DESA was also hiring armed thugs to follow her every step. "They follow me. They threaten to kill me, to kidnap me; they threaten my family. That is what we face," she later described.

The anti-dam movement scored a major victory in late 2013 when Sinohydro and the IFC withdrew from the project, appearing to blame its erstwhile partner DESA for its mendacity and its viciousness toward the protestors. Not surprisingly, construction came to a halt, even if DESA remained committed to finishing the job. There were also still pro-dam actors who continued to bash Cáceres and her movement; indeed, there were Lenca, in Río Bravo and elsewhere, who supported the dam for a variety of reasons.

THE POPE AND A PRIZE

Her fight against the dam brought Cáceres international fame, especially within the global environmental movement. In October 2014, acting as a delegate to the World Meeting of Popular Movements, she was received by Pope Francis (see Chapter 32, "Becoming Pope Francis: Jorge Mario Bergoglio and the Dirty War"). The following year, Cáceres was awarded the 2015 Goldman Environmental Prize for spearheading the anti-Agua Zarca struggle and casting light on how the dam would alter the Lenca realm and spirit. In April, she went to the United States to, among other tasks, formally accept her prize at a ceremony in San Francisco. "We must shake our conscience free of the rapacious capitalism, racism, and patriarchy that will only assure our own self-destruction," she said in her trademark defiance. "Our Mother Earth—militarized, fenced-in, poisoned, a place where basic rights are systematically violated—demands that we take action." Her speech also seemed to foreshadow her killing. "Giving our lives in various ways for the protection of rivers is giving our lives for the well-being of humanity and of this planet."

DEATH COMES FOR THE GUARDIAN

Down but not out, DESA resumed work on the dams in late 2015, although the project had been moved to the opposite side of Gualcarque, which allowed the construction company to contend that Río Blanco was no longer affected. (Cáceres and COPINH saw the relocation as an insufficient mitigation measure.) The resumption of the project also likely explains why the number of death threats aimed at Cáceres started soaring again. The ICHR brought Cáceres's dire situation to the attention of Honduran president Juan Orlando Hernández, pleading with him to take sufficient "precautionary measures" to ensure her safety.

Undaunted, Cáceres led a COPINH protest near La Esperanza that turned into a melee with police, soldiers, and DESA operatives. She used an emotional press conference to denounce the deaths of four fellow marchers. Just days later, in the early morning of March 3, 2016, a hit squad broke in through the backdoor of Cáceres's safe house and shot her repeatedly before fleeing. Despite the high-level pleas from regional rights bodies, the valiant social and environmental activist in Honduras had no personal protection from the security forces at the time of her murder. Knowing full well that she was likely to be murdered, Cáceres even told daughter Laura to start imagining a life with her mother gone.

The cold-blooded assassination sparked domestic and international outrage and tributes for this martyr who had defended Lenca and Mother Earth despite all risks. Three thousand mourners appeared at her funeral in La

A group of indigenous people hold a protest outside a court, during a hearing of Roberto David Castillo, eventually convicted on charges of helping plan the murder of Berta Cáceres, in Tegucigalpa, Honduras, on March 3, 2018. Placard reads: "Berta will come back again and she will be millions." *(Jorge Cabrera/Alamy)*

Esperanza. President Hernández promised swift justice for this "crime against Honduras, a blow for the people of Honduras," but his government was criticized by rock-tossing students in Tegucigalpa for failing to protect her in the first place. Here is how author and activist Dana Frank described Cáceres's postmortem transformation. "Berta wasn't just about Honduras any more [sic]. In her afterlife, she became a potent global symbol of people's struggles from below and repression from above. Her image moved, like Che Guevara's, all over the world." Within days, fifty international organizations had signed a joint letter urging Honduran officials to locate and punish the killers. By early 2017, at least seventy members of the US Congress had co-sponsored the Berta Cáceres Human Rights in Honduras Act.

In what surprised many observers inside and outside the country, a certain level of justice was meted out in the months and years following the gruesome murder. Within a year, eight individuals—several with direct links to security forces and/or DESA—had been arrested, including one in Mexico. Before 2019, the Honduran courts had sentenced seven defendants, handing down prison terms that ranged between thirty and fifty years.

The country's justice system also determined that DESA executives were the intellectual masterminds behind the killing. To this end, Honduran authorities apprehended former military intelligence officer and DESA president Roberto Castillo Mejía as he was attempting to flee the country at a provincial city airport. After a lengthy trial, a court convicted him of plotting the Cáceres operation. As of this writing, no one from the DESA board of directors had been charged with crimes.

In the months and years following Cáceres's murder, foreign corporations such as Voith and Siemens announced that they would no longer cooperate with the dam project. Banks and other sources of financing also followed suit. The woman known as "the guardian of the rivers" had triumphed.

Bibliography

Listed chapter-by-chapter for readers' piece of mind and forest preservation, the following sources contain sufficient material to reconstruct our stories for this book. All quotations can be found in at least one of the sources listed. Additional source material related to this book can be found at: russellcrandall.com.

INTRODUCTION

Belém Lopez, Dawisson. "Latin America: A Desert of New Ideas." *Al Jaezeera*, April 6, 2017.
Kozloff, Max. "Diego Rivera's Dream of a Sunday Afternoon in the Alameda Park." *MoMA* no. 14 (Summer 1993): 8–11.
Krauze, Enrique. *Redeemers: Power and Ideas in Latin America*. New York: Harper, 2012.

CHAPTER 1: AMERIGO VESPUCCI

Anderson, Jon Lee. "Why Spain Was Long in Denial about Franco—and Still Stands by Columbus." *New Yorker*, November 2, 2021.
Arciniegas, Germán. *Amerigo and the New World: The Life and Times of Amerigo Vespucci*. Translated from the Spanish by Harriet de Onís. New York: Knopf, 1955.
Carlyle, Thomas. *On Heroes, Hero-Worship, and the Heroic in History*. Edited by David R. Sorensen and Brent E. Kisner. New Haven, CT: Yale University Press, 2013.
Fernández-Armesto, Felipe. *Amerigo: The Man Who Gave His Name to America*. New York: Random House, 2007.
Formisano, Luciano. *Letters from a New World: Amerigo Vespucci's Discovery of America*. Translated from the Italian by David Jacobson. New York: Marsilio, 1992.
Hessler, John. *The Naming of America: Martin Waldseemüller's 1507 Map and the Cosmographiae Introductio*. Washington, DC: Library of Congress, 2008.
"Is There Still Value in 'Great Man' of History?" *History Today* 69, no. 9 (September 2019).
Lester, Toby. *The Fourth Part of the World: The Race to the Ends of the Earth, and the Epic Story of the Map That Gave America Its Name*. New York: Free Press, 2009.
———. "Putting America on the Map." *Smithsonian Magazine* 40, no. 9 (December 2009).
"Library of Congress Completes Purchase of Waldseemüller Map." *News from the Library of Congress*, June 18, 2003, https://www.loc.gov/item/prn-03-110/.

Markham, Clements R. *The Letters of Amerigo Vespucci and Other Documents Illustrative of His Career.* London: Hakluyt Society, 1894.
Maxwell, Kenneth A. "¡Adiós Columbus!" *New York Review of Books*, January 28, 1993.
Ober, Frederick A. *Amerigo Vespucci.* New York: Harper & Brothers, 1907.

CHAPTER 2: BARTOLOMÉ DE LAS CASAS

Alcina Franch, José. *Bartolomé de las Casas.* Madrid: Historia 16, 1986.
Burkholder, Mark, and Lyman L. Johnson. *Colonial Latin America.* 10th ed. Oxford, UK: Oxford University Press, 2018.
Cárdenas Bunsen, José Alejandro. *Escritura y Derecho Canónico en la obra de fray Bartolomé de las Casas.* Madrid: Iberoamericana, 2011.
Clayton, Lawrence A. *Bartolomé de Las Casas: A Biography.* Cambridge, UK: Cambridge University Press, 2012.
De las Casas, Bartolomé. *The Devastation of the Indies: A Brief Account.* Translated by Herma Briffault. Baltimore, MD: Johns Hopkins University Press, 1992.
———. *Historia de las Indias selección.* Barcelona: Linkgua-digital, 2016.
———. *In Defense of the Indians.* Translated by Stafford Poole. DeKalb, IL: Northern Illinois University Press, 1992.
Fernández-Santamaria, José A. "Juan Ginés De Sepúlveda on the Nature of the American Indians." *The Americas* 31, no. 4 (1975): 434–51.
Gibson, Charles, ed. *The Black Legend: Anti-Spanish Attitudes in the Old World and the New.* New York: Random House, 1971.
Hanke, Lewis. *The Spanish Struggle for Justice in the Conquest of America.* 2nd ed. Dallas, TX: Southern Methodist University, 2015.
Pagden, Anthony. *The Fall of Natural Man: The American Indian and the Origins of Comparative Ethnology.* Cambridge, UK: Cambridge University Press, 1986.
Restall, Matthew, and Kris Lane. *Latin America in Colonial Times.* Cambridge, UK: Cambridge University Press, 2012.
Ricard, Robert. *The Spiritual Conquest of Mexico: An Essay on the Apostolate and the Evangelizing Methods of the Mendicant Orders in New Spain, 1523–1572.* Berkeley, CA: University of California Press, 1974.
Starn, Orin, et al. *The Peru Reader.* 2nd ed. Durham, NC: Duke University Press, 2005.
Tierney, Brian. *The Idea of Natural Rights: Studies on Natural Rights, Natural Law, and Church Law, 1150–1625.* Grand Rapids, MI: William B. Eerdmans Publishing Company, 1997.

CHAPTER 3: SOR JUANA INÉS DE LA CRUZ

A Sor Juana Anthology. Translation by Alan S. Trueblood; foreword by Octavio Paz. Cambridge, MA: Harvard University Press, 1988.
"Biography of Juana Inés de la Cruz, Mexican poet." *Salient Women.*
Bryant, William C. *A Woman of Genius: The Intellectual Autobiography of Sor Juana Inés de La Cruz.* Translated by Margaret Sayers Peden. Salisbury, CT: Lime Rock Press, 1982.
De la Cruz, Sor Juana Inés. *Sor Juana's Love Poems.* Madison, WI: University of Wisconsin Press, 2003.
Glantz, Margo. *Sor Juana Inés de la Cruz: hagiografía o autobiografía?* Mexico City: Grijalbo, 1995.

Harvey, Tamara. *Figuring Modesty in Feminist Discourse across the Americas, 1633–1700.* London: Routledge, 2009.
Kirk, Stephanie, "The Gendering of Knowledge in New Spain." *The Routledge Research Companion to the Works of Sor Juana Inés de la Cruz.* New York: Routledge, 2017.
Merrim, Stephanie. *Early Modern Women's Writing and Sor Juana Inés de La Cruz.* Nashville, TN: Vanderbilt University Press, 1999.
Paz, Octavio. *Sor Juana Inés de la Cruz o las trampas de la fe.* Mexico: Fondo de Cultura Económica, 1995.
———. "The Passionate Rebellion of Sor Juana Inés de la Cruz: Octavio Paz on Latin America's Greatest Baroque Poet." July 6, 1997.
Poot Herrera, Sara, ed. *Y diversa de mí misma entre vuestras plumas ando.* Mexico City: El Colegio de México, 1993.
Schmidhuber, Guillermo, ed. *The Three Secular Plays of Sor Juana Inés de La Cruz.* Translated by Shelby B. Thacker. Lexington, KY: University Press of Kentucky, 2000.
Stavans, Ilan. "Introduction." *Sor Juana Inés de la Cruz: Poems, Protests, and a Dream.* New York: Penguin, 1997.
Thomas, George Antony. *The Politics and Poetics of Sor Juana Ines de La Cruz.* London: Routledge, 2016.

CHAPTER 4: TÚPAC AMARU II AND THE GREAT ANDEAN REBELLION

Burkholder, Mark A., and Johnson, Lyman L. *Colonial Latin America.* 4th ed. Oxford: Oxford University Press, 2001.
Campbell, Leon. "Women and the Great Rebellion in Peru, 1780–1783." *The Americas* 42, no. 2 (1984): 163–96.
Elliott, J. H. "The Huge, Ignored Uprising in the Andes." *New York Review of Books*, October 23, 2014.
Flores Galindo, Alberto. *Buscando un Inca.* Lima: Instituto de Apoyo Agrario, 1987.
Garrett, David. *Shadows of Empire: The Indian Nobility of Cusco, 1750–1825.* Cambridge: Cambridge University Press, 2005.
Lewin, Boleslao. *La rebellion de Túpac Amaru y los orígenes de la independencia de hispanoamérica.* Buenos Aires: Sociedad Editora Latino Americana, 1967.
Restall, Matthew, and Kris Lane. *Latin America in Colonial Times.* Cambridge: Cambridge University Press, 2011.
Serulnikov, Sergio. *Rebellion in the Andes: The Age of Túpac Amaru.* Durham, NC: Duke University Press, 2013.
———. *Subverting Colonial Authority: Challenges to Colonial Rule in Eighteenth-Century Southern Andes.* Durham, NC: Duke University Press, 2003.
Sinclair, Thomas. *We Alone Will Rule: Andean Politics in the Age of Insurgency.* Madison, WI: University of Wisconsin Press, 2002.
Starn, Orin, et al., eds. *Peru Reader: History, Culture, Politics.* 2nd ed. Durham, NC: Duke University Press, 2005.
Stavig, Ward. *The World of Túpac Amaru: Conflict, Community, and Identity in Colonial Peru.* Lincoln, NE: University of Nebraska Press, 1999.
Stavig, Ward, and Ella Schmidt. *The Túpac Amaru and Catarista Rebellions: An Anthology of Sources.* Indianapolis, IN: Hackett, 2008.

Thomson, Sinclair. *We Alone Will Rule: Native Andean Politics in the Ange of Insurgency*. Madison, WI: University of Wisconsin Press, 2003.
Valcárcel, Daniel. *Túpac Amaru: El Revolucionario*. Lima: Moncloa Campodónico, 1970.
Walker, Charles F. *The Túpac Amaru Rebellion*. Cambridge, MA: Harvard University Press 2014.

CHAPTER 5: TOUSSAINT LOUVERTURE

Baptist, Edward E. "The Bittersweet Victory at Saint-Domingue." *Slate*, August 6, 2015.
Bell, David A. "The Contagious Revolution." *New York Review of Books*, December 19, 2019.
———. *Men on Horseback: The Power of Charisma in the Age of Revolution*. New York: Farrar, Straus, and Giroux, 2020.
Crandall, Russell. "The Black Bonaparte." *Survival* 59, no. 4 (September 2018): 183–90.
Forsdick, Charles, and Christian Høgsbjerg. "Black Jacobin Ascending: 1793-98." In *Toussaint Louverture: A Black Jacobin in the Age of Revolutions*, 54–80. London: Pluto Press, 2017.
French, Howard W. "Slavery, Empire, Memory." *New York Review of Books*, April 7, 2022.
Furstenberg, Francois. *In the Name of the Father: Washington's Legacy, Slavery, and the Making of a Nation*. New York: Penguin Books, 2007.
Geggus, David. "The Changing Faces of Toussaint Louverture: Literary and Pictorial Depictions." The John Carter Brown Library.
———. "The French Slave Trade: An Overview." *The William and Mary Quarterly* 58, no. 1 (2001): 119–38.
Girard, Philippe. "Black Talleyrand: Toussaint Louverture's Diplomacy, 1798–1802." *The William and Mary Quarterly* 66, no. 1 (2009): 87–124.
———. *Toussaint Louverture: A Revolutionary Life*. New York: Basic Books, 2016.
Gonzalez, Johnhenry. *Maroon Nation: A History of Revolutionary Haiti*. New Haven, CT: Yale University Press, 2019
Hazareesingh, Sudhir. *Black Spartacus: The Epic Life of Toussaint Louverture*. London: Allen Lane, 2020.
"Hispaniola Smallpox Epidemic of 1507." *Encyclopedia of Plague and Pestilence: From Ancient Times to the Present*. New York: Facts of File, 2008.
James, C. L. R. *The Black Jacobins: Toussaint L'Ouverture and the San Domingo Revolution*. New York: Vintage, 1989.
Lepore, Jill. "The Age of Content." *New Yorker*, March 29, 2021.
———. *These Truths: A History of the United States*. New York: Norton, 2019.
Mount, Ferdinand. "Democracy's Demagogues." *New York Review of Books*, January 14, 2021.
Peterson, Robert K. D. "Insects, Disease, and Military History: The Napoleonic Campaigns and Historical Perception." *American Entomologist* 41 (1995): 147–60.
Schuller, Mark. "Haiti's 200-Year Ménage-à-Trois: Globalization, the State, and Civil Society." *Caribbean Studies* 35, no. 1 (2007): 141–79.
Scott, Julius S. *The Common Wind: Afro-American Currents in the Age of the Haitian Revolution*. New York: Verso, 2019.

CHAPTER 6: SIMÓN BOLÍVAR

Arana, Marie. *Bolívar: American Liberator*. New York: Simon & Schuster, 2014.
Bell, David A. *Men on Horseback: The Power of Charisma in the Age of Revolution*. New York: Farrar, Straus, and Giroux, 2020.
Davis, Wade. *Magdalena: River of Dreams*. New York: Penguin, 2020.
Elliott, J. H. "The First Bolivarian Revolution." *New York Review of Books*, July 13, 2006.
Farah, Douglas. "Secret of Bolivar's Sword." *Washington Post*, February 1, 1991.
"The Flickering Light of Latin American Liberalism." *The Economist*, April 18, 2020.
Helg, Aline. "Simón Bolívar and the Spectre of 'Pardocracia': José Padilla in the Post-Independence Cartagena." *Journal of Latin American Studies* 35, no. 3 (August 2003): 447–71.
Kinsbruner, Jay. *Independence in Latin America: Civil Wars, Revolutions, and Underdevelopment*. 2nd ed. Albuquerque: University of New Mexico Press, 2000.
Krauze, Enrique. "Bolívar: What Price Glory?" *New York Review of Books*, June 6, 2013.
Lewis, William F. "Simón Bolívar and Xavier Mina: A Rendezvous in Haiti." *Journal of Inter-American Studies* 11, no. 1 (July 1969): 458–65.
Lynch, John. *Simón Bolívar: A Life*. New Haven, CT: Yale University Press, 2006.
May, Rachel, et al. *Caribbean Revolutions: Cold War Armed Movements*. New York: Cambridge University Press, 2018.
Triviño Anzola, Consuelo. "Manuela Sáenz: la libertadora del Libertador." *Centro Virtual Cervantes*.
Vargas Llosa, Álvaro. "Democracy's Caudillo." *New Republic*, June 19, 2006.
"Venezuela's Chavez Exhumes Hero Simon Bolivar's Bones." *BBC*, July 17, 2010.

CHAPTER 7: ANTONIO LÓPEZ DE SANTA ANNA

Clary, David A. *Eagles and Empire: The United States, Mexico, and a Struggle for a Continent*. New York: Bantam, 2009.
Fowler, Will. *Santa Anna of Mexico*. Lincoln, NE: University of Nebraska Press, 2007.
González Pedrero, Enrique. *País de un solo hombre: el México de Santa Anna*. Mexico City: Fondo de Cultura Económica, 2013.
López de Santa Anna, Antonio. *The Eagle: The Autobiography of Santa Anna*. Edited by Ann F. Crawford. Austin, TX: Pemberton Press, 1967.

CHAPTER 8: BENITO JUÁREZ

Bazant, Jan, ed. *Alienation of Church Wealth in Mexico: Social and Economic Aspects of the Liberal Revolution, 1856–1875*. UK: Cambridge University Press, 1971.
Benjamin, Thomas. "The Life, Myth, and Commemoration of Benito Juárez." *Latin American History*, June 25, 2018.
Halperín Donghi, Tulio. *The Contemporary History of Latin America*. Durham, NC: Duke University Press, 1993.
Hamnett, Brian R. "Benito Juárez, Early Liberalism, and the Regional Politics of Oaxaca, 1828–1853." *Bulletin of Latin American Research* 10, no. 1 (1991): 3–21.
———. "Liberalism Divided: Regional Politics and the National Project during the Mexican Restored Republic, 1867–1876." *The Hispanic American Historical Review* 76, no. 4 (1996): 659–89.

Knapp, Frank A. "Parliamentary Government and the Mexican Constitution of 1857: A Forgotten Phase of Mexican Political History." *The Hispanic American Historical Review* 33, no. 1 (1953): 65-87.
Krauze, Enrique. *Mexico: Biography of Power*. New York: Harper, 1998.
Mares, José Fuentes. *Juárez: El Imperio y La República*. Barcelona: Grijalbo, 1982.
———. *Juárez y la República*. Mexico: Editorial Jus, 2003.
Meyer, Michael C., et al. *The Course of Mexican History*. 10th ed. New York: Oxford University Press, 2013.
Scholes, Walter V. *Mexican Politics during the Juárez Regime, 1855-1877*. Columbia, MO: University of Missouri Press, 1957.
Thomson, P. C. "Popular Aspects of Liberalism in Mexico, 1848-1888." *Bulletin of Latin American Research* 10, no. 3 (1991): 265-92.
Weeks, Charles A. "Use of a Juárez Myth in Mexican Politics." *Il Politico* 39, no. 2 (1974): 210-33.

CHAPTER 9: JUAN MANUEL DE ROSAS AND DOMINGO SARMIENTO

Ardao, Arturo. "Assimilation and Transformation of Positivism in Latin America." *Journal of the History of Ideas* 24, no. 4 (1963): 515-22.
Crowley, Frances G. *Domingo Faustino Sarmiento*. New York: Twayne, 1972.
Criscenti, Joseph T., ed. *Sarmiento and His Argentina*. Boulder, CO: Lynne Rienner, 1993.
"The Flickering Light of Latin American Liberalism." *The Economist*, April 18, 2020.
Franco, Jean. "Coping with Taliban." *New York Times*, May 22, 1988.
Genova, Thomas. "Beyond Civilization and Barbarism: Culture and Politics in Postrevolutionary Argentina." *Hispanic Review* 83, no. 4 (2015).
Goñi, Uki. "The Hidden History of Black Argentina." *New York Review of Books*, February 8, 2021.
Halperín Donghi, Tulio, ed. *Sarmiento, Author of a Nation*. Berkeley, CA: University of California Press, 1994.
Katra, William H. *The Argentine Generation of 1837: Echeverría, Alberdi, Sarmiento, Mitre*. Madison, NJ: Fairleigh Dickinson University Press, 1996.
Lynch, John. *Argentine Caudillo: Juan Manuel de Rosas*. Lanham, MD: Scholarly Resources Books, 2006.
———. "Argentine Dictator: Juan Manuel de Rosas, 1829-1852 Reviewed by Tulio Halpern Donghi." *Journal of Latin American Studies* 14, no. 1 (1982).
Massot, Vicente Gonzalo. *Matar Y Morir: La Violencia Política En La Argentina (1806-1980)*. Buenos Aires: Emecé Editores, 2003.
Nouzeilles, Gabriela, and Graciela R. Montaldo, eds. *The Argentina Reader: History, Culture, and Society*. Durham, NC: Duke University Press, 2002.
O'Donnell, Pacho. *Juan Manuel de Rosas: el maldito de la historia oficial*. Buenos Aires: Grupo Editorial Norma, 2009.
Patton, Elda Clayton. *Sarmiento in the United States* Evansville, IN: University of Evansville Press, 1976.
Rock, David. *Argentina, 1516-1987: From Spanish Colonization to the Falklands War*. Berkeley, CA: University of California Press, 1987.

Sarmiento, Domingo Faustino. *Facundo: Civilization and Barbarism.* Berkeley, CA: University of California Press, 2004.

———. *Obras de Domingo Faustino Sarmiento.* Paris: Ediciones la Biblioteca Digital, 2012.

Solberg, Carl E. "Argentine Dictator: Juan Manuel de Rosas, 1829-1852." *The American Historical Review* 87, no 4 (1982).

Varela, Fernando. "Thomas Jefferson, Domingo Sarmiento, and the Baroque Wild Man." *Romance Notes* 59, no. 2 (2019): 383-93.

Yamandú Acosta. "'Ariel' de Rodó: un comienzo de la filosofía latinoamericana." *Confluencia* 18, no. 2 (2003).

CHAPTER 10: DOM PEDRO II

Adams, Jerome R. *Latin American Heroes: Liberators and Patriots from 1500 to the Present.* New York: Ballantine Books, 1991.

Barman, Roderick J. *Citizen Emperor: Pedro II and the Making of Brazil, 1825-91.* Stanford, CA: Stanford University Press, 1999.

Bethell, Leslie. *Brazil: Essays on History and Politics.* London: University of London Press, 2018.

Bieber, Judy. "Citizen Emperor: Pedro II and the Making of Brazil, 1825-91, by Roderick J. Barman." *Canadian Journal of History* 36, no. 3 (2001): 609-10.

Conrad, Robert, ed. *Children of God's Fire: A Documentary History of Black Slavery in Brazil.* University Park, PA: Pennsylvania State University Press, 1984.

Cribelli, Teresa. "A Modern Monarch: Dom Pedro II's Visit to the United States in 1876." *Journal of the Historical Society* 9, no. 2 (June 2009): 223-54.

Diario do Imperador D. Pedro II: 1840-91. Esboço Biográfico Lilia Moritz Schwarcz. Museu Imperial 1999.

Gonçalves, João Felipe. "Citizen Emperor: Pedro II and the Making of Brazil, 1825-91. By Roderick J. Barman." Stanford, CA: Stanford University Press, 2000. *The Americas* 58, no. 2 (2001): 313-15.

Grinberg, Keila. "The Emperor and the Abolitionist: A Brazilian Royal Visits the U.S." *Americas Quarterly*, January 13, 2020.

Harvey, Robert. *Liberators: Latin America's Struggle for Independence* Woodstock, NY: Overlook Press, 2000.

Levine, Robert M. *The History of Brazil.* New York: Palgrave Macmillan, 2003.

Macaulay, Neill. "Roderick Barman. Citizen Emperor: Pedro II and the Making of Brazil, 1825-91. Stanford, CA: Stanford University Press. 1999." *The American Historical Review.* Stanford, CA: Oxford University Press, 2002.

Maxwell, Kenneth. "Citizen Emperor: Pedro II and the Making of Brazil, 1825-1891." *Foreign Affairs.* July/August 2000.

Roberts, Phil. "'All Americans Are Hero-Worshippers': American Observations on the First U.S. Visit by a Reigning Monarch, 1876." *The Journal of the Gilded Age and Progressive Era* 7, no. 4 (October 2008): 453-77.

Viotti da Costa, Emilia. *The Brazilian Empire: Myths and Histories.* Chapel Hill, NC: University of North Carolina Press, 1985.

Williams, Mary Wilhemine. *Dom Pedro the Magnanimous: Second Emperor of Brazil.* New York: Octagon Books, 1966.

CHAPTER 11: JOSÉ MARTÍ

Fountain, Anne. *José Martí, the United States, and Race*. Gainesville, FL: University Press of Florida, 2014.
Guadarrama González, Pablo. *José Martí y el humanismo en América Latina*. Bogotá: Convenio Andrés Bello, 2003.
"José Martí." *The Bronx Museum of the Arts*.
Kirk, John M. "Jose Marti and the United States: A Further Interpretation." *Journal of Latin American Studies* 9, no. 2 (1977): 275–90.
———. *José Martí, Mentor of the Cuban Nation*. Tampa, FL: University Presses of Florida, 1983.
Martí y Pérez, José. *Escenas latinoamericanas*. Barcelona: Linkgua, 2013.
———. *Nuestra América*. Havana: Rambla y Bouza, 1910.
Ripoll, Carlos. "Jose Marti: Inside the Monster and the Marxist Interpretation of Cuban History." *World Affairs* 140, no. 3 (Winter 1977): 217–30.
Rodríguez-Luis, Julio. *Re-Reading José Martí (1853–1895): One Hundred Years Later*. Albany, NY: State University of New York Press, 1999.
Rotker, Susana. *The American Chronicles of José Martí: Journalism and Modernity in Spanish America*. Hanover, NH: University Press of New England, 2000.
Shnookal, Deborah, and Mirta Muñiz, eds. *José Martí Reader: Writings on the Americas*. 2nd ed. Melbourne: Ocean Press, 2007.
Turton, Peter. *José Martí: Architect of Cuba's Freedom*. London: Zed Books, 1986.

CHAPTER 12: JOSÉ ENRIQUE RODÓ

"Liberalism in Latin America." *Stanford Encyclopedia of Philosophy*.
Miller, Nicola. *In the Shadow of the State: Intellectuals and the Quest for National Identity in Twentieth-Century Spanish America*. London: Verso, 1999.
Posada-Carbó, Eduardo, and Iván Jaksić. "Shipwrecks and Survivals: Liberalism in Nineteenth-Century Latin America." *Intellectual History Review* 23, no. 4 (2013): 479–98.
Real de Azúa, Carlos. *Medio siglo de Ariel. Su significación y transcendencia literariofilosófica*. Montevideo: Academia Nacional de Letras, 2001.
Rodó, José Enrique. *Ariel*. Translated by Margaret Sayers Peden. Austin, TX: University of Texas Press, 1988.
———. *Obras Completas*. Madrid: Aguilar, 1967.
Salles, Arleen, and Elizabeth Millán-Zaibert. *The Role of History in Latin American Philosophy: Contemporary Perspectives*. Albany, NY: State University of New York Press, 2006.
Schutte, Ofelia. *Cultural Identity and Social Liberation in Latin American Thought*. Albany, NY: State University of New York Press, 1993.

CHAPTER 13: JOSÉ VASCONCELOS

Encinas, Rosario. "José Vasconcelos." *Prospects* 34, no. 3–4 (2002).
Hart, John M. *Revolutionary Mexico: The Coming and Process of the Mexican Revolution*. Berkeley, CA: University of California Press, 1987.
Phillips, R. B., ed. *José Vasconcelos and the Mexican Revolution of 1910*. Stanford, CA: Stanford University, 1953.

Robles, M., ed. *Entre el poder y las letras: Vasconcelos en sus memorias*. Mexico City: Fondo de Cultura Económica, 1989.
Sarabia Viejo, María Justina. *José Vasconcelos*. Madrid: Instituto de Cooperación Iberoamericana, 1989.
Stavans, Ilan. *José Vasconcelos the Prophet of Race*. New Brunswick, NJ: Rutgers University Press, 2011.
Vasconcelos, José. *Antología de textos sobre educación*. Mexico City: Fondo de Cultura Económica, 1981.
———. *A Mexican Ulysses: An Autobiography*. Translated by W. Rex Crawford. Bloomington, IN: Indiana University Press, 1963.
———. *Obras completas*. 4 vols. Mexico City: Libreros Mexicanos Unidos, 1957–61.

CHAPTER 14: DIEGO RIVERA AND FRIDA KAHLO

Cardona Peña, Alfredo. *Conversations with Diego Rivera: The Monster in His Labyrinth*. Translated by Alvaro Cardona-Hine. New York: New Village Press, 2018.
Dickerman, Leah, et al. *Diego Rivera: Murals for the Museum of Modern Art*. Museum of Modern Art, 2011.
Espinoza, Javier. "Frida Kahlo's Last Secret Finally Revealed." *Guardian*, August 11, 2007.
———. "Secret Letters Unravel Kahlo Legend." *Guardian*, December 11, 2007.
Fine Collins, Amy. "Diary of a Mad Artist." *Vanity Fair*, September 1995.
Folgarait, Leonard. *Mural Painting and Social Revolution in Mexico, 1920–1940: Art of the New Order*. Cambridge, UK: Cambridge University Press, 1998.
———. "Revolution as Ritual: Diego Rivera's National Palace Mural." *Oxford Art Journal*, 14, no. 1 (1991): 18–33.
Herrera, Hayden. *Frida*. New York: Harper, 2002.
Kahlo, Frida. *Diary*. New York: Henry N. Abrams, 1998.
Kettenmann, Andrea. *Frida Kahlo, 1907–1954: Pain and Passion*. Germany: Taschen, 1999.
Keyes, Allison. "Destroyed by Rockefellers, Mural Trespassed on Political Vision." *NPR*, March 9, 2014.
Kimmelman, Michael. "Sleeping with the Enemy." *New York Times*, December 20, 1998.
Lee, Anthony W. *Painting on the Left: Diego Rivera, Radical Politics, and San Francisco's Public Murals*. Berkeley, CA: University of California Press, 1999.
Marnham, Patrick. *Dreaming with His Eyes Open: A Life of Diego Rivera*. New York: Knopf, 1998.
Monsiváis, Carlos. *Frida Kahlo: una vida, una obra*. Mexico City: Consejo Nacional para la Cultura y las Artes, 1992.
———. *Frida Kahlo: un homenaje*. Mexico City: Artes de México, 2004.
Sánchez, Carlos Alberto, and Robert Eli Sanchez Jr. "The Philosophy of Mexicanness." *Aeon*.
Souter, Gerry. *Diego Rivera*. New York: Parkstone Press International, 2016.
———. *Frida Kahlo and Diego Rivera*. New York: Parkstone Press, 2007.
———. *Frida Kahlo: Beneath the Mirror*. New York: Parkstone International, 2015.
Rivera Marín, Guadalupe. *Diego Rivera the Red*. Translated by Dick Gerdes. Houston, TX: Arte Público Press, 2004.
Tuer, Dot, and Elliot King, eds. *Frida and Diego: Passion, Politics, and Painting*. Ontario: Art Gallery of Ontario, 2013.

CHAPTER 15: BERTA LUTZ

Besse, Susan K. *Restructuring Patriarchy: The Modernization of Gender Inequality in Brazil, 1914–1940*. Chapel Hill, NC: University of North Carolina Press, 1996.
Hahner, June E. *Emancipating the Female Sex: The Struggle for Women's Rights in Brazil, 1850–1940*. Durham, NC: Duke University Press, 1990.
———. "Feminism, Women's Rights, and The Suffrage Movement in Brazil, 1850–1930." *Latin American Research Review* 15, no. 1 (1980): 65–111.
Kennedy, J. P. "Bertha Lutz, 1894–1976." *Copeia* 1 (1977): 208–209.
Miller, Francesca. *Latin American Women and the Search for Social Justice*. Hanover, NH: University Press of New England, 1991.
Lôbo, Yolanda Lima. *Bertha Lutz*. Brazil: Editora Massangana, 2010.
Rachum, Ilan. "Feminism, Woman Suffrage, and National Politics in Brazil: 1922–1937." *Luso-Brazilian Review* 14, no. 1 (Summer 1977): 118–34.

CHAPTER 16: AUGUSTO SANDINO VERSUS THE UNITED STATES

Blandón, Miguel Jesús. *Entre Sandino y Fonseca Amador*. Managua: Impresiones y Troqueles, 1980.
Crandall, Britta H., and Russell C. Crandall. *"Our Hemisphere"?: The United States in Latin America, from 1776 to the 21st Century*. New Haven, CT: Yale University Press, 2021.
Crandall, Russell. *America's Dirty Wars: The United States and Irregular Warfare from 1776 to the War on Terror*. Cambridge, UK: Cambridge University Press, 2014.
Dospital, Michelle, et al. *Siempre más allá: el movimiento Sandinista en Nicaragua 1927–1934* Mexico: Centro de estudios mexicanos y centroamericanos, 2014.
Hodges, Donald C. *Intellectual Foundations of the Nicaraguan Revolution*. Austin, TX: University of Texas Press, 1986.
———. "Sandino's Mexican Awakening." *Canadian Journal of Latin American and Caribbean Studies / Revue canadienne des études latino-américaines et caraïbes* 19, no. 37–38 (1994): 7–34.
Macaulay, Neill. *The Sandino Affair*. Durham, NC: Duke University Press, 1985.
McPherson, Alan L. *The Invaded: How Latin Americans and Their Allies Fought and Ended U.S. Occupations*. Oxford, UK: Oxford University Press, 2016.
Navarro-Génie, Marco. *Augusto César Sandino: Messiah of Light and Truth*. Syracuse, NY: Syracuse University Press, 2002.
Ramírez, Sergio. *El Pensamiento vivo de Sandino*. Havana: Casa de las Américas, 1980.
Schmidt, Blake. "Nourishing Family Roots to Help a Campaign Bloom." *New York Times*, February 15, 2011.
Schroeder, Michael J. "Social Memory and Tactical Doctrine: The Air War in Nicaragua during the Sandino Rebellion." *The International History Review* 29, no. 3 (September 2007): 508–49.
Selser, Gregorio. *Sandino: General de los hombres libres*. Zurich: Diogenes, 1979.
Wells, Allen. *Latin America's Democratic Crusade: The Transnational Struggle against Dictatorship, 1920s–1960s*. New Haven, CT: Yale University Press, 2023.
Wünderich, Volker. *Sandino: una biografía política*. Managua: IHNCA-UCA, 2009.

CHAPTER 17: LÁZARO CÁRDENAS

Balderrama, Francisco E., and Raymond Rodríguez. *Decade of Betrayal: Mexican Repatriation in the 1930s*. Albuquerque, NM: University of New Mexico Press, 1995.

Becker, Marjorie. *Setting the Virgin on Fire: Lázaro Cárdenas, Michoacán Peasants, and the Redemption of the Mexican Revolution*. Berkeley, CA: University of California Press, 1995.

Cala, Andrés. "The Revolution That Almost Wasn't." *Oy*, August 3, 2015.

Cárdenas, Lázaro. "Discurso con motive del VI Aniversario de la iniciación del movimiento revolucionario '26 de Julio' La Habana, Cuba, 26 de Julio de 1959." In *Mexico y Cuba: dos pueblos Unidos en la historia*, edited by Martha López Portillo et al. Mexico City: Centro de Investigación Científica Jorge L. Tamayo, 1982.

———. "Document #7: 'Speech to the Nation, 1938.'" *Brown University Library Center for Digital Scholarship*.

Dickter, Arturo Grunstein. "In the Shadow of Oil." *Mexican Studies/Estudios Mexicanos* 21, no. 1 (2005): 1–32.

Dwyer, John J. "The End of U.S. Intervention in Mexico: Franklin Roosevelt and the Expropriation of American-Owned Agricultural Property." *Presidential Studies Quarterly* 28, no. 3 (1998): 495–509.

Holden, Robert, and Eric Zolov, eds. *Latin America and the United States: A Documentary History*. 2nd ed. New York: Oxford University Press, 2011.

Keller, Renata Nicole. *Mexico's Cold War: Cuba, the United States, and the Legacy of the Mexican Revolution*. New York: Cambridge University Press, 2015.

Lorenzo Meyer, *The Mexican Revolution and the Anglo-American Powers: The End of Confrontation and the Beginning of Negotiation*. Translated by Sandra del Castillo. La Jolla, CA: University of California, San Diego, 1985.

Mateos, Abdón. *De la Guerra Civil al exilio*. Madrid: Biblioteca Nueva, 2005.

Maurer, Noel. "The Empire Struck Back: Sanctions and Compensation in the Mexican Oil Expropriation of 1938." *Journal of Economic History* 71, no. 3 (September 2011); 590–615.

Montes, Juan. "A New Oil Boom in Mexico's Aging 'Golden Belt.'" *Wall Street Journal*, November 4, 2014.

CHAPTER 18: RAFAEL TRUJILLO

Bishop, Marlon. "80 Years On, Dominicans and Haitians Revisit Painful Memories of Parsley Massacre." *NPR*, October 7, 2017.

Committee on Intelligence Activities. *Alleged Assassination Plots Involving Foreign Leaders: Interim Report of the Select Committee to Study Governmental Operations with Respect to Intelligence Activities*. The Mary Ferrell Foundation, 2007.

Crandall, Britta H., and Russell C. Crandall. *"Our Hemisphere"?: The United States in Latin America, from 1776 to the 21st Century*. New Haven, CT: Yale University Press, 2021.

Crandall, Russell. *Gunboat Democracy: U.S. Interventions in the Dominican Republic, Grenada, and Panama*. Lanham, MD: Rowman & Littlefield, 2006.

Crassweller, Robert D. *Trujillo: The Life and Times of a Caribbean Dictator*. New York: Macmillan, 1966.

Diederich, Bernard. *Trujillo: The Death of the Goat*. London: Bodley Head, 1978.
Drum, Kevin. "'But He's Our Son of a Bitch.'" *Washington Monthly*, May 16, 2006.
Fatalski, Marcin. "The United States and the Fall of the Trujillo Regime." *Journal of American Studies* 14, no. 14 (2013): 7–18.
Haggerty, Richard A., ed. *Dominican Republic: A Country Study*. Washington, DC: GPO for the Library of Congress, 1989.
Horrock, Nicholas M. "C.I.A. Is Reported to Have Helped in Trujillo Death." *New York Times*, June 13, 1975.
"'I Shot the Cruelest Dictator in the Americas.'" *BBC News*, May 28, 2011.
Montgomery, Paul L. "Plotters against Trujillo Doubt Any C.I.A. Involvement in Assassination of Dictator." *New York Times*, June 23, 1975.
Pulley, Raymond H. "The United States and the Trujillo Dictatorship, 1933–1940: The High Price of Caribbean Stability." *Caribbean Studies* 5, no. 3 (October 1965): 22–31.
Rabe, Stephen G. *Eisenhower and Latin America: The Foreign Policy of Anticommunism*. Chapel Hill, NC: University of North Carolina Press, 1988.
———. "Eisenhower and the Overthrow of Rafael Trujillo." *Journal of Conflict Studies* 6, no. 1 (January 1, 1986).
———. *The Killing Zone: The United States Wages Cold War in Latin America*. 2nd ed. New York: Oxford University Press, 2016.
Tierney, Dominic. "'Our S.O.B.s' and America's Revolutionary Dilemma Abroad." *The Atlantic*, February 1, 2011.
Wells, Allen. *Tropical Zion: General Trujillo, FDR, and the Jews of Sosúa*. Durham, NC: Duke University Press, 2009.
Young, Thomas. "40 Years Ago, Church Committee Investigated Americans Spying on Americans." *Brookings*, May 6, 2015.

CHAPTER 19: JOSÉ CARLOS MARIÁTEGUI AND VICTOR RAÚL HAYA DE LA TORRE

Alarcón, Daniel. "What Led Peru's Former President to Take His Own Life?" *New Yorker*, July 1, 2019.
Becker, Marc. *Mariátegui and Latin American Marxist Theory*. Athens, OH: Ohio University Press, 1993.
Becker, Marc, and Harry E. Vanden, eds. *José Carlos Mariátegui: An Anthology*. New York: Monthly Review Press, 2011.
Cozart, Dan. "The Rise of APRA in Peru: Victor Raúl Haya de la Torre and Inter-American Intellectual Connections, 1918–1935." *The Latin Americanist* 58, no. 1 (March 2014): 77–88.
Crabtree, John. "The Consolidation of Alan García's Government in Peru." *Third World Quarterly* 9, no. 3 (July 1987): 804–24.
Davies, Thomas M. "The Indigenismo of the Peruvian Aprista Party: A Reinterpretation." *The Hispanic American Historical Review* 51, no. 4 (1971): 626–45.
De Castro, Juan E. *Bread and Beauty: The Cultural Politics of José Carlos Mariátegui*. The Netherlands: Brill, 2020.
Dix, Robert H. "Cleavage Structures and Party Systems in Latin America." *Comparative Politics* 22, no. 1 (1989): 23–37.
García-Bryce, Iñigo. *Haya de La Torre and the Pursuit of Power in Twentieth-Century Peru and Latin America*. Chapel Hill, NC: University of North Carolina Press, 2018.

Graham, Carol. *Peru's APRA: Parties, Politics, and the Elusive Quest for Democracy.* Boulder, CO: Lynne Rienner, 1992.
Hilliker, Grant. *The Politics of Reform in Peru: The Aprista and Other Mass Parties of Latin America* Baltimore, MD: Johns Hopkins University Press, 1971.
Lomnitz, Claudio. *Nuestra América: My Family in the Vertigo of Translation.* New York: Other Press, 2021.
Kantor, Harry. *The Ideology and Program of the Peruvian Aprista Movement.* Berkeley, CA: University of California Press, 1953.
Klaiber, Jeffrey L. "The Popular Universities and the Origins of Aprismo, 1921–1924." *The Hispanic American Historical Review* 55, no. 4 (1975): 693–715.
Klarén, Peter F. *Modernization, Dislocation, and Aprismo: Origins of the Peruvian Aprista Party, 1870–1932.* Austin, TX: University of Texas Press, 2014.
Mariátegui, José Carlos. *Siete ensayos de interpretación de la realidad peruana.* Barcelona: Linkgua ediciones, 2009.
Salisbury, Richard V. "The Middle American Exile of Víctor Raúl Haya de La Torre." *The Americas* 40, no. 1 (1983): 1–15.
Starn, Orin, et al. *The Peru Reader: History, Culture, Politics.* 2nd ed. Durham, NC: Duke University Press, 2005.
Vanden, Harry. *José Carlos Mariátegui: An Anthology.* New York: Monthly Review Press, 2011.

CHAPTER 20: JUAN AND EVA PERÓN

Alexander, Robert J. *Juan Domingo Perón: A History.* Boulder, CO: Westview Press, 1979.
Ara, Pedro. *El Caso Eva Perón.* Madrid: CVS, 1974.
Bell, Lawrence. "The Jews and Peron: Communal Politics and National Identity in Peronist Argentina, 1946–1955." Electronic Thesis or Dissertation. Ohio State University, 2002.
Castagnola, G. H. *Body of Evidence: Juan Domingo Perón's Discourse during His Political Exile (1955–1972).* University of Essex: United Kingdom, 2002.
Cox, Robert. "The Second Death of Perón?" *New York Review of Books,* December 8, 1983.
Crassweller, Robert D. *Perón and the Enigmas of Argentina.* New York: Norton, 1987.
Davis, William Columbus. "Perón and Argentina." *World Affairs* 118, no. 4 (1955): 107–108.
Falcoff, Mark, and Ronald H. Dolkart, eds. *Prologue to Perón: Argentina in Depression and War, 1930–1943.* Berkeley, CA: University of California Press, 1975.
Hodges, Donald C. *Argentina 1943–1976: The National Revolution and Resistance.* Albuquerque, NM: University of New Mexico Press, 1976.
Lewis, Paul H. "Was Perón a Fascist? An Inquiry into the Nature of Fascism." *Journal of Politics* 42, no. 1 (1980): 242–56.
Nouzeilles, Gabriela, and Graciela Montaldo, eds. *The Argentina Reader: History, Culture, Politics.* Durham, NC: Duke University Press, 2002.
Page, Joseph A. *Perón: A Biography.* New York: Random House, 1983.
Perón, Juan Domingo. "What Is Peronism?" Brown University Center for Digital Scholarship.
Pigna, Felipe. *Mitos de la historia argentina.* Spain: Planeta, 2008.
Smith, Peter H. *The Social Base of Peronism.* Durham, NC: Duke University Press, 1972.
———. "Social Mobilization, Political Participation, and the Rise of Juan Peron." *Political Science Quarterly* 84, no. 1 (1969): 30–49.
Turner, Frederick C., and José Enrique Miguens, eds. *Juan Perón and the Reshaping of Argentina.* Pittsburgh, PA: University of Pittsburgh Press, 1983.

Weyland, Kurt. "Clarifying a Contested Concept: Populism in the Study of Latin American Politics." *Comparative Politics* 34, no. 1 (2001): 1–22.

CHAPTER 21: RÓMULO BETANCOURT

Alexander, Robert J. *Prophets of the Revolution: Profiles of Latin American Leaders.* New York: MacMillan, 1966.
———. *Rómulo Betancourt and the Transformation of Venezuela.* New Brunswick, NJ: Transaction Books, 1982.
———. *Venezuelan Democratic Revolution: A Profile of the Regime of Rómulo Betancourt.* New Brunswick, NJ: Rutgers University Press, 1964.
———. "Venezuela's New Regime: The Inauguration of Romulo Betancourt on January 23, 1959, Will Mark the Country's Return to Rule by a Democratically Elected Government after a Decade of Dictatorship." *The New Leader* 42 (1959): 3–5.
Betancourt, Rómulo, *Trayectoria democrática de una revolución*, Caracas, 1948.
Brown-John, C. L. "The Case of the OAS and the Dominican Republic, 1960–1962." *Caribbean Studies* 15, no. 2 (July 1975): 73–105.
Ewell, Judith. *The Indictment of a Dictator: The Extradition and Trial of Marcos Pérez Jiménez.* College Station, TX: Texas A&M University Press, 1981.
"Injured President of Venezuela Says Trujillo Helped Plotters." *New York Times*, June 26, 1960.
Langue, Frédérique, "El padre de la revolución democrática y la leyenda del tiempo." *Araucaria* 16, no. 31 (2014): 213–15.
Ledbetter, Les. "Betancourt, Ex-Venezuela Chief Dies." *New York Times*, September 29, 1981.
Lieuwen, Edwin. "Review of 'Venezuela: Política y Petróleo' by Rómulo Betancourt." *Hispanic American Historical Review* 37, no. 4 (1957): 513–15.
Martz, John. *Acción Democrática: Evolution of a Modern Political Party in Venezuela.* Princeton, NJ: Princeton University Press, 1966.
Rabe, Stephen. "The Caribbean Triangle: Betancourt, Castro, and Trujillo and U.S. Foreign Policy." *Diplomatic History* 20, no. 1 (Winter 1996): 55–78.
Ramos Pismataro, Francesca, and Ronal F. Rodríguez. *Carlos Lleras Restrepo y Rómulo Betancourt: dos transformadores democráticos* Bogotá: Editorial Universidad del Rosario, 2012.
Rivas, Ricardo Alberto. "Rómulo Betancourt, Juan D. Perón y el 17 de octubre de 1945." *Sociohistórica* no. 17–18 (2005).
Schwartzberg, Steven. "Rómulo Betancourt: From a Communist Anti-Imperialist to a Social Democrat with US Support." *Journal of Latin American Studies* 29, no. 3 (1997): 613–65.
Straka, Tomás. "When Caracas Was a Safe Have from Tyranny." *Americas Quarterly*, April 20, 2020.
Vargas Llosa, Álvaro. "Desperately Calling Romulo Betancourt." *Independent Institute*, July 29, 2009.

CHAPTER 22: JACOBO ÁRBENZ

Anderson, Jon Lee. *Che Guevara: A Revolutionary Life.* New York: Grove Press, 1997.
"Cleaning up America's Backyard." Association for Diplomatic Studies and Training: Moments in U.S. Diplomatic History (blog), June 7, 2016.
Coy Moulton, Aaron. "Amplia ayuda externa contra 'la gangrena comunista': las fuerzas regionales anticomunistas y la finalización de la operación PBFortune, Octubre de 1952." *Revista de historia de América*, 149 (2013): 45–58.

Crandall, Britta H., and Russell C. Crandall. *"Our Hemisphere"?: The United States in Latin America, 1776 to the 21st Century.* New Haven, CT: Yale University Press, 2021.
Crandall, Russell. *America's Dirty Wars.* New York: Cambridge University Press, 2014.
Cullather, Nicholas. "Operation PBSUCCESS: The United States and Guatemala 1952-1954." CIA Historical Review Program, Washington, DC, 1997.
———. *Secret History: The CIA's Classified Account of Its Operations in Guatemala, 1952-1954.* 2nd ed. Stanford, CA: Stanford University Press, 2006.
Eisenhower, Dwight D. "Eisenhower on Guatemala, 1954." In *Mandate for Change: The White House Years, 1953-1956,* 421-26. New York: Doubleday, 1963.
"Ex-President Arbenz of Guatemala Dies." *Reuters,* January 28, 1971.
"Foreign Relations of the United States, 1950, The United Nations; The Western Hemisphere; Volume II." U.S. Department of State, Office of the Historian.
García Añoveros, Jesús M. *Jacobo Arbenz.* Madrid: Historia 16, 1987.
García Ferreira, Roberto. "El caso Árbenz y las acciones encubiertas de las CIA." *Revista de historia de América* 137 (2006): 105-30.
Longley, Kyle. "Resistance and Accommodation: The United States and the Nationalism of José Miguel Figueres, 1953-1957." *Diplomatic History* 18, no. 1 (Winter 1994): 1-28.
Schlesinger, Stephen, and Steven Kinzer. *Bitter Fruit: The Story of the American Coup in Guatemala.* Cambridge, MA: Harvard University Press, 2005.

CHAPTER 23: FIDEL CASTRO

Crandall, Russell. "The Cold War and Cuban Intelligence." *Survival* 55, no. 2 (2013): 191-98.
———. "Fidel's Secret." *American Interest,* February 2015.
———. "Irreconcilable Differences." *Survival* 54, no. 3 (2012): 179-88.
———. "Rebel with a Cause." *Survival* 63, no. 2 (2021): 171-80.
Crandall, Russell, and Frederick Richardson. "Castro's Revolutionary Coming of Age." *Survival* 62, no. 2 (2020): 153-64.
LeoGrande, William M., and Peter Kornbluh. *Back Channel to Cuba: The Hidden History of Negotiations between Washington and Havana.* Chapel Hill, NC: University of North Carolina Press, 2014.
Quirk, Robert E. *Fidel Castro.* New York: Norton, 1995.
Ramonet, Ignacio, ed. *Fidel Castro: A Spoken Autobiography.* New York: Scribner, 2009.
Rasenberger, Jim. *The Brilliant Disaster: JFK, Castro, and America's Doomed Invasion of Cuba's Bay of Pigs.* New York: Scribner, 201.
Solomon, Daniel F. *Breaking Up with Cuba: The Dissolution of Friendly Relations between Washington and Havana, 1956-61.* London: McFarland, 2011.

CHAPTER 24: ERNESTO GUEVARA

Anderson, Jon Lee. *Che Guevara: A Revolutionary Life.* New York: Grove Press, 1997.
Castañeda, Jorge. *Compañero: The Life and Death of Che Guevara.* New York: Vintage, 1998.
Crandall, Britta H., and Russell C. Crandall. *"Our Hemisphere"?: The United States in Latin America, from 1776 to the 21st Century.* New Haven, CT: Yale University Press, 2021.
Crandall, Russell. *America's Dirty Wars: The United States and Guerrilla Warfare from 1776 to the War on Terror.* Cambridge, UK: Cambridge University Press, 2014.

Deutschmann, David, ed. *The Che Guevara Reader: Writings on Politics and Revolution.* New York: Ocean Press, 2005.
Drinot, Paulo, ed. *Che's Travels: The Making of a Revolutionary in 1950s Latin America.* Durham, NC: Duke University Press, 2010.
Guevara, Ernesto. *The Motorcycle Diaries.* New York: Ocean Press, 2003.
Vargas Llosa, Álvaro, "The Killing Machine." *New Republic,* July 10, 2005.
Walters, Robert S. "Soviet Economic Aid to Cub: 1959 to 1964." *International Affairs* 42, no. 1 (January 1966): 74–86.

CHAPTER 25: MANUEL MARULANDA

Crandall, Russell. *Drugs and Thugs: The History and Future of America's War on Drugs.* New Haven, CT: Yale University Press, 2020.
———. "Requiem for the FARC?" *Survival* 53, no. 4 (August–September 2011): 233–40.
Dudley, Stephen. *Walking Ghosts: Murder and Guerrilla Politics in Colombia.* New York: Routledge, 2006.
Guillermoprieto, Alma. *Looking for History: Dispatches from Latin America.* New York: Vintage, 2002.
———. "Our New War in Colombia." *New York Review of Books,* April 13, 2000.
"Manuel Marulanda: Commander of the Farc Guerrilla Army during Four Decades of Insurgency against the Colombian State." *The Independent,* May 26, 2008.
"Manuel Marulanda: Obituary." *Guardian,* May 26, 2008.
"Manuel Marulanda, Top Commander of Colombia's Largest Guerrilla Group, Is Dead." *New York Times,* May 26, 2008.
Otis, Jon. "The FARC and Colombia's Illegal Drug Trade." *Woodrow Wilson Center,* November 2014.
Reid, Michael. *Forgotten Continent: The Battle for Latin America's Soul.* New Haven, CT: Yale University Press, 2007.
"Revolutionary Armed Forces of Colombia—People's Army." *Stanford University Mapping Militant Organizations,* August 15, 2015.

CHAPTER 26: SALVADOR ALLENDE

"Allende, a Man of the Privileged Class Turned Radical Politician." *New York Times,* September 12, 1973.
Cockcroft, James D., and Jane Canning, eds. *Salvador Allende Reader: Chile's Voice of Democracy.* Melbourne: Ocean Press, 2000.
Collier, Simon, and William F. Sater. *A History of Chile, 1808–1994.* UK: Cambridge University Press, 1996.
Crandall, Britta, and Russell C. Crandall. *"Our Hemisphere"?: The United States in Latin America, from 1776 to the 21st Century.* New Haven, CT: Yale University Press, 2021.
Crandall, Russell. "A Hot Cold War." *Survival* 54, no. 6 (December 2012): 183–90.
———. *America's Dirty Wars.* New York: Cambridge University Press, 2014.
Davis, Nathaniel. *The Last Two Years of Salvador Allende.* Ithaca, NY: Cornell University Press, 1985.
Debray, Régis. *The Chilean Revolution: Conversations with Salvador Allende.* New York: Random House, 1971.

Devine, Jack. "What Really Happened in Chile." *Foreign Affairs*. Accessed September 11, 2018.
Devine, Jack, and Peter Kornbluh. "Showdown in Santiago." *Foreign Affairs* 93, no. 5 (2014): 168–74.
Falcoff, Mark. "Kissinger and Chile: The Myth That Will Not Die." *Commentary*, November 2003.
Figueroa Clark, Victor. *Salvador Allende: Revolutionary Democrat*. London: Pluto Press, 2013.
Garcés, Joan E. *El Estado y los problemas tácticos en el gobierno de Salvador Allende*. Madrid, Siglo XXI, 2018.
Gewen, Barry. *The Inevitability of Tragedy: Henry Kissinger and His World*. New York: Norton, 2020.
Gustafson, Kristian C. "CIA Machinations in Chile in 1970: Reexamining the Record." *Studies in Intelligence* 47, no. 3 (2003): 35–49.
Harmer, Tanya. *Allende's Chile and the Inter-American Cold War*. Chapel Hill, NC: University of North Carolina Press, 2014.
Haslam, Jonathan. *The Nixon Administration and the Death of Allende's Chile: A Case of Assisted Suicide*. New York: Verso, 2005.
Hersh, Seymour M. "The C.I.A. Is Linked to Strikes in Chile That Beset Allende." *New York Times*, September 20, 1974.
———. "The Price of Power." *The Atlantic*, December 1, 1982.
Hitchens, Christopher. *The Trial of Henry Kissinger*. London: Verso, 2001.
Howe, Marvine. "Chile Calls Truck Strike 'Catastrophic.'" *New York Times*, August 18, 1973.
Kornbluh, Peter. "Chile and the United States: Declassified Documents Relating to the Military Coup, September 11, 1973." National Security Archive.
———. *The Pinochet File: A Declassified Dossier on Atrocity and Accountability*. New York: New Press, 2004.
Maxwell, Kenneth. "The Other 9/11: The United States and Chile, 1973." *Foreign Affairs*, December 2003.
Navia, Patricio, and Rodrigo Osorio. "'Make the Economy Scream'? Economic, Ideological and Social Determinants of Support for Salvador Allende in Chile, 1970–3." *Journal of Latin American Studies* 49, no. 4 (2017): 771–97.
Nogee, Joseph L., and John W. Sloan. "Allende's Chile and the Soviet Union: A Policy Lesson for Latin American Nations Seeking Autonomy." *Journal of Interamerican Studies and World Affairs* 21, no. 3 (1979): 339–68.
"Papers Show I.T.T Urged U.S. to Help Oust Allende." *New York Times*, July 3, 1972.
Powell, Colin. "U.S. 'Not Proud' of 1973 Covert Action in Chile." Black Entertainment Television's Youth Town Hall, February 20, 2003.
Rogers, William. "Crisis Prevention." *Foreign Affairs*, March 2004.
Rogers, William D., and Kenneth Maxwell. "Fleeing the Chilean Coup: The Debate over U.S. Complicity." *Foreign Affairs*, January 2004.
Sigmund, Paul E. "The 'Invisible Blockade' and the Overthrow of Allende." *Foreign Affairs*, January 1974.
Winn, Peter. *Weavers of Revolution: The Yarur Workers and Chile's Road to Socialism*. New York: Oxford University Press, 1989.

CHAPTER 27: AUGUSTO PINOCHET

Anderson, Jon Lee. "Archbishop Óscar Romero Becomes a Saint, but His Death Still Haunts Salvador." *New Yorker*, October 22, 2018.

———. "The Dictator." *New Yorker*, October 11, 1998.

"Augusto Pinochet Ugarte (Obituary)." *The Economist*, December 13, 2006.

Ayuso, Silvia. "CIA Still Refuses to Reveal Everything It Knows about Pinochet Coup in Chile." *El País*, September 12, 2016.

———. "The Day That Chile's Augusto Pinochet Turned His Sights on Washington, DC." *El País*, September 22, 2016.

Bartlett, John. "Lucía Hart, Powerful Wife of Chile's Dictator, Dies at 98." *New York Times*, December 19, 2021.

Childress, Diana. *Augusto Pinochet's Chile*. 2nd ed. Minneapolis, MN: Lerner, 2012.

Coad, Malcolm. "Pinochet." *Guardian*, December 11, 2006.

Constable, Pamela, and Arturo Valenzuela. *A Nation of Enemies: Chile Under Pinochet*. New York: Norton, 1993.

Crandall, Britta H., and Russell Crandall. *"Our Hemisphere"?: The United States in Latin America, from 1776 to the 21st Century*. New Haven, CT: Yale University Press, 2021.

Dinges, John. *The Condor Years: How Pinochet and His Allies Brought Terrorism to Three Continents*. New York: New Press, 2005.

Evans, Rebecca. "Pinochet in London: Pinochet in Chile: International and Domestic Politics in Human Rights Policy." *Human Rights Quarterly* 28, no. 1 (2006): 207–44.

Kornbluh, Peter. *The Pinochet File: A Declassified Dossier on Atrocity and Accountability*. New York: New Press, 2013.

Lawner, Miguel. *Orlando Letelier: el que lo advirtió: los Chicago Boys en Chile*. Santiago, Chile: LOM Ediciones, 2011.

McMahon, Colin. "Augusto Pinochet: 1915–2006." *Chicago Tribune*, December 11, 2006.

McSherry, JP. "Tracking the Origins of a State Terror Network: Operation Condor." *Latin American Perspectives* 29, no. 1 (January 2002): 38–60.

Morley, Morris, and Chris McGillion. *Reagan and Pinochet: The Struggle over U.S. Policy toward Chile*. Cambridge: Cambridge University Press, 2015.

Miller, Mark Crispin, et al. *Assassination on Embassy Row*. Open Road Integrated Media, 2014.

Muñoz, Heraldo. *The Dictator's Shadow: Life under Augusto Pinochet*. New York: Basic Books, 2008.

Opazo, Tania. "The Boys Who Got to Remake an Economy." *Slate*, January 12, 2016.

O'Shaughnessy, Hugh. *Pinochet: The Politics of Torture*. New York: New York University Press, 2000.

"Pinochet Faces 'Death Caravan' Charges." *BBC*, March 7, 2000.

Soto Gamboa, Ángel. "Review of "Pinochet: La Bibliografía" by Gonzalo Vial. *Historia* 36 (August 2003): 450–58.

Suro, Roberto. "Pope, On Latin Trip, Attacks Pinochet Regime." *New York Times*, April 1, 1987.

Valdivia Ortiz de Zárate, Verónica, et al. *Su revolución contra nuestra revolución izquierdas y derechas en el Chile de Pinochet (1973–1981)*. Santiago: Chile: LOM Ediciones, 2006.

Verdugo, Patricia. *Chile, Pinochet, and the Caravan of Death*. Boulder, CO: Lynne Rienner, 2001.

Vergara, Eva. "Lucía Hiriart, Widow of Chilean Dictator Pinochet, Dies at 99." *Washington Post*, December 17, 2021.
Vial, Gonzalo. *Pinochet: La Biografía*. Santiago: El Mercurio, 2002.

CHAPTER 28: EDUARDO GALEANO

Clark, Andrew. 2009. "Chávez Creates Overnight Bestseller with Book Gift to Obama." *Guardian*, April 19, 2009.
Dabashi, Hamid. 2015. "A Triumphant Voice: Eduardo Galeano (1940–2015)." *Al Jazeera*, April 16, 2015.
Engler, Mark. "The World of Eduardo Galeano." *The Nation*, August 16, 2018.
Ferraro, Vincent. "Dependency Theory: An Introduction." In *The Development Economics Reader*, edited by Giorgio Secondi, 58–64. London: Routledge, 2008.
Fischlin, Daniel, and Martha Nandorfy. *Eduardo Galeano: Through the Looking Glass*. Montreal: Black Rose Books, 2002.
Galeano, Eduardo. *Open Veins of Latin America Five Centuries of the Pillage of a Continent*. New York: Monthly Review Press, 1997.
———. *Guatemala: Occupied Country*. Translated by Cedric Belfrage. New York: Monthly Review Press, 1969.
"The Gods That Failed." *The Economist*, June 13, 2014.
Gott, Richard. "Galeano, Obituary." *Guardian*, April 15, 2015.
Garsd, Jasmine. "Uruguayan Author Eduardo Galeano, Critic of Capitalism, Dies at 74." *NPR*, April 14, 2015.
Love, Joseph L. "Raul Prebisch and the Origins of the Doctrine of Unequal Exchange." *Latin American Research Review* 15, no. 3 (1980): 45–72.
———. "The Rise and Decline of Economic Structuralism in Latin America: New Dimensions." *Latin American Research Review* 40, no. 3 (2005): 100–25.
Lovell, W. George. "Fire of Memory: The Geographical Legacy of Eduardo Galeano." *Journal of Latin American Geography* 16, no. 2 (2017): 199–205.
Martin, Gerald. "Hope Springs Eternal: Eduardo Galeano and the History of Latin America." *History Workshop* no. 34 (1992): 148–58.
Montaner, Carlos Alberto. "The Idiots Lose Their Religion." *National Review*, May 31, 2014.
Reid, Michael. *Forgotten Continent: A History of the New Latin America*. 2nd ed. New Haven, CT: Yale University Press, 2007.
Rohter, Larry. "Galeano Disavows His Book." *New York Times*, May 23, 2014.
Todaro, Lenora. "A World Cup without Eduardo Galeano, Soccer's Poet Laureate." *The Atlantic*, June 15, 2018.
Topic, Steven C., and Allen Wells. *The Second Conquest of Latin America: Coffee, Henequen, and Oil during the Export Boom, 1850–1930*. Austin, TX: University of Texas Press, 1998.

CHAPTER 29: GABRIEL GARCÍA MÁRQUEZ

Apuleyo Mendoza, Plinio. *El olor de la guayaba*. Barcelona: Mondadori, 1994.
Bell-Villada, Gene H. *García Márquez: The Man and His Work*. 2nd ed. Chapel Hill, NC: University of North Carolina Press, 2010.
Caistor, Nick. "Heberto Padilla." *Guardian*, October 13, 2000.

Caistor, Nick, and Katharine Viner. "Gabriel García Márquez: Obituary." *Guardian*, April 17, 2014.
Crandall, Russell. "Colombia's River of Life and Death." *Survival* (2021).
Davis, Wade. *Magdalena: River of Dreams*. New York: Norton, 2021.
Day, Anthony, and Marjorie Miller. "Gabo Talks." *LA Times*, September 2, 1990.
Esteban, Ángel, and Stéphanie Panichelli. *Fidel and Gabo: A Portrait of the Legendary Friendship between Fidel Castro and Gabriel García Márquez*. Translated by Diane Stockwell. New York: Norton, 2009.
García Márquez, Gabriel. *Living to Tell the Tale*. Translated by Edith Grossman. New York: Knopf, 2003.
———. *News of a Kidnapping*. Translated by Edith Grossman. New York: Doubleday, 1996.
Green, Penelope. "Mercedes Barcha, Gabriel García Márquez's Wife and Muse, Dies at 87." *New York Times*, August 23, 2020.
Hart, Stephen M. *Gabriel García Márquez*. London: Reaktion Books, Limited, 2010.
Kennedy, William. "Stunning Portrait of a Monstrous Caribbean Tyrant." *New York Times Book Review*, October 31, 1976.
Krauze, Enrique. *Redeemers: Power and Ideas in Latin America*. New York: Harper, 2012.
Marcial Pérez, David. "When Gabriel García Márquez Was Investigated over His Links to Communism." *El País*, January 27, 2022.
Martin, Gerald. *Gabriel García Márquez: A Life*. New York: Knopf, 2009.
Osorio, Camila. "The Last Days of Gabriel García Márquez." *El País*, May 28, 2021.
Rey, Daniel. "The Story of Cuba's Difficult Relationship with Revolutionary Writers." *Prospect*, August 25, 2021.
Saldívar, Dasso. *García Márquez: El Viaje a la semilla*. Madrid: Alfaguara, 1997.
Sorela, Pedro. *El otro García Márquez: Los años difíciles*. Spain: Mondadori, 1975.
Stavans, Ilan. *Gabriel García Márquez: The Early Years*. New York: Palgrave Macmillan, 2010.
Vargas Llosa, Mario. *García Márquez: historia de un deicidio*. Spain: Barral Editores, 1971.
Wells, Allen. "Interpreting the Past through the Prism of the Present: The Banana Strike, La Violencia and the Cuban Revolution's Impact on García Márquez." *Maine Humanities Council's Winter Weekend*, March 12, 2016.

CHAPTER 30: ÓSCAR ROMERO

Crandall, Russell. *The Salvador Option: The United States in El Salvador, 1977–1992*. New York: Cambridge University Press, 2016.
Domonoske, Camila. "Oscar Romero, Pope Paul VI Elevated to Sainthood." *NPR*, October 14, 2018.
"Y el Vaticano dio la razón a quienes veneran a san Óscar Romero." *ElFaro.net*, October 14, 2018.

CHAPTER 31: THE MOTHERS AND GRANDMOTHERS OF THE PLAZA DE MAYO

Anderson, Jon Lee. "Pope Francis and the Dirty War." *New Yorker*, March 14, 2013.
———. "The Pope of Latin America." *New Yorker*, July 17, 2015.
"Argentina Declassification Project: History." *Intel.gov*.

"Argentina Revokes 'Dirty War' Amnesty." *AP*, June 15, 2005.
"Argentine Sentenced to Life for 'Dirty War' Role." *Reuters*, September 20, 2006.
Barco de Surghi, Susana. *Corredores de la memoria: del campo de la Ribera a los juicios.* Argentina: Villa María, 2015.
Bennett, Dashiell. "Pope Francis Can't Escape Argentina's Dark Past." *Atlantic*, March 15, 2013.
Blakemore, Erin. "Argentinian Grandmothers Are Using DNA to Track Down Stolen Children." *Smithsonian Magazine*, September 3, 2015.
Bosco, Fernando J. "The Madres de Plaza de Mayos and Three Decades of Human Rights' Activism: Embeddedness, Emotions, and Social Movements." *Annals of the Association of American Geographers* 96, no. 2 (June 2006): 342–65.
Christian, Shirley. "Argentina Frees Ex-Junta Leaders." *New York Times*, December 30, 1990.
"Erasing the Kirchner Cult." *The Economist*, July 2, 2016.
Feitlowitz, Marguerite. *Lexicon of Terror: Argentina and the Legacies of Torture.* New York: Oxford University Press, 1999.
Goldman, Francisco. "The Children of the Dirty War." *New Yorker*, March 19, 2012.
Goñi, Uki. "40 Years Later, the Mothers of Argentina's 'Disappeared' Refuse To Be Silent." *Guardian*, April 28, 2017.
———. "Jews Targeted in Argentina's Dirty War." *Guardian*, March 24, 1999.
Hodges, Donald C. *Argentina's "Dirty War": An Intellectual Biography.* Austin: University of Texas Press, 1991.
Kelly, Annie. "Scandal Hits Argentina's Mothers of the Disappeared." *Guardian*, June 12, 2011.
Longoni, Ana, et al. *El Siluetazo.* Buenos Aires: Adriana Hidalgo Editora, 2008.
McNamara, Jason. "Iconic Grandmother of Plaza de Mayo 'Chicha' Mariani Dies Aged 94." *BA Times*, August 21, 2018.
O'Grady, Mary A. "Argentina's Forgotten Terror Victims." *Wall Street Journal*, January 3, 2011.
Sillato, María del Carmen. *Huellas: memorias de resistencia, Argentina 1974–1983.* Argentina: Nueva Editorial Universitaria, 2008.

CHAPTER 32: BECOMING POPE FRANCIS

Agren, David. "Prominent Jesuit, Murdered in '80, Hailed for Aiding Bolivian Democracy." *America*, July 7, 2015.
Anderson, Jon Lee. "The Pope of Latin America." *New Yorker*, July 17, 2015.
———. "Pope Francis and the Dirty War." *New Yorker*, March 14, 2014.
Balza, Martín. "Bergoglio y Francsico: pastor argentine y líder mundial." *Perfil*, March 3, 2021.
Bennett, Dashiell. "Pope Francis Can't Escape Argentina's Dark Past." *Atlantic*, March 15, 2013.
Carroll, James. "Who Am I to Judge?" *New Yorker*, December 2013.
Duffy, Eamon. "Who Is the Pope?" *New York Review of Books*, February 19, 2015.
Elie, Paul. "What Óscar Romero's Canonization Says about Pope Francis." *Atlantic*, November 2018.
Ferguson, Sam. "When Pope Francis Testified about the Dirty War." *New Republic*, March 14, 2013.

Gillespie, Richard. *The Soldiers of Perón: Argentina's Montoneros*. UK: Oxford University Press, 1982.
Goldman, Francisco. "Children of the Dirty War." *New Yorker*, March 19, 2012.
Ivereigh, Austen. *The Great Reformer: Francis and the Making of a Radical Pope*. New York: Henry Holt, 2015.
Neuman, William. "Dirty War Victim Rejects Pope's Connection to Kidnapping." *New York Times*, March 21, 2013.
O'Connell, Gerard. "Antonio Spadaro on His Article about 'The Ecumenism of Hate' in the U.S." *America*, July 14, 2017.
"Pérez Esquivel: 'El Papa no tenía vínculos con la dictadura.'" *BBC*, March 14, 2013.
Spadaro, Antonio. *A Big Heart Open to God: A Conversation with Pope Francis*. New York: HarperOne, 2013.
Tóibín, Colm. "The Bergoglio Smile." *London Review of Books* 43, no. 2 (January 21, 2021).
Vallely, Paul. "How Pope Francis Learned Humility." *Atlantic*, August 23, 2015.
———. *Pope Francis: Untying the Knots*. New York: Bloomsbury, 2013.
Watts, Jonathan. "Vatican Bewildered by Bolivia's 'Communist Crucifix' Gift to Pope Francis." *Guardian*, July 9, 2015.

CHAPTER 33: EFRAÍN RÍOS MONTT

Alterman, Eric. "The Upside of Genocide." *The Nation*. June 19, 2013.
Bonner, Raymond. "Behind the Guatemala Coup: A General Takes Over and Changes Its Course." *New York Times*, March 29, 1982.
———. "Guatemala Enlists Religion in Battle." *New York Times*, July 18, 1982.
Broder, Tanya, and Bernard Lambek. "Military Aid to Guatemala." *Yale Journal of International Law* 13 (1988).
Carmel, Jeremy J. "Rios Montt: Family Man, Disciplinarian." *Christian Science Monitor*, April 29, 1982.
Carothers, Thomas. *In the Name of Democracy: U.S. Policy toward Latin America in the Reagan Years*. Berkeley: University of California Press, 1991.
Crandall, Britta H., and Russell C. Crandall. *"Our Hemisphere"?: The United States in Latin America, from 1776 to the 21st Century*. New Haven, CT: Yale University Press, 2021.
Crandall, Russell. *America's Dirty Wars: Irregular Warfare from 1776 to the War on Terror*. New York: Cambridge University Press, 2014.
Culpepper, Miles. "Ronald Reagan's Genocidal Secret: A True Story of Right-Wing Impunity in Guatemala." *Salon*, March 24, 2015.
Doyle, Kate. "Guatemala's Genocide on Trial." *The Nation*, May 22, 2013.
———. "Indicted for Genocide: Guatemala's Efraín Ríos Montt." National Security Archive.
Gall, Norman. "Slaughter in Guatemala." *New York Review of Books*, May 20, 1971.
Garrard-Burnett, Virginia. *Terror in the Land of the Holy Spirit: Guatemala under General Efraín Ríos Montt, 1982–1983*. UK: Oxford University Press, 2011.
"Genocidal General." *The Economist*. May 11, 2013.
Grandin, Greg. *Denegado en su totalidad: documentos estadounidenses liberados*. Guatemala City: AVANCSO, 2001.
Interview with Judge Yassmín Barrios. "The Door to Impunity and Corruption Is Being Opened." *Network in Solidarity with the People of Guatemala*.

Malkin, Elisabeth. "Former Leader of Guatemala Is Guilty of Genocide against Mayan Group." *New York Times*, May 10, 2013.

———. "Trial on Guatemalan Civil War Carnage Leaves Out U.S. Role." *New York Times*, May 16, 2013.

Meislin, Richard J. "Guatemalan Chief Says War Is Over." *New York Times*, December 11, 1982.

Neier, Aryeh. "Reckoning with Genocide." *New York Review of Books*, March 27, 2013.

Reagan, Ronald. "Question-and-Answer Session with Reporters on the President's Trip to Latin America." December 4, 1982, *American Presidency Project*.

Schirmer, Jennifer G. *The Guatemalan Military Project: A Violence Called Democracy*. Philadelphia, PA: University of Pennsylvania Press, 1998.

Sikkink, Kathryn. *Mixed Messages: U.S. Human Rights Policy and Latin America*. Ithaca, NY: Cornell University Press, 2007.

"U.S. Ambassador Frederic Chapin Says the Government of Guatemala. . . ." *UPI*, April 16, 1982.

"Who Is Elliott Abrams, US Special Envoy for Venezuela?" *Al Jazeera*, February 12, 2019.

Wilkinson, Daniel. *Silence on the Mountain: Stories of Terror, Betrayal, and Forgetting in Guatemala*. Durham, NC: Duke University Press, 2004.

Wills, Santiago. "Did U.S. Back Genocide in Guatemala?" *ABC News*, May 14, 2013.

Stoll, David. "Why They Like Ríos Montt" *NACLA Report on the Americas*, June 2016.

CHAPTER 34: RIGOBERTA MENCHÚ

Arias, Arturo, ed. *The Rigoberta Menchú Controversy*. Minneapolis, MN: University of Minnesota Press, 2001.

Brill, Marlene Targ. *Journey for Peace: The Story of Rigoberta Menchú*. New York: Dutton, 1996.

Calvert, Peter. *Guatemala. A Nation in Turmoil*. Boulder, CO: Westview Press, 1985.

Canby, Peter. "The Truth about Rigoberta Menchú." *New York Review of Books*, April 8, 1999.

Hooks, Margaret, ed. *Guatemalan Women Speak*. Introduction by Rigoberta Menchú Tum. London: Catholic Institute for International Relations, 1991.

Pallister, Kevin. "Why No Mayan Party? Indigenous Movements and National Politics in Guatemala." *Latin American Politics and Society* 55, no. 3 (Fall 2013): 117–38.

Perera, Victor. *Unfinished Conquest. The Guatemalan Tragedy*. Berkeley, CA: University of California Press, 1993.

Menchú, Rigoberta. *Crossing Borders*. Edited by Ann Wright. London: Verso, 1998.

"Menchú Tum, Rigoberta, Guatemala, 1992." *Nobel Women's Initiative*.

Rohter, Larry. "Tarnished Laureate: Nobel Winner Finds Her Story Challenged." *New York Times*, December 15, 1998.

Sanford, Victoria D. L. "The Rigoberta Menchu Controversy: The Rigoberta Menchu Controversy." *American Anthropologist* 105, no. 2 (2003): 384–86.

Stoll, David. *Rigoberta Menchú and the Story of All Poor Guatemalans*. Boulder, CO: Westview Press, 1999.

"World Social Forum Renews Peace Calls, Amid Harsh Criticism of US." *AFP*, February 4, 2002.

CHAPTER 35: ABIMAEL GUZMÁN AND SHINING PATH

"El peor terrorista de la historia peruana." *El Tiempo*, September 11, 2021.
Alarcón, Daniel "Peru Processes the Death of Abimael Guzmán." *New Yorker*, September 19, 2021.
Barbier, Chrystelle. "Victims of Alberto Fujimori's Death Squads Unearthed in Peru." *Guardian*, September 6, 2011.
"Barrios Altos." *Center for Justice and International Law* (CEJIL).
Brooke, James. "Peru Convicts Maoist Rebel Leader and Sentences Him to Life." *New York Times*, October 8, 1992.
Crandall, Russell. "Shining Pathology." *Survival* 61, no. 6 (December 2019–January 2020): 177–84.
"Fifty-Four Adults and Children 'Captive for Decades' Rescued from Shining Path." *Guardian*, August 1, 2015.
Moncada, Andrea. "Is Pedro Castillo's Presidency Doomed?" *Americas Quarterly*, August 2, 2021.
"Peru." *International Center for Transitional Justice* (ICTJ).
"Peru: Shining Path." *InSight Crime*, May 23, 2021.
Roncagliolo, Santiago. *La Cuarta Espada: La Historia de Abimael Guzmán y Sendero Luminoso*. New York: Debate, 2007.
Starn, Orin, et al., eds. *The Peru Reader: History, Culture, Politics*. 2nd ed. Durham, NC: Duke University Press, 2005.
Throssell, Liz. "Peru: The Killings of Lucamarca." *BBC*, October 14, 2006.

CHAPTER 36: CHICO MENDES AND MARINA SILVA

Blair, Leonardo. "Devout Evangelical Christian Marina Silva Started Life Illiterate in the Amazon; Now She's Primed to Become Brazil's First Black President." *Christian Post*, August 28, 2014.
Cowell, Adrian. *The Decade of Destruction: The Crusade to Save the Amazon Rainforest*. New York: Holt, 1990.
"Dilma Rousseff to Face Aecio Neves in Run-Off." *BBC*, October 6, 2014.
Dwyer, August. *Into the Amazon: The Struggle for the Rain Forest*. San Francisco, CA: Sierra Club Books, 1991.
Harberman, Clyde. "The Lasting Legacy of a Fighter for the Amazon." *New York Times*, November 27, 2016.
Hect, Susanna, and Alexander Cockburn. *The Fate of the Forest: Developers, Destroyers and Defenders of the Amazon*. New York: Verso, 1990.
Maxwell, Kenneth. "The Mystery of Chico Mendes." *New York Review of Books*, March 28, 1991.
Mendes, Angela, et al. "Chico Mendes Lives: Amazon Women in Defense of Life." *Ambiente & Sociedade* 24 (2021).
Mendes, Chico. *Fight for the Forest: Chico Mendes in His Own Words*. UK: Latin American Bureau, 1989.
Revkin, Andrew. *The Burning Season: The Murder of Chico Mendes and the Fight for the Amazon Rain Forest*. Washington, DC: Island Press, 2004.
Rodrigues, Gomercindo, and Linda Rabben. *Walking the Forest with Chico Mendes Struggle for Justice in the Amazon*. Austin, TX: University of Texas Press, 2007.

Shoumatoff, Alex. *The World Is Burning: Murder in the Rainforest.* New York: Little, Brown, and Company, 1990.
Souza, Márcio. *O Empate contra Chico Mendes.* Marco Zero, 1990.
"This Is Not a Speech. It Is a Life." *The Economist,* September 18, 2014.
Vadjunec, Jacqueline M. "Extracting a Livelihood: Institutional and Social Dimensions of Deforestation in the Chico Mendes Extractive Reserve, Acre, Brazil." *Journal of Latin American Geography* 10, no. 1 (2011): 151–74.
Vidal, John, et al. "50 People Who Could Save the Planet." *Guardian,* January 5, 2008.
Watts, Jonathan. "Brazil Salutes Chico Mendes 25 Years after His Murder." *Guardian,* December 20, 2013.

CHAPTER 37: MARIO VARGAS LLOSA

Bensoussan, Albert, and Susana Corcuera Martínez del Río. *Mario Vargas Llosa: vida que es palabra.* Mexico City: Nueva Imagen, 2006.
Crandall, Russell. "Letter from Arequipa: Mario Vargas Llosa and His Authoritarians." *The American Interest,* December 2016.
Krauze, Enrique. *Redeemers: Ideas and Power in Latin America.* New York: Harper, 2011.
Kristal, Efraín, and John King, eds. *The Cambridge Companion to Mario Vargas Llosa.* UK: Cambridge University Press, 2012.
Oliva Vega, Carlos. "Gabriel Garcia Marquez: Una vida." *Taller de Letras* 46, no. 46 (2010).
Vargas Llosa, Mario. *A Fish in the Water.* Translated by Helen R. Lane. New York: Picador, 1993.

CHAPTER 38: PABLO ESCOBAR

Crandall, Britta H., and Russell C. Crandall. *"Our Hemisphere"? The United States in Latin America, from 1776 to the 21st Century.* New Haven, CT: Yale University Press, 2021.
Crandall, Russell. *Drugs and Thugs: The History and Future of America's War on Drugs.* New Haven, CT: Yale University Press, 2020.
———. *The United States and Latin America after the Cold War.* New York: Cambridge University Press, 2008.
Escobar, Juan Pablo. *Pablo Escobar: My Father.* New York: Thomas Dunne, 2017.
Stone, Robert. "The Autumn of the Drug Lord." *New York Times,* June 15, 1997.

CHAPTER 39: SUBCOMMANDER MARCOS

Carrigan, Ana. "Chiapas: The First Post-Modern Revolution." *The Fletcher Forum of World Affairs* (Winter/Spring 1995): 71–98.
Evans, Brad. "Revolution without Violence." *Peace Review* 21, no 1 (2009): 85–94.
Henck, Nick. *Subcommander Marcos: The Man and the Mask.* Durham, NC: Duke University Press, 2007.
La Grange, Bertrand de, and Maite Rico. *Subcomandante Marcos: la genial impostura.* Mexico City: Aguilar, 1997.
"Mexican Rebel Leader Marcos Retires, Says 'No Longer Exists.'" *Reuters,* May 26, 2014.
Monsiváis, Carlos. *EZLN Documentado y comunicados.* Mexico: Ediciones Era, 2003.
Romero, César. *Marcos: ¿Un profesional de la esperanza?* Mexico City: Planeta, 1994.

CHAPTER 40: HUGO CHÁVEZ

Anderson, Jon Lee. "Fidel's Heir." *New Yorker*, June 16, 2008.
———. "Nicolás Maduro's Accelerating Revolution." *New Yorker*, December 11, 2017.
———. "The Revolutionary." *New Yorker*, September 10, 2001.
———. "Slumlord." *New Yorker*, January 28, 2013.
Crandall, Russell. "Reports from the Revolution." *Survival* 50, no. 6 (December 2008–January 2009): 193–98.
Crandall, Russell, and Savannah Haeger. "Venezuela's Post-Chavez Torment." *IISS Strategic Comments*, June 2016.
"Devolution of State Power: The 'Colectivos.'" *InSight Crime*, May 2018.
Dobson, William J. "Wanna Beat Hugo Chavez?" *Slate.com*, June 5, 2012.
Faiola, Anthony, and Rachelle Krygier. "In Venezuela's Oil Capital, Life Is a Struggle." *Washington Post*, September 19, 2019.
Finnegan, William. "Venezuela: A Failing State." *New Yorker*, November 6, 2016.
Foer, Franklin. "The Talented Mr. Chávez." *Atlantic*, May 2006.
Jones, Bart. *¡Hugo!: The Hugo Chávez Story from Mud Hut to Perpetual Revolution.* Hanover, NH: Steerforth Press, 2007.
Kozloff, Nikolas. *Revolution! South America and the Rise of the New Left*. New York: Palgrave Macmillan, 2008.
Krauze, Enrique. "Hugo Chávez and Venezuela: A Leader's Destiny." *Open Democracy*, July 24, 2009.
———. "The Shah of Venezuela." *New Republic*, April 1, 2009.
Lemann, Nicholas. "The Anointed." *New Yorker*, December 2011.
López, Leopoldo. "Even in Jail, I Will Fight for a Free Venezuela." *New York Times*, September 25, 2015.
Wilpert, Gregory. *Changing Venezuela by Taking Power: The History and Policies of the Chávez Government*. London: Verso, 2007.

CHAPTER 41: YOANI SÁNCHEZ

14ymedio.com
"A Conversation with Yoani Sánchez." *Cuba and the Caribbean*, University of Miami.
Brenner, Philip, et al. *A Contemporary Cuba Reader: The Revolution under Raúl Castro*. 2nd ed. Lanham, MD: Rowman & Littlefield, 2014.
"Cuban Blogger Blocked from Travelling to Film Premiere in Brazil." *Amnesty International*, 2012.
"Cuban Revolution." *Wall Street Journal*, December 22, 2007.
de Córdoba, José. "Cuban Dissident Starts Website, Which Is Promptly Hacked." *Wall Street Journal*, May 21, 2014.
Kahn, Carrie. "In Cuba, Growing Number of Bloggers Manage to Operate in a Vulnerable Gray Space." *NPR*, July 2, 2017.
"Husband of Cuban Blogger Yoani Sanchez Attacked." *Reuters*, November 21, 2009.
Lamrani, Salin. *Cuba, The Media, and the Challenge of Impartiality*. New York: New York University Press, 2015.
Oppmann, Patrick. "Dissident Blogger Allowed to Leave Cuba." *CNN*, February 18, 2013.
Rohter, Larry. "Yoani Sánchez: Virtually Outspoken in Cuba." *New York Times*, October 17, 2009.

Sánchez, Yoani. *Havana Real: One Woman Fights to Tell the Truth about Cuba Today*. Translated by M. J. Porter. New York: Melville House, 2011.
———. "Country for Old Men." *Foreign Policy* (November 2011): 36–38.
Vicari, Stefania. "Blogging Politics in Cuba: The Framing of Political Discourse in the Cuban Blogosphere." *Media, Culture & Society* 36, no. 7 (2014): 998–1015.
"Yoani Sánchez." *Oslo Freedom Forum*.

CHAPTER 42: MICHELLE BACHELET

Anderson, Jon Lee. "Neruda, Pinochet, and the Iron Lady." *New Yorker*, April 9, 2013.
Cea, Rodrigo. "Bachelet revela que fue interrogada por el jefe de la policía secreta de Pinochet." *El País*, October 7, 2013.
Delfau, Antonio, and Juan Rauld. "Michelle Bachelet: 'ante la finitud humana, no entiendo la soberbia.'" *Mensaje* (Santiago, Chile) 57, no. 575 (2008).
"Education in Chile Slowly Overcomes Pinochet-era Divisions." *The Borgen Project*.
Franklin, Jonathan. "Chileans Elected Socialist as First Female President." *Guardian*, January 15, 2006.
Jiménez, Fernando. "La vida de Bachelet, la historia de Chile en sus espaldas." *24 Horas*. December 15, 2013.
Rohter, Larry. "Jailed by Pinochet, She Now Runs the Military." *New York Times*, January 4, 2003.
———. "A Leader Making Peace with Chile's Past." *New York Times*, January 16, 2006.
———. "Visit to U.S. Isn't a First for Chile's First Female President." *New York Times*, June 8, 2006.
Sepúlveda, Alfredo. "Bachelet en tierra de hombres." *Mensaje* 60, no. 596 (2011).
Skard, Torild. *Women of Power: Half a Century of Female Presidents and Prime Ministers Worldwide*. England: Policy Press, 2014.
Valdés, Teresa. "El chile de Michelle Bachelet: ¿género en le poder? *Latin American research review* 45, no. 4 (2010): 248–73.
Valenzuela Somogyi, Mariana. "La figura de la madre en los casos de las presidentas latinoamericanas: Michelle Bachelet (Chile), Cristina Fernández (Argentina) y Dilma Rousseff (Brasil)." *Revista de estudios sociales* 69 (2019): 67–78.
Waylen, G. *Gender. Institutions and Change in Bachelet's Chile*. New York: Palgrave Macmillan, 2016.

CHAPTER 43: EVO MORALES

Anderson, Jon Lee. "The Fall of Evo Morales." *New Yorker*, March 23, 2020.
———. "The Pope of Latin America." *New Yorker*, July 17, 2015
Crandall, Britta H., and Russell C. Crandall. *"Our Hemisphere"? The United States in Latin America, from 1776 to the 21st Century*. New Haven, CT: Yale University Press, 2021.
Dvoskin, Gabriel. "Finding Evo." *PBS Frontline World Rough Cut*.
Guillermoprieto, Alma. "Bolivia's New Order." *New York Review of Books*, July 2008.
———. "The New Bolivia: II." *New York Review of Books*, September 21, 2006.
Hall, Thomas D., and James V. Fenelon. *Indigenous Peoples and Globalization: Resistance and Revitalization*. New York: Routledge, 2015.
Harten, Sven. *The Rise of Evo Morales and the MAS*. London: Zed, 2010.

Mayorga, Fernando. *Mandato y contingencia: estilo de gobierno de Evo Morales.* Argentina: CLACSO, 2020.
Webber, Jeffery R. *From Rebellion to Reform in Bolivia Class Struggle, Indigenous Liberation, and the Politics of Evo Morales.* Chicago, IL: Haymarket Books, 2011.

CHAPTER 44: JOSÉ "PEPE" MUJICA

Address by Mr. José Mujica, President of the Eastern Republic of Uruguay." September 24, 2013, *Records of the United Nations, General Assembly, 68th Session, 7th Plenary Meeting* A/68/PV.7. New York: United Nations, 2013.
Brands, Hal. *Latin America's Cold War.* Cambridge, MA: Harvard University Press, 2010.
Crandall, Russell. "Is the U.S. the Last Country Fighting the War on Drugs?" *New Republic*, January 1, 2014.
———. "Drug War Divide." *The American Interest*, October 3, 2014.
———. "Drug Wars." *Survival* 55, no. 4 (2013): 229–40.
Gregory, Stephen. *José "Pepe" Mujica: Warrior, Philosopher President.* UK: Academic Press, 2016.
Lissardy, Gerardo. "Uruguay: cuánto ha cambiado realmente el mercado de las drogas en el país con la legalización de la marihuana." *BBC*, December 19, 2019.
Nahum, Benjamín. *El Fin Del Uruguay Liberal.* Montevideo: Ediciones de la Banda Oriental, 1991.
"Pascasio Báez, el trabajador rural." *El Ojo Digital*, May 2, 2013.
Percy, Allan. *Mujica: una biografía inspiradora* Barcelona: Grupo Zeta, 2015.
Romero, Simon. "After Years in Solitary, an Austere Life as Uruguay's President." *New York Times*, January 4, 2013.
Sharnak, Debbie. "The Human Rights Abuses Uruguay Doesn't Want You to Know About." *Foreign Policy*, July 29, 2015.
"The Sage of Montevideo." *The Economist*, August 14, 2014.
Watts, Jonathan. "Uruguay Makes Dramatic Shift to Nearly 95 Percent Electricity from Clean Energy." *Guardian*, December 3, 2015.

CHAPTER 45: LUIZ INÁCIO LULA DA SILVA

Amann, Edmund and Werner Baer, "The Macroeconomic Record of the Lula Administration, the Roots of Brazil's Inequality, and Attempts to Overcome Them." In *Brazil Under Lula: Economy, Politics, and Society under the Worker President*, edited by Joseph Love and Werner Baer, 27–43. London: Palgrave Macmillan, 2009.
Bourne, Richard. *Lula of Brazil: The Story So Far.* London: Zed Books, 2008.
"Em Entrevista a jornal, Lula diz que não crê na existência do mensalão." *Globo*, August 26, 2012.
French, John. *Lula and His Politics of Cunning: From Metalworker to President of* Brazil. Chapel Hill, NC: University of North Carolina Press, 2020.
Hiane de Moura, Mauro. "Never Before in the History of This Country?": The Rise of Presidential Power in the Lula da Silva and Rousseff Administrations (2003–2016)." *Washington International Law Journal* 28, no. 2 (2019).
Lula da Silva, Luiz Inácio. *Truth Will Prevail: Why I was Condemned.* New York: OR Books, 2018.
Schwarcz, Lilia M., "Brazil in the Shadow of Lula." *New York Review of Books*, November 19, 2010.

Skidmore, Thomas E. *Brazil, Five Centuries of Change*. 2nd ed. UK: Oxford University Press, 2009.
Tas, Marcelo. *Nunca Antes Na História Deste País*, Panda Books, 2009.
Tepperman, Jonathan. "Brazil's Antipoverty Breakthrough." *Foreign Affairs* 95, no. 1 (January/February 2016): 34–45.

CHAPTER 46: DANIEL ORTEGA AND ROSARIO MURILLO

Anderson, Jon Lee. "Populists Inflame the Coronavirus Outbreak across Latin America." *New Yorker*, July 2, 2020.
Bay-Meyer, Kelly. "Do Ortega's Citizen Power Councils Empower the Poor in Nicaragua? Benefits and Costs of Local Democracy." *Polity* 45, no. 3 (2013): 393–421.
Berg, Ryan C. "Restoring Democracy in Nicaragua." *AEI Report*, July 28, 2020.
Crandall, Britta H., and Russell C. Crandall. *"Our Hemisphere"?: The United States in Latin America, 1776 to the 21st Century*. New Haven, CT: Yale University Press, 2021.
Crandall, Russell. *America's Dirty Wars*. New York: Cambridge University Press, 2014.
——. *The Salvador Option: The United States in El Salvador, 1977–1992*. New York: Cambridge University Press, 2016.
Cruz Feliciano, Héctor. "The Perils of Reconciliation: Achievements and Challenges of Daniel Ortega and the Modern FSLN." *Latin American Perspectives* 46, no. 1 (2019): 247–62.
Gooren, Henri. 2010. "Ortega for President: The Religious Rebirth of Sandinismo in Nicaragua." *European Review of Latin American & Caribbean Studies*, no. 89 (October).
Jonas, Susanne, and Nancy Stein. "The Construction of Democracy in Nicaragua." *Latin American Perspectives* 17 (July 1990): 10–37.
Kagan, Robert. *A Twilight Struggle: American Power and Nicaragua, 1977–1990*. New York: Free Press, 1996.
Lake, Anthony. *Somoza Falling*. Amherst, MA: University of Massachusetts Press, 1990.
LeoGrande, William M. *Our Own Backyard: The United States in Central America, 1977–1992*. Chapel Hill, NC: University of North Carolina Press, 2007.
Martí i Puig, Salvador. "The Adaptation of the FSLN: Daniel Ortega's Leadership and Democracy in Nicaragua." *Latin American Politics & Society* 52, no. 4 (2010): 79–106.
Medina Sánchez, Fabián. *El Preso 198: Un perfil de Daniel Ortega*. Self-published, 2018.
Morris, Kenneth Earl. *Unfinished Revolution: Daniel Ortega and Nicaragua's Struggle for Liberation*. Chicago, IL: Lawrence Hill Books, 2010.
"Nicaragua: Cruel Response to Hunger Strikes." *Human Rights Watch*, November 22, 2019.
Partlow, Joshua. "From the Rebel to Strongman: How Daniel Ortega Became the Things He Fought Against." *Washington Post*, August 24, 2018.
Robles, Frances. "Wife and Running Mate: A Real-Life 'House of Cards' in Nicaragua." *New York Times*, October 30, 2016.
Thaler, Kai M. "Nicaragua: A Return to Caudillismo." *Journal of Democracy* 28, no. 2 (2017): 157–69.

CHAPTER 47: BERTA CÁCERES

Blitzer, Jonathan. "The Death of Berta Cáceres." *New Yorker*, March 11, 2016.
Frank, Dana. *The Long Honduran Night: Resistance, Terror, and the United States in the Aftermath of the Coup*. Chicago, IL: Haymarket Books, 2018.
Fraser, Barbara J. "Honduran Activists Hope Pope's Climate Encyclical Gives Them Boost." *Catholic Philly.com*, April 22, 2015.

"How Many More?" *Global Witness*, April 20, 2015.
Mackey, Danielle, and Chiara Eisner. "Inside the Plot to Murder Honduran Activist Berta Cáceres." *The Intercept*, December 21, 2019.
Malkin, Elisabeth, and Alberto Arce. "Indigenous Activist Is Killed in Honduras." *New York Times*, March 3, 2016.
Pearce, Fred. "Honduras, Where Defending Nature Is a Deadly Business." *Guardian*, March 22, 2017.
Watts, Jonathan. "Honduran Indigenous Rights Campaigner Wins Goldman Prize." *Guardian*, April 19, 2015.
———. "Murder of Activist Berta Cáceres Sparks Violent Clashes in Honduras." *Guardian*, March 4, 2016.

Index

14ymedio (digital newspaper), 473

Abbes García, Johnny, 192
Abuelas de Plaza de Mayo, 354, 357, 360, 361, 366
Acheson, Dean, 236
Adams, John, 54–55
Adrade de Carvalho, Rubens, 402
Ahmadinejad, Mahmoud, 460, 464
Alamán, Lucas, 77, 80, 82, 88
Alarcón, Daniel, 204–5
Alberdi, Juan Bautista, 103, 106, 107–8
Alckmin, Geraldo, 506
Alemán, Arnoldo, 178, 515
Alessandri, Jorge, 293, 296, 297
Alexander, Robert J., 212
Alfonsín, Raúl, 358–59
Allende, Isabel, 321
Allende, Salvador, 313, 339, *352*, 442, 476, 477, 480; Castro, friendship with, 291–93; coup against, 301–4, 321, 476; government of, 293–96; Pinochet and, 304, 305, 308–9, 310, 315; presidential ambitions, 290–91; as a socialist, 289, 299–301, 306, 312, 337, 478; US-Allende relations, 296–99
Alliance for the Peoples of Our America (ALBA), 459
Álvarez, Juan, 90–91
Álvarez de Toledo, Antonio S., 27
Alves da Silva, Darly and Darci, 405

Amauta (periodical), 200, 204
American Popular Revolutionary Alliance (APRA), 200, 202–7, 224, 417
Anderson, Jon Lee, 268, 270, 315; on Hugo Chávez, 454, 455, 457, 460; on Pope Francis, 368, 369–70
Apaza, Julián, 43
Apologética historia (Las Casas), 22
Apuleyo Mendoza, Plinio, 323, 330, 336
Aramburu, Juan Carlos (Father Carlos), 364, 367
Arana, Marie, 64, 66, 69
Árbenz, Jacobo: communist ties, 236–38, 239–41, 243; in exile, 243–44, 274; overthrow of, 158, 233, *242*, 255, 267–68, 302–3, 372–73; reform proposals, 233, 234–36; Vargas Llosa writing on, 418–19
Arce, Luis, 493
Areche, José Antonio de, 40
ARENA political party, 350, 351, 352–53, 370
Arenas, Reinaldo, 339–40
Arévalo, Juan J., 227, 233–34, 267
Ariel (Rodó), 5, 132–37, 495
Armas Pérez, Ramón, 230, 239, 240–41, 268
Arriaga, Antonio de, 37, 38, 39
The Arsenal (painting), 152
Arzuaga Javier, 271–72
Asbaje, Pedro de, 27

559

Asbaje de Ramírez, Juana de, 27
Aunt Julia and the Scriptwriter (Vargas Llosa), 412, 413
Autonomous Municipal University (UAM), 444–45
Autumn of the Patriarch (García Márquez), 334, 337
Avilés, Gabriel de, 40
Aylwin, Patricio, 314–15
Ayo, Diego, 491

Bachelet, Alberto, 475
Bachelet, Verónica Michelle, 311, 474–82
Baduel, Raúl, 458
Balaguer, Joaquín, 197
Balbín, Ricardo, 214, 219
Banana massacre, 328, 330
Ban Ki-moon, 361
Bañuelos, Juan, 439
Baptist, Edward, 57
Barcha, Mercedes, 334–35, 338
Barco, Virgilio, 430
Barnes, Michael, 375
Barrientos, René, 276
Barríos, Yassmín, 380
Barrios Altos massacre, 396–97
Bartulín, Danilo, 339
The Bases (Alberdi), 107
Bastidas, Micaela, 35, 39, 40, 41, 44
The Bather of Tehuantepec (painting), 150
Batista, Fulgencio, 146, 194, 231, 267, 269, 271, 333; Castro revolt against, 245, 247–48, 250–51; loathing for, 254, 275; Operation Truth, Batista defendants and, 335; ouster of, 186, 246, 292
Battle of Carabobo, 66
Battle of Caseros, 107
Battle of Ocotal, 170–72
Battle of San Jacinto, 82
Battle y Ordóñez, José, 133, 499
Bay of Pigs, 195, 196, 245, 253, 255–57, 336
Beals, Carleton, 174, 190
Belaúnde Terry, Fernando, 205, 392
Belém Lopes, Dawisson, 6
Bell, Alexander Graham, 111
Bell, David A., 49

Bellido, Guido, 397
Beloff, Angelina, 149, 150, 152
Bergoglio, Jorge Mario, 5, 362–70. *See also* Francis, Pope
Bernardino, Minerva, 166
Betancourt, Rómulo, 194, 195, 223–32, 323, 429
Betancur, Belisario, 427, 429, 430
Biden, Joe, 521
Bishop, Abraham, 54
Bissell, Richard, 240
Blair, Tony, 456
Blanco, Antonio Guzmán, 124
Boff, Clodovis, 406
Bogotazo riots, 330–33, 335
Bolívar, Simón, 4, 53, 78, 202, 263; Chávez as inspired by, 60, 451–57, 462, 465; early years, 61–63; fall of regime, 71–73; on Latin American identity, 135, 169; Venezuela, battle for, 63–71
Bolivarian Revolutionary Movement 200 (MRB-200), 454, 456
Bolsonaro, Jair, 409, 502, 509
Bonafini, Hebe de, 360–61
Bonaparte, Joseph, 63
Bonaparte, Napoleon, 56, 57, 63, 70, 76, 80, 96, 113, 306
Bonner, Raymond, 376
Bonner, Robert, 431
Bordon, Geraldo, 402
Borge, Tomás, 338
Borges, Jorge Luis, 214, 362
Bourget, Paul, 133
Bourne, Richard, 503
Boves, José Tomás, 64
Bowden, Mark, 436
Bradock, Daniel, 274
Brands, Hal, 496
Broad Front (FA) coalition, 498
Brown, John, 58
Buchanan, James, 93
Bundy, McGeorge, 256, 292, 293
Bunel, Joseph, 54–55
Burgos Debray, Elisabeth, 384
Burnet, David, 82
Burt, Jo-Marie, 381
Busby, Morris, 433

Bush, George H. W., 351, 431, 433, 514
Bush, George W., 206, 386, 460, 461, 462, 507
Bustamante y Rivero, José L., 205
Butters, Charles, 176

Caballero, Manuel, 226
Cáceres Flores, Berta I., 522–28
Cali cartel, 283, 422, 425, 435
Calles, Plutarco E., 144, 151, 152, 181
Camacho, Manuel Á., 185
Cámpora, Héctor J., 220
Campos, Eduardo, 408
Canby, Peter, 384–85
Cantillo, Eulogio, 271
Capriles, Henrique, 463–64
Caracazo riots, 454
Cardenal, Ernesto, 339
Cárdenas, Cuauhtémoc, 448
Cárdenas, Lázaro, 156, 187, 226, 241, 448;
  Castro, releasing from prison, 247–48;
  PEMEX, founding, 185–86; petroleum ties, 179–81, 183–85; as a reformist, 179, 181–83
Cardoso, Fernando H., 505–6
Carlos III, King, 41
Carlyle, Thomas, 9–10
Carmona, Pedro, 458
Carranza, Venustiano, 140
Carreto, Leonor de, 27, 28, 29
Carroll, James, 363
Carter, Jimmy, 313, 338, 346, 348, 351, 375, 427, 513, 514
Casey, Michael, 265
Castaño, Fidel, 426–27
Castillo, Ramón, 211
Castillo Armas, Carlos, 238, 240–41, 268, 397
Castillo Mejía, Roberto D., *527*, 528
Castro, Ángel, 245
Castro, Fidel, 73, 128, 243, 281, 331, 335, 414, 456, 460; activist support for, 167, 186–87, 501; Allende and, 291–93, 296, 310; Bay of Pigs Invasion, 255–57; Betancourt-Castro relations, 231–32; Chávez and, 457, 458, 462; Chilean radical left, backing, 312, 313;
  criticisms of regime, 391, 473; cutbacks and scarcity, enduring, 466–67;
  Fidelmania, 251–53; García Márquez, friendship with, 5, 326, 338, 339–41;
  Guevarra and, 248, 250, 269, 271, 274, 275, 390; imprisonment of, 186, 247–48, 267; missiles of October, reacting to, 257–59; in photographs, *308, 455, 463, 490*; as a revolutionary, 245–48, 248–51, 259–61, 335, 496, 514; Trujillo and, 194–96, 230; at the United Nations, 254–55; Vargas Llosa and, 412, 415
Castro, Raúl, 186, 248, 250, 261, 269, 370, 470, 473, 514
Castro Gil, Tulio M., 430
Catholic Church, 348, 379, 428, 481, 505;
  Argentine Catholic Church, 102, 109, 363–64; Bourbon monarchs and, 36, 39; Chilean Catholic Church, 299, 313; guerrillas, relationship with, 335, 447; Mexican government and, 76, 78, 79, 91, 92, 95; natives, Church stance on, 20; Ortega, link with, 511, 516–17, 520. *See also* liberation theology
caudillos, 6, 116, 202, 214, 294, 314;
  Argentine caudillos, 100–102, 105–6, 108, 219; Bolívar, installing the rule of, 61, 70; Chávez on, 452–53, 462; Cuban caudillismo, 124, 128, 338; in Mexico, 90, 98–99, 138, 144, 146; Santa Anna as a caudillo, 77, 80, 83; Sarmiento on, 105–6, 122; Spanish caudillos, 64, 229
Cera, J. M. Francisco de la, 26
Cerda y Aragón, Tomás Antonio de la, 30
Cerezo, Vinicio, 377–78
Chamorro, Pedro J., 512–13, 516
Chamorro, Violeta, 515
Chapin, Frederic, 375
Chapman Catt, Carrie, 162–63, *165*
Charles IV, King, 63
Charles V, King, 19, 21, 24
Chávez Frías, Hugo R., 60, 261, 288, 518;
  background, 451–54; *chavismo*, 459, 462, 464, 465; as a civilian, 456–58; coup, launching, 454–56; Morales and, *463, 490, 517*; Obama and, 206, 318, 325; popularity and authority of, 460–62

Chávez y González, Luis, 343
Cheney, Richard, 433
Che's Afterlife (Casey), 265
Cheyre, Juan E., 478
Chomsky, Noam, 419, 462
Christian Democratic Party (PDC), 293–94
Chrobik de Mariani, María I. (Chicha), 356, 360
Church, Frank, 196
Church Committee, 196, 294
Church of the Word, 373, 376, 377
Cinco de Mayo holiday, 96
Clary, David A., 80
Clayton, Lawrence A., 18, 25
Clemente Orozco, José, 143, 150
Clinton, Bill, 286, 341, 456
Cockburn, Andrew, 431
Collor de Mello, Fernando, 505
Colom, Álvaro, 244
Columbus, Christopher, 3, 6, 8–11, 13–15, 17, 47, 192, 385
Comonfort, Ignacio, 91, 92
Comte, Auguste, 139
Condorcanqui, José G. (Túpac Amaru II), 4, 34–45, 390, 496
Constant, Benjamin, 70
Constantino, Rodrigo, 325
Contreras, Manuel, 311, 317
Conversation in the Cathedral (Vargas Llosa), 412, 414
Coolidge, Calvin, 173, 175
COPEI party, 45, 229
Corbyn, Jeremy, 492
Cordano, Ángel, 495
Cordona, Lucía, 495
Cortázar, Julio, 319, 336
Cortés, Hernán, 1, 17, 84, 323
Corvalán, Luis, 301
Cosío Villegas, Daniel, 91–92
The Cosmic Race (Vasconcelos), 144
Cousin, Victor, 103
Crassweller, Robert, 217, 218
Cribelli, Teresa, 110–11
Crisis (periodical), 322
Cristóbal, Diego, 41
"Cry of Dolores," 77

Cuban Missile Crisis, 245, 252, 257, 259
Cullen, Henry, 64–65

Da Costa, Luiz F., 286
Daniel, Jean, 259
Darío, Rubén, 132
D'Aubuisson, Roberto, 349–50, 352
Dávalos, Jorge, 477
Dávalos, Sebastián, 481
Davis, Wade, 66–67, 71, 72, 291, 328
Dearborn, Henry, 195–96
Debray, Régis, 291, 442
De la Cuadra, Alicia Zubasnabar de, 356–57, 366
De la Cuadra, Elena, 366, *368*
De la Cuadra, Estela, 366, 368
Democrates Alter (Sepúlveda), 21–22
DePalma, Anthony, 260
DESA construction, 524–25, 526, 527–28
Dessalines, Jean-Jacques, 57–58
Devine, Jack, 301–3
Díaz, Adolfo, 167, 177
Díaz, Carmen Romero Rubio de, 148–49
Díaz, Porfirio, 1, 96, 180; Juárez, electoral race against, 98–99; opposition to, 124, 139–40, 146, 169; Rivera and, 148–49; as a strongman, 124, 138
Díaz-Balart, Mirta, 246
Dillon, C. Douglas, 195
Dirceu, José, 507–8
Doheny, Edward L., 179
Douglass, Frederick, 58
Draper, Theodore, 256–57
Dream of a Sunday Afternoon at Alameda Central Park (mural), 1–3
Dudley, Steven, 378, 381
Dulles, Allen, 237, 239, 251, 253, 302
Dulles, John Foster, 237, 239, 302
Dunlop, John, 400
Dwyer, Augusta, 402

Echeverría, Esteban, 103–4
Echeverría, Luis, 438
"Economic Plan" (poem), 469–70
Eisenhower, Dwight, 196, 229; Árbenz, stance against, 233, 236–38, 239–40, 243; anti-Castro policies, 194, 251,

253–54, 255, 259; anti-Trujillo policies, 192–93, 195, 230; United Fruit Company and, 233, 236–38
Elbrick, Charles, 507–8
Elliott, John H., 37
Elpidio, Luis, 230
Emerson, Ralph Waldo, 13, 107, 125
Enríquez de Ribera, Payo, 30
Erro, Enrique, 495
Escalante, Salvador Borrego, 146
Escobar, Juan Pablo, 435
Escobar, Pablo, 327, 341, 426, 430; as a drug lord, 5, 283, 423–25, 432, 436, 484; early years, 423–24; *El Espectador*, news stories on, 428–29; as a Liberal Party candidate, 427–28; Los Pepes as acting in the interests of, 434–35; prison escape, 432–34; Search Bloc, special operation against, 430–31
Escobar, Reinaldo, 468, 470–71, 472, 473
Escobar, Roberto, 423
Escobar, Teo, 468
Espinal, Luis, 370
Espino Negro agreement, 167–68, 169, 175
Estrella Ureña, Rafael, 189
Ezeiza Massacre, 221

Falcoff, Mark, 297
Farabundo Martí National Liberation Front (FMLN), 351, 352–53, 438
Farland, Joseph S., 195
Farrell, Edelmiro, 212
Faulkner, William, 336
Federation for Feminine Progress (FBPF), 162–63, 164
Feitlowitz, Marguerite, 357
Feland, Logan, 172–73
Ferdinand I, King, 9
Ferdinand VII, King, 63–64
Fernandes Távora, Euclides, 401
Fernández de Santa Cruz y Sahagún, Manuel ("Sor Filotea"), 31–32
Fidel, Ernesto, 491, 492
Figueres, José, 193–94, 227, 243
Firmenich, Mario, 363
"First Dream" (poem), 30
Fischer, Joseph, 14

A Fish in the Water (Vargas Llosa), 412, 417
Fletcher, James, 115
Flores, Aline, 524
Flores, Austra B., 523
Flores Galindo, Alberto, 39
Ford, Henry, 153, 400
The Forgotten Continent (Reid), 323
Fortuny, José M., 235
Fox, Vicente, 449
Francis, Pope, 5, 353, 361, 362–70, 526
Franco, Francisco, 145, 190, 229
Frank, Dana, 527
Frei Montalvo, Eduardo, 293–96, 299, 300, 302, 316
Friedman, Milton, 311–12
Fuentes, Carlos, 319, 336
Fujimori, Alberto, 197, 393–94, 395, 397, 412, 416–17, 418
Fujimori, Keiko, 397
Funes, Mauricio, 352
Furtado, Celso, 506

Gadea, Hilda, 267, 268, 269
Gaitán, Jorge E., 281, 330–31
Galán, Luis C., 428, 430–32
Galdames, Alicia, 475
Galeano, Eduardo, 265, 318–25
Galeano, Fernando and Mario, 433
Galíndez, Jesús, 162
Gallegos, Rómulo, 228, 230, 336
Galtieri, Leopoldo, 358
Gálvez, Juan M., 238
García, Alan, 198, 206–7, 392, 412, 415–17
García, Tomás, 525
García-Bryce, Iñigo, 202
García Linera, Álvaro, 45, *488*, 491
García Márquez, Gabriel, 5, 319, 326–43, *419*, 422, 426
García Márquez, Patricio, 340
Garrido, Alfredo, 452
Gastelú, Haydeé, 356
Gaviria, César, 73, 432, 433
Gaviria, Gustavo, 423
General Confederation of Labor (CGT), 213, 218
The General in His Labyrinth (García Márquez), 340

Geographical Journal, 14
Gewen, Barry, 291, 293
Ginés de Sepúlveda, Juan, 21
Girard, Philippe, 55
Goldman, Francisco, 358–59, 361
Goldman Environmental Prize, 407, 526
Gómez, Juan V., 144, 224, 225, 228
Gómez, Máximo, 124, 127
Gómez Farías, Valentín, 79
Goodyear, Charles, 400
Granado, Alberto, 263
Grande, Rutilio, 344
Grant, Ulysses S., 97, *119*
Greenberg, Michael, 412
Greene, Graham, 445
Grosso, Matto, 116
Guatemala: Occupied Country (Galeano), 320
Guerra, Eutimio, 270
Guerrero, Vicente, 77–78
Guerrero, Xavier, 150
Guevara, Aleida, 265
Guevara, Ángel Aníbal, 292
Guevara de la Serna, Ernesto (Che), 186, 233, 243, 442, 475, 527; activists as inspired by, 385, 390–91, 439, 444, 445, 446, 466; Bolivia, final days in, *277*; Castro and, 248, 250, 269, 271, 274, 275, 390; communism, on the road to, 262–66; coup, as a witness to, 267–68; Cuba, visiting, 269–71; death, aftermath of, 278–79; *foco* strategy, 273–76, 278, 446, 497; *Guerrilla Warfare*, 273, 321; last adventures of, 275–78; *Latin Press*, working for, 335–36; as ruthless and idealistic, 271–73
Guide to the Perfect Latin American Idiot (Galeano), 323
Guillén, Nicolás, 271, 333, 335
Guillén Vicente, Rafael S., 443–45, 446. *See also* Marcos, Subcommander
Guillermoprieto, Alma, 415, 426, 427, 435, 442
Gutiérrez, Gustavo, 342
Gutiérrez Cruz, Carlos, 151
Guzmán Reynoso, M. R. Abimael, 201, 388–98, 415–16

Habeaus foundation, 339–40
Harberger, Arnold, 311
Harrington, Oliver Wendell, *303*
Harsh Times (Vargas Llosa), 418–19
Hatfield, G. D., 170
Hatuey, 16, 17–18
Haya de la Torre, Victor R., 198–209, 224, 267
Hazareesingh, Sudhir, 47, 53
Heflin, J. Thomas, 174
Hegemony or Survival (Chomsky), 461
Helms, Richard, 296–97
Henck, Nick, 438–39, 447
Herter, Christian, 251, 254
Hidalgo y Costilla, Miguel, 77–78
Hiriart, Lucía, 305, 307, 310, 311, 317
Hitler, Adolf, 145, 191, 211
Hobart, Robert, 53
Hoover, Herbert, 177, 189
Houston, Sam, 82, 83
Huerta, Victoriano, 140
Hugo, Victor, 115
Hull, Cordell, 183, 184, 190
Humboldt, Alexander von, 78, 115
Hurtado, Emma, 158
Hussein, Saddam, 460, 507
Hutchison Norris, William, 118

Ickes, Harold, 184
The Ides of March (Wilder), 337–38
Imbert Barrera, Antonio, 196
Immerman, Richard, 237
Institutional Revolutionary Party (PRI), 145, 181, 185, 186, 443, 448
Inter-American Development Bank (IADB), 402–3
International Finance Corporation (IFC), 524, 525
International Monetary Fund (IMF), 206, 454, 459, 462
International Telephone and Telegraph Corporation (ITT), 299
Iparraguirre, Elena, 391, 392, 395–96, 398
Iron Guard, 363
Isabella II, Queen, 9
Isabel of Bragança, 111, 118
Isaza, Luis, 434

Iturbide, Agustin de, 78, 79
Iwasaki, Fernando, 201

Jackson, Geoffrey, 496
Jalics, Francisco, 364–65, 369
Jefferson, Thomas, 53, 55, 58
Jeria, Ángela, 475, *480*
Jiménez de Cisneros, Francisco, 19
João VI, Emperor, 113
John Paul II, Pope, 313
Juana Inés de la Cruz (Sor Juana), 1, 26–33, 388
Juan Carlos, King, 461
Juárez, Benito, 1, 89–99, 132–33, 323

Kádár, János, 334
Kahlo, Guillermo, 154
Kahlo, Matilde, 154
Kahlo y Calderón, M. C. Frida, 1, 5, 147, 152, 154–59
Kant, Immanuel, 247, 389
Katari, Tomás, 41, 43, 45
Kennedy, John F., 195, 252, 260, 292, 323; Bay of Pigs invasion, 196, 253, 255–59, 336; Betancourt and, *231*, 232
Khrushchev, Nikita, 253, 254–55, 257, 391
King, J. C., 239
King, Martin Luther, Jr., 475
King, Mary-Claire, 361
Kinzer, Stephen, 237
Kirchner, Cristina Fernández de, 360, 367
Kirchner, Néstor, 359, 360, 367, 487
Kirk, Robin, 392
Kissinger, Henry, 296, 298, 302–3
Kornbluh, Peter, 302–3
Korry, Edward, 291, 298
Krauze, Enrique, 3, 61, 95, 185, 275, 445; on Chávez, 452, 457, 462; on Evita Perón, 215, 217; on Marcos, 446, 449

Lacalle, Luis Alberto, 498
Lacerda de Moura, Maria, 162
Lagos, Ricardo, 478
Langley (CIA headquarters), 294, 297, 298, 302
Lanusse, Alejandro, 220

La Prensa (periodical), 199–200, 213, 512, 516
Lara Bonilla, Rodrigo, 428–29, 430
Las Casas, Bartolomé de, 13, 16, 17, 18–25, 438
Las Casas, Pedro de, 17
La Serna, Miguel, 390
La Torre, Augusta, 391, 392, 395
Latin American Boom, 319, 336
Latrille, Charles, 96
Leclerc, Charles V., 56–57
Leguía, Augusto B., 200, 201, 202, 204
Lehder Rivas, Carlos, 422, 430
Lehman, William, 348
Le Moyne, August, 71
Lemoyne, James, 350
Lenin, Vladimir, 153, 203, 225, 247, 330, 391, 414
Lenov, Nikolai, 269
Leopoldina, Maria, 116
Lerdo de Tejada, Miguel, 91
Lerdo de Tejada, Sebastián, 98
Lester, Toby, 9, 11
Letelier, Orlando, 305–6, 311, 315, *316*, 317
Ley Juarez and *Ley Lerdo*, 381
Liberation theology, 24, 178, 363, 401, 406; anticommunist sentiments against, 369–70; rise of, 342–45; social inequality and repression, focus on, 5, 383
Lima, Ariel, 272
Lincoln, Abraham, 58
Liniers, Santiago de, 101
Litanies of the Evening (Vasconcelos), 146
Livingstone, Ken, 464
Living to Tell the Tale (García Márquez), 327
Lodge, Henry Cabot, 237
Lomnitz, Claudio, 200
Lonardi, Eduardo, 219
Longfellow, Henry Wadsworth, 107, 115
López, Francisco, 447
López, Rodolfo, 521
López de Santa Anna, Antonio, 76–88, 90–91, 99
López Portillo, Luis, 352–53
Louverture, Toussaint, 5, 46–59

Love in the Time of Cholera (García Márquez), 328
Loyola, Ignatius, 363
Lucanamarca Massacre, 393
Lucas García, Fernando R., 373–74, 375
Luisi, Paulina, 162
Lula. *See* Silva, Luiz Inácio Lula da
Lumumba, Patrice, 275
Lutz, Adolfo, 160–61
Lutz, Amy Fowler, 160–61
Lutz, Berta M. J., 160–66

MacArthur, Douglas, 228
Maceo, Antonio, 124
El Machete (periodical), 150, 152
Macmillan, Harold, 253
MacQuarrie, Kim, 423
Madero, Francisco I., 1, 99, 139–40, 149
Maduro, Nicolás, 451, 456, 464–65
Maitland, Thomas, 55
Majano, Adolfo, 350
Mallon, Thomas, 416
"Man at the Crossroads" commission, 153–54
Mandela, Nelson, *455*
Mann, Horace, 106–7
Mann, Mary, 107
Manrique de Lara y Gonzaga, María L., 30
Manuel Rodríguez Patriotic Front, 477
Mao Zedong, 273, 292, 391, 398
March, Aleida, 265, 268
Marcos, Subcommander, 437–50
María Eva Duarte de Perón Foundation, 215, 216
Mariana, Daniel, 355–56, 361
Mariani, Clara Anahí, 355–56, 361
Maríategui, José C., 5, 198–207, 224, 319, 391
Marín, Guadalupe, 150, 152
Marín, Pedro Antonio. *See* Marulanda Vélez, Manuel
Marín, Refugio, 443–44
Marnham, Patrick, 150
Márquez, Leonardo, 94
Márquez Mejía, Nicolás R., 327
Marsé Carbó, Juan, 337
Martin, Gerald, 335

Martínez, Gerson, 351
Martí y Peréz, José J., 122–29, 133, 200, 202, 263, 265, 271
Marty, Martin E., 25
Marulanda Vélez, Manuel, 280–88, 426
Marx, Karl, 246, 247, 414
Masetti, Jorge R., 275, 335
"El Matadero" (Echeverría), 103–4
Matamoros, Mariano, 77
Mattei, Fernando, 314
Matthei, Evelyn, 314, 479–80
Matthews, Herbert, 250
Maximilian I, Emperor, 1, 96–97
Maxwell, Kenneth, 304, 401, 402
Maza, Antonio de la, 196
Maza, Margarita, 90, 98
Maza, Octavio de la, 192
McCoy, Frank, 175
McHugh, Matthew, 348
Medellín cartel, 283, 422, 424–25, 427, 430, 434, 484
Medina Angarita, Isaías, 226
Mein Kampf (Hitler), 145, 211
Mejía, Óscar, 385
Memory of Fire (Galeano), 322–23
Menchú, Vicente, 383, 384
Menchú Tum, Rigoberta, 4, *324*, 378, 382–87, 449, *488*
Mendes Filho, Francisco A. (Chico), 399–409
Mendoza, Antonio de, 21
Menen, Carlos, 358
Mercader, Ramón, 157
Mercado, Manuel, 127
Mercator, Gerardus, 11
Merkel, Angela, 14–15
Mesa, Carlos, 486, 492
A Mexican Ulysses (Vasconcelos), 145
Mier y Terán, Manuel, 79
Miguel Etchecolatz, 359
Miranda, Francisco de, 62–63
Mistral, Gabriela, 5
Mitre, Bartolomé, 108
Mitrione, Dan, 496, 497
Moffitt, Michael, 306
Moffitt, Ronni, 306, *316*, 317
Moncada, Gerardo and William J., 433

INDEX 567

Moncada, José M., 168, 169, 175, 243, 247, 250
Moncada Barracks attack, 267
Monroe Doctrine, 79, 97, 184, 239
Montaner, Carlos Alberto, 323, 325
Montealegre, Eduardo, 517, 519
Montecristi Manifesto, 127
Montesinos, Antonio, 18
Montesinos, Vladimiro, 418
Montoneros guerrillas, 355, 363
Montoya, Marina, 431
Montt, Manuel, 106
Mora, J. M. Luis, 76, 79
Morales Ayma, Evo, 45, 370, *463*, 483–93, 517
Morelos, José M., 77–78
Moro, Sérgio, 509
Mossadegh, Mohammad, 239
Motorcycle Diaries (Guevara), 263–65
Movement of Popular Participation (MPP), 498
Movement to Socialism (MAS), 486, 489, 493
Moyano, Dolores, 263
Moyano, María Elena, 263, 393
Muerte a Secuestradores (MAS), 426–27
Mujica, Demetrio, 495
Mujica Cordano, José A. (Pepe), 494–501
Munguía, Clemente de Jesús, 92
Murillo Zambrana, Rosario, 511, 516–17, 519, *520*, 521
Murphy, Gerald, 192
Murphy, Robert, 239
Mussolini, Benito, 145, 200, 211

Nabuco, Joaquim, 118
Nagy, Imre, 334
Nasser, Gamal A., 253
National Autonomous University of Mexico (UNAM), 138, 141, 387, 443, 444
National Council of Popular and Indigenous Organizations of Honduras (COPINH), 523, 524–25, 526
National Liberation Forces (FLN), 444–47
National University of Saint Augustine (UNSA), 389

The Neighborhood (Vargas Llosa), 412, 418
Neruda, Pablo, 5, 45, 330, 334
Neves, Aecio, 408
Neves, Tancredo, 505
News of a Kidnapping (García Márquez), 327, 341
Nicaragua Opposition Union, 514–15
Nietzsche, Friedrich, 115, 201
Nieves Ochoa, Marta, 426, 430
Nixon, Richard: Allende and, 296–99, 304; Castro-Nixon relations, 251, 253; Chile, assessing US role in, 302–3; Trujillo presidency and, 192–93
Notes about Military History (Perón), 211
Nuñez de Miranda, Antonio, 28, 30, 62

Obama, Barack, 206, 318, 352, 465, 470, 491, 495, 507
Oblotas, Antonio, 38
Obregón, Álvaro, 140, 141, 144, 145, 149, 152
Ocampo, Melchor, 90
Ochoa, Arnaldo, 340
Ochoa Brothers, 422, 426
Odría, Manuel, 414
O'Higgins, Bernardo, 310
O'Kelley, James J., 111
O'Leary, Daniel F., 70
One Hundred Years of Solitude (García Márquez), 326–27, 328, 336
Open Veins of Latin America (Galeano), 318–25
Operation Carwash, 502, 509
Operation Condor, 311
Operation Zapata, 255–56
Oppenheimer, J. Robert, 442
Organization of American States (OAS), 194, 230, 236, 331, 463, 492, 520
Orlando Hernández, Juan, 526, 527
Orozco, Pascual, 149
Ortega, Jairo, 427–28
Ortega Saavedra, Humberto, 512, 514, 515
Ortega Saavedra, J. Daniel, 178, 259, 438, 511, 512–21
Our America (Martí), 126, 265
Outre Mer (Bourget), 133
Ovando, Nicolás de, 17

Pacheco, Amaury, 469–70
Pacheco, Jorge, 496
Pacheco, Máximo, 143–44
Pachón de Villamizar, Maruja, 431
Pact of Punto Fijo, 229, 453
Padilla, Herberto, 336–37, 414
Páez, José A., 66, 70
Pagden, Anthony, 24
Page, Joseph A., 221
Pan-American feminist movement, 160, 162–66
Parejo, Enrique, 430
Parra, Guido A., 434
Parsley Massacre, 191
Partlow, Joshua, 519–20
Pastor, Edén, 338
Pastrana, Andrés, 284–85, 286, 288
Pastry War, 83
Patterson, Richard, 238
Paul III, Pope, 20
Paz, Octavio, 30, 339, 416, 440–41
PBSUCCESS covert operation, 238
Pearson, Weetman, 180
Peasant Unity Committee (CUC), 383–84
Pedro II, Emperor, 110–21
Peñaloza, Ángel V. (Chacho), 108
Penn, Sean, 464
Pérez, Carlos Andrés (CAP), 453–55, 463
Pérez Esquivel, Adolfo, 368
Pérez Jiménez, Marcos, 220, 228–29, 230, 333, 334, 453
Perón, Isabel, 210, 218, 220, 221, 322, 333, 355
Perón, Juan D., 146, 191, 210–22, 226, 519
Perón, María Eva (Evita), 4, 210–22, 234, 354, 519
Peronism, 4, 210–22, 354, 355, 360, 363, 367
Perrottet, Tony, 247
Persons, Albert C., 255
Pétion, Alexandre, 65
Petrik, Joan, 343
PetroCaribe alliance, 518
Petróleos Mexicanos (PEMEX), 185–86
Peurifoy, John, 238, 268
Phelps, John, 429

Philip II, King, 23
Philip IV, King, 28
Piar, Manuel, 340
Pickering, Thomas, 54–55
Pike, Frederick B., 291
Piñera, Sebastián, 478
Pinheiro, Wilson, 403
Pink Tide, 487, 518
Pinochet Ugarte, Augusto J. R., 314, 374; Allende, coup against, 289, 305, 321, 337–38; Bachelet and, 474–77, 480; as a Chicago Boy, 311–12; downfall of, 315–17; as a Junta general, 310–11; military career, pursuing, 306–7; Penguin's Revolution against, 479; Reagan-Pinochet relations, 313; *Tanquetazo* coup, attempting, 308–9
Pinochet Vera, Augusto, 306
Plan de Iguala, 78
Plaza de Mayo movement, 4, 354–61, 366
Plekhanov, Georgi, 452
Poniatowska, Elena, 446
Pope Francis: The Struggle for the Soul of Catholicism (Vallely), 366
Popular Unity (UP) coalition, 296, 299, 300– 301, 302, 304
Portillo, Alfonso, 379
Posada, José G., 1
Powell, Colin, 433
Powers, Francis G., 254
Prats, Carlos, 298, 302, 309, 310, 315
Prebisch, Raúl, 320
Ptolemy, 10–11

Quiroga, Facundo, 105

Ramírez, Isabel, 27
Ramírez, Rafael, 259
Ramírez Amaya, Atilio, 350
Ramírez Durand, Óscar, 397
Reagan, Ronald, 128, 313, 351, 375, 514
Redeemers (Krauze), 3
La Reforma agenda, 91, 94, 97, 98, 99
Reform War, 92–93
Reid, Michael, 323–24
René II, Duke of Lorraine, 10
Restrepo, Fabio, 423

INDEX 569

Revolutionary Armed Forces of Colombia (FARC), 280–88, 425, 426, 427, 430
Revolution of Ayutla, 86, 90–91
Revuelta, Naty, 247
Reyes, Raúl, 288
Reyes Echandía, Alfonso, 430
Reynoso, Berenice, 388
Ribeiro, Maria de Lourdes, 503–4
Rice, Condoleezza, 461
Rigaud, André, 56
"The Rights of Black Men" (Louverture), 54
Ringmann, Matthias, 10–11
Rio Blanco village, 524, 525, 526
Ríos Montt, Efraín, 371–81, 385–86
Ríos Montt, Mario, 372
Rivas, Carlos Lehder, 422
Rivera, Diego, 1–3, 5, 139, 143–44, 147–59, 242
Roa Serra, Juan, 331
Robinson, Jackie, 252
Robles, Frances, 519
Rockefeller, John D., Jr., 153–54
Rodó, José E., 5, 132–37, 141, 495
Rodrigues, Gomercindo, 403, 405, 409
Rodrigues, Ilzamar and Elenira, 403
Rodríguez, Félix, 278
Rodríguez, Miguel Á., 389
Rodríguez del Toro, María T., 62
Rodriguez Gacha, José G., 422, 427
Rogers, Will, 173
Rojas Pinilla, Gustavo, 333
Role of the Individual in History (Plekhanov), 452
Romagoza, Juan, 352
Román, Edwin, 521
Romero, Carlos H., 344
Romero, Óscar, 5, 342–53, 362, 370
Romero, Simon, 498
Romo, Osvaldo, 311
Romo, Pablo, 443
Roncagliolo, Santiago, 389
Roosevelt, Franklin D., 153, 183–85, 187, 190, 227, 233
Rosas, Juan Manuel de, 100–105, 107, 109, 116, 191, 219
Rosseau, Jean-Jacques, 62, 247

Roume, Philippe, 51
Rouseff, Dilma, 408
Royal Commentaries of the Incas (Vega), 38
Rudder (periodical), 145
Ruiz, Samuel, 447, 521
Rus, Sara, 357
Rusk, Dean, 256

Sabato, Ernesto, 219
Sacasa, Juan, 177
Sáenz, Manuela, 71
Salanueva, Antonio, 89
Salinas de Gortari, Carlos, 437–38, 440–41, 443, 448
San Andrés Accords, 437, 449
San Carlos de La Cabaña citadel, 271–72
Sánchez, Celia, 250
Sánchez, Luis A., 202
Sánchez Cerro, Luis Miguel, 204–5
Sánchez Cordero, Yoani M., 466–73
Sánchez de Lozada, Gonzalo, 487
Sandinistas, 178, 374, 448; in Nicaragua, 373, 445, 513–16; Ortega-era Sandinistas, 259, 275, 438, 511, 521; Sandinista National Liberation Front, 167, 338, 512, 515, 518; Sandino-era movement, 167, 170, 172, 175, 177–78
Sandino, Augusto César, 4, 167–78, 190, 403, 457, 512, 516
Sandoval, Miguel Á., 379
Sanguinetti, Eduardo, 501
San Martin, José de, 67, 271
Santa Anna. *See* López de Santa Anna, Antonio
Santa Clara, Battle of, 270
Santander, Francisco de Paula, 70
Santos, Francisco, 431
Santos, Juan M., 286, 288, 326
Saravia, Álvaro R., 349
Sarmiento, Domingo: Argentina, as president of, 108–9; on *caudillismo*, 105–6, 122; early years, 103–4; education and, 136, 198; *Facundo: Civilization and Barbarism*, 105–6, 109, 126; Mann, friendship with, 106–7; as a reformist, 100, 107–8, 144, 323; United States and, 125, 132–33

Schlesinger, Arthur, Jr., 252, 259
Schneider, René, 297–99
Schoelcher, Victor, 58
Schoklender, Sergio, 360–61
Schöner, Joannes, 14
Schwarcz, Lilia, 504
Schwartzberg, Steven, 225
Sedova, Natalia, 156–57
Self Portrait with Stalin (painting), 158
Sendic, Raúl, 319, 496, 497
Serpa, Horacio, 284
Serrano Elias, Jorge, 379
Seven Interpretive Essays on Peruvian Reality (Mariátegui), 5, 201, 204
Seward, William Henry, 86, 97
Shakespeare, William, 134
Shakur, Túpac Amaru, 45
Shining Path (Sendero Luminoso), 201, 206, 280, 388–98, 415
A Short Account of Destruction of the Indies (Las Casas), 23–24
Silva, Aristides Inácio da, 503
Silva, Euridice da, 503
Silva, Luiz Inácio Lula da, 402, 407, 409, 487, 502–10
Silva, Maria Osmarina da (Marina), 399, 405–9
Siqueiros, David A., 150, 157
Smith, Walter Bedell, 238
Soccer in Sun and Shadow (Galeano), 319
Social Darwinism, 109, 135, 139, 144
Solano López, Francisco, 116–17
Somoza García, Anastasio, 190, 333, 457, 521; dictatorship of, 177–78, 227, 519; revolution following reign of, 167, 338, 374, 518; Somoza dynasty as loathed, 511, 512; US-Somoza relations, 238, 513–14
Souter, Gerry, 152
Spring, Karen, 523
Stalin, Josef, 147, 151–52, 156, 157–59, 225, 268
Stanton, James V., 196
Starn, Orin, 390, 392
Stavans, Ilan, 444–45
Stoll, David, 378, 381, 386
Stone, Robert, 422

Streeter, Stephen, 238
Stroessner, Alfredo, 219, 220, 333
Suárez, Victor J., 288
Sucre, Antonio José de, 67, 69
Sumulong, Lorenzo, 255

Taber, Robert, 250, 254
Tanquetazo coup attempt, 308–9
Tapia, Carlos, 390–91
Taylor, Simon, 53
Taylor, Zachary, 84
Teapot Dome scandal, 184
Téllez, Dora M., 521
The Tempest (play), 134
Teresa Cristina, Empress, 111, 116, 121
Terrugi, Diana, 355–56
Thatcher, Margaret, 315, 415
Time of the Hero (Vargas Llosa), 413
Tinoco, Victor H., 521
Tizón, Aurelia, 211
Toft, Joe, 435
Toledo, Francisco de, 38
Topolansky, Lucía, 494
Torres, Camilo, 334–35, *352*
Torres, Hugo, 521
Torrijos, Omar, 338
Travis, William Barrett, 80
Treaty of Guadalupe Hidalgo, 86
Trincado Mateo, Joaquín, 175
Trotsky, Leon, 147, 156–57, 159, 225, 290
Trujillo, Ramfis, 194, 196
Trujillo Molina, Rafael L., 227, 231, 246, 333; Cuban communism and, 192–95; Dominican Republic, offering sanctuary in, 194, 220, 229, 270; *Feast of the Goat* as depicting, 412, 418; powers backing, 190–91; regime change, 195–96; rise of, 188–89; as a strongman, 146, 294; *trujillismo*, 195, 197, 230
Truman, Harry S., 227, 236
Trump, Donald, 6, 493, 521
Túpac Amaru I, 34, 38–39, 40–41, 43, *44*, 45, 390
Túpac Amaru II (J. G. Condorcanqui), 4, 34–45, 390, 496
Túpac Katari, 43

Túpac Katari Guerrilla Army, 45
Tupamaro revolutionaries, 319, 496–97
Turbay, Diana, 431
Turbay, Diego, 285
Turbay, Julio C., 427, 431
Turner, Nat, 58

Ubico, Jorge, 233, 372
Ugarte Martínez, Avelina, 306
United Fruit Company, 168, 419; Eisenhower support for, 233, 236–38, 241; García Márquez writing on, 327–28; Guevarra and, 267, 268
El Universal (periodical), 333
Uribe, Álvaro, 286–87
Uribe Uribe, Rafael, 327
Uriburu, José Féliz, 210
Urquiza, José de, 107

Valenzuela, Camilo, 298
Valle, José del, 41
Vallely, Paul, 366–67
Valverde de Betancourt, Carmen, *231*
Vance, Cyrus, 346
Vargas, Ernesto, 413
Vargas, Getúlio, 163, 165, 226, 400, 440
Vargas Llosa, Álvaro, 270, 275, 323, 326
Vargas Llosa, Mario, 202, 236, 271, 448, 473; Castro, disdain for, 340–41; *Feast of the Goat*, 197, 412, 418; ideological flip-flop, 414–15; Latin American Boom, as part of, 319, 336, 412; as a Nobel laureate, 413, *419*, 420; political ambitions, 5, 415–18
Vasconcelos, José, 138–46, 149–50, 151, 330
Vásquez, Horacio, 189
Vásquez, Pascualita, 523
Vásquez, Tabaré, 498–99, 500
Vatican II, 342–44, 363
Vega, Garcilaso, 38
Velázquez, Diego, 16, 17
Vernich, Christian von, 364
Vespucci, Amerigo, 6, 8–11, 13, 15
Viaux, Roberto, 297–98
Victoria, Guadalupe, 78
Videla, Jorge Rafael, 354, 358, 360

Vieyra, António de, 27, 31
Vilanova, María, 234–35
Villa, Francisco (Pancho), 5, 140, 149, 322
Villamizar, Alberto, 431–32
La Violencia civil war, 281, 331, 333, 442
Viscardo y Guzmán, Juan Pablo, 62
Vitier, Cinio, 263
Vivanco, José Miguel, 462
Vojkovic Trier, Alex, 477
VRAEM rebel faction, 397

Waldeseemüller, Martin, 10–11, 13
Waldeseemüller map, 11–14
Weavers of Revolution (Winn), 304
Wells, Allen, 170
Whidden, Benjamin F., 58
Whitman, Ann, 237
Why the Kremlin Hates Bananas (film), 237
Wilder, Thornton, 337
Winn, Peter, 304
Wolf, Navarro, 73
Wolfensohn, James, 507
Workers' Party (PT), 402, 502, 505
World Bank, 402–3, 454, 504, 507, 524
Worldwide Defeat (Borrego), 146

X, Malcolm, 254

Yorio, Graciela, 368
Yorio, Orlando (Father Yorio), 364–65, 369
Yrigoyen, Hipólito, 210

Zamora, Mario, 350
Zapata, Carlos E., 441
Zapata, Emiliano, 140, 149, 441–42, 449, 457
Zapata, Gabriela, 491–92
Zapatista Army of National Liberation (EZLN): Chiapas, founded in, 437, 438, 445, 447; landless campesinos, championing, 439, 441; Subcommander Marcos and, 437, 442, 443, 449, *450*
Zavala, Lorenzo de, 87–88
Zedillo, Ernesto, 443, 449
Zelaya, Manuel, 523
Zuloaga, Félix, 93

www.ingramcontent.com/pod-product-compliance
Lightning Source LLC
Chambersburg PA
CBHW051842300426
44117CB00006B/235